A-Z

C000059036

Key to Map Pages	
Large Scale City Centre	262
Map Pages	263-264

REFERENCE

Motorway	**M57**	Car Park (selected)	P
A Road	A562	Church or Chapel	†
Proposed		Cycleway (selected)	
Tunnel		Fire Station	■
B Road	B5174	Hospital	H
Dual Carriageway		House Numbers (A & B Roads only)	18 25
One-way Street	→	Information Centre	i
Traffic flow on A Roads is indicated by a heavy line on the driver's left.		National Grid Reference	³40
All one-way streets are shown on Large Scale Pages 4-5		Police Station	▲
Restricted Access		Post Office	★
Pedestrianized Road		Toilet:	
Track & Footpath		without facilities for the Disabled	▽
		with facilities for the Disabled	▽
Railway	Station / Tunnel / Level Crossing	Disabled facilities only	▽
		Viewpoint	
Built-up Area	BOOTH ST.	Educational Establishment	
Local Authority Boundary	—·—·—	Hospital or Hospice	
Posttown Boundary		Industrial Building	
Postcode Boundary		Leisure or Recreational Facility	
		Place of Interest	
		Public Building	
		Shopping Centre or Market	
Map Continuation	18 Large Scale 4	Other Selected Buildings	

SCALE

Map Pages 6-175
1:15840   4 inches to 1 mile

0 ¼ Mile

0 250 Metres

6.31cm to 1km   10.16cm to 1 mile

Map Pages 4-5
1:10560   6 inches to 1 mile

0 ⅛ ¼ Mile

0 100 200 300 Metres

9.46cm to 1km   15.24cm to 1 mile

Copyright of Geographers' A-Z Map Company Limited

Head Office:
Fairfield Road, Borough Green, Sevenoaks, Kent TN15 8PP
Telephone: 01732 781000 (Enquiries & Trade Sales)
01732 783422 (Retail Sales)
www.a-zmaps.co.uk

Ordnance Survey® This product includes mapping data licensed from Ordnance Survey® with the permission of the Controller of Her Majesty's Stationery Office.

© Crown Copyright 2004. All rights reserved.
Licence number 100017302

Edition 4 2005

2 KEY TO MAP PAGES

Formby

B5195 · A5741 · B5195 · A59

IRISH SEA

B5193 · River Alt

Crosby Channel

Lydiate
6 | **7**
MAGHULL

| Little Crosby **8** | **9** Great Crosby | Lunt **10** | Sefton **11** | **12** | Kennessee Green **13** | **14** Mellin |

LIVERPOOL BAY

Blundellsands **16** | **17** **CROSBY** | Netherton **18** | **19** **Litherland** | **20** | **21** Aintree | **22** Waddic

| LARGE SCALE **4** **5** LIVERPOOL CITY CENTRE |

Seaforth **32** | **33** **BOOTLE** | Orrell **34** | **35** | Fazakerley **36** | **37** Walton | **38** Dog & Gu

New Brighton **50** **51** | **52** | **53** | Kirkdale **54** | **55** | Norris Green **56** | **57** Anfield | **58**

Everton

WALLASEY Leasowe **70** | **71** Moreton **72** | **73** | Egremont *(Kingsway)* Liscard **74** | **75** | **LIVERPOOL** Mersey Tunnel **76** | **77** | **78** | **79** Stanley | **80** Kno As Old Swan

HOYLAKE **90** | **91** Meols | Bidston **92** | **93** Greasby | **94** | **95** Upton **BIRKENHEAD** | Seacombe Claughton **96** | **97** | *(Queensway)* **98** | **99** Toxteth | **Wavertree** **100** | **101** Sefton Park | **10**

Newton **112** | **113** **West Kirby** Grange | Frankby **114** | **115** Irby Hill | Woodchurch **116** | **117** Prenton | **Tranmere** **118** | **119** Dacre Hill | Rock Ferry **120** | **121** **New Ferry** | Dingle **122** | Mossley Hill **123** Aigburth | **12** Grassend

Caldy **134** | **135** | Irby Heath **136** | Irby **137** Pensby | **Thingwall** **138** | **139** Barnston | Storeton **140** | **141** | **BEBINGTON** **142** | **143** Spital | **RIVER** | **14**

HESWALL **156** | **157** | **158** | **159** Gayton | Thornton Hough **160** | **161** | Poulton **Bromborough** **162** | **163** Brookhurst | **MERSEY**

NESTON | B5135 · B5157 | B5133 · A540 | Eastham **170** | **17 1** Willaston | **5** **6** **7** M53 **8** B5463

RIVER DEE (AFON DYFRDWY)

ENGLAND WALES

B5134 · A550 · A41 · B5132

| SCALE |
| 0 — 1 — 2 Miles |
| 0 — 1 — 2 — 3 Kilometres |

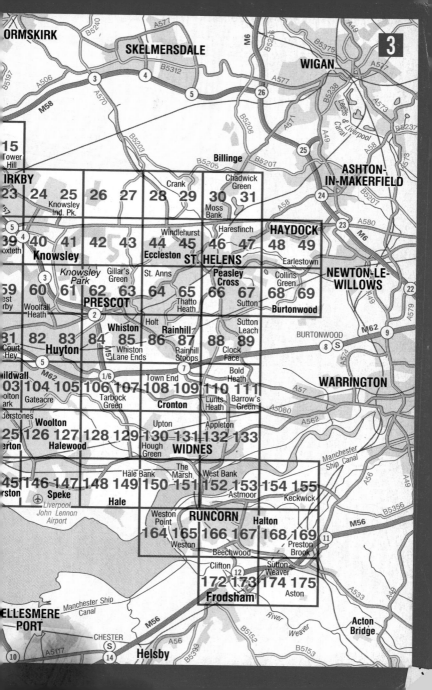

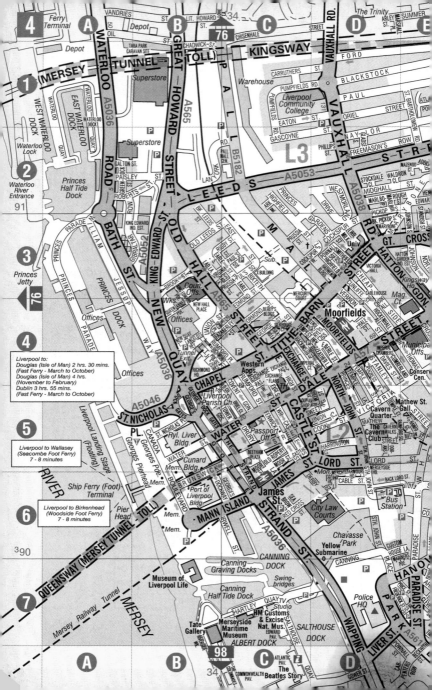

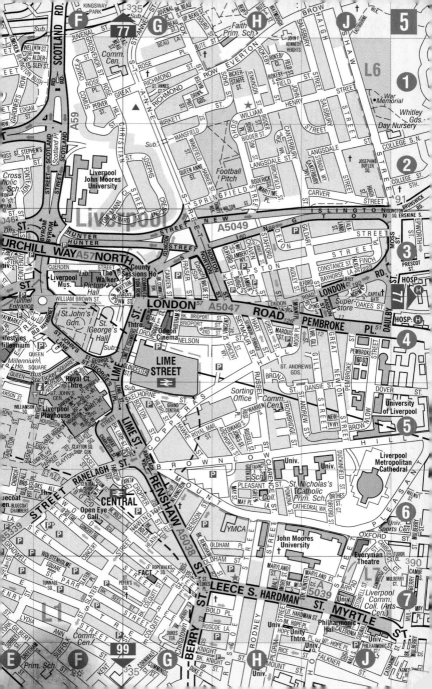

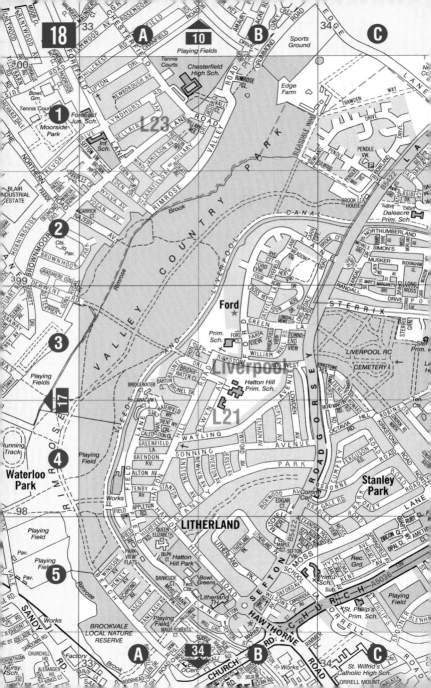

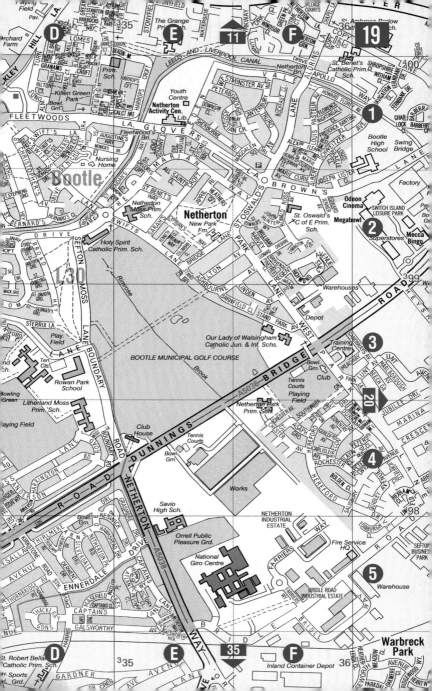

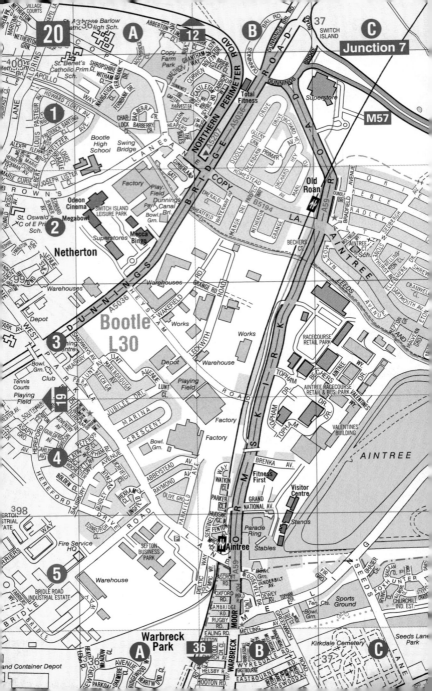

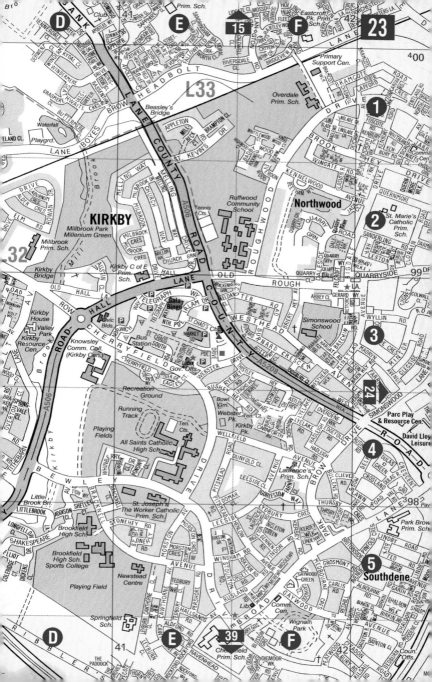

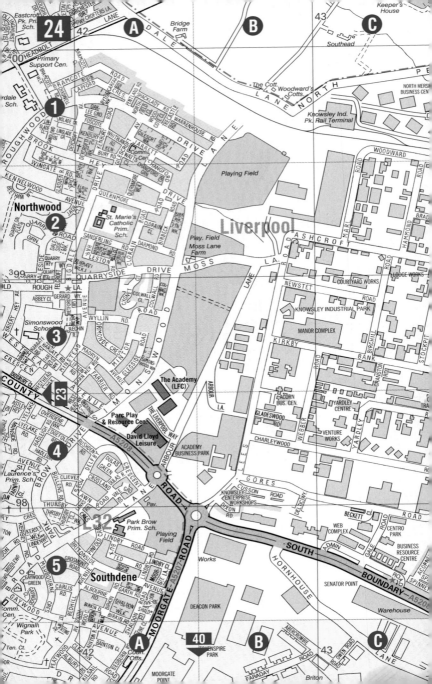

SIMONSWOOD MOSS ⁴00

Eccleston House

Spencer's House Farm

Acorn Venture Urban Farm

Works

ROAD

MOSS END WAY

ROAD

ROAD

ROAD

ROAD

WELL

DRAW

L33

BOUNDARY LANE

Top House Farm

WEST LANCASHIRE KNOWSLEY

MOSS PLANTATION

26

Kirkby Moss

CHARLEY WOOD

Playing Field

PARK

RIMETER

Sandy Brow

Private Road

CUT

LANE RED

LANE CUT

Acornfield Plantation Local Nature Reserve

Sandy Brow Cottage

BROW

SANDY

LANE

CUT

NEW

LANE

New Cut House

ROAD

PINNEY VW.

Cooper's Farm

LANE

MOLLY

Sandy Lane Farm

Electricity Sub Station

Cooper's Moss Farm

K n o w s l e y

NEW CUT

1

2

³99

3

4

98

5

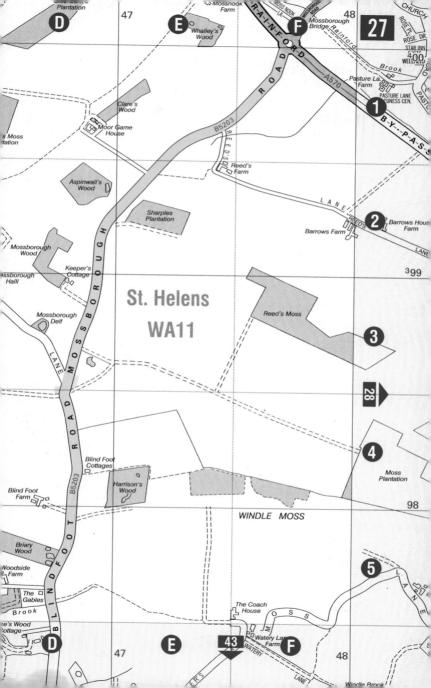

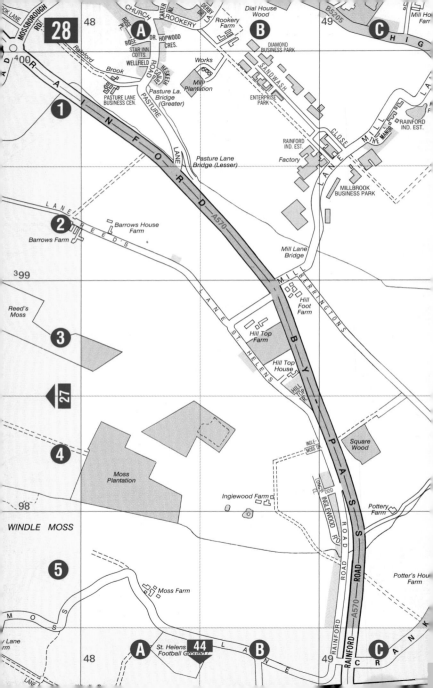

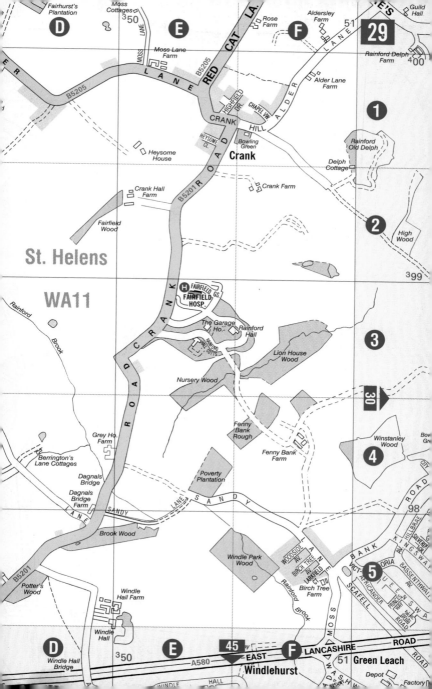

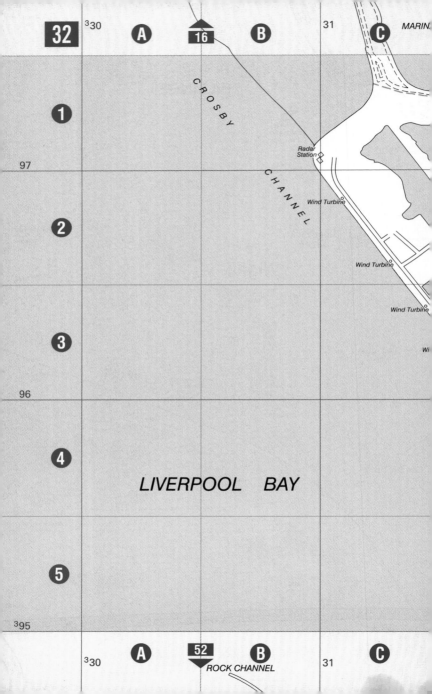

32 ³30 **A** **16** **B** 31 **C** MARIN.

CROSBY

1

97

CHANNEL

Radar
Station

2

Wind Turbine

Wind Turbine

3

Wind Turbine

96

Wi

4

LIVERPOOL   BAY

5

³95

³30 **A** **52** **B** 31 **C**

ROCK CHANNEL

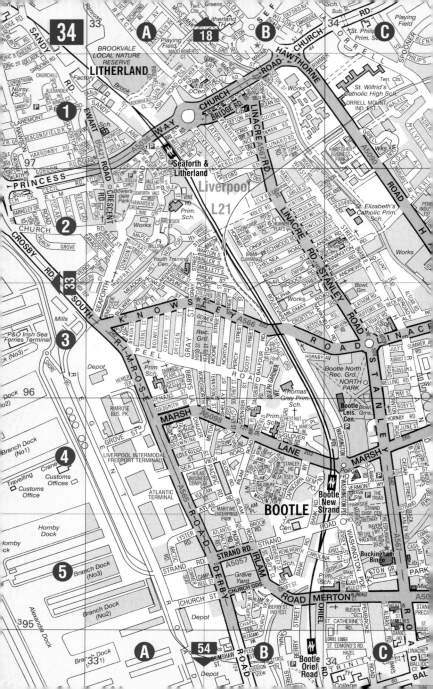

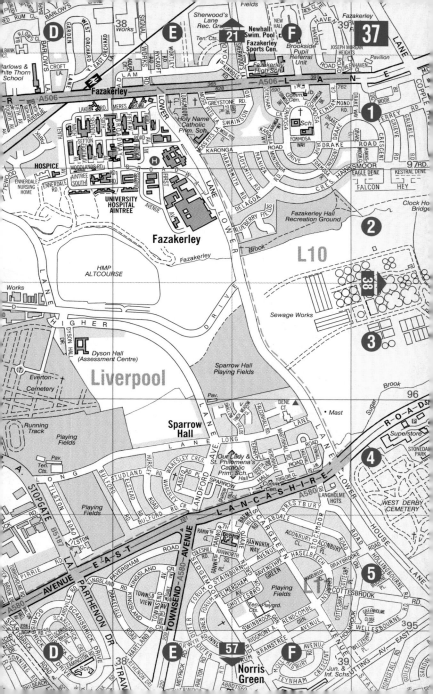

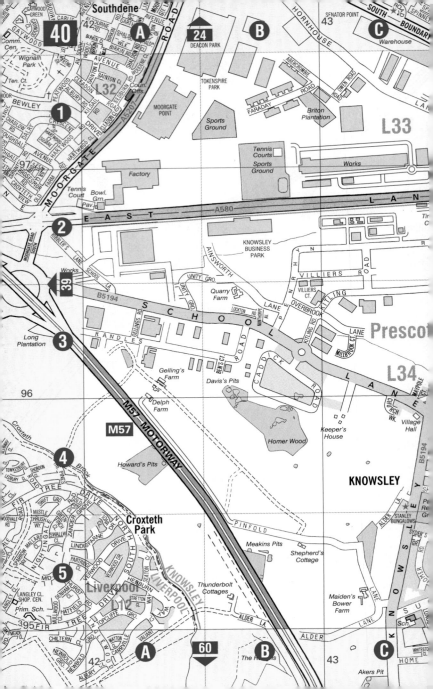

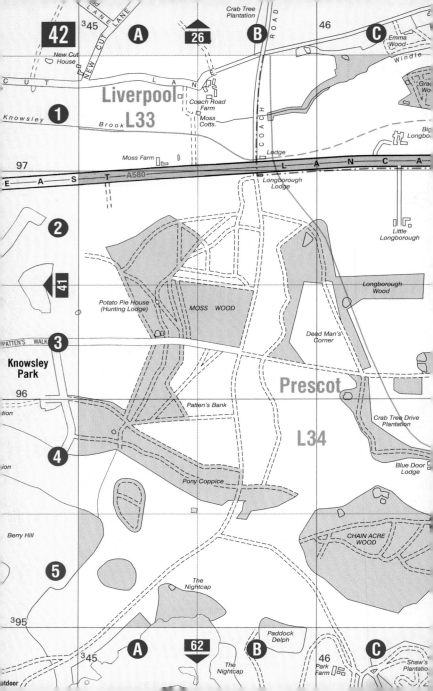

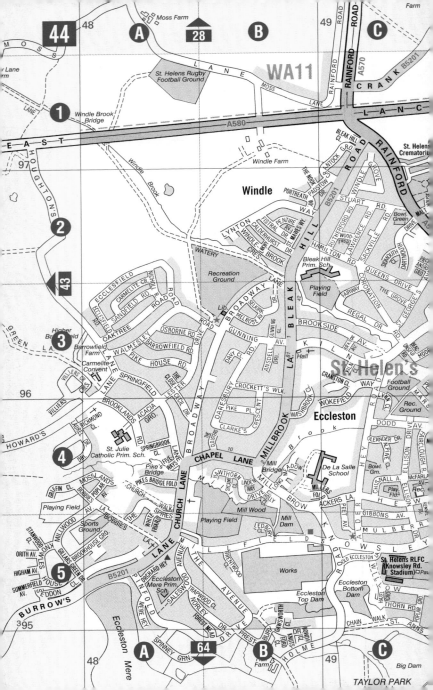

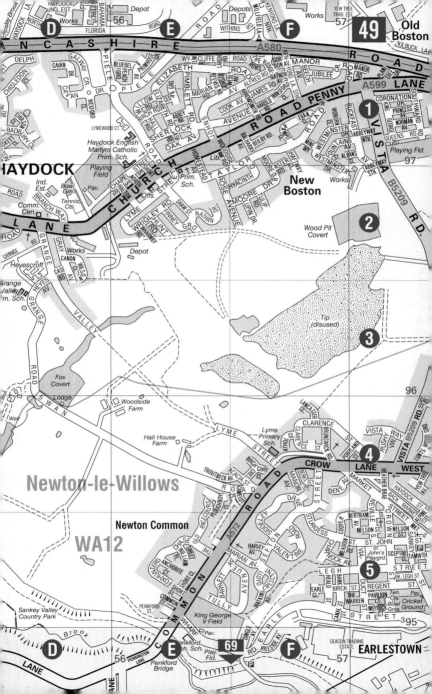

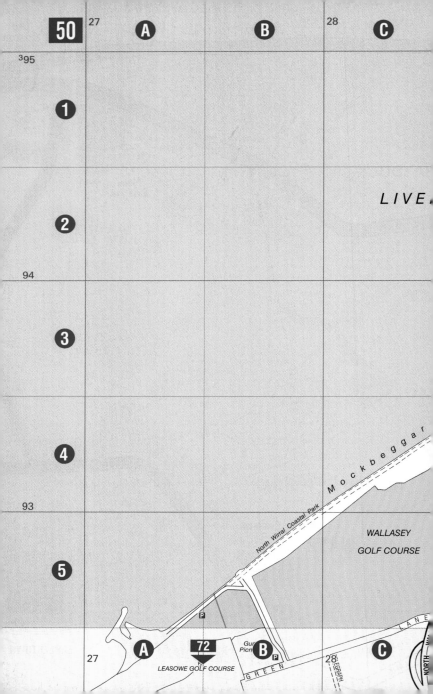

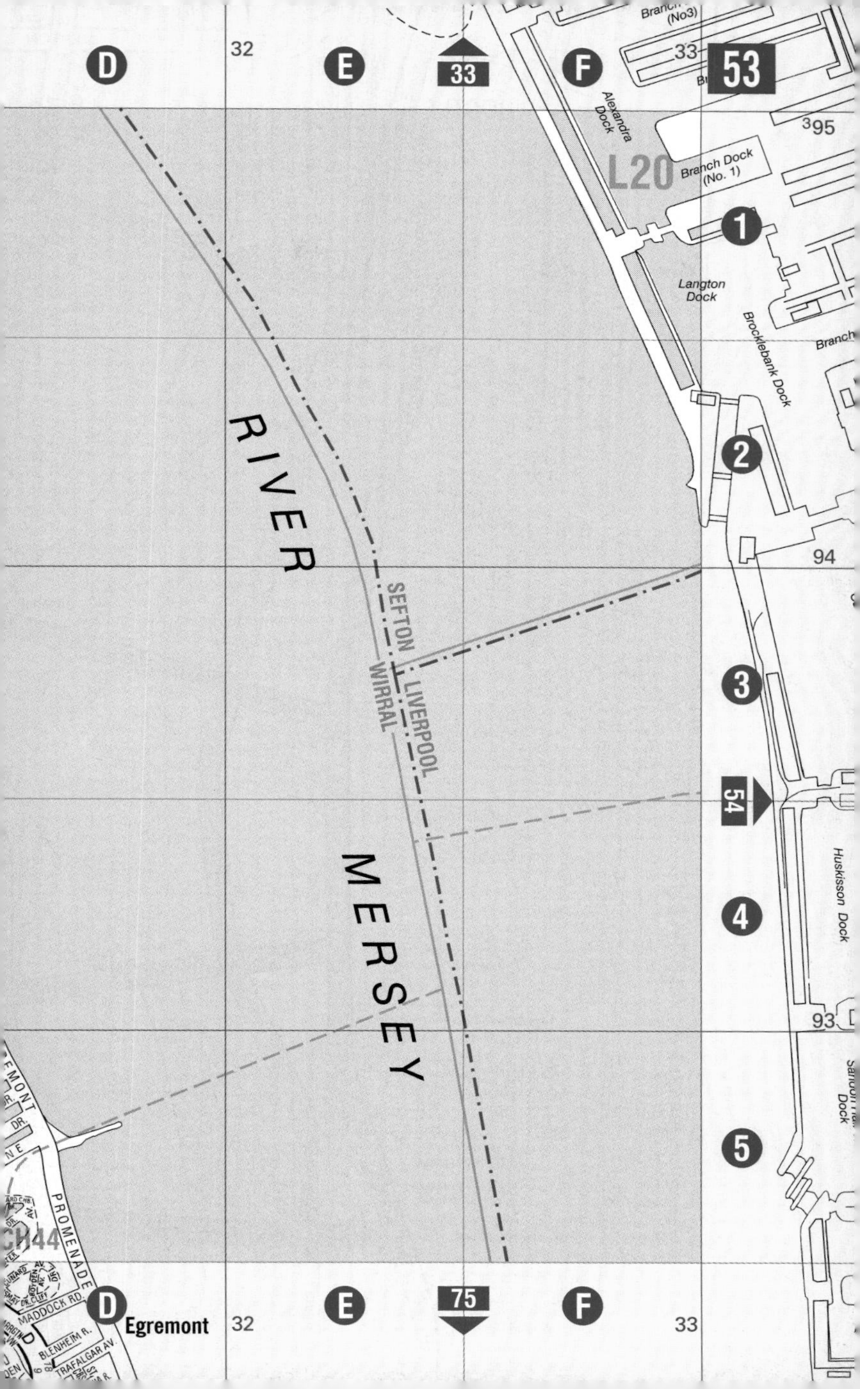

395

Branch
(No3)

33

Alexandra
Dock

L20

Branch Dock
(No. 1)

1

Langton
Dock

Brocklebank Dock

Branch

2

94

R I V E R

SEFTON
WIRRAL · LIVERPOOL

3

54

Huskisson Dock

M E R S E Y

4

93

Sandon
Dock

5

PROMENADE

CH44

EGREMONT

MADDOCK RD.

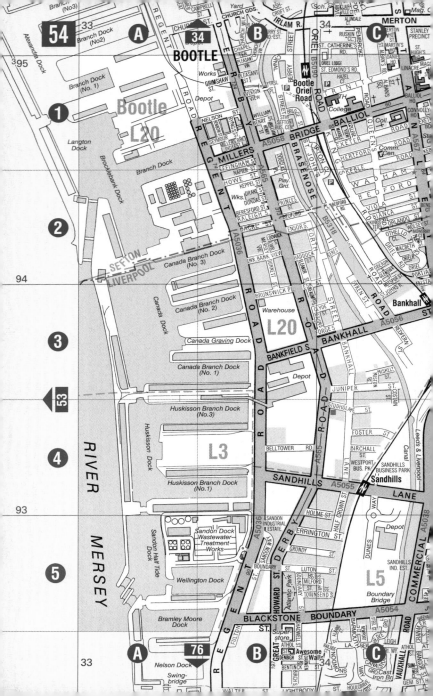

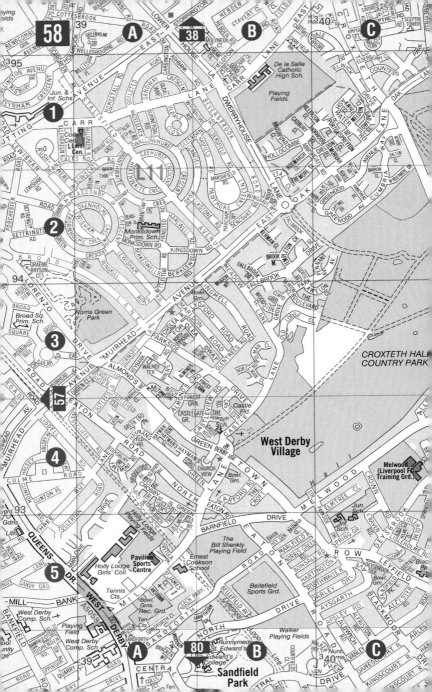

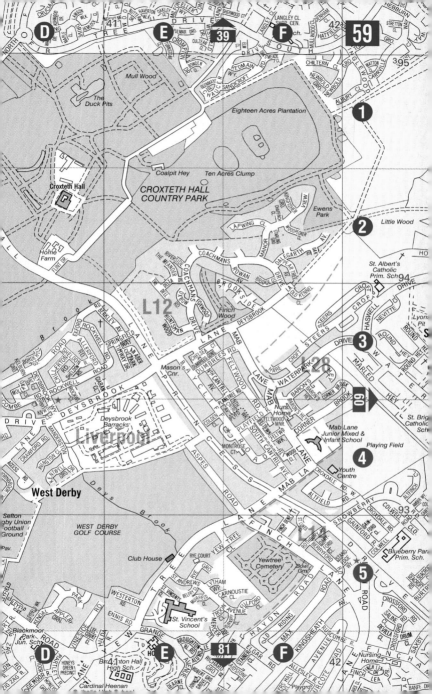

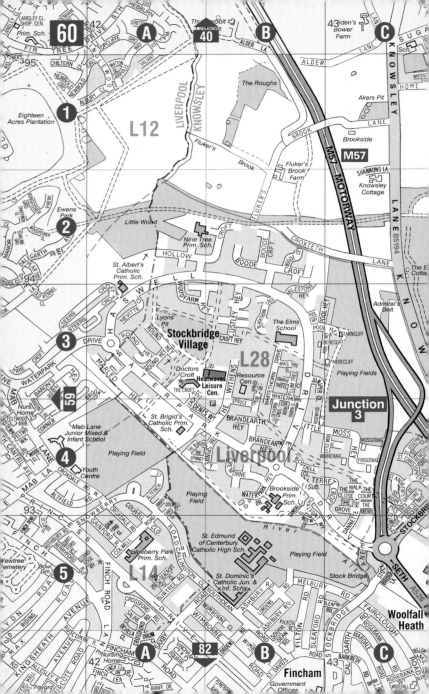

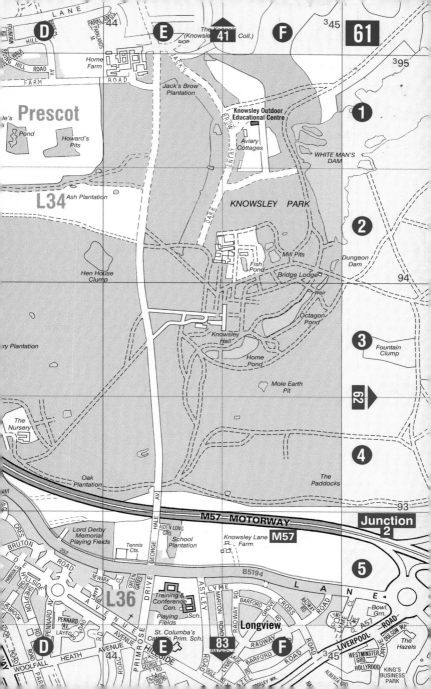

GILLAR'S LANE

SUMMERFIELD HOUSE
AV.
SEDDON

Eccleston Mere

395

B5203

Burgesses Farm

B5201

Gillar's Green

St. Helen's
WA10

Eccleston Mere

1

Trap Wood

Burrow's Lane Farm

Mere View Farm

2

Trapwood Cottage

Trap Lodge

KNOWSLEY

ST. HELENS

Ivy House

Roughley's Brow Farm

Sale's Wood

94

Gorse Plantation

BURROW'S

B5201

No. 4 RESERVOIR

Cricket Ground

No. 3 RESERVOIR

3

No. 2 Reservoir

Roughley's Brow House

Works

Yates Plantation

No. 1 Reservoir

Prescot

Valencia Farm

64

VALENCIA

NEW

ST.

HELENS

A58

ROAD

B-Y--P-A-S-S

FERN GDNS.

CENTRAL

PARK

AVENUE

WEST

CL.

Recreation Ground

Our Lady's Catholic Prim. Sch.

THE GREEN

ALBANY

ELM

GROVE

WOODLANDS

AVENUE

INGLEHOLME GDNS.

ORC

MIDDLE

HURST CL.

Prescot ables AFC (Valerie Pk.)

A58

Stands

RD.

LLOYD
CANTERBURY
CHAPMAN

ST. JAMES'S RD.

HILARY

CL.

FOREST

HEATH

GORSEY

Eccleston Lane Ends Prim. Sch.

Tennis Cts.

Eccleston Park

THE PADDOCK

CROFT

AVENUE

93

BELVEDERE
HARVARD
YALE CL.
FLETCHER
RD.

Evelyn Prim. Sch.

B5201

FAIRHOLME

THE CABLES

GROVE

THE BROOM

Eccle

HIGH ST.

WARRING

ST. HELENS

CROSS

ROWSON S.

GROSVENOR

Prescot Centre

GREENWOOD

RD.

PRESCOT TRADE CENTRE

HAWTHORN

ALDER

DERWENT

RYDAL AV.

CONISTON

ROAD

LIME TREE CL.

GEORGIAN CL.

PORTICO

AV.

Eccle

The Lodge

5

RIO ST.

JACK'S

COLUMBIA RD.

ALBANY

MARYVILLE

Prescot Prim. Sch.

Playing Field

SINCLAIR

AVENUE

L35

McVINNIE

HONEYBOURNE

FAR

RINGSTONE

Civic Hall

ASPINALL

OLIVER
LYME RD.
MENAI

BRETHERTON

LAVENDER CR.

LAUREL

GRASMERE

COOK S.

VININS

RD.

RYDALE

WATLING

PORTICO LA.

PRESCOT

KEMBLE

B5200 STREET

SMITH

SCOTCHBARN

LADY

Scotchbarn Sports Centre

SCOTCHBARN

LANE

Ten. Cts.

DELPH LANE

BUTT

MYERS

Supermarket

CABLES RETAIL PARK

Club Sports Gr.

DELPH LANE

Prescot Leisure Centre

85

St. Edmund Arrowsmith Catholic High Sch.

Ten. Cts.

STELEY

ROAD

Bowl. Grns.

BROADLAND

SINCLAIR

ROAD

TWO

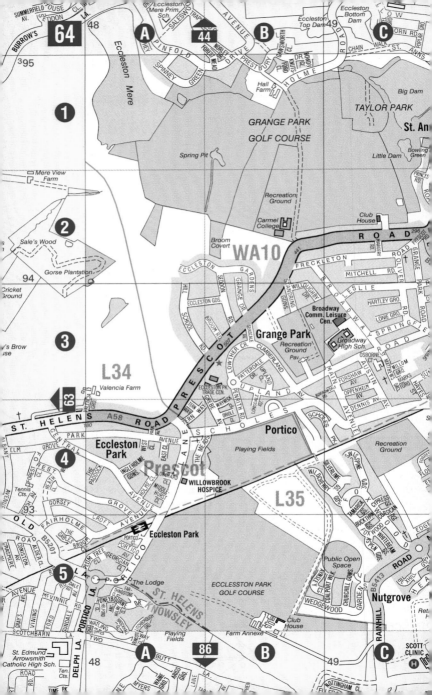

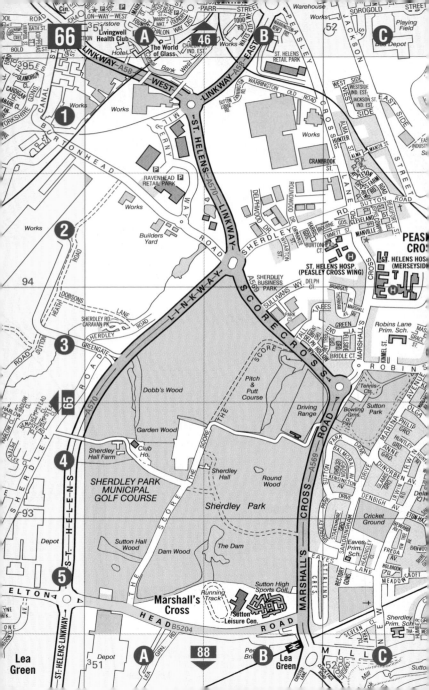

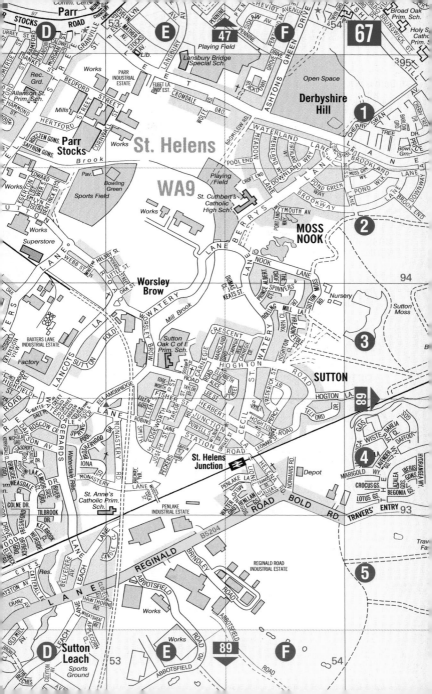

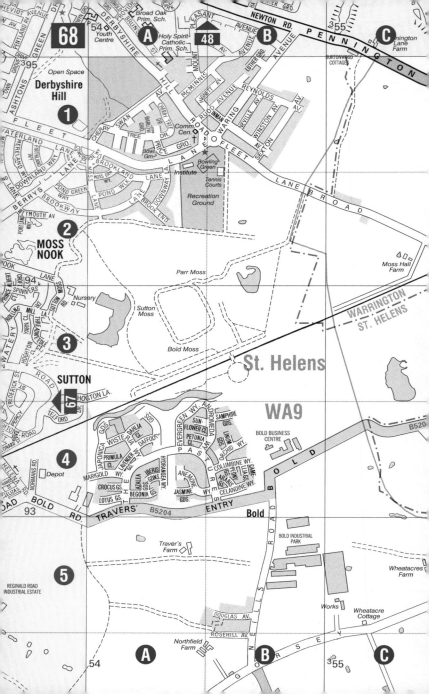

24

A

B

3 25

C

1

LIVERPOOL

92

2

3

Wallasey

LANE

Lighthouse
(Disused)

Th

91

North Wirral Coastal Park

Parkfield
House

LINGHAM

LA.

LINGHAM

Eve-a-lyn
Farm

Wirral

Birket

PARK

4

PARKFIELDS

guard
ion

CH47

91

The

PARK RD CARR

Sewage
Works

Great
Meols

5

L A.

CARR LANE

TERN

TERN WAY

TERN WAY

CURLEW WAY

CURLEW WAY

WASTDALE AV

WASTWATER

WASTDALE AV

CURLEW CT.

DREW WAY

WASTWATER WAY

MALLARD
WAY

BERMUDA DR

MALLARD WAY

MEADOW

SMITHY

LINEAR BROOK

HARDIE AV

BURTON

MILLHOUSE

MILLHOUSE
CLOSE

BESFORD

BLENFIELD

ARROW

ASBY CL.

BRANTFIELD

MILLHOUSE LANE

MAPLE CL.

GLENCROFT CL.

BERRY CL.

BELBY

OAKHAM

AUSTELL CL.

DARLING CL.

KEARNS

MORPETH CL.

FELTON CL.

ROTHWORT CL.

OAKHAM

TANWORTH

KESTREL

HUNTINGDON

ALNWICK CL.

HUXLEY CL.

KENNERTON

REDWOOD DR

BEDFORD

ALNWICK LANE

3 25

STOTFORD

SNOWDEN CL.

KESTREL

KESTREL

MACCOIN

A

24

92

RS

B

Clay Pit

C

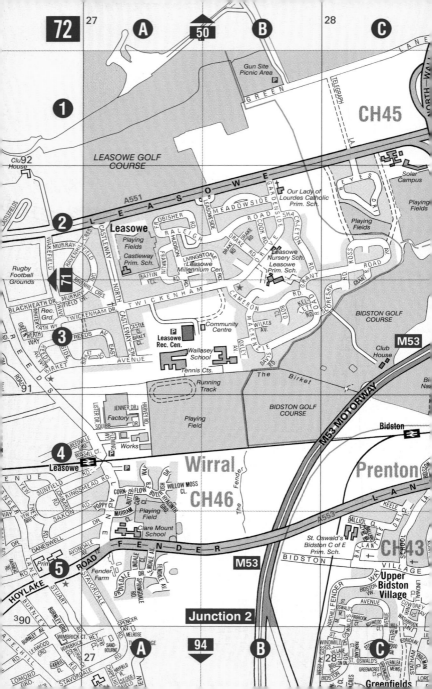

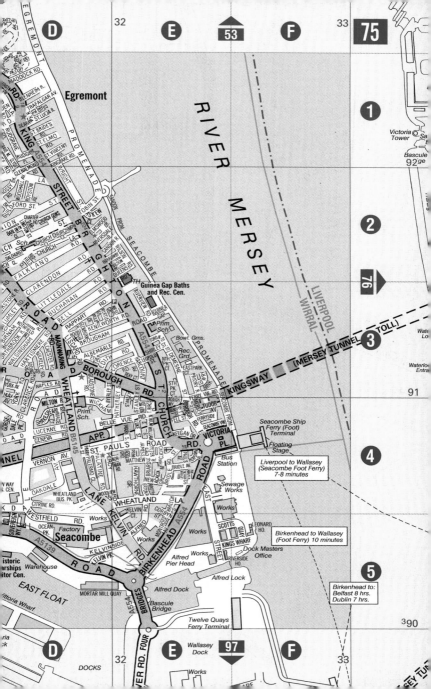

1

2

▶ **76**

3

91

4

5

390

Egremont

RIVER MERSEY

LIVERPOOL WIRRAL

KINGSWAY (MERSEY TUNNEL) [TOLL]

Victoria Tower

Bascule 92 ge

Wate Lo

Waterlo Entra

Guinea Gap Baths and Rec. Cen.

Seacombe Ship Ferry (Foot) Terminal

Floating Stage

Victoria PL.

Bus Station

Liverpool to Wallasey (Seacombe Foot Ferry) 7-8 minutes

Sewage Works

Works

Seacombe

Works

Works

Works

LEONARD HO.

SCOTTS QUAY

KINGS WHARF

Birkenhead to Wallasey (Foot Ferry) 10 minutes

Dock Masters Office

RIVERSIDE HO.

Alfred Pier Head

Alfred Lock

Factory

OCEAN PK.

CITRINE RD.

WHEATLAND BUS. PK.

Warehouse

istoric arships itor Cen.

EAST FLOAT

ittoria Wharf

MORTAR MILL QUAY

Alfred Dock

Bascule Bridge

Twelve Quays Ferry Terminal

Birkenhead to: Belfast 8 hrs. Dublin 7 hrs.

ria

Wallasey Dock

DOCKS

Works

MERSEY TUN

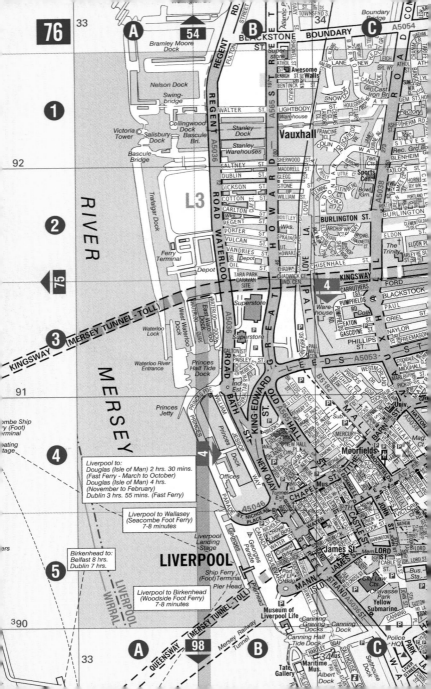

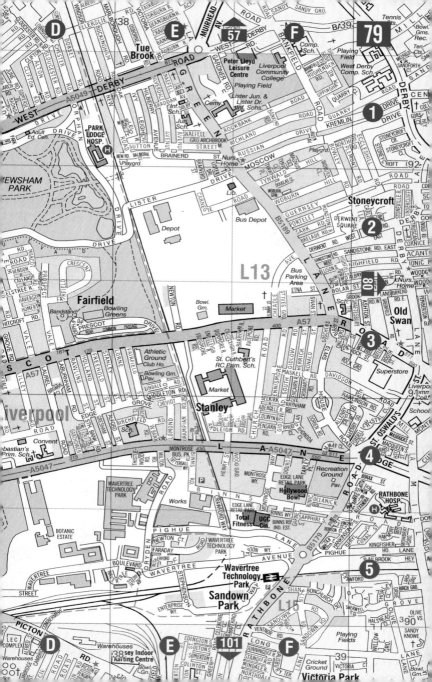

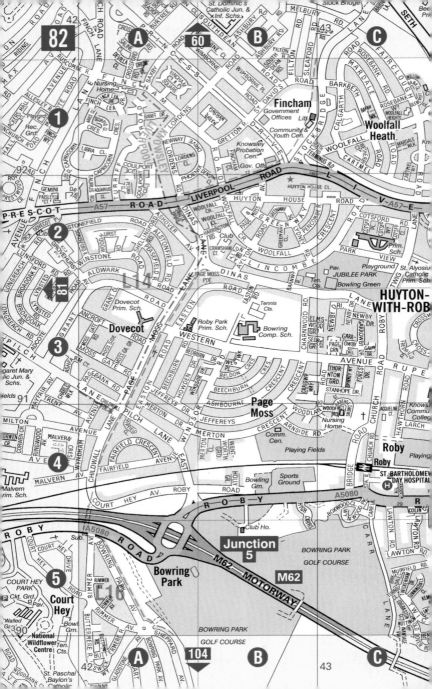

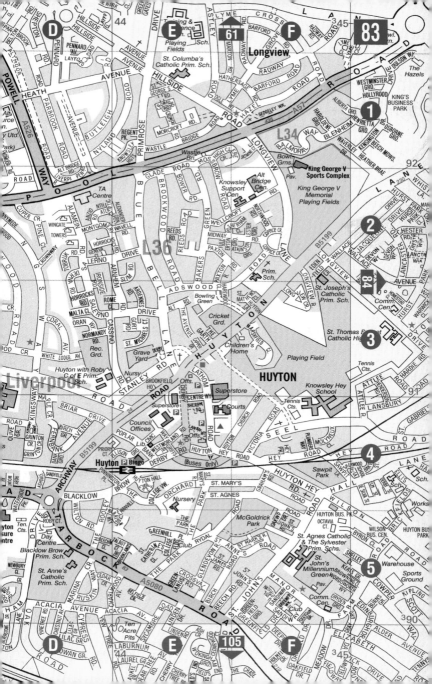

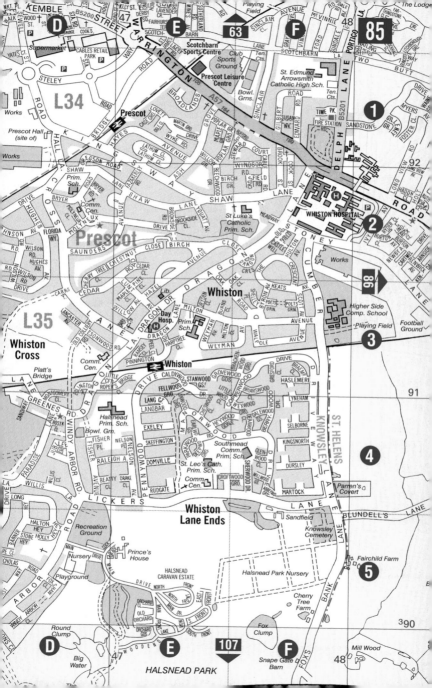

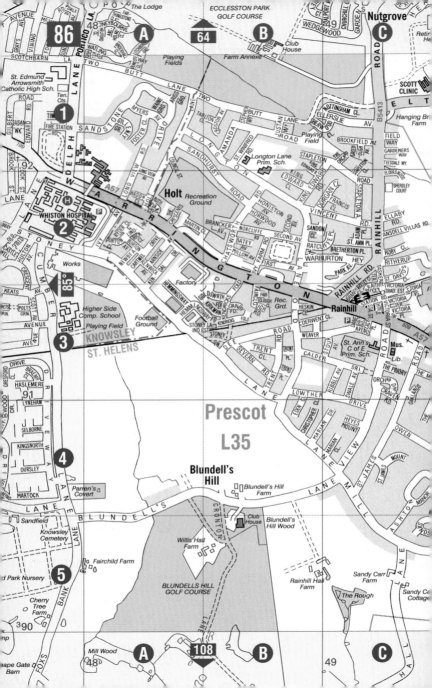

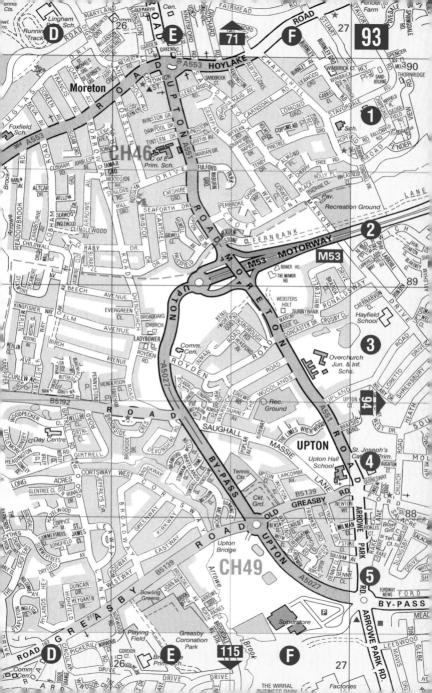

A

B 34 **C**

Birkenhead to Wallasey (Foot Ferry) 10 minutes

Birkenhead to: Belfast 8 hrs. Dublin 7 hrs.

1

76

(Foot Terminal)
Pier Head

Museum of Liverpool Life

Canning Graving Docks

Canning Dock

LIVERPOOL

Canning Half Tide Dock

Hartley Quay

Maritime Mus.

Tate Gallery

4

COMMON-WEALTH PAV.

ATLANTIC PAV.

BRITANNIA PAV.

Studio

The Beatles Story

Wapping Basin

Duke's Dock

ROYAL QUAY

Birkenhead Transport Mus.

WOODSIDE BUS. PARK

Liverpool to Birkenhead (Woodside Foot Ferry) 7-8 minutes

2

WOODSIDE FERRY BUS. STA.

GREAT WESTERN HOUSE

ROSEBRAE CT.

89

R I V E R

Wapping Dock

Customs & Excise

QUEENS

KINGS

PARADE

L3

Liverpool Watersports Centre

BIRKENHEAD

HORNBY ST
CASTLE ST.
WATER ST.
PILGRIM ST. Sch.

CHURCH ST

Monk's Ferry

3

Birkenhead Priory

PRIORY STREET

97

Works

Graving Docks

MARINERS

COBURG

WHARF

QUEBEC QUAY

4

Outer Basin

L I V E R P O O L   W I R R A L

M E R S E Y

88

Shipbuilding & Engineering Works

5

CAMPBELTOWN

Corporation Yard

Lairdside Maritime Cen.

TRANMERE

VANGUARD WY.

A

Floating Stage

120

B

34

C

RING ROAD

Pier

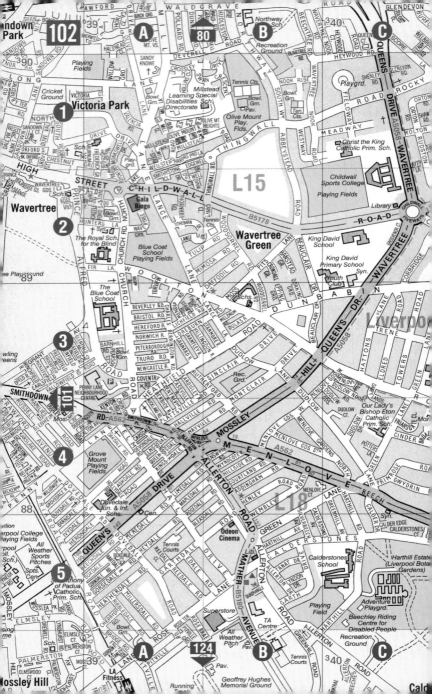

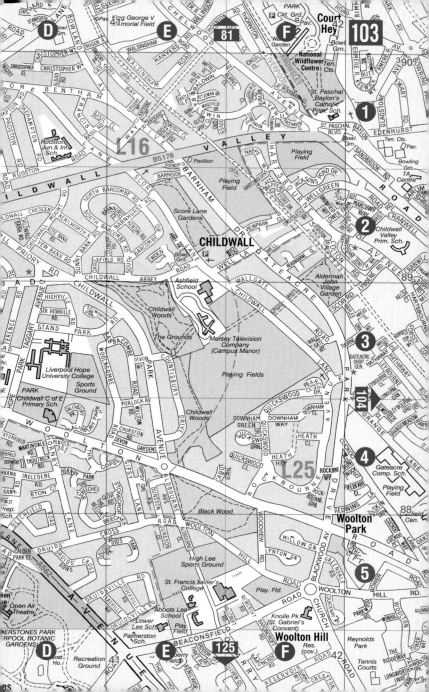

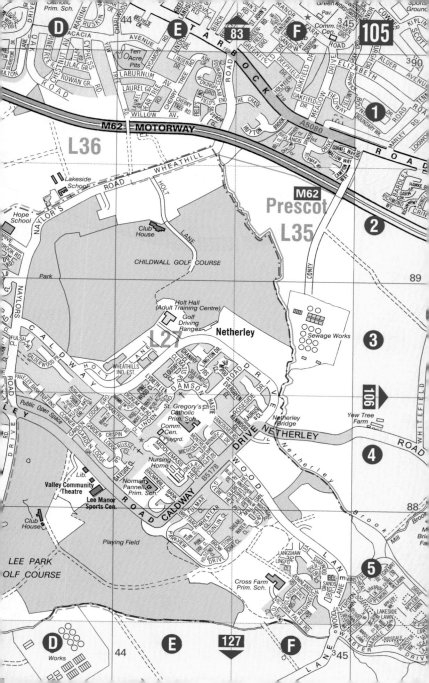

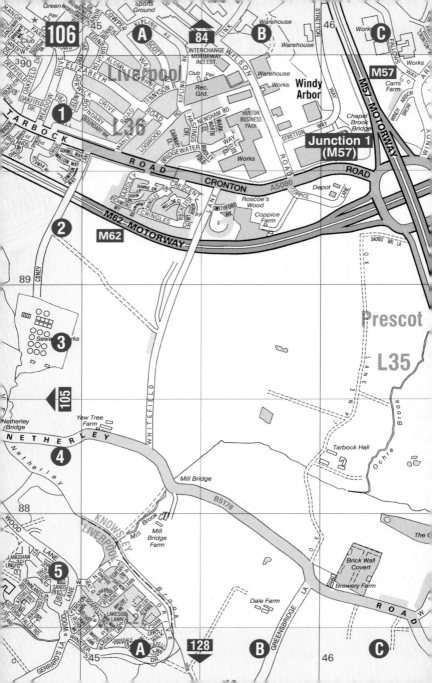

108 48

A

86

B

49 The Rough

C

Sandy Car Cottage

Cherry Tree Farm

390

Lape Gate Barn

BLUNDELLS HILL GOLF COURSE

Mill Wood

Prescot

L35

HALL LANE

1

SHAW

M62

M62 MOTORWAY

ST. HELENS

Brick Wood

ENTRY

CRONTON

KNOWSLEY

Higher Shaw Farm

Rough Head

BANK

2

Little Foxshaw

Bluebell Farm

PENNY LANE

Fox's - Bank Brook

HALL LANE

89

FOXS

Fox's Bank Farm

PENNY

Penny Lane Farm

LA.

LANE

PENNY

Town End

Town End Farm

3

C

A5080

R

O

N

T

O

N

TUE

LANE

LANE

THE RIDGEWAY

SMITHY

BROOK CL.

CRONTON IVER Prim. Sch.

HALL LANE

107

Gorse Lodge Nursery

George's Wood

WHEATFIELD RD.

SMITHY FORGE

HAMPTON

LAMBOURL

Lower House Farm

George's Hall

Welchman's Farm

WHEATFIELD RD.

4

Smaller Gorse Farm

LODGE LANE

Caxton Lodge

LANE

385

Rosewood Farm

CHAPE

88

Tan House Farm

ALDER

Dog Clog Bridge

5

STOCKSWELL

Stock's Well House

LODGE LANE

Alder Wood

COLUMBINE CL.

SUTTON

REDBOURNE DR.

NEWSHAM CL.

CHINWORTH DR.

OXINGTON

DR

HADDON

BROXTON CL.

BLAIR

BURNALL

RAVENFIELD

WORTH DR

HAMBL

A

130

B

ROAD

CHERRY

NORTHER

CHERRYS

SUTTON

All Saints Upton C of E Prim. Sch.

MADELEINE McKENNA

49

48

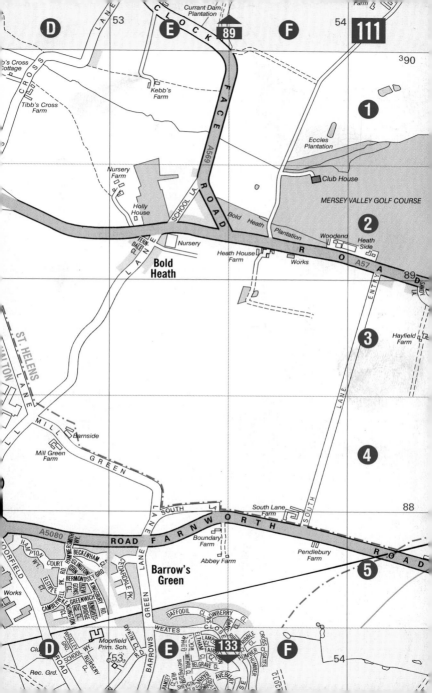

D

Tibb's Cross Cottage

Kebb's Farm

Tibb's Cross Farm

1

Eccles Plantation

Currant Dam Plantation

Farm

C L O C K F A C E

Nursery Farm

Holly House

CROSS LANE

A569 ROAD

SCHOOL LA.

Club House

MERSEY VALLEY GOLF COURSE

2

Nursery

FERN DALE CL

Bold Heath

Bold Heath Plantation

Heath House Farm

Works

Woodend

Heath Side

R O A D A57

89 D

SANDY L.

ST. HELENS

HATTON LANE

3

Hayfield Farm

ENTRY LANE

MILL GREEN

Barnside

Mill Green Farm

4

SOUTH LANE

South Lane Farm

88

A5080

Works

MOORFIELD

HAMPTON WY.

COURT

ESTREL CL.

CAMBERWELL

KENSINGTON

BECKENHAM WY.

ISLINGTON GRO.

KEW

BERMONDSEY GRO.

GREENWICH RO.

BRIDGE

LINGSBURY RD.

KIMBERLEY

CEDARDALE PK.

R O A D F A R N W O R T H R O A D

Barrow's Green

Boundary Farm

Abbey Farm

Pendlebury Farm

5

GREEN LANE

SOUTH LANE

DAFFODIL CL

COWBERRY CL.

CLOSE

WEATES

BARROWS

DYKIN CL

WHITLEY RD.

SCHOOL WY.

NURSERY CL.

Moorfield Prim. Sch.

Club

Rec. Grd.

D 53 **E** **133** **F** 54

LAMBOURN

FAIRBANK

W.M.

ELTHAM

MITRE CL.

BELGRAVE CL.

SHEVINGTON

RAMSEY

AVEBURY

MIRRAL CL.

CROSS GATES

PREBLE

HUMBER

PRIMULA

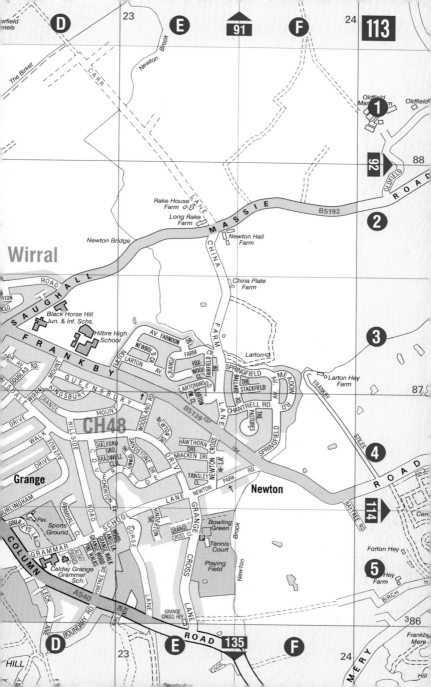

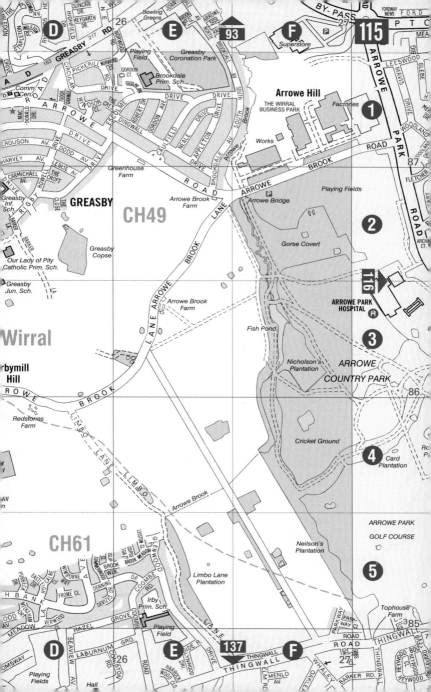

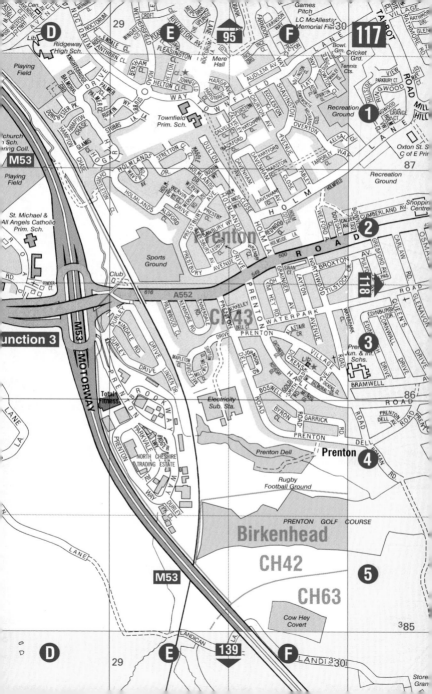

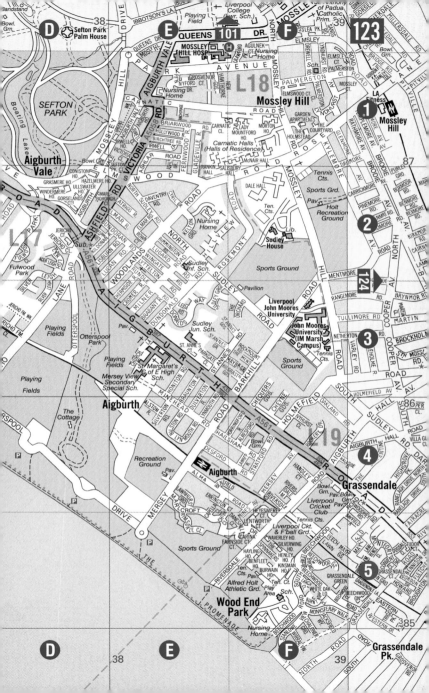

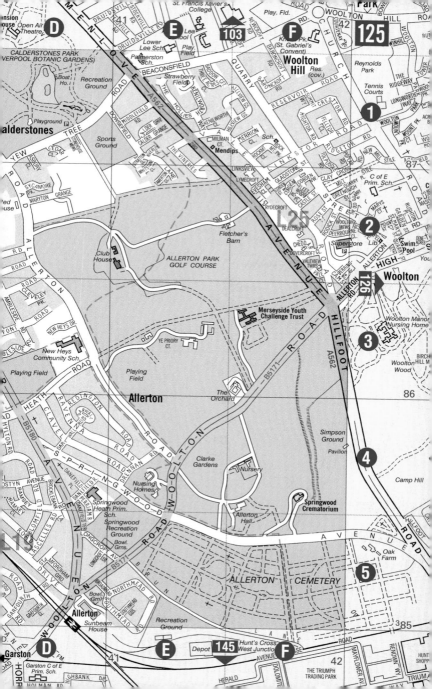

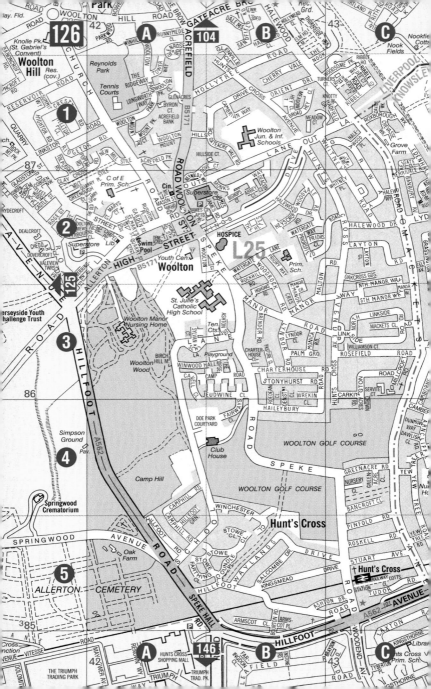

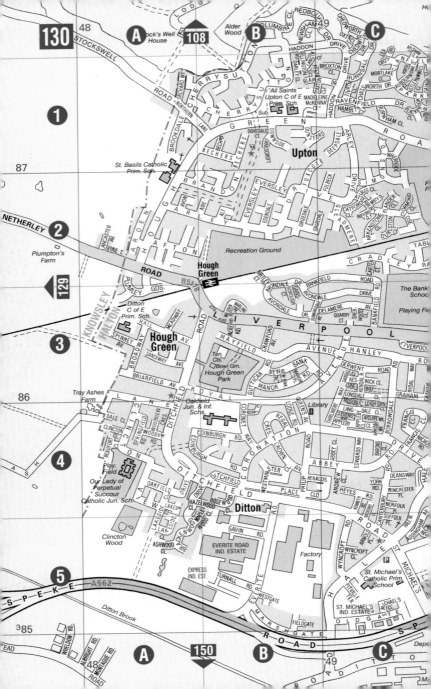

130

48

STOCKSWELL ROAD

A ock's Well House

▲ 108

B Alder Wood

COLUMBIA CL

REDBOLTH

NEWSHAM CL DR

CHEPWORTH

OXING CL

49

C

1

87

SUTTON

CHERRYDALE DR

ORCHARD DR

CHERRY

HADDON

BROXTON CL

BLAIR

WELLINGTON CL

BURTONWOOD

MADELEINE McKENNA

All Saints Upton C of E Prim. Sch.

Sub.

RAVENFIELD

HAMBLE

BURNSALL

WORTH DR

MORTLAKE CL

ROAD

BURNHAM CL

G R E E N

DOVEDALE CT.

DOWNSIDE

KESSINGTON

★

DEEPDALE

DUNSFORD

ARLEY

FOLCOTE

DEEPDALE

Upton

CATFORD

ARKENSTONE CLOSE

WAPENSIDE

St. Basils Catholic Prim. Sch.

BRANDON

BROUGH ARDEN ARLEY

EVERSLEY

EVERSLEY

EDENDALE

GRIZEDALE

GRAPEDALE

RUFFORD

DURLSTON

ORMOND CLOSE

DRIVE

AONDALE

NETHERLEY

2

Plumpton's Farm

LANCASTER AV.

VINE T

HOUGH ROAD

Recreation Ground

CRADLEY

CARTER AV

TABL

CRADLEY RA

▲ 129

PLUMLEY GDNS.

KNOWSLEY HALTON

Ditton C of E Prim. Sch.

MEADWAY

B5178

Hough Green

BRITELEY

MONDALE DR

AVONDALE

DELAMERE

BANKFIELD

AVONDALE DR.

SHER.

QUARRY AV.

BANKFIELD

ROAD

DRIVE

The Bank Schoo

Playing Fie

3

SPINNEY AV.

BROADWAY

HALL

SANDWAY

Hough Green

MAYFIELD AV

CRAWFORD AV

L I V E R P O O L

A V E N U E

HANLEY

ROAD

LIVERPOOL

BRIARFIELD AV.

Ten. Cts. Bowl Gm. Hough Green Park

GUTTICAR RD

NEW MANOR BANK RD

RAVEN

DERWENT

WICK CL

KENDAL

LONSDALE

LANG

APPLEBY

WAY

GRAHAM

WAY

4

86

Tray Ashes Farm

DALE CL

SPRINGHILL

WOODVIEW RD.

CLINCTON CL

BEAUFORT CL

ROYAL

DITCHFIELD

Oakfield Jun. & Inf. Schs.

★

CORONET CRES.

EDINBURGH RD.

DINBURGH

ROYK

CROWN

C O R O N A T I O N

WESTMINSTER

PLACE

QUEENS AV.

REGAL CL

LODGE RD

Library

THIRLMERE

BORROWDALE

ABBEY CL

ABBEY

FRANCIS CL

FRANCIS DR

Play Field

Our Lady of Perpetual Succour Catholic Jun. Sch.

OAKFIELD CL

LAKESIDE

LAKES

DRIVE

DITCHFIELD

HAZELWOOD CL

ROSEWAY

WOOD CL

MAPLE

Ditton

PHILIP HERALDS CLO

ANDREW

HEYES

EDWARDS WAY

BARONS

YORK RD.

DEANSWAY

WINCHESTER PL.

CANTERBURY

NORFOLK PL.

SUFFOLK PL.

Clinton Wood

ASHWOOD CL.

GAVIN RD.

EVERITE ROAD IND. ESTATE

Factory

WYNCROFT

ROAD

ST. MICHAEL'S

St. Michael's Catholic Prim. School

5

A562

S P E K E

EXPRESS IND. EST.

TURNALL

RD

EVERITE

LIMESGATE

MARSHGATE

FIELDGATE

ST. MICHAEL'S IND. ESTATE

MICHAEL'S

S P

Ditton Brook

R O A D

DITTON

Depo

385

48

WHELDON RD.

ALBRIGHT RD.

MONTAGUE RD.

ROAD

EAD

A

▼ 150

B

49

C

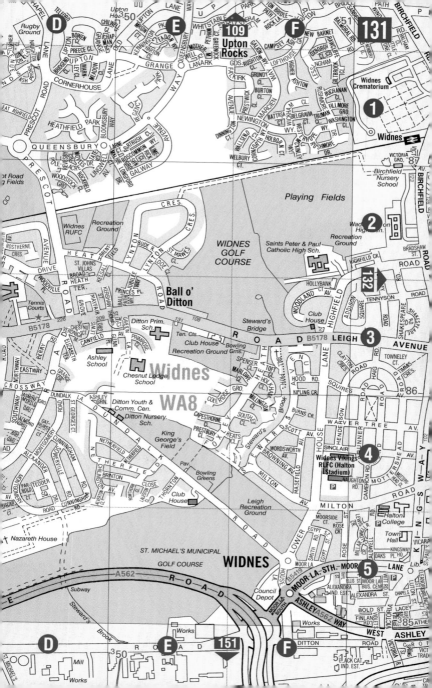

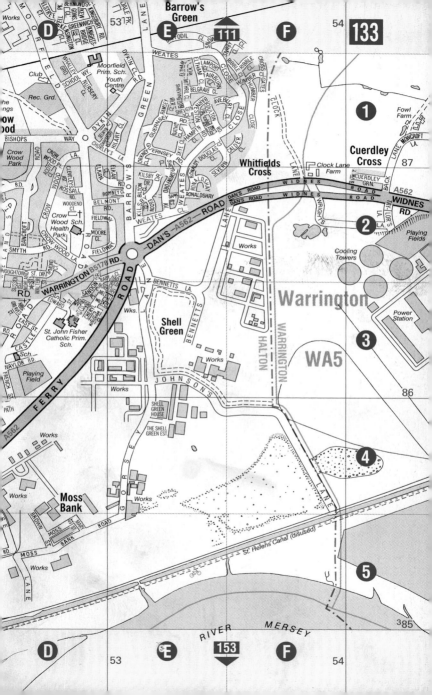

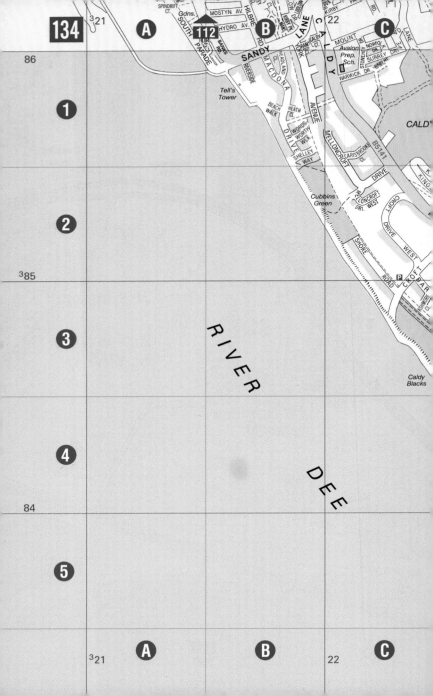

³21

A

SPINDRIFT CT.
Gdns.

MOSTYN AV.
HYDRO AV.

112

B

HILBRE RD.
BANKS RD.

YORK

LANE

CALDY

22

C

GLYN
KIRBY
RD.

MOUNT
Avalon DR.
Prep.
Sch.

NORFO
STONEHEY DR
SURREY DRI.
MINSTE CT.

WARWICK DR.

SANDY

RIVERSIDE

MACDONA

86

1

Tell's
Tower

BEACH
WALK

HEATH
CL.

AVENUE

WORDS-
WORTH
WLK.

SHELLEY
WAY

DRIVE

MELLONCROFT

CARISBROOKE
CL.

BS141

DRIVE

CALD*

CALD*

2

Cubbins
Green

DRI. WEST

CONCROFT

DRIVE

WEST

CROFT

SHORE

ROAD

KING

³85

P

BAR

3

R I V E R

Caldy
Blacks

84

4

D E E

5

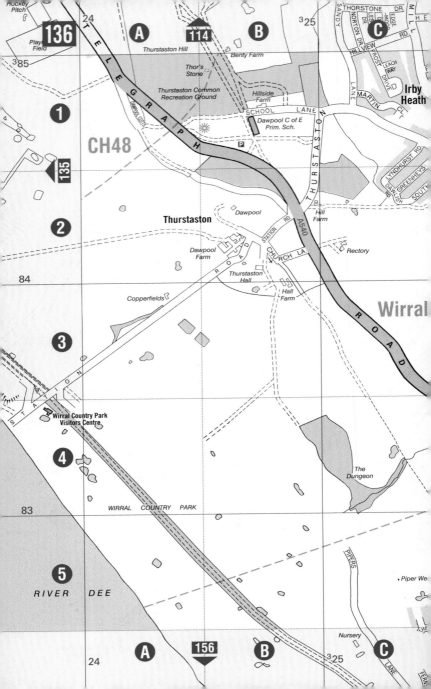

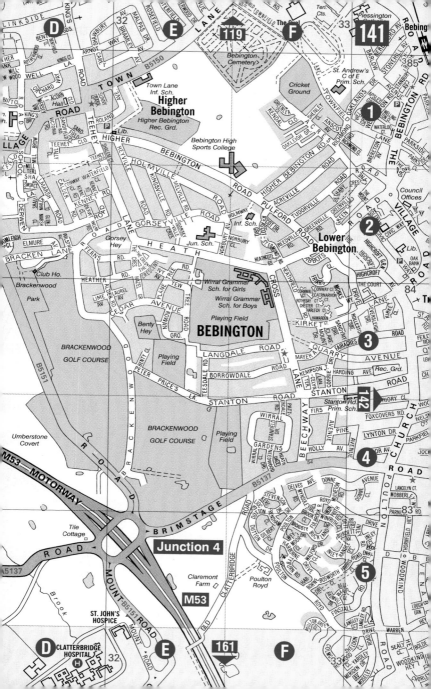

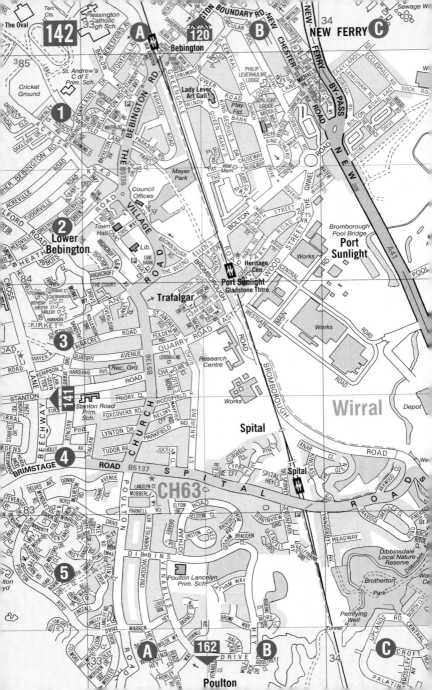

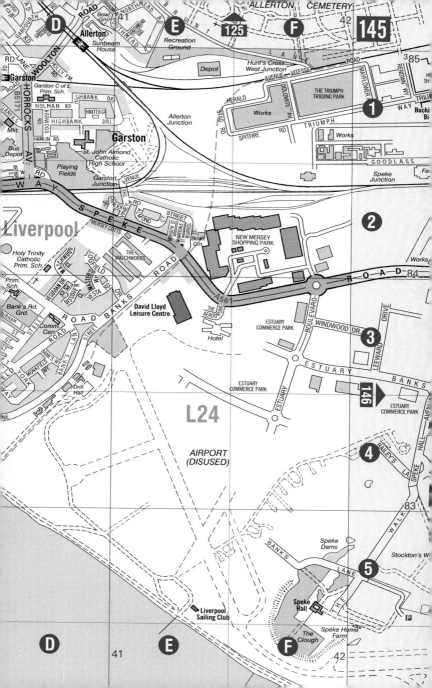

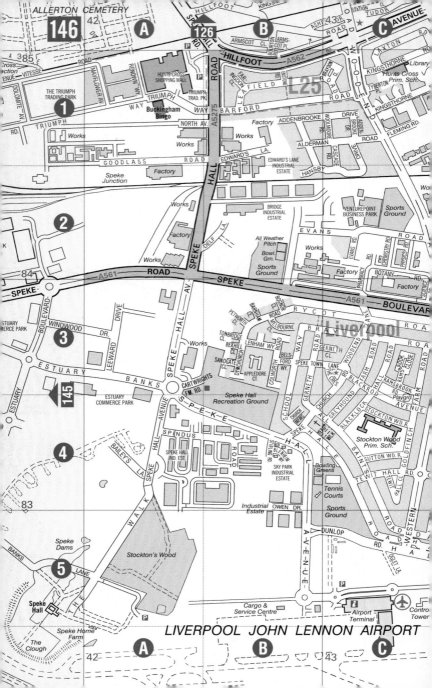

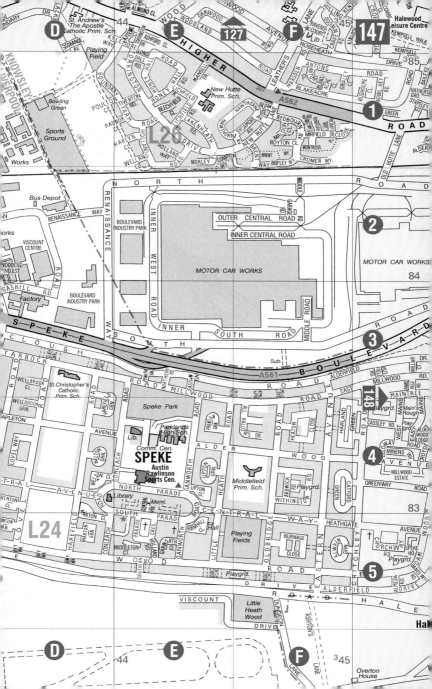

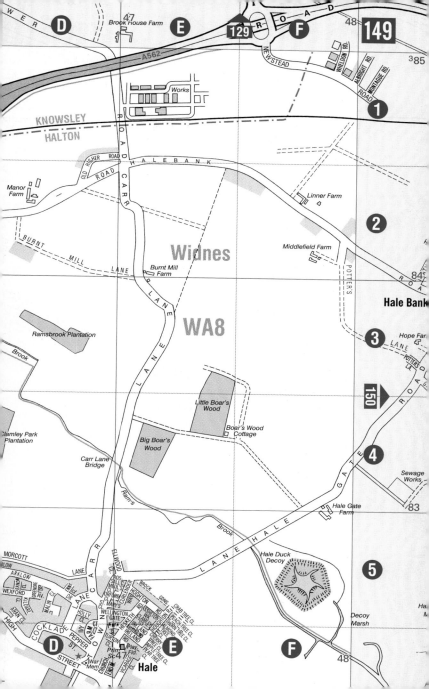

WER

D

Brook House Farm

E

129

NEWSTEAD

F

48

WHELDON RD.

ALBRIGHT RD.

MONTAGUE RD.

385

A562

Works

1

ROAD

KNOWSLEY

HALTON

OLD HIGHER ROAD

HALEBANK

Manor Farm

ROAD CARR

Linner Farm

2

Middlefield Farm

POTTER'S

ROAD

84

Hale Bank

BURNT

MILL

LANE

Burnt Mill Farm

Widnes

Ramsbrook Plantation

LANE

WA8

3

Hope Far

LANE

POTTER'S LA

Brook

Clamley Park Plantation

LANE

Little Boar's Wood

ROAD

150

Boar's Wood Cottage

Big Boar's Wood

4

Carr Lane Bridge

Ram's

Sewage Works

83

Brook

Hale Gate Farm

HALE

GATE

MORCOTT

ARKLOW

WEXFORD

Brook

LANE

ELWOOD

Hale Duck Decoy

LANE

5

HIGH

CARR

HOLLY

BROCK GDNS.

CRAB TREE CL.

PEACH TREE CL.

Decoy Marsh

Ha

COCKLADE

PEPPER ST.

WELLINGTON GATE

D

STREET

War Mem

Prim Sc

E

Play Fld.

F

48

Hale

48

A

130 **B**

49 **C**

St. Michael's School

ST. MICHAEL'S IND. ESTATE

MARSHGATE

WESTGATE

FIELDGATE

ROAD A562

SPEKE

HALE RD.

PITVILLE TER.

St. Michael's

OLDGATE

Depot

385 NEWSTEAD

WHELDON RD.

ALBRIGHT RD.

MONTAGUE RD.

ROAD

Ditton Brook

Widnes

1

ROAD

DITTON

Mill

WA8

Mills

CLAPGATE

CLAPGATE

LOVEL TER.

CRES.

STAPLETON WAY

HARRISON ST.

GOLDEN TRIANGLE INDUSTRIAL ESTATE

LANE

Halebank Rec. Grd.

BLACKBURN

CR.

HOWLING WAY

P

LANE

FOUNDRY

WATERSIDE LA.

DITTON

Ditton Brook

BAGULEY

BLACKBURN

AV.

MEADOW LINK

BROUGHTON WAY

FOUNDRY

LANE

2

HEATHVIEW

CHURCH

AVENUE

PICKERINGS

Works

HALE

Middlefield Farm

84

Linner Farm

HALEBANK

POTTER'S

CL.

KENVIEW CL.

Halebank Prim. Sch.

FREDERICK TER.

MEADOW CL.

PICKERINGS

Hale Road IND. EST.

ROAD

ROAD

Hale Bank

ROAD

MERSEY

COCK LANE ENDS

3

Hope Farm

LANE

POTTERS LA.

VIEW

Shore House

Pickerings Pasture Visitor Centre

149

GATE

GARNETT'S LA.

ROAD

4

Sewage Works

Pickerings Pasture Local Nature Reserve

83

HALE

Hale Gate Farm

R I V E R

Duck Decoy

5

Decoy Marsh

Hale Gate Marsh

Hale Gate Marsh

48

A

164 **B**

49

C

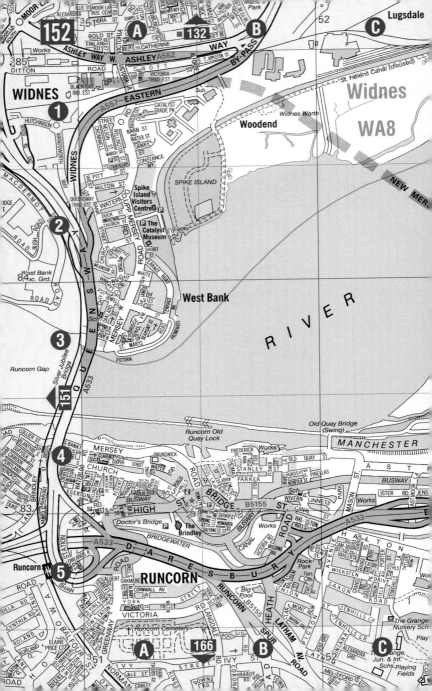

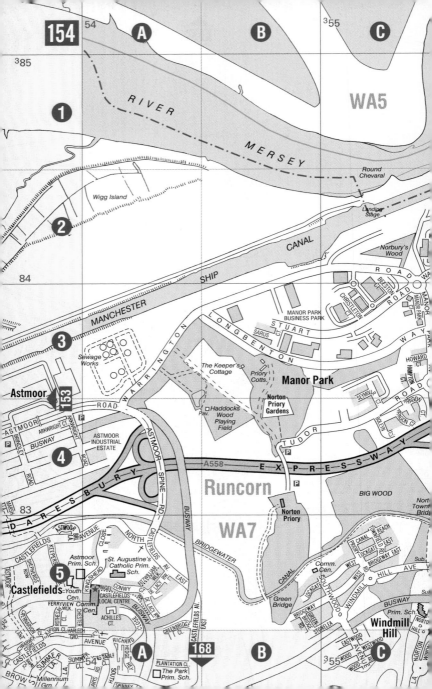

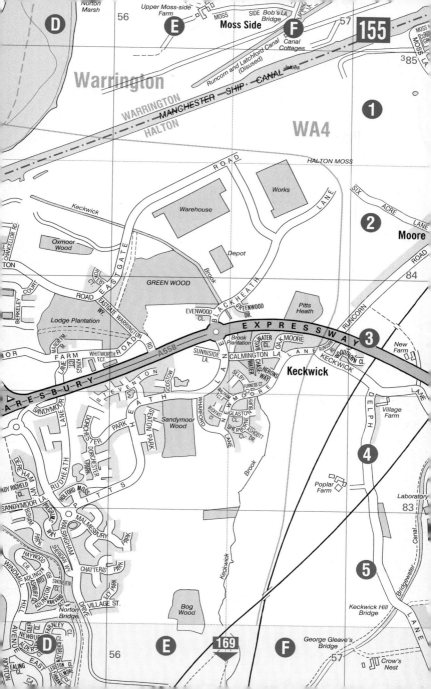

Brimstage

Brimstage Hall

160

The Brooklet

BRIMSTAGE ROAD

A5137

MANOR ROAD

TALBOT AVENUE

Boat House

Manor House

Pav.

159

Fish Ponds

Copley House

Westmead

Hesketh Grange

Lodge

GRANGE DR.

Croft Bank Cottages

Crofts Bank

COMMON

Wirra

CH63

Hill Top Farm

Lodge

Sch.

Thornton Hough

ST GEORGE'S

ST. MANOR

THORNTON

CHURCH RD.

Thornton House

SMITHY HILL

ROAD

R A B Y

Pav.

Recreation Ground

THE

FOUR

Lodge Farm

ETON DRIVE

OXFORD DRIVE

AUDLEY DRIVE

DRIVE

B5136

NESTON

ROAD

Nursery

Sewage Works

Thornton Farm Coach House

Fish Pond

NESTON LANE

WIDGEONS COVERT

Hotel

Westwood Farm

R O A D

Pear Tree Farm

Hillyard Farm

White Co

R A B Y

THE GREEN

Raby

Westwood Grange

ROAD

CROSSNA

Grange Farm

30

31

30

31

82

81

80

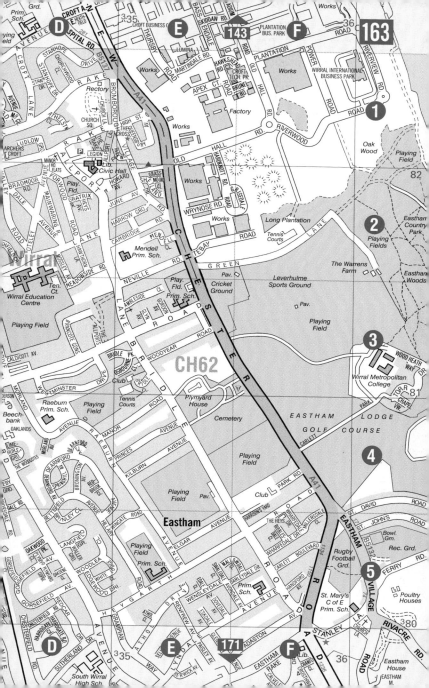

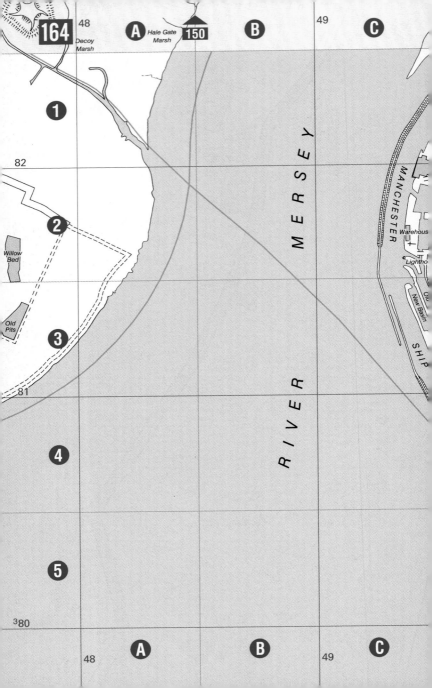

48

Hale Gate Marsh **150** **B** 49 **C**

Decoy Marsh

1

82

2

Willow Bed

Old Pits

3

81

4

5

³80

48 **A** **B** 49 **C**

MERSEY

RIVER

SHIP

MANCHESTER

Warehous

Lightho

Old New Basin

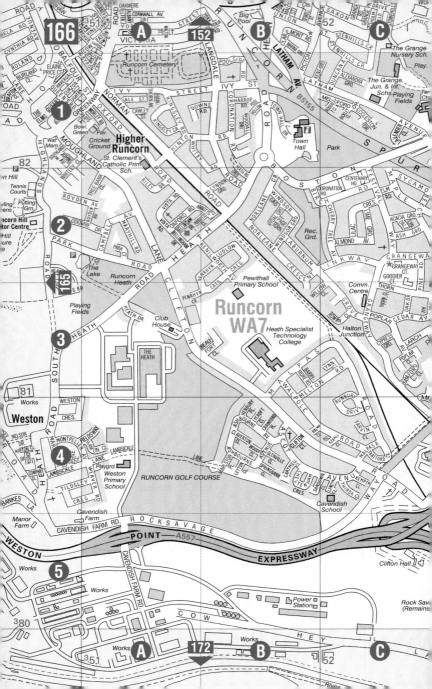

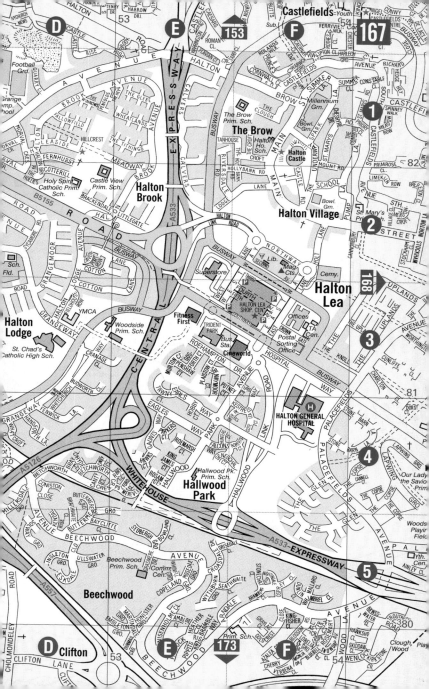

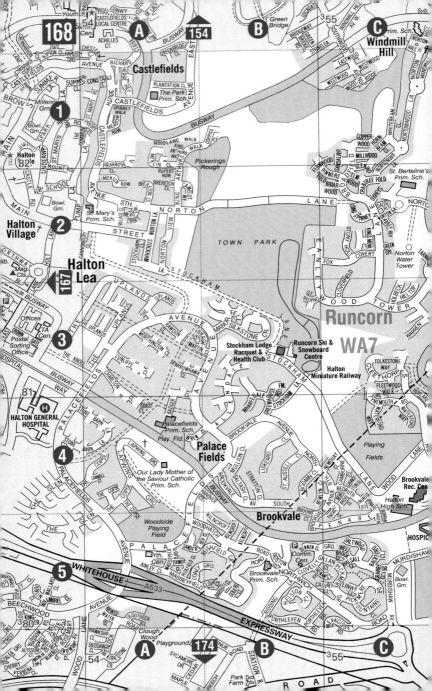

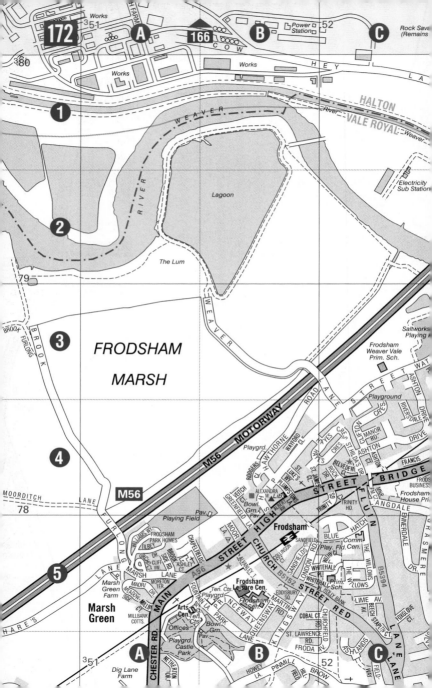

INDEX

Including Streets, Places & Areas, Industrial Estates, Selected Flats & Walkways,
Stations and Selected Places of Interest.

HOW TO USE THIS INDEX

1. Each street name is followed by its Postcode District and then by its Locality abbreviation(s) and then by its map reference; e.g. **Abacus Rd.** L13: Liv . . . .2A **80** is in the L13 Postcode District and the Liverpool Locality and is to be found in square 2A on page **80**. The page number is shown in bold type.

2. A strict alphabetical order is followed in which Av., Rd., St., etc. (though abbreviated) are read in full and as part of the street name; e.g. **Abbey St.** appears after **Abbeystead Rd.** but before **Abbeyvale Dr.**

3. Streets and a selection of flats and walkways too small to be shown on the maps, appear in the index with the thoroughfare to which it is connected shown in brackets; e.g. **Alexander Way** L8: Liv . . . .5F **99** (off Park Hill Rd.)

4. Addresses that are in more than one part are referred to as not continuous.

5. Places and areas are shown in the index in **BLUE TYPE** and the map reference is to the actual map square in which the town centre or area is located and not to the place name shown on the map; e.g. **AIGBURTH VALE** 2D **123**

6. An example of a selected place of interest is **Aintree Racecourse** 4C **20**

7. An example of a station is **Aigburth Station (Rail)** . . . .4E **123**. Included are Rail **(Rail)** and Park and Ride **(Park and Ride)**

8. Map references shown in brackets; e.g. **Addison St.** L3: Liv . . . .3D **77** (2E **4**) refer to entries that also appear on the large scale pages **4** & **5**.

GENERAL ABBREVIATIONS

All. : Alley	**Fld.** : Field	**Pde.** : Parade
App. : Approach	**Flds.** : Fields	**Pk.** : Park
Arc. : Arcade	**Gdn.** : Garden	**Pas.** : Passage
Av. : Avenue	**Gdns.** : Gardens	**Pav.** : Pavilion
Bk. : Back	**Gth.** : Garth	**Pl.** : Place
Blvd. : Boulevard	**Ga.** : Gate	**Pct.** : Precinct
Bri. : Bridge	**Gt.** : Great	**Prom.** : Promenade
B'way. : Broadway	**Grn.** : Green	**Ri.** : Rise
Bldg. : Building	**Gro.** : Grove	**Rd.** : Road
Bldgs. : Buildings	**Hgts.** : Heights	**Shop.** : Shopping
Bus. : Business	**Ho.** : House	**Sth.** : South
Cvn. : Caravan	**Ind.** : Industrial	**Sq.** : Square
C'way. : Causeway	**Info.** : Information	**Sta.** : Station
Cen. : Centre	**Intl.** : International	**St.** : Street
Chu. : Church	**Junc.** : Junction	**Ter.** : Terrace
Cl. : Close	**La.** : Lane	**Twr.** : Tower
Comn. : Common	**Lit.** : Little	**Trad.** : Trading
Cnr. : Corner	**Lwr.** : Lower	**Up.** : Upper
Cott. : Cottage	**Mnr.** : Manor	**Va.** : Vale
Cotts. : Cottages	**Mans.** : Mansions	**Vw.** : View
Ct. : Court	**Mkt.** : Market	**Vs.** : Villas
Cres. : Crescent	**Mdw.** : Meadow	**Vis.** : Visitors
Cft. : Croft	**Mdws.** : Meadows	**Wlk.** : Walk
Dr. : Drive	**M.** : Mews	**W.** : West
E. : East	**Mt.** : Mount	**Yd.** : Yard
Ent. : Enterprise	**Mus.** : Museum	
Est. : Estate	**Nth.** : North	

LOCALITY ABBREVIATIONS

Aig : **Aigburth**	Caldy : **Caldy**	Gars : **Garswood**
Ain : **Aintree**	Cas : **Castlefields**	Gate : **Gateacre**
Aller : **Allerton**	Chil T : **Childer Thornton**	Gras : **Grassendale**
Ast : **Astmoor**	Child : **Childwall**	Grea : **Greasby**
Aston : **Aston**	C'ton : **Claughton**	Hale : **Hale**
Augh : **Aughton**	Clftn : **Clifton**	Hale B : **Hale Bank**
Barn : **Barnston**	Clock F : **Clock Face**	Halew : **Halewood**
Beb : **Bebington**	C Grn : **Collins Green**	Halt : **Halton**
Beech : **Beechwood**	Crank : **Crank**	Hay : **Haydock**
Bic : **Bickerstaffe**	Cron : **Cronton**	Hel : **Helsby**
Bid : **Bidston**	C'by : **Crosby**	Hes : **Heswall**
Bil : **Billinge**	Crox : **Croxteth**	High B : **Higher Bebington**
Birk : **Birkenhead**	Cuerd : **Cuerdley**	H Walt : **Higher Walton**
Blun : **Blundellsands**	Dares : **Daresbury**	High : **Hightown**
Bold : **Bold**	Dutt : **Dutton**	Hoot : **Hooton**
Bold H : **Bold Heath**	East : **Eastham**	Hoy : **Hoylake**
Boot : **Bootle**	Eccl : **Eccleston**	Hunts X : **Hunts Cross**
Brim : **Brimstage**	Ecc P : **Eccleston Park**	Huy : **Huyton**
B Grn : **Broad Green**	Faz : **Fazakerley**	Ince B : **Ince Blundell**
Brom : **Bromborough**	Ford : **Ford**	Irby : **Irby**
Brook : **Brookvale**	Frank : **Frankby**	K'by : **Kirkby**
Burt : **Burton**	Frod : **Frodsham**	Kirk : **Kirkdale**
B'wood : **Burtonwood**	Gars : **Garston**	K Ash : **Knotty Ash**

Know : **Knowsley**
Know I : **Knowsley Industrial Park**
Know P : **Knowsley Park**
Leas : **Leasowe**
Lith : **Litherland**
Lit C : **Little Crosby**
Lit Sut : **Little Sutton**
Liv : **Liverpool**
Lyd : **Lydiate**
Mag : **Maghull**
Mnr P : **Manor Park**
Mell : **Melling**
Meols : **Meols**
Moore : **Moore**
More : **Moreton**
Moss H : **Mossley Hill**
Murd : **Murdishaw**
Nest : **Neston**
N'ley : **Netherley**
N'ton : **Netherton**
New B : **New Brighton**
New F : **New Ferry**
New W : **Newton-le-Willows**
Noct : **Nocturum**
N Grn. : **Norris Green**
Nort : **Norton**

O'ton : **Oxton**
Pal F : **Palace Fields**
Park : **Parkgate**
Penk : **Penketh**
Pens : **Pensby**
Port S : **Port Sunlight**
Pren : **Prenton**
Prsct : **Prescot**
Pres B : **Preston Brook**
Pres H : **Preston on the Hill**
Raby : **Raby**
Raby M : **Raby Mere**
R'ford : **Rainford**
R'hill : **Rainhill**
Roby : **Roby**
R Ferr : **Rock Ferry**
Run : **Runcorn**
St. H : **St Helens**
Sea : **Seaforth**
Seft : **Sefton**
Sim : **Simonswood**
Speke : **Speke**
Spit : **Spital**
Stock V : **Stockbridge Village**
Store : **Storeton**
Sut L : **Sutton Leach**

Sut M : **Sutton Manor**
Sut W : **Sutton Weaver**
Tar G : **Tarbock Green**
Thing : **Thingwall**
Thorn : **Thornton**
Thorn H : **Thornton Hough**
Thurs : **Thurstaston**
Tran : **Tranmere**
Upton : **Upton**
Wall : **Wallasey**
Walt : **Walton**
Water : **Waterloo**
W'tree : **Wavertree**
W Der : **West Derby**
W Kir : **West Kirby**
West : **Weston**
West P : **Weston Point**
Whis : **Whiston**
Wid : **Widnes**
Will : **Willaston**
Windle : **Windle**
Wind H : **Windmill Hill**
W'chu : **Woodchurch**
Wltn : **Woolton**

20, Forthlin Road
(Childhood Home of Paul McCartney)
. . . . .3C **124**

A

A41 Expressway CH42: Tran 1F **119**
Abacus Rd. L13: Liv 2A **80**
Abberley Cl. WA10: St. H 5F **45**
Abberley Rd. L25: Hunts X 5C **126**
Abberton Pk. L30: N'ton 5A **12**
Abbey Cl. CH41: Birk 4F **97**
 L33: K'by 3F **23**
 WA8: Wid 4C **130**
Abbey Ct. L25: Wltn 2B **126**
Abbeyfield Dr. L12: Crox 4D **39**
Abbey Hey WA7: Nort 2C **168**
Abbey Rd. CH48: W Kir 4B **112**
 L6: Liv 5B **56**
 WA8: Wid 4C **130**
 WA10: St. H 1D **45**
 WA11: Hay 1E **49**
Abbeystead Av. L30: N'ton 4A **20**
Abbeystead Rd. L15: W'tree 1B **102**
Abbey St. CH41: Birk 4F **97**
Abbeyvale Dr. L25: Gate 5F **127**
Abbey Vw. L16: Child 2E **103**
Abbeyway Nth. WA11: Hay 1F **49**
Abbeyway Sth. WA11: Hay 1F **49**
Abbeywood Gro. L35: Whis 4F **85**
Abbot Cl. CH43: Bid 3C **94**
Abbotsbury Way L12: Crox 5E **39**
Abbots Bus. Pk. WA7: Pres B . . .5E **169**
Abbots Dr. CH63: Beb 2F **141**
Abbotsfield Rd. WA9: St. H 5E **67**
 (not continuous)
Abbotsford Ct. L23: Blun 2C **16**
Abbotsford Gdns. L23: C'by 2C **16**
Abbotsford Rd. L11: N Grn. 1E **57**
 L23: Blun 2C **16**
Abbotsford St. CH44: Wall 4E **75**
Abbots Hall Av. WA9: Clock F . . .3D **89**
Abbots Way CH48: W Kir 3C **112**
 WN5: Bil 2D **31**
Abbott Dr. L20: Boot 3E **35**
Abbotts Cl. L18: Moss H 1B **124**
 WA7: Run 2A **166**
Abbottshey Av. L18: Moss H 1B **124**
Abdale Rd. L11: N Grn. 5F **37**
Abercrombie Rd. L33: Know I 1B **40**
Abercromby Sq. L7: Liv 5F **77**
 (not continuous)
Aberdale Rd. L13: Liv 3B **80**

Aberdeen St. CH41: Birk 2C **96**
Aberford Av. CH45: Wall 1E **73**
Abergele Rd. L13: Liv 4F **79**
Aber St. L6: Liv 3A **78**
Abingdon Gro. L4: Walt 1C **56**
 L26: Halew 3A **128**
Abingdon Rd. CH49: Grea 1B **114**
 L4: Walt 1C **56**
Abington Wlk. WA7: Brook 5C **168**
Abney Cl. L7: Liv 1B **100**
Aboyne Cl. L9: Walt 4A **36**
Abram Cl. L5: Liv 1E **77**
Abyssinia Cl. L15: W'tree 2E **101**
Acacia Av. L36: Huy 5D **83**
 WA8: Wid 1B **132**
Acacia Cl. CH49: Grea 3C **114**
Acacia Gro. CH44: Wall 4E **75**
 CH48: W Kir 4A **112**
 L9: Ain 2B **36**
 WA7: Run 2C **166**
 WA10: Eccl 4A **44**
Acacia St. WA12: New W 4F **49**
Academy Bus. Pk. L33: Know I . . .4A **24**
Academy, The (LFC) 3A **24**
Acanthus Rd. L13: Liv 2A **80**
Access Rd. L19: W Der 4D **59**
Acer Leigh L17: Aig 2D **123**
Acheson Rd. L13: Liv 5E **57**
Achilles Ct. WA7: Cas 5A **154**
Ackers Hall Av. L14: K Ash 2F **81**
Ackers Hall Cl. L14: K Ash 1F **81**
Ackers La. L23: Lit C 3C **8**
 WA10: St. H 4C **44**
Ackers Rd. CH49: W'chu 2C **116**
Ackers St. L34: Prsct 5D **63**
Acland Rd. CH44: Wall 2B **74**
Aconbury Cl. L11: N Grn. 5F **37**
Aconbury Pl. L11: N Grn. 5F **37**
Acorn Bus. Cen.
 L33: Know I 4B **24**
Acorn Cl. CH63: High B 1D **141**
 WA9: Clock F 2C **88**
Acorn Ct. L8: Liv 3E **99**
Acornfield Cl. L33: Know I 5C **24**
Acornfield Rd. L33: Know I 4D **25**
Acorn Venture Urban Farm 1D **25**
Acorn Way L20: Boot 3D **35**
Acrefield Bank L25: Wltn 1A **126**
Acrefield Ct. CH42: Tran 3B **118**
Acrefield Pk. L25: Wltn 1A **126**
Acrefield Rd. CH42: Tran 3B **118**
 L25: Wltn 5A **104**
 WA8: Wid 3B **130**
Acre Grn. L26: Halew 1A **148**
Acre La. CH60: Hes 1C **158**
 CH62: Brom 5A **142**
 CH63: Brom 3C **162**

Acres Cl. L25: Gate 2A **104**
Acresfield L13: Liv 4B **80**
Acresgate Ct. L25: Gate 3A **104**
Acres La. L31: Lyd 1A **6**
Acres Rd. CH47: Meols 4F **91**
 CH63: Beb 1F **141**
Acreville Rd. CH63: Beb 2F **141**
Acton Cl. WA11: Hay 2C **48**
Acton Gro. L6: Liv 5C **56**
Acton La. CH46: More 2C **92**
Acton Rake L30: N'ton 5D **11**
Acton Rd. CH42: R Ferr 3A **120**
 L32: K'by 3C **22**
 WA5: B'wood 5E **69**
Acton Way L7: Liv 1C **100**
Acuba Gro. CH42: Tran 5E **97**
Acuba Rd. L15: W'tree 5C **80**
Adair Pl. L13: Liv 4E **57**
Adair Rd. L13: Liv 4E **57**
Adam Cl. L19: Gars 2C **144**
Adam St. L5: Liv 5F **55**
Adaston Av. CH62: East 1F **171**
Adcote Cl. L14: K Ash 3F **81**
Adcote Rd. L14: K Ash 3F **81**
Addenbrooke Dr. L24: Speke 1B **146**
Adderley Av. WA7: Run 1C **166**
Adderley St. L7: Liv 4B **78**
Addingham Av. WA8: Wid 5C **130**
Addingham Rd. L18: Moss H 4B **102**
Addington St. CH44: Wall 3D **75**
Addison Cl. L32: K'by 5D **23**
Addison Sq. WA8: Wid 3F **131**
Addison St. L3: Liv 3D **77** (2E **4**)
 L20: Boot 3A **34**
Addison Way L3: Liv 3D **77** (2E **4**)
Adelaide Av. WA9: St. H 4E **65**
Adelaide Rd. WA8: Wid 5A **132**
Adelaide Pl. L5: Liv 2E **77**
Adelaide Rd. CH42: Tran 5C **96**
 L7: Liv 4A **78**
 (not continuous)
 L21: Sea 1F **33**
Adelaide St. CH44: Wall 3B **74**
Adelaide Ter. L22: Water 4C **16**
Adela Rd. WA7: Run 5F **151**
Adele Thompson Dr. L8: Liv 2A **100**
Adelphi St. CH41: Birk 3E **97**
Adkins St. L5: Liv 5A **56**
Adlam Cres. L9: Faz 1E **37**
Adlam Rd. L9: Faz 1E **37**
 L10: Faz 1E **37**
Adlington Ho. L3: Liv 3D **77** (2E **4**)
Adlington Rd. WA7: Wind H 5D **155**
Adlington St. L3: Liv 2E **4**
Admin Rd. L33: Know I 5C **24**
Admiral Gro. L8: Liv 3A **100**

Admiral St. L8: Liv 4F 99
Adrian's Way L32: K'by 3E 23
Adshead Rd. L13: Liv 4E 57
Adstone Rd. L25: Gate 4C 104
Adswood Rd. L36: Huy 3E 83
Aerodrome, The
    L24: Speke 3E 145
Africander Rd. WA11: St. H 5A 30
Afton WA8: Wid 2A 130
Agar Rd. L11: N Grn. 4F 57
Agate St. L5: Liv 1A 78
Agincourt Rd. L12: W Der 1C 80
Agnes Gro. CH44: Wall 1C 74
Agnes Jones Ho. L8: Liv 1F 99 (7J 5)
Agnes Rd. CH42: Tran 1D 119
    L23: Blun 2C 16
Agnes St. WA9: Clock F 3C 88
Agnes Way L7: Liv 5B 78
Aguinek Cl. L18: Moss H 5F 101
Aiden Long Gro.
    L34: Know P 5E 61
AIGBURTH .4E 123
Aigburth Dr. L17: Aig 4C 100
Aigburth Gro. CH46: More 1D 93
Aigburth Hall Av. L19: Aig 4F 123
Aigburth Hall Rd. L19: Aig 4A 124
Aigburth Ho. L17: Aig 1E 123
Aigburth Rd. L17: Aig 5B 100
    L19: Aig 3E 123
Aigburth Station (Rail) 4E 123
Aigburth St. L7: Liv 1B 100
AIGBURTH VALE 2D 123
Aigburth Va. L17: Aig 2D 123
                    (not continuous)
Ailsa Rd. CH45: Wall 1A 74
Ainley Cl. WA7: Brook 5A 168
Ainsdale Cl. CH61: Thing 2A 138
    CH63: Brom 5C 162
    L10: Faz 5F 21
Ainsdale Rd. L20: Boot 2D 35
Ainsworth Av. CH46: More 3C 92
Ainsworth La. L34: Know 2B 40
Ainsworth Rd. WA10: St. H 3D 45
Ainsworth St. L3: Liv 5E 77 (5H 5)
AINTREE 3D 21
Aintree Cl. CH46: Leas 3F 71
Aintree Ct. L10: Ain 2C 20
Aintree La. L10: Ain 2C 20
    L10: Faz 4F 21
Aintree Racecourse 4C 20
Aintree Racecourse Retail & Bus. Pk.
    L9: Ain .3B 20
Aintree Rd. L9: Ain 2D 37
    L20: Boot 4D 35
Aintree Station (Rail) 5B 20
Aintree Vis. Cen. &
    Grand National Experience
    . . . . .4B 20
Aintree Way L9: Ain 3C 20
Airdale Cl. CH43: Bid 3C 94
Airdale Rd. L15: W'tree 3E 101
Airdrie Cl. CH62: East 2D 171
Aire WA8: Wid 2B 130
Airegate L31: Mag 5B 6
Airlie Gro. L13: Liv 5D 57
Airlie Rd. CH47: Hoy 5B 90
Aisthorpe Gro. L31: Mag 3D 13
Akbar, The CH60: Hes 1C 158
Akenside Ct. L20: Boot 2A 34
Akenside St. L20: Boot 2A 34
Alabama Way CH41: Birk 3F 97
Alamein Rd. L36: Huy 2D 83
Alan's Way L33: K'by 1E 23
Alastair Cres. CH43: Pren 3F 117
Alban Rd. L16: Child 1D 103
Albany Av. L34: Ecc P 4F 63
Albany Rd. CH42: R Ferr 2E 119
    L7: Liv .4A 78
    L9: Ain .1B 36
    L13: Liv 2A 80
    L34: Prsct 5E 63
Albany Ter. WA7: Run 5A 152
Albemarle Rd. CH44: Wall 3D 75
Alberta Gro. L34: Prsct 1F 83
Albert Dr. L9: Walt 2F 35

Albert Edward Rd. L7: Liv 4A 78
                    (not continuous)
Albert Gro. L15: W'tree 1A 102
    L23: C'by 1D 17
Albert Pk. L17: Aig 4B 100
Albert Rd. CH42: Tran 5C 96
    CH47: Hoy 5B 90
    CH48: W Kir 5A 112
    L13: Liv 5D 57
    L22: Water 4D 17
    WA8: Wid 4B 132
Albert Row WA6: Frod 4B 137
Albert Schweitzer Av. L30: N'ton . . .2F 19
Albert Sq. WA8: Wid 4B 132
Albert St. CH45: New B 2C 52
    L7: Liv .5A 78
    WA7: Run 5A 152
    WA10: St. H 3A 46
Albert Ter. WA5: C Grn 2E 65
Albion Pl. CH45: New B 3B 52
Albion St. CH41: Birk 3F 97
                    (not continuous)
    CH45: New B 3A 52
    L5: Liv .5E 55
    WA10: St. H 5E 45
                    (not continuous)
Albourne Rd. L32: K'by 5A 24
Albright Rd. WA8: Wid 1A 150
Albury Cl. L12: Crox 1F 59
    WA11: Hay 1C 48
Albury Rd. L32: K'by 1F 39
Alcester Rd. L12: W Der 5C 58
Alcock St. WA7: Run 4A 152
Aldams Gro. L4: Kirk 2E 55
Aldbourne Av. L25: Wltn 4E 103
Aldbourne Cl. L25: Wltn 5E 103
Alder Av. L36: Huy 1A 106
    WA8: Wid 1A 132
Alder Cl. L34: Prsct 5F 63
Alder Cres. L32: K'by 2D 23
Alderfield Dr. L24: Speke 3F 147
Alder Gro. L22: Water 3D 17
Alder Hey Rd. WA10: St. H 5C 44
Alder La. L34: Know 5B 40
                    (not continuous)
    WA5: B'wood 4F 69
    WA8: Cron 5F 107
    WA11: Crank 1F 29
Alderley Av. WA7: Wind H 1D 169
Aldergate Rd. CH42: R Ferr 2F 119
Aldersgate Av. WA7: Murd 3D 169
Aldersgate Dr. L26: Halew 1A 148
Aldersley St. L3: Liv 3D 77 (1F 5)
Alderson Rd. L15: W'tree 2D 101
Alderton Cl. L26: Halew 5A 128
Alderville Rd. L4: Walt 1C 56
Alder Wood Av. L24: Speke 4E 147
Alderwood Ct. WA8: Wid 5E 109
Alderwood Lodge L24: Speke 4A 148
Aldford Cl. CH43: O'ton 2E 117
    CH63: Brom 4B 162
Aldford Rd. L32: K'by 1E 39
Aldridge Cl. L12: Crox 5E 39
Aldridge Dr. WA5: B'wood 4F 69
Aldrins La. L30: N'ton 1F 19
Aldwark Rd. L14: K Ash 2A 82
Aldwych Rd. L12: W Der 5C 58
Aldykes L31: Mag 2E 13
Alexander Dr. CH61: Pens 4E 137
    L31: Lyd 4D 7
    WA8: Wid 4D 131
Alexander Fleming Av.
    L30: N'ton 1F 19
Alexander Grn. L36: Huy 2E 83
Alexander Ho. L21: Sea 1F 33
    L34: Prsct 4D 63

Alexander Wlk. L4: Walt 3F 55
Alexander Way L8: Liv 5F 99
                    (off Park Hill Rd.)
Alexandra Cl. L6: Liv 3B 78
Alexandra Ct. CH45: New B 3A 52
    L23: C'by 1D 17
    WA9: St. H 3D 65
Alexandra Dr. CH42: R Ferr 3E 119
    L17: Aig 5B 100
    L20: Boot 2E 35
    WA10: St. H 2D 65
Alexandra Grn. L17: Aig 5B 100
Alexandra Gro. WA7: Run 1C 166
Alexandra Ho. L17: Aig 5B 100
Alexandra Ind. Est.
    WA8: Wid 5F 131
Alexandra M. WA6: Frod 4B 172
Alexandra Mt. L21: Lith 5B 18
Alexandra Pk. L17: Aig 1B 122
Alexandra Rd. CH43: O'ton 4B 96
    CH45: New B 3A 52
    CH48: W Kir 1C 100
    L7: Liv .4A 80
    L13: Liv 5C 124
    L19: Gars 5E 17
    L22: Water 5E 17
    L23: C'by 1D 17
Alexandra St. WA8: Wid 5A 132
    WA10: St. H 2D 65
Alexandra Ter. L8: Liv 2F 99
                    (off Princes Rd.)
Alexandra Vs. L21: Lith 5B 18
Alex Cl. L8: Liv 3F 99
Alfonso Rd. L4: Kirk 3D 55
Alford Av. WA9: Sut M 2B 88
Alforde St. WA8: Wid 5A 132
                    (not continuous)
Alfred Cl. WA8: Wid 4B 132
Alfred M. L1: Liv 2E 99
Alfred Pl. L8: Liv 5A 100
Alfred Rd. CH43: O'ton 4C 96
    CH44: Wall 5E 75
    WA11: Hay 1F 49
Alfred Stocks Ct. L8: Liv 1A 122
Alfred St. L15: W'tree 1D 101
    WA8: Wid 4B 132
    WA10: St. H 4B 46
Alfriston Rd. L12: W Der 5C 58
Algernon St. WA7: Run 4F 151
Alice Ct. WA8: Wid 3A 152
Alice St. WA9: St. H 3E 67
Alicia Wlk. L10: Faz 1B 38
Alison Av. CH42: R Ferr 1F 119
Alison Pl. L13: Liv 4E 57
Alison Rd. L13: Liv 4E 57
Alistair Dr. CH63: Brom 5C 162
Allangate Cl. CH49: Grea 2C 114
Allangate Rd. L19: Gras 4A 124
Allan Rd. WA11: St. H 1C 46
Allanson St. WA9: St. H 1D 67
Allcot Av. CH42: Tran 2D 119
Allenby Av. L23: C'by 3F 17
Allenby Sq. L13: Liv 4E 57
Allendale WA7: Pal F 4B 168
Allendale Av. L9: Ain 1B 36
    L35: R'hill 3D 87
Allengate L23: C'by 1F 17
Allen Rd. WA7: West P 3D 165
Allerford Rd. L12: W Der 4C 58
ALLERTON .4D 125
Allerton Beeches L18: Moss H 1C 124
Allerton Dr. L18: Moss H 5B 102
Allerton Gro. CH42: Tran 1D 119
Allerton Rd. CH42: Tran 5D 97
    CH45: Wall 5A 52
    L18: Aller, Moss H 4A 102
    L25: Wltn 2A 126
    WA8: Wid 3B 132
Allerton Station (Rail) 5D 125
Allesley Rd. L14: K Ash 1F 81
Alleyne Rd. L4: Walt 3D 57
All Hallows Dr. L24: Speke 4F 147
Allington Dr. L17: Aig 1B 122
Allonby Cl. CH43: Noct 5E 95

Allport La. CH62: Brom 2D 163
          (not continuous)
Allport Rd. CH62: Brom 4C 162
  CH63: Brom 4C 162
Allports, The CH62: Brom 3D 163
All Saints Cl. L30: N'ton 2E 19
All Saints Rd. L24: Speke 4C 146
Allysum Cl. WA7: Beech 1F 173
Alma Cl. L12: Faz 1B 38
Almacs Cl. L23: Blun 2B 16
Alman Cl. L17: Aig 1B 122
Alma Pl. WA9: St. H 1C 66
Alma Rd. L17: Aig 4E 123
Alma St. CH41: Birk 3E 97
  CH62: New F 5A 120
  WA9: St. H 1C 66
Alma Ter. L15: W'tree 1F 101
Almeda Rd. L24: Speke 5A 148
Almond Av. L30: N'ton 2C 18
  WA7: Run 2C 166
Almond Cl. L26: Halew 5E 127
  WA11: Hay 3F 47
Almond Ct. L19: Gars 2E 145
Almond Dr. WA5: B'wood 5F 69
Almond Gro. WA8: Wid 4D 131
Almond Pl. CH46: More 1F 93
Almonds, The L26: Halew 5E 127
Almond's Grn. L12: W Der 3A 58
Almond's Gro. L12: W Der 4A 58
Almond's Pk. L12: W Der 3A 58
Almonds Turn L30: N'ton 1D 19
Almond Tree Cl. L24: Hale 5E 149
Almond Way CH49: Grea 2C 114
Alness Dr. L35: R'hill 4D 87
Alnwick Dr. CH46: More 1B 92
Aloeswood Cl. L6: Liv 3F 78
Alpass Rd. L17: Aig 1B 122
Alpha Dr. CH42: R Ferr 3A 120
Alpha St. L21: Lith 3B 34
Alpine Cl. WA10: St. H 4C 44
Alpine St. WA12: New W 5F 49
Alresford Rd. L19: Aig 4F 123
Alroy Rd. L4: Walt 4A 56
Alscot Av. L10: Faz 1A 38
Alscot Cl. L31: Mag 2D 13
Alsop Community Sports Cen. 1F 55
Alston Cl. CH62: Brom 1C 162
Alstonfield Rd. L14: K Ash 2A 82
Alston Rd. L17: Aig 4E 123
Alt WA8: Wid 2B 130
Alt Av. L31: Mag 3C 12
Altbridge Pk. L11: Crox 4A 38
          (not continuous)
Altbridge Rd. L36: Huy 2D 83
Altcar Av. L15: W'tree 2C 100
Altcar Dr. CH46: More 2D 93
Altcar La. L31: Lyd 2A 6
Altcar Rd. L20: Boot 3C 34
Altcross Rd. L11: Crox 4C 38
Altcross Way L11: Crox 4C 38
Altfield Rd. L14: K Ash 4F 59
Altfinch Cl. L14: K Ash 4A 60
Altham Rd. L11: N Grn 4F 37
Althorp St. L8: Liv 1F 121
Altmoor Rd. L36: Huy 1D 83
Alton Av. L21: Lith 4A 18
Alton Rd. CH43: O'ton 4A 96
  L6: Liv 1D 79
Alt Rd. L20: Boot 3C 34
  L36: Huy 3E 83
Altside Ct. L10: Faz 1B 38
Alt St. L8: Liv 2B 100
Altway L10: Ain 2C 20
Altway Ct. L10: Ain 2C 20
          (off Altway)
Alundale Ct. L20: Boot 5C 34
Alundale Rd. L12: W Der 1E 81
Alvanley Grn. L32: K'by 2C 22
Alvanley Pl. CH43: O'ton 3C 96
Alvanley Rd. L12: W Der 1C 80
  L32: K'by 3C 22
Alvanley Ter. WA6: Frod 5B 172
Alva Rd. L35: R'hill 4D 87
Alvega Cl. CH62: New F 5C 120

Alverstone Av. CH41: Birk 2F 95

Alverstone Rd. CH44: Wall 3D 75
  L18: Moss H 3D 101
Alverton Cl. WA8: Wid 4D 131
Alvina La. L4: Walt 4E 55
  L33: K'by 5F 15
Alwain Grn. L24: Speke 5F 147
Alwen St. CH41: Birk 5F 73
Alwyn Av. L21: Lith 4B 18
Alwyn Cl. L17: Aig 1B 122
Alwyn Gdns. CH46: More 1F 93
Alwyn St. L17: Aig 1B 122
Amanda Rd. L10: Faz 1B 38
  L35: R'hill 1B 86
Amanda Way L31: Mell 1B 22
Amaury Cl. L23: Thorn 5B 10
Amaury Rd. L23: Thorn 5B 10
Ambassador Dr. L26: Halew 3A 128
Ambergate Cl. WA9: St. H 4D 67
Ambergate Rd. L19: Gras 5B 124
Amberley Av. CH46: More 2C 92
Amberley Cl. CH46: More 2C 92
  L6: Liv 4D 57
Amberley St. L8: Liv 2A 100
Amber Way L14: K Ash 4A 60
Ambleside Av. CH46: More 1D 93
Ambleside Cl. CH61: Thing 1A 138
  CH62: Brom 3E 163
  WA7: Beech 5E 167
Ambleside Pl. WA11: St. H 4B 30
Ambleside Rd. L18: Aller 3D 125
  L31: Mag 5D 7
Amelia Cl. L6: Liv 3F 77
  WA8: Wid 5B 110
Amersham Rd. L4: Walt 1C 56
          (not continuous)
Amery Gro. CH42: Tran 2B 118
Amethyst Cl. L6: Liv 2B 78
  L21: Lith 5C 18
Amherst Rd. L17: Aig 2C 122
Amity St. L8: Liv 4F 99
Amos Av. L21: Lith 5C 18
Ampleforth Cl. L32: K'by 4C 22
Ampthill Rd. L17: Aig 2C 122
Ampulla Rd. L11: Crox 5C 38
Amy Wlk. L10: Faz 1B 38
Ancaster Rd. L17: Aig 2C 122
Ancholme Cl. L35: Whis 5A 64
Anchorage, The L3: Liv 3D 99
Anchorage La. L18: Moss H 1E 123
Anchor Cl. WA7: Murd 4D 169
Anchorite Cl. WA12: New W 5E 49
Ancient Mdws. L9: Ain 1B 36
Ancroft Rd. L14: K Ash 3A 82
Ancrum Rd. L33: K'by 4D 15
Anders Dr. L33: K'by 5F 15
Anderson Cl. CH61: Thing 1A 138
  L35: R'hill 5D 87
Anderson Ct. CH62: Brom 4D 163
Anderson Rd. L21: Lith 4D 19
Anderson St. L5: Liv 5E 55
          (not continuous)
Anderson Way L21: Lith 4D 19
Anderton Ter. L36: Roby 4C 82
Andover Way L25: Hunts X 5D 127
Andrew Cl. L31: Mell 2A 22
Andrew Cl. WA8: Wid 4C 130
Andrew Ho. L8: Liv 2F 99
          (off Birley Ct.)
Andrew St. L4: Walt 2F 55
Andrew's Wlk. CH60: Hes 2B 158
Andromeda Way WA9: Bold 4A 68
Anemone Way WA9: Bold 4A 68
ANFIELD 4A 56
Anfield 4A 56
Anfield Ct. L4: Walt 4A 56
Anfield Crematorium L4: Walt 3A 56
Anfield Rd. L4: Walt 4F 55
Angela St. L7: Liv 1B 100
Angers La. L31: Mell 4B 14
Anglesea Rd. L9: Walt 5F 35
Anglesea Way L8: Liv 5F 99
Anglesey Rd. CH44: Wall 1B 74
  CH48: W Kir 3A 112
Anglezark Cl. L7: Liv 4B 78
Anglia Way L25: Hunts X 4C 126

Anglican Ct. L8: Liv 2E 99
Anglo Cl. L9: Ain 5C 20
Angus Rd. CH63: Brom 4C 162
  L11: N Grn. 3F 57
Annandale Cl. L33: K'by 4D 15
Ann Conway Ho. L15: W'tree 2D 101
          (off Garmoyle Cl.)
Anne Gro. WA9: St. H 4C 66
Annesley Rd. CH44: Wall 3C 74
  L17: Aig 2C 122
Anne St. WA9: Clock F 3D 89
Annie Rd. L20: Boot 2D 35
Ann St. WA7: Run 4B 152
Ann St. W. WA8: Wid 5B 132
Anscot Av. CH63: Beb 1F 141
Ansdell Rd. WA10: Eccl 3B 44
Ansdell Dr. WA10: Eccl 3B 44
Ansdell Vs. Rd. L35: R'hill 2C 86
Anson St. L3: Liv 4E 77 (4J 5)
Anstey Cl. CH46: More 5B 70
Anstey Rd. L13: Liv 3B 80
Anthony's Way CH60: Hes 3A 158
Anthorn Cl. CH43: Noct 5D 95
Antonio St. L20: Boot 2D 55
Antons Cl. L26: Halew 1F 147
Antons Rd. L26: Halew 1F 147
Antrim Cl. WA11: Hay 2C 48
Antrim St. L13: Liv 4E 57
Anvil Cl. L20: Boot 4B 34
Anzacs, The CH62: Port S 1C 142
Anzio Rd. L36: Huy 2D 83
Apex Ct. CH62: Brom 1E 163
Apollo Cres. L33: K'by 1E 23
Apollo Way L6: Liv 1B 78
  L30: N'ton 1F 19
Apostles Way L33: K'by 5D 15
Appin Rd. CH41: Birk 4E 97
Appleby Cl. WA8: Wid 4C 130
Appleby Dr. L30: N'ton 2C 18
Appleby Grn. L12: W Der 5D 59
Appleby Gro. CH62: Brom 4D 163
Appleby Lawn L27: N'ley 5A 106
Appleby Rd. L33: K'by 1D 23
  WA8: Wid 4C 130
Appleby Wlk. L27: N'ley 5A 106
  WA8: Wid 4C 130
Applecorn Cl. WA9: Sut L 5D 67
Apple Ct. L6: Liv 3B 78
          (off Coleridge St.)
Appledore Ct. L24: Speke 3B 146
Appledore Gro. WA9: Sut L 1C 88
Appledore Rd. CH46: More 3C 92
APPLETON 2B 132
Appleton Dr. CH49: Grea 1E 115
Appleton Rd. L4: Walt 2A 56
  L21: Lith 4A 18
  L33: K'by 1E 23
  WA8: Wid 3B 132
  WA9: St. H 2C 66
Appleton St. WA8: Wid 1B 152
Appleton Village WA8: Wid 3A 132
Apple Tree Cl. L24: Hale 5E 149
  L28: Stock V 3B 60
Appletree Ct. L18: Aller 3B 124
April Gro. L6: Liv 1D 79
April Ri. L30: N'ton 2E 19
Apsley Av. CH45: Wall 5B 52
Apsley Brow L31: Mag 1B 12
Apsley Gro. CH63: Beb 1A 142
Apsley Rd. CH62: New F 4B 120
  L12: W Der 5C 58
Aqua Complex, The 4E 55
Aquarius Cl. L14: K Ash 2A 82
Arabis Gdns. WA9: Bold 4B 68
Aragon Cl. L31: Lyd 4E 7
Aragon Ct. WA7: Mnr P 4C 154
Aran Cl. L24: Hale 5D 149
Arborn Dr. CH49: Upton 3A 94
Arbour La. L33: Know I 4A 24
Arbury Av. WA11: St. H 2D 47
Arcadia Av. L31: Lyd 4D 7
Archbishop Warlock Ct. L3: Liv . . .2C 76
Archbrook M. L13: Liv 1E 79

Archer Cl. L4: Kirk 4E 55
Archerfield Rd. L18: Aller 3B 124
Archer Gro. WA9: St. H 4E 47
Archers Ct. CH49: W'chu 2A 116
Archers Cft. CH62: Brom 1D 163
Archers Fold L31: Mell 1B 22
Archers Grn. CH62: East 1E 171
Archers St. L4: Kirk 4E 55
Archers Way
    CH49: W'chu 2A 116
Arch La. WN4: Gars 2F 31
Arch Vw. Cres. L1: Liv 1E 99
Archway Rd. L36: Huy 4D 83
Arctic Rd. L20: Boot 5A 34
Arden WA8: Wid 2A 130
Ardennes Rd. L36: Huy 3E 83
Arderne Cl. CH63: Spit 5B 142
Ardleigh Cl. L13: Liv 4F 79
Ardleigh Gro. L13: Liv 4F 79
Ardleigh Pl. L13: Liv 4F 79
Ardleigh Rd. L13: Liv 4F 79
Ardmore Rd. L18: Moss H 2A 124
Ardrossan Rd. L4: Walt 3C 56
Ardville Rd. L11: N Grn. 5D 37
Ardwick Rd. L24: Speke 4F 147
Ardwick St. WA9: St. H 5C 46
Argo Rd. L22: Water 4D 17
Argos Pl. L20: Kirk 2D 55
Argos Rd. L20: Kirk 2D 55
Argyle Rd. L4: Walt 5B 56
    L19: Gars 1C 144
Argyle St. CH41: Birk 3E 97
    L1: Liv 1D 99 (7E 4)
    WA10: St. H 3F 45
Argyle St. Sth. CH41: Birk 4D 97
Argyll Av. CH62: East 1D 171
Aries Cl. L14: K Ash 1A 82
Ariss Gro. L35: Whis 1A 86
Arkenstone Cl. WA8: Wid 2C 130
Arkle Rd. CH41: Birk 1F 95
Arkles La. L4: Walt 4A 56
Arkles Rd. L4: Walt 5A 56
Arklow Dr. L24: Hale 5D 149
Ark Royal Way
    CH41: Tran 5F 97
Arkwood Cl. CH62: Spit 4C 142
Arkwright Ct. WA7: Ast 4F 153
Arkwright Rd. WA7: Ast 4F 153
Arkwright St. L5: Liv 1E 77
Arlescourt Rd. L12: W Der 1C 80
Arley Cl. CH43: Bid 3C 94
Arley Dr. WA8: Wid 2A 130
Arley St. L3: Liv 2C 76 (1D 4)
Arlington Av. L18: Moss H 4E 101
Arlington Ct. CH43: O'ton 4F 95
Arlington Rd. CH45: Wall 5E 51
Armill Rd. L11: Crox 5C 38
Armitage Gdns. L18: Aller 3B 124
Armley Rd. L4: Walt 4B 56
Armour Gro. L13: Liv 4A 80
Armour Ho. L1: W'tree 5D 4
Armoury, The L12: W Der 4B 58
Armscot Cl. L25: Hunts X 5B 126
Armscot Pl. L25: Hunts X 5B 126
Armstrong Quay L3: Liv 1E 121
Arncliffe Dr. WA5: B'wood 5F 69
Arncliffe Rd.
    L25: Hunts X, Wltn 4C 126
Arndale WA7: Beech 5E 167
Arnhem Rd. L36: Huy 2E 83
Arno Cl. CH43: O'ton 1B 118
Arnold Av. WA10: St. H 3D 45
Arnold Cl. WA9: St. H 2C 66
Arnold Cres. L8: Liv 3F 99
Arnold Gro. L15: W'tree 1A 102
Arnold Pl. WA8: Wid 5C 130
Arnold St. CH45: Wall 1B 74
Arno Rd. CH43: O'ton 1B 118
Arnot Cl. WA10: St. H 3F 45
Arnot St. L4: Walt 2F 55
Arnot Way CH63: High B 1D 141
Arnside L21: Lith 5D 19
Arnside Av. L35: R'hill 2A 86
    WA11: Hay 2B 48

Arnside Rd. CH43: O'ton 5A 96
    CH45: Wall 1B 74
    L7: Liv 5C 78
    L36: Huy 4B 82
Aron Ct. L34: Prsct 5D 63
Arrad St. L7: Liv 1F 99 (7J 5)
Arran Cl. WA11: St. H 2E 47
Arranmore Rd. L18: Moss H 2A 124
Arrowe Av. CH46: More 2D 93
Arrowe Brook La. CH49: Grea 3D 115
Arrowe Brook Rd. CH49: W'chu 2F 115
Arrowe Country Pk. 3F 115
Arrowe Pk. Rd.
    CH49: Upton, W'chu 4A 94
Arrowe Rd. CH49: Grea 1D 115
Arrowe Side CH49: Grea 5E 93
Arrowe Vw. CH49: Upton 4A 94
Arrowsmith Rd. WA11: Hay 1F 49
Arthur St. CH41: Birk 2C 96
    (not continuous)
    L9: Walt 5F 35
    L19: Gars 2D 145
    WA7: Run 5F 151
Arundel Av. CH45: Wall 5F 51
    L17: Liv 3C 100
Arundel Cl. CH61: Pens 2F 137
    L8: Liv 3A 100
Arundel Cl. WA5: B'wood 5F 69
Arundel St. L4: Walt 2E 55
Arvon St. L20: Boot 2D 35
Asbridge St. L8: Liv 2B 100
Asbury Cl. L18: Aller 1D 125
Asbury Rd. CH45: Wall 5D 51
Ascot Av. L21: Lith 5A 18
    WA7: Run 4B 166
Ascot Dr. CH63: Beb 2F 141
    L33: K'by 5E 15
Ascot Gro. CH63: Beb 2F 141
Ascot Pk. L23: C'by 1F 17
Ashbank Rd. L11: N Grn. 1A 58
Ashbourne Av. L23: Blun 1C 16
    L30: N'ton 2E 19
    WA7: Run 4B 166
Ashbourne Cres. L36: Huy 4B 82
Ashbourne Rd. L17: Aig 2C 122
Ashbrook Av. WA7: Sut W 2F 173
Ashbrook Dr. L9: Ain 2C 36
Ashbrook Ter. CH63: Beb 1A 142
Ashburn Av. L33: K'by 1E 23
Ashburton Av. CH43: C'ton 3F 95
Ashburton Rd. CH43: C'ton 3F 95
    CH44: Wall 2B 74
    CH48: W Kir 3B 112
Ashbury Cl. WA7: Wind H 5D 155
Ashbury Dr. WA11: Hay 1C 48
Ashby Cl. L14: K Ash 5B 60
Ashby Cl. CH46: More 5B 70
Ash Cl. L15: W'tree 1E 101
Ashcombe Rd. L14: K Ash 3B 80
Ash Cres. L36: Huy 1E 105
Ashcroft Rd. L33: Know I 2B 24
Ashcroft Rd. L20: Boot 5B 34
    WA9: St. H 5C 46
Ashdale L36: Huy 4D 83
Ashdale Pk. CH49: Grea 1B 114
Ashdale Rd. L9: Walt 4A 36
    L18: Moss H 4A 102
    L22: Water 3D 17
Ashdown Cres. WA9: Clock F 2C 88
Ashdown Dr. CH49: Grea 2C 114
Ashdown Gro. L26: Halew 3A 128
Ashfarm Ct. L14: K Ash 3F 81
Ashfield L15: W'tree 1D 101
    L35: R'hill 3D 87
Ashfield Cres. CH62: Brom 2D 163
    WN5: Bil 1E 31
Ashfield Rd. CH62: Brom 2C 162
    L17: Aig 2D 123
Ashfield St. L5: Liv 1C 76
Ashford Cl. L26: Halew 5E 127

Ashford Rd. CH41: Birk 5C 96
    CH47: Meols 3C 90
Ashford Way WA8: Wid 3D 133
Ash Grange L14: K Ash 3D 81
Ash Gro. CH45: New B 4C 52
    L15: W'tree 1D 101
    L21: Sea 2A 34
    L35: Prsct 2E 85
    WA7: Run 2C 166
    WA8: Wid 4D 131
    WA9: Clock F 2C 88
Ashlands Rd. CH46: Frod 5C 172
Ashlar Gro. L17: Aig 1E 123
Ashlar Rd. L17: Aig 1E 123
    L22: Water 3E 17
Ashlea Rd. CH61: Pens 4F 137
Ashleigh Rd. L31: Mag 3F 13
Ashley Av. CH47: Meols 2F 91
Ashley Cl. L33: K'by 5E 15
    L35: R'hill 4D 87
Ashley Ct. WA6: Frod 5A 172
Ashley Grn. WA8: Wid 4D 131
Ashley Retail Pk. WA8: Wid 5B 132
Ashley Rd. WA7: Run 5D 153
Ashley St. CH42: R Ferr 2F 119
Ashley Way WA8: Wid 1A 152
Ashley Way W. WA8: Wid 5F 131
Ashmore Cl. CH48: Caldy 3C 134
Ashmuir Hey L32: K'by 4F 23
Ashover Av. L14: K Ash 2A 82
Ashridge St. WA7: Run 4F 151
Ash Rd. CH42: Tran 5C 96
    CH63: High B 5F 119
    L21: Lith 1A 34
    WA11: Hay 1E 49
Ash St. L20: Boot 4C 34
Ashton Av. L35: R'hill 5C 86
Ashton Cl. CH62: East 2E 171
    WA6: Frod 4C 172
    WA7: West 4F 165
Ashton Ct. WA6: Frod 4C 172
Ashton Dr. CH48: W Kir 4A 112
    L25: Hunts X 5B 126
    WA6: Frod 3C 172
Ashton Pk. L25: Hunts X 4D 127
ASHTON'S GREEN 5F 47
Ashtons Grn. Dr. WA9: St. H 1F 67
Ashton's La. L24: Hale 5F 147
Ashton Sq. L25: Wltn 3B 126
Ashton St. L3: Liv 4F 77
    L13: Liv 3A 80
Ashtree Cft. CH64: Will 5A 170
Ashtree Farm Ct. CH64: Will 5A 170
Ashtree Gro. L12: Crox 4E 39
Ashurst Cl. L25: Gate 5B 104
    WA11: St. H 2E 47
Ashurst Dr. WA11: St. H 2D 47
Ash Va. L15: W'tree 1D 101
Ash Vs. CH44: Wall 4C 74
Ashville Ind. Est. WA7: Sut W 2E 173
Ashville Rd. CH41: Birk 3A 96
    CH43: C'ton 3A 96
    CH44: Wall 3C 74
Ashville Way WA7: Sut W 2E 173
Ashwater Rd. L12: W Der 1C 58
Ash Way CH60: Hes 4B 158
Ash Wharf L8: Liv 2E 99
Ashwell St. L8: Liv 2E 99
Ashwood Cl. L27: N'ley 4E 105
    L33: K'by 5E 15
    WA8: Wid 5A 130
Ashwood Dr. CH43: Bid 5C 72
Ashwood Dr. L12: Crox 5D 39
Askern Rd. L32: K'by 5F 23
Askett Cl. WA11: Hay 1D 49
Askew Cl. CH44: Wall 2D 75
Askew St. L4: Walt 2F 55
Askham Cl. L8: Liv 2B 100
Aspen Cl. CH60: Hes 3D 159
    L33: K'by 4F 15
Aspen Gro. L8: Liv 3B 100
Aspendale Rd. CH42: Tran 5D 97
Aspen Gdns. WA9: St. H 5C 64
Aspen Gro. L8: Liv 3B 100
Aspes Rd. L12: W Der 4E 59

Aspinall St. CH41: Birk 2C 96
   L34: Prsct 5D 63
Apsley Ho. L22: Water 4E 17
Asquith Av. CH41: Birk 2B 96
Asser Rd. L11: N Grn. 3E 57
Assheton Wlk. L24: Hale 5E 149
Assissian Cres. L30: N'ton 1E 19
Aster Cl. L31: Lyd 4C 6
Aster Cres. WA7: Beech 5F 167
Aster Dr. L33: K'by 5D 15
Asterfield Av. CH63: High B 5E 119
Aster Rd. WA11: Hay 1F 49
Astley Cl. WA8: Wid 1C 130
Astley Rd. L36: Huy 5E 61
ASTMOOR 4F 153
Astmoor Bri. La. WA7: Cas 5F 153
Astmoor Ind. Est. WA7: Ast 4F 153
   (Brindley Rd.)
   WA7: Ast 4E 153
   (Goddard Rd.)
Astmoor La. WA7: Ast 4C 152
   WA7: Cas 5F 153
Astmoor Rd. WA7: Ast 4C 152
Astmoor Spine Rd. WA7: Ast ...4A 154
ASTON 4D 175
Aston Cl. CH43: O'ton 1F 117
Aston Fields Rd. WA7: Pres B ...1D 175
Aston Grn. WA7: Pres B 4E 169
ASTON HEATH 3D 175
Aston La. WA7: Aston, Sut W ...2B 174
   WA7: Pres B 5E 169
Aston La. Nth. WA7: Pres B 1E 175
Aston La. Sth. WA7: Pres B 2E 175
Aston St. L19: Gars 2C 144
Astonwood Rd. CH42: Tran 1D 119
Astor Cl. L4: Walt 1F 55
Atheldene Rd. L4: Walt 1C 56
Athelstan Cl. CH62: Brom 1D 163
Atherton Cl. L5: Liv 1E 77
Atherton Ct. CH45: New B 3A 52
Atherton Dr. CH49: W'chu 1A 116
Atherton Rake L30: N'ton 1D 19
Atherton Rd. L9: Ain 2C 36
Atherton St. CH45: New B 2A 52
   L34: Prsct 5D 63
   WA10: St. H 3F 45
Athol Cl. CH62: East 5E 163
   WA12: New W 4F 49
Athol Dr. CH62: East 1E 171
Atholl Cres. L10: Ain 3D 21
Athol St. CH41: Birk 2E 97
   L5: Liv 1B 76
   (Gt. Howard St.)
   L5: Liv 1C 76
   (Vauxhall Rd., not continuous)
Atkinson Gro. L36: Huy 2F 83
Atlanta Ct. L33: K'by 3D 15
Atlantic Pav. L3: Liv 1C 98 (7C 4)
Atlantic Point L3: Liv 3D 77 (1E 4)
Atlantic Rd. L20: Boot 5B 34
Atlantic Terminal L20: Boot ...4A 34
Atlantic Way L3: Liv 4D 99
   L30: Boot 5E 19
Atlas Bus. Complex
   L20: Boot 4A 34
Atlas Cl. WA9: St. H 5B 46
Atlas Rd. L20: Boot 5B 34
Atlas St. WA9: St. H 5B 46
Atterbury Cl. WA8: Wid 2C 130
Atterbury St. L8: Liv 4D 99
Attlee Rd. L36: Huy 3A 84
Attwood St. L4: Walt 4F 55
Atwell St. L6: Liv 2A 78
Atworth Ter. CH64: Will 5A 170
   (off Neston Rd.)
Aubourn Cl. WA8: Wid 1C 130
Aubrey Cl. L6: Liv 2A 78
Aubrey St. L6: Liv 2F 77
Auburn Rd. CH45: Wall 4A 52
   L13: Liv 5E 57
Aubynes, The CH45: Wall 4E 51
Auckland St. L18: Moss H 4A 102
Audlem Av. CH43: O'ton 1F 117
Audlem Cl. WA7: Sut W 1F 173
Audley St. L3: Liv 4E 77 (3H 5)

Audrey Wlk. L10: Faz 1B 38
Aughton Cl. WN5: Bil 1E 31
Aughton Ct. CH49: Upton 4A 94
Aughton Rd. L20: Boot 3D 35
Augusta Cl. L13: Liv 4A 80
August Rd. L6: Liv 1C 78
August St. L20: Boot 3C 34
Aukland Gro. WA9: St. H 5D 65
Aurorean Cl. L27: N'ley 3D 105
Austell Cl. WA11: St. H 1D 47
Austin Av. WA10: St. H 3C 64
Austin Cl. L32: K'by 2D 23
Austin Rawlinson Sports Cen. ...4E 147
Austin St. CH44: Wall 1F 75
Autumn Gro. CH42: R Ferr 4E 119
Autumn Way L20: Boot 3C 34
   WA9: Clock F 3C 88
Avalon Ter. L20: Boot 4B 34
Avebury Cl. WA8: Wid 1E 133
Avelon Cl. CH43: Noct 4D 95
   L31: Lyd 2B 6
Avenue, The CH62: Brom 2C 162
   L19: Gars 2E 145
   L26: Halew 5E 127
   L36: Huy 3E 83
   WA10: Eccl 5A 44
Avery Cres. WA11: Hay 1C 48
Avery Rd. WA11: Hay 1C 48
Avery Sq. WA11: Hay 1C 48
Aviary Ct. L9: Walt 2F 35
Aviemore Rd. L13: Liv 3F 79
Avington Cl. L12: W Der 4D 59
Avis Wlk. L10: Faz 1B 38
Avolon Rd. L12: W Der 1D 81
Avon Cl. L4: Kirk 3E 55
   L33: K'by 4F 15
Avon Ct. L23: C'by 5E 9
Avondale Av. CH46: More 5F 71
   CH62: East 5E 163
   L31: Mag 2C 12
Avondale Dr. WA8: Wid 3B 130
Avondale Rd. CH47: Hoy 4B 90
   L15: W'tree 3E 101
   WA1: Hay 1A 48
Avonmore Av. L18: Moss H 1A 124
Avon Rd. WN5: Bil 2D 31
Avon St. CH41: Birk 5F 73
   L6: Liv 1B 78
Awelon Cl. L12: W Der 3B 58
Awesome Walls Climbing Cen. ...1B 76
Axbridge Av. WA9: Sut L 1D 89
Axholme Cl. CH61: Thing 2B 138
Axholme Rd. CH61: Thing 1B 138
Ayala Cl. L9: Walt 1F 35
Aycliffe Rd. WA9: St. H 5D 65
Aycliffe Wlk. WA8: Wid 4C 130
Aylesbury Av. CH43: O'ton 2E 117
Aylesbury Rd. CH45: New B 4C 52
Aylesford Rd. L13: Liv 3A 80
Aylsham Cl. WA8: Wid 5C 108
Aylsham Dr. CH49: Upton 2A 94
Aylton Rd. L36: Huy 2B 82
Aylward Pl. L20: Boot 4B 34
Aynsley Cl. WA9: St. H 5B 64
Ayr Rd. L4: Walt 1A 56
Ayrshire Gdns. WA10: St. H 1E 65
Ayrshire Rd. L4: Walt 3C 56
Aysgarth Av. L12: W Der 5C 58
Aysgarth Rd. CH45: Wall 5F 51
Ayton La. L16: Child 1C 102
Azalea Gro. L26: Halew 2D 127
   WA7: Beech 1F 173

B

Babbacombe Rd. L16: Child 3E 103
Bk. Barlow La. L4: Kirk 3E 55
Bk. Beau St. L5: Liv 2E 77 (1G 5)
Bk. Bedford St. L7: Liv 1F 99
   (not continuous)
Bk. Belmont Rd. L6: Liv 1B 78
Bk. Berry St. L1: Liv 1E 99 (7G 5)
Bk. Blackfield Ter. L4: Kirk 4D 55

Bk. Bold St. L1: Liv 5E 77 (6F 5)
Bk. Boundary Cl. L5: Kirk 5D 55
Back Bri. Rd. L23: Blun 2C 16
   (off Riverslea Rd.)
Bk. Bridport St. L3: Liv 4G 5
Back B'way. L11: N Grn. 2E 57
Bk. Canning St. L8: Liv 1E 99
Bk. Catharine St. L8: Liv 1F 99
Bk. Chadwick Mt. L5: Liv 4E 55
Bk. Chatham Pl. L7: Liv 5B 78
Bk. Colquitt St. L1: Liv ...1D 99 (7G 5)
Bk. Commutation Row
   L3: Liv 4E 77 (3G 5)
Bk. Dovecot Pl. L14: K Ash 2F 81
Bk. Egerton St. Nth. L8: Liv 2F 99
Bk. Egerton St. Sth. L8: Liv 2F 99
Bk. Falkner St. Sth. L8: Liv 1F 99
Backford Cl. CH43: O'ton 1E 117
   WA7: Brook 5C 168
Backford Rd. CH61: Irby 2D 137
Bk. Gillmoss La. L11: Crox 2C 38
Bk. Granton Rd. L5: Liv 5A 56
Bk. Guildford St. L6: Liv 2F 77
Bk. Hadfield Pl. L25: Wltn 2A 126
   (off Church Rd.)
Bk. High St. L25: Wltn 2A 126
   (off High St.)
Bk. Holland Pl. L7: Liv 5B 78
Bk. Hope Pl. L1: Liv 1E 99 (7H 5)
Bk. Huskisson St. L8: Liv 2F 99
Bk. Irvine St. L7: Liv 5A 78
Bk. Kelvin Gro. L8: Liv 3A 100
Bk. Knight St. L1: Liv 1E 99 (7G 5)
Back La. L23: Lit C 2E 9
   L39: Augh 1E 7
   WA5: C Grn 4D 69
   WA5: Cuerd 2F 133
Bk. Langham St. L4: Walt 3F 55
Bk. Leeds St. L3: Liv 3B 76 (2B 4)
Bk. Legh St. WA12: New W 5F 49
Bk. Lime St. L1: Liv 5F 5
Back Lit. Canning St. L8: Liv ...2F 99
Bk. Lord St. L1: Liv 5C 76 (6D 4)
Bk. Luton Gro. L4: Walt 3E 55
   (off Walton Rd.)
Bk. Market St. WA12: New W 4F 49
Bk. Maryland St. L1: Liv ..1E 99 (7H 5)
Bk. Menai St. CH41: Birk 3C 96
Bk. Mersey Vw. L22: Water 3C 16
Back Mt. L22: Water 4D 17
Back Mt. Vernon Vw. L7: Liv 4A 78
Bk. Mulberry St. L7: Liv ...1F 99 (7J 5)
Bk. Oliver St. CH41: Birk 3E 97
Bk. Orford St. L15: W'tree 1F 101
Bk. Penny La. WA5: C Grn 2D 69
Bk. Percy St. L8: Liv 2F 99
Bk. Pickop St. L3: Liv 3C 76 (3D 4)
Bk. Price St. CH41: Birk 2D 97
Bk. Renshaw St. L1: Liv ...5E 77 (6G 5)
Bk. Rockfield Rd. L4: Walt 4F 55
Bk. St Bride St. L8: Liv 1F 99
Bk. Sandon St. L8: Liv 2F 99
Bk. Sandown La. L15: W'tree 1F 101
Bk. Seaman Rd. L15: W'tree 2E 101
   (off Seaman Rd.)
Bk. Seaview CH47: Hoy 4B 90
Bk. Seel St. L1: Liv 1D 99 (7F 5)
Bk. Sir Howard St. L8: Liv 1F 99
Back Sth. Rd. L22: Water 4E 17
Bk. Stanley Rd. L20: Boot 5C 34
Bk. Towerlands St. L7: Liv 5B 78
Bk. Wellesley Rd. L8: Liv 5A 100
Bk. Westminster Rd. L4: Kirk ...3E 55
Bk. Windsor Vw. L8: Liv 2B 100
Bk. Winstanley Rd. L22: Water ..3E 17
Bk. York Ter. L5: Liv 5E 55
Badbury Cl. WA11: Hay 1D 49
Badby Wood L33: K'by 1F 23
Baddow Cft. L25: Wltn 1E 125
Baden Rd. L13: Liv 3B 80
Bader Cl. CH61: Pens 4F 137
Badger Cl. WA7: Pal F 4A 168
Badger's Set CH48: Caldy 3D 135
Badger Way CH43: Pren 4E 117

Badminton St.—Baskervyle Cl.

Badminton St. L8: Liv 1F **121**
Baffin Cl. CH46: Leas 2A **72**
Bagnall St. L4: Walt 4F **55**
Bagot St. L15: W'tree 2D **101**
Baguley Av. WA8: Hale B 2A **150**
Bahama Cl. WA11: Hay 1D **49**
Bahama Rd. WA11: Hay 1D **49**
Bailey Ct. L20: Boot 1E **35**
Bailey Dr. L20: Boot 2E **35**
Baileys Cl. WA8: Wid 4A **110**
Bailey's La. L24: Speke 4A **146**
L26: Halew 4A **128**
Bailey St. L1: Liv 1D **99**
Bailey Way L31: Mag 3C **12**
Bainton Cl. L32: K'by 1A **40**
Bainton Rd. L32: K'by 1A **40**
Baker Rd. WA7: West P 3D **165**
Bakers Grn. Rd. L36: Huy 2E **83**
Baker St. L6: Liv 3A **78**
L36: Huy 4A **84**
WA9: St. H 5C **46**
Baker Way L6: Liv 3A **78**
Bakewell Gro. L9: Ain 1B **36**
Bakewell Rd. WA5: B'wood 4F **69**
Bala Gro. CH44: Wall 3A **74**
Bala St. L4: Walt 5B **56**
Balcarres Av. L18: Moss H 4F **101**
Baldwin Av. L16: Child 1E **103**
Baldwin St. WA10: St. H 4A **46**
Bales, The L30: N'ton 1A **20**
Balfe St. L21: Sea 2A **34**
Balfour Av. L20: Boot 3B **34**
Balfour Rd. CH43: O'ton 4B **96**
CH44: Wall 3A **74**
L20: Boot 3B **34**
Balfour St. L4: Walt 4F **55**
WA7: Run 1F **165**
WA10: St. H 5D **45**
Balham Cl. WA8: Wid 5A **110**
Balharry Av. WA11: Hay 1F **49**
Balker Dr. WA10: St. H 3F **45**
Ballantrae Rd. L18: Moss H 1B **124**
Ballantyne Dr. CH43: Bid 5C **72**
Ballantyne Gro. L13: Liv 4E **57**
L20: Boot 2E **35**
Ballantyne Pl. L13: Liv 5E **57**
Ballantyne Rd. L13: Liv 5E **57**
Ballantyne Wlk. CH43: Bid 5C **72**
Ballard Rd. CH48: W Kir 3E **113**
Ball Av. CH45: New B 3A **52**
Balliol Cl. CH43: Bid 5C **72**
BALL O'DITTON 3E 131
Balliol Gro. L23: Blun 3B **16**
Balliol Ho. L20: Boot 1C **54**
Balliol Rd. L20: Boot 1C **54**
Balliol Rd. E. L20: Boot 1D **55**
Ball Path WA8: Wid 3F **131**
Ball Path Way WA8: Wid 3E **131**
Ball's Rd. CH43: O'ton 5B **96**
Balls Rd. E. CH41: Birk 4C **96**
Ball St. WA9: St. H 4D **47**
Balmer St. WA9: St. H 3D **65**
Balmoral Av. L23: C'by 2E **17**
WA9: St. H 4C **66**
Balmoral Cl. L33: K'by 5E **15**
Balmoral Ct. L13: Liv 1E **79**
Balmoral Gdns. CH43: Pren 3F **117**
Balmoral Gro. CH43: Noct 1D **117**
Balmoral Rd. CH45: New B 2C **52**
L6: Liv 2C **78**
L9: Walt 2A **36**
L31: Mag 1C **12**
WA8: Wid 5F **109**
Balmoral Way L34: Prsct 1F **83**
Balm St. L7: Liv 4B **78**
Balniel St. WA9: Clock F 3D **89**
Balsham Cl. L25: Hunts X 5D **127**
Baltic Rd. L20: Boot 5B **34**
Baltic St. L4: Walt 4F **55**
Baltimore St. L1: Liv 1E **99** (7H **5**)
Bamboo Cl. L27: N'ley 3E **105**
Bamford Cl. WA7: Run 3C **166**
Bampton Av. WA11: St. H 4B **30**
Bampton Rd. L16: Child 1D **103**
Banbury Av. L25: Wltn 2C **126**
Banbury Way CH43: O'ton 2E **117**
Bancroft Cl. L25: Hunts X 4C **126**
Bancroft Rd. WA8: Wid 2D **133**
Bandon Cl. L24: Hale 5D **149**
Banff Av. CH63: East 5D **163**
Bangor Rd. CH45: Wall 5D **51**
Bangor St. L5: Liv 1C **76**
Bankburn Rd. L13: Liv 5E **57**
Bank Dene CH42: R Ferr 4A **120**
Bankes La. WA7: West P 4E **165**
(not continuous)
Bankfield Ct. L13: Liv 1F **79**
Bankfield Rd. L13: Liv 5F **57**
WA8: Wid 3B **130**
Bankfield St. L20: Kirk 3B **54**
Bankhall La. L20: Kirk 3C **54**
Bankhall Station (Rail) 3C **54**
Bankhall St. L20: Kirk 3C **54**
Bankland Rd. L13: Liv 1F **79**
Bank La. L33: K'by 3C **14**
Bank Rd. L20: Boot 5B **34**
Banks, The CH45: Wall 4E **51**
Bank's Av. CH47: Meols 3D **91**
Bankside WA7: Murd 3E **169**
Bankside Ct. L21: Lith 5A **18**
Bankside Rd. CH42: R Ferr 4F **119**
Bank's La. L19: Gars 3D **145**
L24: Speke 5F **145**
Banks Rd. CH48: W Kir 4A **112**
CH60: Hes 3D **157**
L19: Gars 2C **144**
Bank St. CH41: Birk 3E **97**
WA8: Wid 3A **152**
WA10: St. H 5E **45**
WA12: New W 5F **49**
Bank's Way L19: Gars 3D **145**
Bankville Rd. CH42: Tran 1D **119**
Banner Hey L35: Whis 5D **85**
Bannerman St. L7: Liv 1C **100**
Banner St. L15: W'tree 2D **101**
WA10: St. H 5F **45**
Banner Wlk. *WA10: St. H* *5E* ***45***
(off Banner St.)
Banning Cl. CH41: Birk 2D **97**
Banstead Gro. L15: W'tree 2B **102**
Barbara Av. L10: Faz 1A **38**
Barbara St. WA9: Clock F 3E **89**
Barberry Cl. CH46: More 1B **92**
Barberry Cres. L30: N'ton 1A **20**
Barber St. WA9: St. H 4C **46**
Barbour Dr. L20: Boot 2E **35**
Barbrook Way L9: Walt 5B **36**
Barchester Dr. L17: Aig 3C **122**
Barclay St. L8: Liv 5F **99**
Barcombe Rd. CH60: Hes 1D **159**
Bardley Cres. L35: Tar G 2A **106**
Bardon Cl. L25: Gate 4C **104**
Bardsay Rd. L4: Walt 2F **55**
Barford Cl. CH43: Bid 3B **94**
Barford Grange CH64: Will 5B **170**
Barford Rd. L25: Hunts X 1B **146**
L36: Huy 5F **61**
Bargate Water WA9: St. H 5D **65**
Barington Dr. WA7: Murd 3E **169**
Barkbeth Rd. L36: Huy 1C **82**
Barkbeth Wlk. L36: Huy 1C **82**
Barkeley Dr. L21: Sea 2F **33**
Barker Cl. L36: Huy 1F **105**
Barker La. CH49: Grea 2C **114**
(not continuous)
Barker Rd. CH61: Irby 1F **137**
Barker's Hollow Rd.
WA4: Dutt, Pres H 4F **169**
Barkerville Cl. L13: Liv 4D **57**
Barker Way L6: Liv 1B **78**
Barkhill Rd. L17: Aig 3F **123**
Barkin Cen., The WA8: Wid 4C **132**
Barkis Cl. L8: Liv 4F **99**
Bark Rd. L21: Lith 4C **18**
Barleyfield CH61: Pens 3F **137**
Barlow Av. CH63: Beb 1A **142**
Barlow Gro. WA9: St. H 1A **68**
Barlow La. L4: Kirk 3E **55**
Barlows Cl. L9: Ain 5D **21**
Barlow's La. L9: Ain 5D **21**
Barlow St. L4: Kirk 3E **55**
Barmouth Rd. CH45: Wall 5D **51**
Barmouth Way L5: Liv 5C **54**
Barnacre La. CH46: More 3C **92**
Barnard Rd. CH43: O'ton 4B **96**
Barn Cl. L30: N'ton 1A **20**
Barncroft WA7: Nort 2D **169**
Barncroft, The CH49: Grea 5D **93**
Barncroft Pl. L23: C'by 4E **9**
Barn Cft. Rd. L26: Halew 5A **128**
Barndale Rd. L18: Moss H 5F **101**
Barnes Cl. L33: K'by 4E **15**
WA8: Wid 2D **133**
Barnes Dr. L31: Lyd 3C **6**
Barnes Grn. CH63: Spit 5A **142**
Barnes Rd. WA8: Wid 2C **132**
Barnes St. L6: Liv 1A **78**
Barneston Rd. WA8: Wid 1E **133**
Barnet Cl. L7: Liv 1C **100**
Barnett Av. WA12: New W 5E **49**
Barnfield Av. WA7: Murd 5C **168**
Barnfield Cl. CH47: Meols 2E **91**
L12: W Der 5B **58**
L30: N'ton 3E **19**
Barnfield Dr. L12: W Der 5B **58**
Barnham Cl. L24: Speke 3B **146**
Barnham Dr. L16: Child 2E **103**
Barn Hey CH47: Hoy 1A **112**
Barn Hey Cres. CH47: Meols 3F **91**
Barn Hey Grn. L12: W Der 5B **58**
Barn Hey Rd. L33: K'by 3A **24**
Barnhill Rd. L15: W'tree 3A **102**
Barnhurst Cl. L16: Child 2E **103**
Barnhurst Rd. L16: Child 2E **103**
Barn La. WA5: B'wood 5F **69**
Barnmeadow Rd. L25: Gate 4A **104**
Barnsbury Rd. L4: Walt 1B **56**
Barnsdale Av. CH61: Thing 2B **138**
Barnside Ct. L16: Child 2E **103**
BARNSTON 3C 138
Barnston La. CH46: More 5E **71**
Barnston Rd. CH60: Hes 3B **158**
CH61: Barn, Thing 5B **116**
L9: Ain 1A **36**
Barnston Towers Cl. CH60: Hes 2C **158**
Barnstream Cl. L27: N'ley 3C **104**
Barn St. WA8: Wid 1A **152**
Barnwell Av. CH44: Wall 1B **74**
Barnwood Rd. L36: Huy 2B **82**
Baroncroft Rd. L25: Wltn 5F **103**
Barons Cl. WA7: Cas 1F **167**
WA8: Wid 4C **130**
Barons Hey L28: Stock V 3F **59**
Barren Gro. CH43: O'ton 5B **96**
Barrington Rd. CH44: Wall 3C **74**
L15: W'tree 3E **101**
Barrow Cl. L12: W Der 2C **58**
Barrowfield Rd. WA10: Eccl 3A **44**
Barrows Cotts. L35: Whis 3E **85**
BARROW'S GREEN 5D 111
Barrows Grn. La. WA8: Wid 2E **133**
Barrow's Row WA8: Wid 5B **110**
Barrow St. WA10: St. H 5A **46**
Barr St. L20: Kirk 3C **54**
Barrymore Rd. L13: Liv 3F **79**
WA7: Run 3B **166**
Barrymore Way CH63: Brom 4B **162**
Bartholomew Cl. L35: R'hill 5E **87**
Bartlegate Cl. WA7: Brook 5B **168**
Bartlett St. L15: W'tree 2D **101**
Barton Cl. CH47: Hoy 5A **90**
L21: Lith 3A **18**
WA7: Murd 3D **169**
WA10: St. H 4F **45**
Barton Hey Dr. CH48: Caldy 3C **134**
Barton Rd. CH47: Hoy 5A **90**
L9: Walt 4F **35**
Barton St. CH41: Birk 3C **96**
CH43: O'ton 4C **96**
Barwell Av. WA11: St. H 2C **46**
Basil Cl. L16: Child 1D **103**
Basildon Cl. WA9: St. H 4E **65**
Basil Rd. L16: Child 1D **103**
Basing St. L19: Gars 5C **124**
Baskervyle Cl. CH60: Hes 4A **158**

Baskervyle Rd. CH60: Hes 4A 158
Basnett St. L1: Liv 5D 77 (5E 5)
Bassendale Rd. CH62: Brom 5E 143
Bassenthwaite Av. CH43: Noct . . .4D 95
L33: K'by 1D 23
WA11: St. H 5A 30
Bates Cres. WA10: St. H 3D 65
Batey Av. L35: R'hill 2B 86
Batherton Cl. WA8: Wid 5B 132
Bathgate Way L14: W Der 4D 15
Bath St. CH62: Port S 2B 142
L3: Liv 4B 76 (3A 4)
L22: Water 5D 17
WA10: St. H 5F 45
Bathurst Rd. L19: Gras 5B 124
Batley St. L13: Liv 3A 80
Battenberg St. L7: Liv 4A 78
Battersea Ct. WA8: Wid 1F 131
Battery Cl. L17: Aig 2C 122
Baucher Dr. L20: Boot 1E 35
Baumville Dr. CH63: Spit 5F 141
Baxter St. L7: Murd 3D 169
(not continuous)
Baxters La. WA9: St. H 3D 67
Baxters La. Ind. Est. WA9: St. H . .3D 67
Baycliffe Cl. CH43: Beech 5D 167
Baycliff Rd. L12: W Der 3E 59
Bayfield Rd. L19: Gras 5A 124
Bayhorse La. L3: Liv 4F 77 (3J 5)
Baysdale Cl. L8: Liv 5F 99
Bayswater Cl. WA7: Nort 3F 155
Bayswater Ct. CH45: Wall 5D 51
Bayswater Gdns. CH45: Wall 4D 51
Bayswater Rd. CH45: Wall 5D 51
Baythorne Rd. L4: Walt 1C 56
Bay Tree Gro. WA9: St. H 3C 66
Baytree Gro. L31: Mell 2A 22
Baytree Rd. CH42: Tran 1E 119
CH48: Frank 4F 113
Bay Vw. Dr. CH45: Wall 4D 51
Bayvil Cl. WA7: Murd 3E 169
Beach Bank L22: Water 3C 16
Beachcroft Rd. CH47: Meols 2E 91
Beach Gro. CH45: Wall 4C 52
Beach Lawn L22: Water 4C 16
Beach Rd. CH47: Hoy 5A 90
L21: Lith 5A 18
(not continuous)
Beach Wlk. CH48: W Kir 1B 134
Beacon Ct. CH60: Hes 2A 158
Beacon Dr. CH48: W Kir 4C 112
Beacon Gro. WA11: St. H 2D 47
Beacon Hill Vw. WA7: West P . . .2D 165
Beacon Ho. L5: Liv 2E 77
Beacon La. CH60: Hes 2A 158
L5: Liv 5F 55
Beacon Pde. CH60: Hes 2A 158
Beacons, The CH60: Hes 3A 158
Beaconsfield L34: Prsct 5D 63
Beaconsfield Cl. CH42: Tran 1E 119
Beaconsfield Cres. WA8: Wid . . .5A 110
Beaconsfield Gro. WA8: Wid 5B 110
Beaconsfield Rd. CH62: New F . . .5B 120
L21: Sea 1F 33
L25: Wltn 1E 125
WA7: Run 2E 165
WA8: Wid 1B 132
WA10: St. H 3C 44
Beaconsfield St. L8: Liv 3A 100
Beaconsfield Ter. L19: Gars 1B 144
(off St Mary's Rd.)
Beames Cl. L7: Liv 5C 78
Beamont St. WA8: Wid 3A 152
Beatles Story, The 1C 98 (7C 4)
Beatrice Av. CH63: High B 5E 119
Beatrice St. L20: Boot 2D 55
Beattock Cl. L33: K'by 4D 15
Beatty Cl. CH48: Caldy 3C 134
L35: Whis 4D 85
Beatty Rd. L13: Liv 3A 80
Beauclair Dr. L15: W'tree 2B 102
Beaufort Cl. WA7: Run 3B 166
WA8: Wid 4A 130
Beaufort Dr. CH44: Wall 1E 73
Beaufort Rd. CH41: Birk 5F 73

Beaufort St. L8: Liv 3E 99
(Hill St.)
L8: Liv 4E 99
(Northumberland St.)
L8: Liv 3E 99
(Stanhope St.)
WA9: Sut M 2C 66
Beau La. L3: Liv 2E 77 (1G 5)
Beaumaris Ct. CH43: O'ton 4B 96
Beaumaris Dr. CH61: Thing 1B 138
Beaumaris Rd. CH45: Wall 5D 51
Beaumaris St. L20: Kirk 3B 54
(not continuous)
Beaumont Av. WA10: St. H 4C 44
Beaumont Dr. L10: Ain 4E 21
Beaumont St. L8: Liv 2B 100
Beau St. L3: Liv 2E 77 (1G 5)
Beauworth Av. CH49: Grea 1C 114
Beaver Gro. L9: Ain 2A 36
BEBINGTON 3F 141
Bebington Rd. CH42: Tran 2D 119
CH62: New F 5A 120
CH63: Beb 1A 142
Bebington Station (Rail) 5A 120
Bechers WA8: Wid 1B 130
Bechers Ct. L30: N'ton 2B 20
Bechers Dr. L9: Ain 3C 20
Bechers Row L9: Walt 2F 35
Beck Cl. L10: Faz 1B 38
Beckenham Av. L18: Moss H 4F 101
Beckenham Cl. WA8: Wid 5D 111
Beckenham Rd. CH45: New B 2B 52
Becket St. L4: Kirk 3D 55
(not continuous)
Beckett Cl. L33: Know I 5C 24
Beckett Gro. CH63: High B 5D 119
Beck Gro. WA11: St. H 5B 30
Beckinsale Cl. L26: Halew 3A 128
Beck Rd. L20: Boot 3C 34
Beckwith St. CH41: Birk 1B 96
L1: Liv 1C 98 (7E 4)
Beckwith St. E. CH41: Birk 2D 97
Becky St. L6: Liv 1B 78
Becontree Rd. L12: W Der 2D 81
Bective St. L7: Liv 1C 100
Bedale Wlk. L33: K'by 1F 23
Bedburn Dr. L36: Huy 3A 82
Bede Cl. L33: K'by 4E 15
Bedford Av. CH42: R Ferr 3E 119
L31: Mell 4E 13
Bedford Cl. L7: Liv 1F 99
L36: Huy 3A 84
Bedford Ct. CH42: R Ferr 3D 119
Bedford Pl. CH42: R Ferr 2A 120
L20: Boot 2B 54
L21: Sea 1F 33
Bedford Rd. CH42: R Ferr 2F 119
CH45: Wall 5B 52
L20: Boot 2C 54
Bedford Rd. E. CH42: R Ferr 2A 120
Bedford St. WA9: St. H 1D 67
Bedford St. Nth. L7: Liv 5F 77
Bedford St. Sth. L7: Liv 1F 99
(not continuous)
Bedford Wlk. L7: Liv 1F 99
Beecham Cl. L36: Huy 5D 83
Beech Av. CH49: Upton 3D 93
CH61: Pens 3A 138
L17: Aig 2A 122
L23: C'by 4A 10
L31: Mell 2A 22
L34: Ecc P 4F 63
WA6: Frod 5C 172
WA9: Clock F 1F 49
WA11: Hay 1F 49
Beechbank Rd. L18: Moss H 4E 101
Beechburn Cres. L36: Huy 3B 82
Beechburn Rd. L36: Huy 3A 82
Beech Cl. L12: Crox 5D 39
L32: K'by 2C 22
Beech Ct. CH42: Tran 5D 97
L18: Moss H 1C 124
Beechcroft L31: Mag 1C 12
Beechcroft Rd. CH44: Wall 4C 74

Beechdale Rd. L18: Moss H 5A 102
Beechdene Rd. L4: Walt 4B 56
Beeches, The CH42: R Ferr 3F 119
CH46: Leas 3E 71
L18: Moss H 4D 103
Beechfield L31: Mag 1E 13
Beechfield Cl. CH60: Hes 3A 158
L26: Halew 1E 147
Beechfield Rd. L18: Moss H 5D 103
Beech Grn. L12: W Der 3A 58
Beech Gro. L9: Ain 2B 36
L21: Sea 2F 33
L30: N'ton 3A 20
Beech Hey La. CH64: Will 4B 170
Beechill Cl. L25: Gate 5C 104
Beech La. L18: Moss H 4C 102
Beech Lawn L19: Gras 5F 123
Beech Lodge CH43: Noct 4D 95
Beech Mdws. L34: Prsct 1A 84
Beech Pk. L12: W Der 5A 58
L23: C'by 4F 9
Beech Rd. CH42: Tran 5C 96
CH60: Hes 2C 158
CH63: High B 5F 119
L4: Walt 1A 56
L36: Huy 5E 83
WA7: Run 2C 166
WA7: Sut W 1B 174
Beech St. L7: Liv 4C 78
L20: Boot 4C 34
WA10: St. H 3D 65
Beech Ter. L7: Liv 4C 78
WA8: Wid 3A 152
Beechtree Rd. L15: W'tree 5B 80
Beechurst Cl. L25: Gate 4B 104
Beechurst Rd. L25: Gate 4B 104
Beechwalk, The L14: K Ash 2B 80
Beechway CH63: Beb 4F 141
L31: Mag 1B 14
Beechway Av. L31: Mag 1B 14
BEECHWOOD
    Bidston 1C 94
    Runcorn 5E 167
Beechwood Av. CH45: Wall 1E 73
L26: Halew 5E 127
WA7: Beech 4C 166
Beechwood Cl. L19: Gras 5F 123
WA9: Clock F 2C 68
Beechwood Ct. CH49: W'chu 3B 116
L31: Mag 1E 13
Beechwood Dr. CH43: Bid 2C 94
Beechwood Gdns. L19: Gras 5F 123
Beechwood Grn. L19: Gras 5A 124
Beechwood Gro. L35: Prsct 2E 85
Beechwood Recreation Cen. 2B 94
Beechwood Rd. CH62: Brom 2C 162
L19: Gras 5F 123
L21: Lith 2B 34
Beechwood Rd. Sth. L19: Gras . . .5F 123
Beesands Cl. L27: N'ley 5F 105
Beesley Rd. L34: Prsct 5C 62
Beeston Cl. CH43: Bid 3C 94
Beeston Ct. WA7: Mnr P 3C 154
Beeston Dr. CH61: Pens 3F 137
L30: N'ton 5B 12
Beeston Gro. L19: Gras 5A 124
Beeston St. L4: Kirk 2E 55
Beetham Plaza L2: Liv 5C 4
Beetham Way L33: K'by 2F 23
Begonia Gdns. WA9: Bold 4A 68
Beilby Rd. WA11: Hay 1F 49
Beldale Pk. L32: K'by 1B 22
Beldon Cres. L36: Huy 3B 82
Belem Cl. L17: Aig 4C 100
Belem Twr. L17: Aig 4B 100
Belfast Rd. L13: Liv 3B 80
Belfield Cres. L36: Huy 5E 83
Belfield Dr. CH43: O'ton 1B 118
Belford Dr. CH46: More 1B 92
Belfort Rd. L25: Gate 5B 104
Belfry Cl. CH46: More 5B 70
L12: W Der 5E 59
Belgrave Av. CH44: Wall 2C 74
Belgrave Cl. WA8: Wid 1E 133

Belgrave Rd. L17: Aig 1B 122
L21: Sea 1F 33
Belgrave St. CH44: Wall 1B 74
Belgravia Ct. WA8: Wid 1F 131
Belhaven Rd. L18: Moss H 4F 101
Bellair Av. L23: C'by 1A 18
Bellairs Rd. L11: N Grn. 3E 57
Bellamy Rd. L4: Walt 1E 55
Bell Cl. L36: Huy 1F 105
Belldene Rd. CH61: Hes 5F 137
Bellefield Av. L12: W Der 5B 58
BELLE VALE 3B 104
Belle Va. Rd. L25: Gate 5B 104
Belle Va. Shop. Cen. L25: Gate . .3B 104
Belle Vue Rd. CH44: Wall 4D 75
L25: Gate 5B 104
Bellew Rd. L11: N Grn. 4F 57
Bellfield Cres. CH45: New B 3A 52
Bellflower Cl. WA8: Wid 5E 109
Bellgreen Rd. L11: N Grn. 1A 58
Bell Ho. WA8: Wid 3C 132
Bellingham Dr. WA7: Run 2A 166
Bellini Cl. L21: Sea 2F 33
Bellis Gro. L33: K'by 5D 15
Bell La. L35: R'hill 4A 88
WA9: Sut M 4A 88
Bellmore St. L19: Gars 5B 124
Bell Rd. CH44: Wall 3D 75
Bell's Cl. L31: Lyd 3B 6
Bells La. L31: Lyd 4A 6
Bell St. L13: Liv 3A 80
Belltower Rd. L20: Kirk 4B 54
Bellward Cl. CH63: Spit 5F 141
Belmont Av. CH41: Birk 4C 96
Belmont Av. CH62: Brom 1C 162
Belmont Dr. CH61: Pens 4A 138
L6: Liv 1C 78
Belmont Gro. CH43: O'ton 4C 96
L6: Liv 1B 78
Belmont Pl. L19: Gars 1C 144
Belmont Rd. CH45: New B 2B 52
CH48: W Kir 3B 112
L6: Liv 1B 78
WA8: Wid 2D 133
Belmont St. WA10: St. H 5D 45
Belmont Vw. L6: Liv 1C 78
(off Bk. Belmont Rd.)
Beloe St. L8: Liv 5F 99
Belper St. L19: Gars 1B 144
Belsford Way L24: Speke 3B 146
Belston Rd. L16: Child 1C 102
Belton Rd. L36: Huy 5D 61
(not continuous)
Belvedere Av. WA9: Sut L 5D 67
Belvedere Cl. L34: Prsct 4E 63
WA6: Frod 4C 172
Belvedere Ct. CH49: W'chu 3B 116
(off Childwall Grn.)
Belvidere Pk. L23: C'by 2E 17
Belvidere Rd. CH45: Wall 5F 51
L8: Liv 4A 100
L23: C'by 2D 17
Belvoir Rd. L18: Aller 4C 124
WA8: Wid 3B 132
Bembridge Cl. WA8: Wid 5F 109
Bempton Rd. L17: Aig 2B 122
Benbow Cl. CH43: Bid 1F 95
Benbow St. L20: Boot 1B 54
Benedict Ct. L20: Boot 2C 54
Benedict St. L20: Boot 2D 55
Benfleet Ho. L19: Aig 5F 123
Bengel St. L7: Liv 4A 78
Benledi St. L5: Liv 1D 77
Benmore Rd. L18: Moss H 2A 124
Bennet's La. CH47: Meols 1E 91
Bennett Cl. CH64: Will 5A 170
Bennetts Hill CH43: O'ton 5B 96
Bennetts La. WA8: Wid 3E 133
Bennett St. L19: Gars 1C 144
Bennett Wlk. CH61: Pens 4F 137
Ben Nevis Rd. CH42: Tran 2D 119
Bennison Dr. L19: Gras 5A 124
Ben's Ct. L34: Know 3B 40
Benson Cl. CH49: Upton 5F 93
Benson St. L1: Liv 5E 77 (6G 5)

Bentfield Cl. L17: Aig 4E 123
Bentfield Cl. CH63: High B 5D 119
Bentfield Gdns. CH63: High B 5D 119
Bentham Cl. CH43: Noct 1E 117
Bentham Dr. L16: Child 1D 103
Bentinck Cl. CH41: Birk 3C 96
Bentinck Pl. CH41: Birk 3C 96
Bentinck St. CH41: Birk 3C 96
(not continuous)
L5: Liv 1B 76
WA7: Run 4F 151
Bentley Rd. CH43: O'ton 5B 96
CH61: Pens 2A 138
L8: Liv 3B 100
Bentley St. WA9: Clock F 2C 88
Benton Cl. L5: Liv 5D 55
Bent Way CH60: Hes 1A 158
Benty Cl. CH63: High B 3E 141
Benty Farm Gro. CH61: Pens 2A 138
Benty Heath La. CH64: Will 2A 170
CH66: Hoot 2A 170
Benwick Rd. L32: K'by 3B 22
Berbice Rd. L18: Moss H 3A 102
Beresford Av. CH63: Beb 5A 120
Beresford Cl. CH43: O'ton 4A 96
Beresford Ct. CH43: O'ton 4A 96
Beresford Rd. CH43: O'ton 4F 95
CH45: Wall 4F 51
L8: Liv 3D 99
Beresford St. L5: Liv 2E 77 (1H 5)
L20: Boot 2B 54
WA9: St. H 4E 65
Berey's Bldgs. L3: Liv 4C 4
Bergen Cl. L20: Boot 1E 55
Berkeley Av. CH43: Pren 3F 117
Berkeley Ct. CH49: W'chu 3A 116
(off Childwall Grn.)
WA7: Mnr P 3D 155
WA12: New W 4F 49
Berkeley Dr. CH45: New B 4C 52
Berkeswell Rd. L11: N Grn. 2A 58
Berkley Av. L12: W Der 3D 59
Berkley Cl. L8: Liv 3F 99
Berkley St. L8: Liv 2F 99
Berkshire Gdns. WA10: St. H 1F 65
Bermondsey Gro. WA8: Wid 5D 111
Bermuda Rd. CH46: More 5C 70
Bernard Av. CH45: New B 4C 52
Bernard Wood Ct. WN5: Bil 1C 82
Berner's Rd. L19: Gras 5B 124
Berner St. CH41: Birk 1D 97
Berrington Av. L25: Wltn 2F 125
Berringtons La. WA11: R'ford 3B 28
Berryford Rd. L14: K Ash 5F 59
Berry Hill Av. L34: Know 5C 40
Berrylands Cl. CH46: More 5D 71
Berrylands Rd. CH46: More 4D 71
Berry Rd. WA8: Wid 3D 131
Berrys La. WA9: St. H 2F 67
Berry St. L1: Liv 1E 99 (7G 5)
L20: Boot 1B 54
Berry St. Ind. Est. L20: Boot 5B 34
Berrywood Dr. L35: Whis 4F 85
Bertha Gdns. CH41: Birk 1F 95
Bertha St. CH41: Birk 1F 95
Bertram Dr. CH47: Meols 3C 90
Bertram Dr. Nth. CH47: Meols 3D 91
Bertram Rd. L17: Aig 5C 100
Bertram St. WA12: New W 5F 49
Berwick Av. CH62: East 1E 171
Berwick Cl. CH43: Bid 3C 94
CH46: More 1B 92
L6: Liv 2B 78
Berwick Dr. L23: C'by 5C 8
Berwick St. L6: Liv 2B 78
Berwyn Av. CH47: Hoy 4C 90
CH61: Thing 1A 138
Berwyn Blvd. CH63: High B 4E 119
Berwyn Dr. CH61: Hes 5A 138
Berwyn Gro. WA9: St. H 5F 47
Berwyn Rd. CH44: Wall 1C 74
L4: Walt 3C 56
Beryl Rd. CH43: Noct 4C 94

Beryl St. L13: Liv 5A 80
Beryl Wlk. L10: Faz 1B 38
Besford Ho. L25: Gate 4B 104
Besford Rd. L25: Gate 4B 104
Bessborough Rd. CH43: O'ton 5B 96
Bessbrook Rd. L17: Aig 2D 123
Bessemer St. L8: Liv 5F 99
Beta Cl. CH62: New F 5A 120
Betchworth Cres. WA7: Beech 4D 167
Bethany Cl. WA11: Hay 1A 48
Bethany Cres. CH63: Beb 2F 141
Bethel Gro. L15: Liv 3D 101
Betjeman Gro. L16: Child 1E 103
Betony Cl. L26: Halew 3E 127
Bettisfield Av. CH62: Brom 5D 163
Betula Cl. L9: Walt 4B 36
Beulah Av. WN5: Bil 1D 31
Bevan Cl. WA9: St. H 5D 65
Bevan's La. L12: W Der 4C 58
Beverley Dr. CH60: Hes 4B 158
Beverley Gdns. CH61: Thing 1B 138
Beverley Rd. CH45: Wall 5F 51
CH62: New F 4B 120
L15: W'tree 3A 102
Beversbrook Rd. L11: N Grn. 1B 58
Bevington Bush L3: Liv 3D 77 (1E 5)
Bevington Hill L3: Liv 2D 77
Bevington St. L3: Liv 2D 77
Bewey Cl. L8: Liv 5E 99
Bewley Dr. L32: K'by 4D 23
Bewsey St. WA10: St. H 2D 65
Bexhill Cl. L24: Speke 3B 146
Bexhill Gdns. WA9: St. H 5C 64
Bianca St. L20: Boot 2C 54
Bibbys La. L20: Boot 3A 34
Bibby St. L13: Liv 3F 79
Bickerstaffe St. L3: Liv 3E 77 (1H 5)
WA10: St. H 5A 46
Bickerton Av. CH63: High B 4D 119
Bickerton St. L17: Aig 1C 122
Bickley Cl. WA7: Run 1C 166
Bidder St. L3: Liv 3E 77 (1H 5)
Bideford Av. WA9: Sut L 1C 88
Bidson Link Rd. CH44: Wall 4D 73
BIDSTON 1D 95
Bidston Av. CH41: Birk 2F 95
CH45: Wall 5E 51
WA11: St. H 3D 47
Bidston Cn. CH43: Noct 2E 95
Bidston Grn. Ct. CH43: Bid 1C 94
Bidston Grn. Dr. CH43: Bid 1C 94
Bidston Ind. Est. CH44: Wall 3D 73
Bidston Link Rd. CH43: Bid 4D 73
Bidston Moss CH44: Wall 3D 73
Bidston Moss Nature Reserve 3E 73
Bidston Rd. CH43: C'ton, O'ton . . .3E 95
L4: Walt 3B 56
Bidston Sta. App. CH43: Bid 4C 72
Bidston Station (Rail) 4C 72
Bidston Vw. CH43: Bid 5C 72
Bidston Village Rd. CH43: Bid 5B 72
Bidston Way WA11: St. H 3D 47
Bigdale Dr. L33: K'by 2F 23
Bigham Rd. L6: Liv 3C 78
Biglands Dr. L36: Huy 1F 105
Big Mdw. Rd. CH49: W'chu 5A 94
BILLINGE 1E 31
Billinge Cres. WA11: St. H 2D 47
Billingham Rd. WA9: St. H 4D 65
Billings Cl. L5: Kirk 5C 54
Billington Rd. WA8: Wid 1B 130
Bilston Rd. L17: Aig 4E 123
Bilton Cl. WA8: Wid 2E 133
Bingley Rd. L4: Walt 4B 56
Binns Rd. L7: Liv 4E 79
L13: Liv 4E 79
Binns Rd. Ind. Est. L13: Liv 5F 79
Binns Way L13: Liv 5F 79
Binsey Cl. CH49: Upton 4D 93
Birbeck Rd. L33: K'by 2A 24
Birbeck Wlk. L33: K'by 2A 24
Birchall St. L20: Kirk 4C 54
Birch Av. CH49: Upton 3D 93
L9: Ain 2B 36
WA10: St. H 2F 45

Birch Cl. CH43: O'ton 1B 118
L31: Mag 1F 13
L35: Whis 2E 85
Birch Ct. L8: Liv 5A 100
(off Weller Way)
Birch Cres. WA12: New W 4F 49
Birchdale Cl. CH49: Grea 4D 93
Birchdale Rd. L9: Walt 4A 36
L22: Water 3D 17
Birchen Rd. L26: Halew 5A 128
L28: Stock V 4A 60
Birches, The CH44: Wall 4E 75
Birches Cl. CH60: Hes 2A 158
Birchfield CH46: More 2C 92
Birchfield Av. WA8: Wid 2A 132
Birchfield Cl. CH46: More 2C 92
L7: Liv 4E 79
Birchfield Rd. L4: Walt 1A 56
L7: Liv 4E 79
WA8: Wid 4A 110
Birchfield St. L3: Liv 3E 77 (2H 5)
WA9: St. H 4D 65
Birchfield Way L31: Lyd 2B 6
Birch Gdns. WA10: St. H 2F 45
Birch Gro. CH45: New B 4C 52
L15: W'tree 5A 80
L35: Prsct 2E 85
L36: Huy 4D 83
Birch Heys CH48: Frank 3A 114
Birch Hill M. L25: Wltn 3A 126
Birchill Rd. L33: Know I 3C 24
Birchley Av. WN5: Bil 2C 30
Birchley Rd. WN5: Bil 2B 30
Birchley St. WA10: St. H 4A 46
Birchley Vw. WA11: St. H 3B 30
Birchmere CH60: Hes 5E 137
Birchmuir Hey L32: K'by 4F 23
Birchridge Cl. CH62: Spit 5C 142
Birch Rd. CH43: O'ton 1B 118
CH47: Meols 3E 91
CH63: Beb 3A 142
L36: Huy 5E 83
WA7: Run 2B 166
WA8: Wid 1B 132
WA11: Hay 1E 49
Birch St. L5: Liv 1B 76
Birch Tree Av. WA11: St. H 5F 29
Birch Tree Ct. L12: W Der 5A 58
Birchtree Dr. L31: Mell 2A 22
Birchtree Rd. L17: Aig 1E 123
Birchview Way WN5: Noct 4D 95
Birchway CH60: Hes 5C 158
Birchwood Av. CH41: Birk 2D 97
Birchwood Cl. CH41: Birk 2D 97
Birchwood Way L33: K'by 5F 15
Birdcage Cotts. WA11: Hay 1E 49
(off Church Rd.)
Bird St. L7: Liv 2C 100
Birdwood Rd. L11: N Grn. 3F 57
Birkdale Av. CH63: Brom 4C 162
Birkdale Cl. L6: Liv 5D 57
L36: Roby 5C 82
Birkdale Rd. WA8: Wid 4B 110
BIRKENHEAD 3F 97
Birkenhead Central Station (Rail)
. . . . .4E 97
Birkenhead North Station (Rail) . .5F 73
Birkenhead Park Station (Rail) . . .1B 96
Birkenhead Priory 3F 97
Birkenhead Rd. CH44: Wall 5E 75
CH47: Hoy, Meols 3C 90
Birkenhead Transport Mus. 2F 97
Birkenshaw Av. L23: Blun 5B 8
Birket Av. CH46: Leas 3F 71
Birket Cl. CH46: Leas 3A 72
Birket Ho. CH41: Birk 2D 97
Birket Sq. CH46: Leas 3A 72
Birkett Rd. CH42: R Ferr 3E 119
CH48: W Kir 2B 112
Birkett St. L3: Liv 3E 77 (1G 5)
Birkin Cl. L32: K'by 5A 24
Birkin Rd. L32: K'by 5A 24
Birkin Wlk. L32: K'by 5A 24
Birley Ct. L8: Liv 2F 99
Birnam Dr. L35: R'hill 4D 87

Birnam Rd. CH44: Wall 3D 75
Birstall Av. WA11: St. H 3C 46
Birstall Ct. WA7: Run 3D 167
Birstall Rd. L6: Liv 3B 78
Birt Cl. L8: Liv 2A 100
Birtley St. WA8: Wid 2B 130
Bisham Pk. WA7: Nort 5D 155
Bishopdale Dr. L35: R'hill 3D 87
Bishop Dr. L35: Whis 5C 84
Bishopgate St. L15: W'tree 1D 101
Bishop Reeves Rd. WA11: Hay . . .1E 49
Bishop Rd. CH44: Wall 4B 74
L6: Liv 4C 56
WA10: St. H 3E 45
Bishops Ct. CH43: O'ton 1A 118
L25: Wltn 2B 126
Bishop Sheppard Ct. L3: Liv 2C 76
Bishops Way WA8: Wid 1D 133
Bisley St. CH45: Wall 1B 74
L15: W'tree 2E 101
Bispham Dr. CH47: Meols 4E 91
Bispham Ho. L3: Liv 3D 77 (2E 5)
Bittern Cl. WA7: Nort 2D 169
Bixteth St. L3: Liv 4C 76 (3C 4)
Blackberry Gro. L26: Halew 2D 127
Blackboards La. CH66: Chil T 5F 171
BLACKBROOK 2F 47
Blackbrook Cl. L9: Walt 5A 36
WA8: Wid 1C 130
Blackbrook Rd. WA11: St. H 3E 47
Blackburne Av. WA8: Hale B 2B 150
Blackburne Dr. L25: Hunts X 5D 127
Blackburne Pl. L8: Liv 1F 99
Blackburne St. L19: Gars 3C 144
Blackburne Ter. L8: Liv 1F 99
Black Cat Ind. Est. WA8: Wid 1F 151
Black Denton's Pl. WA8: Wid 3D 132
Blackdown Gro. WA9: St. H 1F 67
Blackfield St. L5: Kirk 5D 55
Blackheath Dr. CH46: Leas 3F 71
Blackheath La. WA7: Mnr P 3E 155
Black Horse Cl. CH48: W Kir 3C 112
Black Horse Hill CH48: W Kir 4C 112
Black Horse La. L13: Liv 2B 80
Black Horse Pl. L13: Liv 3B 80
Blackhorse St. WA9: St. H 4D 47
Blackhouse Wlk. L5: Walt 5E 35
Blackhurst Rd. L31: Lyd 2C 6
Blackley Gro. L33: K'by 5F 15
(off Carl's Way)
Blackleyhurst Av. WN5: Bil 1E 31
Blacklock Hall Rd. L24: Speke . . .4C 146
Blacklow Brow L36: Huy 4D 83
Blackmoor Dr. L12: W Der 5C 58
Blackpool St. CH41: Birk 4C 96
Blackrod Av. L24: Speke 3C 146
Blacksmith Pl. L25: Hunts X 4D 127
Blackstock St. L30: N'ton 1D 19
Blackstock St. L3: Liv 3C 76 (1D 4)
Blackstone Av. WA11: St. H 3D 47
Blackstone St. L5: Liv 5B 54
Blackthorn Cres. L28: Stock V 3B 60
Blackthorne Cl. CH46: More 2F 93
Blackthorne Rd. L9: Walt 4B 36
Blackwater Rd. L11: Crox 4D 39
Blackwood Av. L25: Wltn 5F 103
Blair Ct. CH43: C'ton 3A 96
Blair Dr. WA8: Wid 1B 130
Blair Ind. Est. L23: C'by 2F 17
Blair Pk. CH63: Spit 4B 142
Blair St. L8: Liv 2E 99
Blair Wlk. L26: Halew 1F 147
Blaisdon Cl. L11: N Grn. 2A 58
Blakeacre Cl. L26: Halew 1F 147
Blakeacre Rd. L26: Halew 1F 147
Blake Ct. L19: Gars 2C 144
Blakefield Rd. L23: Thorn 4C 10
Blakeley Brow CH63: Raby M 4A 162
Blakeley Ct. CH63: Raby M 4A 162
Blakeley Dell CH63: Raby M 4B 162
Blakeley Dene CH63: Raby M 3B 162
Blakeley Rd. CH63: Raby M 3A 162
Blakeney Cl. CH49: Upton 2A 94
Blakenhall Way CH49: Upton 3D 93
Blaking Dr. L34: Know 4D 41

Blantyre Rd. L15: W'tree 3D 101
Blantyre St. WA7: Run 4F 151
Blay Cl. L25: Hunts X 4D 127
Blaydon Cl. L30: N'ton 4F 19
Blaydon Gro. WA9: St. H 4D 65
Blaydon Wlk. CH43: C'ton 3E 95
Bleak Hill Cl. WA10: Windle 1C 44
Bleak Hill Rd.
WA10: Eccl, Windle 3B 44
Bleasdale Av. L10: Ain 3E 21
Bleasdale Cl. CH49: Upton 3E 93
Bleasdale Rd. L18: Moss H 5A 102
Bleasdale Way L21: Ford 1B 18
Blenheim Av. L21: Lith 5C 18
Blenheim Dr. L34: Prsct 1F 83
Blenheim Rd. CH44: Wall 1D 75
L18: Moss H 4F 101
Blenheim St. L5: Liv 1C 76
Blenheim Way L24: Speke 4B 146
WA11: St. H 2B 46
Blessington Rd. L4: Walt 4F 55
Bletchley Av. CH44: Wall 2F 73
Bligh St. L15: W'tree 2D 101
Blindfoot Rd. WA10: R'ford 1D 43
WA11: R'ford 1D 43
Blisworth St. L21: Lith 2B 34
Blomfield Rd. L19: Aller 5D 125
Bloomfield Grn. L17: Aig 5C 100
Bloomsbury Way WA8: Wid 1D 131
Blossom Gro. L32: K'by 1F 39
Blossom St. L20: Boot 3C 34
Blucher St. L22: Water 4C 16
Bluebell Av. CH41: Birk 1F 95
WA11: Hay 1E 49
Bluebell Cl. L22: Water 4E 17
Bluebell Ct. WA7: Beech 1F 173
Blue Bell La. L36: Huy 2E 83
Blueberry Flds. L10: Faz 2F 37
Bluecoat Arts Cen. 5D 77 (6E 5)
Bluecoat Chambers L1: Liv 6E 5
Bluecoat Display Cen. 5D 77 (6E 5)
Bluefields St. L8: Liv 2F 99
Blue Hatch WA6: Frod 5C 172
Blue Jay Cl. L27: N'ley 4E 105
Bluestone La. L31: Mag 1E 13
Bluewood Dr. CH41: Birk 5D 73
Blundell Rd. L38: High 1A 8
WA8: Wid 4C 130
BLUNDELLSANDS 1C 16
Blundellsands & Crosby Station (Rail)
. . . . .1C 16
Blundellsands Classic L23: Blun . .2B 16
Blundellsands Ct. L23: Blun 2B 16
(off Blundellsands Rd. W.)
Blundellsands Rd. E. L23: Blun . . .1C 16
Blundellsands Rd. W. L23: Blun . . .2B 16
Blundells Dr. CH46: More 5F 71
BLUNDELL'S HILL 4B 86
Blundell's La. L35: R'hill 5A 86
Blundell St. L1: Liv 2D 99
Blyth Cl. WA7: Murd 5D 169
Blythe Av. WA8: Wid 5B 110
Blyth Hey L30: N'ton 1D 19
Blyth Rd. CH63: Brom 3C 162
Blythswood St. L17: Aig 1A 122
Boaler St. L6: Liv 3A 78
Boaler St. Ind. Est. L6: Liv 2B 78
Boardmans La. WA9: St. H 4E 47
WA11: St. H 4E 47
Boathouse La. CH64: Park 5C 158
Bobbies La. WA10: Eccl 4F 43
Bob Paisley Ct. L5: Liv 5F 55
Bodden St. WA9: Clock F 2D 89
Bodley St. L4: Walt 4F 55
Bodmin Av. WA7: Brook 4B 168
Bodmin Gro. WA11: St. H 1D 47
Bodmin Rd. L4: Walt 2F 55
Bodmin Way L26: Halew 4E 127
Bognor Cl. L24: Speke 3B 146
Bolan St. L13: Liv 3F 79
BOLD .4B 68
Bold Bus. Cen. WA9: Bold 4B 68
Bolden Cl. L30: N'ton 4F 19
Bolde Way CH63: Spit 1A 162
BOLD HEATH 2E 111

Bold Ind. Est. WA8: Wid 4C 110
Bold Ind. Pk. WA9: Bold 5B 68
Bold La. WA5: C Grn 4B 68
   WA9: Bold 4B 68
Bold Pl. L1: Liv 1E 99 (7H 5)
Bold Rd. WA9: St. H 4F 67
Bold St. L1: Liv 5D 77 (6F 5)
   WA7: Run 4B 152
               (not continuous)
   WA8: Wid 5A 132
   WA10: St. H 5F 45
Boleyn, The L31: Lyd 4E 7
Boleyn Ct. WA7: Mnr P 4C 154
Bollington Cl. CH43: O'ton 1F 117
Bolton Av. L32: K'by 3C 22
Bolton Cl. WA9: St. H 4C 46
Bolton Rd. CH62: Port S 2B 142
Bolton Rd. E. CH62: Port S 1C 142
Bolton St. L3: Liv 5D 77 (5G 5)
   WA9: St. H 4C 46
               (not continuous)
Bolton Wlk. L32: K'by 3C 22
Bonchurch Dr. L15: W'tree 5F 79
Bond St. L3: Liv 2D 77
   L34: Prsct 5D 63
Bonnington Av. L23: C'by 5C 8
Bonsall Rd. L12: W Der 5B 58
Boode Cft. L28: Stock V 2B 60
Booker Av. L18: Moss H, Aller 3A 124
Booth St. L13: Liv 3A 80
   WA9: St. H 4D 65
Boothwood Cl. L7: Liv 1B 100
BOOTLE .5D 35
Bootle Leisure Cen. 4C 34
Bootle New Strand Station (Rail)
   . . . . .4C 34
Bootle Oriel Road Station (Rail)
   . . . . .1B 54
Borax St. L13: Liv 4A 80
Bordehill Gdns. L12: W Der 3D 59
Border Rd. CH60: Hes 2B 158
Border Way L5: Liv 5E 55
Borella Rd. L13: Liv 5F 57
Borough Pavement CH41: Birk 3D 97
Borough Pl. CH41: Birk 3E 97
Borough Rd. CH41: Birk 1C 118
   CH42: Tran 1C 118
   CH44: Wall 3D 75
   WA10: St. H 1E 65
Borough Rd. E. CH41: Birk 3E 97
               (not continuous)
Borough Way CH44: Wall 4E 75
Borrowdale Cl. WA6: Frod 5D 173
Borrowdale Rd. CH46: More 1E 93
   CH63: Beb 3E 141
   L15: W'tree 3E 101
   WA8: Wid 4C 130
   WA10: St. H 3C 64
Bosco Cl. L11: Crox 4B 38
Boscow Cres. WA9: St. H 4D 67
Bosnia St. L8: Liv 1A 122
Bossom Ct. L22: Water 5D 17
Bostock St. L5: Liv 1D 77
Boston Av. WA7: Run 2B 166
Boswell Rd. CH43: Pren 3F 117
Boswell St. L8: Liv 2B 100
   L20: Boot 3A 34
Bosworth Cl. CH63: Spit 5F 141
Bosworth Rd.
   WA11: St. H 2C 46
Botanic Est. L7: Liv 5D 79
Botanic Gro. L7: Liv 5C 78
Botanic Pl. L7: Liv 4C 78
Botanic Rd. L7: Liv 4C 78
Botany Rd. L24: Speke 2C 146
Botley Cl. CH49: Upton 4D 93
Boulevard L6: Liv 2C 78
Boulevard, The L8: Liv 3A 100
   L12: W Der 3B 58
Boulevard Industry Pk.
   L24: Halew 2E 147
               (not continuous)
Boulton Av. CH48: W Kir 2B 112
   CH62: New F 4B 120

Boundary Dr. L23: C'by 4D 9
   L25: Hunts X 5D 127
Boundary Farm Rd. L26: Halew . . .1D 147
Boundary La. CH60: Hes 2A 158
   L6: Liv 2A 78
   L33: Know 3E 25
Boundary Rd. CH43: Bid 5D 73
   CH48: W Kir 1D 135
   CH62: Port S 5B 120
   L21: Lith 3D 19
               (not continuous)
   L36: Huy 1A 106
   WA10: St. H 5E 45
Boundary St. L5: Liv 5B 54
Boundary St. E. L5: Liv 5D 55
Boundary Wlk. L36: Huy 1A 106
Bourne Gdns. WA9: St. H 2C 66
Bournemouth Ct. WA7: Murd 4D 169
Bourne St. L6: Liv 3B 78
Bourton Rd. L25: Hunts X 5B 126
Bousfield St. L4: Walt 4E 55
Bowden Cl. L12: Crox 1E 59
Bowden Rd. L19: Gars 1B 144
Bowden St. L21: Lith 2B 34
Bowdon Cl. WA10: Eccl 1B 64
Bowdon Rd. CH45: Wall 5A 56
Bowen Cl. WA8: Wid 5D 109
Bower Gro. L21: Sea 1F 33
Bower Ho. CH49: Upton 2F 93
Bower Rd. CH60: Hes 3C 158
   L25: Wltn 5A 104
   L36: Huy 2E 83
Bowers Bus. Pk. WA8: Wid 5B 132
Bowers Pk. Ind. Est. WA8: Wid 5C 132
Bower St. WA8: Wid 3D 132
Bowfell Cl. CH62: East 2D 171
Bowfield Rd. L19: Gras 5B 124
Bowgreen Cl. CH43: Bid 2C 94
Bowland Av. L16: Child 5D 81
   WA9: Sut M 3B 88
Bowland Cl. CH62: Brom 1C 162
   WA7: Beech 5E 167
Bowland Dr. L21: Ford 1B 18
Bowles St. L20: Boot 2A 34
Bowley Rd. L13: Liv 1F 79
Bowness Av. CH43: Pren 2A 118
   CH63: Brom 5C 162
   WA11: St. H 5B 30
Bowood St. L8: Liv 1F 121
BOWRING PARK 5A 82
Bowring Pk. Av. L16: Child 5A 82
Bowring Pk. Rd. L14: B Grn 5C 80
Bowring St. L8: Liv 5F 99
Bowscale Cl. CH49: Upton 4E 93
Bowscale Rd. L11: N Grn. 2A 58
Boxdale Cl. L18: Moss H 5A 102
Boxdale Rd. L18: Moss H 5A 102
Boxgrove Cl. WA8: Wid 1B 132
Boxmoor Rd. L18: Moss H 2A 124
Boxtree Cl. L12: Crox 4F 39
Boxwood Cl. L36: Roby 4C 82
Boycott St. L5: Liv 5A 56
Boyd Cl. CH46: Leas 3B 72
Boydell Cl. L28: Stock V 4B 60
Boyer Av. L31: Mag 3D 13
Boyes Brow L33: K'by 1D 23
Boyton Ct. L7: Liv 1C 100
Brabant Rd. L17: Aig 3E 123
Braby Rd. L21: Lith 2C 34
Bracken Ct. WA9: St. H 5C 66
Brackendale CH49: W'chu 1C 116
   WA7: Run 2D 167
Brackendale Av. L9: Ain 1B 36
Bracken Dr. CH48: W Kir 4E 113
Brackenhurst Dr. CH45: New B 4C 52
Brackenhurst Grn. L33: K'by 3E 23
Bracken La. CH63: High B 2D 141
Brackenside CH60: Hes 5F 137
Bracken Wlk. L32: K'by 4D 23
Bracken Way L12: W Der 1A 80
Bracken Wood L12: Crox 4E 39
Brackenwood Dr. WA8: Wid 5A 130
Brackenwood Gro. L35: Whis 3F 85
Brackenwood Rd. CH63: High B . . .4E 141

Brackley Cl. CH44: Wall 3A 74
   WA7: Run 4F 151
Brackley St. WA7: Run 4F 151
Bracknell Av. L32: K'by 4D 23
Bracknell Cl. L32: K'by 4D 23
Bradbourne Cl. L12: Crox 5E 39
Bradda Cl. CH49: Upton 2F 93
Braddan Av. L13: Liv 1E 79
Braddan Cl. CH63: Spit 5B 142
Bradewell Cl. L4: Kirk 3E 55
Bradewell St. L4: Kirk 3E 55
Bradfield Av. L10: Ain 2C 20
Bradfield St. L7: Liv 4C 78
Bradgate Cl. CH46: More 5B 70
Bradkirk Ct. L30: N'ton 5D 11
Bradley Fold L36: Huy 1B 106
Bradley La. WA5: B'wood 1F 69
Bradley Rd. L21: Lith 4B 18
Bradley Way WA8: Wid 3B 132
Bradman Cl. CH45: Wall 1B 74
Bradman Rd. CH46: More 5C 70
   L33: Know I 2C 24
Bradmoor Rd. CH62: Brom 2D 163
Bradshaw Cl. WA10: St. H 4D 45
Bradshaw St. WA8: Wid 2A 132
Bradshaw Wlk. L20: Boot 4B 34
Bradstone Cl. L10: Faz 2B 38
Bradville Rd. L9: Ain 1C 36
Bradwell Cl. CH48: W Kir 4D 113
Braehaven Rd. CH45: New B 4C 52
Braemar Cl. L35: Whis 3F 85
Braemar St. L20: Kirk 2D 55
Braemore Rd. CH44: Wall 2F 73
Braeside Cres. WN5: Bil 1D 31
Braeside Gdns. CH49: Upton 4F 93
Brae St. L7: Liv 4B 78
Brahms Cl. L8: Liv 3B 100
Braid St. CH41: Birk 1D 97
Brainerd St. L13: Liv 1E 79
Braithwaite Cl. L35: R'hill 3C 86
   WA7: Beech 4D 167
Bramberton Pl. L4: Walt 2C 56
Bramberton Rd. L4: Walt 2C 56
Bramble Av. CH41: Birk 1F 95
Bramble Way CH46: More 4D 71
   WA7: Beech 1E 173
Bramblewood Cl. CH43: Noct 5D 95
   L27: N'ley 4E 105
Brambling Cl. WA7: Beech 5F 167
Brambling Pk. L26: Halew 3E 127
Bramcote Av. WA11: St. H 1C 46
Bramcote Cl. L33: K'by 1A 24
Bramcote Rd. L33: K'by 1F 23
Bramcote Wlk. L33: K'by 1F 23
Bramerton Ct. CH48: W Kir 3A 112
Bramford Cl. CH49: Upton 4E 93
Bramhall Cl. CH48: W Kir 5D 113
   L24: Speke 5E 147
Bramhall Dr. CH62: East 2F 171
Bramhall Rd. L22: Water 5E 17
Bramley Av. CH63: High B 5E 119
Bramley Cl. L27: N'ley 4D 105
Bramleys, The L31: Mag 3C 12
Bramley Wlk. L24: Speke 5D 147
Bramley Way L32: K'by 2C 22
Brampton Cl. L33: K'by 1E 23
Brampton Ct. WA9: St. H 5B 48
Brampton Dr. L8: Liv 1A 100
Bramwell Av. CH43: Pren 3A 118
Bramwell St. WA9: St. H 4E 47
Branch Way WA11: Hay 2D 49
Brancker Av. L35: R'hill 2B 86
Brancote Ct. CH43: C'ton 3E 95
Brancote Gdns. CH62: Brom 3D 163
Brancote Mt. CH43: C'ton 3F 95
Brancote Rd. CH43: C'ton 3F 95
Brandearth Hey L28: Stock V 4B 60
Brandearth Ho. L28: Stock V 4B 60
Brandon WA8: Wid 2A 130
Brandon St. CH41: Birk 3F 97
Brandreth Cl. L35: R'hill 3C 86
Branfield Cl. L12: Crox 4E 39
Branstree Av. L11: N Grn. 1F 57
Bran St. L8: Liv 4E 99
Branthwaite Cl. L11: N Grn. 2A 58

Branthwaite Cres. L11: N Grn. 1A 58
Branthwaite Gro. L11: N Grn. 2A 58
Brasenose Rd. L20: Boot 1B 54
Brassey St. L41: Birk 1A 96
  L8: Liv 3E 99
Brattan Rd. L41: Birk 5C 96
Braunton Rd. CH45: Wall 5A 52
  L17: Aig 3E 123
Braybrooke Rd. L11: N Grn. 5F 37
Bray Cl. WA7: Beech 4D 167
Braydon Cl. L25: Hunts X 1C 146
Brayfield Rd. L4: Walt 2D 57
Bray Rd. L24: Speke 3B 146
Bray St. L41: Birk 1B 96
Brechin St. L33: K'by 3F 23
Breckfield Pl. L5: Liv 1F 77
Breckfield Rd. Nth. L5: Liv 5F 55
Breckfield Rd. Sth. L6: Liv 1A 78
Breck Pl. CH44: Wall 3A 74
Breck Rd. CH44: Wall 2F 73
  L4: Walt 2F 57
  L5: Liv 2F 77
  WA8: Wid 3B 132
Breckside Av. CH44: Wall 2E 73
Breckside Pk. L6: Liv 5C 56
Brecon Av. L30: N'ton 4F 19
Brecon Rd. CH42: Tran 3C 118
Brecon St. L6: Liv 2B 78
Brecon Wlk. L30: N'ton 4A 20
Breeze Cl. L9: Walt 5F 35
Breeze Hill L9: Walt 1F 55
  L20: Boot 5D 35
Breeze La. L9: Walt 5F 35
Brelade Rd. L13: Liv 2F 79
Bremhill Rd. L11: N Grn. 5F 37
Bremner Cl. L7: Liv 5C 78
Brenda Cres. L23: Thorn 3A 10
Brendale Av. L11: Mag 2C 12
Brendan's Way L30: N'ton 2E 19
Brendon Av. L21: Lith 4A 18
Brendon Gro. WA9: St. H 4A 48
Brendor Rd. L25: Wltn 3B 126
Brenig St. CH41: Birk 5F 73
Brenka Av. L9: Ain 4B 20
Brentfield WA8: Wid 2D 131
Brent Way L26: Halew 1F 147
       (not continuous)
Brentwood Av. L17: Aig 1C 122
  L23: C'by 5F 9
Brentwood Ct. WA10: Eccl 5B 44
Brentwood Ct. CH49: W'chu 2A 116
       (off Childwall Grn.)
Brentwood Gro. L33: K'by 4E 15
Brentwood St. CH44: Wall 3C 74
Brereton Av. CH63: Beb 1A 142
  L15: W'tree 2A 102
Brereton Cl. WA7: Cas 2A 168
       (not continuous)
Bretherton Pl. L35: R'hill 2C 86
Bretherton Rd. L34: Prsct 5E 63
Bretlands Rd. L23: Thorn 4B 10
Brett Cl. L33: K'by 5D 15
Brett St. CH41: Birk 1B 96
Brewery La. L31: Mell 1E 21
       (not continuous)
Brewster St. L4: Boot 2E 55
  L20: Walt 2E 55
Breydon Gdns. WA9: St. H 5E 65
Brian Av. CH61: Irby 1F 137
Brian Cummings Ct. L21: Lith 2B 34
Briardale Rd. CH42: Tran 5C 96
  CH44: Wall 4E 75
  CH63: High B 5F 119
  CH64: Will 5A 170
  L18: Moss H 4F 101
Briar Dr. CH46: Hes 2A 158
  L36: Huy 4D 83
Briarfield Av. WA8: Wid 3A 130
Briarfield Rd. CH60: Hes 2B 158
Briars Cl. L35: R'hill 5D 87
Briars Grn. WA10: St. H 3F 45
Briars La. L31: Mag 1E 13
Briar St. L4: Kirk 4D 55
Briarswood CH42: R Ferr 4F 119
  L35: Whis 3F 85

Briarwood L23: Blun 4B 8
  WA7: Nort 2C 168
Briarwood Rd. L17: Aig 1E 123
Briary Cl. CH60: Hes 1B 158
Brickfields L36: Huy 5A 84
Brick St. L1: Liv 2D 99
  WA12: New W 5F 49
Brickwall Grn. L29: Seft 3F 11
Brickwall La. L29: Seft 5D 11
Bride St. L4: Walt 1F 55
Bridge Ct. CH48: W Kir 3A 112
  L30: N'ton 1D 19
  WA9: Clock F 4D 89
Bridgecroft Rd. CH45: Wall 5B 52
Bri. Farm Cl. CH49: W'chu 5B 94
Bri. Farm Dr. L31: Mag 5F 7
Bridgefield Cl. L25: Gate 2B 104
Bridgefield Forum Leisure Cen. . . .2A 128
Bridgeford Av. L12: W Der 4A 58
Bridge Gdns. L12: W Der 2F 59
Bridge Ind. Est. L24: Speke 2B 146
Bridge La. L30: N'ton 2E 19
  WA6: Frod 4C 172
Bridgeman St. WA10: St. H 5D 45
       (not continuous)
Bridgemere Cl. L7: Liv 3D 79
Bridgemere Ho. L17: Aig 2D 123
       (off Mossley Hill Dr.)
Bridgenorth Rd. CH61: Pens 3E 137
Bridge Rd. CH48: W Kir 3A 112
  L7: Liv 1C 100
  L18: Moss H 1A 124
  L21: Lith 1A 34
  L23: Blun 2C 16
  L31: Mag 3D 13
  L34: Prsct 1D 85
  L36: Roby 4C 82
  WA9: Clock F 4D 89
Bridges La. L29: Seft 3F 11
Bridge St. CH41: Birk 2E 97
       (not continuous)
  CH62: Port S 2B 142
       (not continuous)
  L20: Boot 1B 54
  WA7: Run 4B 152
  WA10: St. H 5A 46
Bridge Vw. Cl. WA8: Wid 3A 152
Bridgeway Dr. L33: K'by 1F 23
Bridge Wlk. WA7: Pal F 3F 167
     (off Halton Lea Shop. Cen.)
Bridgewater Cl. L21: Lith 3A 18
Bridgewater Ct. L21: Lith 3A 18
Bri. Water Grange WA7: Pres B . . .5F 169
Bridgewater St. L1: Liv 2D 99
  WA7: Run 4A 152
Bridgeway Way L36: Huy 1A 106
Bridgeway E. WA7: Wind H 2E 57
Bridgeway E. WA7: Wind H 5C 154
Bridgeway W. WA7: Wind H 5B 154
Bridle Av. CH44: Wall 4E 75
Bridle Cl. CH43: Bid 3B 94
  CH62: Brom 3E 163
Bridle Ct. WA9: St. H 3C 66
Bridle Pk. CH62: Brom 3D 163
Bridle Rd. CH44: Wall 4E 75
  CH62: Brom 3E 163
  L30: N'ton 5E 19
Bridle Rd. Ind. Est. L30: N'ton 5F 19
Bridle Way L30: N'ton 5F 19
  L33: K'by 4E 15
Bridport St. L3: Liv 4E 77 (4G 5)
Brierfield Rd. L15: W'tree 3F 101
Brierley Cl. L30: N'ton 1B 20
Briery Hey Av. L33: K'by 3F 23
Brightgate Cl. L7: Liv 1B 100
BRIGHTON LE SANDS 2B 16
Brighton Rd. L22: Water 4D 17
  L36: Huy 3B 84
Brighton St. CH44: Wall 2D 75
Brighton Va. L22: Water 3C 16
Bright St. CH41: Birk 3C 96
       (not continuous)
  L6: Liv .3F 77

Bright Ter. L8: Liv 1F 121
Brightwell Cl. CH49: Upton 5F 93
Brill St. CH41: Birk 1B 96
BRIMSTAGE 5B 140
Brimstage Av. CH63: High B 4D 119
Brimstage Cl. CH60: Hes 3C 158
Brimstage Grn. CH60: Hes 2D 159
Brimstage Hall
  CH63: Brim, Store 3B 140
Brimstage Rd. CH60: Hes 3C 158
  CH63: Beb, Brim, High B 3C 158
  L4: Walt 1E 55
Brimstage St. CH41: Birk 4C 96
Brindley, The 5A 152
Brindley Cl. L21: Lith 3A 18
Brindley Rd. L32: K'by 3C 22
  WA7: Ast 4F 153
  WA9: St. H 5E 67
Brindley St. L8: Liv 3D 99
  WA7: Run 4F 151
Brindley Wharf
  WA4: Dutt, Pres H 5F 169
Brinley Cl. CH62: Brom 5D 163
Brinton Cl. L27: N'ley 3C 104
Brisbane Av. CH45: New B 3A 52
Brisbane St. WA9: St. H 4D 65
Briscoe Av. CH46: More 2E 93
Briscoe Dr. CH46: More 2E 93
Bristol Av. CH44: Wall 2C 74
  WA7: Murd 4E 169
Bristol Rd. L15: W'tree 3A 102
Britannia Av. L5: Liv 2C 100
Britannia Cres. L8: Liv 1F 121
Britannia Pav. L3: Liv 1C 98
Britannia Rd. CH45: Wall 1A 74
Britonside Av. L32: K'by 5F 23
Brittarge Brow L27: N'ley 5E 105
Britten Cl. L8: Liv 3B 100
Broadacre Cl. L18: Moss H 4C 102
Broadbelt St. L4: Walt 1F 55
Broadbent Ho. L31: Mag 3D 13
       (off Boyer Av.)
Broadfield Av. CH43: Bid 1B 94
Broadfield Cl. CH43: Bid 2C 94
Broadgate Av. WA9: St. H 3C 66
BROAD GREEN 5D 81
Broad Grn. Rd. L13: Liv 3A 80
Broad Green Station (Rail) 5D 81
Broadheath Av. CH43: Bid 2C 94
Broadheath Ter. WA8: Wid 3D 131
Broad Hey L30: N'ton 2D 19
Broad Hey Cl. L25: Wltn 1B 126
Broadhurst St. L17: Aig 1B 122
Broadlands L35: Prsct 1E 85
Broad La. CH60: Hes 1C 156
  L4: Walt 2D 57
  L29: Thorn 1C 10
  L32: K'by 5F 23
  WA5: C Grn 2C 68
  WA11: St. H 3B 30
Broad La. Pct. L11: N Grn. 2F 57
Broadleaf Rd. L19: Gras 5F 123
Broadmead CH60: Hes 3C 158
  L19: Aller 5D 125
BROAD OAK 4E 47
Broad Oak Av. WA11: Hay 2B 48
Broad Oak Rd. WA9: St. H 5E 47
Broadoak Rd. L14: K Ash 3F 81
  L31: Mag 1E 13
Broadoaks CH49: Upton 3E 93
Broad Pl. L11: N Grn. 3F 57
Broads, The WA9: St. H 5E 65
Broad Sq. L11: N Grn. 3F 57
Broadstone Dr. CH63: Spit 5F 141
Broad Vw. L11: N Grn. 3F 57
Broadway CH45: Wall 1F 73
  CH49: Grea 4E 93
  CH63: High B 5D 119
Broadway L9: Ain 1E 37
  L11: N Grn. 2E 57
  WA8: Wid 3A 130

Broadway—Buckingham Av.

Broadway WA10: Eccl 4A **44**
WA10: St. H 3C **64**
Broadway Av. CH45: Wall 1F **73**
Broadway Community Leisure Cen. 3B **64**
Broadway Mkt. L11: N Grn. 2E **57**
Broadwood Av. L31: Mag 3C **12**
Broadwood St. L15: W'tree 2E **101**
Brock Av. L31: Mag 5E **7**
Brockenhurst Rd. L9: Walt 3A **36**
Brock Gdns. L24: Hale 5E **149**
Brock Hall Cl. WA9: Clock F 2C **88**
Brockhall Cl. L35: Whis 5A **64**
Brockholme Rd. L18: Moss H 3A **124**
Brocklebank La. L19: Aller 4D **125**
Brockley Av. CH45: New B 2B **52**
Brockmoor Twr. L4: Kirk 3D **55**
Brock St. L4: Kirk 3E **55**
Brodie Av. L18: Moss H 1A **124**
L19: Aig, Aller 2A **124**
BROMBOROUGH 2C **162**
BROMBOROUGH POOL 2D **143**
BROMBOROUGH PORT 4F **143**
Bromborough Rake Station (Rail) 2C **162**
Bromborough Rd. CH63: Beb 2A **142**
Bromborough Station (Rail) 3C **162**
Bromborough Village Rd.
CH62: Brom 1D **163**
Brome Way CH63: Spit 5B **142**
Bromilow Rd. WA9: St. H 1F **67**
Bromley Av. L18: Moss H 4F **101**
Bromley Cl. CH60: Hes 3E **157**
L26: Halew 3A **128**
Bromley Rd. CH45: New B 4A **52**
Brompton Av. CH44: Wall 2C **74**
L17: Liv 3C **100**
L23: C'by 2C **16**
L33: K'by 5F **15**
Brompton Ct. L17: Liv 3C **100**
Brompton Ho. L17: Aig 4C **100**
Bromsgrove Rd. CH49: Grea 5C **92**
Bromyard Cl. L20: Boot 4B **34**
Bronington Av. CH62: Brom 4D **163**
Bronshill Ct. L23: Blun 1A **16**
Bronte Cl. L23: Blun 1B **16**
Bronte St. L3: Liv 4E **77** (4H **5**)
WA10: St. H 4D **45**
Brookbank Ct. L10: Faz 1B **38**
Brookbridge Rd. L13: Liv 5E **57**
Brook Cl. CH44: Wall 1C **74**
WA8: Cron 3C **108**
Brookdale WA8: Wid 1A **130**
Brookdale Av. Nth. CH49: Grea 5E **93**
Brookdale Av. Sth. CH49: Grea 5E **93**
Brookdale Cl. CH49: Grea 5E **93**
Brookdale Rd. L15: W'tree 3E **101**
Brook End WA9: St. H 2A **68**
Brooke Rd. E. L22: Water 3D **17**
Brooke Rd. W. L22: Water 3C **16**
Brookfield Av. L22: Water 5F **17**
L23: C'by 2D **17**
L35: R'hill 1C **86**
WA7: Run 5D **153**
Brookfield Cen. L9: Ain 3C **36**
Brookfield Dr. L9: Ain 3C **36**
Brookfield Gdns. CH48: W Kir 4B **112**
Brookfield Ho. L36: Huy 3E **83**
Brookfield La. L39: Augh 3F **7**
Brookfield Rd. CH48: W Kir 4B **112**
BROOKFIELDS GREEN 2F **7**
Brook Furlong WA6: Frod 3A **172**
Brook Hey Dr. L33: K'by 1F **23**
Brook Hey Wlk. L33: K'by 2A **24**
Brookhill Cl. L20: Boot 5D **35**
Brookhill Rd. L20: Boot 4D **35**
Brookhouse Gro. WA10: Eccl 5F **43**
BROOKHURST 5C **162**
Brookhurst Av. CH62: East 4C **162**
CH63: Brom, East 4C **162**
Brookhurst Cl. CH63: Brom 5C **162**
Brookhurst Rd. CH63: Brom 4C **162**
Brookland La. WA9: St. H 1A **68**
Brookland Rd. CH41: Birk 4D **97**
Brookland Rd. E. L13: Liv 3A **80**
Brookland Rd. W. L13: Liv 3A **80**
Brooklands CH41: Birk 2D **97**
Brooklands, The L36: Huy 5E **83**
Brooklands Av. L22: Water 5E **17**
Brooklands Dr. L31: Mag 2D **13**
Brooklands Pk. WA8: Wid 2C **132**
Brooklands Rd. WA10: Eccl 4A **44**
Brook Lea Ho. L21: Ford 2C **18**
Brooklet Rd. CH60: Hes 2C **158**
Brook Mdw. CH61: Irby 5E **115**
Brook Pk. L31: Mag 3C **12**
Brook Rd. L9: Walt 4A **36**
L20: Boot 5B **34**
L23: Thorn 4A **10**
L31: Mag 2E **13**
Brooks, The WA11: St. H 1A **46**
Brooks All. L1: Liv 5D **77** (6E **5**)
Brookside L12: W Der 3F **59**
L31: Mag 1E **13**
Brookside Av. L14: K Ash 3D **81**
L22: Water 5F **17**
WA10: Eccl 3B **44**
Brookside Cl. L35: Prsct 2E **85**
WA11: Hay 1B **48**
WN5: Bil 1E **31**
Brookside Ct. L23: C'by 1E **17**
Brookside Cres. CH49: Upton 4D **93**
Brookside Dr. CH49: Upton 4E **93**
Brookside Rd. L35: Prsct 2E **85**
WA6: Frod 5A **172**
Brookside Vw. WA11: Hay 1B **48**
Brookside Way WA11: Hay 1B **48**
Brook St. CH41: Birk 1C **96**
CH62: Port S 1A **142**
L3: Liv 4B **76** (3B **4**)
L35: Whis 1F **85**
WA7: Run 4A **152**
WA8: Wid 4B **132**
WA10: St. H 5A **46**
Brook St. E. CH41: Birk 2E **97**
Brook Ter. CH48: W Kir 4B **112**
WA7: Run 5E **153**
Brookthorpe Cl. CH45: Wall 5B **52**
BROOKVALE 5C **168**
Brook Va. L22: Water 5F **17**
Brookvale Av. Nth. WA7: Brook 4B **168**
Brookvale Av. Sth. WA7: Brook 4B **168**
Brookvale Cl. WA5: B'wood 5F **69**
Brookvale Local Nature Reserve 5A **18**
Brookvale Recreation Cen. 4C **168**
Brook Wlk. CH61: Irby 5D **115**
Brookway CH43: Pren 3E **117**
CH45: Wall 1A **74**
CH49: Grea 4E **93**
Brookway La. WA9: St. H 2F **67**
Brookwood Rd. L36: Huy 2E **83**
Broom Cl. L34: Ecc P 5F **63**
Broome Ct. WA7: Brook 4B **168**
Broomfield Cl. CH60: Hes 1D **157**
Broomfield Gdns. L9: Walt 3F **35**
Broomfield Rd. L9: Walt 3F **35**
(not continuous)
Broom Hill CH43: C'ton 2F **95**
Broomhill Cl. L27: N'ley 3C **104**
Broomlands CH60: Hes 2F **157**
Broomleigh Cl. CH63: High B 2D **141**
Broom Rd. WA10: St. H 3B **64**
Brooms Gro. L10: Ain 3E **21**
Broom Way L26: Halew 5E **127**
Broseley Av. CH62: Brom 1C **162**
Broster Av. CH46: More 1C **92**
Broster Cl. CH46: More 1C **92**
Brosters La. CH47: Meols 2E **91**
Brotherhood Dr. WA9: St. H 4D **67**
Brotherton Cl. CH62: Brom 1C **162**
Brotherton Rd. CH44: Wall 4E **75**
Brougham Av. CH41: Tran 5F **97**
Brougham Rd. CH44: Wall 3D **75**
Brougham Ter. L6: Liv 3A **78**
Broughton Av. CH48: W Kir 3A **112**
Broughton Dr. L19: Gras 5A **124**
Broughton Hall Rd. L12: W Der 1E **81**
Broughton Rd. CH44: Wall 3B **74**
Broughton Way WA8: Hale B 2B **150**
BROW, THE 1F **167**
Brow La. CH60: Hes 3F **157**
Brownbill Bank L27: N'ley 4E **105**
BROWN EDGE 4D **65**
Brown Heath Av. WN5: Bil 2D **31**
Browning Av. CH42: R Ferr 3F **119**
WA8: Wid 4F **131**
Browning Cl. L36: Huy 5F **83**
Browning Rd. CH45: Wall 1D **73**
L13: Liv 5F **57**
L22: Water 3D **17**
Browning St. L20: Boot 4A **34**
Brownlow Arc. WA10: St. H 5A **46**
Brownlow Hill L3: Liv 5E **77** (5G **5**)
Brownlow Rd. CH62: New F 5B **120**
Brownlow St. L3: Liv 5F **77** (5J **5**)
Brownmoor Cl. L23: C'by 1A **18**
Brownmoor La. L23: C'by 2F **17**
Brownmoor Pk. L23: C'by 2F **17**
Brown's La. L30: N'ton 2F **19**
Brown St. WA8: Wid 5D **133**
Brownville Rd. L13: Liv 4D **57**
Brow Rd. CH43: Bid 5D **73**
Brow Side L5: Liv 2F **77**
Broxholme Way L31: Mag 3D **13**
Broxton Av. CH43: Pren 2F **117**
CH48: W Kir 3C **112**
Broxton Cl. WA8: Wid 1C **130**
Broxton Rd. CH45: Wall 5F **51**
Broxton St. L15: W'tree 1E **101**
Bruce Cres. CH63: Brom 4C **162**
Bruce St. L8: Liv 5A **100**
WA10: St. H 4E **45**
Brunel Dr. L21: Lith 3A **18**
Brunel M. L5: Liv 1A **78**
Brunel Rd. CH62: Brom 1F **163**
Brunner Rd. WA8: Wid 4A **132**
Brunsborough Cl.
CH62: Brom 4C **162**
Brunsfield Cl. CH46: More 2C **92**
Brunstath Cl. CH60: Hes 1C **158**
Brunswick WA7: Run 4A **152**
Brunswick Bus. Pk. L3: Liv 4D **99**
(not continuous)
Brunswick Cl. L4: Kirk 3E **55**
Brunswick Ct. CH41: Birk 2E **97**
Brunswick Ent. Cen. L3: Liv 4D **99**
Brunswick M. CH41: Birk 2E **97**
L22: Water 5E **17**
Brunswick Pde. L22: Water 5D **17**
Brunswick Pl. L20: Kirk 3B **54**
Brunswick Rd. L6: Liv 3F **77** (2J **5**)
WA12: New W 4F **49**
Brunswick Station (Rail) 5E **99**
Brunswick St. L2: Liv 5C **76** (6B **4**)
L3: Liv 5B **76** (6B **4**)
L19: Gars 4C **144**
WA9: St. H 5A **48**
Brunswick Way L3: Liv 4D **99**
Brunt La. L19: Aller 5E **125**
Brushford Cl. L12: W Der 1B **58**
Bruton Rd. L36: Huy 5D **61**
(not continuous)
Bryanston Rd. CH42: Tran 2A **118**
L17: Aig 1B **122**
Bryant Rd. L21: Lith 2B **34**
Bryceway, The L12: W Der 2D **81**
Brydges St. L7: Liv 5A **78**
Bryer Rd. L35: Prsct 2D **85**
Bryn Bank CH44: Wall 2C **74**
Brynmor Rd. L18: Moss H 3A **124**
Brynmoss Av. CH44: Wall 2F **73**
Brynn St. WA8: Wid 4B **132**
WA10: St. H 4A **46**
Bryony Way CH42: R Ferr 4F **119**
Brythen St. L1: Liv 5D **77** (5F **5**)
Buccleuch St. CH41: Birk 5F **73**
Buchanan Cl. WA8: Wid 1F **131**
Buchanan Rd. CH44: Wall 3D **75**
L9: Walt 5F **35**
Buckfast Av. WA11: Hay 1F **49**
Buckfast Cl. L30: N'ton 1F **19**
Buckfast Ct. WA7: Nort 4E **155**
Buckingham Av. CH43: C'ton 2F **95**
CH63: High B 5E **119**

Buckingham Av. L17: Liv 3D **101**
  WA8: Wid 5A **110**
Buckingham Bingo
  Bootle 5C **34**
  Hunt's Cross 1A **146**
  Huyton 4E **83**
Buckingham Cl. L30: N'ton 2C **18**
Buckingham Ct. L33: K'by 1F **23**
Buckingham Dr. WA11: St. H 1A **46**
Buckingham Ho. L17: Aig 4D **101**
Buckingham Rd. CH44: Wall 2F **73**
  L9: Walt 2A **36**
  L13: Liv 5D **57**
  L31: Mag 1C **12**
Buckingham St. L5: Liv 1E **77**
Buckland Cl. WA8: Wid 5C **130**
Buckland Dr. CH63: Spit 5F **141**
Buckland St. L17: Aig 1B **122**
Buckley Hill La. L29: Seft 1D **19**
Buckley La. CH64: Will 5A **170**
Buckley Wlk. L24: Speke 5D **147**
Buckley Way L30: N'ton 5D **11**
Buckthorn Cl. L28: Stock V 4B **60**
Buckthorn Gdns. WA9: St. H 5C **64**
Bude Cl. CH43: Bid 3C **94**
Bude Rd. WA8: Wid 2E **131**
Budworth Av. WA8: Wid 2D **131**
  WA9: Sut M 3B **88**
Budworth Cl. CH43: O'ton 5E **95**
  WA7: Run 3D **167**
Budworth Ct. CH43: O'ton 4F **95**
Budworth Dr. L25: Wltn 2C **126**
Budworth Rd.
  CH43: Noct, O'ton 5E **95**
Buerton Cl. CH43: Noct 5E **95**
Buffs La. CH60: Hes 1B **158**
Bulford Rd. L9: Faz 4D **37**
Bulkeley Rd. CH44: Wall 3D **75**
Bull Bri. La. L10: Ain 3E **21**
Bullens Rd. L4: Walt 3F **55**
  L32: K'by 4F **23**
Bullfinch Ct. L26: Halew 3E **127**
Bull La. L9: Ain 1A **36**
  L9: Walt 2F **35**
Bullrush Dr. CH46: More 4A **72**
Bulrushes, The L17: Aig 1F **121**
Bulwer St. CH42: R Ferr 2F **119**
  L5: Liv 1A **78**
  L20: Boot 3A **34**
Bunbury Dr. WA7: Run 4C **166**
Bundoran Rd. L17: Aig 2D **123**
Bungalows, The *CH63: Thorn H* *4B* **160**
  (off Raby Rd.)
Bunter Rd. L32: K'by 1F **39**
Bunting Ct. L26: Halew 2D **127**
Burbo Bank Rd. L23: Blun 1A **16**
Burbo Bank Rd. Nth. L23: Blun . . .5A **8**
Burbo Bank Rd. Sth. L23: Blun . . .2B **16**
Burbo Cres. L23: Blun 2B **16**
Burbo Mans. L23: Blun 2B **16**
Burbo Way CH45: Wall 3E **51**
Burden Rd. CH46: More 1C **92**
Burdett Av. CH63: Spit 5F **141**
Burdett Cl. CH63: Spit 5A **142**
Burdett Rd. CH45: Wall 1D **73**
  L22: Water 3D **17**
Burdett St. L17: Aig 1B **122**
Burford Av. CH44: Wall 3F **73**
Burford Rd. L16: Child 5C **80**
Burgess Gdns. L31: Mag 5C **6**
Burgess St. L3: Liv 4E **77** (3H **5**)
Burghill Rd. L12: Crox 4F **39**
Burgundy Cl. L17: Aig 2C **122**
Burland Cl. WA7: Run 1F **165**
Burland Rd. L26: Halew 1A **148**
Burleigh M. L5: Liv 4F **55**
Burleigh Rd. Nth. L5: Liv 4F **55**
Burleigh Rd. Sth. L5: Liv 5F **55**
Burley Cl. L32: K'by 4F **23**
Burlingham Av. CH48: W Kir 5D **113**
Burlington Ho. L22: Water 4E **17**
Burlington Rd. CH45: New B 2B **52**
Burlington St. CH41: Birk 3E **97**
  L3: Liv 2C **76**
Burman Cres. L19: Gars 5C **124**

Burman Rd. L19: Gars 5C **124**
Burnage Av. WA9: Clock F 2C **88**
Burnage Cl. L24: Speke 5F **147**
Burnand St. L4: Walt 4F **55**
Burnard Cl. L33: K'by 3F **23**
Burnard Cres. L33: K'by 3F **23**
Burnard Wlk. L33: K'by 3F **23**
Burnell Cl. WA10: St. H 4F **45**
Burnham Cl. WA8: Wid 1C **130**
Burnham Rd. L18: Moss H 1C **124**
Burnie Av. L20: Boot 2E **35**
Burnley Av. CH46: More 1F **93**
Burnley Cl. L6: Liv 2A **78**
Burnley Gro. CH46: More 5F **71**
Burnley Rd. CH46: More 5F **71**
Burnsall Dr. WA8: Wid 1C **130**
Burnsall St. L19: Gars 2E **145**
Burns Av. CH45: Wall 1A **74**
Burns Cl. L16: Child 1F **103**
  L35: Whis 3E **85**
Burns Cres. WA8: Wid 4F **131**
Burns Gro. L36: Huy 5A **84**
Burnside Av. CH44: Wall 4B **74**
Burnside Rd. CH44: Wall 4B **74**
Burns Rd. WA9: Sut M 3A **88**
Burns St. L20: Boot 3A **34**
Burnt Ash Cl. L19: Gras 5F **123**
Burnthwaite Rd. L14: K Ash 3C **80**
Burnt Mill La. WA8: Hale B 2D **149**
Burrell Cl. CH42: Tran 3C **118**
Burrell Ct. CH42: Tran 3C **118**
Burrell Dr. CH46: More 2D **93**
Burrell Rd. CH42: Tran 4B **118**
Burrell St. L4: Walt 3F **55**
Burroughs Gdns. L3: Liv 2D **77**
Burrow's Av. WA11: Hay 3F **47**
Burrows Ct. L3: Liv 1C **76**
  WA9: St. H 5E **47**
Burrows La. L34: Ecc P 4E **63**
  WA10: Eccl 4E **63**
Burrows St. WA11: Hay 2A **48**
Burton Av. CH45: Wall 1E **73**
  L35: R'hill 2A **86**
Burton Cl. L1: Liv 1D **99**
  L35: R'hill 2A **86**
  WA8: Wid 1F **131**
Burtonhead Cl. WA9: St. H 2B **66**
Burtonhead Rd. WA9: St. H 1F **65**
  WA10: St. H 1F **65**
Burton St. L5: Kirk 5B **54**
Burtons Way L32: K'by 5C **22**
BURTONWOOD 5E **69**
Burtonwood Ind. Cen.
  WA5: B'wood 4F **69**
Burtree Rd. L14: K Ash 5A **60**
Burwain Ho. L19: Aig 5F **123**
Burwell Cl. L33: K'by 2A **24**
Burwell Wlk. L33: K'by 2A **24**
Burwen Dr. L9: Walt 2F **35**
Busby's Cotts. CH45: New B 3B **52**
Bushell Cl. CH43: O'ton 5A **96**
Bushel's Dr. WA9: Clock F 3E **89**
Bushey Rd. L4: Walt 1C **56**
Bushley Cl. L20: Boot 4A **34**
Bush Rd. WA8: Wid 2F **151**
Bush Way CH60: Hes 2E **157**
Bus. Resource Cen. L33: Know I . .5C **24**
Butcher's La. L39: Augh 2F **7**
Bute St. L5: Liv 2E **77** (1G **5**)
  (not continuous)
Butleigh Rd. L36: Huy 1D **83**
Butler Cres. L6: Liv 3B **78**
Butler St. L6: Liv 2B **78**
  (not continuous)
Buttercup Cl. CH46: More 4A **72**
  L22: Water 4F **17**
Buttercup Way L9: Walt 4B **36**
Butterfield St. L4: Walt 4F **55**
Buttermere Av. CH43: Noct 3C **94**
  WA11: St. H 5A **30**
Buttermere Cl. L31: Mag 1E **13**
  L33: K'by 1D **23**
  WA6: Frod 5D **173**
Buttermere Ct. *CH41: Birk* *4C* **96**
  (off Penrith St.)

Buttermere Gdns. L23: C'by 3F **17**
Buttermere Gro. WA7: Beech 4D **167**
Buttermere Rd. L16: Child 5A **82**
Buttermere St. L8: Liv 2B **100**
Butterton Av. CH49: Upton 3D **93**
Butterwick Dr. L12: Crox 5B **58**
Button St. L2: Liv 5C **76** (5E **4**)
Butts, The WA7: Cas 5F **153**
Buxted Rd. L32: K'by 5A **24**
Buxted Wlk. L32: K'by 5A **24**
Buxton La. CH44: Wall 1E **73**
Buxton Rd. CH42: R Ferr 2A **120**
Byerley St. CH44: Wall 4D **75**
Byland Cl. WA8: Wid 4C **110**
Byles St. L8: Liv 5A **100**
Byng Pl. L4: Walt 3D **57**
Byng Rd. L4: Walt 3D **57**
Byng St. L20: Boot 1B **54**
By-Pass, The L23: C'by 1E **17**
Byrne Av. CH42: R Ferr 3F **119**
Byrne Avenue Recreation Cen. . . .3F **119**
Byrom St. L3: Liv 3D **77** (3F **5**)
Byron Av. L12: W Der 4A **58**
  L35: Whis 3F **85**
Byron Cl. CH43: Pren 4F **117**
  L36: Huy 5A **84**
  WA10: St. H 3A **46**
Byron Ct. L25: Wltn 1A **126**
Byron Rd. L23: Blun 1C **16**
  L31: Lyd 4D **7**
Byron St. L19: Gars 2C **144**
  L20: Boot 3A **34**
  WA7: Run 1A **166**
Byron Ter. L23: C'by 1C **16**
Byton Wlk. L33: K'by 1A **24**
Bywater Way L10: Faz 1B **38**
Byway, The L23: C'by 5E **9**

C

CABBAGE HALL 5B **56**
Cabes Cl. L14: K Ash 4A **60**
Cabin La. L31: Lyd 3A **6**
Cablehouse L2: Liv 3D **4**
Cable Rd. CH47: Hoy 4B **90**
  L35: Whis 1F **85**
Cables Retail Pk. L34: Prsct 1D **85**
Cable St. L1: Liv 5C **76** (6D **4**)
Cabot Grn. L25: Wltn 4E **103**
Cadbury Cl. L12: W Der 1B **58**
Caddick Rd. L34: Know 3B **40**
Cadmus Wlk. L6: Liv 2F **77**
Cadnam Rd. L25: Gate 4D **105**
Cadogan St. L15: W'tree 1D **101**
Cadwell Rd. L31: Lyd 2B **6**
Caecars Cl. WA7: Cas 1E **167**
Caernarvon Cl. CH49: Upton 3A **94**
  WA7: Cas 5F **153**
Caernarvon Ct. CH63: Beb 3F **141**
Caerwys Gro. CH42: Tran 5E **97**
Caesars Cl. WA7: Cas 5E **153**
Caird St. L6: Liv 3A **78**
Cairn Ct. WA9: St. H 3D **65**
Cairnmore Rd. L18: Moss H 2A **124**
Cairns St. L8: Liv 3A **100**
Cairo St. L4: Kirk 2E **55**
  WA10: St. H 2D **65**
Caithness Dr. WA7: Run 5B **152**
Caithness Dr. CH45: Wall 5C **52**
  L23: C'by 2F **17**
Caithness Gdns. CH43: Pren 3F **117**
Caithness Rd. L18: Aller 3B **124**
Calcott Rake L30: N'ton 1E **19**
  (not continuous)
Calday Grange Cl.
  CH48: W Kir 5D **113**
Caldbeck Gro. WA11: St. H 4C **30**
Caldbeck Rd. CH62: Brom 5D **143**
Calder Av. CH43: Pren 2F **117**
Calder Cl. L33: K'by 4F **15**
  WA8: Wid 1F **133**
Calder Dr. L18: Moss H 4C **102**
  L31: Mag 5E **7**
  L35: R'hill 3B **86**

Calder Edge L18: Moss H 5C 102
Calderfield Rd. L18: Moss H ...4D 103
Calder Grange L18: Aller 1E 125
Calderhurst Dr. WA10: Windle ..2B 44
Calder Pk. Ct. L18: Moss H 5D 103
Calder Rd. CH63: High B 2D 141
  L5: Liv 5F 55
Calders, The L18: Moss H 1C 124
Calderstone Pk.
  (Liverpool Botanic Gardens)
  ....1D 125
CALDERSTONES 1C 124
Calderstones Av. L18: Moss H ..4B 102
Calderstones Ct. L18: Moss H ..5C 102
Calderstones Rd.
  L18: Moss H 5B 102
Calderwood Pk. L27: N'ley 3D 105
Caldicott Av. CH62: Brom 3D 163
Caldon Cl. L21: Lith 4A 18
Caldway Dr. L27: N'ley 3D 105
Caldwell Cl. L33: K'by 1F 23
Caldwell Dr. CH49: W'chu 2B 116
Caldwell Rd. L19: Aller 4C 124
  WA8: Wid 5A 132
Caldwell St. WA9: St. H 5D 47
CALDY 2D 135
Caldy Chase Dr.
  CH48: Caldy 2D 135
Caldy Ct. CH48: W Kir 5B 112
Caldy Gro. WA11: Hay 1A 48
  WA11: St. H 3D 47
Caldy Rd. CH45: Wall 1B 74
  CH48: Caldy, W Kir 5B 112
  L9: Ain 1A 36
Caldy Wood CH48: Caldy 2D 135
Caldywood Dr. L35: Whis 3E 85
Caledonian Cres. L21: Lith 4A 18
Caledonia St. L7: Liv ...1F 99 (7J 5)
Calgarth Rd. L36: Huy 1C 82
California Rd. L13: Liv 4D 57
Callaghan Cl. L5: Liv 1D 77
Callander Rd. L6: Liv 3D 79
Callard Cl. L27: N'ley 3C 104
Callestock Cl. L11: Crox 3C 38
Callington Cl. L14: K Ash 5A 60
Callon Av. WA11: St. H 3E 47
Callow Rd. L15: W'tree 2D 101
Calmet Cl. L5: Liv 5E 55
Calmington La. WA7: Nort 3F 155
Calne Cl. CH61: Irby 5D 115
Calthorpe St. L19: Gars 1B 144
Calthorpe Way CH43: Noct 3D 95
Calvados Cl. L17: Aig 3C 122
Calveley Av. CH62: East 1F 171
Calveley Cl. CH43: O'ton 1A 148
Calveley Gro. L26: Halew 5B 168
Calverley Rd. WA7: Brook 5B 168
Calvers WA7: Halt 1E 167
Camberley Dr. L25: Hunts X ...4C 126
Camberwell Pk. Rd.
  WA8: Wid 5D 111
Camborne Av. L25: Wltn 3C 126
Camborne Cl. WA7: Brook 4C 168
Camborne Rd. WA5: B'wood 5F 69
Cambourne Av. WA11: St. H 1D 47
Cambrian Cl. CH46: More 2C 92
Cambrian Rd. CH46: More 2C 92
Cambrian Way L25: Wltn 1B 126
Cambria St. Nth. L6: Liv 3B 78
Cambria St. Sth. L6: Liv 3B 78
Cambridge Av. L21: Lith 5B 18
  L23: C'by 5D 9
Cambridge Dr. L23: C'by 5C 8
  L26: Halew 4F 127
Cambridge Rd. CH42: Tran 2B 118
  CH45: New B 4B 52
  CH62: Brom 2E 163
  L9: Ain 5B 20
  L20: Boot 1D 55
  L21: Sea 5F 17
  L22: Water 1E 33
  L23: C'by 5C 8
  WA10: St. H 4E 45

Cambridge St. L7: Liv 1F 99
  (not continuous)
  L15: W'tree 1D 101
  (not continuous)
  L34: Prsct 5D 63
  WA7: Run 5C 152
  WA8: Wid 5B 132
Camdale Cl. L28: Stock V 4B 60
Camden Cl. WA7: Nort 1D 169
Camden Pl. CH41: Birk 3D 97
Camden St. CH41: Birk 2E 97
  L3: Liv 4E 77 (3G 5)
Camelford Rd. L11: Crox 3C 38
Camelia Ct. L17: Aig 2A 122
Camellia Gdns. WA9: Bold 4B 68
Camellia Ct. WA12: New W 4F 49
Camelot Ter. L20: Boot 4B 34
  (off Tennyson St.)
Camelot Way WA7: Cas 2A 168
Cameo Cl. L6: Liv 2B 78
Cameron Av. WA7: Run 2E 165
Cameron Rd. CH46: Leas 3B 72
  WA8: Wid 4A 132
Cameron St. L7: Liv 4C 78
Cammell Ct. CH43: C'ton 3B 96
Campania St. L19: Gars 3C 144
Campbell Av. WA7: Run 2A 166
Campbell Cres. L33: K'by 4D 15
Campbell Dr. L14: B Grn 3E 81
Campbell Sq. L1: Liv 7E 5
Campbell St. L1: Liv 1D 99 (7E 5)
  L20: Boot 5A 34
  WA10: St. H 4E 45
Campbeltown Rd. CH41: Tran ...4F 97
Camperdown St. CH41: Birk 3F 97
Camphill Rd. L25: Wltn 4A 126
Campion Cl. WA11: St. H 1B 46
Campion Way L36: Huy 2F 105
Camp Rd. L25: Wltn 3B 126
Campsey Ash WA8: Wid 5F 109
Camp St. CH44: Wall 4C 166
  WA7: Run 4F 152
Cam St. L25: Wltn 2F 125
Canada Blvd. L3: Liv 5B 76 (5B 4)
Canal Bank L31: Lyd 1C 6
Canal Bank Cotts. L31: Lyd 1C 6
Canal Reach WA7: Wind H 5C 154
Canal St. WA7: West P 3D 165
Canalside Gro. L5: Liv 1C 76
Canal St. L20: Boot 1B 54
  (not continuous)
  WA7: Run 4B 152
  WA10: St. H 1F 65
  WA12: New W 5F 49
Canal Vw. L31: Mell 2A 22
Canal Vw. Ct. L21: Lith 3A 18
Canberra Av. WA9: St. H 4E 65
Canberra La. L11: Crox 3C 38
Candia Towers L5: Liv 5E 55
Cannell St. CH64: Will 5A 170
  WA7: Pal F 4A 168
Canning Pl. L1: Liv 5C 76 (7D 4)
Canning St. CH41: Birk 1F 99
  L8: Liv 1F 99
  L22: Water 4D 17
Cannington Rd. WA9: St. H 1B 66
Canniswood Rd. WA11: Hay 2A 48
Cannock Grn. L31: Mag 1B 12
Cannonbury Cl. WA7: Halt 2A 168
Cannon Hill CH43: C'ton 3B 96
Cannon Mt. CH43: C'ton 3B 96
Cannon St. WA9: Clock F 3C 88
Canon Rd. L6: Liv 4C 56
Canon St. WA7: Run 4A 152
Canon Wilson Cl. WA11: Hay ...2D 49
Canova Cl. L27: N'ley 5F 105
  (off Victoria Falls Rd.)
Canrow La. L34: Know 3D 41
Cansfield St. WA10: St. H 4A 46
Canterbury Av. L22: Water 2D 17
Canterbury Cl. L10: Ain 3E 21
  L34: Prsct 4E 63
Canterbury Pk. L18: Aller 4C 124
Canterbury Rd. CH42: R Ferr ...3A 120
  CH44: Wall 3C 74
  WA8: Wid 5C 130

Canterbury St. L3: Liv 3E 77 (2H 5)
  L19: Gars 3C 144
  WA10: St. H 3E 45
Canterbury Way L3: Liv ...3E 77 (2J 5)
  L30: N'ton 1F 19
Canter Cl. L9: Ain 5D 21
Cantley Cl. WA7: Beech 4D 167
Cantsfield St. L7: Liv 2C 100
Canvey Cl. L15: W'tree 2B 102
Capella Cl. L17: Aig 4E 123
Cape Rd. L9: Ain 2C 36
Capesthorne Cl. WA8: Wid 4E 131
Capital Ga. L3: Liv 3J 5
Capitol Trad. Pk. L33: Know I ...4C 24
Caplin Cl. L33: K'by 4E 15
Capper Gro. L36: Huy 3E 83
Capricorn Cres. L14: K Ash 1F 81
Capricorn Way L20: Boot 4B 34
Capstick Cres. L25: Gate 3B 104
Captains Cl. L30: Boot 5D 19
Captains Grn. L30: Boot 5D 19
Captains La. L30: Boot 5E 19
Caradoc Rd. L21: Sea 2A 34
Caraway Cl. L23: Thorn 5B 10
Caraway Gro. WA10: St. H 4D 45
Carbis Cl. L10: Faz 2A 38
Carden Cl. L4: Kirk 4E 55
Cardeston Cl. WA7: Sut W 2F 173
Cardigan Av. CH41: Birk 3D 97
Cardigan Cl. WA10: St. H 1F 65
Cardigan Rd. CH45: New B 4B 52
Cardigan St. L15: W'tree 1D 101
Cardigan Way L6: Liv 2B 78
  L30: N'ton 1B 20
Cardinal Heenan Leisure Cen. ..1D 81
Cardus Cl. CH46: More 1B 92
Cardwell Rd. L19: Gars 1C 144
Cardwell St. L7: Liv 1A 100
Carey Av. CH63: High B 1D 141
Carey St. WA8: Wid 3B 132
Carfax Rd. L33: K'by 1A 24
Cargill Gro. CH42: R Ferr 4B 120
Carham Rd. CH47: Hoy 5C 90
Carina Ct. L19: Aig 5F 123
Carisbrooke Cl. CH48: Caldy ...1C 134
Carisbrooke Pl. L4: Kirk 2F 55
Carisbrooke Rd. L4: Kirk, Walt ..1E 55
  L20: Boot 1E 55
Carkington Rd. L25: Wltn 3C 126
Carlake Gro. L9: Ain 5C 36
Carland Cl. L10: Faz 2B 38
Carlaw Rd. CH42: Tran 2A 118
Carleen Cl. L17: Aig 2B 122
Carlett Blvd. CH62: East 5F 163
Carlett Pk. CH62: East 4F 163
Carley Wlk. L24: Speke 5E 147
Carlile Way L33: K'by 4F 15
Carlingford Cl. L8: Liv 2A 100
Carlisle Av. L30: N'ton 4F 19
Carlisle Cl. CH43: O'ton 4C 96
  L4: Walt 3D 57
Carlisle M. CH43: O'ton 4C 96
Carlis Rd. L32: K'by 5F 23
Carlow Cl. L24: Hale 5D 149
Carlow St. WA10: St. H 2D 65
Carlsruhe Ct. L8: Liv 4A 100
Carl's Way L33: K'by 4F 15
Carlton Av. L18: Moss H 4A 102
  WA7: Run 5D 153
Carlton Bingo Club 2F 35
Carlton La. CH47: Meols 3C 90
  L13: Liv 2A 80
Carlton Mt. CH42: Tran 1E 119
Carlton Rd. CH42: Tran 5C 96
  CH45: New B 3B 52
  CH63: Beb 3B 142
Carlton St. L3: Liv 2B 76
  L34: Prsct 4E 63
  WA8: Wid 4A 132
  WA10: St. H 5E 45
Carlton Ter. CH47: Meols 3C 90
  L23: C'by 1D 17
Carlyon Way L26: Halew 3E 127
Carmarthen Cres. L8: Liv 3D 99
Carmel Cl. CH45: New B 3B 52

Carmel Ct. WA8: Wid 5B **110**
Carmelite Cres. WA10: Eccl 3A **44**
Carmichael Av. CH49: Grea 2D **115**
Carnaby Cl. L36: Huy 1A **106**
Carnarvon Cl. L9: Walt 5F **35**
Carnarvon Rd. L9: Walt 5F **35**
Carnarvon St. WA9: St H 4D **65**
Carnatic Cl. L18: Moss H 1E **123**
Carnatic Rd. L18: Moss H 1E **123**
Carnation Rd. L4: Walt 4B **36**
Carnegie Av. L23: C'by 2D **17**
Carnegie Cres. WA9: St H 3E **67**
Carnegie Rd. L13: Liv 2E **79**
Carnegie Wlk. WA9: St H 3F **67**
Carnforth Av. L32: K'by 4F **23**
Carnforth Cl. CH41: Birk 4C **96**
  L12: W Der 2B **58**
Carnforth Rd. L18: Moss H 2C **124**
Carno St. L15: W'tree 1E **101**
Carnoustie Ct. CH46: More 5B **70**
  L12: W Der 5F **59**
Carnoustie Gro. WA11: Hay 3B **48**
Carnsdale Rd. CH46: More 1F **93**
Carol Dr. CH60: Hes 2C **158**
Carole Cl. WA9: Sut L 5E **67**
Carolina St. L20: Boot 5B **34**
Caroline Pl. CH43: O'ton 4B **96**
Caroline St. WA8: Wid 5B **132**
Caronia St. L19: Gars 3C **144**
Carpathia St. L19: Gars 3C **144**
Carpenter's La. CH48: W Kir 4B **112**
Carpenters Row L1: Liv 1C **98** (7E **4**)
Carraway Rd. L11: Crox 2B **38**
Carr Bri. Rd. CH49: W'chu 5B **94**
Carr Cft. L21: Ford 2B **18**
Carr Cl. L11: N Grn. 1B **58**
Carrfield Av. L23: C'by 2A **18**
Carr Ga. CH46: More 1B **92**
Carr Hey CH46: More 1B **92**
Carr Hey Cl. CH49: W'chu 2C **116**
Carr Ho. La. CH46: More 1B **92**
Carrick Ct. L23: C'by 2A **18**
Carr La. CH46: More 5B **70**
  CH47: Hoy 5B **90**
  CH47: Meols 5A **70**
  CH47: W Kir 1D **113**
  CH48: W Kir 1D **113**
  L11: N Grn. 1F **57**
  L24: Hale 5D **149**
  L31: Lyd .2A **6**
  L34: Prsct 1B **84**
  L36: Roby 4C **82**
  WA8: Hale B 2E **149**
Carr La. E. L11: N Grn. 1B **58**
Carr La. Ind. Est. CH47: Hoy 5C **90**
Carr Mdw. Hey L30: N'ton 3C **18**
CARR MILL 5B **30**
Carr Mill Cres. WN5: Bil 1E **31**
Carr Mill Rd. WA11: St H 1C **46**
  WN5: Bil 1D **31**
Carrock Rd. CH62: Brom 5E **143**
Carrow Cl. CH46: More 2B **92**
Carr Rd. L20: Boot 1D **35**
Carrs St. L35: Whis 3D **85**
Carr St. WA10: St H 3D **45**
Carruthers St. L3: Liv 3C **76** (1C **4**)
Carrville Way L12: Crox 1A **60**
Carrwood Cl. WA11: Hay 2A **48**
Carsdale Rd. L18: Moss H 4A **102**
Carsgoe Rd. CH47: Hoy 5C **90**
Carsington Rd. L11: N Grn. 1A **58**
Carstairs Rd. L6: Liv 2C **78**
Carsthorne Rd. CH47: Hoy 5C **90**
Cartbridge La. L26: Halew 3F **127**
Carter Av. WA11: R'ford 1A **28**
Carters, The CH49: Grea 5C **92**
  L30: N'ton 1A **20**
Carter St. L8: Liv 2F **99**
Carterton Rd. CH47: Hoy 5C **90**
Cartmel Av. L31: Mag 5E **7**
Cartmel Cl. CH41: Birk 4C **96**

Cartmel Dr. CH46: More 2E **93**
  L12: W Der 2C **58**
  L35: R'hill 2A **86**
Cartmell Av. WA10: St H 1E **45**
Cartmell Cl. WA7: Run 4B **166**
Cartmel Rd. L36: Huy 1C **82**
Cartmel Ter. L11: N Grn. 5B **38**
Cartmel Way L36: Huy 2C **82**
Cartwrights Farm Rd.
  L24: Speke 3A **146**
Cartwright St. WA7: Run 5C **152**
Carver St. L3: Liv 3F **77** (2J **5**)
Caryl Gro. L8: Liv 5E **99**
Caryl St. L8: Liv 4E **99**
                              (Park St.)
  L8: Liv .3D **99**
                              (Stanhope St.)
  L8: Liv .4D **99**
                              (Warwick St.)
Cascade Rd. L24: Speke 1C **146**
Case Gro. L35: Prsct 1E **85**
Case Rd. WA11: Hay 2D **49**
Cases St. L1: Liv 5D **77** (5F **5**)
Cashel Rd. CH41: Birk 4B **74**
Caspian Pl. L20: Boot 5C **34**
Caspian Rd. L4: Walt 1C **56**
Cassia Cl. L9: Walt 4B **36**
Cassino Rd. L36: Huy 3D **83**
Cassio St. L20: Boot 1E **55**
Cassley Rd. L24: Speke 4A **148**
Cassville Rd. L18: Moss H 4A **102**
Castell Gro. WA10: St H 5F **45**
Castle Av. WA9: St H 5E **47**
Castle Cl. CH46: Leas 3A **72**
Castle Dr. CH60: Hes 2F **157**
Castlefield Cl. L12: W Der 4A **58**
Castlefield Rd. L12: W Der 4A **58**
CASTLEFIELDS 5A **154**
Castlefields CH46: More 2F **71**
Castlefields Av. E. WA7: Cas 1A **168**
Castlefields Av. Nth. WA7: Cas . . .5E **153**
Castlefields Av. Sth. WA7: Cas . . .1F **167**
Castlefields Local Cen.
  WA7: Cas 5A **154**
Castleford Ri. CH46: Leas 3E **71**
Castleford St. L15: W'tree 2A **102**
Castlegate Gro. L12: W Der 4A **58**
Castlegrange Cl. CH46: Leas 2E **71**
Castleheath Cl. CH46: Leas 3E **71**
Castle Hill L2: Liv 5C **4**
Castle Keep L12: W Der 4B **58**
Castle La. L12: W Der 4B **58**
Castle Mt. CH60: Hes 2F **157**
Castle Pk. 5A **172**
Castle Pk. Arts Cen. 5A **172**
Castle Ri. WA7: Run 5D **153**
Castle Rd. CH45: Wall 5A **52**
  WA7: Halt 2F **167**
Castlesite Rd. L12: W Der 4B **58**
Castle St. CH41: Birk 3F **97**
  L2: Liv 5C **76** (5C **4**)
  L25: Wltn 2F **125**
  WA8: Wid 3D **133**
Castleton Dr. L30: N'ton 1B **20**
Castletown Cl. L16: Child 1E **103**
Castleview Rd. L12: W Der 4B **58**
Castleway Nth. CH46: Leas 2A **72**
Castleway Sth. CH46: Leas 3A **72**
Castlewell L35: Whis 2F **85**
Castlewood Rd. L6: Liv 1B **78**
Castner Av. WA7: West P 3E **165**
Castor St. L6: Liv 1B **78**
Catalyst Mus., The 2A **152**
Catalyst Trade Pk. WA8: Wid 1A **152**
Catchdale Moss La. WA10: Eccl 4E **43**
Catford Cl. WA8: Wid 2C **130**
Catford Grn. L24: Speke 4F **147**
Catharine St. L8: Liv 2F **99** (7J **5**)
Cathcart St. CH41: Birk 2D **97**
Cathedral Cl. L1: Liv 1E **99**
Cathedral Ga. L1: Liv 1E **99**
                          (off Gambier Ter.)
Cathedral Rd. L6: Liv 5C **56**
Cathedral Wlk. L3: Liv 5E **77** (6H **5**)

Catherine Ct. L21: Lith 2B **34**
                          (off Linacre Rd.)
Catherine St. CH41: Birk 3D **97**
  L21: Lith 2B **34**
  WA8: Wid 5A **132**
Catherine Way WA11: Hay 2F **47**
Catkin Rd. L26: Halew 2D **127**
Catonfield Rd. L18: Moss H 4D **103**
Catterall Av. WA9: Sut L 5D **67**
Catterick Cl. L26: Halew 4F **127**
Caulfield Dr. CH49: Grea 1E **115**
Caunce Av. WA11: Hay 2B **48**
Causeway, The CH62: Port S 2B **142**
                              (not continuous)
  L12: W Der 2D **81**
Causeway Cl. CH62: Port S 1B **142**
Causeway Ho. CH46: Leas 2E **71**
Cavalier Dr. L19: Gars 2D **145**
Cavan Dr. WA11: Hay 1D **49**
Cavan Rd. L11: N Grn. 3E **57**
Cavell Cl. L25: Wltn 3A **126**
Cavendish Ct. L18: Moss H 1C **124**
Cavendish Dr. CH42: R Ferr 3D **119**
  L9: Walt 5A **36**
Cavendish Farm Rd.
  WA7: West 5F **165**
Cavendish Gdns. L8: Liv 4A **100**
Cavendish Retail Pk. L9: Walt 5A **36**
Cavendish Rd. CH41: Birk 2B **96**
  CH45: New B 2B **52**
  L23: Blun 2C **16**
Cavendish St. CH41: Birk 1B **96**
  WA7: Run 5F **151**
                              (not continuous)
Cavern Club, The 5D **4**
Cavern Ct. L6: Liv 3B **78**
                          (off Coleridge St.)
Cavern Quarter 5D **4**
Cavern Walks L2: Liv 5D **4**
Cawdor St. L8: Liv 3A **100**
  WA7: Run 4F **151**
Cawfield Av. WA8: Wid 3D **131**
Cawley St. WA7: Run 1A **166**
Cawthorne Av. L32: K'by 5E **23**
Cawthorne Cl. L32: K'by 5E **23**
Cawthorne Wlk. L32: K'by 5E **23**
Caxton Cl. CH43: Bid 3C **94**
  WA8: Wid 1C **130**
Caxton Rd. L35: R'hill 5E **87**
Cazneau St. L3: Liv 2D **77** (1F **5**)
Cearns Rd. CH43: O'ton 4A **96**
Cecil Dr. WA10: Eccl 3A **44**
Cecil Rd. CH42: Tran 2B **118**
  CH45: Wall 2A **74**
  CH62: New F 4B **120**
  L21: Sea 2F **33**
Cecil St. L15: W'tree 1D **101**
  WA9: St H 4F **47**
Cedar Av. CH63: High B 3E **141**
  WA7: Run 3C **166**
  WA7: Sut W 1A **174**
  WA8: Wid 2B **132**
Cedar Cl. L18: Aller 1D **125**
  L35: Whis 2E **85**
Cedar Ct. L34: Know 4D **41**
Cedar Cres. L36: Huy 5D **83**
Cedar Dale Pk. WA8: Wid 5E **111**
Cedardale Rd. L9: Walt 4A **36**
Cedar Gro. L8: Liv 3B **100**
  L22: Water 3D **17**
  L31: Mag 4D **13**
  WA11: Hay 1E **49**
Cedar Rd. L9: Ain 2B **36**
  L35: Whis 3D **85**
Cedars, The CH46: More 2C **92**
  L12: Crox 5F **39**
Cedar St. CH41: Birk 4D **97**
  L20: Boot 4C **34**
  WA10: St H 1D **65**
Cedar Ter. L8: Liv 3B **100**
Cedarway CH60: Hes 5B **158**
Cedarwood Cl. CH49: Grea 5B **92**
Cedarwood Ct. L36: Huy 1E **105**
Celandine Way WA9: Bold 4B **68**
Celebration Dr. L6: Liv 1C **78**

Celendine Cl. L15: W'tree 1E 101
Celia St. L20: Kirk 2D 55
Celtic Rd. CH47: Meols 2E 91
Celtic St. L8: Liv 3A 100
Celt St. L6: Liv 2B 78
Cemeas Cl. L5: Liv 1C 76
Centec Bus. Cen. L10: Faz 3B 38
Centenary Ho. WA7: Run 2C 166
Centenary Rd. L4: Walt 3C 56
Central Av. CH62: Brom 1C 162
   L24: Speke 4C 146
   L34: Ecc P 4F 63
   L34: Prsct 5C 62
Central Bldgs. L23: C'by 1D 17
                                (off Church Rd.)
Central Dr. L12: W Der 1A 80
   WA11: Hay 2B 48
Central Expressway WA7: Run 3E 167
Central Library 3F 5
                               (off Cuerden St.)
Central Pde. L24: Speke 4E 147
Central Pk. Av. CH44: Wall 2C 74
Central Rd. CH62: Port S 5B 120
                                 (Primrose Hill)
   CH62: Port S 2B 142
                                   (Wood St.)
Central Shop. Cen.
   L1: Liv 5D 77 (6F 5)
Central Sq. L31: Mag 5D 7
Central Station (Rail) 5D 77 (6F 5)
Central St. WA10: St. H 4A 46
Central Way L24: Speke 4E 147
Centreville Rd. L18: Moss H 3A 102
Centre Way L36: Huy 4E 83
Centro Pk. L33: Know I 5C 24
Centurion Cl. CH47: Meols 2E 91
Centurion Dr. CH47: Meols 2E 91
Centurion Row WA7: Cas 5F 153
Century Bldgs. L3: Liv 5D 99
Century Rd. L23: C'by 1D 17
Ceres Cl. CH43: Bid 2C 94
Ceres St. L20: Kirk 2C 54
Cestrian Dr. CH61: Thing 2A 138
Chadlow Rd. L32: K'by 1F 39
Chadwell Rd. L33: K'by 1F 23
Chadwick Ct. Ind. Cen.
   L3: Liv 2B 76 (1B 4)
CHADWICK GREEN 2D 31
Chadwick Rd. WA7: Ast 4E 153
   WA11: St. H 1C 46
Chadwick St. CH46: More 1E 93
   L3: Liv 2B 76 (1B 4)
Chadwick Way L33: K'by 4E 15
Chaffinch Cl. L12: W Der 2F 59
Chaffinch Glade L26: Halew 3E 127
Chainhurst Cl. L27: N'ley 4D 105
Chain La. WA11: St. H 1D 47
Chain Wlk. WA10: St. H 5C 44
Chalfont Rd. L18: Aller 3D 125
Chalfont Way L28: Stock V 4B 60
Chalgrave Cl. WA8: Wid 1E 133
Chalkwell Dr. CH60: Hes 3C 158
Challis St. CH41: Birk 5E 73
Challoner Cl. L36: Huy 1F 105
Chaloner Gro. L19: Gars 5F 123
Chaloner St. L3: Liv 2D 99
Chalon Way E. WA10: St. H 5A 46
Chalon Way Ind. Est. WA9: St. H . . .5A 46
Chalon Way W. WA10: St. H 5F 45
Chamberlain Dr. L33: K'by 5F 15
Chamberlain St. CH41: Tran 5E 97
   CH44: Wall 4A 74
   WA10: St. H 5D 45
Chancellor Ct. L8: Liv 1A 100
                                (off Crown St.)
Chancellor Rd. WA7: Mnr P 2D 155
Chancel St. L4: Kirk 4D 55
Chancery La. WA9: St. H 5E 47
Chandlers Ct. WA7: Run 1E 165
Chandos St. L7: Liv 5B 78
Change La. CH64: Will 5B 170
Changford Grn. L33: K'by 2A 24
Changford Rd. L33: K'by 2A 24
Channel, The CH45: Wall 4E 51
Channell Rd. L6: Liv 3C 78

Channel Reach L23: Blun 2B 16
Channel Rd. L23: Blun 2B 16
Chantrell Rd. CH48: W Kir 4E 113
Chantry Cl. CH43: Bid 3C 94
Chantry Wlk. CH60: Hes 4A 158
Chapel Av. L9: Walt 2A 36
Chapel Cl. WA10: St. H 2D 65
Chapelfields WA6: Frod 5A 172
Chapel Gdns. L5: Liv 1D 77
Chapelhill Rd. CH46: More 1F 93
Chapel Ho. L22: Water 5D 17
   L31: Mag 2D 13
Chapel La. L30: N'ton 5F 11
   L31: Mell 1A 22
   L35: R'hill 5E 87
   WA5: B'wood 5E 69
   WA8: Cron 4C 108
   WA10: Eccl 4B 44
Chapel Pde. CH47: Hoy 3C 90
   L6: Liv 5C 56
   L19: Gars 1C 144
Chapel St. L3: Liv 4B 76 (4B 4)
   L34: Prsct 5D 63
   WA8: Wid 5A 132
   WA10: St. H 3F 45
   WA11: Hay 2E 49
Chapel Ter. L20: Boot 5B 34
Chapel Vw. CH62: East 4F 163
   WA11: Crank 1F 29
Chapel Walks L3: Liv 4B 4
Chapel Yd. L15: W'tree 3A 102
                               (off Waterloo St.)
Chapman Cl. L8: Liv 4E 99
   WA8: Wid 5D 109
Charlecombe St. CH42: Tran 5D 97
Chardstock Dr. L25: Gate 5C 104
Charing Cross CH41: Birk 3C 96
Charlecombe St. CH42: Tran 5D 97
Charlecote St. L8: Liv 1F 121
Charles Berrington Rd.
   L15: W'tree 3A 102
Charles Best Grn. L30: N'ton 1F 19
Charles Rd. CH47: Hoy 5B 90
Charles St. CH41: Birk 2D 97
   WA8: Wid 4A 132
   WA10: St. H 4A 46
Charleston Rd. L8: Liv 5E 99
Charlesville CH43: O'ton 4B 96
Charlesville Ct. CH43: O'ton 4B 96
Charles Wlk. L14: B Grn 3F 81
Charlesworth Cl. L31: Lyd 2B 6
Charleywood Rd. L33: Know I 4B 24
Charlock Cl. L30: N'ton 1A 20
Charlotte Rd. CH44: Wall 1C 74
Charlotte's Mdw. CH63: Beb 3A 142
Charlotte Wlk. WA8: Wid 5B 132
Charlotte Way L1: Liv 5F 5
Charlton Cl. WA7: Pal F 3A 168
Charlton Ct. CH43: C'ton 3F 95
   L25: Hunts X 5D 127
Charlton Pl. L13: Liv 5A 80
Charlton Rd. L13: Liv 5A 80
Charlwood Av. L36: Huy 5D 83
Charlwood Cl. CH43: Bid 3C 94
Charmalue Av. L23: C'by 1F 17
Charmouth Cl. L12: Crox 4E 39
Charnock Av. WA11: New W 5F 49
Charnock Rd. L9: Ain 5C 36
Charnwood Cl. L12: Crox 5D 39
Charnwood Rd. L36: Huy 3B 82
Charnwood St. WA9: St. H 4E 47
Charter Ho. CH44: Wall 2D 75
Charterhouse Cl. L25: Wltn 3B 126
Charterhouse Dr. L10: Ain 3E 21
Charterhouse Rd. L25: Wltn 3B 126
Chartmount Way L25: Gate 5B 104
Chartwell Gro. L26: Halew 3A 128
Chase, The CH60: Hes 2A 158
   CH63: Brom 5C 162
   L36: Huy 1F 105
Chaser Cl. L9: Ain 5C 20
Chasewater WA7: Nort 3F 155
Chase Way L5: Liv 2E 77

Chatbrook Cl. L17: Aig 5E 123
Chater Cl. L35: Whis 5A 64
Chatham Cl. L21: Sea 1F 33
Chatham Ct. L22: Water 5E 17
Chatham Pl. L7: Liv 5B 78
Chatham Rd. CH42: R Ferr 2A 120
Chatham St. L7: Liv 1F 99
Chatsworth Av. CH44: Wall 2C 74
   L9: Walt 2F 35
Chatsworth Dr. L7: Liv 1B 100
   WA8: Wid 1C 130
Chatsworth Rd. CH42: R Ferr 2A 120
   CH61: Pens 2F 137
   L35: R'hill 2B 86
Chatteris Pk. WA7: Nort 5D 155
Chatterton Dr. WA7: Murd 2E 169
Chatterton Rd. L14: K Ash 2B 80
Chaucer Dr. L12: Crox 1E 59
Chaucer Rd. WA10: St. H 2D 45
Chaucer St. L3: Liv 3D 77 (1F 5)
   L20: Boot 4A 34
   WA7: Run 1A 166
Cheadle Av. L13: Liv 3F 79
Cheapside L2: Liv 4C 76 (3D 4)
Cheapside All. L2: Liv 4D 4
Cheddar Cl. L25: Wltn 2F 125
Cheddar Gro. L32: K'by 1E 39
   WA5: B'wood 4F 69
Cheddon Way CH61: Pens 3E 137
Chedworth Dr. WA8: Wid 5C 108
Chedworth Rd. L14: K Ash 2E 81
Cheldon Rd. L12: W Der 1C 58
Chelford Cl. CH43: Bid 2C 94
Chellow Dene L23: Thorn 4A 10
Chelmsford Cl. L4: Kirk 4D 55
Chelsea Ct. L12: W Der 3E 59
Chelsea Lea L9: Walt 2A 36
Chelsea Rd. L9: Walt 2A 36
   L21: Lith 2B 34
Cheltenham Av. L17: Liv 3D 101
Cheltenham Cl. L10: Ain 4E 21
Cheltenham Cres. CH46: Leas 3E 71
   L36: Roby 5C 82
   WA7: Run 4B 166
Cheltenham Rd. CH45: Wall 5E 51
Chelwood Av. L16: Child 5E 81
Chemistry Rd. L24: Speke 2C 146
Chenotrie Gdns. CH43: Noct 4D 95
Chepstow Av. CH44: Wall 2C 74
Chepstow St. L4: Walt 2E 55
Chequers Gdns. L19: Aig 4F 123
Cheriton Av. CH48: W Kir 4D 113
Cheriton Cl. L26: Halew 4E 127
Chermside Rd. L17: Aig 3E 123
Cherry Av. L4: Walt 2B 56
Cherrybank CH44: Wall 4B 74
Cherry Blossom Rd.
   WA7: Beech 1F 173
Cherry Brow Ter. CH64: Will 5A 170
                               (off Hadlow Rd.)
Cherry Cl. L4: Walt 2B 56
   WA12: New W 4F 49
Cherrydale Rd. L18: Moss H 3A 102
Cherryfield Cres. L32: K'by 3E 23
Cherryfield Dr. L32: K'by 3D 23
Cherry Gdns. CH47: Hoy 4B 90
   L32: K'by 1F 39
Cherry La. L4: Walt 2A 56
Cherry Sq. CH44: Wall 2B 74
Cherry Tree Av. WA7: Run 2C 166
Cherrysutton WA8: Wid 1A 130
Cherry Tree Cl. L24: Hale 5E 149
   L35: Whis 3D 85
   WA11: Hay 3A 48
Cherry Tree Dr. WA9: St. H 1A 68
Cherry Tree La. WA11: St. H 3A 30
Cherry Tree M. CH60: Hes 2A 158
Cherry Tree Rd. CH46: More 2F 93
   L36: Huy 1E 105
Cherry Va. L25: Wltn 1B 126
Cherry Vw. L33: K'by 5F 15
Cheryl Dr. WA8: Wid 3D 133
Cheshire Acre CH49: W'chu 2A 116
Cheshire Av. L10: Faz 1B 38
Cheshire Gdns. WA10: St. H 1E 65

Cheshire Gro. CH46: More 2E 93
Cheshire Way CH61: Pens 4F 137
Cheshyre Dr. WA7: Halt 1F 167
Cheshyres La.
  WA7: West, West P 3E 155
           (not continuous)
Chesnell Rd. L33: K'by 5F 15
Chesney Cl. L8: Liv 3E 99
Chesnut Rd. L21: Sea 5F 17
Chester Av. L30: N'ton 4F 19
Chester Cl. L23: C'by 1B 18
Chester Cas. 5F 153
Chester Ct. CH63: Beb 3F 141
Chesterfield Dr. L12: K'by 5E 15
Chesterfield Rd. CH62: East . . .1D 171
  L23: C'by 5A 10
Chesterfield St. L8: Liv 2E 99
Chester High Rd.
  CH64: Burt, Will, Nest 5D 159
Chester La. WA9: Sut M, St. H . . .2B 88
Chester Rd. CH60: Hes 3B 158
  L6: Liv 1D 79
  L36: Huy 2A 84
  WA4: Dares 3F 169
  WA6: Frod, Hel 5A 172
  WA7: Sut W, Pres B 3F 173
Chester St. CH41: Birk 4F 97
  CH44: Wall 3A 74
  L8: Liv 2E 99
  L34: Prsct 5D 63
  WA8: Wid 3B 132
Chesterton St. L19: Gars 3C 144
Chester Wlk. L36: Huy 2A 84
Chestnut Av. L23: C'by 4F 9
  L36: Huy 1D 105
  WA8: Wid 2B 132
  WA11: Hay 3F 47
Chestnut Cl. CH49: Grea 3C 114
  L35: Whis 2E 85
Chestnut Ct. L20: Boot 4B 34
  WA8: Wid 3D 131
Chestnut Gro. CH42: Tran 5D 97
  CH62: Brom 2C 162
  L15: W'tree 1F 101
  L20: Boot 3B 34
          (not continuous)
  WA11: St. H 1D 47
Chestnut Ho. L20: Boot 4B 34
Chestnut Rd. L9: Walt 5B 36
Chestnut Wlk. L31: Mell 1A 22
Cheswood Cl. L35: Whis 4E 85
Cheswood Ct. CH49: W'chu 3A 116
      (off Childwall Grn.)
Chetton Dr. WA7: Murd 3D 169
Chetwood Av. L23: C'by 5F 9
Chetwood Dr. WA8: Wid 4F 109
Chetwynd Cl. CH43: O'ton 5F 95
Chetwynd Rd. CH43: O'ton 4A 96
Chetwynd St. L17: Aig 1B 122
Chevasse Wlk. L25: Wltn 1C 126
Cheverton Cl. CH49: W'chu 1B 116
Chevin Rd. L9: Walt 3A 36
Cheviot Av. WA9: St. H 5F 47
Cheviot Cl. CH42: Tran 3D 119
Cheviot Rd. CH42: Tran 3C 118
  L7: Liv 4E 79
Cheviot Way L33: K'by 4F 15
Cheyne Cl. L23: Blun 2A 16
Cheyne Gdns. L19: Aig 4F 123
Cheyne Wlk. WA9: St. H 5F 65
Chichester Cl. L15: W'tree 1D 101
  WA7: Murd 4D 169
Chidden Cl. CH49: Grea 1C 114
Chidlow Cl. WA8: Wid 2A 152
Chigwell Cl. L12: Crox 5E 39
Chilcott Rd. L14: K Ash 3C 80
Childers St. L13: Liv 3F 79
CHILDWALL 2E 103
Childwall Abbey Rd. L16: Child . .2D 103
Childwall Bank Rd. L16: Child . . .2D 103
  L15: W'tree 2C 100
Childwall Cres. L16: Child 2D 103
Childwall Fiveways L15: W'tree . .2C 102

Childwall Grn. CH49: W'chu 2A 116
Childwall La. L14: B Grn 4A 82
  L25: Child 3F 103
Childwall Mt. Rd. L16: Child 2D 103
Childwall Pk. Av. L16: Child 3D 103
Childwall Priory Rd.
  L16: Child 2C 102
Childwall Rd. L15: W'tree 2A 102
Childwall Valley Rd. L16: Child . .2D 103
  L25: Gate 3B 104
  L27: N'ley 3B 104
Chilham Cl. L8: Liv 5F 99
Chilington Av. WA8: Wid 4D 131
Chillerton Rd. L12: W Der 3D 59
Chillingham St. L8: Liv 5A 100
Chiltern Cl. L12: Crox 1F 59
  L32: K'by 1C 22
Chiltern Dr. L32: K'by 1C 22
Chiltern Rd. CH42: Tran 3C 118
  WA9: St. H 5F 47
Chilton Cl. L31: Mag 1D 13
Chilton Ct. L31: Mag 1D 13
Chilton M. L31: Mag 1D 13
Chilwell Cl. WA8: Wid 5D 109
China Farm La. CH48: W Kir . . .2E 113
Chippenham Av. CH49: Grea . . .5C 92
Chirkdale St. L4: Kirk 2E 55
Chirk Way CH46: More 2F 93
Chirton Cl. WA11: Hay 1D 49
Chisenhale St. L3: Liv 2C 76 (1C 4)
Chisledon Cl. WA11: Hay 1D 49
Chislehurst Av. L25: Gate 3A 104
Chislet Cl. WA8: Wid 5E 109
Chisnall Av. WA10: St. H 4C 44
Chiswell St. L7: Liv 4C 78
Chiswick Cl. WA7: Murd 3D 169
Cholmondeley Rd. CH48: W Kir . .4B 112
  WA7: Clftn 1D 173
Cholmondeley St. WA8: Wid . . .3A 152
Cholsey Cl. CH49: Upton 5F 93
Chorley Rd. L34: Prsct 5B 62
Chorley's La. WA8: Wid 1D 133
Chorley St. WA10: St. H 4F 45
Chorley Way CH63: Spit 1A 162
Chorlton Cl. L16: Child 1F 103
  WA7: Wind H 1D 169
Chorlton Gro. CH45: Wall 1D 73
Christchurch Rd. CH43: O'ton . . .5B 96
Christian St. L3: Liv 3D 77 (2F 5)
Christie St. WA8: Wid 3D 133
Christleton Cl. CH43: O'ton 2D 117
Christleton Ct. WA7: Mnr P 3C 154
Christmas St. L20: Kirk 2D 55
Christopher Cl. L16: Child 1D 103
  L35: R'hill 4B 86
Christophers Cl. CH61: Pens . . .3A 138
Christopher Taylor Ho. L31: Mag . .3D 13
Christopher Way L16: Child 1D 103
Christowe Wlk. L11: Crox 3C 38
Chriswaard Cl. L7: Liv 5C 78
Chudleigh Cl. L26: Halew 3E 127
Chudleigh Rd. L13: Liv 3E 79
Chung Hok Ho. L1: Liv 5D 77
         (off Pine M.)
Church All. L1: Liv 5D 77 (6E 5)
Church Av. L9: Ain 1B 36
Church Cl. CH44: Wall 2D 75
Church Cotts. L25: Gate 4C 104
Church Ct. CH49: Upton 3E 93
Church Cres. CH44: Wall 4E 75
Churchdown Cl. L14: K Ash 2F 81
Churchdown Gro. L14: K Ash . . .2E 81
Churchdown Rd. L14: K Ash 2E 81
Church Dr. CH62: Port S 1B 142
Church End M. L24: Hale 5D 149
Church Farm CH60: Hes 3F 157
  CH64: Will 5A 170
Churchfield L25: Gate 5C 104
     (off Jones Farm Rd.)
Churchfield Rd. L25: Gate 4C 104
  WA6: Frod 5C 172
Churchfields WA8: Wid 4B 110
  WA9: Clock F 2C 88
Church Flats L4: Walt 1F 55

Church Gdns. CH44: Wall 2D 75
  L20: Boot 5B 34
Church Grn. L16: Child 2F 103
  L32: K'by 2E 23
Church Gro. L21: Sea 2F 33
Church Hill CH45: Wall 1F 73
Churchill Av. CH41: Birk 2B 96
Churchill Gdns. WA9: St. H 5C 64
Churchill Gro. CH44: Wall 1C 74
Churchill Ho. L21: Sea 1F 33
Churchill Ind. Est. L9: Ain 5C 20
Churchill Mans. WA7: Run 4A 152
      (off Cooper St.)
Churchill Way Nth.
  L3: Liv 4D 77 (3E 5)
Churchlands CH44: Wall 4E 75
       (off Bridle Rd.)
Church La. CH44: Wall 2D 75
      (not continuous)
  CH49: W'chu 2B 116
  CH61: Thurs 2B 136
  CH62: Brom 1D 163
  CH62: East 5F 163
  L4: Walt 1F 55
  L17: Aig 3E 123
  L34: Know 4C 40
  L39: Augh 1F 7
  WA10: Eccl 5A 44
Churchmeadow CH44: Wall 2D 75
Church Mdw. La. CH60: Hes 3E 157
Church Mdw. Wlk. WA8: Hale B . .2B 150
Church Mt. L7: Liv 5B 78
Church M. CH42: R Ferr 3A 120
  L24: Speke 4B 146
Church Pl. CH42: Tran 1D 119
Church Rd. CH42: Tran 1D 119
  CH44: Wall 4E 75
  CH48: W Kir 5A 112
  CH49: Upton 4A 94
  CH63: Beb 4A 142
  CH63: Thorn H 4B 160
  L4: Walt 1A 56
  L13: Liv 4F 79
  L15: W'tree 2A 102
  L19: Gars 2C 144
  L20: Boot 2D 35
  L21: Lith 1B 34
      (not continuous)
  L21: Sea 2F 33
  L22: Water 4D 17
  L23: C'by 1E 17
  L25: Wltn 5F 103
  L26: Halew 2E 127
  L31: Mag 3D 13
  WA11: Hay 2E 49
  WA11: R'ford 1A 28
Church Rd. Nth. L15: W'tree 2A 102
Church Rd. Roby L36: Roby 4C 82
Church Rd. Sth. L25: Wltn 2A 126
Church Rd. W. L4: Walt 1F 55
  WA10: St. H 5A 46
Church Sq. CH62: Brom 1D 163
  WA10: St. H 5A 46
Church St. CH41: Birk 3F 97
      (not continuous)
  CH44: Wall 2D 75
  L1: Liv 5D 77 (5E 4)
  L20: Boot 5A 34
  L34: Prsct 5D 63
  WA6: Frod 5B 172
  WA7: Run 4A 152
  WA8: Wid 2A 152
  WA10: St. H 5A 46
Church Ter. CH42: Tran 1D 119
Church Vw. L12: W Der 4B 58
  L20: Boot 5B 34
Churchview Rd. CH41: Birk 1B 96
Church Wlk. CH48: W Kir 5B 112
  L20: Boot 5B 34
  L34: Know 4C 40
  WA10: Eccl 4A 44
Churchward Ct. L25: Wltn 2A 126
      (off Garden St.)
Church Way L30: N'ton 1D 19
  L32: K'by 2E 23
Churchway Rd. L24: Speke 5A 148

Churchwood Cl. CH62: Brom 1D 163
Churchwood Ct. WA7: W'chu 3B 116
Churnet St. L4: Kirk 3E 55
Churn Way CH49: Grea 5D 93
Churston Rd. L16: Child 4E 103
Churton Av. CH43: O'ton 1F 117
Churton Cl. L6: Liv 3F 77
Ciaran Cl. L12: W Der 3D 59
Cicely St. L7: Liv 5B 78
Cinder La. L18: Moss H 4C 102
   L20: Boot 1D 35
Cineworld Cinema
   Runcorn 3F 167
   St Helens 5F 45
Circular Dr. CH49: Grea 1D 115
   CH60: Hes 1F 157
   CH62: Port S 5B 120
Circular Rd. CH41: Birk 4D 97
Circular Rd. E. L11: N Grn 3F 57
Circular Rd. W. L11: N Grn 3F 57
Cirencester Av. CH49: Grea 5C 92
Citrine Rd. CH44: Wall 4D 75
Citron Cl. L9: Walt 4B 36
City Gdns. WA10: St. H 1F 45
City Rd. L4: Walt 2F 55
   WA10: St. H 2F 45
City Vw. WA11: St. H 4A 30
Civic Way CH63: Beb 2A 142
   L36: Huy 4E 83
Clairville Cl. L20: Boot 5C 34
Clairville Ct. L20: Boot 5C 34
Clairville Way L13: Liv 1E 79
Clamley Ct. L24: Speke 4A 148
Clamley Gdns. L24: Hale 5E 149
Clandon Rd. L18: Aller 3C 124
Clanfield Av. WA8: Wid 1C 130
Clanfield Rd. L11: N Grn 1A 58
Clapgate Cres. WA8: Hale B 2B 150
Clapham Rd. L4: Walt 5B 56
Clare Cl. WA9: St. H 4E 65
Clare Cres. CH44: Wall 1F 73
Claremont Av. L31: Mag 2B 12
   WA8: Wid 5C 110
Claremont Cl. L21: Sea 1F 33
Claremont Ct. CH45: Wall 5F 51
Claremont Dr. WA8: Wid 5B 110
Claremont Rd. CH48: W Kir 3B 112
   L15: W'tree 3E 101
   L21: Sea 1F 33
   L23: C'by 1E 17
   WA7: Run 5B 152
Claremont Way CH63: High B 4D 119
Claremount Dr. CH63: Beb 3F 141
Claremount Rd. CH45: Wall 4F 51
Clarence Av. WA8: Wid 5A 110
Clarence Cl. WA9: St. H 1C 66
Clarence Rd. CH42: Tran 1C 118
   CH44: Wall 4D 75
Clarence St. L3: Liv 5E 77 (5H 5)
   WA7: Run 4F 151
   WA12: New W 4F 49
Clarence Ter. WA7: Run 4A 152
Clarendon Cl. CH43: O'ton 4C 96
   WA7: Murd 3D 169
Clarendon Gro. L31: Lyd 2C 6
Clarendon Rd. CH44: Wall 3D 75
   L6: Liv 5C 56
   L19: Gars 1C 144
   L21: Sea 2F 33
Clare Rd. L20: Boot 1D 55
Claret Cl. L17: Aig 3C 122
Clare Wlk. L10: Faz 1B 38
Clare Way CH45: Wall 1F 73
Claribel St. L8: Liv 3A 100
Clarke Av. CH42: R Ferr 2E 119
Clarke Gardens 4E 125
Clarke Gdns. WA8: Wid 5B 132
Clarke's Cres. WA10: Eccl 4B 44
Clarks Ter. WA7: West P 2D 165
Classic Rd. L13: Liv 2A 80
Clatterbridge Rd. CH63: Spit 2D 161
Claude Rd. L6: Liv 5C 56
CLAUGHTON 2F 95
Claughton Cl. L7: Liv 5C 78
Claughton Dr. CH44: Wall 3B 74

Claughton Firs CH43: O'ton 5B 96
Claughton Grn. CH43: O'ton 4A 96
Claughton Pl. CH41: Birk 3C 96
Claughton Rd. CH41: Birk 3C 96
Claughton St. WA10: St. H 4A 46
Clavell Rd. L19: Aller 4D 125
Claverton Cl. WA7: Run 4B 166
Clay Cross Rd. L25: Wltn 2F 125
Claydon Ct. L26: Halew 3A 128
Clayfield Cl. L20: Boot 5D 35
Clayford Cres. L14: K Ash 2B 80
Clayford Pl. L14: K Ash 2B 80
Clayford Rd. L14: K Ash 2B 80
Clayford Way L14: K Ash 2C 80
Clay La. WA5: B'wood 5E 69
   WA10: Eccl 5D 43
Claypole Cl. L7: Liv 1C 100
Clay St. L3: Liv 2B 76
Clayton Cl. WA10: St. H 5E 45
Clayton Cres. WA7: Run 1F 165
   WA8: Wid 3F 131
Clayton La. CH44: Wall 4A 74
Clayton Pl. CH41: Birk 4C 96
Clayton Sq. L1: Liv 5D 77 (5F 5)
Clayton Sq. Shop. Cen. L1: Liv 5F 5
Clayton St. CH41: Birk 4C 96
Cleadon Cl. L32: K'by 1A 40
Cleadon Rd. L32: K'by 1F 39
Cleadon Way WA8: Wid 5E 109
Clearwater Cl. L7: Liv 4B 78
Cleary St. L20: Boot 4B 34
Clee Hill Rd. CH42: Tran 3C 118
Cleethorpes Rd. WA7: Murd 3C 168
Clegg St. L5: Liv 2E 77
Clematis Rd. L27: N'ley 3E 105
Clement Gdns. L3: Liv 2C 76
Clementina Rd. L23: Blun 1B 16
Clements Way L33: K'by 5D 15
Clemmey Dr. L20: Boot 2E 35
Clent Av. L31: Lyd, Mag 4C 6
Clent Gdns. L31: Lyd 4C 6
Clent Rd. L31: Mag 4C 6
Cleopas St. L8: Liv 5F 99
Cleveland Bldgs. L1: Liv 1C 98 (7E 4)
Cleveland Cl. L32: K'by 1C 22
Cleveland Sq. L1: Liv 1D 99 (7E 4)
Cleveland St. CH41: Birk 1B 96
   WA9: St. H 2C 66
Cleveley Pk. L18: Aller 3D 125
Cleveley Rd. CH47: Meols 3E 91
   L18: Aller 3C 124
Cleveleys Av. WA8: Wid 2D 133
Cleves, The L31: Lyd 4E 7
Clieves Rd. L32: K'by 4F 23
Cliff, The CH45: New B 2F 51
Cliff Dr. CH44: Wall 1D 75
Cliffe St. WA8: Wid 3C 132
Clifford Rd. CH44: Wall 3B 74
Clifford St. CH41: Birk 1A 96
   L3: Liv 4E 77 (3H 5)
Cliff Rd. CH44: Wall 3F 73
Cliff St. L7: Liv 4C 78
Cliff Vw. WA6: Frod 5A 172
CLIFTON 1D 173
Clifton Av. CH62: East 2E 171
   L26: Halew 3E 127
Clifton Ct. CH41: Birk 4D 97
   L19: Aller 4C 124
Clifton Cres. CH41: Birk 3E 97
   WA6: Frod 4C 172
   WA10: St. H 1D 65
Clifton Dr. L10: Ain 3D 21
Clifton Ga. CH41: Birk 4D 97
Clifton Gro. CH44: Wall 2C 74
   L5: Liv 2E 77
Clifton La. WA7: Clftn 1D 173
   (not continuous)
CLIFTON PARK 4D 97
Clifton Rd. CH41: Birk 4D 97
   L6: Liv 1D 79
   WA7: Run 3A 166
   WA7: Sut W 2E 173
   WN5: Bil 1D 31
Clifton Rd. E. L6: Liv 1D 79

Clifton St. L19: Gars 1C 144
   WA10: St. H 4A 46
Clifton Ter. WA10: St. H 1D 65
Cliftonville Rd. L34: Prsct 5E 63
Clincton Cl. WA8: Wid 4A 130
Clincton Vw. WA8: Wid 4A 130
CLINKHAM WOOD 4A 30
Clinton Pl. L12: W Der 4F 57
Clinton Rd. L12: W Der 4F 57
Clint Rd. L7: Liv 5C 78
Clint Rd. W. L7: Liv 5C 78
Clint Way L7: Liv 5C 78
Clipper Vw. CH62: New F 4B 120
Clipsley Brook Vw. WA11: Hay 2F 47
Clipsley Cres. WA11: Hay 1A 48
Clipsley La. WA11: Hay 2B 48
Clive Rd. CH43: O'ton 5B 96
CLOCK FACE 3D 89
Clock Face Colliery Country Pk. . . .2F 89
Clock Face Rd. WA8: Bold H 1C 88
   WA9: Clock F 1C 88
Clock La. WA8: Wid 1F 133
Clock Tower St. WA10: St. H 5F 45
Cloisters, The L23: C'by 2D 17
   WA10: Eccl 4B 44
Clorain Cl. L33: K'by 2A 24
Clorain Rd. L33: K'by 2A 24
Close, The CH49: Grea 2D 115
   CH61: Irby 1D 137
   CH63: High B 3D 119
   L9: Walt 4F 35
   L23: C'by 2D 17
   L28: Stock V 4C 60
   WA10: Eccl 3A 44
   WA11: Hay 3F 47
Closeburn Av. CH60: Hes 4E 157
Close St. WA9: St. H 4E 65
Cloudberry Cl. L27: N'ley 3E 105
Clough, The WA7: Halt 1F 167
Clough Rd. L24: Speke 3D 147
   L26: Halew 3A 128
Clovelly Av. WA9: Sut L 5D 67
Clovelly Gro. WA7: Brook 5B 168
Clovelly Rd. L4: Walt 5B 56
Clover Av. L26: Halew 2D 127
Clover Ct. WA7: Brook 5B 168
Cloverdale Rd. L25: Gate 2A 104
Clover Dr. CH41: Birk 5E 73
Cloverfield WA7: Nort 3C 168
Clover Hey WA11: St. H 1B 46
CLUBMOOR 4E 57
Club St. WA11: St. H 4A 30
Clwyd Gro. L12: W Der 3B 58
Clwyd St. CH41: Birk 3D 97
   CH45: New B 4A 52
Clyde Rd. L7: Liv 4E 79
Clydesdale Rd. CH44: Wall 1D 75
   CH47: Hoy 3B 90
Clyde St. CH42: R Ferr 2F 119
   L20: Kirk 3C 54
Coach Ho. Ct. L29: Seft 4E 11
Coachmans Dr. L12: W Der 2E 59
Coach Rd. L33: Know 1B 42
   WA11: R'ford, Bic 1B 26
Coalgate La. L35: Whis 4C 84
Coalport Wlk. WA9: St. H 5C 64
Coal St. L1: Liv 4E 77 (4G 5)
Coalville Rd. WA11: St. H 2D 47
Coastal Dr. CH45: Wall 3D 51
Cobal Ct. WA6: Frod 5B 172
Cobb Av. L21: Lith 2B 34
Cobbles, The L26: Halew 2D 127
Cobblestone Cnr. L19: Gras 5A 124
Cobden St. CH42: Tran 1F 119
   CH42: Tran 1E 119
Cobden Pl. CH42: Tran 1F 119
   L25: Wltn 2F 125
Cobden St. L6: Liv 3F 77
   L25: Wltn 2F 125
Cobden Vw. L25: Wltn 2F 125
Cobham Av. L9: Walt 2F 35
Cobham Rd. CH46: More 2D 93
Cobham Wlk. L30: N'ton 1D 19
Coburg St. CH41: Birk 3D 97
Coburg Wharf L3: Liv 3C 98

Cochrane St. L5: Liv 1F 77
Cockburn St. L8: Liv 5F 99
Cockerell Cl. L4: Walt 4F 55
Cockerham Way L11: Crox 3B 38
Cock Glade L35: Whis 5D 85
Cocklade La. L24: Hale 5D 149
Cock La. Ends WA8: Hale B 3B 150
Cocksfield Rd. L25: Gate 3B 104
Cockshead Rd. L25: Gate 4B 104
Cockshead Way L25: Gate 3B 104
Cockspur St. L3: Liv 4C 76 (3D 4)
Cockspur St. W. L3: Liv 4C 76 (3C 4)
Coerton Rd. L9: Ain 1B 36
Cokers, The CH42: High B 4E 119
Colbern Cl. L31: Mag 1E 13
Colby Cl. L16: Child 1E 103
Colden Cl. L12: W Der 4E 59
Colebrooke Rd. L17: Aig 1A 122
Coleman Dr. CH49: Grea 1C 114
Colemere Dr. CH61: Thing 1B 138
Coleridge Av. WA10: St. H 4D 45
Coleridge Cl. L32: K'by 5D 23
Coleridge Dr. CH62: New F 5A 120
Coleridge Gro. WA8: Wid 4E 131
Coleridge St. L6: Liv 3B 78
L20: Boot 4A 34
Colesborne Rd. L11: N Grn 1A 58
Coles Cres. L23: Thorn 4B 10
Coleshill Rd. L11: N Grn 5E 37
Cole St. CH43: O'ton 3C 96
Colette Rd. L10: Faz 1B 38
Coleus Cl. L9: Walt 4B 36
Colin Cl. L36: Roby 4C 82
Colindale Rd. L16: Child 2E 103
Colin Dr. L3: Liv 1C 76
Colinton St. L15: W'tree 1E 101
College Av. L23: C'by 2D 17
College Cl. CH43: Bid 3B 94
CH45: Wall 5E 51
College Cl. L12: W Der 1A 80
College Dr. CH63: Beb 5A 120
College Flds. L36: Huy 5E 83
College Grn. Flats L23: C'by 2D 17
College La. L1: Liv 5D 77 (6E 4)
College Rd. L23: C'by 1C 16
College Rd. Nth. L23: Blun 5C 8
College St. WA10: St. H 4A 46
         (not continuous)
College St. Nth. L6: Liv ...3F 77 (2J 5)
College St. Sth. L6: Liv ...3F 77 (2J 5)
College Vw. L20: Boot 1C 54
L36: Huy 4E 83
Collier's Row WA7: West 3E 165
Collier St. WA7: Run 4F 151
Collingwood Rd. CH63: Beb 3B 142
Collin Rd. CH43: Bid 1E 95
Collins Cl. L20: Boot 3A 34
COLLINS GREEN 2D 69
Collins Grn. La. WA5: C Grn 2E 69
Collins Ind. Est. WA9: St. H 3C 46
Collinson Ct. WA6: Frod 5B 172
Colmoor Cl. L33: K'by 4F 15
Colmore Av. CH63: Spit 1F 161
Colmore Rd. L11: N Grn 1E 57
Colne Dr. WA9: St. H 4D 67
Colne Rd. WA5: B'wood 5F 69
Colonnades, The L3: Liv ...1B 98 (7C 4)
Colquitt St. L1: Liv 1E 99 (7G 5)
Coltart Rd. L8: Liv 3B 100
Colton Rd. L25: Gate 2F 103
Colton Wlk. L25: Gate 2F 103
Columban Cl. L30: N'ton 2E 19
Columbia La. CH43: O'ton 5B 96
Columbia Rd. CH43: O'ton 5B 96
L4: Walt 1A 56
L34: Prsct 5E 63
Columbine Cl. L31: Mell 2A 22
WA8: Wid 5B 108
Columbine Way WA9: Bold 4B 68
Columbus Dr. CH61: Pens 4E 137
Columbus Quay L3: Liv 1E 121
Columbus Way L21: Lith 1A 34
Column Rd. CH48: Caldy, W Kir ...4C 112
Colville Rd. CH44: Wall 2A 74
Colville St. L15: W'tree 1E 101

Colwall Cl. L33: K'by 3A 24
Colwall Rd. L33: K'by 3A 24
Colwall Wlk. L33: K'by 3A 24
Colwell Cl. L14: K Ash 4A 60
Colwell Ct. L14: K Ash 4A 60
Colwell Rd. L14: K Ash 5A 60
Colworth Rd. L24: Speke 3B 146
Colwyn Rd. L13: Liv 4F 79
Colwyn St. CH41: Birk 1A 96
Colyton Av. WA9: Sut L 1D 89
Combermere St. L8: Liv 3E 99
L15: W'tree 1D 101
Comely Av. CH44: Wall 2C 74
Comely Bank Rd. CH44: Wall 2D 75
Comer Gdns. L31: Lyd 4C 6
Comfrey Gro. L26: Halew 2E 127
Commerce Way L8: Liv 2B 100
Commercial Rd. CH62: Brom 4E 143
L5: Kirk 5C 54
Common, The WA7: Halt 1A 168
Common Fld. Rd. CH49: W'chu ...3B 116
Common Rd. WA12: New W 1E 69
Common St. WA9: St. H 4D 65
WA12: New W 5E 49
Commonwealth Pav.
L3: Liv 1C 98 (7C 4)
Commutation Row
L1: Liv 4D 77 (3G 5)
Company's Cl. WA7: West 4F 165
Compass Cl. WA7: Murd 5D 169
Compass Cl. WA5: Wall 3F 51
Compton Cl. WA11: Hay 1C 48
Compton Rd. CH41: Birk 5D 73
L6: Liv 2A 78
Compton Wlk. L20: Boot 4B 34
Compton Way L26: Halew 1E 147
Comus St. L3: Liv 3D 77 (1F 5)
Concert Sq. L1: Liv 6F 5
Concert St. L1: Liv 5D 77 (6F 5)
Concordia Av. CH49: Upton 4A 94
Concourse, The CH48: W Kir 3A 112
Concourse Way WA9: St. H 1F 67
Condor Cl. L19: Gars 1C 144
Condron Rd. Nth. L21: Lith 4C 18
Condron Rd. Sth. L21: Lith 4C 18
Coney Cres. L23: Thorn 5B 10
Coney La. L35: Tar G 2F 105
L36: Huy 2F 105
Coney Wlk. CH49: Upton 3D 93
Congress Gdns. WA9: St. H 4D 65
Conifer Cl. L9: Walt 4B 36
L33: K'by 5E 15
Conifers, The L31: Mag 4C 6
Coningsby Dr. CH45: Wall 2A 74
Coningsby Rd. L4: Walt 4A 56
Coniston Av. CH43: Noct 4C 94
CH45: Wall 4E 51
CH63: East 1C 170
L34: Prsct 5F 63
Coniston Cl. L9: Ain 1B 36
L33: K'by 1D 23
WA7: Beech 4D 167
Coniston Dr. WA6: Frod 5C 172
Coniston Gro. WA11: St. H 1A 46
Coniston Ho. L17: Aig 2D 123
Coniston Rd. CH61: Irby 1D 137
L31: Mag 5D 7
Coniston St. L5: Liv 5A 56
Conleach Rd. L24: Speke 5D 147
Connaught Cl. CH41: Birk 1A 96
Connaught Rd. L7: Liv 4A 78
Connaught Way L41: Birk 1F 95
Connolly Av. L20: Boot 3E 35
Connolly Ho. L20: Boot 1C 54
Conservation Cen. 4D 77 (4E 4)
Consett Rd. WA9: St. H 5D 65
Constables Cl. WA7: Cas 1A 168
Constance St. L3: Liv 4F 77 (3J 5)
WA10: St. H 1D 65
Constance Way WA8: Wid 1A 152
Constantine Av. CH60: Hes 1A 158
Convent Cl. CH42: Tran 5D 97
L19: Gras 5A 124
Conville Blvd. CH63: High B 4D 119

Conway Cl. CH63: High B 2D 141
L33: K'by 5D 15
Conway Ct. CH63: Beb 3F 141
WA7: Cas 5A 154
Conway Dr. CH41: Birk 3D 97
Conway Ho. L6: Liv 2C 78
Conway Park Station (Rail) 2E 97
Conway St. CH41: Birk 2C 96
         (not continuous)
L5: Liv 1E 77
WA10: St. H 1D 65
Conwy Dr. L6: Liv 1B 78
Cook Av. WA11: Hay 1E 49
Cook Rd. CH46: Leas 2B 72
Cookson Rd. L21: Sea 2A 34
Cookson St. L1: Liv 2E 99
Cooks Rd. L23: C'by 5D 9
Cook St. CH41: Birk 4C 96
L2: Liv 5C 76 (5D 4)
L34: Prsct 5D 63
L35: Whis 2F 85
Coombe Dr. WA7: Run 2F 165
Coombe Rd. CH61: Irby 5E 115
Cooperage Cl. L8: Liv 5E 99
Cooper Av. WA12: New W 5F 49
Cooper Av. Nth. L18: Moss H 3A 124
Cooper Av. Sth. L19: Aig 3A 124
Cooper Cl. L19: Aig 4A 124
Cooper La. WA11: Hay 3B 48
Cooper's La. L33: Know I 2D 41
Coopers Row L22: Water 5E 17
Cooper St. WA7: Run 4A 152
WA8: Wid 3B 132
WA10: St. H 4F 45
Copeland Cl. CH61: Pens 3E 137
Copeland Gro. WA7: Beech 5E 167
Copperas Hill L3: Liv 5E 77 (5G 5)
Copperas St. WA10: St. H 5F 45
Copperfield Cl. L8: Liv 4F 99
Copperwood WA7: Nort 1C 168
Copperwood Dr. L35: Whis 4E 85
Coppice, The CH45: Wall 4A 52
L4: Walt 5C 56
L34: Know 5D 41
Coppice Cl. CH43: Bid 3B 94
WA7: Cas 1B 168
Coppice Cres. L36: Huy 2F 83
Coppice Grange CH46: More 2C 92
Coppice Gro. CH49: Grea 2C 114
Coppice La. L35: Tar G 2B 106
Copple Ho. La. L10: Faz 1A 38
Coppull Rd. L31: Lyd 3C 6
Copse, The L18: Moss H 4D 103
L25: Wltn 3B 126
WA7: Pal F 4A 168
         (not continuous)
Copse Gro. CH61: Irby 5E 115
Copsmead CH46: More 1F 93
Copthorne Rd. L32: K'by 3B 22
Copthorne Wlk. L32: K'by 3B 22
Copy Cl. L30: N'ton 5F 11
Copy La. L30: N'ton 5F 11
Copy Way L30: N'ton 5F 11
Coral Av. L36: Huy 3D 83
WA9: St. H 4F 65
Coral Cl. L32: K'by 3C 22
Coral Dr. L20: Boot 5C 34
Coral Ridge CH43: Bid 3D 95
Coral St. L13: Liv 5A 80
Corbet Cl. L32: K'by 3C 22
Corbet Wlk. L32: K'by 3C 22
Corbet Cl. L32: K'by 3C 22
Corbridge Rd. L16: Child 2C 102
Corbyn St. CH44: Wall 4E 75
Corfu St. CH41: Birk 3C 96
Corinthian Av. L13: Liv 2A 80
Corinthian St. CH42: R Ferr 2F 119
L21: Sea 1F 33
Corinth Twr. L5: Liv 5E 55
Corinto St. L8: Liv 2E 99
Corkdale Rd. L9: Walt 4B 36
Cormorant Cen., The WA7: Run ...5E 151
Cormorant Ct. CH45: Wall 3E 51
Cormorant Dr. WA7: Run 5E 151
Corncroft L34: Know 5D 41
Corndale Rd. L18: Moss H 5A 102

Cornelius Dr.—Cresttor Rd.

Cornelius Dr. CH61: Pens 2F 137
Cornel Way L36: Huy 1F 105
Corner Brook L28: Stock V 4F 59
Cornerhouse La. WA8: Wid 1D 131
Cornett Rd. L9: Ain 1B 36
Corney St. L7: Liv 2C 100
Cornfields Cl. L19: Gars 1B 144
Cornflower Way CH46: More 4A 72
Cornforth Way WA8: Wid 1F 131
Cornhill L1: Liv 1C 98
Cornice Rd. L13: Liv 2A 80
Corniche Rd. CH62: Port S 1B 142
Cornmill Lodge L31: Mag 5C 6
Corn St. L8: Liv 4E 99
Cornubia Rd. WA8: Wid 5C 132
Cornwall Av. WA7: Run 5A 152
Cornwall Cl. CH62: New F 4B 120
WA7: Cas 1F 167
Cornwall Ct. CH63: Beb 3F 141
Cornwall Dr. CH43: Pren 3A 118
Cornwallis St. L1: Liv 1D 99 (7G 5)
(not continuous)
Cornwall Rd. WA8: Wid 1B 132
Cornwall St. WA9: St. H 1D 67
Cornwood Cl. L25: Gate 2B 104
Corona Av. L31: Lyd 2C 6
Corona Rd. CH62: Port S 1C 142
L13: Liv 2A 80
L22: Water 4D 17
Coronation Av. CH45: New B 4B 52
L14: B Grn 3E 81
Coronation Bldgs. CH45: Wall 2A 74
CH48: W Kir 2C 112
Coronation Ct. L9: Faz 4F 37
(off Ternhall Rd.)
Coronation Dr. CH62: Brom 4D 143
L14: B Grn 3E 81
L23: C'by 2D 17
L35: Prsct 2C 84
WA6: Frod 4D 173
WA8: Wid 4B 130
WA11: Hay 1F 49
Coronation Ho. WA7: Run 2C 166
Coronation Rd. CH47: Hoy 5A 90
L23: C'by 2D 17
L31: Lyd 4C 6
WA7: Pres B 4F 169
WA7: Run 1B 166
WA10: Windle 2C 44
Coronation Wlk. WN5: Bil 1D 31
Coroner's La. WA8: Wid 4A 110
Coronet Rd. L11: Crox 5C 38
Coronet Way WA8: Wid 4B 130
Corporation Rd. CH41: Birk 1F 95
Corporation St. WA9: St. H 5A 46
WA10: St. H 4A 46
(not continuous)
Corrie Dr. CH63: Beb 3F 141
Corsewall St. L7: Liv 1D 101
Corsican Gdns. WA9: St. H 4C 64
Cortsway CH49: Grea 4E 93
Cortsway W. CH49: Grea 4D 93
Corwen Cl. CH43: Bid 3B 94
CH46: More 2F 93
Corwen Cres. L14: B Grn 4F 81
Corwen Dr. L30: N'ton 1A 20
Corwen Rd. CH47: Hoy 4C 90
L4: Walt 3C 56
Cosgrove Cl. L6: Liv 4D 57
Costain St. L20: Kirk 3C 54
Cote Lea Ct. WA7: Pal F 4F 167
Cotham St. WA10: St. H 5A 46
Coton Way L32: K'by 2C 22
Cotsford Cl. L36: Huy 2C 82
Cotsford Pl. L36: Huy 2C 82
Cotsford Rd. L36: Huy 2C 82
Cotsford Way L36: Huy 2C 82
Cotswold Gro. WA9: St. H 5A 48
Cotswold Rd. CH42: Tran 3C 118
Cotswolds Cres. L26: Halew 5E 127
Cotswold St. L7: Liv 4B 78
Cottage Cl. CH63: Brom 5C 162
L32: K'by 1E 39
Cottage Dr. E. CH60: Hes 5F 157
Cottage Dr. W. CH60: Hes 5F 157
Cottage La. CH60: Hes 5F 157
Cottage Pl. WA9: Clock F 2C 88
Cottage St. CH41: Birk 2D 97
Cottenham St. L6: Liv 3B 78
Cotterdale Cl. WA9: St. H 5C 66
Cotterill WA7: Run 2D 167
Cottesbrook Cl. L11: N Grn. 5F 37
Cottesbrook Pl. L11: N Grn. 5F 37
Cottesbrook Rd. L11: N Grn. 5F 37
Cottesmore Dr. CH60: Hes 2D 159
Cotton La. WA7: Run 2D 167
Cotton St. L3: Liv 2B 76
Cottonwood L17: Aig 1F 121
Cottrell Cl. L19: Gars 3C 144
Coulport Cl. L14: K Ash 1A 82
Coulsdon Pl. L8: Liv 5A 100
Coulthard Rd. CH42: R Ferr 4A 120
Coulton Rd. WA8: Wid 1E 133
Council St. L35: R'hill 1A 86
Countess Pk. L11: Crox 1C 58
Countisbury Dr. L16: Child 3E 103
County Dr. WA10: St. H 1E 65
County Rd. L4: Walt 2F 55
L32: K'by 1E 23
County Sessions House 3G 5
Court, The CH63: Beb 3A 142
L28: Stock V 4C 60
Court Av. L26: Halew 3A 128
Courtenay Av. L22: Water 3C 16
Courtenay Rd. CH47: Hoy 4A 90
L22: Water 3C 16
L25: Wltn 5F 103
Courtfields Cl. L12: W Der 1B 80
COURT HEY 5F 81
Court Hey L31: Mag 1E 13
Ct. Hey Av. L36: Roby 4A 82
Ct. Hey Dr. L16: Child 5F 81
Court Hey Pk. 5F 81
Ct. Hey Rd. L16: Child 5F 81
Courthope Rd. L4: Walt 1B 56
Courtland Rd. L18: Moss H 4B 102
Courtney Av. CH44: Wall 3A 74
Courtney Rd. CH42: R Ferr 4A 120
Courtyard, The CH64: Will 5A 170
L18: Moss H 1F 123
Courtyard Works L33: Know I 3C 24
Covent Gdn. L2: Liv 4B 76 (4C 4)
Coventry Av. L30: N'ton 4F 19
Coventry Rd. L15: W'tree 3A 102
Coventry St. CH41: Birk 3D 97
Coverdale Av. L35: R'hill 3D 87
Covertside CH48: W Kir 4D 113
Cowan Dr. L6: Liv 2A 78
Cowan Way WA8: Wid 5F 109
Cowdrey Av. CH43: Bid 5C 72
Cow Hey La. WA7: Clftn 5A 166
Cowley Cl. CH49: Upton 4D 93
COWLEY HILL 3F 45
Cowley Hill La. WA10: St. H 3E 45
Cowley Rd. L4: Walt 2F 55
Cowley St. WA10: St. H 3A 46
Cowper Rd. L13: Liv 3B 80
Cowper St. L20: Boot 3A 34
WA9: St. H 2C 66
Cowper Way L36: Huy 5A 84
Coylton Av. L35: R'hill 4D 87
Crab St. WA10: St. H 4F 45
Crab Tree Cl. L24: Hale 5E 149
Crabtree Cl. L27: N'ley 4D 105
Crabtree Fold WA7: Nort 2C 168
Cradley WA8: Wid 2C 130
Crag Gro. WA11: St. H 4B 30
Craigburn Rd. L13: Liv 5E 57
Craighurst Rd. L25: Gate 2A 104
Craigleigh Gro. CH62: East 1F 171
Craigmore Rd. L18: Moss H 3A 124
Craigside Av. L12: W Der 4A 58
Craigs Rd. L13: Liv 5E 57
Craigwood Way L36: Huy 3B 82
Craine Cl. L4: Walt 3B 56
Cramond Av. L18: Moss H 4F 101
Cranage Cl. WA7: Run 3D 167
Cranberry Cl. L27: N'ley 3E 105
WA10: St. H 3F 45
Cranborne Av. CH47: Meols 2E 91
Cranborne Rd. L15: W'tree 2C 100
Cranbourne Av. CH41: Birk 2A 96
CH46: More 2D 93
Cranbrook St. WA9: St. H 1B 66
Crane Av. WA9: Sut L 5D 67
Cranehurst Rd. L4: Walt 1B 56
Cranfield Rd. L23: C'by 5A 10
Cranford Cl. CH62: East 1F 171
Cranford Rd. L19: Gras 4B 124
Cranford St. CH44: Wall 4C 74
CRANK 1E 29
Crank Hill WA11: Crank 1E 29
Crank Rd. WA11: Crank, St. H 1C 44
Cranleigh Gdns. L23: C'by 1D 17
Cranleigh Pl. L25: Gate 3A 104
Cranleigh Rd. L25: Gate 3A 104
Cranmer St. L5: Liv 1C 76
(not continuous)
Cranmore Av. L23: C'by 3E 17
Cranshaw Av. WA9: Clock F 3D 89
Cranshaw La. WA8: Wid 4B 110
Cranstock Gro. WA10: Windle 2C 44
Cranston Cl. WA10: St. H 3C 44
Cranston Rd. L33: Know I 3C 24
Crantock Cl. L11: Crox 4C 38
L26: Halew 4F 127
Cranwell Cl. L10: Ain 3C 20
Cranwell Rd. CH49: Grea 1B 114
L25: Gate 2A 104
Cranwell Wlk. L25: Gate 2A 104
Crask Wlk. L33: K'by 1F 23
Craven Cl. CH41: Birk 3D 97
Craven Lea L12: Crox 5E 39
Craven Rd. L12: W Der 5C 58
L35: R'hill 3C 86
Craven St. CH41: Birk 3C 96
L3: Liv 4E 77 (3H 5)
Cravenwood Rd. L26: Halew 5F 127
Crawford Av. L18: Moss H 4F 101
L31: Mag 4B 6
WA8: Wid 3B 130
Crawford Cl. L12: W Der 4D 59
WA9: Clock F 2D 89
Crawford Dr. L15: W'tree 5A 80
Crawford Pk. L18: Moss H 1F 123
Crawford Pl. WA7: Run 4B 166
Crawford St. WA9: Clock F 2E 89
Crawford Way L7: Liv 4E 79
Crawshaw Ct. L36: Huy 2B 82
Crediton Cl. L11: Crox 3C 38
Creek, The CH45: Wall 3E 51
Creer St. L5: Liv 2E 77
Cremona Cnr. L22: Water 4E 17
Cremorne Hey L28: Stock V 4B 60
Crescent, The CH48: W Kir 4A 112
CH49: Grea 1D 115
CH60: Hes 4B 158
CH61: Pens 1F 137
CH63: High B 2E 141
L20: Boot 2E 35
L22: Water 4E 17
L23: Thorn 4A 10
L24: Speke 3C 146
L31: Mag 3C 12
L35: Whis 2F 85
L36: Huy 4A 84
Crescent Ct. L21: Sea 2A 34
Crescent Rd. CH44: Wall 2C 74
L9: Walt 4B 36
L21: Sea 2A 34
L23: Blun 5B 8
Crescents, The L35: R'hill 2A 86
Cressida Av. CH63: High B 5E 119
Cressingham Rd. CH45: New B 3B 52
Cressington Av. CH42: Tran 3D 119
Cressington Esplanade
L19: Gras 1A 144
CRESSINGTON PARK 1A 144
Cressington Station (Rail) 5A 124
Cresson Ct. CH43: O'ton 4F 95
Cresswell Cl. L26: Halew 3A 128
Cresswell St. L6: Liv 2F 77
(not continuous)
Cresta Dr. WA7: West 4F 165
Cresttor Rd. L25: Wltn 1F 125

Creswell St. WA10: St. H 5E 45
Cretan Rd. L15: W'tree 2D 101
Crete Towers L5: Liv 5E 55
Crewe Grn. CH49: W'chu 2A 116
Cricket Cl. L19: Gars 3D 145
Cricklade Cl. L20: Boot 4B 34
Cringles Dr. L35: Tar G 2A 106
Crispin Rd. L27: N'ley 4D 105
Crispin St. WA10: St. H 5E 45
Critchley Rd. L24: Speke 5A 148
Critchley Way L33: K'by 1F 23
Croasdale Dr. WA7: Beech 5E 167
Crockett's Wlk. WA10: Eccl 3B 44
Crocus Av. CH41: Birk 5C 73
Crocus Gdns. WA9: Bold 4A 68
Crocus St. L5: Kirk 4D 55
Croft, The CH49: Grea 2D 115
   L12: W Der 4B 58
   L28: Stock V 3A 60
   L31: Lyd 2B 6
   L32: K'by 1F 39
   WA7: Halt 1F 167
   WA9: St. H 2F 67
Croft Av. CH62: Brom 1C 162
Croft Av. E. CH62: Brom 5D 143
Croft Bus. Cen. CH62: Brom 5E 143
Croft Bus. Pk. CH62: Brom 5D 143
Croft Cl. CH43: Noct 5E 95
Croft Dr. CH46: More 2F 93
   CH48: Caldy 2C 134
Croft Dr. E. CH48: Caldy 2D 135
Croft Dr. W. CH48: Caldy 2C 134
Croft Edge CH43: O'ton 1B 118
Croft End WA9: St. H 2F 67
Crofters, The CH49: Grea 5D 93
Crofters La. L33: K'by 5F 15
Croftfield L31: Mag 1E 13
Croft Grn. CH62: Brom 4D 143
Croft La. CH62: Brom 1D 163
   L9: Ain 1D 37
Crofton Cres. L13: Liv 3B 80
Crofton Rd. CH42: Tran 1E 119
   L13: Liv 3B 80
   WA7: Run 1E 165
Croft St. WA8: Wid 1A 152
Croft Technology Pk.
   CH62: Brom 1E 163
Croft Trade Pk. CH62: Brom 5E 143
Croft Way L23: Thorn 4B 10
Croftwood Gro. L35: Whis 4E 85
Cromarty Rd. CH44: Wall 2F 73
   L13: Liv 3F 79
Cromdale Gro. WA9: St. H 1E 67
Cromer Dr. CH45: Wall 1A 74
Cromer Rd. CH47: Hoy 4A 90
   L17: Aig 3E 123
Cromer Way L26: Halew 1F 147
Cromford Rd. L36: Huy 1E 83
Crompton Ct. L18: Moss H 4D 103
Crompton Dr. L12: Crox 5E 39
Cromptons La. L18: Moss H 5C 102
Crompton St. L5: Liv 1D 77
Cromwell Rd. L4: Walt 1E 55
Cromwell St. WA8: Wid 1A 152
Crondall Gro. L15: W'tree 2B 102
CRONTON 4C 108
Cronton Av. CH46: Leas 3F 71
   L35: Whis 5C 84
Cronton Farm Ct. WA8: Wid 5E 109
Cronton La. L35: R'hill 4B 86
   WA8: Cron 1B 108
   WA8: Wid 4E 109
Cronton Pk. Av. WA8: Cron 3C 108
Cronton Pk. Cl. WA8: Cron 3C 108
Cronton Rd. L15: W'tree 4A 102
   L35: Tar G 2B 106
   WA8: Cron 2D 107
Croome Dr. CH48: W Kir 4C 112
Croppers Hill Ct. WA10: St. H 5E 45
Cropper St. L1: Liv 5D 77 (6G 5)
CROSBY 4C 16
Crosby Cl. CH49: Upton 3F 93
Crosby Coastal Pk.
    . . . . .1A 8
Crosby Grn. L12: W Der 4A 58

Crosby Gro. CH64: Will 4B 170
   WA10: St. H 2D 65
Crosby Leisure Cen. 3B 16
Crosby Rd. Nth. L22: Water 3E 17
Crosby Rd. Sth. L21: Sea 2F 33
   L22: Water 5E 17
Crosby Sailing Club 5D 17
Crosender Rd. L23: C'by 2C 16
Crosfield Cl. L7: Liv 5C 78
Crosfield Rd. CH44: Wall 3C 74
   L7: Liv 5C 78
   L35: Prsct 2F 85
Crosfield Wlk. L7: Liv 5C 78
Crosgrove Rd. L4: Walt 2B 56
Crosland Rd. L32: K'by 4A 24
Cross, The CH62: Brom 1E 163
Cross Acre Rd. L25: Gate 2B 104
Crossdale Rd. CH62: Brom 4D 163
   L23: C'by 2C 16
Crossdale Way WA11: St. H 4B 30
Cross Farm Rd. WA9: St. H 2C 66
Crossfield St. WA9: St. H 5B 46
Crossford Rd. L14: K Ash 5A 60
Cross Gates WA8: Wid 1F 133
Crosshall St. L1: Liv 4D 77 (4E 4)
Cross Hey L21: Ford 3B 18
   L31: Mag 3E 13
Cross Hey Av. CH43: Noct 4D 95
Cross Hillocks La. WA8: Wid 2E 129
Cross La. CH45: Wall 1D 73
   CH63: Beb 3F 141
   L35: Prsct, Whis 2D 85
Crossledge Way L25: Gate 2F 103
Crossley Dr. CH60: Hes 2D 157
   L15: W'tree 1A 102
Crossley Rd. WA10: St. H 3D 65
Cross Mdw. Ct. WA9: St. H 2C 66
               (off Appleton Rd.)
Cross St. CH41: Birk 3F 97
   CH62: Port S 2B 142
   L22: Water 4D 17
   L34: Prsct 4D 63
   WA7: Run 4A 152
   WA8: Wid 3B 132
              (not continuous)
   WA10: St. H 5F 45
Crossvale Rd. L36: Huy 5E 83
Crossway CH43: Bid 1E 95
   WA8: Wid 3D 131
Crossway, The CH63: Raby 5C 160
Crossways CH62: Brom 4D 143
   L25: Gate 3F 103
Crosswood Cres. L36: Huy 3C 82
Crosthwaite Av. CH62: East 1F 171
Croston Av. L35: R'hill 1B 86
Croston Cl. WA8: Wid 1C 130
Crouch St. L5: Liv 5A 56
   WA9: St. H 3D 67
Crow La. W. WA12: New W 4F 49
Crowmarsh Cl. CH49: Upton 5F 93
Crown Acres Rd. L25: Wltn 4C 126
Crown Av. WA8: Wid 4B 130
Crown Ga. WA7: Pal F 3F 167
Crown Rd. L12: W Der 4C 58
Crown Sta. Pl. L7: Liv 1A 100
Crown St. L7: Liv 4F 77
              (not continuous)
   L8: Liv 1A 100
   WA9: St. H 4D 65
   WA12: New W 5F 49
Crownway L36: Huy 2D 83
Crow St. L8: Liv 3D 99
Crowther St. WA10: St. H 5D 45
CROW WOOD 2D 133
Crow Wood La. WA8: Wid 2D 133
Crow Wood Pl. WA8: Wid 1D 133
Croxdale Rd. L14: K Ash 4A 60
Croxdale Rd. W. L14: K Ash 4F 59
Croxeth Ga. L17: Aig 4C 100
CROXTETH 4C 38
Croxteth Av. CH44: Wall 2B 74
   L21: Lith 1A 34
Croxteth Cl. L31: Mag 4E 7
Croxteth Ct. L8: Liv 3B 100
Croxteth Dr. L17: Aig 4C 100

Croxteth Gro. L8: Liv 3B 100
Croxteth Hall 2D 59
Croxteth Hall Country Pk. 2E 59
Croxteth Hall La. L11: Crox 5C 38
   L12: Crox, W Der 5C 38
Croxteth La. L34: Know 2B 60
CROXTETH PARK 5F 39
Croxteth Rd. L8: Liv 3B 100
   L20: Boot 3B 34
Croxteth Sports Cen. 4C 38
Croxteth Vw. L32: K'by 1F 39
              (not continuous)
Croyde Pl. WA9: Sut L 2C 88
Croyde Rd. L24: Speke 4A 148
Croydon Av. L18: Moss H 4F 101
Croylands St. L4: Kirk 3E 55
Crucian Way L12: Crox 5D 39
Crump St. L1: Liv 2E 99
Crutchley Av. CH41: Birk 1B 96
Crystal Cl. L13: Liv 4A 80
Cubbin Cres. L5: Kirk 5D 55
Cubert Rd. L11: Crox 4C 38
Cuckoo Cl. L25: Gate 5A 104
Cuckoo La. L25: Gate 4A 104
Cuckoo Way L25: Gate 5A 104
Cuerden St. L3: Liv 4D 77 (3F 5)
CUERDLEY CROSS 2F 133
Cuerdley Grn. WA5: Cuerd 2F 133
Culford Cl. WA7: Wind H 1D 169
Cullen Av. L20: Boot 3D 35
Cullen Cl. CH63: East 1C 170
Cullen Dr. L21: Lith 1A 34
Cullen Rd. WA7: West P 3D 165
Cullens La. CH62: Brom 2C 162
Cullen St. L8: Liv 2C 100
Culme Rd. L12: W Der 4F 57
Culzean Cl. L12: Crox 5E 39
Cumberland Av. CH43: Pren 2A 118
   L17: Liv 3D 101
   L30: N'ton 2C 18
   WA10: St. H 3B 64
Cumberland Cl. L6: Liv 5D 57
Cumberland Cres. WA11: Hay 2A 48
Cumberland Ga. L30: N'ton 1A 20
Cumberland Rd. CH45: New B 4C 52
Cumberland St. L1: Liv 4C 76 (4D 4)
Cumber La. L35: Whis 2F 85
Cumbria Way L12: W Der 2C 58
Cummings St. L1: Liv 1E 99 (7G 5)
Cumpsty Rd. L21: Lith 4C 18
Cunard Av. CH44: Wall 1D 75
Cunard Cl. CH43: Bid 3C 94
Cunard Rd. L21: Lith 1B 34
Cunliffe Cl. WA7: Pal F 3A 168
Cunliffe St. L2: Liv 4C 76 (3D 4)
Cunningham Cl. CH48: Caldy 3C 134
Cunningham Dr. CH63: Brom 2C 162
   WA7: Run 2E 165
Cunningham Rd. L13: Liv 4A 80
   WA8: Wid 4D 131
Cuper Cres. L36: Huy 2D 83
Curate Rd. L6: Liv 4C 56
Curlender Cl. CH41: Birk 5E 73
Curlender Way L24: Hale 5E 149
Curlew Av. CH49: Upton 3D 93
Curlew Cl. CH49: Upton 3D 93
Curlew Ct. CH46: More 5C 70
Curlew Gro. L26: Halew 3E 127
Curlew Way CH46: More 5C 70
Curran Way L33: K'by 4D 15
Curtana Cres. L11: Crox 5C 38
Curtis Rd. L4: Walt 2C 56
Curwell Cl. CH63: Spit 4B 142
Curzon Av. CH41: Birk 2B 96
   CH45: New B 3B 52
Curzon Rd. CH42: Tran 2B 118
   CH47: Hoy 4A 90
   L22: Water 4E 17
Curzon St. WA7: Run 1F 165
Cusson Rd. L33: Know I 4B 24
Custley Hey L28: Stock V 3B 60
Custom Ho. La. L1: Liv 5C 76 (6D 4)
Cut La. L33: Know 1E 41
Cygnet Ct. L33: K'by 3A 24
Cynthia Rd. WA7: Run 5F 151
Cypress Av. WA8: Wid 1B 132

Cypress Cl. L31: Mell 2A 22
Cypress Cft. CH63: Spit 4B 142
Cypress Gdns. WA9: St. H 4C 64
Cypress Gro. WA7: Run 3C 166
Cypress Rd. L36: Huy 1D 105
Cyprian's Way L30: N'ton 2E 19
Cyprus Gro. L8: Liv 5A 100
Cyprus St. L34: Prsct 5D 63
Cyprus Ter. CH45: New B 4B 52
Cyril Gro. L17: Aig 2E 123

D

DACRE HILL 4F 119
Dacres Bri. La. L35: Tar G 2C 106
                              (not continuous)
Dacre St. CH41: Birk 3E 97
    L20: Boot 2B 54
Dacy Rd. L5: Liv 5A 56
Daffodil Cl. WA8: Wid 5E 111
Daffodil Gdns. WA9: Bold 4A 68
Daffodil Rd. CH41: Birk 2B 102
    L15: W'tree 2B 102
Dagnall Rd. L32: K'by 4C 22
Dahlia Cl. L9: Walt 4B 36
    WA9: Bold 4A 68
Dairy Lands Cl. L18: Moss H 3C 102
Daisy Gro. L7: Liv 5B 78
Daisy M. L21: Lith 2B 34
Daisy Mt. L31: Mag 2E 13
Daisy St. L5: Kirk 4D 55
Dakin Wlk. L33: K'by 3F 23
Dalby Cl. WA11: St. H 3C 46
Dale Acre Dr. L30: N'ton 2C 18
Dale Av. CH60: Hes 1F 157
    CH62: Brom 2D 163
Dalebrook Cl. L25: Gate 2B 104
Dale Cl. L31: Mag 5C 6
    WA8: Wid 4A 130
Dale Cres. WA9: Sut L 5D 67
Dale End Rd. CH61: Barn 3C 138
Dale Gdns. CH60: Hes 1D 157
Dalegarth Av. L12: W Der 2F 59
Dale Hall L18: Moss H 2F 123
Dalehead Pl. WA11: St. H 4B 30
Dale Hey CH44: Wall 3B 74
    CH66: Hoot 3E 171
Dalehurst Cl. CH44: Wall 2D 75
Dale La. L33: K'by . . . . . . .1A 24 & 5F 15
Dalesmeadow Rd.
    L14: K Ash 3D 81
Dale M. L25: Gate 5B 104
Dale Rd. CH62: Brom 4D 163
DALES, THE 1F 137
Daleside Cl. CH61: Irby 1F 137
Daleside Rd. L33: K'by 2F 23
Daleside Wlk. L33: K'by 2F 23
Dales Row L36: Huy 4B 84
Dale St. L2: Liv 4C 76 (5C 4)
    L3: Liv 4D 77 (4E 4)
    L19: Gars 2C 144
    WA7: Run 1A 166
Dalesway CH60: Hes 2E 157
Dale Vw. Cl. CH61: Pens 3A 138
Dalewood L12: Crox 5E 39
Dalewood Gdns. L35: Whis 4F 85
Daley Pl. L20: Boot 1E 35
Daley Rd. L21: Lith 4C 18
Dallas Gro. L9: Ain 2A 36
Dallinton Ct. L13: Liv 4B 80
Dalmeny St. L17: Aig 1B 122
Dalmorton Rd. CH45: New B 3B 52
Dalry Cres. L32: K'by 1F 39
Dalrymple St. L5: Liv 1D 77
Dalry Wlk. L32: K'by 1F 39
Dalston Dr. WA11: St. H 1C 58
Dalton Cl. L12: W Der 4B 60
Dalton St. WA7: Ast 4E 153
Dalton Rd. CH45: New B 4C 52
Dalton St. WA7: Murd 5D 153
Daltry Cl. L12: W Der 4A 58
Dalwood Cl. WA7: Murd 3E 169
Damerham Cft. L25: Gate 2A 104
Damerham M. L25: Gate 2A 104
Damfield La. L31: Mag 1C 12
Damson Rd. L27: N'ley 3E 105
Dam Wood Rd. L24: Speke 5C 146
Danby Cl. L5: Liv 1F 77
    WA7: Beech 4D 167
Danby Fold L35: R'hill 3B 86
Dane Cl. CH61: Irby 1F 137
Dane Ct. L35: R'hill 3C 86
Danefield Pl. L19: Aller 4D 125
Danefield Rd. CH49: Grea 2C 114
    L19: Aller 4D 125
Danefield Ter. L19: Aller 4D 125
Dane Rd. L31: Mag 1B 36
Danesbury Cl. WN5: Bil 1E 31
Danescourt Rd. CH41: Birk 1A 96
    L12: W Der 1C 80
Danescroft WA8: Wid 1B 130
Daneshill Cl. L17: Aig 5F 123
Daneson St. L4: Walt 2F 55
Daneswell Rd. CH46: More 5F 71
Danes Well Rd.
    L24: Speke 5A 148
Daneville Rd. L4: Walt 1D 57
Danger La. CH46: More 4F 71
Daniel Cl. L20: Boot 2A 34
Daniel Davies Dr. L8: Liv 2A 100
Daniel Ho. L20: Boot 1C 54
Dannette Hey L28: Stock V 5C 60
Dansie St. L3: Liv 4E 77 (5J 5)
Dan's Rd. WA8: Wid 2E 133
Dante Cl. L9: Ain 5C 20
Danube St. L8: Liv 2B 100
Dapple Heath Av. L31: Mell 2A 22
Darby Gro. L19: Gars 1B 144
Darby Rd. L19: Gras 4A 124
D'Arcy Cotts. CH63: Thorn H 4B 160
                              (off Raby Rd.)
Darent Rd. WA11: Hay 1B 48
Daresbury Cl. L32: K'by 3C 22
Daresbury Rd. CH65: Ell P . . . . . .

Daresbury Expressway
    WA4: Moore, Dares 4D 155
    WA7: Run, Wind H, Nort, Ast
                              . . . . .5A 152
Daresbury Pk. WA4: Dares 2F 169
Daresbury Rd. CH44: Wall 2A 74
    WA10: Eccl 4B 44
Dark Entry L34: Know P 2E 61
Dark La. L31: Mag 1D 13
Darley Cl. WA8: Wid 1B 130
Darleydale Dr. CH62: East 5F 163
Darley Dr. L12: W Der 5C 58
Darlington Cl. CH44: Wall 2D 75
Darlington St. WA8: Wid 5A 132
Darlington St. CH44: Wall 2D 75
Darmond Rd. L33: K'by 2A 24
Darmond's Grn. CH48: W Kir 3B 112
Darmonds Grn. Av. L6: Liv 4C 56
Darnley St. L8: Liv 4E 99
Darrel Dr. L7: Liv 2C 100
Darsefield Rd. L16: Child 2D 103
Dartford Cl. L14: K Ash 5F 59
Dartington Rd. L16: Child 1C 102
Dartmouth Av. L10: Ain 3C 20
Dartmouth Dr. L30: N'ton 1C 18
    WA10: Windle 2C 44
Darwall Rd. L19: Aller 4D 125
Darwen St. L5: Liv 1B 76
Darwick Dr. L36: Huy 1F 105
Darwin Gro. WA9: St. H 4E 65
Daryl Rd. CH60: Hes 1A 158
Daulby St. L3: Liv 4F 77 (4J 5)
Dauntsey Brow L25: Gate 2B 104
Dauntsey M. L25: Gate 2B 104
Davenham Av. CH43: O'ton 1F 117
Davenham Cl. CH43: O'ton 2F 117
Davenham Ct. L15: W'tree 2A 102
Davenhill Pk. L10: Ain 3C 20
Davenport Cl. CH48: Caldy 3D 135
Davenport Gro. L33: K'by 1E 23
Davenport Rd. CH60: Hes 3E 157
Davenport Row WA7: Run 2D 167
Daventree Rd. CH45: Wall 1B 74
Daventry Rd. L17: Aig 2E 123

David Lloyd Leisure Cen.
    Knowsley 4A 24
    Speke 3E 145
Davidson Rd. L13: Liv 3F 79
David St. L8: Liv 5F 99
Davids Wlk. L25: Wltn 1C 126
Davies Cl. WA8: Wid 3A 152
Davies St. L1: Liv 4C 76 (4D 4)
    L20: Boot 4D 35
    WA9: St. H 4C 46
Davis Rd. CH46: Leas 3B 72
Davy Cl. WA10: Eccl 3B 44
Davy Rd. WA7: Ast 4E 153
Davy St. L5: Liv 5A 56
Dawber Cl. L6: Liv 2A 78
Dawlish Cl. L25: Hunts X 4C 126
Dawlish Rd. CH44: Wall 2F 73
    CH61: Irby 2C 136
Dawn Cl. WA9: St. H 4E 65
Dawn Wlk. L10: Faz 1B 38
Dawpool Cotts. CH48: Caldy 1A 136
Dawpool Dr. CH46: More 1E 93
    CH62: Brom 3C 162
Dawson Av. CH41: Birk 1B 96
    WA9: St. H 4D 67
Dawson Gdns. L31: Mag 5C 6
Dawson St. L1: Liv 4D 77 (5E 5)
Dawson Way L1: Liv 5F 5
Dawstone Ri. CH60: Hes 3F 157
Dawstone Rd. CH60: Hes 3F 157
Days Mdw. CH49: Grea 1C 114
Day St. L13: Liv 3F 79
Deacon Cl. L22: Water 5D 17
Deacon Ct. L22: Water 5D 17
    L25: Wltn 2B 126
Deacon Pk. L33: Know I 5A 24
Deacon Rd. WA8: Wid 3B 132
Deacon Trad. Est. WA12: New W . .1F 69
Deakin St. CH41: Birk 1F 95
Dealcroft L25: Wltn 2F 125
Dean Av. CH45: Wall 5E 51
Dean Cl. WA8: Wid 4B 132
    WN5: Bil 2D 31
Dean Dillistone Ct. L1: Liv 2E 99
Deane Rd. L7: Liv 4C 78
Dean Ho. L22: Water 5D 17
Dean Patey Ct. L1: Liv 1E 99
Deansburn Rd. L13: Liv 5E 57
Deanscales Rd. L11: N Grn. 1F 57
Dean St. L22: Water 5D 17
    WA8: Wid 4B 132
Deans Way CH41: Birk 1F 95
Deansway WA8: Wid 4C 130
Dean Way WA9: Sut M 4B 88
Deanwood Cl. L35: Whis 4F 85
Dearham Av. WA11: St. H 1A 46
Dearne Cl. L12: W Der 1E 81
Dearnford Av. CH62: Brom 4D 163
Dearnford Cl. CH62: Brom 4D 163
Dearnley Av. WA11: St. H 3E 47
Deauville Rd. L9: Ain 1C 36
Debra Cl. L31: Mell 1B 22
Dee Cl. L33: K'by 4F 15
Dee Ct. L25: Gate 1C 126
Dee Ho. L25: Gate 1C 126
                              (off Woodsome Cl.)
Deelands Pk. CH46: More 5C 70
Dee La. CH48: W Kir 4A 112
Deeley Cl. L7: Liv 5C 78
Dee Pk. Cl. CH60: Hes 4B 158
Dee Pk. Rd. CH60: Hes 4B 158
Deepdale WA8: Wid 1C 130
Deepdale Av. L20: Boot 3A 34
    WA11: St. H 4C 30
Deepdale Cl. CH43: Bid 3C 94
Deepdale Dr. L35: R'hill 3D 87
Deepdale Rd. L25: Gate 2A 104
Deepfield Dr. L36: Huy 1F 105
Deepfield Rd. L15: W'tree 3F 101
Deepwood Gro. L35: Whis 4E 85
Deerbarn Dr. L30: N'ton 1B 20
Deerbolt Cl. L32: K'by 2C 22
Deerbolt Cres. L32: K'by 2C 22
Deerbolt Way L32: K'by 2C 22
Deerbourne Cl. L25: Wltn 2F 125

Dee Rd. L35: R'hill 3B 86
Deer Pk. Ct. WA7: Pal F 4F 167
Dee Sailing Club 4E 135
Deeside CH60: Hes 2C 156
Deeside Cl. CH43: Bid 3B 94
Dee Vw. Rd. CH60: Hes 2F 157
De Grouchy St. CH48: W Kir . . . 3B 112
Deirdre Av. WA8: Wid 3A 132
Dekker Rd. L33: K'by 4E 15
Delabole Rd. L11: Crox 3D 39
De Lacy Row WA7: Cas 5A 154
Delagoa Rd. L10: Faz 2F 37
Delamain Rd. L13: Liv 5E 57
Delamere Av. CH62: East 1E 171
 WA8: Wid 3C 130
 WA9: Sut M 3A 88
Delamere Cl. CH43: Bid 3C 94
 CH62: East 1E 171
 L12: Crox 5D 39
Delamere Gro. CH44: Wall 4E 75
Delamore Pl. L4: Kirk 2E 55
Delamore's Acre CH64: Will . . . 5A 170
Delamore St. L4: Kirk 2E 55
Delavor Cl. CH60: Hes 2E 157
Delavor Rd. CH60: Hes 2E 157
Delaware Cres. L32: K'by 2C 22
Delaware Rd. L20: Boot 4C 34
Delfby Cres. L32: K'by 4A 24
Delf La. L4: Walt 1A 56
 L24: Speke 2B 146
Dell, The CH42: R Ferr 3A 120
 L12: W Der 3E 59
Dell Cl. CH63: Brom 4B 162
Dell Ct. CH43: Pren 3F 117
Dellfield La. L31: Mag 1E 13
Dell Gro. CH42: R Ferr 4A 120
Dell La. CH60: Hes 3B 158
Dellside Gro. WA9: St. H 3C 66
Dell St. L7: Liv 4C 78
Delph Cl. L21: Lith 5A 18
 WA9: St. H 2B 66
Delphfield WA7: Nort 2D 169
Delph Hollow Way WA9: St. H . . 3B 66
Delph La. L35: Whis 1F 85
 WA4: Dares 4F 155
Delph Mdw. Gdns. WN5: Bil . . . 1D 31
Delph Rd. L23: Lit C 2D 9
Delphwood Dr. WA9: St. H 2B 66
Delta Dr. L12: W Der 3E 59
Delta Rd. L21: Lith 1B 34
 WA9: St. H 4F 47
Delta Rd. E. CH42: R Ferr 3B 120
Delta Rd. W. CH42: R Ferr 3B 120
Deltic Way L30: N'ton 5B 20
 L33: Know I 5B 24
Delves Av. CH63: Spit 4F 141
Delyn Cl. CH42: R Ferr 3E 119
Demesne St. CH44: Wall 3E 75
Denbigh Av. WA9: St. H 4C 66
Denbigh Rd. CH44: Wall 3C 74
 L9: Walt 5F 35
Denbigh St. L5: Liv 1B 76
Dencourt Rd. L11: N Grn 2B 58
Deneacres L25: Wltn 2A 126
Dene Av. WA12: New W 4F 49
Denebank Rd. L4: Walt 4B 56
Denecliff L28: Stock V 3C 60
Dene Ct. L9: Faz 4F 37
Deneshey Rd. CH47: Meols . . . 3C 90
Denes Way L28: Stock V 4A 60
Denford Rd. L14: K Ash 1F 81
Denham Cl. L12: Crox 5F 39
Denise Rd. L10: Faz 1B 38
Denison Gro. WA9: St. H 4E 65
Denman Dr. L6: Liv 2C 78
Denman Gro. CH44: Wall 4E 75
Denman St. L6: Liv 3B 78
Denman Way L6: Liv 2C 78
Denmark St. L22: Water 4D 17
Dennett Cl. L31: Mag 3D 13
Dennett Rd. L35: Prsct 2C 84
Denning Dr. CH61: Irby 5D 115
Dennis Av. WA10: St. H 4C 64
Dennis Rd. WA8: Wid 5C 132
Denny Cl. CH49: Upton 5F 93

Denston Cl. CH43: Bid 2B 94
Denstone Av. L10: Ain 3D 21
Denstone Cl. L14: K Ash 2B 82
 L25: Wltn 4B 126
Dentdale Dr. L5: Liv 2E 77
Denton Dr. CH45: Wall 5C 52
Denton Gro. L6: Liv 1C 78
DENTON'S GREEN 3E 45
Dentons Grn. La. WA10: St. H . . 3D 45
Denton St. L8: Liv 5F 99
 WA8: Wid 3C 132
Dentwood St. L8: Liv 5A 100
Denver Rd. L32: K'by 4C 22
Depot Rd. L33: Know I 1D 25
Derby Bldgs. L7: Liv 5A 78
Derby Dr. WA11: R'ford 1B 28
Derby Gro. L31: Mag 4D 13
Derby Hall L17: Aig 5E 101
Derby La. L13: Liv 2A 80
Derby Rd. CH42: Tran 1D 119
 CH45: Wall 5A 52
 L5: Kirk 5B 54
 L20: Boot 5B 34
 L36: Huy 3E 83
 WA8: Wid 1A 132
DERBYSHIRE HILL 1F 67
Derby Sq. L2: Liv 5C 76 (6D 4)
 L34: Prsct 5E 63
Derby St. L19: Gars 3C 144
 L34: Prsct 5C 62
 L36: Huy 4A 84
Derby Ter. L36: Huy 3E 83
Dereham Av. CH49: Upton 2A 94
Dereham Cres. L10: Faz 1F 37
Dereham Way W7: Nort 4D 155
Derna Rd. L36: Huy 2D 83
Derrington Cl. WA10: St. H 2D 65
Derrylea L9: Ain 1C 36
Derwent Av. L34: Prsct 5F 63
Derwent Cl. CH63: High B 2D 141
 L31: Mag 5F 7
 L33: K'by 1D 23
 L35: R'hill 3B 86
Derwent Dr. CH45: Wall 5A 52
 CH61: Pens 3F 137
 L21: Lith 5D 19
Derwent Rd. CH43: O'ton 5B 96
 CH47: Meols 3E 91
 CH63: High B 2D 141
 L23: C'by 2F 17
 WA8: Wid 3C 130
 WA11: St. H 1B 46
Derwent Rd. E. L13: Liv 2A 80
Derwent Rd. W. L13: Liv 2F 79
Derwent Sq. L13: Liv 2F 79
Desborough Cres. L12: W Der . . 4A 58
Desford Av. WA11: St. H 2D 47
Desford Cl. CH46: More 5B 70
Desford Rd. L19: Aig 4E 123
De Silva St. L36: Huy 4A 84
Desmond Cl. CH43: Bid 2C 94
Desmond Gro. L23: C'by 2F 17
Desoto Rd. WA8: Wid 2D 151
Desoto Rd. E. WA8: Wid 1F 151
(not continuous)
Desoto Rd. W. WA8: Wid 1F 151
Deva Cl. L33: K'by 3E 15
Deva Rd. CH48: W Kir 4A 112
Devereux Dr. CH44: Wall 3B 74
Deverell Gro. L15: W'tree 5B 80
Deverell Rd. L15: W'tree 1A 102
Deverill Rd. CH42: R Ferr 3E 119
Devilla Cl. L14: K Ash 5A 60
De Villiers Av. L23: C'by 5E 9
Devisdale Gro. CH43: Bid 2C 94
Devizes Cl. L25: Gate 2B 104
Devizes Dr. CH61: Irby 5D 115
Devoke Av. WA11: St. H 4A 30
Devon Cl. L23: Blun 1C 74
Devon Ct. L5: Liv 1A 78
Devondale Rd. L18: Moss H . . . 4A 102
Devon Dr. CH61: Pens 3E 137

Devonfield Rd. L9: Walt 3F 35
Devon Gdns. CH42: R Ferr 3E 119
 L16: Child 4E 103
Devon Pl. WA8: Wid 1A 132
Devonport St. L8: Liv 4F 99
Devonshire Cl. CH43: O'ton . . . 4B 96
 L33: K'by 1E 23
DEVONSHIRE PARK 1C 118
Devonshire Pl. CH43: O'ton . . . 4A 96
 L5: Liv 5E 55
(not continuous)
 WA7: Run 4A 152
Devonshire Rd. CH43: O'ton . . 4B 96
 CH44: Wall 2B 74
 CH48: W Kir 5C 112
 CH49: Upton 4E 93
 CH61: Pens 3E 137
 L8: Liv 4A 100
 L22: Water 3C 16
 WA10: St. H 3D 45
Devonshire Rd. W. L8: Liv 4A 100
Devon St. L3: Liv 4E 77 (3H 5)
 WA10: St. H 4D 45
Devonwall Gdns. L8: Liv 4B 100
Devon Way L16: Child 3E 103
 L36: Huy 2A 84
(not continuous)
Dewar St. WA7: Ast 4E 153
Dewberry Cl. CH42: Tran 5D 97
Dewey Av. L9: Ain 5B 20
Dewlands Rd. L21: Sea 5F 17
Dewsbury Rd. L4: Walt 5B 56
Dexter St. L8: Liv 3E 99
Deycroft Av. L33: K'by 1F 23
Deycroft Wlk. L33: K'by 1A 24
Deyes Cl. L31: Mag 1E 13
Deyes End L31: Mag 1D 13
Deyes La. L31: Mag 1D 13
Deyes Lane Swimming Pool . . . 1D 13
Deysbrook La. L12: W Der 5C 58
(not continuous)
Deysbrook Side L12: W Der . . . 5C 58
Deysbrook Way L12: W Der . . . 3D 59
Dial Rd. CH42: Tran 1D 119
Dial St. L7: Liv 4C 78
Diamond Bus. Pk. WA11: R'ford . 1B 28
Diamond St. L5: Liv 2D 77
Diana St. L4: Walt 3F 55
Diane Ho. L8: Liv 2F 99
(off Birley Ct.)
Dibbinsdale Local Nature Reserve
 . . . . 5C 142
Dibbinsdale Rd. CH63: Brom . . 2B 162
Dibbins Grn. CH63: Brom 4B 162
Dibbins Hey CH63: Spit 5A 142
Dibbinview Gro. CH63: Spit . . . 5B 142
Dibb La. L23: Lit C 3C 8
Dicconson St. WA10: St. H 4A 46
Dickens Av. CH43: Pren 3F 117
Dickens Cl. CH43: Pren 3F 117
 L32: K'by 5D 23
Dickenson Cl. WA11: Hay 2A 48
Dickenson St. L1: Liv 1D 99
(off Up. Frederick St.)
Dickens Rd. WA10: St. H 3C 64
Dickens St. L8: Liv 3F 99
Dickson Cl. WA8: Wid 4B 132
Dickson St. L3: Liv 2B 76
 WA8: Wid 4A 132
(not continuous)
Didcot Cl. L25: Hunts X 4D 127
Didsbury Cl. L33: K'by 3F 23
Digg La. CH46: More 5D 71
Digmoor Rd. L32: K'by 1F 39
Digmoor Wlk. L32: K'by 1F 39
Dignum Mead L27: N'ley 4E 105
Dilloway St. WA10: St. H 4D 45
Dinas La. L36: Huy 2A 82
Dinas La. Pde. L14: K Ash 2A 82
Dinesen Rd. L19: Gars 5C 124
DINGLE 1A 122
Dingle Av. WA12: New W 1F 69
Dinglebrook Rd. L9: Ain 5C 36
Dingle Brow L8: Liv 1A 122

Dingle Grange L8: Liv 1A 122
Dingle Gro. L8: Liv 5A 100
Dingle La. L8: Liv 1A 122
Dingle Mt. L8: Liv 1A 122
Dingle Rd. CH42: Tran 5C 96
   L8: Liv 1F 121
Dingle Ter. L8: Liv 5A 100
Dingle Va. L8: Liv 1A 122
Dingley Av. L9: Walt 2F 35
Dingwall Dr. CH49: Grea 1E 115
Dinmore Rd. CH44: Wall 2B 74
Dinnington Ct. WA8: Wid 1E 131
Dinorben Av. WA9: St. H 4C 66
Dinorwic Rd. L4: Walt 5A 56
Dinsdale Rd. CH62: Brom 5E 143
Discovery Cl. L19: Gars 3D 145
Ditchfield Pl. WA8: Wid 4B 130
Ditchfield Rd. WA8: Wid 4B 130
DITTON 4C 130
Ditton La. CH46: Leas 3D 71
Ditton Rd. WA8: Wid 1C 150
             (not continuous)
Dixon M. L30: N'ton 5E 11
Dixon Rd. L33: Know I 5B 24
Dobsons La. WA9: St. H 3F 65
Dobson St. L6: Liv 2F 77
Dobson Wlk. L6: Liv 2A 78
Dock Rd. CH41: Birk 4A 74
   L19: Gars 2B 144
   WA8: Wid 2F 151
Dock Rd. Nth. CH62: Port S 1C 142
Dock Rd. Sth. CH62: Brom 3D 143
Docks Link CH44: Wall 3F 73
Dock St. WA8: Wid 2A 152
Dodd Av. CH49: Grea 1D 115
   WA10: St. H 4C 44
Doddridge Rd. L8: Liv 4E 99
Dodds La. L31: Mag 5C 6
Dodleston Cl. CH43: Noct 5D 95
Dodman Rd. L11: Crox 3D 39
Doe Pk. Courtyard L25: Wltn . . .4A 126
Doe's Mdw. Rd. CH63: Brom . . .3B 162
DOG & GUN 5A 38
Dolomite Av. L24: Speke 1F 145
Domar Cl. L32: K'by 4E 23
Dombey Pl. L8: Liv 3F 99
Dombey St. L8: Liv 3F 99
Domingo Dr. L33: K'by 5D 15
Dominic Cl. L16: Child 1E 103
Dominic Rd. L16: Child 1E 103
Dominion St. L6: Liv 1C 78
Domville L35: Whis 4E 85
Domville Dr. CH49: W'chu 1A 116
Domville Rd. L13: Liv 5A 56
Donaldson Ct. L5: Liv 5A 56
Donaldson St. L5: Liv 5A 56
Donalds Way L17: Aig 3E 123
Doncaster Dr. CH49: Upton 3F 93
Donegal Rd. L13: Liv 3B 80
Donne Av. CH63: Spit 4F 141
Donne Cl. CH63: Spit 4A 142
Donnington Cl. L36: Roby 1D 105
Donsby Rd. L9: Ain 2B 36
Dooley Dr. L30: N'ton 1B 20
Doon Cl. L4: Kirk 3E 55
Dorans La. L2: Liv 5C 76 (5D 4)
Dorbett Dr. L23: C'by 3F 17
Dorchester Cl. CH49: Upton 5F 93
Dorchester Dr. L33: K'by 5F 15
Dorchester Pk. CH43: Noct 1D 117
   WA7: Nort 4D 155
Dorchester Rd. L25: Gate 3B 104
Dorchester Way WA5: B'wood . . .5F 69
Doreen Av. CH46: More 1D 93
Dorgan Cl. L35: R'hill 2B 86
Doric Rd. L13: Liv 2A 80
Doric St. CH42: R Ferr 2F 119
   L21: Sea 1F 33
Dorien Rd. L13: Liv 4F 79
Dorin Ct. CH43: O'ton 5A 96
Dorking Gro. L15: W'tree 3B 102
Dorney Cl. L12: W Der 4D 59
Dorothy St. L7: Liv 5B 78
   WA9: St. H 4E 65
Dorrington Cl. WA7: Murd 2D 169

Dorrit St. L8: Liv 3F 99
Dorset Av. L15: W'tree 2C 100
Dorset Cl. L20: Boot 5D 35
Dorset Ct. L25: Gate 3B 104
   WA7: Pal F 4A 168
Dorset Dr. CH61: Pens 3E 137
Dorset Gdns. CH42: R Ferr 3E 119
Dorset Rd. CH45: New B 4A 52
   CH48: W Kir 3C 112
   L6: Liv 5D 57
   L36: Huy 3A 84
   WA10: St. H 2D 65
Douglas Arc. CH41: Birk 3E 97
             (off Douglas St.)
Douglas Av. WA9: Bold 5B 68
   WN5: Bil 2D 31
Douglas Cl. L13: Liv 2F 79
   WA8: Wid 1E 133
Douglas Dr. CH46: More 1D 93
   L31: Mag 5F 7
Douglas Pl. L20: Boot 1B 54
Douglas Rd. CH48: W Kir 3D 113
   L4: Walt 5B 56
Douglas St. CH41: Birk 3E 97
   WA10: St. H 5D 45
Douglas Way L33: K'by 4F 15
Doulton Cl. CH43: Bid 2B 94
Doulton Pl. L35: Whis 3C 84
Doulton St. WA10: St. H 5D 45
Douro Pl. L13: Liv 4F 79
Douro St. L5: Liv 2E 77 (1G 5)
DOVECOT 2F 81
Dovecot Av. L14: K Ash 3F 81
Dovecote Dr. WA11: Hay 1C 48
Dovecot Pl. L14: K Ash 2F 81
          (off Dovecot Av.)
Dove Ct. L25: Wltn 1A 126
Dovedale Av. CH62: East 5E 163
   L31: Mag 5C 6
Dovedale Cl. CH43: Pren 2F 117
Dovedale Ct. WA8: Wid 1B 130
Dovedale Rd. CH45: Wall 4A 52
   CH47: Hoy 3B 90
   L18: Moss H 4F 101
Dovepoint Rd. CH47: Meols 2E 91
Dovercliffe Rd. L13: Liv 3B 80
Dover Cl. CH41: Birk 2D 97
   WA7: Murd 4E 169
Dovercroft L25: Wltn 2F 125
Dove Rd. L9: Walt 2F 35
Dover Rd. L31: Mag 4C 12
Dover St. L3: Liv 4F 77 (5J 5)
   WA7: Run 4B 152
Dovesmead Rd. CH60: Hes 3D 159
Dovestone Cl. L7: Liv 1B 100
Dove St. L8: Liv 2B 100
Dovey St. L8: Liv 4F 99
Doward St. WA8: Wid 2C 132
Dowhills Dr. L23: Blun 5B 8
Dowhills Pk. L23: Blun 4B 8
Dowhills Rd. L23: Blun 4B 8
Downes Grn. CH63: Spit 1A 162
Downham Cl. L25: Wltn 4F 103
Downham Dr. CH60: Hes 2A 158
Downham Grn. L25: Wltn 4F 103
Downham Rd. CH42: Tran 1D 119
Downham Rd. Nth. CH61: Hes . . .5A 138
Downham Rd. Sth. CH60: Hes . . .2A 158
Downham Way L25: Wltn 4F 103
Downing Cl. CH43: O'ton 1B 118
Downing Rd. L20: Boot 1D 55
Downing St. L5: Liv 1F 77
Downlands Rd. L27: N'ley 5F 105
Downland Way WA9: St. H 2F 67
Downs, The L23: Blun 2B 16
Downside WA8: Wid 1B 130
Downside Cl. L30: N'ton 1E 19
Downs Rd. WA7: Run 1A 166
   WA10: St. H 1D 65
Downway La. WA9: St. H 2A 68
Dowsefield La. L18: Aller 1E 125
Dragon Cl. L11: Crox 4C 38
Dragon Cres. L35: Whis 2F 85

Dragon Dr. L35: Whis 3E 85
Dragon La. L35: Whis 4D 85
Dragon Wlk. L11: Crox 4C 38
Dragon Yd. WA8: Wid 5B 110
Drake Cl. L10: Faz 1A 38
   L35: Whis 4E 85
Drake Cres. L10: Faz 1F 37
Drakefield Rd. L11: N Grn. 5D 37
Drake Gdns. WA9: St. H 5E 65
Drake Pl. L10: Faz 1F 37
Drake Rd. CH46: Leas 2B 72
   L10: Faz 1F 37
Drake St. L20: Boot 2B 54
   WA10: St. H 4D 45
Drake Way L10: Faz 1A 38
Draw Well Rd. L33: Know I 3D 25
Draycott St. L8: Liv 1F 121
Drayton Cl. CH61: Irby 2D 137
   WA7: Run 1F 165
Drayton Cres. WA11: St. H 2D 47
Drayton Rd. CH44: Wall 3C 74
   L4: Walt 1A 56
Drennan Rd. L19: Aller 4E 125
Drewell Rd. L18: Moss H 5F 101
Driffield Rd. L34: Prsct 5C 62
Drinkwater Gdns. L3: Liv . .3E 77 (1G 5)
Drive, The L12: W Der 1B 80
Driveway L35: Whis 4F 85
Droitwich Av. CH49: Grea 5C 92
Dromore Av. L18: Moss H 1F 123
Dronfield Way L25: Gate 2F 103
            (not continuous)
Droxford Dr. L25: Gate 2F 103
Druids' Cross Gdns.
   L18: Moss H 5D 103
Druids' Cross Rd. L18: Moss H . . .5D 103
Druids Pk. L18: Moss H 5E 103
Druidsville Rd. L18: Moss H 5D 103
Druids Way CH49: W'chu 2A 116
Drum Cl. L14: K Ash 1A 82
Drummond Ct. WA8: Wid 2D 133
Drummond Rd. CH47: Hoy 1A 112
   L4: Walt 2C 56
   L23: Thorn 1B 18
Drummoyne Ct. L23: Blun 5A 8
Drury La. L2: Liv 5C 76 (5C 4)
Drybeck Gro. WA9: St. H 5D 67
Dryburgh Way L4: Kirk 3E 55
Dryden Cl. CH43: Bid 2C 94
   L35: Whis 3E 85
Dryden Gro. L36: Huy 5F 83
Dryden Rd. L7: Liv 5E 79
Dryden St. L5: Liv 2D 77
   L20: Boot 3A 34
Dryfield Cl. CH49: Grea 5D 93
Dublin St. L3: Liv 2B 76
Ducie St. L8: Liv 3A 100
Duckinfield St. L3: Liv 5F 77 (5J 5)
Duck Pond La. CH42: Tran 2A 118
Duddingston Av. L18: Moss H 4F 101
   L23: C'by 3E 17
Duddon Av. L31: Mag 5F 7
Duddon Cl. CH43: O'ton 1F 117
Dudley Av. WA7: Run 5D 153
Dudley Cl. CH43: O'ton 5B 96
Dudley Gro. L23: C'by 3E 17
Dudley Pl. WA9: St. H 5C 46
Dudley Rd. CH45: New B 3A 52
   L18: Moss H 4F 101
Dudley St. WA9: St. H 5C 46
Dudlow Ct. L18: Moss H 4C 102
Dudlow Dr. L18: Moss H 4C 102
Dudlow Gdns. L18: Moss H 3C 102
Dudlow La. L18: Moss H 3B 102
Dudlow Nook Rd. L18: Moss H . . .3C 102
Dugdale Cl. L19: Gars 5A 124
Duke Cl. WA7: Run 4F 151
Duke of York Cotts.
   CH62: New F 1A 142
Dukes Rd. L5: Liv 2C 58
Dukes Ter. L1: Liv 1E 99 (7G 5)
Duke St. CH41: Birk 5C 74
   CH45: New B 3B 52
   L1: Liv 1D 99 (7E 4)
   L19: Gars 1C 144

Duke St. L22: Water 5D 17
  L34: Prsct 4D 63
  WA10: St. H 4F 45
Duke St. Bri. CH41: Birk 5C 74
Duke St. La. L: Liv 1D 99 (7E 4)
Dukes Wharf WA7: Pres B 4E 169
Dulas Grn. L32: K'by 4A 24
Dulas Rd. L15: W'tree 3B 102
  L32: K'by 4A 24
Dulson Way L34: Prsct 1A 84
Dulverton Rd. L17: Aig 4E 123
Dumbarton St. L4: Walt 2E 55
Dumbrees Gdns. L12: W Der 3E 59
Dumbrees Rd. L12: W Der 3E 59
Dumbreeze Gro. L34: Know 3D 41
Dumfries Way L33: K'by 4D 15
Dunacre Way L26: Halew 5F 127
Dunbabin Rd. L15: W'tree 3B 102
  L16: Child 3B 102
Dunbar St. L4: Walt 1F 55
Dunbeath Av. L35: R'hill 5D 87
Dunbeath Cl. L35: R'hill 5D 87
Duncan Av. WA7: Run 1C 166
Duncan Cl. WA10: St. H 1E 65
Duncan Dr. CH49: Grea 5D 93
Duncansby Dr. CH63: East 1C 170
Duncan St. CH41: Birk 3F 97
  L1: Liv 2E 99
  WA10: St. H 5E 45
Dunchurch Rd. L14: K Ash 1F 81
Duncombe Rd. Nth. L19: Gras 5B 124
Duncombe Rd. Sth. L19: Gars 5B 124
Duncote Cl. CH43: O'ton 5A 96
  L35: Whis 1A 86
Dundale Rd. L13: Liv 3B 80
Dundalk La. WA8: Wid 4D 131
Dundalk Rd. WA8: Wid 4D 131
Dundas St. L20: Boot 2B 54
Dundee Gro. CH44: Wall 3A 74
Dundonald Rd. L17: Aig 3E 123
Dundonald St. CH41: Birk 1A 96
Dunedin St. WA9: St. H 4E 65
Dunes Way L5: Kirk 5C 54
Dunfold Cl. L32: K'by 4F 23
Dungeon La. L24: Hale 5F 147
Dunham Cl. CH62: East 2F 171
Dunham Rd. L15: W'tree 5A 80
Dunkeld Cl. L6: Liv 3A 78
Dunkeld St. L6: Liv 3A 78
Dunkerron Cl. L27: N'ley 2C 104
Dunlin Cl. L27: N'ley 5E 105
  WA7: Beech 5F 167
Dunlin Ct. L25: Gate 4A 104
Dunlop Dr. L31: Mell 1B 22
Dunlop Rd. L24: Speke 5C 146
Dunluce St. L4: Walt 2E 55
Dunmail Av. WA11: St. H 4C 30
Dunmail Gro. WA7: Beech 1E 173
Dunmore Rd. L13: Liv 3E 79
Dunmow Way L25: Hunts X 4C 126
Dunnerdale Rd. L11: N Grn. 1A 58
Dunnett St. L20: Kirk 2B 54
Dunning Cl. CH49: Upton 4E 93
Dunnings Bri. Rd. L30: N'ton 4E 19
  L31: Mag 5B 12
Dunnings Wlk. L30: N'ton 1A 20
Dunnock Cl. L25: Gate 4A 104
Dunraven Rd. CH48: W Kir 4A 112
Dunriding La. WA10: St. H 5D 45
Dunscroft WA9: St. H 4D 67
Dunsdon Cl. L25: Wltn 5E 103
Dunsdon Rd. L25: Wltn 4E 103
Dunsford WA8: Wid 1B 130
Dunsmore Cl. WA11: Hay 1C 48
Dunsop Av. WA9: Clock F 2D 69
Dunstall Cl. CH46: Leas 3E 71
Dunstan La. L7: Liv 1C 100
Dunstan St. L15: W'tree 1E 101
Dunster Gro. CH60: Hes 3B 158
  WA9: Sut L 2D 89
Durants Cotts. L31: Mag 3E 13
Durban Av. L23: C'by 5E 9
Durban Rd. CH45: Wall 5B 52
  L13: Liv 4B 80

Durden St. L7: Liv 2C 100
Durham Av. L30: N'ton 4F 19
Durham E. L30: N'ton 4A 20
Durham M. E. L30: N'ton 4A 20
Durham M. W. L30: N'ton 4F 19
Durham Rd. L21: Sea 1E 33
  WA8: Wid 1B 132
Durham St. L19: Gars 3D 145
Durham Way L30: N'ton 4A 20
  L36: Huy 3A 84
Durley Dr. CH43: Pren 3E 117
Durley Pk. Cl. CH43: Pren 4E 117
Durley Rd. L9: Ain 2B 36
Durlston Cl. WA8: Wid 2C 130
Durning Rd. L7: Liv 5B 78
Durrant Rd. L11: N Grn. 3E 57
Dursley L35: Whis 4F 85
Durston Rd. L16: Child 1D 103
DUTTON 2F 175
Dutton Dr. CH63: Spit 5F 141
Duxbury Cl. L31: Mag 4E 7
Dwerryhouse La. L11: N Grn. 1B 58
Dwerryhouse St. L8: Liv 3D 99
Dyke St. L6: Liv 2A 78
Dykin Cl. WA8: Wid 1E 133
Dykin Rd. WA8: Wid 1D 133
Dymchurch Rd. L24: Speke 3B 146
Dymoke Rd. L11: Crox 5C 38
Dymoke Wlk. L11: Crox 5C 38
Dyson Hall Dr. L9: Faz 3D 37
Dyson St. L4: Walt 2F 55

E

Eagle Dene L10: Faz 2A 38
Eaglehall Rd. L9: Faz 4F 37
Eaglehurst Rd. L25: Gate 5B 104
Eagles Ct. L20: Boot 3E 23
Eaglesfield Cl. WA9: St. H 4D 67
Eagles Way WA7: Pal F 4E 167
Ealing Cl. WA7: Nort 1D 169
Ealing Rd. L9: Ain 1B 36
Eanleywood La. WA7: Nort 2B 168
Eardisley Rd. L18: Moss H 3A 102
Earle Cl. WA12: New W 5F 49
Earle Ho. CH62: New F 4B 120
Earle Rd. L7: Liv 1C 100
  WA8: Wid 5C 132
EARLESTOWN 1F 69
Earle St. L3: Liv 4C 76 (3B 4)
  (not continuous)
  WA12: New W 1F 69
Earl Rd. L20: Boot 4D 35
Earl's Cl. L23: C'by 2D 17
Earlsfield Rd. L15: W'tree 3F 101
Earlston Rd. CH45: Wall 5A 52
Earl St. CH62: New F 4B 120
  WA9: St. H 4C 46
Earls Way WA7: Pal F 3E 167
Earlswood Cl. CH46: More 1B 92
Earlwood Gdns. L35: Whis 4E 85
Earp St. L19: Gars 1C 144
Easby Cl. WA7: Run 5C 152
Easby Rd. L4: Kirk 4D 55
  (not continuous)
Easby Wlk. L4: Kirk 4D 55
Easedale Wlk. L33: K'by 1D 23
Easenhall Cl. WA8: Wid 5B 110
Easington Rd. WA9: St. H 5D 65
E. Albert Rd. L17: Aig 5B 100
East Bank CH42: Tran 1C 118
Eastbourne M. L9: Ain 1B 36
Eastbourne Rd. CH41: Birk 3C 96
  L9: Ain 1B 36
  L22: Water 3B 16
Eastbourne Wlk. L6: Liv 2F 77 (1J 5)
E. Brook St. L5: Liv 5A 56
Eastbury Cl. WA8: Wid 4C 110
Eastcliffe Rd. L13: Liv 3B 80
East Cl. L34: Ecc P 4A 64
Eastcote Rd. L19: Aller 4B 124
Eastcott Cl. CH49: Grea 1C 114
Eastcroft Rd. CH44: Wall 3C 74
Eastdale Rd. L15: W'tree 1F 101
E. Dam Wood Rd. L24: Speke 5A 148

Eastern Av. CH62: Brom 3D 143
  L24: Speke 5F 147
Eastern Dr. L19: Gras 5A 124
E. Farm M. CH48: Caldy 1F 135
Eastfield Dr. L17: Aig 1C 122
Eastfield Wlk. L32: K'by 4B 22
East Front L35: Whis 5E 85
Eastgate Way WA7: Mnr P 3D 155
EASTHAM 5E 163
Eastham Cl. L16: Child 5F 81
Eastham Cres. WA9: Clock F 2B 88
Eastham Grn. L24: Speke 3E 147
Eastham M. CH62: East 1F 171
Eastham Rake CH62: East 2D 171
  CH66: East, Hoot 3C 170
Eastham Rake Station (Rail) 2D 171
Eastham Village Rd.
  CH62: East 5F 163
Eastlake Av. L5: Liv 1F 77
E. Lancashire Rd. L11: N Grn. 5E 37
  L32: K'by 2E 39
  L33: Know I 2A 40
  L34: Know 2A 40
  WA10: Eccl, R'ford, St. H 2A 40
  WA11: Hay 1B 48
East La. L35: Thorn 1B 10
  WA7: Pal F 3F 167
Eastleigh Dr. CH61: Irby 5D 115
East Mains L24: Speke 4A 148
Eastman Rd. L13: Liv 4E 57
East Meade L31: Mag 5C 6
E. Millwood Rd. L24: Speke 3F 147
Easton Rd. CH62: New F 4B 120
  L36: Huy 3A 82
E. Orchard La. L9: Ain 1D 37
East Side WA9: St. H 1C 66
E. Side Ind. Est. WA9: St. H 1C 66
East St. CH41: Birk 4E 75
  L3: Liv 4B 76 (3C 4)
  L22: Water 4D 17
  L34: Prsct 5E 63
  WA8: Wid 3D 133
Eastview Cl. CH43: Noct 5D 95
East Way CH46: More 5E 71
Eastway CH49: Grea 5E 93
  L31: Mag 5D 7
  (not continuous)
  WA7: Pal F 3F 167
  WA8: Wid 3D 131
Eastwood L17: Aig 1A 122
Eastwood WA5: B'wood 4F 69
  WA7: Wind N 1C 168
Eaton Av. CH44: Wall 2C 74
  L20: Boot 2D 35
  L21: Lith 1B 34
Eaton Cl. L12: W Der 4A 58
  L36: Roby 4C 82
Eaton Gdns. L12: W Der 2D 81
Eaton Grange L12: W Der 1C 80
Eaton Rd. CH43: O'ton 4B 96
  CH48: W Kir 5A 112
  L12: W Der 4B 58
  (not continuous)
  L19: Gras 1A 144
  L31: Mag 4D 13
  WA10: St. H 2D 45
Eaton Rd. Nth. L12: W Der 4F 57
Eaton St. CH44: Wall 1B 74
  L3: Liv 3C 76 (1C 4)
  L34: Prsct 4D 63
  WA7: Run 5A 152
Eaves La. WA9: St. H 5B 66
Ebenezer Howard Rd. L21: Ford . . .3C 18
Ebenezer Rd. L7: Liv 4C 78
Ebenezer St. CH42: R Ferr 2A 120
  WA11: Hay 2F 47
Eberle St. L2: Liv 4C 76 (4D 4)
Ebony Cl. CH46: More 1B 92
Ebony Way L33: K'by 5E 15
Ebor La. L5: Liv 2E 77

Ebrington St. L19: Gars 5C 124
Ecclesall Av. L21: Lith 5D 19
Eccles Dr. L25: Gate 2B 104
Ecclesfield Rd. WA10: Eccl 3A 44
Eccles Gro. WA9: Clock F 3E 89
Eccleshall Rd. CH62: Port S 1C 142
Eccleshill Rd. L13: Liv 1A 80
ECCLESTON 3B 44
Eccleston Av. CH62: Brom 1C 162
Eccleston Cl. CH43: O'ton 1F 117
Eccleston Dr. WA7: Run 1C 166
Eccleston Gdns. WA10: St. H 2A 64
(not continuous)
ECCLESTON PARK 4A 64
Eccleston Park Station (Rail) 5A 64
Eccleston Pk. Trade Cen.
  WA10: St. H 3B 64
Eccleston Rd. L9: Walt 2F 35
Eccleston St. L34: Prsct 5D 63
  WA10: St. H 5E 45
Echo La. CH48: W Kir 5C 112
Edale Cl. CH62: East 5E 163
Edale Rd. L18: Moss H 5A 102
Eddarbridge Est. WA8: Wid 2F 151
Eddisbury Rd. CH44: Wall 1C 74
  CH47: Hoy 2A 112
  CH48: W Kir 2A 112
Eddisbury Sq. WA6: Frod 5B 172
Eddisbury Way L12: W Der 4A 58
Eden Cl. L33: K'by 4F 15
  L35: R'hill 4B 86
Edendale WA8: Wid 2B 130
Eden Dr. Nth. L23: C'by 1A 18
Eden Dr. Sth. L23: C'by 2A 18
Edenfield Cres. L36: Huy 2F 83
Edenfield Rd. L15: W'tree 3F 101
Edenhall Dr. L25: Wltn 1C 126
  L16: Child 1A 104
Edenhurst Av. CH44: Wall 1C 74
  L36: Huy 2B 82
Edenpark Rd. CH42: Tran 1C 118
Eden St. L8: Liv 2B 100
Eden Va. L30: N'ton 1E 19
Edgar Ct. CH41: Birk 2D 97
  L21: Lith 4B 18
Edgar St. CH41: Birk 2D 97
  L3: Liv 3D 77 (1E 5)
Edgbaston Cl. L36: Roby 5C 82
Edgbaston Way CH43: Bid 1C 94
Edgefield Cl. CH43: Noct 5D 95
Edgefold Rd. L32: K'by 4F 23
Edge Gro. L7: Liv 4D 79
EDGE HILL 5B 78
Edgehill Rd. CH46: More 1C 92
Edge Hill Station (Rail) 1C 100
Edge La. L7: Liv 5B 78
  L13: Liv 5B 78
  L23: Thorn 4A 10
Edge La. Dr. L13: Liv 4A 80
Edge La. Retail Pk. L13: Liv 4F 79
(not continuous)
Edgeley Gdns. L9: Walt 2F 35
Edgemoor Cl. CH43: Bid 2B 94
  L12: W Der 1D 81
  L23: Thorn 5B 10
Edgemoor Dr. CH61: Irby 5C 114
  L10: Faz 1A 38
  L23: Thorn 4A 10
Edgemoor Rd. L12: W Der 1D 81
Edge St. WA9: St. H 5C 64
Edgewood Dr. CH62: Brom 5D 163
Edgewood Rd. CH47: Meols 2D 91
  CH49: Upton 3F 93
Edgeworth Cl. WA9: St. H 3E 67
Edgeworth St. WA9: St. H 4E 67
Edgworth Rd. L4: Walt 5B 56
Edinburgh Cl. L30: N'ton 5A 8
Edinburgh Dr. CH43: Pren 3A 118
  L36: Huy 5A 84
Edinburgh Rd. CH45: Wall 1B 74
  L7: Liv .4A 78
  WA8: Wid 4A 130
Edington St. L15: W'tree 1E 101
Edison Rd. WA7: Ast 4D 153

Edith Cl. CH44: Wall 3D 75
  L4: Walt 5A 56
  L20: Boot 2D 35
Edith Rd. WA7: Run 4F 151
  WA9: St. H 4F 67
Edmondson St. WA9: St. H 5F 47
Edmonton Cl. L5: Kirk 5D 55
Edna Av. L10: Faz 1A 38
Edrich Av. CH43: Bid 1C 94
Edward Jenner Av. L30: N'ton 2F 19
Edward Pav. L3: Liv 1C 98 (7C 4)
Edward Rd. CH47: Hoy 5C 90
  L35: Whis 1F 85
Edward's La. L24: Speke 1B 146
Edward's La. Ind. Est.
  L24: Speke 1B 146
Edward St. L3: Liv 5E 77 (5H 5)
  WA8: Wid 3D 133
  WA9: St. H 2D 67
  WA11: Hay 2A 48
Edwards Way WA8: Wid 4C 130
Edwin St. WA8: Wid 3C 132
Effingham St. L20: Boot 1B 54
Egan Rd. CH43: Bid 1E 95
Egbert Rd. CH47: Meols 3C 90
Egdon Cl. WA8: Wid 2E 133
Egerton Dr. CH48: W Kir 4B 112
Egerton Gdns. CH42: R Ferr 3E 119
Egerton Gro. CH45: Wall 1B 74
Egerton Pk. CH42: R Ferr 3E 119
Egerton Pk. Cl. CH42: R Ferr 3E 119
Egerton Rd. CH43: C'ton 3A 96
  CH62: New F 5B 120
  L15: W'tree 2D 101
  L34: Prsct 4C 62
Egerton St. CH45: New B 3B 52
  L8: Liv .2F 99
  WA7: Run 4F 151
  WA9: St. H 2D 67
Egerton Wharf CH41: Birk 2E 97
Eglington Av. L35: Whis 3D 85
EGREMONT 1D 75
Egremont Cl. L27: N'ley 5A 106
Egremont Lawn L27: N'ley 5A 106
(not continuous)
Egremont Prom. CH44: Wall 5D 53
  CH45: Wall 5D 53
Egypt St. WA8: Wid 5F 131
Eighth Av. L9: Ain 1D 37
Eilian Gro. L14: K Ash 4D 81
Elaine Cl. WA8: Wid 2C 132
Elaine Norris Sports Cen. 2C 76
Elaine Price Ct. WA7: Run 1F 165
Elaine St. L8: Liv 3F 99
Elderberry Cl. L11: Crox 1C 58
Elderdale Rd. L4: Walt 4B 56
Elderflower Rd. WA9: St. H 3E 45
Elder Gdns. L19: Gras 4B 124
Elder Gro. CH48: W Kir 4B 112
Eldersfield Rd. L11: N Grn. 1B 58
Elderswood Rd. CH42: Tran 1E 119
Eldon Cl. WA10: St. H 1E 65
Eldon Gro. L3: Liv 2D 77
Eldonian Way L3: Liv 2C 76
Eldon Pl. L3: Liv 2C 76
Eldon Rd. CH42: R Ferr 2F 119
  CH44: Wall 2B 74
Eldon St. L3: Liv 2C 76
  WA10: St. H 1E 65
Eldred Rd. L16: Child 3C 102
Eleanor Pk. CH43: Bid 1C 94
Eleanor Rd. CH43: Bid 5D 73
  CH46: More 5D 71
  L20: Boot 2D 35
Eleanor St. L20: Kirk 2B 54
  WA8: Wid 5A 132
Elephant La. WA9: St. H 4D 65
Elfet St. CH41: Birk 1F 95
Elgar Av. CH62: East 5E 163
Elgar Rd. L14: K Ash 1F 81
Elgin Ct. L35: R'hill 4D 87
Elgin Dr. CH45: Wall 5C 52
Elgin Way CH41: Birk 2E 97

Eliot Cl. CH62: New F 5A 120
Eliot St. L20: Boot 3B 34
Elizabeth Cl. WA8: Wid 5B 132
Elizabeth Rd. L10: Faz 1B 38
  L20: Boot 2D 35
  L36: Huy 1F 105
  WA11: Hay 1E 49
Elizabeth St. L3: Liv 4F 77
  WA9: Clock F 3E 89
  WA9: St. H 3E 67
Elizabeth Ter. WA8: Wid 3D 131
Eliza St. WA9: St. H 4F 67
Elkan Cl. WA8: Wid 2E 133
Elkan Rd. WA8: Wid 2D 133
Elkstone Rd. L11: N Grn. 2B 58
Ellaby Rd. L35: R'hill 2C 86
Ellamsbridge Rd. WA9: St. H 4D 67
Ellel Gro. L6: Liv 1C 78
Ellen Gdns. WA9: St. H 4E 67
Ellens Cl. L6: Liv 4A 78
Ellen's La. CH63: Beb 2A 142
Ellen St. WA9: St. H 4E 67
Elleray Dr. L8: Liv 5F 99
Elleray Pk. Rd. CH45: Wall 4A 52
Ellerby Cl. WA7: Murd 3E 169
Ellergreen Rd. L11: N Grn. 1F 57
Ellerman Rd. L3: Liv 1E 121
Ellerslie Av. L35: R'hill 1B 86
Ellerslie Rd. L13: Liv 5D 57
Ellerton Cl. WA8: Wid 1C 130
Ellerton Way L12: Crox 5E 39
Ellesmere Dr. L10: Ain 3C 20
Ellesmere Gro. CH45: Wall 5B 52
Ellesmere St. WA7: Run 5B 152
Elliot Dr. L32: K'by 5D 23
Elliot St. L1: Liv 5D 77 (5F 5)
  WA8: Wid 4B 132
  WA10: St. H 5E 45
  L36: Huy 4A 84
Ellis La. WA6: Frod 4D 173
Ellison Dr. WA10: St. H 4C 44
Ellison Gro. L36: Huy 4E 83
Ellison St. L13: Liv 2F 79
Ellis Pl. L8: Liv 4F 99
Ellis Rd. WN5: Bil 1D 31
Ellis St. WA8: Wid 5A 132
Ellon Av. L35: R'hill 4D 87
Elloway Rd. L24: Speke 4A 148
Ellwood Cl. L24: Hale 5E 149
Elmar Rd. L17: Aig 2E 123
(not continuous)
Elm Av. CH49: Upton 3D 93
  L23: C'by 5F 9
  WA8: Wid 2B 132
Elm Bank L4: Walt 4F 55
Elmbank Rd. CH62: New F 1B 142
  L18: Moss H 4E 101
Elmbank St. CH44: Wall 3C 74
Elm Cl. CH61: Pens 3A 138
  L12: Crox 5F 39
Elm Ct. CH63: High B 1D 141
  L23: Blun 1C 16
Elmcroft Cl. L9: Ain 2D 37
Elmdale Rd. L9: Walt 4A 36
Elmdene Cl. CH49: Grea 2C 114
Elm Dr. CH49: Grea 1C 114
  L21: Sea 2F 33
Elmfield Cl. WA9: St. H 3E 65
Elmfield Rd. L9: Walt 3A 36
Elm Gdns. L21: Sea 2A 34
(off Elm Rd.)
Elm Grn. CH64: Will 5A 170
Elm Gro. CH42: Tran 5D 97
  CH47: Hoy 4C 90
  L7: Liv .5A 78
  L34: Ecc P 4F 63
  WA8: Wid 3B 132
Elm Hall Dr. L18: Moss H 4A 102
Elmham Cres. L10: Faz 1F 37
Elm Ho. L34: Prsct 5C 62
Elm Ho. M. L25: Gate 5B 104
Elmhurst Rd. L25: Gate 2A 104
Elmore Cl. L5: Liv 1F 77
  WA7: Wind H 1D 169

ELM PARK 3C 78
Elm Pk. Rd. CH45: Wall 4A 52
Elm Rd. CH42: Tran 1D 119
(Derby Rd.)
CH42: Tran 2B 118
(Waterpark Rd.)
CH61: Irby 1F 137
CH63: High B 5F 119
CH64: Will 5A 170
L4: Walt 1A 56
L21: Sea 2F 33
L32: K'by 2D 23
WA7: Run 2C 166
WA9: St. H 3D 65
WA10: St. H 3D 65
WA11: Hay 1E 49
Elm Rd. Nth. CH42: Tran 2B 118
Elms, The L8: Liv 5A 100
L31: Lyd 4D 7
WA7: Run 1F 165
Elmsdale Rd. L18: Moss H 4A 102
Elmsfield Cl. L25: Gate 4A 104
Elmsfield Pk. L39: Augh 1F 7
Elmsfield Rd. L23: Thorn 4B 10
Elms Ho. Rd. L13: Liv 3F 79
Elmsley Ct. L18: Moss H 1F 123
Elmsley Rd. L18: Moss H 5F 101
Elms Pk. CH61: Thing 2A 138
Elms Rd. L31: Mag 4C 12
Elm St. CH41: Birk 3D 97
L36: Huy 4A 84
Elmswood Av. L35: R'hill 4D 87
Elmswood Ct. L18: Moss H 1F 123
Elmswood Gro. L36: Huy 3B 82
Elmswood Rd. CH42: Tran 5C 96
CH44: Wall 2D 75
L17: Aig 2D 123
L18: Moss H 2D 123
Elm Ter. CH47: Hoy 4C 90
L7: Liv 4C 78
Elmtree Cl. L12: W Der 4C 58
Elmtree Gro. CH43: Bid 1E 95
Elmure Av. CH63: High B 2D 141
Elm Va. L6: Liv 2D 79
Elmway Cl. L13: Liv 4F 79
Elmwood WA7: Nort 2C 168
Elmwood Av. L23: C'by 5F 9
Elmwood Dr. CH61: Hes 5F 137
Elphin Gro. L4: Walt 2A 56
Elric Wlk. L33: K'by 2A 24
Elsbeck Gro. WA9: St. H 5D 67
Elsie Rd. L4: Walt 5A 56
Elsmere Av. L17: Aig 1C 122
Elstead Rd. L9: Faz 4E 37
L32: K'by 4C 22
Elstow St. L5: Kirk 4D 55
Elstree Ct. WA8: Wid 5D 111
Elstree Rd. L6: Liv 3D 79
Elswick St. L8: Liv 1F 121
Eltham Av. L21: Lith 4B 18
Eltham Cl. CH49: W'chu 2B 116
WA8: Wid 1E 133
Eltham Grn. CH49: W'chu 2B 116
Eltham St. L7: Liv 4D 79
Eltham Wlk. WA8: Wid 1E 133
Elton Av. L23: Blun 1C 16
L30: N'ton 2E 19
Elton Cl. CH62: East 2E 171
Elton Dr. CH63: Spit 4A 142
Elton Head Rd. WA9: St. H 1C 86
Elton St. L4: Walt 1F 55
Elvington Cl. WA7: Sut W 2F 173
Elvington Rd. L38: High 1A 8
Elwick Dr. L11: Crox 1C 58
Elwood Cl. L33: K'by 4E 15
Elworth Av. WA8: Wid 4A 110
Elworthy Av. L26: Halew 3F 127
Elwyn Dr. L26: Halew 4F 127
Elwyn Gdns. L26: Halew 4A 128
Elwyn Rd. CH47: Meols 2E 91
Elwy St. L8: Liv 4A 100
Ely Av. CH46: More 1C 92
Ely Cl. L30: N'ton 4F 19
Ely Pk. WA7: Nort 5E 155
Ember Cres. L6: Liv 2F 77

Embledon St. L8: Liv 2B 100
Embleton Gro. WA7: Beech 5E 167
Emerald Cl. L30: N'ton 2B 20
Emerald St. L8: Liv 1F 121
Emerson St. L8: Liv 2F 99
Emery St. L4: Walt 2F 55
Emily St. WA8: Wid 5A 132
WA9: St. H 4C 64
Emlyn St. WA9: St. H 2D 67
Emmett St. WA9: St. H 2C 66
Empire Bri. L3: Liv 4B 4
(off Union St.)
Empire Rd. L21: Lith 2B 34
Empress Cl. L31: Mag 1C 12
Empress Rd. CH44: Wall 2C 74
L6: Liv 5C 56
L7: Liv 4A 78
Emstrey Wlk. L32: K'by 3C 22
Endborne Rd. L9: Walt 2A 36
Endbutt La. L23: C'by 1E 17
Enderby Av. WA11: St. H 2C 46
Endfield Pk. L19: Gras 4A 124
Endmoor Rd. L36: Huy 1D 83
Endsleigh Rd. L13: Liv 3E 79
L22: Water 3B 16
Enerby Cl. CH43: Bid 2C 94
Enfield Av. L23: C'by 1E 17
Enfield Rd. L13: Liv 4B 80
Enfield St. WA10: St. H 1E 65
Enfield Ter. CH43: O'ton 4B 94
Enford Dr. WA9: St. H 4D 67
Enid St. L8: Liv 3F 99
Ennerdale Av. CH62: East 1F 171
L31: Mag 5E 7
WA11: St. H 5B 30
Ennerdale Cl. L33: K'by 5D 15
Ennerdale Dr. L21: Lith 5D 19
WA6: Frod 5C 172
Ennerdale Nursing Home
L9: Ain 2D 37
Ennerdale Rd. CH43: Pren 3E 117
CH45: Wall 3F 51
L9: Ain 2D 37
Ennerdale St. L3: Liv 2D 77
Ennis Cl. L24: Hale 5D 149
Ennis Ct. L11: N Grn. 5B 38
Ennisdale Dr. CH48: W Kir 3D 113
Ennismore Rd. L13: Liv 3F 79
L23: C'by 5C 8
Ennis Rd. L12: W Der 5E 59
Ensor St. L20: Boot 2B 34
Enstone Av. L21: Lith 4A 18
Enstone Rd. L25: Hunts X 1B 146
Ensworth Rd. L18: Moss H 4B 102
Enterprise Pk. WA11: R'ford 1B 28
Enterprise Way L13: W'tree 5E 79
Epping Av. WA9: Sut M 3B 88
Epping Cl. L35: R'hill 4D 87
Epping Ct. CH60: Hes 2A 158
Epping Gro. L15: W'tree 3B 102
Epsom Cl. L10: Ain 4E 21
Epsom Gro. L33: K'by 5F 15
Epsom Rd. CH46: Leas 3F 71
Epsom St. WA9: St. H 4E 47
Epsom Way L5: Liv 1D 77
Epstein Ct. L6: Liv 3B 78
(off Coleridge St.)
Epworth Cl. CH43: C'ton 3A 96
WA5: B'wood 4F 69
Epworth Grange CH43: C'ton 3A 96
(off Park Rd. W.)
Epworth St. L6: Liv 4F 77 (3J 5)
Eremon Cl. L9: Ain 5D 21
Erfurt Av. CH63: Beb 3A 142
Erica Ct. CH60: Hes 1E 157
Eric Gro. CH44: Wall 2A 74
Eric Rd. CH44: Wall 2A 74
Eric St. WA8: Wid 2C 132
Eridge St. L8: Liv 5A 100
Erin Cl. L8: Liv 3E 99
Erl St. L9: Ain 2A 36
Ermine Cres. L5: Liv 1F 77
Errington Cl. L17: Aig 4E 123
Errington St. L5: Kirk 5B 54
Errol St. L17: Aig 1B 122

Erskine Cl. WA11: St. H 2E 47
Erskine Ind. Est. L6: Liv 3F 77
Erskine Rd. CH44: Wall 3E 51
Erskine St. L6: Liv 3F 77 (3J 5)
Erskine St. Ind. Est. L6: Liv 4F 77
(off Erskine St.)
Erylmore Rd. L18: Moss H 3A 124
Escolme Dr. CH49: Grea 1D 115
Escor Rd. L25: Gate 3F 103
Escort Cl. L25: Hunts X 4C 126
Eshelby Cl. L22: Water 4E 17
Esher Cl. CH43: Bid 2C 94
CH62: New F 4B 120
Eshe Rd. L23: Blun 1C 16
Eshe Rd. Nth. L23: Blun 5B 8
Esher Rd. CH62: New F 4B 120
L6: Liv 3C 78
Eskburn Rd. L13: Liv 5E 57
Eskdale Av. CH46: More 5C 70
CH62: East 5E 163
WA11: St. H 5B 30
Eskdale Cl. WA7: Beech 5D 167
Eskdale Dr. L31: Mag 5E 7
Eskdale Rd. L9: Walt 2A 36
Esk St. L20: Kirk 3B 54
Eslington St. L19: Gras 5A 124
Esmond St. L6: Liv 1B 78
Esonwood Rd. L35: Whis 3D 85
Espin St. L4: Walt 2F 55
Esplanade CH42: R Ferr 2A 120
Esplanade, The CH62: New F 3B 120
L20: Boot 5C 34
L22: Water 5D 17
Esplen Av. L23: C'by 5F 9
Essex Rd. CH48: W Kir 3C 112
L36: Huy 2A 84
Essex St. L8: Liv 4E 99
Essex Way L20: Boot 4D 35
Esthwaite Av. WA11: St. H 5C 30
Estuary Banks L24: Speke 3F 145
Estuary Blvd. L24: Speke 4F 145
Estuary Commerce Pk.
L24: Speke 3F 145
(not continuous)
Etal Cl. L11: N Grn. 2B 58
Ethelbert Rd. CH47: Meols 3C 90
Ethel Rd. CH44: Wall 3D 75
Etna St. L13: Liv 3F 79
Eton Cl. L18: Moss H 4D 103
Eton Dr. CH63: Thorn H 4F 159
L10: Ain 3C 20
Etonhall Dr. WA9: St. H 4C 66
Eton St. L4: Walt 2F 55
Etruria St. L19: Gars 3C 144
Etruscan Rd. L13: Liv 2A 80
Ettington Rd. L4: Walt 5A 38
Ettrick Cl. L33: K'by 4D 15
Eurolink WA9: St. H 2F 87
Europa Blvd. CH41: Birk 3E 97
Europa Cen., The CH41: Birk 3D 97
Europa Pools 2D 97
Europa Sq. CH41: Birk 3D 97
Euston Gro. CH43: O'ton 4B 96
Euston St. L4: Walt 1F 55
Evans Cl. WA11: Hay 1F 49
Evans Rd. CH47: Hoy 4B 90
L24: Speke 2B 146
Evans St. L34: Prsct 4D 63
Evellynne Cl. L32: K'by 3C 22
Evelyn Av. L34: Prsct 5E 63
WA9: St. H 5E 47
Evelyn Rd. CH44: Wall 3C 74
Evelyn St. L5: Kirk 5D 55
WA9: St. H 5E 47
Evenson Way L13: Liv 2B 80
Evenwood WA9: St. H 5C 66
Evenwood Cl. WA7: Mnr P 3E 155
Everdon Wood L33: K'by 2F 23
Evered Av. L9: Walt 4A 36
Everest Rd. CH42: Tran 2D 119
L23: C'by 1E 17
Evergreen Cl. CH49: Upton 3E 93
L27: N'ley 3E 105
Evergreen Way WA9: Bold 4A 68
Everite Rd. WA8: Wid 5B 130

Everite Rd. Ind. Est.
  WA8: Wid 5B **130**
Everleigh Cl. CH43: Bid 2C **94**
Eversleigh Dr. CH63: Beb 3A **142**
Eversley WA8: Wid 2B **130**
Eversley Pk. CH43: O'ton 1B **118**
Eversley St. L8: Liv 3A **100**
  (not continuous)
EVERTON .1E **77**
Everton Brow L3: Liv 3E **77** (1H **5**)
Everton FC 2F **55**
Everton Gro. WA11: St. H 3D **47**
Everton Pk. Sports Cen. 1E **77**
Everton Rd. L6: Liv 2F **77**
Everton Valley L4: Walt 4E **55**
Everton Vw. L20: Boot 1B **54**
Everyman Theatre 5F **77** (6J **5**)
Every St. L6: Liv 2B **78**
Evesham Cl. L25: Wltn 2F **125**
Evesham Rd. CH45: Wall 5F **51**
  L4: Walt 2D **57**
Ewanville L36: Huy 5E **83**
Ewart Rd. L16: Child 1A **104**
  L21: Sea 1A **34**
  WA11: St. H 2B **46**
Ewden Cl. L16: Child 2E **103**
Exchange Flags L2: Liv 4C **4**
Exchange Pas. E. L2: Liv . .4C **76** (4C **4**)
Exchange Pas. W. L2: Liv . .4C **76** (4C **4**)
Exchange Pl. L35: R'hill 3C **86**
Exchange St. WA10: St. H 5A **46**
Exchange St. E. L2: Liv . . .4C **76** (4C **4**)
Exchange St. W. L2: Liv . . .4C **76** (5C **4**)
Exeley L35: Whis 4E **85**
Exeter Cl. L10: Ain 4E **21**
Exeter Rd. CH44: Wall 1C **74**
  L20: Boot 1C **54**
Exeter St. WA10: St. H 4D **45**
Exford Rd. L12: W Der 3D **59**
Exmoor Cl. CH61: Pens 2F **137**
Exmouth Cl. CH41: Birk 3D **97**
Exmouth Cres. WA7: Murd 4E **169**
Exmouth Gdns. CH41: Birk 3D **97**
Exmouth St. CH41: Birk 3D **97**
Exmouth Way CH41: Birk 3D **97**
  WA5: B'wood 5F **69**
Express Ind. Est. WA8: Wid 5A **130**
Extension Vw. WA9: St. H 3D **67**
Exwood Gro. L35: Whis 4F **85**

F

FACT Cen. 1D **99** (7G **5**)
Factory La. WA8: Wid 1B **132**
Factory Row WA10: St. H 2E **65**
Fairacre Rd. L19: Gras 5A **124**
Fairacres Rd. CH63: Beb 3F **141**
Fairbairn Rd. L22: Water 4E **17**
Fairbank St. L15: W'tree 2E **101**
Fairbeech Cl. CH43: Bid 2C **94**
Fairbeech M. CH43: Bid 2C **94**
Fairbrook Dr. CH41: Birk 5E **73**
Fairburn Cl. WA8: Wid 1E **133**
Fairburn Rd. L13: Liv 5E **57**
Fairclough Cl. L35: R'hill 3B **86**
Fairclough Cres. WA11: Hay 2A **48**
Fairclough La. CH43: O'ton 5B **96**
Fairclough Rd. L35: R'hill 3B **86**
  L36: Huy 5C **60**
  WA10: St. H 4C **44**
Fairclough St. L1: Liv 5D **77** (6F **5**)
  WA5: B'wood 5E **69**
Fairfax Dr. WA7: Run 5D **153**
Fairfax Pl. L11: N Grn. 1D **57**
Fairfax Rd. CH41: Tran 5E **97**
  L11: N Grn. 1D **57**
FAIRFIELD 3D **79**
Fairfield L23: C'by 1E **17**
  (not continuous)
Fairfield Av. L36: Huy 4A **82**
Fairfield Cl. L36: Huy 4A **82**
Fairfield Cres. CH46: More 1D **93**
  L6: Liv .3D **79**
  L36: Huy 4A **82**

Fairfield Dr. CH48: W Kir 3E **113**
Fairfield Gdns.
  WA11: Crank 3E **29**
Fairfield Rd. CH42: Tran 2E **119**
  WA8: Wid 3B **132**
  WA10: St. H 3C **44**
Fairfield St. L7: Liv 3E **79**
Fairford Cres. L14: K Ash 2B **80**
Fairford Rd. L14: K Ash 2B **80**
Fairhaven Cl. CH42: R Ferr 2F **119**
Fairhaven Dr. CH63: Brom 5C **162**
Fairhaven Ho. L19: Aig 5F **123**
  (off Spinnakers, The)
Fair Havens Ct. WA8: Wid 2C **132**
Fairholme Av. L34: Ecc P 5B **132**
Fairholme Cl. L12: W Der 3A **58**
Fairholme M. L23: C'by 1E **17**
Fairholme Rd. L23: C'by 1E **17**
Fairhurst Ter. L34: Prsct 5E **63**
Fairlawn Cl. CH63: Raby M 4A **162**
Fairlawn Ct. CH43: O'ton 4F **95**
Fairlawne Cl. L33: K'by 5E **15**
Fairlie Cres. L20: Boot 1D **35**
Fairlie Dr. L35: R'hill 4D **87**
Fairmead Rd. CH46: More 5E **71**
  L11: N Grn. 1E **57**
Fairoak Cl. CH43: Bid 2C **94**
Fairoak Ct. WA7: Pres B 2F **175**
Fairoak La. WA7: Pres B 2F **175**
Fairthorn Wlk. L33: K'by 2A **24**
Fair Vw. CH41: Tran 5E **97**
  WN5: Bil 1D **31**
Fair Vw. Av. WN5: Bil 1D **31**
Fairview Av. CH45: Wall 1A **74**
Fairview Cl. CH43: O'ton 1B **118**
Fairview Rd. CH43: O'ton 2B **118**
Fairview Way CH61: Pens 4F **137**
Fairway L36: Huy 2A **84**
  WA10: Windle 3C **44**
Fairway, The L12: K Ash 2D **81**
Fairway Cres. CH62: Brom 3D **143**
Fairway Nth. CH62: Brom 3D **143**
Fairways CH42: Tran 4B **118**
  L23: C'by 5D **9**
  WA6: Frod 5D **173**
Fairways, The CH48: Caldy 3D **135**
  L25: Hunts X 4D **127**
Fairways Cl. L25: Wltn 4B **126**
Fairway Sth. CH62: Brom 3D **143**
Falcon Cres. L27: N'ley 5F **105**
Falcon Ct. L20: Boot 2A **34**
Falconers Grn.
  CH44: Wall 5C **74**
  (off Old Gorsey La.)
Falconhall Rd. L9: Faz 4F **37**
Falcon Hey L10: Faz 2A **38**
Falcon Rd. CH41: Birk 5C **96**
Falcons Way WA7: Pal F 4E **167**
Falkirk Av. WA8: Wid 1E **131**
Falkland Rd. CH44: Wall 2D **75**
Falklands App. L11: N Grn. 1E **57**
Falkland St. CH41: Birk 1A **96**
  L3: Liv 4F **77** (3J **5**)
  (not continuous)
Falkner Sq. L8: Liv 1F **99**
Falkner St. L7: Liv 1F **99**
  L8: Liv 1F **99** (7J **5**)
  (not continuous)
Falkner Ter. L8: Liv 2A **100**
  (off Up. Parliament St.)
Fallbrook Dr. L12: W Der 3B **58**
  (not continuous)
Fallow Cl. WA9: Clock F 2C **88**
Fallowfield L33: K'by 1E **23**
  WA7: Run 1D **167**
Fallowfield Rd. CH46: More 1A **94**
  L15: W'tree 3F **101**
Falls La. L26: Halew 2E **127**
Falmouth Pl. WA7: Murd 4E **169**
Falmouth Rd. L11: Crox 3C **38**
Falstaff St. L20: Kirk 2C **54**
Falstone Dr. WA7: Murd 3E **169**

Faraday Rd. L13: W'tree 5E **79**
  L33: Know I 1B **40**
  WA7: Ast 4D **153**
Faraday St. L5: Liv 1A **78**
Fareham Cl. CH49: Upton 3E **93**
Fareham Rd. L7: Liv 4C **78**
Faringdon Cl. L25: Hunts X 1B **146**
Farley Av. CH62: Brom 1C **162**
Farlow Rd. CH42: R Ferr 3F **119**
Farmbrook Rd. L25: Gate 2B **104**
Farm Cl. CH49: Grea 5C **92**
  WA9: Clock F 3D **89**
Farmdale Cl. L18: Moss H 1B **124**
Farmdale Dr. L31: Mag 1E **13**
Farmer Pl. L20: Boot 1E **35**
Farmers La. WA5: B'wood 5F **69**
Farmfield Dr. CH43: Bid 2C **94**
Far Moss Rd. L23: Blun 4B **8**
Farm Rd. WA9: Clock F 3D **89**
Farmside CH46: Leas 3F **71**
Farm Vw. L21: Ford 3B **18**
Farmview Cl. L27: N'ley 2C **104**
Farnborough Gro. L26: Halew 3F **127**
Farndale WA8: Wid 4A **110**
Farndon Av. CH45: Wall 5E **51**
  WA9: Sut M 2B **88**
Farndon Dr. CH48: W Kir 3E **113**
Farndon Way CH43: O'ton 5F **95**
Farnham Cl. L32: K'by 4F **23**
Farnhill Cl. WA7: Nort 2D **169**
Farnley Rd. WA7: Wind H 1D **169**
Farnside Ct. L17: Aig 5E **123**
Farnworth Av. CH46: Leas 2F **71**
Farnworth Cl. WA8: Wid 5B **110**
Farnworth Gro. L33: K'by 5E **15**
Farnworth Rd. WA8: Wid 5E **111**
Farnworth St. L6: Liv 3B **78**
  WA8: Wid 5B **110**
  WA9: St. H 4C **46**
Farrant St. WA8: Wid 4B **132**
Farrar St. L13: Liv 4D **57**
Farrell Cl. L31: Mell 1B **22**
Farr Hall Dr. CH60: Hes 3E **157**
Farr Hall Rd. CH60: Hes 2E **157**
Farrier Rd. L33: K'by 3A **24**
Farriers Wlk. WA9: Clock F 2C **88**
Farriers Way CH48: Frank 2B **114**
  L30: N'ton 5F **19**
Farringdon Cl. WA9: St. H 1F **87**
Farthing Cl. L25: Hunts X 5A **126**
Farthingstone Cl. L35: Whis 5A **64**
Fatherside Dr. L30: N'ton 2C **18**
Faversham Rd. L11: N Grn. 5E **37**
Fawcett Rd. L31: Lyd 4D **7**
Fawley Rd. L18: Moss H 2C **124**
  L35: R'hill 5E **87**
FAZAKERLEY 1F **37**
Fazakerley Bri. L3: Liv 4B **4**
  (off Fazakerley St.)
Fazakerley Cl. L9: Walt 4A **36**
Fazakerley Rd. L9: Walt 4A **36**
  L35: Prsct 2E **85**
Fazakerley Sports Cen. 5F **21**
Fazakerley St. L3: Liv 4B **76** (4B **4**)
Fearnley Hall CH41: Birk 4D **97**
Fearnley Rd. CH41: Birk 4D **97**
Fearnside St. L7: Liv 1C **100**
Feather La. CH60: Hes 2F **157**
  (not continuous)
Feeny St. WA9: Sut M 4B **88**
Feilden Rd. CH63: Beb 3A **142**
Felcroft Way L33: K'by 3F **23**
Felicity Gro. CH46: More 5D **71**
Fell Gro. WA11: St. H 5A **30**
Fell St. CH44: Wall 4E **75**
  L7: Liv .4B **78**
Felltor Cl. L25: Wltn 1F **125**
Fellwood Gro. L35: Whis 3E **85**
Felmersham Av. L11: N Grn. 5E **37**
Felspar Rd. L32: K'by 1E **39**
Felstead Av. L25: Wltn 2C **126**
Felsted Av. L25: Wltn 2C **126**
Felsted Dr. L10: Ain 4E **21**
Felthorpe Cl. CH49: Upton 2B **94**

Felton Cl. CH46: More 1C 92
Felton Gro. L13: Liv 2F 79
Feltree Ho. CH43: Bid 2C 94
Feltwell Rd. L4: Walt 5B 56
Feltwood Cl. L12: W Der 4F 59
Feltwood Mnr. L12: W Der 4F 59
Feltwood Pl. L12: W Der 3F 59
Feltwood Wlk. L12: W Der 4F 59
Fendale Av. CH46: More 5A 72
Fender Ct. CH49: W'chu 3D 117
   CH46: More 5A 72
Fender La. CH43: Bid 5A 72
Fenderside Rd. CH43: Bid 1C 94
Fender Vw. Rd. CH46: More 1A 94
Fender Way CH43: Bid 2B 94
Fenderway CH61: Pens 3A 138
Fenton Cl. L24: Speke 4D 147
   L30: N'ton 5B 20
   WA8: Wid 1B 130
   WA10: St. H 4F 45
Fenton Grn. L24: Speke 5D 147
Fenwick La. WA7: Run 4D 167
Fenwick St. L2: Liv 5C 76 (5C 4)
Ferguson Av. CH49: Grea 1D 115
Ferguson Rd. L11: N Grn. 3E 57
   L21: Lith 4C 18
Fern Bank L31: Mag 1D 13
Fernbank Av. L36: Huy 4D 83
Fernbank Dr. L30: N'ton 1A 20
Fernbank La. CH49: Upton 2F 93
Fern Cl. L27: N'ley 5E 105
Ferndale Av. CH44: Wall 2C 74
   CH48: Frank 3B 114
Ferndale Cl. L9: Walt 1A 36
   WA8: Bold H 2E 111
Ferndale Rd. CH47: Hoy 4B 90
   L15: W'tree 3E 101
   L22: Water 3D 17
Fern Gdns. L34: Ecc P 4F 63
Fern Gro. CH43: Noct 4D 95
   L8: Liv 3B 100
   L20: Boot 4C 34
Fern Hey L23: Thorn 5B 10
Fernhill CH45: New B 3B 52
Fernhill Av. L20: Boot 5E 35
Fernhill Cl. L20: Boot 5E 35
   (not continuous)
Fernhill Dr. L8: Liv 3A 100
Fernhill Gdns. L20: Boot 5E 35
Fernhill M. E. L20: Boot 5E 35
Fernhill M. W. L20: Boot 5E 35
Fernhill Rd. L20: Boot 2D 35
Fernhill Sports Cen. 2D 35
Fernhill Wlk. WA9: Clock F 2C 88
Fernhill Way L20: Boot 5E 35
Fernhurst WA7: Run 1D 167
Fernhurst Rd. L32: K'by 4C 22
Fernie Cres. L8: Liv 4E 99
Fernlea Av. WA9: St. H 4D 65
Fernlea M. CH43: Bid 1C 94
Fernlea Rd. CH60: Hes 2A 158
Fernleigh CH43: O'ton 1B 118
Fernleigh Rd. L13: Liv 3B 80
Fern Lodge L8: Liv 3B 100
Ferns Cl. CH60: Hes 1C 156
Ferns Rd. CH63: High B 2D 141
Fernwood WA7: Nort 2B 168
Fernwood Dr. L26: Halew 4E 127
Fernwood Rd. L17: Aig 1E 123
Ferny Brow Rd. CH49: W'chu 1A 116
Ferrey Rd. L10: Faz 1A 38
Ferries Cl. CH63: R Ferr 4A 120
Ferry Rd. CH62: East 5F 163
Ferryside CH44: Wall 4E 75
Ferry Vw. Rd. CH44: Wall 4E 75
Ferryview Wlk. WA7: Cas 5F 153
Festival Ct. L11: N Grn. 5A 38
Festival Way WA7: Run 2C 166
Ffrancon Dr. CH63: High B 5F 119
Fiddlers Ferry Rd. WA8: Wid 4C 132
Fidler St. WA10: St. H 2D 65
Field Cl. CH62: New F 4B 120
   WA9: Clock F 3D 89
Fieldfare Cl. L25: Gate 4A 104

Fieldgate WA8: Wid 5B 130
Field Hey La. CH64: Will 4B 170
   (not continuous)
Field Ho. L12: W Der 4A 58
Fieldhouse Row WA7: Run 3D 167
Fieldings, The L31: Lyd 3B 6
Fielding St. L6: Liv 3A 78
Field La. L10: Faz 2A 38
   L21: Lith 4A 18
Field Rd. CH45: New B 4B 52
   WA9: Clock F 3D 89
Field's End L36: Huy 1E 105
Fieldsend Cl. L27: N'ley 5E 105
Fieldside Rd. CH42: R Ferr 2A 121
Field St. L3: Liv 3E 77 (1H 5)
   (not continuous)
Fieldsway WA7: West 4A 166
Fieldton Rd. L11: N Grn. 1B 58
Field Vw. L21: Lith 4A 18
Field Wlk. L23: Thorn 5A 10
Field Way L35: R'hill 1C 86
Fieldway CH45: Wall 1A 74
   CH47: Meols 4F 91
   CH60: Hes 1C 158
   CH63: High B 4D 119
   L15: W'tree 1C 102
   L31: Mag 3D 13
   L36: Huy 1F 105
   WA6: Frod 5C 172
   WA8: Wid 2D 133
Fieldway Ct. CH41: Birk 1C 96
Fifth Av. CH43: Bid 2B 94
   L9: Ain 1E 37
   (Meres Av.)
   L9: Ain 1D 37
   (Park Av.)
   WA7: Pal F 3F 167
Filbert Cl. L33: K'by 4F 15
Filby Gdns. WA9: St. H 5E 65
Fillmore Gro. WA8: Wid 1F 131
Filton Rd. L14: K Ash 1B 82
Finborough Rd. L4: Walt 1C 56
FINCHAM 1B 82
Fincham Cl. L14: K Ash 1B 82
Fincham Grn. L14: K Ash 1B 82
Fincham Rd. L14: K Ash 1A 82
Fincham Sq. L14: K Ash 1A 82
Finch Cl. WA9: Clock F 3D 89
Finch Ct. CH41: Birk 2D 97
Finchdean Cl. CH49: Grea 1C 114
Finch Dene L14: K Ash 5F 59
Finch La. L14: K Ash 5F 59
   L26: Halew 1B 148
Finch Lea Dr. L14: K Ash 1A 82
Finchley Dr. WA11: St. H 1C 46
Finchley Rd. L4: Walt 4B 56
Finch Mdw. Cl. L9: Faz 4F 37
Finch Pl. L3: Liv 4F 77 (3J 5)
Finch Rd. L14: K Ash 5A 60
Finch Way L14: K Ash 1F 81
Findley Dr. CH46: Leas 3F 71
Findon Rd. L32: K'by 5F 23
Fingall Rd. L15: W'tree 3A 102
Finger Ho. La. WA8: Bold H 5D 89
Fingland Rd. L15: W'tree 2E 101
Finlan Rd. WA8: Wid 5A 132
Finlay Ct. L30: N'ton 1F 19
Finlay St. L6: Liv 3C 78
Finney, The CH48: Caldy 3D 135
Finney Gro. WA11: Hay 2C 48
Finsbury Pk. WA8: Wid 4C 110
Finstall Rd. CH63: Spit 5F 141
Finvoy Rd. L13: Liv 4E 57
Fiona Wlk. L10: Faz 1D 38
Firbank Cl. WA7: Wind H 1D 169
Firbrook Ct. CH43: Bid 5C 72
Fir Cl. L26: Halew 4A 128
Fir Cotes L31: Mag 1E 13
Firdale Rd. L9: Walt 4A 36
Firdene Cres. CH43: Noct 5E 95
Fire Sta. Rd. L35: Whis 1F 85
Firethorne Rd. L26: Halew 2D 127
Fir Gro. L9: Ain 5C 20
Fir La. L15: W'tree 2A 102

Fir Rd. L22: Water 3E 17
Firs, The CH43: Bid 1E 95
Firs Av. CH63: Beb 4F 141
Firscraig L28: Stock V 4C 60
Firshaw Rd. CH47: Meols 2C 90
First Av. CH43: Bid 3C 94
   L9: Ain 2E 37
   (Lower La.)
   L9: Ain 1C 36
   (Park Av.)
   L23: C'by 1D 17
   L35: R'hill 2B 86
Firthland Way WA9: St. H 1F 67
Fir Tree Dr. Nth. L12: Crox 5D 39
Fir Tree Dr. Sth. L12: Crox 5D 39
Fir Tree La. WA5: B'wood 4F 69
Fir Way CH60: Hes 5B 158
Fisher Av. L35: Whis 4D 85
Fisher Pl. L35: Whis 4D 85
Fishers La. CH61: Pens 3E 137
Fisher St. L8: Liv 3D 99
   WA7: Run 3D 152
   WA9: St. H 3E 67
Fishguard Cl. L6: Liv 2F 77
Fishwicks Ind. Est. WA9: St. H 3C 66
Fistral Cl. L10: Faz 2B 38
Fistral Dr. WA10: Windle 2B 44
Fitness First
   Bootle 4B 20
   Bromborough 4E 143
   Runcorn 3E 167
Fitzclarence Wlk. L6: Liv 2F 77
Fitzclarence Way L6: Liv 2F 77
Fitzgerald Rd. L13: Liv 3A 80
Fitzpatrick Ct. L3: Liv 2C 76
Fitzroy Way L6: Liv 3A 78
Fitzwilliam Wlk. WA7: Cas 5A 154
Fiveways WA10: Eccl 4A 44
Flail Cl. CH49: Grea 5D 93
Flambards CH49: W'chu 1C 116
Flander Cl. WA8: Wid 2C 130
Flatfield Way L31: Mag 1E 13
Flatt La. CH43: O'ton 1F 117
Flavian Ct. WA7: Cas 1E 167
Flawn Rd. L11: N Grn. 3E 57
Flaxhill CH46: More 5D 71
Flaxman St. L7: Liv 4C 78
Flaybrick Cl. CH43: Bid 1E 95
Fleck La. CH48: Caldy, W Kir 5D 113
Fleet Cft. Rd. CH49: W'chu 2A 116
Fleet La. WA9: St. H 5E 47
Fleet La. Ind. Est. WA9: St. H 1E 67
Fleet St. L1: Liv 5D 77 (6F 5)
Fleetwood Gdns. L33: K'by 5F 15
   (not continuous)
Fleetwood Pl. L25: Wltn 2F 125
Fleetwoods La. L30: N'ton 1D 19
Fleetwood Wlk. WA7: Murd 3C 168
Fleming Cl. L3: Liv 2C 76
Fleming Rd. L24: Speke 1C 146
Flemington Av. L4: Walt 2D 57
Fleming Way CH46: Leas 4A 72
Fletcher Av. CH42: R Ferr 2E 119
   L34: Prsct 4E 63
Fletcher Cl. CH49: W'chu 2A 116
Fletcher Dr. L19: Gras 5A 124
Flint Dr. L12: Crox 2D 59
Flintshire Gdns. WA10: St. H 1F 65
Flint St. L1: Liv 2D 99
Flixton Gdns. WA9: St. H 5E 65
Floral Pavilion Theatre 2C 52
Floral Wood L17: Aig 2F 121
Florence Av. CH60: Hes 1F 157
Florence Cl. L9: Walt 5F 35
Florence Nightingale Cl.
   L30: N'ton 1F 19
Florence Rd. CH44: Wall 3E 75
Florence St. CH41: Birk 3D 97
   L4: Walt 3F 55
   WA9: St. H 4C 64
Florentine Rd. L13: Liv 2A 80
Florida Ct. L19: Gras 4B 124

Florida Way L35: Prsct 2D 85
Flowermead Cl. CH47: Meols 2F 91
Fluin La. WA6: Frod 4C 172
Fluker's Brook La. L34: Know 2B 60
Foinavon Cl. L9: Walt 1F 35
Folds, The CH63: Thorn H 4A 160
Folds La. WA11: St. H 1A 46
Folds Rd. WA11: Hay 2F 47
Foley Cl. L4: Kirk 4E 55
Foley St. L4: Kirk 4E 55
                              (not continuous)
Folkestone Way WA7: Murd 3C 168
Folly La. CH44: Wall 1E 73
    WA7: Run 1D 165
Fontenoy St. L3: Liv 4D 77 (2E 5)
Fonthill Cl. L4: Kirk 4D 55
Fonthill Rd. L4: Kirk 3D 55
Forbes Ho. L7: Liv 4C 78
FORD
    Bootle 3B 18
    Prenton 4C 94
Ford Av. L33: K'by 4E 15
Ford Cl. CH49: Upton 5B 94
    L20: Boot 1E 35
    L21: Ford 3B 18
Fordcombe Rd. L25: Gate 5C 104
Ford Dr. CH49: Upton 4B 94
Fordham St. L4: Kirk 3E 55
Fordhill Vw. CH46: More 1A 94
Ford La. CH49: Upton 4B 94
    L21: Ford 3B 18
Fordlea Rd. L12: W Der 3A 58
Fordlea Way L12: W Der 3A 58
Ford Rd. CH49: Upton 4A 94
    L35: Prsct 5F 63
Ford St. L3: Liv 3C 76 (1D 4)
Ford Vw. L21: Ford 2B 18
Ford Way CH49: Upton 5A 94
Fordway M. CH49: Upton 5A 94
Forefield La. L23: C'by 5F 9
Forest Cl. CH47: Meols 2D 91
Forest Ct. CH43: C'ton 3F 95
Forest Dr. L36: Huy 3C 82
Forest Grn. L34: Ecc P 4F 63
Forest Gro. L34: Ecc P 4F 63
Forest Lawn L12: W Der 3B 58
Forest Mead WA10: Eccl 5A 44
Forest Rd. CH43: C'ton 2A 96
    CH47: Meols 2D 91
    CH60: Hes 1A 158
    WA9: Sut M 3A 88
Forest Wlk. WA7: Pal F 3F 167
          (off Halton Lea Shop. Cen.)
Forfar Rd. L13: Liv 5D 57
Forge Cl. WA8: Cron 4C 108
Forge Cotts. L17: Aig 5C 100
Forge St. L20: Kirk 3C 54
Formby Av. WA10: St. H 2D 65
Formosa Dr. L10: Faz 1F 37
Formosa Rd. L10: Faz 1F 37
Formosa Way L10: Faz 1F 37
Fornalls Grn. La. CH47: Meols 4E 91
Forrester Av. WA9: St. H 4C 64
Forshaw Av. WA10: St. H 3C 64
Forshaw's La. WA5: C Grn 3E 69
Forsythia Cl. L9: Walt 5C 36
Forthlin Rd. L18: Aller 3C 124
                              (not continuous)
Forth St. L20: Kirk 2B 54
Forton Lodge Flats L23: Blun 1C 16
          (off Blundellsands Rd. E.)
Fort Perch Rock 2C 52
Fort St. CH45: New B 4C 52
Forwood Rd. CH62: Brom 2D 163
Foscote Rd. L33: K'by 1A 24
Foster Cl. L35: Whis 1A 86
Fosters Gro. WA11: Hay 2F 47
Fosters Rd. WA11: Hay 2F 47
Foster St. L20: Kirk 4C 54
    WA8: Wid 3B 132
Foundry La. WA8: Hale B 2B 150
Foundry St. WA10: St. H 5A 46
                              (not continuous)

Fountain Ct. L23: Blun 5A 8
Fountain La. WA6: Frod 5A 172
Fountain Rd. CH45: New B 4B 52
    L34: Know 5D 41
Fountains Av. WA11: Hay 1F 49
Fountains Cl. L4: Walt 4F 55
    WA7: Brook 5C 168
Fountains Ct. L5: Kirk 4D 55
Fountains Rd. L4: Kirk 4D 55
                              (not continuous)
Fountain St. CH42: Tran 1C 118
    WA9: St. H 5C 64
Four Acre Dr. L21: Ford 2B 18
Four Acre La. WA9: Clock F 2B 88
Four Acre Pct. WA9: Clock F 2B 88
Fouracres L31: Mag 3B 12
Four Bridges CH41: Birk 1E 97
Fourth Av. CH43: Bid 2B 94
    L9: Ain 1E 37
                                    (Lower La.)
    L9: Ain 1D 37
                                    (Park Av.)
    WA7: Pal F 3F 167
Fowell Rd. CH45: New B 3B 52
Fowler Cl. L7: Liv 5C 78
Fowler St. L5: Liv 1A 78
Fox Bank Cl. WA8: Wid 5F 109
Foxcote WA8: Wid 2B 130
Foxcover Rd. CH60: Hes 3C 158
Foxcovers Rd. CH63: Beb 4A 142
Fox Covert WA7: Nort 2C 168
Foxdale Cl. CH43: O'ton 4A 96
Foxdale Rd. L15: W'tree 3E 101
Foxdell Cl. L13: Liv 4A 80
Foxes, The CH61: Thing 1B 138
Foxfield Rd. CH47: Meols 3D 91
Foxglove Av. L26: Halew 3E 127
Foxglove Cl. L9: Faz 4F 37
Foxglove Ct. WA6: Frod 5C 172
Foxglove Rd. CH41: Birk 2F 95
Fox Hey Rd. CH44: Wall 2F 73
Foxhill Cl. L8: Liv 3A 100
Foxhill La. L26: Halew 2E 127
Foxhouse La. L31: Mag 2E 13
Foxhunter Dr. L9: Ain 5C 20
Foxhunters Chase WA12: New W . . .5E 49
Foxleigh L26: Halew 3D 127
Foxleigh Grange CH41: Birk 5F 73
Foxley Heath WA8: Wid 4E 131
Fox Pl. WA10: St. H 4A 46
Foxshaw Cl. L35: Whis 5D 85
Fox St. CH41: Birk 3C 96
    L3: Liv 2E 77 (1G 5)
    WA7: Run 5A 152
Foxton Cl. CH46: More 5B 70
    WA11: St. H 3D 47
Foxwood L12: W Der 3E 59
    WA9: St. H 4C 64
Foxwood Cl. CH48: W Kir 3E 113
Frampton Rd. L4: Walt 1D 57
Franceys St. L3: Liv 5E 77 (5H 5)
Francine Cl. L3: Liv 1C 76
Francis Av. CH43: C'ton 3B 96
    CH46: More 1D 93
Francis Cl. L35: R'hill 2C 86
    WA8: Wid 4C 130
Francis Rd. WA6: Frod 4C 172
Francis St. WA9: St. H 4F 67
Francis Way L16: Child 1D 103
FRANKBY .2B 114
Frankby Av. CH44: Wall 2A 74
Frankby Cl. CH49: Grea 1B 114
Frankby Grn. CH48: Frank 2B 114
Frankby Gro. CH49: Upton 4F 93
Frankby Rd. CH47: Meols 3D 91
    CH48: Frank, W Kir 3D 113
    CH49: Grea 3D 113
    L4: Walt 3B 56
Frankby Stiles CH48: Frank 3F 113
Frankby Vs. L33: K'by 4E 15
Franklin Pl. L6: Liv 1B 78
Franklin Rd. CH46: Leas 2A 72
Frank St. L8: Liv 4E 99
    WA8: Wid 3C 132

Franton Wlk. L32: K'by 3C 22
Fraser St. L3: Liv 4E 77 (3G 5)
Freckleton Dr. L33: K'by 5F 15
Freckleton Rd. WA10: St. H 2B 64
Freda Av. WA9: St. H 5C 66
Frederick Banting Cl.
    L30: N'ton 1F 19
Frederick Gro. L15: W'tree 1A 102
Frederick Lunt Av. L34: Know 5C 40
Frederick St. L1: Liv 7D 4
    WA8: Wid 3B 132
    WA9: St. H 3F 67
Fredric Pl. WA7: Run 4B 152
Freedom Cl. L7: Liv 1A 100
Freehold St. L7: Liv 3D 79
Freehold St. L4: Kirk 4E 55
Freeman St. CH41: Birk 2E 97
    L7: Liv 1C 100
Freemantle Av. WA9: St. H 4E 65
Freemason's Row L3: Liv . .3C 76 (2D 4)
                              (not continuous)
Freemont Rd. L12: W Der 4A 58
Freeport Gro. L9: Ain 1B 36
Freesia Av. L9: Walt 4B 36
Freme Cl. L11: N Grn. 5B 38
Frenchfield St. WA9: Clock F 3D 89
French St. WA8: Wid 3D 133
    WA10: St. H 2D 65
Frensham Cl. CH63: Spit 5F 141
Freshfield Rd.
    L15: W'tree 3F 101
Freshford WA9: St. H 5D 67
Friars Cl. CH63: Beb 2F 141
Friarsgate Cl. L18: Moss H 4C 102
Friar St. WA10: St. H 2F 45
Frinsted Rd. L11: N Grn. 2A 58
Frobisher Rd. CH46: Leas 2A 72
Froda Av. WA6: Frod 5B 172
FRODSHAM 5B 172
Frodsham Bus. Cen.
    WA6: Frod 4C 172
Frodsham Dr.
    WA11: St. H 3D 47
Frodsham Leisure Cen. 5B 172
Frodsham Pk. Homes
    WA6: Frod 5A 172
Frodsham Station (Rail) 5B 172
Frodsham St. CH41: Tran 5E 97
                              (not continuous)
Frogmore Rd. L13: Liv 3E 79
Frome Cl. CH61: Irby 5D 115
Frome Way L25: Hunts X 4D 127
Frontfield Ct. WA9: St. H 1C 66
          (off Appleton Rd.)
Frost Dr. CH61: Irby 1C 136
Frost St. L7: Liv 4C 78
Fryer St. WA7: Run 4A 152
Fry St. WA9: St. H 5E 47
                              (not continuous)
Fuchsia Wlk. CH49: Grea 2C 114
Fulbeck WA8: Wid 2C 130
Fulbrook Cl. CH63: Spit 4F 141
Fulbrook Rd. CH63: Spit 5F 141
Fulford Cl. L12: W Der 5F 59
Fulford Pk. CH46: More 1E 93
Fulford Rd. L17: Aig 2D 123
Fulwood Cl. L17: Aig 2D 123
Fulwood Dr. L17: Aig 2C 122
Fulwood Pk. L17: Aig 3C 122
Fulwood Rd. L17: Aig 2C 122
Fulwood Way L21: Ford 1C 18
Furlong Cl. L9: Ain 5C 20
Furness Av. L12: W Der 2C 58
    WA10: St. H 1E 45
Furness Cl. CH49: Upton 3E 93
Furness Ct. WA7: Nort 3F 155

Furness St. L4: Walt 4E 55
Furze Way CH46: More 5E 71

G

Gable Ct. L11: N Grn. 5E 37
Gables, The L31: Mag 3E 13
  L34: Ecc P 5F 63
Gable Vw. L11: N Grn. 5E 37
Gabriel Cl. CH46: More 1F 93
Gainford Cl. L14: K Ash 5A 60
  WA8: Wid 1C 130
Gainford Rd. L14: K Ash 5A 60
Gainsborough Av. L31: Mag 2B 12
Gainsborough Cl. L12: W Der 1E 81
Gainsborough Ct. WA8: Wid 3B 130
Gainsborough Rd. CH45: Wall 1E 73
  CH49: Upton 3F 93
  L15: W'tree 3D 101
Gaisgill Ct. WA8: Wid 3C 130
Gala Bingo
  Bromborough 4E 143
  Croxteth 4A 38
  Kirkby .3E 23
  Wavertree 2A 102
  Widnes 4B 132
Gala Cl. L14: K Ash 2E 81
Galbraith Cl. L17: Aig 2C 122
Galemeade L11: N Grn. 5B 38
Gale Rd. L21: Lith 4C 18
  L33: Know I 5C 24
Galion Way WA8: Wid 5F 109
Gallagher Ind. Est. CH41: Birk 5B 74
Gallopers La. CH61: Thing 1C 138
Galloway Rd. L32: Water 3E 17
Galloway St. L7: Liv 1D 101
Galston Av. L35: R'hill 4D 87
Galston Cl. L33: K'by 4D 15
Galsworthy Av. L30: Boot 5D 19
Galsworthy Pl. L30: Boot 5E 19
Galsworthy Wlk. L30: Boot 1E 35
Galton St. L3: Liv 3B 76 (2A 4)
Galtres Ct. CH63: High B 4E 119
Galtres Pk. CH63: High B 4E 119
Galway Av. WA8: Wid 2E 131
Galway Cres. WA11: Hay 1D 49
Gambier Ter. L1: Liv 2E 99
Gamble Av. WA10: St. H 2E 45
Gamlin St. CH41: Birk 1F 95
Gamston Wood L32: K'by 4C 22
Ganney's Mdw. Rd.
  CH49: W'chu 2C 116
Gannock St. L7: Liv 4C 78
Ganton Cl. WA8: Wid 5B 110
Ganworth Cl. L24: Speke 5E 147
Ganworth Rd. L24: Speke 5E 147
Garage Rd. L24: Halew 2F 147
Garden Apartments
  L18: Moss H 1F 123
Garden Cotts. L12: W Der 2D 81
Garden Ct. CH42: Tran 3C 118
Gardeners Vw. L33: K'by 4F 15
Gardeners Way L35: R'hill 1C 86
Garden Hey Rd. CH46: More 2B 92
  CH47: Meols 3C 90
Gardenia Gro. L17: Aig 2A 122
Garden La. CH46: More 5E 71
  L5: Liv .2E 77
  L9: Ain .5D 21
Garden Lodge Gro. L27: N'ley 4D 105
Gardenside CH46: Leas 2B 72
Gardenside St. L6: Liv 3F 77
Gardens Rd. CH63: Beb 3B 142
Garden St. L25: Wltn 2A 126
Garden Wlk. L34: Prsct 1D 85
Gardiner Av. WA11: Hay 2C 48
Gardner Av. L20: Boot 1D 35
Gardner Rd. L13: Liv 1E 79
Gardner's Dr. L6: Liv 2C 78
Gardner's Row L3: Liv 3D 77 (1E 5)
Gareth Av. WA11: St. H 2B 46
Garfield Ter. CH49: Upton 4A 94
Garfourth Cl. L19: Gars 5D 125
Garfourth Rd. L19: Gars 5D 125

Garmoyle Cl. L15: W'tree 2D 101
Garmoyle Rd. L15: W'tree 2E 101
Garnet St. L13: Liv 5F 79
  WA9: St. H 4D 67
Garnett Av. L4: Kirk 3D 55
Garnetts La. L35: Tar G 3D 129
  WA8: Hale B 3A 150
Garnge Wood CH48: W Kir 5D 113
Garrick Av. CH46: More 1C 92
Garrick Rd. CH43: Pren 4F 117
Garrick St. L7: Liv 2C 100
Garrigill Cl. WA8: Wid 4B 110
Garrison Cl. L8: Liv 3B 100
Garrowby Dr. L36: Huy 3C 82
Garsdale Av. L35: R'hill 4D 87
Garsfield Rd. L4: Walt 2D 57
GARSTON 1D 145
Garston Ind. Est. L19: Gars 3C 144
Garston Old Rd. L19: Gras 5A 124
Garston Sports Cen. 5C 124
Garston Station (Rail) 1D 145
Garston Way L19: Gars 1B 144
Garswood Cl. CH46: Leas 2F 71
  L31: Mag .4E 7
Garswood Cres. WN5: Bil 1E 31
Garswood Old Rd. WA11: St. H 5C 30
  WN4: Gars 5C 30
Garswood Rd. WN5: Bil 1E 31
Garswood St. L8: Liv 1F 121
  WA10: St. H 4A 46
Garter Cl. L11: Crox 5C 38
Garth, The L36: Huy 3E 83
Garth Blvd. CH63: High B 4E 119
Garth Ct. L22: Water 4E 17
Garthdale Rd. L18: Moss H 5A 102
Garth Dr. L18: Moss H 5B 102
Garthowen Rd. L7: Liv 4D 79
Garth Rd. L32: K'by 5A 24
Garth Wlk. L32: K'by 5A 24
Gartons La. WA9: Clock F, Sut M . . .3C 88
Garway L25: Wltn 1C 126
Gascoyne St. L3: Liv 3C 76 (2C 4)
Gaskell Ct. WA9: St. H 5F 47
Gaskell Rake L30: N'ton 5D 19
Gaskell St. WA9: St. H 2C 66
Gaskill Rd. L24: Speke 3D 147
Gas St. WA7: Run 5B 152
Gatclif Rd. L13: Liv 3E 57
GATEACRE 4B 104
Gateacre Brow L25: Gate 5A 104
Gateacre Pk. Dr. L25: Gate 2F 103
Gateacre Ri. L25: Gate 5A 104
Gateacre Shop. Cen. L25: Gate 3A 104
Gateacre Va. L25: Wltn 1B 126
Gateside Cl. L27: N'ley 4E 105
Gates La. L29: Thorn 2B 10
Gathurst Ct. WA8: Wid 4D 131
Gatley Dr. L31: Mag 5E 7
Gatley Wlk. L24: Speke 3F 147
Gaunts Way WA7: Pal F 4E 167
Gautby Rd. CH41: Birk 5E 73
Gavin Rd. WA8: Wid 5B 130
Gawsworth Cl. CH43: O'ton 1F 117
  WA10: Eccl 5B 44
Gaybeech Cl. CH43: Bid 1B 94
Gayhurst Cres. L11: N Grn. 1A 58
Gaynor Av. WA11: Hay 1F 49
GAYTON .3B 158
Gayton Av. CH45: New B 3B 52
  CH63: High B 4C 118
Gayton Farm Rd. CH60: Hes 5A 158
Gayton La. CH60: Hes 4B 158
Gayton Mill Cl. CH60: Hes 3B 158
Gayton Parkway CH60: Hes 5C 158
Gayton Rd. CH60: Hes 4F 157
Gaytree Ct. CH43: Bid 2C 94
Gaywood Av. L32: K'by 5F 23
Gaywood Cl. CH43: Bid 2C 94
  L32: K'by 5F 23
Gaywood Ct. L23: Blun 2B 16
Gaywood Grn. L32: K'by 5F 23
Gellings Rd. L34: Know 3A 40
Gelling St. L8: Liv 4E 99
Gemini Cl. L20: Boot 4B 34
Gemini Dr. L14: K Ash 2F 81

Gem St. L5: Liv 1C 76
Geneva Cl. L36: Huy 2D 83
Geneva Rd. CH44: Wall 4D 75
  L6: Liv 3C 78
Genoa Cl. L25: Gate 2B 104
Gentwood Pde. L36: Huy 2D 83
Gentwood Rd. L36: Huy 2C 82
George Hale Av. L34: Know P 5E 62
George Harrison Cl. L6: Liv 3B 78
George Moore Ct. L23: Thorn 4C 10
George Rd. CH47: Hoy 5C 90
George's Dock Gates
  L3: Liv 4B 76 (5B 4)
Georges Dockway L3: Liv . .5B 76 (6C 4)
George's Pk. L6: Liv 1B 78
George St. CH41: Birk 2E 97
  L3: Liv 4C 76 (4C 4)
  WA10: St. H 5A 46
Georgia Av. CH62: Brom 4E 143
Georgia Cl. L20: Boot 5C 34
Georgian Cl. L26: Halew 1F 147
  L35: Ecc P 5A 64
Geraint St. L8: Liv 3F 99
Gerald Rd. CH43: O'ton 5A 96
Gerard Av. CH45: Wall 4A 52
Gerard Rd. CH45: Wall 5F 51
  CH48: W Kir 3B 112
GERARD'S BRIDGE 3A 46
Gerards Ct. WA11: St. H 5C 30
Gerards La. WA9: St. H, Sut L 4D 67
Gerard St. L3: Liv 3D 77 (3F 5)
Gerard Way L33: K'by 3F 23
Germander Cl. L26: Halew 3E 127
Gerneth Cl. L24: Speke 3C 146
Gerneth Rd. L24: Speke 3B 146
Gerrard Av. WN5: Bil 1E 31
Gerrard's La. L26: Halew 2E 127
Gerrard St. WA8: Wid 4B 132
Gertrude Rd. L4: Walt 5A 56
Gertrude St. CH41: Birk 3F 97
  WA9: St. H 4C 64
Geves Gdns. L22: Water 4E 17
Ghyll Gro. WA11: St. H 4B 30
Gibbons Av. WA10: St. H 5C 44
Gibbs Ct. CH61: Irby 1A 138
Gibraltar Row L3: Liv 4B 76 (3B 4)
Gibson Cl. CH61: Pens 4F 137
  L33: K'by 5D 15
Gibson Rd. L8: Liv 2F 99
Giddygate La. L31: Mag, Mell 1B 14
Gidlow Rd. L13: Liv 3F 79
Gidlow Rd. Sth. L13: Liv 4F 79
Gilbert Cl. L33: Spit 5F 141
Gilbert Rd. L35: Whis 1F 85
Gilbert St. L1: Liv 1D 99 (7E 5)
Gildarts Gdns. L3: Liv 2C 76
Gildart St. L3: Liv 4E 77 (3J 5)
Gilead St. L7: Liv 4B 78
Gilescroft Av. L33: K'by 1A 24
Gilescroft Wlk. L33: K'by 1A 24
Gillan Cl. WA7: Brook 5C 168
GILLAR'S GREEN 1E 63
Gillars Grn. Dr. WA10: Eccl 5F 43
Gillar's La. WA10: Eccl 3D 43
  (not continuous)
Gillbrook Sq. CH41: Birk 1F 95
  (off Vaughan St., not continuous)
Gilleney Gro. L35: Whis 1A 86
GILLMOSS 3D 39
Gillmoss Cl. L11: Crox 4C 38
Gillmoss Ind. Est. L10: Faz 2B 38
Gillmoss La. L11: Crox 3C 38
Gills La. CH61: Barn, Pens 3A 138
Gill St. L3: Liv 4E 77 (4J 5)
Gilman St. L4: Walt 4A 56
Gilmartin Gro. L6: Liv 3A 78
Gilmour Mt. CH43: O'ton 5B 96
Gilpin Av. L31: Mag 5E 7
Gilroy Rd. CH48: W Kir 3C 112
  L6: Liv 3B 78
Gilwell Av. CH46: More 2E 93
Gilwell Cl. CH46: More 2E 93
Ginnel, The CH62: Port S 2B 142

Gipsy Gro. L18: Moss H 4E **103**
Gipsy La. L18: Moss H 4E **103**
Girton Av. L20: Boot 1E **55**
Girtrell Cl. CH49: Upton 4D **93**
Girtrell Rd. CH49: Upton 4D **93**
Givenchy Cl. L16: Child 1E **103**
Glade, The CH47: Meols 2D **91**
Glade Pk. Cl. L8: Liv 5B **100**
Glade Rd. L36: Huy 2E **83**
Gladeswood Rd. L33: Know I 4B **24**
Gladeville Rd. L17: Aig 1E **123**
Gladica Cl. L36: Huy 4B **84**
Gladstone Av. L16: Child 1A **104**
   L21: Sea 1A **34**
Gladstone Cl. CH41: Birk 3C **96**
Gladstone Cl. L8: Liv 2F **99**
   (off Up. Parliament St.)
Gladstone Hall Rd.
   CH62: Port S 2B **142**
Gladstone Rd. CH44: Wall 3D **75**
   L7: Liv 5B **78**
   L9: Walt 5F **35**
   L19: Gars 1C **144**
   L21: Sea 1F **33**
Gladstone St. L3: Liv 3C **76** (2D **4**)
   L25: Wltn 2F **125**
   WA8: Wid 4B **132**
   WA10: St. H 5D **45**
Gladstone Ter. CH64: Will 5A **170**
   (off Neston Rd.)
Gladstone Theatre 3B **142**
Gladsville Rd. L27: N'ley 5F **105**
Glaisher St. L5: Liv 5A **56**
Glamis Gro. WA9: St. H 4C **66**
Glamis Rd. L13: Liv 5D **57**
Glamorgan Cl. WA10: St. H 1F **65**
Glanaber Pk. L12: W Der 3E **59**
Glasgow St. CH42: R Ferr 2F **119**
Glasier Rd. CH46: More 5C **70**
Glaslyn Way L9: Walt 5A **36**
Glassonby Cres. L11: N Grn. 2A **58**
Glassonby Way L11: N Grn. 2A **58**
Glastonbury Cl. L6: Liv 4D **57**
   WA7: Nort 4F **155**
Glasven Rd. L33: K'by 2F **23**
Gleadmere WA8: Wid 2C **130**
Gleaner Cl. WA7: Run 4F **151**
Gleaston Cl. CH62: Brom 1D **163**
Gleave Cl. WA5: B'wood 5F **69**
Gleave Cres. L6: Liv 2F **77**
Gleave St. WA10: St. H 4A **46**
Glebe, The WA7: Run 1F **167**
Glebe Cl. L31: Mag 1B **12**
Glebe End L29: Seft 3E **11**
Glebe Hey L27: N'ley 4E **105**
Glebe Hey Rd. CH49: W'chu 1A **116**
Glebelands Rd. CH46: More 1E **93**
Glebe La. WA8: Wid 4A **110**
Glebe Rd. CH45: Wall 5A **52**
Gleggside CH48: W Kir 4C **112**
Glegg St. L3: Liv 2B **76**
Glegside Rd. L33: K'by 3A **24**
Glen, The CH63: Spit 4C **142**
   L18: Moss H 1C **124**
   WA7: Pal F 4F **167**
Glenacres L25: Wltn 1A **126**
Glenalmond Rd. CH44: Wall 2D **75**
Glenathol Rd. L18: Moss H 2C **124**
Glenavon Rd. CH43: Pren 3A **118**
   L16: Child 5C **80**
Glenbank L22: Water 3C **16**
Glenbank Cl. L9: Walt 1A **36**
Glenburn Av. CH62: East 1E **171**
Glenburn Rd. CH44: Wall 3D **75**
Glenby Av. L23: C'by 3F **17**
Glencairn Rd. L13: Liv 3F **79**
Glencoe Rd. CH45: Wall 5B **52**
Glenconner Rd. L16: Child 5E **81**
Glencourse Rd. WA8: Wid 4A **110**
Glencroft Cl. L36: Huy 1C **82**
Glendale Cl. L8: Liv 1F **121**
Glendale Gro. CH63: Spit 5B **142**
   L33: K'by 5F **15**
   (off Dorchester Dri.)
Glendale Gro. WA11: St. H 1A **46**

Glendevon Rd. L16: Child 5C **80**
   L36: Huy 5E **83**
Glendower Rd. L22: Water 4E **17**
Glendower St. L20: Kirk 2C **54**
Glendyke Rd. L18: Moss H 2C **124**
Gleneagles Cl. CH61: Pens 4F **137**
   L33: K'by 4D **15**
Gleneagles Dr. WA8: Wid 3A **48**
Gleneagles Rd. L16: Child 5D **81**
Glenfield Cl. CH43: Bid 1C **94**
   CH46: More 5B **70**
Glenfield Rd. L15: W'tree 3F **101**
Glengariff St. L13: Liv 4D **57**
Glenham Cl. CH47: Meols 3E **91**
Glenhead Rd. L19: Aller 4B **124**
Glenholm Rd. L31: Mag 3C **12**
Glenista Cl. L9: Walt 5A **36**
Glenluce Rd. L19: Aig 3A **124**
Glenlyon Rd. L16: Child 1C **102**
Glenmarsh Cl. CH63: High B 2D **141**
   L12: W Der 5C **58**
Glenmaye Cl. L12: Crox 1E **59**
Glenmore Av. L18: Moss H 1F **123**
Glenmore Rd. CH43: O'ton 5A **96**
Glenn Pl. WA8: Wid 3E **131**
Glen Pk. Rd. CH45: Wall 4A **52**
Glen Rd. L13: Liv 4B **80**
Glen Ronald Dr. CH49: Grea 4D **93**
Glenrose Rd. L25: Wltn 5A **104**
Glenside L18: Aller 2C **124**
Glentree Cl. CH49: Grea 4D **93**
Glentrees Rd. L12: W Der 3B **58**
Glentworth Cl. L31: Mag 2D **13**
Glenville Cl. L25: Wltn 5B **104**
   WA7: Run 4B **166**
Glen Vine Cl. L16: Child 1E **103**
Glen Way L33: K'by 4F **15**
Glenway Cl. L12: Crox 4F **39**
Glenwood WA7: Nort 2C **168**
Glenwood Cl. L35: Whis 4F **85**
Glenwood Dr. CH61: Irby 5E **115**
Glenwyllin Rd. L22: Water 3C **16**
Globe Rd. L20: Boot 4B **34**
Globe St. L4: Walt 4E **55**
Gloucester Cl. L6: Liv 3A **78**
Gloucester Rd. CH45: Wall 5E **51**
   L6: Liv 1D **79**
   L20: Boot 4D **35**
   L36: Huy 3A **84**
   WA8: Wid 1B **132**
Gloucester Rd. Nth. L6: Liv 5D **57**
Gloucester St. L1: Liv 4D **77** (4G **5**)
   WA9: St. H 1D **67**
Glover Pl. L20: Boot 4B **34**
Glover's Brow L32: K'by 1C **22**
Glover's La. L30: N'ton 1E **19**
Glover St. CH42: Tran 5C **96**
   L8: Liv 3D **99**
   WA10: St. H 1F **65**
Glyn Av. CH62: Brom 3E **163**
Glynne Gro. L16: Child 1A **104**
Glynne St. L20: Boot 2D **35**
Glynn St. L15: W'tree 2F **101**
Glyn Rd. CH44: Wall 1B **74**
Goddard Rd. WA7: Ast 4E **153**
Godetia Cl. L9: Faz 4F **37**
Godstow WA7: Nort 3E **155**
Goldcrest Cl. L12: Crox 4F **39**
   WA7: Beech 1F **173**
Goldcrest M. L26: Halew 3E **127**
Golden Gro. L4: Walt 2A **56**
Golden Triangle Ind. Est.
   WA8: Hale B 2B **150**
Goldfinch Cl. L26: Halew 3E **127**
Goldfinch Farm Rd. L24: Speke . . .4C **146**
Goldie St. L4: Walt 4F **55**
Goldsmith Rd. CH43: Pren 3F **117**
Goldsmith St. L6: Liv 3B **78**
   L20: Boot 4A **34**
Goldsmith Way CH43: Pren 3F **117**
Goldsworth Fold L35: R'hill 3B **86**
Golf Links Rd. CH42: Tran 3B **118**
Gondover Av. L9: Walt 2F **35**
Gonville Rd. L20: Boot 1D **55**

Goodacre Rd. L9: Ain 1B **36**
Goodakers Ct. CH49: W'chu 2A **116**
   (off Goodakers Mdw.)
Goodakers Mdw. CH49: W'chu 2A **116**
Goodall Pl. L4: Kirk 2E **55**
Goodall Rd. L4: Kirk 2E **55**
Goodban St. WA9: St. H 3E **67**
Goodier Ct. WA7: Run 2C **166**
Goodison Av. L4: Walt 3F **55**
Goodison Pk. 2F **55**
Goodison Pl. L4: Walt 2F **55**
Goodison Rd. L4: Walt 2F **55**
Goodlass Rd. L24: Speke 1A **146**
Goodleigh Pl. WA9: Sut L 1C **88**
Good Shepherd Cl. L11: N Grn. 1B **58**
Goodwood Cl. L36: Roby 5D **83**
Goodwood Ct. WA9: St. H 5D **65**
Goodwood Dr. CH46: Leas 3F **71**
Goodwood St. L5: Liv 1D **77**
Gooseberry Hollow
   WA7: Wind H 1D **169**
Gooseberry La. WA7: Nort 1D **169**
Goose Grn., The CH47: Meols 2D **91**
Goostrey Cl. CH63: Spit 1B **162**
Gordale Cl. L8: Liv 5A **100**
Gordon Av. CH49: Grea 1E **115**
   CH62: Brom 3E **163**
   L22: Water 3C **16**
   L31: Mag 4C **6**
   WA11: Hay 1F **49**
Gordon Cl. CH49: Grea 1E **115**
Gordon Dr. L14: B Grn 3E **81**
   L19: Gras 5A **124**
Gordon Pl. L18: Moss H 1A **124**
Gordon Rd. CH45: New B 4B **52**
   L21: Sea 2F **33**
Gordon St. CH41: Birk 3C **96**
   L15: W'tree 2E **101**
Gordon Ter. CH64: Will 5A **170**
   (off Neston Rd.)
Goree L2: Liv 5B **76** (5B **4**)
Gore's La. WA11: Crank 1A **30**
Gores Rd. L33: Know I 4B **24**
Gore St. L8: Liv 3E **99**
Gorleston M. L32: K'by 5F **23**
Gorleston Way L32: K'by 4F **23**
Gorran Haven WA7: Brook 5C **168**
Gorse Av. L12: W Der 2B **58**
Gorsebank Rd. L18: Moss H 4E **101**
Gorsebank St. CH44: Wall 3C **74**
Gorseburn Rd. L13: Liv 5E **57**
Gorse Cres. CH44: Wall 4C **74**
Gorsedale Pk. CH44: Wall 4D **75**
Gorsedale Rd. CH44: Wall 4B **74**
   L18: Moss H 5A **102**
Gorsefield WA9: St. H 4D **65**
Gorsefield Av. CH62: Brom 5D **163**
   L23: Thorn 5B **10**
Gorsefield Cl. CH62: Brom 5D **163**
Gorsefield Rd. CH42: Tran 1C **118**
Gorse Hey Ct. L13: W Der 1A **80**
Gorsehill Rd. CH45: New B 4A **52**
   CH60: Hes 1A **158**
Gorselands L17: Aig 2D **123**
Gorse La. CH48: W Kir 5E **113**
Gorse Rd. CH47: Meols 3D **91**
Gorsewood Cl. L25: Gate 4C **104**
   (off Gorsewood Rd.)
Gorsewood Gro. L25: Gate 4B **104**
Gorsewood Rd. L25: Gate 4B **104**
   WA7: Murd 4D **169**
Gorsey Av. L30: N'ton 2C **18**
Gorsey Brow WN5: Bil 1D **31**
Gorsey Cop Rd. L25: Gate 3A **104**
Gorsey Cop Way L25: Gate 3A **104**
Gorsey Cft. L34: Ecc P 4F **63**
Gorsey La. CH44: Wall 3B **74**
   L21: Ford 4B **18**
   L30: N'ton 4C **18**
   L38: High 1A **8**
   WA8: Wid 4E **133**
   WA9: Bold 5B **68**
   WA9: Clock F . . . . . . .3D **89** & 5B **68**
Gorseyville Cres. CH63: High B 2E **141**
Gorseyville Rd. CH63: High B 2E **141**

Gorseywell La. WA7: Pres B 4F 169
Gorst St. L4: Walt 4F 55
Gorton Rd. L13: Liv 4B 80
Gort Rd. L36: Huy 3E 83
Goschen St. L5: Liv 4F 55
  L13: Liv 3F 79
Gosford St. L8: Liv 5F 99
Gosforth Ct. WA7: Pal F 3E 167
Goswell St. L15: W'tree 1E 101
Gotham Rd. CH63: Spit 5A 142
Gothic St. CH42: R Ferr 2F 119
Gough Rd. L13: Liv 4E 57
Goulders Ct. WA7: Brook 5B 168
Gourley Rd. L13: Liv 5A 80
Gourleys La. CH48: W Kir 5D 113
Government Rd. CH47: Hoy 4B 90
Govett Rd. WA9: St. H 4C 64
Gower St. L3: Liv 1C 98 (7D 4)
  L20: Boot 3A 34
  WA9: St. H 2D 67
Gowrie Gro. L21: Lith 1B 34
Goyt Hey Av. WN5: Bil 1E 31
Grace Av. L10: Faz 1A 38
Grace Cl. L35: Wall 1B 74
Grace Rd. L9: Walt 2A 36
Grace St. L8: Liv 5F 99
  WA9: St. H 3C 66
Gradwell St. L1: Liv 5D 77 (6E 5)
Graeme Bryson Ct. L11: N Grn. . . .2F 57
Grafton Wlk. CH48: W Kir 4C 112
Grafton Cl. L8: Liv 3D 99
Grafton Dr. CH49: Upton 5B 94
Grafton Gro. L8: Liv 5E 99
Grafton Rd. CH45: New B 4B 52
Grafton St. CH43: O'ton 4B 96
  L8: Liv 1F 121
    (Beresford Rd.)
  L8: Liv 3D 99
    (Grafton Cres.)
  L8: Liv 4E 99
    (Park St.)
  L8: Liv 3D 99
    (Parliament St.)
  WA10: St. H 5D 45
Graham Cl. WA8: Wid 4C 112
Graham Dr. L26: Halew 4A 128
Graham Rd. CH48: W Kir 3A 112
  WA8: Wid 3C 130
Graham's Rd. L36: Huy 4F 83
Graham St. WA9: St. H 5C 46
Grainger Av. CH43: Pren 2F 117
  CH48: W Kir 2B 112
  L20: Boot 2E 35
Grain Ind. Est. L8: Liv 5E 99
Grain St. L8: Liv 5E 99
Graley Cl. L26: Halew 1F 147
Grammar School La.
  CH48: W Kir 5D 113
Grampian Av. CH46: More 1F 93
Grampian Rd. L7: Liv 4E 79
Grampian Way CH46: More 1E 93
  CH62: East 5E 163
Granams Cft. L30: N'ton 1D 19
Granard Rd. L15: W'tree 3A 102
Granary Mill WA4: Pres H 4F 169
Granary Way L3: Liv 3D 99
Granborne Chase L32: K'by 2B 22
GRANBY .1F 99
Granby Cl. WA7: Brook 5C 168
Granby Cres. CH63: Spit 5A 142
Granby St. L8: Liv 2A 100
Grand Central L3: Liv 5G 5
Grandison Rd. L4: Walt 2B 56
Grand National Av. L9: Ain 4B 20
GRANGE .4D 113
Grange, The CH44: Wall 2C 74
Grange Av. CH44: Wall 5B 52
  L12: W Der 1E 81
  L25: Hunts X 5D 127
Grange Av. Nth. L12: W Der 1E 81
Grange Ct. CH43: O'ton 1A 118
  L15: W'tree 2F 101
Grange Cross Cl. CH48: W Kir 5E 113
Grange Cross Hey CH48: W Kir . . .5E 113
Grange Cross La. CH48: W Kir 5E 113

Grange Dr. CH60: Hes 1A 158
  CH63: Thorn H 3A 160
  WA8: Wid 3D 131
  WA10: St. H 3B 64
Grange Farm Cres.
  CH48: W Kir 3E 113
Grangehurst Ct. L25: Gate 5B 104
Grange La. L25: Gate 4A 104
Grangemeadow Rd. L25: Gate . . .4A 104
Grangemoor WA7: Run 3D 167
Grange Mt. CH43: O'ton 4C 96
  CH48: W Kir 4D 113
  CH60: Hes 1F 157
Grange Old Rd. CH48: W Kir 4C 112
GRANGE PARK 3B 64
Grange Pk. L31: Mag 3E 13
Grange Pk. Av. WA7: Run 5C 152
Grange Pk. Rd. WA10: St. H 2C 64
Grange Pct. CH41: Birk 3D 97
Grange Rd. CH41: Birk 3D 97
    (not continuous)
  CH48: W Kir 4A 112
  CH60: Hes 5F 137
  L30: N'ton 3B 20
  WA7: Run 5C 152
  WA11: Hay 3D 49
    (not continuous)
Grange Rd. E. CH41: Birk 3E 97
Grange Road Sports Cen. 3B 96
Grange Rd. W. CH41: Birk 3C 96
  CH43: O'ton 3B 96
Grangeside L25: Gate 4A 104
Grange St. L6: Liv 1C 78
Grange Ter. L15: W'tree 2F 101
Grange Va. CH42: R Ferr 3A 120
Grange Valley WA11: Hay 2D 49
Grange Vw. CH43: O'ton 4C 96
Grange Wlk. CH48: W Kir 5D 113
Grange Way L25: Gate 4A 104
Grangeway WA7: Run 2C 166
Grangeway Ct. WA7: Run 2C 166
Grange Weint L25: Gate 5A 104
Grangewood L16: Child 5F 81
Granite Ter. L36: Huy 4A 84
Grant Av. L15: W'tree 3F 101
Grant Cl. L14: K Ash 3A 82
  WA10: St. H 4E 45
Grant Ct. L20: Boot 5C 34
Grantham Cl. CH61: Pens 3E 137
Grantham Cres. WA11: St. H 3C 46
Grantham Rd. L33: K'by 5E 15
Grantham St. L6: Liv 3B 78
Grantham Way L30: N'ton 1B 20
Grantley Rd. L15: W'tree 3A 102
Granton Rd. L5: Liv 5F 55
Grant Rd. CH60: Leas 2B 72
  L14: K Ash 3F 81
Granville Av. L31: Mag 5C 6
Granville Cl. CH45: Wall 5E 51
Granville Ct. CH45: Wall 5E 51
Granville Rd. L15: W'tree 2D 101
  L19: Gars 1C 144
Granville St. WA7: Run 4A 152
  WA9: St. H 5D 47
Grappenhall Way CH43: Bid 2C 94
Grasmere Av. CH43: Noct 4C 94
  L34: Prsct 5F 63
  WA11: St. H 1B 46
Grasmere Cl. L33: K'by 1D 23
  WA11: St. H 1B 46
Grasmere Ct. CH41: Birk 4C 96
    (off Penrith St.)
  WA11: St. H 1A 46
Grasmere Dr. CH45: Wall 5A 52
  L21: Lith 1A 34
  WA7: Beech 5E 167
Grasmere Fold WA11: St. H 1B 46
Grasmere Gdns. L23: C'by 2F 17
Grasmere Ho. L17: Aig 2D 123
Grasmere Rd. L31: Mag 5D 7
  WA6: Frod 5C 172
Grasmere St. L5: Liv 3A 56
GRASSENDALE 4A 124
Grassendale Ct. L19: Gras 5A 124

Grassendale Esplanade
  L19: Gras 1A 144
Grassendale Grn. L19: Gras 5F 123
Grassendale La. L19: Gras 5A 124
GRASSENDALE PARK 5F 123
Grassendale Rd. L19: Gras 5A 124
Grassington Cres. L25: Wltn 2C 126
Grassmoor Cl. CH62: Brom 2E 163
Grasswood Rd. CH49: W'chu 2B 116
Grasville Rd. CH42: Tran 1E 119
Gratrix Rd. CH62: Brom 2D 163
Gray Av. WA11: Hay 2D 49
Gray Gro. L36: Huy 1F 105
Graylag Cl. WA7: Beech 5F 167
Graylands Pl. L4: Walt 2C 56
Graylands Rd. CH62: Port S 1C 142
  L4: Walt 2B 56
Graylaw Ind. Est. L9: Ain 2C 36
Grayling Dr. L12: Crox 5D 39
Gray's Av. L35: Prsct 5F 63
Grayson Av. WA9: Sut L 5D 67
Grayson St. L1: Liv 1C 98
Gray St. L20: Boot 3A 34
GREASBY 1D 115
Greasby Hill Rd. CH48: W Kir 5C 112
Greasby Rd. CH44: Wall 2A 74
  CH49: Grea 1C 114
Gt. Ashfield WA8: Wid 1D 131
Gt. Charlotte St. L1: Liv 5D 77 (5F 5)
    (not continuous)
GREAT CROSBY 1E 17
Gt. Crosshall St. L3: Liv 4C 76 (3D 4)
Gt. Delph WA11: Hay 1D 49
Gt. George Pl. L1: Liv 2E 99
Gt. George Sq. L1: Liv 1D 99
Gt. George's Rd. L22: Water 5D 17
Gt. George St. L1: Liv 2E 99
Great Hey L30: N'ton 5D 11
Gt. Homer St. L5: Liv 5D 55
Gt. Homer St. Shop. Cen.
  L5: Liv 1E 77
Gt. Howard St. L3: Liv 3B 76 (1B 4)
  L5: Liv 3B 76
GREAT MEOLS 2E 91
Gt. Mersey St. L5: Kirk 5C 54
    (not continuous)
Gt. Nelson St. L3: Liv 2D 77
Gt. Newton St. L3: Liv 4F 77 (4J 5)
Gt. Orford St. L3: Liv 5F 77 (6J 5)
Gt. Richmond St. L3: Liv 3D 77 (1F 5)
Great Riding WA7: Nort 3B 168
Gt. Western Ho. CH41: Birk 2F 97
Greaves St. L8: Liv 4F 99
Grebe Av. WA10: St. H 4B 64
Grecian St. L21: Sea 5F 17
Grecian Ter. L5: Liv 5E 55
Gredington St. L8: Liv 5A 100
Greek St. L3: Liv 4E 77 (4H 5)
  WA7: Run 4F 151
Green, The CH48: Caldy 2D 135
  CH62: Brom 2D 143
  CH63: Raby 5C 160
  CH64: Will 5A 170
  L13: Liv 4B 80
  L23: C'by 1D 17
  L34: Ecc P 4F 63
Greenacre L25: Hunts X 4C 126
Greenacre Dr. CH63: Brom 3C 162
Greenacre Rd. L25: Hunts X 4C 126
Greenacres Cl. CH43: Bid 1C 94
Greenacres Ct. CH43: Bid 1C 94
Green Acres Est. CH49: Grea 2C 114
Greenall Ct. L34: Prsct 5D 63
Greenall St. WA10: St. H 4D 45
Green Av. CH45: New B 3B 52
GREEN BANK 1E 65
Green Bank CH63: Brim 5A 140
Greenbank L22: Water 5E 17
Greenbank Av. CH45: New B 4B 52
  L31: Mag 4C 6
Greenbank Ct. L17: Aig 4E 101
Greenbank Cres. WA10: St. H 5F 45
Greenbank Dr. CH61: Pens 4A 138
  L10: Faz 1B 38
  L17: Aig 4E 101

Greenbank La. L17: Aig 5E 101
Greenbank Rd. CH42: Tran 1C 118
  CH48: W Kir 2B 112
  L18: Moss H 4E 101
Greenbank Sports Academy 5E 101
Greenbridge Cl. WA7: Cas 5A 154
Greenbridge Rd. WA7: Wind H . .5B 154
Greenburn Av. WA11: St. H 4C 30
Green Coppice WA7: Nort 2C 168
Greencroft Rd. CH44: Wall 3C 74
Greendale Rd. CH62: Port S 1A 142
  L25: Wltn 5F 103
Green End Pk. L12: W Der 4A 58
Greenes Rd. L35: Whis 4D 85
Greenfield Ct. L18: Aller 3B 124
Greenfield Dr. L36: Huy 5F 83
Greenfield Gro. L36: Huy 5F 83
Greenfield La. CH60: Hes 5D 137
  L21: Lith 4A 18
  WA6: Frod 4B 172
Greenfield Rd. L13: Liv 3A 80
  WA10: St. H 3D 45
GREENFIELDS 1C 94
Greenfields Av. CH62: Brom 3C 162
Greenfields Cres. CH62: Brom . .3C 162
Greenfield Vw. WN5: Bil 1D 31
Greenfield Wlk. L36: Huy 5F 83
Greenfield Way CH44: Wall 2B 74
  L18: Aller 3B 124
Greenfinch Cl. L12: Crox 5F 39
Greenfinch Gro. L26: Halew 3E 127
Greengables Cl. L8: Liv 4A 100
Greengate WA9: St. H 3A 66
Green Gates L36: Huy 5E 61
Greenham Av. L33: K'by 4F 15
Green Haven CH43: Noct 4D 95
Greenhaven Cl. L10: Faz 1F 37
Greenheath Way CH46: Leas 3F 71
Greenhey Dr. L30: N'ton 3C 18
Green Heys Dr. L31: Mag 1F 13
Greenheys Gdns. L8: Liv 3B 100
Greenheys Rd. CH44: Wall 2B 74
  CH61: Irby 2C 136
  L8: Liv 3B 100
Greenhill Av. L18: Moss H 4C 102
Greenhill Cl. L18: Moss H 2B 124
Greenhill Pl. L36: Huy 5E 83
Greenhill Rd. L18: Moss H 1B 124
  L19: Aller 4C 124
Greenholme Cl. L11: N Grn. 5A 38
Greenhouse Farm Rd.
  WA7: Pal F 4B 168
Greenhow Av. CH48: W Kir 3B 112
Grn. Jones Brow WA5: B'wood . . .5F 69
Greenlake Rd. L18: Moss H 2B 124
Greenlands L36: Huy 5E 83
Greenland St. L1: Liv 2D 99
Green La. CH41: Tran 5E 97
  CH45: Wall 1B 72
      (not continuous)
  CH62: East 2E 163
  CH63: Beb 2F 141
  L3: Liv 5E 77 (6H 5)
  L13: Liv 1E 79
  L18: Moss H 5B 102
      (not continuous)
  L21: Ford 3B 18
  L21: Sea 1A 34
      (not continuous)
  L22: Water 3B 16
  L23: Thorn 4B 10
  L31: Mag 5A 6
  WA5: B'wood 4E 69
  WA8: Wid 3E 131
  WA10: Eccl 2E 43
Green La. Nth. L16: Child 3C 102
Green Lane Station (Rail) 5E 97
Green Lawn CH42: R Ferr 3F 119
  L36: Huy 2A 84
Green Lawn Gro. CH42: R Ferr . .3F 119
GREEN LEACH 1A 46
Green Leach Av. WA11: St. H 1B 46
Green Leach Ct. WA11: St. H 1B 46
Green Leach La. WA11: St. H 1B 46

Greenlea Cl. CH63: Beb 1F 141
Greenleaf St. L8: Liv 2C 100
Greenleas Cl. CH45: Wall 5D 51
Greenleas Rd. CH45: Wall 5D 51
Greenleigh Rd. L18: Moss H 2B 124
Green Link L31: Mag 5B 6
Green Mt. CH49: Upton 4A 94
Grn. Oaks Path WA8: Wid 4C 132
      (not continuous)
Grn. Oaks Way WA8: Wid 4B 132
Greenock M. WA8: Wid 1E 131
Greenock St. L3: Liv 3B 76 (2A 4)
Greenodd Av. L12: W Der 2C 58
Greenore Dr. L24: Hale 5D 149
Greenough Av. L35: R'hill 1C 86
Greenough St. L25: Wltn 2F 125
Green Pk. L30: N'ton 5F 11
Green Pk. Dr. L31: Mag 1B 12
Green Rd. L34: Prsct 4C 62
Greensbridge La. L26: Halew 3A 128
  L35: Tar G 3A 128
Greens Health & Fitness 1E 121
Greenside L6: Liv 3F 77
Greenside Av. L10: Ain 3D 21
Greenside Cl. L33: K'by 4F 15
Green St. L5: Liv 2C 76
Greens Wlk. L17: Aig 1E 123
Greenville Cl. CH63: Beb 2F 141
Greenville Dr. L31: Mag 1C 12
Greenville Rd. CH63: Beb 2F 141
Green Way CH61: Pens 3E 137
Greenway CH49: Grea 5E 93
  CH62: Brom 4D 143
  L23: C'by 5A 10
  L36: Huy 2B 82
Greenway, The L12: K Ash 2D 81
Greenway Cl. L36: Huy 2B 82
Greenway Rd. CH42: Tran 1D 119
  L24: Speke 4A 148
  WA7: Run 1F 165
  WA8: Wid 2B 132
Greenways CH62: Brom 4C 162
Greenways Sq. L36: Huy 2B 82
Greenwell Rd. WA11: Hay 2C 48
Greenwich Av. WA8: Wid 5D 111
Greenwich Ct. L9: Ain 5B 20
Greenwich Rd. L9: Ain 5B 20
Greenwood Ct. L34: Prsct 5E 63
Greenwood Dr. WA9: Clock F 2C 88
Greenwood La. CH44: Wall 1C 74
Greenwood Rd. CH47: Meols 3E 91
  CH49: W'chu 1B 116
  L18: Aller 3B 124
Greetham St. L1: Liv 1D 99 (7E 5)
Gregory Cl. L16: Child 1D 103
Gregory Way L16: Child 1D 103
Gregson Ct. CH45: New B 3C 52
Gregson Ho. WA10: St. H 4A 46
Gregson Rd. L14: B Grn 3C 80
  L35: Prsct 1D 85
  WA8: Wid 3C 132
Gregson St. L6: Liv 3F 77
Grenfell Rd. L13: Liv 3E 57
Grenfell St. WA8: Wid 4B 132
Grennan, The CH45: New B 3B 52
Grennan Ct. CH45: New B 3B 52
Grenville Cres. CH63: Brom 3C 162
Grenville Dr. CH61: Pens 4E 137
Grenville Rd. CH42: Tran 1F 119
Grenville St. Sth. L1: Liv 1D 99
Grenville Way CH42: Tran 1F 119
Gresford Av. CH43: Pren 2A 118
  CH48: W Kir 3C 112
  L17: Liv 3D 101
Gresford Cl. L35: Whis 3F 85
Gresham St. L7: Liv 4D 79
Gresham Cl. L7: Liv 5C 78
Gresley Cl. L7: Liv 5C 78
Gressingham Rd. L18: Moss H . . .2C 124
Gretton Rd. L14: K Ash 1B 82
Greyhound Farm Rd.
  L24: Speke 4C 146

Grey Rd. L9: Walt 4F 35
Greystoke Cl. CH49: Upton 5F 93
Greystone Cres. L14: B Grn 4E 81
Greystone Pl. L10: Faz 1E 37
Greystone Rd. L10: Faz 1E 37
  L14: B Grn 3E 81
      (not continuous)
Grey St. L8: Liv 2F 99
      (not continuous)
Gribble Rd. L10: Faz 1A 38
Grierson St. L8: Liv 2B 100
Grieve Rd. L10: Faz 1A 38
Griffin Av. CH46: More 1E 93
Griffin Cl. L11: Crox 4C 38
  WA10: Eccl 4F 43
Griffin M. WA8: Wid 1B 132
Griffin St. WA9: St. H 4E 67
Griffin Wlk. L11: Crox 4C 38
Griffiths Cl. CH49: Grea 1C 114
Griffiths Rd. L36: Huy 4E 83
Griffiths St. L1: Liv 1E 99
Grimshaw St. L20: Boot 1B 54
  WA9: Sut L 5C 66
Grinfield St. L7: Liv 5A 78
Grinshill Cl. L8: Liv 3A 100
Grinton Cres. L36: Roby 4D 83
Grisedale Cl. WA7: Beech 5E 167
Grisedale Rd.
  CH62: Brom 2F 163
Grizedale WA8: Wid 2B 130
      (not continuous)
Grizedale Av. WA11: St. H 5B 30
Groes Rd. L19: Gras 5B 124
Grogan Sq. L20: Boot 2D 35
Gronow Pl. L20: Boot 2E 35
Grosmont Rd. L32: K'by 5F 23
Grosvenor Av. CH48: W Kir 4B 112
  L23: C'by 3E 17
Grosvenor Cl. L30: N'ton 4B 96
  CH47: Hoy 5B 90
  L15: W'tree 2C 102
  L18: Moss H 1E 123
  L34: Prsct 5D 63
Grosvenor Dr. CH45: New B 3B 52
Grosvenor Pl.
  CH43: O'ton 4A 96
Grosvenor Rd. CH43: O'ton 3A 96
  CH45: New B 3B 52
  CH47: Hoy 5B 90
  L4: Walt 1E 55
  L15: W'tree 1D 101
  L19: Gras 1A 144
  L31: Mag 4C 12
  L34: Prsct 5D 63
  WA8: Wid 4B 110
  WA10: St. H 1C 64
  WA11: Hay 1B 48
Grosvenor St. CH44: Wall 1B 74
  L3: Liv 2D 77 (1F 5)
  WA7: Run 5A 100
Grosvenor Ter. L8: Liv 5A 100
      (off Belvidere Rd.)
Grove, The CH43: O'ton 1B 118
  CH44: Wall 3C 74
  CH63: Beb 1A 142
  L13: Liv 1F 79
  L28: Stock V 4C 60
  WA10: Windle 3C 44
Grove Av. CH60: Hes 1F 157
Grovedale Dr. CH46: More 5A 72
Grovedale Rd.
  L18: Moss H 4F 101
Grovehurst Av. L14: K Ash 2F 81
Groveland Av. CH45: Wall 5D 51
  CH47: Hoy 4B 90
Groveland Rd. CH45: Wall 4D 51
Grovelands L7: Liv 1F 99
      (off Groveside)
Grove Mead L31: Mag 1F 13
Grove Mt. CH41: Tran 5E 97
Grove Pk. L8: Liv 3B 100
Grove Park Av. L12: W Der 3B 58
Grove Pl. CH47: Hoy 4B 90
  L4: Kirk 4E 55

Grove Rd. CH42: R Ferr	.2F **119**
CH45: Wall	.5E **51**
CH47: Hoy	.4B **90**
L6: Liv	.3D **79**
Groves, The CH43: O'ton	.4A **96**
L32: K'by	.1E **39**
Grove Side L7: Liv	.1F **99**
Groveside CH48: W Kir	.4A **112**
Grove Sq. CH62: New F	.5A **120**
Grove St. CH62: New F	.5B **120**
L7: Liv	.1A **100**
L15: W'tree	.1F **101**
L20: Boot	.4A **34**
WA7: Run	.4F **151**
WA10: St. H	.5F **45**
Grove Ter. CH47: Hoy	.4B **90**
Grove Way L7: Liv	.1A **100**
Grovewood Ct. CH43: O'ton	.1B **118**
Grovewood Gdns. L35: Whis	.3E **85**
Grundy Cl. WA8: Wid	.1F **131**
Grundy St. L5: Kirk	.5B **54**
Guardian Cl. CH48: W Kir	.5C **112**
Guelph Pl. L7: Liv	.4A **78**
Guelph St. L7: Liv	.4A **78**
Guernsey Rd. L13: Liv	.2F **79**
Guest St. WA8: Wid	.1E **133**
	.5A **132**
Guffitts Cl. CH47: Meols	.2E **91**
Guffitt's Rake CH47: Meols	.2E **91**
Guildford Av. L30: N'ton	.4F **19**
Guildford St. CH44: Wall	.2D **75**
Guildhall Rd. L9: Ain	.2A **36**
Guild Hey L34: Know	.4D **41**
Guillemot Way L26: Halew	.3E **127**
Guilsted Rd. L11: N Grn	.1A **58**
Guinea Gap CH44: Wall	.3E **75**
Guinea Gap Baths & Recreation Cen.	
	.3E **75**
Guion Rd. L21: Lith	.1B **34**
Guion St. L6: Liv	.2B **78**
Gulls Way CH60: Hes	.2D **157**
Gunning Av. WA10: Eccl	.3B **44**
Gunning Cl. WA10: Eccl	.3B **44**
Gurnall St. L4: Walt	.4F **55**
Gutticar Rd. WA8: Wid	.3B **130**
Guy Cl. WA8: Wid	.1F **131**
Gwendoline Cl. CH61: Thing	.2B **138**
Gwendoline St. L8: Liv	.3F **99**
Gwenfron Rd. L6: Liv	.3B **78**
Gwent Cl. L6: Liv	.1B **78**
Gwent St. L8: Liv	.3A **100**
Gwladys St. L4: Walt	.2F **55**
Gwydir St. L8: Liv	.4A **100**
Gwydrin Rd. L18: Moss H	.4C **102**

H

Hackett Av. L20: Boot	.2D **35**
Hackett Pl. L20: Boot	.2D **35**
	(not continuous)
Hackins Hey L2: Liv	.4C **76** (4C **4**)
Hackthorpe St. L5: Liv	.4E **55**
Hadassah Gro. L17: Aig	.5C **100**
Hadden Cl. L35: R'hill	.2A **86**
Haddock St. L20: Kirk	.2B **54**
Haddon Av. L9: Walt	.2F **35**
Haddon Dr. CH61: Pens	.3F **137**
WA8: Wid	.5B **108**
Haddon Rd. CH42: R Ferr	.2A **120**
Haddon Wlk. L12: Crox	.5C **39**
Hadfield Av. CH47: Hoy	.4C **90**
Hadfield Cl. WA8: Wid	.2E **133**
Hadfield Gro. L35: Wltn	.1C **126**
Hadleigh Rd. L32: K'by	.4F **23**
Hadley Av. CH62: Brom	.1F **143**
Hadlow La. CH64: Will	.5A **170**
Hadlow Rd. CH64: Will	.5A **170**
Hadlow Ter. CH64: Will	.5A **170**
Hadwens Bldgs. L3: Liv	.4C **76** (3D **4**)
Haggerston Rd. L4: Walt	.1A **56**
Hahneman Rd. L4: Walt	.1E **55**
Haig Av. CH46: More	.1F **93**
Haigh Cres. L31: Lyd	.3C **6**
Haigh Rd. L22: Water	.4E **17**

Haigh St. L3: Liv	.2F **77** (1J **5**)
	(not continuous)
Haig Rd. WA8: Wid	.3A **132**
Haileybury Av. L10: Ain	.3D **21**
Haileybury Rd. L25: Wltn	.4B **126**
Hailsham Rd. L19: Aig	.4E **123**
Halby Rd. L9: Ain	.2B **36**
Halcombe Rd. L12: W Der	.4D **59**
Halcyon Rd. CH41: Birk	.5C **96**
Haldane Av. CH41: Birk	.2F **95**
Haldane Rd. L4: Walt	.1A **56**
HALE	.5D **149**
HALE BANK	.2B **150**
Hale Bank Ter. WA8: Hale B	.1E **149**
Hale Ct. WA8: Hale B	.3A **150**
Hale Dr. L24: Speke	.5C **146**
Halefield St. WA10: St. H	.4F **45**
Hale Ga. Rd. WA8: Hale B	.5F **149**
HALE HEATH	.5A **148**
Hale M. WA8: Wid	.5C **130**
Hale Rd. CH45: Wall	.5C **52**
L4: Walt	.2E **55**
L24: Speke	.4B **146**
WA8: Hale B	.3B **150**
WA8: Wid	.5C **130**
Hale Rd. Ind. Est. WA8: Hale B	.2B **150**
Hale St. L2: Liv	.4C **76** (4D **4**)
Hale Vw. WA7: Run	.2E **165**
Hale Vw. Rd. L36: Huy	.4A **84**
HALEWOOD	.5F **127**
Halewood Caravan Pk.	
L26: Halew	.4C **128**
Halewood Ct. L25: Gate	.5B **104**
Halewood Dr. L25: Wltn	.2C **126**
	(Hunts Cross Av.)
L25: Wltn	.2B **126**
	(Kings Dri.)
HALEWOOD GREEN	.2E **127**
Halewood Leisure Cen.	.5A **128**
Halewood Pl. L25: Wltn	.1C **126**
Halewood Rd. L25: Gate, Wltn	.5B **104**
Halewood Station (Rail)	.4F **127**
Halewood Triangle Country Pk.	
	.4D **127**
Halewood Way L25: Wltn	.2C **126**
Haley Rd. Nth. WA5: B'wood	.5D **69**
Haley Rd. Sth. WA5: B'wood	.5E **69**
Half Crown St. L5: Kirk	.5C **54**
Halfpenny Cl. L19: Gras	.5B **124**
Halidon Ct. L20: Boot	.4A **34**
Halifax Cres. L23: Thorn	.4B **10**
Halkirk Rd. L18: Aller	.3C **124**
Halkyn Av. L17: Liv	.3D **101**
Halkyn Dr. L5: Liv	.1A **78**
Hallam Wlk. L7: Liv	.5C **78**
Hall Av. WA8: Wid	.3A **130**
Hall Dr. CH49: Grea	.1D **115**
L32: K'by	.2E **23**
Hall La. L7: Liv	.4A **78**
L9: Ain	.1B **36**
L31: Mag	.2C **12**
L32: K'by	.3D **23**
L33: Sim	.3F **15**
L34: Prsct	.1D **85**
L35: R'hill	.5C **86**
L36: Huy	.4F **83**
WA5: B'wood	.4F **69**
WA8: Cron	.2C **108**
WA9: Bold	.3F **89**
Hall Rd. WA11: Hay	.1E **49**
Hall Rd. E. L23: Blun	.4B **8**
Hall Road Station (Rail)	.4A **8**
Hall Rd. W. L23: Blun	.4A **8**
Hallsands Rd. L32: K'by	.5E **23**
Hallside Cl. L19: Aig	.4F **123**
Hall St. WA9: Clock F	.3D **89**
WA10: St. H	.5A **46**
Halltine Cl. L23: Blun	.4A **8**
Hallville Rd. CH44: Wall	.3C **74**
L18: Moss H	.4A **102**
Hallwood Cl. WA7: Nort	.4B **166**
Hallwood Link Rd. WA7: Pal F	.4F **167**
HALLWOOD PARK	.4E **167**
Hallwood Pk. Av. WA7: Pal F	.4E **167**

Halsall L23: C'by	.5E **9**
WA7: Brook	.5C **168**
Halsall Grn. CH63: Spit	.1B **162**
Halsall Rd. L20: Boot	.2C **34**
Halsall St. L34: Prsct	.4D **63**
Halsbury Rd. CH45: Wall	.5B **52**
L6: Liv	.3C **78**
Halsey Av. L12: W Der	.4F **57**
Halsey Cres. L12: W Der	.4F **57**
Halsnead Av. L35: Whis	.5C **84**
Halsnead Cvn. Est. L35: Whis	.5C **85**
Halsnead Cl. L15: W'tree	.5A **80**
Halstead Rd. CH44: Wall	.3C **74**
L9: Walt	.2F **35**
Halstead Wlk. L32: K'by	.4C **22**
HALTON BROOK	.2E **167**
Halton Brook Av. WA7: Run	.1D **167**
Halton Brow WA7: Halt	.1E **167**
Halton Castle	.1F **167**
Halton Ct. WA7: Run	.5D **153**
Halton Cres. CH49: Grea	.1B **114**
Halton Hey L35: Whis	.5D **85**
HALTON LEA	.3F **167**
Halton Link Rd. WA7: Pal F	.2E **167**
HALTON LODGE	.2C **166**
Halton Lodge Av. WA7: Run	.3D **167**
Halton Miniature Railway	.3C **168**
Halton Rd. CH45: Wall	.5A **52**
L31: Lyd	.4D **7**
WA7: Run	.5B **152**
Halton Stadium	.4F **131**
Halton Sta. Rd. WA7: Sut W	.2F **173**
Halton St. WA11: Hay	.2E **49**
HALTON VIEW	.3C **132**
Halton Vw. Rd. WA8: Wid	.3C **132**
HALTON VILLAGE	.2F **167**
Halton Wlk. L25: Gate	.3A **104**
Halton Wood L32: K'by	.2B **22**
Hambledon Dr. CH49: Grea	.5C **92**
Hambleton Cl. L11: Crox	.4B **38**
WA8: Wid	.1C **130**
Hambleton Cres. WA11: St. H	.2B **46**
Hamer St. WA10: St. H	.4F **45**
Hamer St. Sth. WA10: St. H	.5F **45**
Hamil Cl. CH47: Meols	.2E **91**
Hamilton Ct. L23: Blun	.1B **16**
Hamilton La. CH41: Birk	.2E **97**
Hamilton Rd. CH45: New B	.3A **52**
L5: Liv	.1F **77**
WA10: Windle	.2C **44**
Hamilton Sq. CH41: Birk	.2F **97**
Hamilton Square Station (Rail)	.2F **97**
Hamilton St. CH41: Birk	.3E **97**
	(not continuous)
Hamlet Ct. L17: Aig	.1C **122**
Hamlet Rd. CH45: Wall	.5F **51**
Hamlin Cl. WA7: West	.4A **166**
Hamlin Rd. L19: Gars	.1D **145**
Hammersley Av. WA9: Clock F	.3C **88**
Hammersley St. WA9: Clock F	.3C **88**
Hammersmith Way	
WA8: Wid	.5D **111**
Hamill St. WA10: St. H	.3D **45**
	(not continuous)
Hammond Rd. L33: Know I	.2C **24**
Hammond St. WA9: St. H	.1D **67**
Hamnett Rd. L34: Prsct	.4E **63**
Hampden Gro. CH42: Tran	.5D **97**
Hampden Rd. CH42: Tran	.5D **97**
Hampden St. L4: Walt	.1F **55**
Hampshire Av. L30: N'ton	.2C **18**
Hampshire Gdns. WA10: St. H	.1F **65**
Hampson St. L6: Liv	.1C **78**
Hampstead Rd. CH44: Wall	.3C **74**
L6: Liv	.3C **78**
Hampton Chase CH43: Noct	.1D **117**
Hampton Cl. WA8: Wid	.1E **133**
Hampton Ct. WA7: Mnr P	.3C **154**
Hampton Ct. Rd. L12: W Der	.1C **80**
Hampton Ct. Way WA8: Wid	.5D **111**
Hampton Dr. WA8: Cron	.4C **108**
Hampton Pl. WA11: St. H	.2B **46**
Hampton St. L8: Liv	.2F **99**
Hanbury Rd. L4: Walt	.3D **57**
Handel Ct. L8: Liv	.3B **100**

Handel Rd.—Hawarden Av.

Handel Rd. L27: N'ley 3C **104**
Handfield Pl. L5: Liv 1A **78**
Handfield Rd. L22: Water 4D **17**
Handfield St. L5: Liv 1A **78**
Handford Av. CH62: East 5F **163**
Handforth La. WA7: Run 4D **167**
Handley Ct. L19: Aig 4F **123**
Handley St. WA7: Run 4F **151**
Hands St. L21: Lith 2B **34**
Hanford Av. L9: Walt 2F **35**
Hankey Dr. L20: Boot 3E **35**
Hankey St. WA7: Run 5F **151**
Hankinson St. L13: Liv 5F **79**
Hankin St. L5: Liv 5D **55**
Hanley Cl. WA8: Wid 3C **130**
Hanley Rd. WA8: Wid 3C **130**
Hanlon Av. L20: Boot 2D **35**
Hanmer Rd. L32: K'by 3B **22**
Hannah Cl. CH61: Pens 4E **137**
Hannan Rd. L6: Liv 3B **78**
Hanover Cl. CH43: C'ton 3F **95**
Hanover Ct. WA7: Brook 4B **168**
Hanover St. L1: Liv 5C **76** (7E **4**)
Hansard Ct. WA9: St. H 4D **65**
Hansby Dr. L24: Speke 2B **146**
Hanson Pk. CH43: O'ton 4E **95**
Hanson Rd. L9: Ain 3C **36**
Hanson Rd. Bus. Pk. L9: Ain 3C **36**
Hans Rd. L4: Walt 2A **56**
Hanwell St. L6: Liv 5B **56**
Hanworth Cl. L12: Crox 5E **39**
Hapsford Rd. L21: Lith 2B **34**
Hapton St. L5: Liv 5E **55**
Harbern Cl. L12: W Der 5C **58**
Harbord Rd. L22: Water 4C **16**
Harbord St. L7: Liv 5B **78**
Harbord Ter. L22: Water 4C **16**
Harborne Dr. CH63: Spit 5F **141**
Harbour Cl. WA7: Murd 4D **169**
Harbreck Gro. L9: Ain 5D **37**
Harcourt Av. CH44: Wall 3E **75**
Harcourt St. CH41: Birk 2C **96**
L4: Kirk 4D **55**
Hardie Av. CH46: More 5C **70**
Hardie Cl. WA9: Sut M 3A **88**
Hardie Rd. L36: Huy 3A **84**
Harding Av. CH63: Beb 3F **141**
Harding Cl. L5: Liv 1A **78**
Hardinge Rd. L19: Aller 4C **124**
Hardknott Rd. CH62: Brom 1E **163**
Hard La. WA10: St. H 2D **45**
Hardman St. L1: Liv 1E **99** (7H **5**)
Hardshaw Cen. WA10: St. H 5A **46**
Hardshaw St. WA10: St. H 5A **46**
Hardwick Rd. WA7: Ast 4D **153**
Hardy St. L1: Liv 2D **99**
(not continuous)
L19: Gars 3C **144**
Harebell Cl. WA8: Wid 5E **109**
Harebell St. L5: Kirk 4D **55**
Hare Cft. L28: Stock V 3F **59**
Harefield Grn. L24: Speke 4D **147**
Harefield Rd. L24: Speke 5D **147**
HARESFINCH 2B **46**
Haresfinch Cl. L26: Halew 3A **128**
Haresfinch Rd. WA11: St. H 2B **46**
Haresfinch Vw. WA11: St. H 2B **46**
Hare's La. WA6: Frod 5A **172**
Harewell Rd. L11: N Grn. 2A **58**
Harewood Cl. L36: Huy 3E **83**
Harewood Rd. CH45: New B 4A **52**
Harewood St. L6: Liv 2A **78**
Hargate Rd. L33: K'by 3F **23**
Hargate Wlk. L33: K'by 3F **23**
Hargrave Av. CH43: O'ton 1E **117**
Hargrave Cl. CH43: O'ton 1E **117**
Hargrave La. CH64: Will 5F **161**
Hargreaves Ct. WA8: Wid 3D **133**
Hargreaves Ho. *WA8: Wid 3D **133***
(off Hargreaves Ct.)
Hargreaves Rd. L17: Aig 1C **122**
Hargreaves St. WA9: St. H 4E **47**
Harker St. L3: Liv 3E **77** (2G **5**)
Harke St. L7: Liv 1B **100**
Harland Grn. L24: Speke 4F **147**
Harland Rd. CH42: Tran 5D **97**
Harlech Ct. CH63: Beb 3F **141**
Harlech Gro. WA7: Cas 1F **167**
Harlech Rd. L23: Blun 2C **16**
Harlech St. CH44: Wall 4E **75**
L4: Kirk, Walt 2E **55**
Harleston Rd. L33: K'by 2A **24**
Harleston Wlk. L33: K'by 2A **24**
Harley Av. CH63: High B 4C **118**
Harley St. L9: Walt 2A **36**
Harlian Av. CH46: More 2D **93**
Harlow Cl. WA9: St. H 4F **65**
Harlow St. L8: Liv 5E **99**
Harlyn Cl. L26: Halew 1E **147**
Harmony Way L13: Liv 5A **80**
Haroldene Gro. L34: Prsct 1F **83**
Harold Rd. WA11: Hay 1F **49**
Harper Rd. L9: Walt 4A **36**
Harpers Pond La. L15: W'tree 1A **102**
Harper St. L6: Liv 4A **78**
Harps Cft. L30: N'ton 2C **18**
Harptree Cl. L35: Whis 3E **85**
Harradon Rd. L9: Ain 1B **36**
Harrier Dr. L26: Halew 3E **127**
Harringay Av. L18: Moss H 4F **101**
Harrington Av. CH47: Hoy 4C **90**
Harrington Rd. L3: Liv 5E **99**
L21: Lith 4D **19**
L23: C'by 1D **17**
L36: Huy 2B **82**
Harrington St. L2: Liv 5C **76** (5D **4**)
Harrington Vw. CH44: Wall 1D **75**
Harris Cl. CH63: Spit 5A **142**
Harris Dr. L20: Boot 2C **34**
L30: Boot 1D **35**
Harris Gdns. WA9: St. H 2B **66**
Harrismith Rd. L10: Faz 1E **37**
Harrison Dr. CH45: Wall 4D **51**
L20: Boot 5E **35**
WA11: Hay 2A **48**
Harrison Hey L36: Huy 5E **83**
Harrison St. WA8: Hale B 1B **150**
WA9: St. H 4D **67**
Harrison's Yd. CH62: East 5F **163**
Harrison Way L3: Liv 5D **99**
Harris St. WA8: Wid 3C **132**
WA10: St. H 4E **45**
Harrocks Cl. L30: N'ton 5D **11**
Harrock Wood Cl. CH61: Irby 1E **137**
Harrogate Cl. CH62: East 1D **171**
Harrogate Dr. L5: Liv 1F **77**
Harrogate Rd. CH42: R Ferr 3A **120**
CH62: East 1D **171**
Harrogate Wlk. CH42: R Ferr 4A **120**
Harron Cl. L32: K'by 3C **22**
Harrop Rd. WA7: Run 1B **166**
Harrops Cft. L30: N'ton 1E **19**
Harrowby Cl. L8: Liv 2A **100**
Harrowby Rd. CH42: Tran 5C **96**
CH44: Wall 2D **75**
L21: Sea 1F **33**
Harrowby Rd. Sth. CH42: Tran 5C **96**
Harrowby St. L8: Liv 2A **100**
(Granby St.)
L8: Liv 2F **99**
(Park Way)
Harrow Cl. CH44: Wall 1F **73**
L30: N'ton 2F **19**
Harrow Dr. L10: Ain 3D **21**
WA7: Run 5E **153**
Harrow Gro. CH62: Brom 2E **163**
Harrow Rd. CH44: Wall 1F **73**
L4: Walt 5B **56**
Hartdale Rd. L18: Moss H 5A **102**
L23: Thorn 4A **10**
Hartford Cl. CH43: O'ton 1F **117**
Harthill Av. L18: Moss H 5B **102**
Harthill M. CH43: Bid 5C **72**
Harthill Rd. L18: Moss H 4C **102**
Hartington Av. CH41: Birk 2B **96**
Hartington Rd. CH44: Wall 2B **74**
L8: Liv 3C **100**
L12: W Der 5B **58**
L19: Gars 1C **144**
WA10: St. H 3C **44**
Hartington Ter. *L19: Gars 1B **144***
(off St Mary's Rd.)
Hartismere Rd. CH44: Wall 3D **75**
Hartland Cl. WA8: Wid 4A **110**
Hartland Gdns. WA9: St. H 5D **65**
Hartland Rd. L11: N Grn. 1E **57**
Hartley Av. L9: Ain 3B **36**
Hartley Cl. L4: Walt 4F **55**
Hartley Gro. L33: K'by 5F **15**
WA10: St. H 3C **64**
Hartley Quay L3: Liv 1B **98** (7C **4**)
HARTLEY'S VILLAGE 2B **36**
Hartnup St. L5: Liv 5F **55**
(not continuous)
Harton Cl. WA8: Wid 1E **131**
Hartopp Rd. L25: Gate 2A **104**
Hartopp Wlk. *L25: Gate 2A **104***
(off Hartopp Rd.)
Hartsbourne Av. L25: Gate 1F **103**
(not continuous)
Hartsbourne Cl. L25: Gate 2F **103**
Hartsbourne Wlk. L25: Gate 2A **104**
Hart St. L3: Liv 4E **77** (4H **5**)
Hartwell St. L21: Lith 2B **34**
Hartwood Cl. L32: K'by 1F **39**
Hartwood Rd. L32: K'by 1F **39**
Hartwood Sq. L32: K'by 1F **39**
Harty Rd. WA11: Hay 3F **47**
Harvard Cl. WA7: Wind H 5D **155**
Harvard Gro. L34: Prsct 4E **63**
Harvester Way CH49: Grea 5C **92**
L30: N'ton 1A **20**
Harvest La. CH46: More 5D **71**
Harvest Way WA9: Clock F 2C **88**
Harvey Av. CH49: Grea 1D **115**
WA12: New W 5F **49**
Harvey Rd. CH45: Wall 5A **52**
CH46: Leas 4A **72**
Harwich Gro. L16: Child 1F **103**
Harwood Rd. L19: Gars 1D **145**
Haselbeech Cl. L11: N Grn. 5F **37**
Haselbeech Cres. L11: N Grn. 5F **37**
Hasfield Rd. L11: N Grn. 1B **58**
Haslemere L35: Whis 3F **85**
Haslemere Rd. L25: Gate 3A **104**
Haslemere Way L25: Gate 3A **104**
Haslingden Cl. L13: Liv 4B **80**
Haslington Gro. L26: Halew 1A **148**
Hassal Rd. CH42: R Ferr 4A **120**
Hastie Cl. L27: N'ley 4E **105**
Hastings Dr. L36: Huy 1A **106**
Hastings Rd. L22: Water 3B **16**
Haswell Dr. L28: Stock V 3A **60**
Hatchmere Cl. CH43: O'ton 1F **117**
Hatfield Cl. L12: Crox 5F **39**
WA9: St. H 4F **65**
Hatfield Gdns. L36: Huy 5F **83**
Hatfield Rd. L20: Boot 5E **35**
Hathaway L31: Mag 3B **12**
Hathaway Cl. L25: Gate 3A **104**
Hathaway Rd. L25: Gate 3A **104**
Hatherley Av. L23: C'by 3E **17**
Hatherley Cl. L8: Liv 2A **100**
(not continuous)
Hatherley St. CH44: Wall 4E **75**
L8: Liv 2A **100**
Hathersage Rd. L36: Huy 1E **83**
Hatherton Gro. L26: Halew 1A **148**
Hatton Av. CH62: East 2E **171**
Hatton Cl. CH60: Hes 2D **157**
Hatton Gdn. L3: Liv 4C **76** (3D **4**)
Hatton Garden Ind. Est. L3: Liv 3E **4**
Hatton Hill Rd. L21: Lith 4A **18**
Hattons La. L16: Child 3C **102**
Hauxwell Gro. WA11: St. H 2B **46**
Havannah La. WA9: St. H 5B **48**
Havelock Cl. WA10: St. H 5F **45**
Haven Rd. L10: Faz 5F **21**
Haven Wlk. L31: Lyd 3C **6**
Havergal St. WA7: Run 1F **165**
Haverstock Rd. L6: Liv 3D **79**
Haverton Wlk. L12: Crox 5E **39**
Hawarden Av. CH43: O'ton 3B **96**
CH44: Wall 2C **74**
L17: Liv 3D **101**

Hawarden Ct. CH63: Beb 3F 141
Hawarden Gro. L21: Sea 2A 34
Hawdon Ct. L7: Liv 1C 100
Hawes Av. WA11: St. H 5C 30
Haweswater Av. WA11: Hay 2A 48
Haweswater Cl. L33: K'by 5D 15
  WA7: Beech 5A 168
Haweswater Gro. L31: Mag 5F 7
Hawgreen Rd. L32: K'by 4B 22
Hawick Cl. L33: K'by 4D 15
Hawke Grn. L35: Tar G 2A 106
Hawke St. L3: Liv 5E 77 (5G 5)
Hawkesworth St. L4: Walt 5A 56
Hawkhurst Cl. L8: Liv 5F 99
Hawkins St. L6: Liv 3B 78
Hawks Cl. WA7: Pal F 4E 167
Hawkshead Av. L12: W Der 2C 58
Hawkshead Cl. L31: Mag 5E 7
  WA7: Beech 1A 174
Hawkshead Dr. L21: Lith 5D 19
Hawkshead Rd.
  CH62: Brom 1E 163
  WA5: B'wood 5E 69
Hawksmoor Cl. L10: Faz 1A 38
Hawksmoor Rd. L10: Faz 2F 37
Hawksmore Cl. CH49: Upton 3D 93
Hawkstone Wlk. L8: Liv 5A 100
     (off Gordale Cl.)
Haworth Dr. L20: Boot 1D 35
Hawthorn Av. WA7: Run 1A 166
  WA8: Wid 2B 132
Hawthorn Cl. WA11: Hay 3A 48
  WN5: Bil 1D 31
Hawthorn Dr. CH48: W Kir 4E 113
  CH61: Hes 5F 137
  WA10: Eccl 4B 44
Hawthorne Av. L26: Halew 1E 147
Hawthorne Ct. L21: Lith 5B 18
Hawthorne Dr. CH64: Will 4B 170
Hawthorne Gro. CH44: Wall 4E 75
Hawthorne Rd. CH42: Tran 1D 119
  L20: Boot 2C 34
  L21: Lith 5B 18
  WA6: Frod 4B 172
  WA9: Sut L 5D 67
Hawthorn Gro. L7: Liv 5B 78
  L12: W Der 5B 58
Hawthorn La. CH62: Brom 2D 163
Hawthorn Rd. L34: Prsct 5E 63
  L36: Roby 4C 82
Haxted Gdns. L19: Gars 1D 145
Haydn Rd. L14: K Ash 5F 59
HAYDOCK 2C 48
Haydock Community Leisure Cen.
   .2B 48
Haydock Ind. Est. WA11: Hay 1D 49
Haydock La. WA11: Hay 2C 48
     (not continuous)
Haydock Pk. Rd. L10: Ain 2E 21
Haydock Rd. CH45: Wall 4C 52
Haydock St. WA10: St. H 5A 46
  WA12: New W 4F 49
Hayes Av. L35: Prsct 1E 85
Hayes Cres. WA6: Frod 4C 172
Hayes Dr. L31: Mell 2A 22
Hayes St. WA10: St. H 3C 64
Hayfield Cl. L26: Halew 3A 128
Hayfield Pl. CH46: More 1A 94
Hayfield St. L4: Walt 4F 55
Hayfield Way WA9: Clock F 2C 88
Hayles Cl. L25: Gate 3A 104
Hayles Grn. L25: Gate 3A 104
Hayles Gro. L25: Gate 3A 104
Hayling Ho. L19: Aig 5F 123
Haylock Cl. L8: Liv 5F 99
Hayman's Cl. L12: W Der 4A 58
Haymans Grn. L12: W Der 4A 58
  L31: Mag 1E 13
Hayman's Gro. L12: W Der 4A 58
Haywood Cres. WA7: Wind H 5D 155
Haywood Gdns. WA10: St. H 1D 65
Hazel Av. L32: K'by 2C 22
  L35: Whis 3E 85
  WA7: Run 2E 165

Hazel Ct. L8: Liv 5A 100
     (off Byles St.)
  L20: Boot 1C 54
Hazeldale Rd. L9: Walt 4A 36
Hazeldene Av. CH45: Wall 1A 74
  CH61: Thing 1B 138
Hazeldene Way
  CH61: Thing 1B 138
Hazelfield Ct. WA9: Clock F 2C 88
Hazel Gro. CH61: Irby 5D 115
  CH63: High B 3E 141
  L9: Ain 2B 36
  L23: C'by 2F 17
  WA10: St. H 5C 44
Hazelmere Ho. L17: Aig 2D 123
Hazel M. L31: Mell 2B 22
Hazel Rd. CH41: Birk 4D 97
  CH47: Hoy 4C 90
  L36: Huy 1F 83
Hazelslack Rd. L11: N Grn 1A 58
Hazelwood CH49: Grea 4D 93
Hazelwood Cl. WA8: Wid 4A 130
  WA9: Sut M 3B 88
Hazelwood Gro. L26: Halew 2D 127
Hazlehurst Rd. L4: Walt 4B 56
Hazleton Rd. L14: K Ash 3C 80
Headbolt La. L33: K'by 1E 23
Headbourne Cl. L25: Gate 2F 103
Headingley Cl. L36: Roby 1C 104
  WA9: St. H 5C 66
Headington Rd. CH49: Upton 4D 93
Headland Cl. CH48: W Kir 1B 134
Headley Cl. WA10: St. H 5F 45
Heald St. L8: Liv 3E 99
Heald St. L19: Gars 1C 144
  WA12: New W 5F 49
Healy Cl. L27: N'ley 5A 106
Hearne Rd. WA10: St. H 4D 45
Hearts Health Club
  Liverpool 5D 9
  Wallasey 2A 74
Heartwood Cl. L9: Walt 1A 36
Heath, The WA7: West 3A 166
Heathbank Av. CH44: Wall 3A 74
  CH61: Irby 5C 114
Heathbank Rd. CH42: Tran 1D 119
Heath Cl. CH48: W Kir 1B 134
  L25: Wltn 4F 103
  L34: Ecc P 4F 63
Heathcote Cl. L7: Liv 1B 100
Heathcote Gdns. CH63: Beb 2F 141
Heathcote Rd. L4: Walt 1F 55
Heath Dale CH63: Beb 4F 141
Heath Dr. CH49: Upton 4A 94
  CH60: Hes 1F 157
  WA7: West 3A 166
Heather Bank CH63: High B 1D 141
Heather Brae L34: Prsct 1A 84
  WA12: New W 4F 49
Heather Brow CH43: C'ton 2F 95
Heather Cl. L4: Walt 3F 55
  L33: K'by 1E 23
  WA7: Beech 5E 167
Heather Ct. L4: Walt 3F 55
Heatherdale Cl. CH42: O'ton 1B 118
Heatherdene Rd. CH48: W Kir 3B 112
Heatherdale Rd. CH42: Tran 5C 96
Heatherland CH49: W'chu 5B 94
Heatherleigh CH48: Caldy 3E 135
  WA9: St. H 5C 64
Heatherleigh Cl. L9: Walt 1A 36
Heather Rd. CH60: Hes 1A 158
  CH63: High B 3D 141
Heathers Cft. L30: N'ton 2E 19
Heather Way L23: Thorn 4C 10
Heathfield CH62: Brom 5D 143
Heathfield Av. WA9: St. H 3E 65
Heathfield Cl. L21: Lith 2C 34
Heathfield Dr. L33: K'by 1E 23
Heathfield Ho. CH61: Thing 1A 138
Heathfield Pk. WA8: Wid 1D 131

Heathfield Rd. CH43: O'ton 5C 96
  CH63: Beb 2F 141
  L15: W'tree 3A 102
  L22: Water 3C 16
  L31: Mag 3F 13
Heathfield St. L1: Liv 5E 77 (6G 5)
Heathgate Av. L24: Speke 5F 147
Heath Hey L25: Wltn 4F 103
Heathland Rd. WA9: Clock F 2C 88
Heathlands, The CH46: Leas 3E 71
Heath La.
  CH64: Chil T, Will, Lit Sut 4C 170
  CH66: Chil T 5E 171
Heathmoor Rd. CH46: More 5D 71
Heath Pk. Gro. WA7: Run 2F 165
Heath Rd. CH63: Beb, High B 2E 141
  L19: Aller 4C 124
  L36: Huy 1B 82
  WA7: Run, West 3F 165
  WA8: Wid 2D 131
Heath Rd. Cres. WA7: Run 2B 166
Heath Rd. Sth. WA7: West 4F 165
Heathside CH60: Hes 1D 157
Heath St. WA9: St. H 4D 65
Heath Vw. L21: Ford 2B 18
Heathview Cl. WA8: Hale B 2A 150
Heathview Rd. WA8: Hale B 2A 150
Heathwaite Cres. L11: N Grn 2A 58
Heathway CH60: Hes 3B 158
Heathwood L12: W Der 1B 80
Hebden Pde. L11: N Grn 5C 38
Hebden Rd. L11: N Grn 5B 38
Hedgebank Cl. L9: Ain 5D 21
Hedgecote L32: K'by 1E 39
Hedgecroft L23: Thorn 4C 10
Hedgefield Rd. L25: Gate 3B 104
Hedgerows, The WA11: Hay 1F 49
Hedges Cres. L13: Liv 4E 57
Hedingham Cl. L26: Halew 3A 128
Hedworth Gdns. WA9: St. H 5D 65
Helena Rd. WA9: St. H 4F 67
Helena St. CH41: Birk 4E 97
  L7: Liv 5B 78
  L9: Walt 5F 35
Helen Ho. L8: Liv 2F 99
     (off Birley Ct.)
Helford Cl. L35: Whis 5A 64
Helford Rd. L11: Crox 3D 39
Heliers Rd. L13: Liv 4B 80
Helmdon Cl. L11: N Grn 2A 58
Helmingham Gro. CH41: Tran 5E 97
Helmsley Rd. L26: Halew 5F 127
Helsby Av. CH62: East 2F 171
Helsby Rd. L9: Ain 1B 36
Helsby St. L7: Liv 5A 78
  WA9: St. H 2D 67
Helston Av. L26: Halew 3F 127
  WA11: St. H 1D 47
Helston Cl. WA7: Brook 5B 168
Helston Grn. L36: Huy 3B 84
Helston Rd. L11: Crox 3D 39
Helton Cl. CH43: Noct 1E 117
Hemans St. L20: Boot 4A 34
Hemer Ter. L20: Boot 3A 34
Hemingford St. CH41: Birk 3D 97
Hemlock Cl. L12: Crox 5D 39
Hemmingsway L35: R'hill 3A 86
Hempstead Cl. WA9: St. H 4F 65
Henbury Pl. WA7: Run 4B 166
Henderson Cl. CH49: Upton 3D 93
Henderson Rd. L36: Huy 3A 84
  WA8: Wid 4F 131
Hendon Rd. L6: Liv 2D 79
Hendon Wlk. CH49: Grea 1C 114
Hengest Cl. L33: K'by 4E 15
Henglers Cl. L6: Liv 3F 77
Henley Av. L21: Lith 5A 18
Henley Cl. CH63: Spit 5A 142
Henley Ct. WA7: Run 5D 153
  WA10: St. H 2D 65

Henley Ho. L19: Aig 5F 123
Henley Rd. L18: Moss H 4B 102
Henllan Gdns. WA9: St. H 4F 67
Henlow Av. L32: K'by 5F 23
Hennawood Cl. L6: Liv 1B 78
Henrietta Gro. L34: Prsct 1A 84
Henry Edward St.
    L3: Liv 3D 77 (2E 4)
Henry Hickman Cl. L30: N'ton . . .1F 19
Henry St. CH41: Birk 3E 97
    L1: Liv 1D 99 (7E 5)
    L13: Liv 4E 79
    WA8: Wid 3C 132
    WA10: St. H 4F 45
Henthorne Rd. CH62: New F 4B 120
Henthorne St. CH43: O'ton 4C 96
Herald Av. L24: Speke 5C 38
Herald Cl. L11: Crox 5C 38
Heralds Cl. WA8: Wid 4B 130
Herbarth Cl. L9: Walt 5F 35
Herberts La. CH60: Hes 3F 157
Herbert St. WA5: B'wood 5E 69
    WA9: St. H 4E 67
Herbert Taylor Cl. L6: Liv 1C 78
Herculaneum Ct. L8: Liv 1F 121
Herculaneum Rd. L8: Liv 5E 99
Herdman Cl. L25: Gate 4B 104
Hereford Av. CH49: Upton 3F 93
Hereford Cl. WA10: St. H 1F 65
Hereford Dr. L30: N'ton 4F 19
Hereford Rd. L15: W'tree 3A 102
    L21: Sea 1E 33
Heriot St. L5: Kirk 5D 55
Hermes Cl. L30: Boot 5E 19
Hermes Rd. L11: Crox 2B 38
Hermitage Gro. L20: Boot 1D 35
Herm Rd. L5: Liv 1C 76
Heron Cl. WA7: Nort 2D 169
Heron Ct. L26: Halew 3E 127
Herondale Rd. L18: Moss H 5F 101
Heronhall Rd. L9: Faz 4F 37
Heronpark Way CH63: Spit 5B 142
Heron Rd. CH47: Meols 4F 91
    CH48: W Kir 4F 91
Herons Ct. L31: Lyd 3B 6
Herons Way WA7: Nort 3F 155
Hero St. L20: Boot 1D 55
Herrick St. L13: Liv 3F 79
Herschell St. L5: Liv 5F 55
Hertford Cl. L26: Halew 5F 127
Hertford Dr. CH45: Wall 5C 52
Hertford Rd. L20: Boot 1C 54
Hertford St. WA9: St. H 1D 67
Hesketh Av. CH42: R Ferr 3D 119
    WA11: R'ford 1A 28
Hesketh Dr. CH60: Hes 1A 158
    L31: Mag 1F 13
Hesketh Rd. L24: Hale 5E 149
Hesketh St. L17: Aig 5C 100
Heskin Cl. L31: Lyd 3D 7
    L32: K'by 1E 39
    L35: R'hill 3B 86
Heskin Rd. L32: K'by 1E 39
Heskin Wlk. L32: K'by 1E 39
Hessle Dr. CH60: Hes 3F 157
Hesslewell Ct. CH60: Hes 1A 158
HESWALL 2A 158
Heswall Av. CH63: High B 4C 118
    WA9: Clock F 2B 88
Heswall Mt. CH61: Thing 2A 138
Heswall Rd. L9: Ain 1B 36
Heswall Station (Rail) 2D 159
Hetherlow Towers L4: Walt 5A 36
Hever Dr. L26: Halew 3F 127
Heward Av. WA9: St. H 5C 66
Hewitson Av. L13: Liv 5F 57
Hewitson Rd. L13: Liv 5F 57
Hewitt Av. WA10: St. H 4C 44
Hewitt's La. L33: Know 2D 41
    L34: Know 2D 41
Hexagon, The L20: Boot 5C 34
Hexham Cl. L30: N'ton 4A 20
    WA9: St. H 5D 65
Heyburn Rd. L13: Liv 5E 57
Heydale Rd. L18: Moss H 5A 102

Heydean Rd. L18: Aller 3C 124
Heydean Wlk. L18: Aller 3C 124
Heydon Av. L32: K'by 4C 22
Heydon Cl. L26: Halew 5A 128
Heyes, The L25: Wltn 2B 126
    WA7: Run 1E 167
Heyes Av. WA11: Hay 3D 49
Heyes Dr. CH45: Wall 2C 72
Heyesmere Ct. L19: Aig 4F 123
Heyes Mt. L35: R'hill 4C 86
Heyes Rd. WA8: Wid 4C 130
Heyes St. L5: Liv 1A 78
Heygarth Dr. CH49: Grea 5D 93
Heygarth Rd. CH62: East 5E 163
Hey Grn. Rd. L15: W'tree 1E 101
Hey Pk. L36: Huy 4F 83
Hey Rd. L36: Huy 4F 83
Heys Av. CH62: East 5F 163
    L36: Huy 4F 83
Heys Ct. L19: Gars 1C 144
Heyscroft Rd. L25: Wltn 2B 126
Heysham Cl. WA7: Murd 4C 168
Heysham Lawn L27: N'ley 5A 106
Heysham Rd. L30: N'ton 3A 20
Heysmoor Hgts. L8: Liv 3B 100
Heysome Cl. WA11: Crank 1E 29
Heythrop Dr. CH60: Hes 2D 159
Heyville Rd. CH63: High B 1E 141
Heywood Blvd. CH61: Thing 1A 138
Heywood Cl. CH61: Thing 1A 138
Heywood Ct. L15: W'tree 5C 80
Heywood Gdns. L35: Whis 4E 85
Heywood Rd. L15: W'tree 1C 102
Heyworth St. L5: Liv 1F 77
Hibbert St. WA8: Wid 4B 132
Hickling Gdns. WA9: St. H 5E 65
Hickmans Rd. CH41: Birk 5B 74
Hickory Gro. L31: Mell 3A 22
Hickson Av. L31: Mag 4C 6
Hicks Rd. L21: Sea 1A 34
    L22: Water 3E 17
Hig-acre Rd. CH45: New B 4A 52
Higham Av. WA10: Eccl 5F 43
Higham Gdns. WA9: St. H 5E 65
Higham Sq. L5: Liv 2E 77
High Bank Cl. CH43: Noct 4D 95
Highbank Dr. L19: Gars 1D 145
Highbanks L31: Lyd 4C 6
High Beeches L16: Child 5F 81
High Carrs L36: Roby 4B 82
High Clere Cres. L36: Huy 1E 83
Highcroft, The CH63: Beb 2A 142
Highcroft Av. CH63: Beb 2A 142
Highcroft Grn. CH63: Beb 2A 142
Higher Ashton WA8: Wid 1F 131
HIGHER BEBINGTON 5D 119
Higher Bebington Rd.
    CH63: High B 1D 141
Higher End Pk. L30: N'ton 5E 11
Higher Heys WA7: Beech 5F 167
Higher La. L9: Ain, Faz 1C 36
    WA11: R'ford 1C 28
Higher Parr St. WA9: St. H 5C 46
Higher Rd. L25: Hunts X 5D 127
    L26: Halew 1B 148
    WA8: Hale B 2C 148
HIGHER RUNCORN 1F 165
Highfield L33: K'by 4F 15
Highfield Cl. CH44: Wall 2A 74
Highfield Ct. CH42: R Ferr 3F 119
Highfield Cres. CH42: R Ferr 3F 119
    WA8: Wid 2A 132
Highfield Dr. CH49: Grea 5D 93
    WA11: Crank 1E 29
Highfield Gro. CH42: R Ferr 3F 119
    L23: C'by 5F 9
Highfield Pk. L31: Mag 1F 13
Highfield Rd. CH42: R Ferr 2F 119
    L9: Walt 4F 35
    L13: Liv 2A 80
    L21: Lith 5A 18
    WA8: Wid 3F 131
Highfields CH60: Hes 1F 157
    L34: Prsct 5C 62
Highfield Sth. CH42: R Ferr 4F 119

Highfield Sq. L13: Liv 2F 79
Highfield St. L3: Liv 3C 76 (2C 4)
                            (not continuous)
    WA9: St. H 3D 67
Highfield Vw. L13: Liv 2F 79
Highgate Cl. CH60: Hes 5F 137
    WA7: Nort 1D 169
Highgate Ct. L7: Liv 5A 78
Highgate Rd. L31: Lyd 4D 7
Highgate St. L7: Liv 5A 78
Highgreen Rd. CH42: Tran 1C 118
Highgrove Pk. L19: Gras 4A 124
Highlands Rd. WA7: Run 1F 165
Highoaks Rd. L25: Wltn 3B 126
Highpark Rd. CH42: Tran 1C 118
High Pk. St. L8: Liv 4F 99
Highsted Gro. L33: K'by 5F 15
High St. CH62: Brom 1E 163
    L2: Liv 4C 76 (4C 4)
    L15: W'tree 1F 101
    L24: Hale 5D 149
    L25: Wltn 1A 126
    L34: Prsct 5D 63
    WA6: Frod 5B 172
    WA7: Run 5A 152
Hightor Rd. L25: Wltn 1F 125
Highville Rd. L16: Child 3D 103
Highwood Ct. L33: K'by 1F 23
Hignett Av. WA9: St. H 1A 68
Higson Ct. L8: Liv 1A 122
Hilary Av. L14: B Grn 4E 81
Hilary Cl. L4: Walt 3C 56
    L34: Ecc P 4E 63
    WA8: Wid 1E 133
Hilary Dr. CH49: Upton 3A 94
Hilary Rd. L4: Walt 3C 56
Hilberry Av. L13: Liv 1E 79
Hilbre Av. CH44: Wall 2A 74
    CH60: Hes 4E 157
Hilbre Ct. CH48: W Kir 5A 112
Hilbre Rd. CH48: W Kir 5B 112
Hilbre St. CH41: Birk 1D 97
    L3: Liv 5E 77 (5G 5)
Hilbre Vw. CH48: W Kir 4C 112
Hilcrest Rd. L4: Walt 2D 57
Hilda Rd. L12: W Der 1D 81
Hildebrand Cl. L4: Walt 3C 56
Hildebrand Rd. L4: Walt 3C 56
Hillaby Cl. L8: Liv 3F 99
Hillam Rd. CH45: Wall 5D 51
Hillary Cres. L31: Mag 1D 13
Hillary Dr. L23: C'by 1A 18
Hillary Rd. CH62: East 5D 163
Hillary Wlk. L23: C'by 1A 18
Hill Bark Rd. CH48: Frank 2B 114
Hillbrae Av. WA11: St. H 5A 30
Hill Brook Dr. L9: Ain 5D 37
Hillburn Dr. CH41: Birk 5E 73
Hill Crest L20: Boot 1E 55
Hillcrest L31: Mag 2F 13
    WA7: Run 1D 167
Hillcrest Av. L36: Huy 4A 84
Hillcrest Dr. CH49: Grea 1C 114
Hillcrest Pde. L36: Huy 4A 84
Hillcrest Rd. L23: C'by 1A 18
Hillcroft Rd. CH44: Wall 3C 74
    L25: Wltn 5F 103
Hillerton Cl. L12: W Der 1B 58
Hillfield WA6: Frod 5B 172
    WA7: Nort 2D 169
Hillfield Dr. CH61: Hes 5F 137
Hillfoot Av. L25: Hunts X 1B 146
Hillfoot Cl. CH43: Bid 1C 94
Hillfoot Grn. L25: Wltn 5A 126
Hillfoot Rd.
    L25: Hunts X, Wltn 3F 125
Hill Gro. CH46: More 2E 93
Hillhead Rd. L20: Boot 1E 55
Hillingden Av. L26: Halew 5F 127
Hillingdon Av. CH61: Hes 5A 138
Hillingdon Rd. L15: W'tree 3A 102
Hill Ridge CH43: Noct 4D 95
Hill Rd. CH43: C'ton 2E 95
Hill School Rd. WA10: St. H 3A 64
Hillside L25: Gate 5A 104

Hillside Av. L36: Huy 5C **60**
  WA7: Run 2E **165**
  WA10: St. H 2E **45**
  WA12: New W 1F **69**
Hillside Cl. CH41: Tran 5E **97**
  L20: Boot 1E **55**
  WN5: Bil 1D **31**
Hillside Ct. CH41: Tran 5E **97**
  L25: Wltn 1A **126**
Hillside Cres. L36: Huy 5C **60**
Hillside Dr. L25: Wltn 1A **126**
Hillside Rd. CH41: Tran 5E **97**
  CH43: Bid 1D **95**
  CH44: Wall 2F **73**
  CH48: W Kir 4D **113**
  CH60: Hes 3A **158**
  L18: Moss H 1E **83**
  L36: Huy 4B **102**
Hillside St. L6: Liv 3F **77**
Hillside Vw. CH43: O'ton 1A **118**
Hills Pl. L15: W'tree 2A **102**
Hill St. L8: Liv 1D **99**
            (not continuous)
  L34: Prsct 5D **63**
  WA7: Run 5A **152**
  WA10: St. H 3A **46**
Hill St. Bus. Cen. L8: Liv 3D **99**
           (off Hill St.)
Hilltop WA7: Nort 3C **168**
Hilltop La. CH60: Hes 2B **158**
Hill Top Rd. WA4: Pres H 2F
  WA11: R'ford 3B **28**
Hilltop Rd. L16: Child 2C **102**
Hill Vw. WA8: Wid 4F **109**
Hillview L17: Aig 2E **123**
Hillview Av. CH48: W Kir 3B **112**
Hillview Ct. CH43: Bid 1C **94**
Hill Vw. Dr. CH49: Upton 3A **94**
Hillview Gdns. L25: Wltn 1E **125**
Hillview Mans. CH48: W Kir 3B **112**
          (off Lang La.)
Hillview Rd. CH61: Irby 5C **114**
Hillwood Cl. CH63: Spit 1F **161**
Hilton Cl. CH41: Birk 3C **96**
Hilton Ct. L30: N'ton 1D **19**
Hilton Gro. CH48: W Kir 3A **112**
Hinchley Grn. L31: Mag 5F **7**
Hinckley Rd. WA11: St. H 3C **46**
Hindburn Av. L31: Mag 5F **7**
Hinderton Cl. CH41: Birk 5E **97**
Hinderton Dr. CH48: W Kir 5E **113**
  CH60: Hes 4F **157**
Hinderton Rd. CH41: Birk 4E **97**
Hindley Beech L31: Mag 5C **6**
Hindley Wlk. L24: Speke 5D **147**
Hindlip St. L8: Liv 1A **122**
Hind St. CH41: Birk 4E **97**
Hinson St. CH41: Birk 3E **97**
Hinton Rd. WA7: Run 1A **166**
Hinton St. L6: Liv 3C **78**
  L21: Lith 2B **34**
Historic Warships Vis. Cen. 5D **75**
Hitchens Cl. WA7: Murd 3D **169**
HM Customs & Excise National Mus.
               .1C **98** (7C **4**)
HMP Altcourse L9: Faz 2D **37**
HMP Liverpool L9: Walt 3F **35**
Hobart Dr. L33: K'by 4E **15**
Hobart St. WA9: St. H 3E **65**
Hobby Cl. WA7: Pal F 4E **167**
Hobhouse Ct. CH43: C'ton 3B **96**
Hob La. Wlk. L32: K'by 3B **22**
Hoblyn Rd. CH43: Bid 1E **95**
Hockenhall All. L2: Liv 4C **76** (4D **4**)
Hockenhull Cl.
  CH63: Spit 5A **142**
Hodder Av. L31: Mag 5F **7**
Hodder Cl. WA11: St. H 1B **46**
Hodder Rd. L5: Liv 5F **55**
Hodder St. L5: Liv 5E **55**
Hodson Pl. L6: Liv 2F **77**
Hogarth Dr. CH43: Noct 1D **117**
Hogarth St. L21: Sea 2A **34**
Hogarth Wlk. L4: Kirk 3D **55**
Hoghton Cl. WA9: St. H 3F **67**

Hoghton Rd. L24: Hale 5E **149**
  WA9: St. H 3F **67**
Holbeck WA7: Nort 3C **168**
Holbeck St. L4: Watt 5B **56**
Holborn Ct. WA8: Wid 1F **131**
Holborn Hill CH41: Tran 5E **97**
Holborn Sq. CH41: Tran 5E **97**
Holborn Sq. Ind. Est. CH41: Tran . . .5E **97**
Holborn St. L7: Liv 4A **78**
Holbrook Cl. WA9: St. H 5C **66**
Holcombe Ct. CH49: Grea 5D **93**
Holden Gro. L22: Water 3C **16**
Holden Rd. L22: Water 3B **16**
  L35: Prsct 2C **84**
Holden Rd. E. L22: Water 3C **16**
Holden Ter. L22: Water 3C **16**
Holdsworth St. L7: Liv 4B **78**
Holford Moss WA7: Nort 4D **155**
Holgate L23: Thorn 3B **10**
  L29: Thorn 3B **10**
Holgate Back La.
  L29: Seft, Thorn 2B **10**
Holgate Pk. L23: Thorn 3B **10**
Holin Ct. CH43: C'ton 2F **95**
Holingsworth Ct. WA10: St. H . . .4B **46**
Holkham Cl. WA8: Wid 3F **131**
Holkham Gdns. WA9: St. H 5D **65**
Holland Cl. L30: N'ton 1D **19**
Holland Gro. CH60: Hes 1F **157**
Holland Pl. L7: Liv 5B **78**
Holland Rd. CH45: Wall 4C **52**
  L24: Speke 5E **147**
  L26: Halew 1E **147**
Holland Way L26: Halew 1E **147**
Holley Ct. L35: R'hill 3C **86**
Holliers Ct. L31: Mag 1D **13**
Hollies, The L25: Wltn 1E **125**
  WA7: Run 2D **167**
Hollies Rd. L26: Halew 5F **127**
Hollingbourne Pl. L11: N Grn. . . .5A **38**
Hollingbourne Rd. L11: N Grn. . . .5A **38**
Hollinghurst Rd. L33: K'by 5F **15**
Hollingworth Cl. L9: Walt 5A **36**
Hollin Hey Cl. WN5: Bil 2D **31**
Hollinhey Cl. L30: N'ton 5A **12**
Hollins Cl. L15: W'tree 1A **102**
Hollins Way WA8: Hale B 2B **150**
Hollocombe Rd. L12: W Der 1B **58**
Holloway WA7: Run 1F **165**
Hollow Cft. L28: Stock V 2A **60**
Holly Av. CH63: Beb 4F **141**
Holly Bank WA6: Frod 5C **172**
Hollybank Ct. CH41: Birk 4D **97**
  WA8: Wid 3F **131**
Holly Bank Gro. WA9: St. H 4C **46**
Hollybank Rd. CH41: Birk 4D **97**
  L18: Moss H 4E **101**
  WA7: Halt 1F **167**
Holly Bank St. WA9: St. H 4C **46**
Holly Cl. L24: Hale 5D **149**
  WA10: Eccl 4B **44**
Holly Ct. L20: Boot 3B **34**
Hollydale Rd. L18: Moss H 4A **102**
Holly Farm Ct. WA8: Wid 5F **109**
Holly Farm Rd. L19: Gars 1D **145**
Hollyfield Rd. L9: Walt 3F **35**
Holly Gro. CH42: Tran 5E **97**
  L21: Sea 2F **33**
  L36: Roby 4B **82**
Holly Hey L35: Whis 5D **85**
Hollyhurst Cl. L8: Liv 4A **100**
Hollymead Cl. L25: Gate 5B **104**
Holly Mt. L12: W Der 5A **58**
Holly Pl. CH46: More 2F **93**
Holly Rd. L7: Liv 4C **78**
  WA11: Hay 3F **47**
Hollyrood L34: Prsct 1A **84**
Holly St. L20: Boot 4C **34**
Hollytree Rd. L25: Wltn 1A **126**
Hollywood Bowl 4F **79**
Hollywood Rd. L17: Aig 1E **123**
Holman Rd. L19: Gars 1D **145**

Holm Cotts. CH43: O'ton 2F **117**
Holme Cl. L34: Ecc P 4A **64**
Holmefield Av. L19: Aig 3A **124**
Holmefield Rd. L19: Aig 4F **123**
Holme Rd. WA10: St. H 1B **64**
Holmes La. L21: Lith 1A **34**
       (off Seaforth Rd.)
Holmes St. L8: Liv 2C **100**
Holme St. L5: Kirk 4B **54**
Holmesway CH61: Pens 3F **137**
Holmfield CH43: O'ton 2F **117**
Holmfield Av. WA7: Run 5C **152**
Holmfield Gro. L31: Mag 1C **12**
  L36: Huy 1F **105**
Holm Hey Rd. CH43: Pren 2F **117**
Holm Hill CH48: W Kir 5C **112**
Holmlands Cres. CH43: O'ton . .2E **117**
Holmlands Dr. CH43: O'ton 2E **117**
Holmlands Way CH43: O'ton . . .2F **117**
Holm La. CH43: O'ton 2F **117**
Holmleigh Rd. L25: Gate 3A **104**
Holmrook Rd. L11: N Grn. 1F **57**
Holmside Cl. CH46: More 1F **93**
Holmside La. CH43: O'ton 2F **117**
Holmstead, The L18: Moss H . . .1F **123**
Holm Vw. Cl. CH43: O'ton 1A **118**
Holmville Rd. CH63: High B 1E **141**
Holmway CH63: High B 2F **141**
Holmwood Av. CH61: Thing 2C **138**
Holmwood Dr. CH61: Thing 2C **138**
HOLT .2A **86**
Holt Av. CH46: More 1E **93**
  WN5: Bil 1D **31**
Holt Coppice L39: Augh 1F **7**
Holt Cres. WN5: Bil 1D **31**
Holt Hill CH41: Birk 5E **97**
Holt Hill Ter. CH42: Tran 4D **97**
Holt La. L27: N'ley 3D **105**
           (not continuous)
  L35: R'hill 2A **86**
  WA7: Halt 2F **167**
Holt Rd. CH41: Tran 5E **97**
  L7: Liv 4C **78**
Holt Way L32: K'by 3D **23**
Holy Cross Cl. L3: Liv 3D **77** (2E **5**)
Holyrood L23: Blun 1A **16**
Holyrood Av. WA8: Wid 5A **110**
Holywell Cl. WA9: St. H 5D **67**
Homedove Ho. L23: Blun 1C **16**
Home Farm Cl. CH49: W'chu . . .2C **116**
Home Farm Rd. CH49: W'chu . .2B **116**
  L34: Know 1C **60**
HOMER GREEN 1C **10**
Homer Rd. L34: Know 5C **40**
Homerton Rd. L6: Liv 3D **79**
Homestall Rd. L11: N Grn. 1A **58**
Homestead Av. L30: N'ton 2B **20**
  WA11: Hay 1E **49**
Homestead Cl. L36: Huy 3A **84**
Homestead M. CH48: W Kir 3B **112**
Honeybourne Dr. L35: Whis 5A **64**
Honey Hall Rd. L26: Halew 1E **147**
Honeys Grn. Cl. L12: W Der 1D **81**
Honeys Grn. La. L12: W Der 1D **81**
Honeys Grn. Pct. L12: W Der . . .1D **81**
Honey St. WA9: St. H 4C **64**
Honeysuckle Cl. L26: Halew 2D **127**
  WA8: Wid 5B **110**
Honeysuckle Dr. L9: Walt 5B **36**
Honister Av. WA11: St. H 5C **30**
Honister Cl. L27: N'ley 1A **128**
Honister Gro. WA7: Beech 5E **167**
Honister Wlk. L27: N'ley 1A **128**
Honiston Av. L35: R'hill 2B **86**
Honiton Rd. L17: Aig 3E **123**
Hood Rd. WA8: Wid 3F **131**
Hood St. CH44: Wall 3D **75**
  L20: Boot 3A **34**
Hoole Rd. CH49: W'chu 1B **116**
Hoose Ct. CH47: Hoy 4C **90**
HOOTON 4F **171**
Hooton Rd. CH64: Will 5A **170**
  CH66: Hoot 5A **170**
  L9: Ain 1B **36**
Hooton Station (Rail) 4D **171**

Hooton Way CH66: Hoot 3F 171
Hooton Works Trad. Est.
  CH66: Hoot 4E 171
Hope Cl. WA10: St. H 4E 45
Hope Pk. L16: Child 4D 103
Hope Pl. L1: Liv 1E 99 (7H 5)
Hope St. CH41: Birk 2D 97
  CH45: New B 3B 52
  L1: Liv 2E 99 (7J 5)
  L34: Prsct 5D 63
Hope Ter. CH42: Tran 1D 119
Hope Way L8: Liv 1F 99
Hopfield Rd. CH46: More 1F 93
Hopkins Cl. WA10: St. H 4D 45
Hopwood Cres.
  WA11: R'ford 1A 28
Hopwood St. L5: Liv 1C 76
   (not continuous)
Horace St. WA10: St. H 4D 45
Horatio St. CH41: Birk 3D 97
Hornbeam Cl. CH46: More 1B 92
  WA7: Wind H 1C 168
  WA11: Hay 2F 47
Hornbeam Rd. L9: Walt 5C 36
  L26: Halew 5A 128
Hornby Av. CH62: Brom 1C 162
  L20: Boot 3B 34
Hornby Blvd. L20: Boot 2B 34
  L21: Lith 2B 34
Hornby Chase L31: Mag 3D 13
Hornby Cl. L9: Walt 4F 35
  CH62: Brom 1C 162
Hornby Cres. WA9: Clock F 2D 89
Hornby Flats L21: Lith 2B 34
Hornby La. L18: Moss H 4D 103
Hornby Pk. L18: Moss H 4D 103
Hornby Pl. L9: Walt 3A 36
Hornby Rd. CH62: Brom 1C 162
  L9: Walt 4F 35
  L20: Boot 3B 34
   (Knowsley Rd.)
  L20: Boot 4C 34
   (Stanley Rd.)
Hornby St. CH41: Birk 3F 97
  L21: Sea 2A 34
  L23: C'by 1E 17
Hornby Wlk. L5: Liv 2C 76
Horne St. L6: Liv 2B 78
Hornet Cl. L11: Liv 1A 78
Hornhouse La. L33: Know I 5B 24
Hornsey Rd. L4: Walt 4B 56
Hornspit La. L12: W Der 4F 123
Horringford Rd. L19: Aig 4F 123
Horrocks Av. L19: Gars 1D 145
Horrocks Cl. L36: Huy 2D 83
Horrocks Rd. L36: Huy 3D 83
Horseman Pl. CH44: Wall 4E 75
Horseshoe Dr. L10: Faz 1B 38
Horsey Mere Gdns.
  WA9: St. H 5E 65
Horsfall Gro. L8: Liv 5E 99
Horsfall St. L8: Liv 5E 99
Horton Cl. L33: K'by 4E 15
Horwood Av. L35: R'hill 2B 86
Horwood Cl. L12: W Der 1C 58
Hoscar Ct. WA8: Wid 5D 131
Hoscote Pk. CH48: W Kir 4A 112
Hose Side Rd. CH45: Wall 4A 52
Hospital Cl. CH62: Port S 1B 142
Hospital St. WA10: St. H 4A 46
Hospital Way WA7: Pal F 3F 167
Hosta Cl. L33: K'by 5D 15
Hostock Cl. L35: Whis 4D 85
Hotham St. L3: Liv 4E 77 (4G 5)
Hothfield Rd. CH44: Wall 3D 75
Hotspur St. L20: Kirk 2C 54
HOUGH GREEN 3A 130
Hough Grn. Rd. WA8: Wid 2A 130
Hough Green Station (Rail) 2B 130
Houghton Cft. WA8: Wid 2C 132
Houghton Cl. WA8: Cron 4C 108
Houghton La. L1: Liv 5D 77 (5F 5)
Houghton Rd.
  CH49: W'chu 5B 94
  L24: Hale 5E 149

Houghton's La. WA10: Eccl 1F 43
Houghton St. L1: Liv 5D 77 (5F 5)
  L34: Prsct 5D 63
  L35: R'hill 3C 86
  WA8: Wid 2D 133
Houghton Way L1: Liv 5F 5
Hougoumont Av. L22: Water 4E 17
Hougoumont Gro. L22: Water 4E 17
Houlding La. L4: Walt 5A 56
Houlgrave Rd. L5: Liv 1C 76
Houlston Rd. L32: K'by 3B 22
Houlston Wlk. L32: K'by 3B 22
Houlton St. L7: Liv 4B 78
House La. WA8: Wid 5F 131
Hove, The WA7: Murd 4D 169
   (not continuous)
Hoveton Gdns. WA9: St. H 5D 65
Howard Av. CH62: Brom 2D 163
Howard Cl. L21: Ford 3C 18
  L31: Mag 1F 13
Howard Ct. WA7: Mnr P 3C 154
Howard Dr. L19: Gras 5A 124
Howard Florey Av. L30: N'ton 1F 19
Howard's La. WA10: Eccl 4E 43
Howards Rd. CH61: Thing 1B 138
Howarth St. WA10: St. H 3C 64
Howarth Ct. WA7: Run 5B 152
Howbeck Cl. CH43: C'ton 3F 95
Howbeck Cl. CH43: O'ton 4F 95
Howbeck Dr. CH43: C'ton 3F 95
Howbeck Rd. CH43: O'ton 4F 95
Howden Dr. L36: Huy 3A 82
Howell Dr. CH49: Grea 2D 115
Howell Rd. CH62: New F 5A 120
Howells Cl. L31: Mag 5D 7
Howe St. L20: Boot 2B 54
Howey La. WA6: Frod 5B 172
Howson St. CH42: R Ferr 2F 119
HOYLAKE 4B 90
Hoylake La. WA7: Murd 3C 168
   (not continuous)
Hoylake Gro. WA9: Clock F 2C 88
Hoylake Rd. CH41: Birk 4D 73
  CH46: More 2B 92
Hoylake Station (Rail) 5B 90
Hoyle Rd. CH47: Hoy 3B 90
Huddleston Cl. CH49: W'chu 1C 116
Hudleston Rd. L15: W'tree 5B 80
Hudson Rd. CH46: Leas 2A 72
  L31: Mag 3D 13
Hudson St. WA9: St. H 5C 46
Hudswell Cl. L30: N'ton 4B 20
Hughenden Rd. L13: Liv 1F 79
Hughes Av. L35: Prsct 2D 85
Hughes Cl. L7: Liv 5C 78
Hughes Dr. L20: Boot 2E 35
Hughes La. CH43: O'ton 1B 118
Hughes St. L6: Liv 2A 78
   (not continuous)
  L19: Gars 2C 144
  WA9: St. H 3D 67
Hughestead Gro. L19: Gars 1B 144
Hughson St. L8: Liv 4E 99
Hulmewood CH63: Beb 5A 120
Hulton Av. L35: Whis 2F 85
Humber Cl. L4: Kirk 3E 55
  WA8: Wid 1F 133
Humber Cres. WA9: Sut L 5C 66
Humber St. CH41: Birk 5F 73
Hume Ct. CH47: Meols 3C 90
Humphrey's Cl. WA7: Murd 3D 169
Humphreys Hey L23: Thorn 5B 10
Humphrey St. L20: Boot 2D 35
Huncote Av. WA11: St. H 2D 47
Hunstanton Cl. CH49: Upton 2A 94
Hunter Cl. L34: Prsct 5E 63
Hunters Ct. WA7: Pal F 4E 167
Hunters La. L15: W'tree 2A 102
Hunter St. L3: Liv 4D 77 (3F 5)
  WA9: St. H 1C 66
Huntingdon Cl. CH46: More 1B 92
Huntingdon Gro. L31: Lyd 3C 6
Huntley Av. WA9: St. H 4C 66
Huntley Gro. WA9: St. H 4C 66

Huntly Rd. L6: Liv 3C 78
Hunt Rd. L31: Mag 5D 7
  WA11: Hay 2E 49
HUNT'S CROSS 5B 126
Hunts Cross Av. L25: Wltn 1B 126
   (not continuous)
Hunts Cross Shop. Mall
  L24: Hunts X 1A 146
Hunt's Cross Station (Rail) 5C 126
Huntsman Cl. L25: Hunts X 3D 127
Huntsman Wood L12: W Der 3E 59
Hurlingham Rd. L4: Walt 1C 56
Hurrell Rd. CH41: Birk 5D 73
Hursley Rd. L9: Faz 4E 37
Hurst Bank CH42: R Ferr 4F 119
Hurst Gdns. L13: Liv 4A 80
Hurstlyn Rd. L18: Aller 3C 124
Hurst Pk. Cl. L36: Huy 2A 84
Hurst Pk. Dr. L36: Huy 2A 84
Hurst Rd. L31: Mag 3E 13
Hurst St. L1: Liv 1C 98
  L13: Liv 4A 80
  WA8: Wid 3A 152
Huskisson St. L8: Liv 2F 99
Hutchinson St. L6: Liv 3A 78
  WA8: Wid 1F 151
Hutchinson Wlk. L6: Liv 3A 78
Hutfield Rd. L24: Speke 3A 148
Huxley Cl. CH46: More 1B 92
Huxley St. L13: Liv 4D 57
HUYTON 4E 83
Huyton Av. WA10: St. H 2E 45
Huyton Brook L36: Huy 1F 105
Huyton Bus. Pk. L36: Huy 5A 84
Huyton Chu. Rd. L36: Huy 4E 83
Huyton Hall Cres. L36: Huy 4E 83
Huyton Hey Rd. L36: Huy 4E 83
Huyton Ho. Cl. L36: Huy 2B 82
Huyton Ho. Rd. L36: Huy 2B 82
Huyton La. L34: Prsct 3E 83
  L36: Huy 3E 83
Huyton Leisure Cen. 5D 83
Huyton Station (Rail) 4E 83
HUYTON-WITH-ROBY 3C 82
Hyacinth Av. L33: K'by 5D 15
Hyacinth Cl. WA11: Hay 2F 49
Hyacinth Gro. CH46: More 4A 72
Hyde Cl. WA7: Beech 4D 167
Hyde Rd. L22: Water 4D 17
Hydrangea Way WA9: Bold 4A 68
Hydro Av. CH48: W Kir 5B 112
Hygeia St. L6: Liv 2A 78
Hylton Av. CH44: Wall 2A 74
Hylton Rd. L19: Aller 4D 125
Hyslop St. L8: Liv 3E 99
Hythe Av. L21: Lith 5C 18
Hythedale Cl. L17: Aig 2C 122

          I

Ibbotson's La. L17: Aig 5E 101
Iberis Gdns. WA9: Bold 4A 68
Ibstock Rd. L20: Boot 3B 34
Iffley Cl. CH49: Upton 4D 93
Ikin Cl. CH43: Bid 5C 72
Ilchester Rd. CH41: Birk 5F 73
  CH44: Wall 3D 75
  L16: Child 5E 81
Ilford Av. CH44: Wall 3B 74
  L23: C'by 5D 9
Ilford Cl. L5: Liv 4E 77 (3H 5)
Ilfracombe Rd.
  WA9: Sut L 1C 88
Iliad St. L5: Liv 2E 77
Ilkley Wlk. L24: Speke 3D 147
Ilsley Cl. CH49: Upton 5F 93
Imber Rd. L32: K'by 5F 23
Imison St. L9: Walt 5E 35
Imison Way L9: Walt 5E 35
Imperial Av. CH45: Wall 5C 52
Imperial Chambers L1: Liv 4D 4
   (off Dale St.)
Imperial Ct. L2: Liv 4C 4
Imrie St. L4: Walt 1F 55

Ince Av. CH62: East 2E **171**
    L4: Walt 3B **56**
    L21: Lith 1B **34**
    L23: C'by 5C **8**
Ince Cl. CH43: O'ton 5F **95**
Ince Cres. CH43: O'ton 1F **117**
Ince La. L23: Thorn 1F **9**
Incemore Rd. L18: Moss H 3A **124**
Ince Rd. L23: Thorn 3A **10**
Inchcape Rd. CH45: Wall 1D **73**
Ingham Rd. WA8: Wid 5F **109**
Ingleborough Rd. CH42: Tran .2D **119**
Ingleby Rd. CH44: Wall 3A **74**
    CH62: New F 4B **120**
Ingledene Rd. L18: Moss H ...4D **103**
Ingle Grn. L23: Blun 5A **8**
Inglegreen CH60: Hes 2B **158**
Ingleholme Gdns. L34: Ecc P ..4A **64**
Ingleholme Rd. L19: Aig 3A **124**
Inglemere Rd. CH42: R Ferr ..2E **119**
Ingleside Ct. L23: Blun 2C **16**
Ingleton Cl. CH49: Grea 5D **93**
Ingleton Dr. WA11: St. H 4B **30**
Ingleton Grn. L32: K'by 5F **23**
Ingleton Gro. WA7: Beech 5D **167**
Ingleton Rd. L18: Moss H 4F **101**
    L32: K'by 5F **23**
Inglewood CH46: More 2D **93**
    L12: Crox 5A **40**
Inglewood Av. CH46: More 2D **93**
Inglewood Rd. WA11: R'ford ..4C **28**
Inglis Rd. L9: Ain 1B **36**
Ingoe Cl. L32: K'by 4B **22**
Ingoe La. L32: K'by 4B **22**
    (not continuous)
Ingrave Rd. L4: Walt 1C **56**
Ingrow Rd. L6: Liv 3B **78**
Inigo Rd. L13: Liv 2A **80**
Inley Cl. CH63: Spit 5A **142**
Inley Rd. CH63: Spit 5F **141**
Inman Av. WA9: St. H 1B **68**
Inman Rd. CH49: Upton 3E **93**
    L21: Lith 1B **34**
Inner Central Rd. L24: Halew .2F **147**
Inner Forum L11: N Grn. 1E **57**
Inner Sth. Rd. L24: Halew 3E **147**
Inner W. Rd. L24: Halew 2E **147**
Insall Rd. L13: Liv 5B **80**
Intake Cl. CH64: Will 5A **170**
Interchange Motorway Ind. Est.
    L36: Huy 5A **84**
Inveresk Cl. CH43: Noct 3E **95**
Invergarry Rd. L11: Crox 4B **38**
Invincible Cl. L30: Boot 5E **19**
Invincible Way L11: Crox 2C **38**
Inwood Rd. L19: Gars 5C **124**
Iona Cl. L12: Crox 5A **40**
Iona Gdns. WA9: St. H 4D **67**
Ionic Rd. L13: Liv 2A **80**
Ionic St. CH42: R Ferr 2F **119**
    L21: Sea 1F **33**
IRBY 1D **137**
Irby Av. CH44: Wall 2A **74**
IRBY HEATH 1C **136**
IRBY HILL 4C **114**
IRBYMILL HILL 3D **115**
Irby Rd. CH61: Irby 2D **137**
    L4: Walt 3B **56**
Irbyside Rd. CH48: Frank 3B **114**
Ireland Rd. L24: Hale 5E **149**
    WA11: Hay 2C **48**
Ireland St. WA8: Wid 2D **133**
Irene Av. WA11: St. H 1C **46**
Irene Rd. L16: Child 3C **102**
Ireton St. L4: Walt 1F **55**
Iris Av. CH41: Birk 1F **95**
Iris Cl. CH43: K'by 5D **15**
Iris Pk. Wlk. L31: Mell 2A **22**
Irlam Dr. L32: K'by 3E **23**

Irlam Ho. L20: Boot 5B **34**
Irlam Pl. L20: Boot 4B **34**
Irlam Rd. L20: Boot 4B **34**
Ironbridge Vw. L8: Liv 5E **99**
Ironside Rd. L36: Huy 2D **83**
Irvine Cl. CH42: Tran 2D **119**
Irvine St. L7: Liv 5A **78**
Irvine Ter. CH62: New F 4B **120**
Irving Cl. L9: Ain 5C **20**
Irwell Chambers L3: Liv 4C **4**
Irwell Cl. L17: Aig 1E **123**
Irwell Ho. L17: Aig 1E **123**
Irwell La. L17: Aig 1E **123**
    WA7: Run 4B **152**
Irwell St. L3: Liv 5B **76** (6C **4**)
    WA8: Wid 3A **152**
Irwin Rd. WA9: St. H 4C **66**
Isaac St. L8: Liv 5F **99**
Isabel Rd. L13: Liv 4E **57**
Island Pl. L19: Gars 1C **144**
Island Rd. L19: Gars 1C **144**
Island Rd. Sth. L19: Gars 1D **145**
Islands Brow WA11: St. H 2B **46**
Isleham Cl. L19: Aller 4C **124**
Islington L3: Liv 4E **77** (3G **5**)
    L23: C'by 5D **9**
Islington Grn. WA8: Wid 5D **111**
Islington Sq. L3: Liv 3F **77** (3J **5**)
Islip Cl. CH61: Irby 5D **115**
Ismay Dr. CH44: Wall 1D **75**
Ismay Rd. L21: Lith 1B **34**
Ismay St. L4: Walt 2F **55**
Ivanhoe Rd. L17: Aig 5C **100**
    L23: Blun 1C **16**
Iveagh Cl. WA7: Pal F 3A **168**
Iver Cl. WA8: Cron 3C **108**
Ivernia Rd. L4: Walt 1B **56**
Ivor Rd. CH44: Wall 1C **74**
Ivory Dr. L33: K'by 5E **15**
Ivy Av. CH63: High B 2E **141**
    L19: Gras 5A **124**
    L35: R'hill 2A **86**
Ivychurch M. WA7: Run 5D **153**
Ivy Cl. WA9: St. H 4C **46**
Ivydale Rd. CH42: Tran 1E **119**
    L9: Walt 4B **36**
    L18: Moss H 5F **101**
Ivy Farm Cl. L24: Hale 5D **149**
Ivy Farm Rd. L35: R'hill 2B **86**
Ivyhurst Cl. L19: Aig 4F **123**
Ivy La. CH46: More 4E **71**
Ivy Leigh L13: Liv 1E **79**
Ivy St. CH41: Birk 3F **97**
    WA7: Run 1A **166**

J

Jack McBain Ct. L3: Liv 2C **76**
Jack's Brow L34: Know P 1E **61**
Jacksfield Way L19: Gras 5F **123**
Jackson Cl. CH63: High B 4F **119**
    L35: R'hill 5D **87**
Jacksons Pond Dr. L25: Gate .2F **103**
Jackson St. CH41: Birk 4E **97**
    L19: Gars 1C **144**
    WA5: B'wood 5E **69**
    WA9: St. H 5C **46**
    WA11: Hay 1A **48**
Jackson St. Ind. Est. WA9: St. H .1C **66**
Jacobs Cl. L21: Lith 2B **34**
Jacob St. L8: Liv 5F **99**
Jacqueline Ct. L36: Roby 4C **82**
Jacqueline Dr. L36: Huy 2A **84**
Jade Cl. L33: K'by 2F **23**
Jade Rd. L6: Liv 2B **78**
Jamaica St. L1: Liv 2D **99**
Jamesbrook Cl. CH41: Birk 1A **96**
James Clarke St. L5: Liv 2C **76**
James Cl. WA8: Wid 3A **152**
James Ct. L25: Wltn 2B **126**
James Ct. Apartments
    L25: Wltn 2A **126**
James Dixon Ct. L30: N'ton .. .5D **11**
James Dunne Av. L3: Liv 1C **76**

James Gro. WA10: St. H 1E **65**
James Holt Av. L32: K'by 4C **22**
James Hopkins Way L4: Kirk .4D **55**
James Horrigan Ct. L30: N'ton ..2C **18**
James Larkin Way L4: Kirk .. .4D **55**
James Rd. L25: Wltn 2B **126**
    WA11: Hay 1F **49**
James Simpson Way L30: N'ton ..1F **19**
James St. CH43: O'ton 5C **96**
    CH44: Wall 4E **75**
    L2: Liv 5C **76** (6C **4**)
    L19: Gars 1C **144**
    WA9: Clock F 3D **89**
James Street Station (Rail)
    .... .5C **76** (6C **4**)
Jamieson Av. L23: C'by 1A **18**
Jamieson Rd. L15: W'tree 2E **101**
Jane St. WA9: St. H 4F **67**
Janet St. L7: Liv 5B **78**
Japonica Gdns. WA9: Bold 4A **68**
Jarrett Rd. L33: K'by 1A **24**
Jarrett Wlk. L33: K'by 1A **24**
Jarrow Cl. CH43: O'ton 5B **96**
Jasmine Cl. CH49: Upton 2D **93**
    L5: Liv 1F **77**
Jasmine Ct. L36: Huy 1F **83**
Jasmine Gdns. WA9: Bold 4A **68**
Jasmine Gro. WA8: Wid 4D **131**
Jasmine M. L17: Aig 1A **122**
Jason St. L5: Liv 5E **55**
Jason Wlk. L5: Liv 5E **55**
Java Rd. L4: Walt 1D **57**
Jay's Cl. WA7: Murd 3E **169**
Jean Wlk. L10: Faz 2B **38**
Jedburgh Dr. L33: K'by 4D **15**
Jeffereys Cres. L36: Huy 4B **82**
Jeffreys Dr. CH49: Grea 4D **93**
    L36: Huy 3A **82**
Jellicoe Cl. CH48: Caldy 3D **135**
Jenkinson St. L3: Liv 3E **77** (1H **5**)
Jenner Dr. L36: Leas 4A **72**
Jensen Ct. WA7: Ast 4C **152**
Jericho Cl. L17: Aig 2D **123**
Jericho Ct. L17: Aig 2D **123**
Jericho Farm Cl. L17: Aig 3D **123**
Jericho Farm Wlk. L17: Aig .. .3D **123**
Jericho La. L17: Aig 3D **123**
Jermyn St. L8: Liv 3A **100**
Jerningham Rd. L11: N Grn. .. .5D **37**
Jersey Av. L21: Lith 4B **18**
Jersey Cl. L20: Boot 5C **34**
Jersey St. L20: Boot 5C **34**
    WA9: Clock F 3C **88**
Jesmond St. L15: W'tree 1D **101**
Jessamine Rd. CH42: Tran 1E **119**
Jessica Ho. L20: Kirk 2D **55**
Jet Cl. L6: Liv 2B **78**
Jeudwine Cl. L25: Wltn 3B **126**
Joan Av. CH46: More 1D **93**
    CH49: Grea 5E **93**
Jocelyn Cl. CH63: Spit 4A **142**
John Bagot Cl. L5: Liv 1E **77**
John F Kennedy Hgts.
    L3: Liv 2E **77** (1H **5**)
John Hunter Way L30: N'ton .. .2F **19**
John Lennon Dr. L6: Liv 3B **78**
John Middleton Cl. L24: Hale .5D **149**
John Moores Cl. L7: Liv 1A **100**
John Moores University
    Avril Robarts Cen. 4C **76** (3D **4**)
    Byrom St. 3D **77** (2F **5**)
    Henry Cotton Campus, The .. .3E **5**
Johns Av. WA7: Run 1F **165**
    WA11: Hay 1E **49**
Johnson Av. L35: Prsct 2D **85**
Johnson Gro. L12: W Der 1E **81**
Johnson Rd. CH43: Pren 3F **117**
Johnson's La. WA8: Wid 3E **133**
Johnson St. L3: Liv 3C **76** (3E **4**)
    WA9: St. H 4C **46**
Johnson Wlk. L7: Liv 5A **78**
    (off Deeley Clo.)
Johnston Av. L20: Boot 2E **35**
John St. CH41: Birk 2F **97**
    L3: Liv 3E **77** (1H **5**)

John Willis Ho. CH42: R Ferr 2A **120**
Jones Farm Rd. L25: Gate 4C **104**
Jones St. L3: Liv 5E **77** (5H **5**)
Jonville Rd. L9: Ain 1C **36**
Jordan St. L1: Liv 2D **99**
Joseph Gardner Way L20: Boot 3B **34**
Josephine Butler Sq.
   L3: Liv 3F **77** (2J **5**)
Joseph Lister Cl. L30: N'ton 2F **19**
Joseph Morgan Hgts. L10: Faz 5A **22**
Joseph St. WA8: Wid 2C **132**
   WA9: St H 4E **67**
Joshua Cl. L5: Liv 5E **55**
Joyce Wlk. L10: Faz 1C **38**
Joy La. WA9: Clock F 4E **89**
Joy Wlk. WA9: Clock F 3E **89**
Jubilee Av. L14: B Grn 5D **81**
Jubilee Ct. WA11: Hay 1B **48**
Jubilee Cres. CH62: Port S 2B **142**
   WA11: Hay 1F **49**
Jubilee Dr. CH48: W Kir 2B **112**
   L7: Liv 4B **78**
   L30: N'ton 4A **20**
   L35: Whis 4D **85**
Jubilee Rd. L21: Lith 1B **34**
   L23: C'by 2C **16**
Jubilee Way WA8: Wid 3E **131**
Jubits La. WA8: Bold H 1A **110**
   WA9: Sut M 1A **110**
Juddfield St. WA11: Hay 2A **48**
Judges Dr. L6: Liv 2C **78**
Judges Way L6: Liv 2C **78**
Julian Way WA8: Wid 5F **109**
Julie Gro. L12: W Der 1E **81**
Juliet Av. CH63: High B 5E **119**
Juliet Gdns. CH63: High B 5E **119**
July Rd. L6: Liv 1C **78**
July St. L20: Boot 3C **34**
Junction La. WA9: St. H 4E **67**
Junc. One Retail Pk. CH44: Wall . . .3D **73**
June Av. CH62: Brom 2E **163**
June Rd. L6: Liv 1D **79**
June St. L20: Boot 4C **34**
Juniper Cl. CH49: Grea 2C **114**
   L28: Stock V 3B **60**
   WA10: St. H 4D **45**
Juniper Gdns. L23: Thorn 4B **10**
Juniper St. L20: Kirk 3C **54**
Justan Way L35: R'hill 1B **86**
Juvenal Pl. L3: Liv 2E **77** (1G **5**)
Juvenal St. L3: Liv 2D **77** (1F **5**)

K

Kaigh Av. L23: C'by 5D **9**
Kale Cl. CH48: W Kir 5B **112**
Kale Gro. L33: K'by 5F **15**
Kara Cl. L20: Boot 5C **34**
Karan Way L31: Mell 2A **22**
Karen Cl. WA5: B'wood 5F **69**
Karonga Rd. L10: Faz 1E **37**
Karonga Way L10: Faz 1F **37**
Karslake Rd. CH44: Wall 3D **75**
   L18: Moss H 4F **101**
Katherine Wlk. L10: Faz 1C **38**
Kearsley Cl. L4: Kirk 4E **55**
Kearsley St. L4: Walt 4E **55**
Keats Av. L35: Whis 3F **85**
Keats Cl. WA8: Wid 4F **131**
Keats Gro. L36: Huy 5F **83**
Keats St. L20: Boot 3B **34**
   WA9: St. H 3F **67**
Keble Dr. CH45: Wall 5D **51**
   L10: Ain 2C **20**
Keble Rd. L20: Boot 2C **54**
Keble St. L6: Liv 3A **78**
   WA8: Wid 5B **132**
KECKWICK 3F **155**
Keckwick La. WA4: Dares 3F **155**
Kedleston St. L8: Liv 5A **100**
Keegan Dr. CH44: Wall 4E **75**
Keele Cl. CH43: Bid 4C **72**
Keel Hey CH64: Will 4B **170**
Keenan Dr. L20: Boot 3E **35**

Keene Ct. L30: N'ton 1D **19**
Keepers La. CH63: Store 2B **140**
Keepers Wlk. WA7: Cas 5F **153**
Keighley Av. CH45: Wall 1E **73**
Keightley St. CH41: Birk 2C **96**
Keir Hardie Av. L20: Boot 3E **35**
Keith Av. L4: Walt 2F **55**
Keith Dr. CH63: East 5C **162**
Keithley Wlk. L24: Speke 3E **147**
Kelbrook Cl. WA9: St. H 5D **67**
Kelburn Gro. L12: W Der 3D **59**
Kelby Cl. L8: Liv 5A **100**
Kelda Ct. L25: Gate 3A **104**
Kelday Cl. L33: K'by 3E **23**
Kelkbeck Cl. L31: Mag 5F **7**
Kellet's Pl. CH42: R Ferr 1F **119**
Kellett Rd. CH46: Leas 3B **72**
Kellitt Rd. L15: W'tree 2E **101**
Kelly Dr. L20: Boot 3E **35**
Kelly St. L34: Prsct 5E **63**
Kelmscott Dr. CH44: Wall 2E **73**
   WA9: Sut M 2B **88**
Kelsall Cl. CH43: O'ton 1F **117**
   CH62: East 2E **171**
   WA8: Wid 2D **131**
Kelsey Cl. WA10: St. H 4D **45**
Kelso Cl. L33: K'by 4D **15**
Kelso Rd. L6: Liv 3C **78**
Kelton Gro. L17: Aig 2E **123**
Kelvin Ct. CH44: Wall 4E **75**
Kelvin Gro. L8: Liv 3A **100**
Kelvin Pk. CH41: Birk 5D **75**
Kelvin Rd. CH41: Tran 5C **97**
   CH44: Wall 5E **75**
Kelvinside CH44: Wall 5D **75**
   L23: C'by 3E **17**
Kemberton Dr. WA8: Wid 4A **110**
Kemble St. L6: Liv 3B **78**
   L34: Prsct 5D **63**
Kemlyn Rd. L4: Walt 4A **56**
Kempsell Wlk. L26: Halew 5A **128**
Kempsell Way L26: Halew 5A **128**
Kempsey Gro. WA9: St. H 4E **65**
Kempson Ter. CH63: Beb 3F **141**
Kempston St. L3: Liv 4E **77** (3H **5**)
Kempton Cl. L36: Roby 5C **82**
   WA7: Run 4C **166**
Kempton Pk. Rd. L10: Ain 2E **21**
Kempton Rd. CH62: New F 4B **120**
   L15: W'tree 1D **101**
Kemsley Rd. L14: K Dash 3F **81**
Kenbury Cl. L33: K'by 1A **24**
Kenbury Rd. L33: K'by 1A **24**
Kendal Cl. CH63: Beb 1F **141**
Kendal Dr. L31: Mag 5D **7**
   L35: R'hill 2A **86**
   WA11: St. H 5B **30**
Kendal Pk. L12: W Der 5D **59**
Kendal Ri. WA7: Beech 5D **167**
Kendal Rd. CH44: Wall 4A **74**
   L16: Child 2E **103**
   WA8: Wid 3C **130**
Kendal St. CH41: Birk 3E **97**
Kendricks Fold L35: R'hill 3B **86**
Kenilworth Av. WA7: Run 2B **166**
Kenilworth Cl. L25: Wltn 1E **125**
Kenilworth Dr. CH61: Pens 2F **137**
Kenilworth Gdns. CH49: Upton 3E **93**
Kenilworth Rd. CH44: Wall 3D **75**
   L16: Child 2D **103**
   L23: Blun 1C **16**
Kenilworth St. L20: Boot 5B **34**
Kenilworth Way L25: Wltn 1E **125**
Kenley Av. WA8: Cron 4D **109**
Kenmare Rd. L15: W'tree 3E **101**
Kenmay Wlk. L33: K'by 2A **24**
Kenmore Rd. CH43: Pren 3E **117**
Kennelwood Av. L33: K'by 2F **23**
Kennessee Cl. L31: Mag 2E **13**
KENNESSE GREEN 2D **13**
Kenneth Cl. L30: N'ton 2E **19**
Kenneth Rd. WA8: Wid 4C **130**
Kennet Rd. CH63: High B 2D **141**
   WA11: Hay 2C **48**

Kennford Rd. L11: Crox 3C **38**
Kennington Pk. WA8: Wid 1E **131**
KENSINGTON 4C **78**
Kensington L7: Liv 4A **78**
Kensington Av. WA9: St. H 4C **66**
Kensington Cl. WA8: Wid 5D **111**
Kensington Dr. L34: Prsct 1A **84**
Kensington Gdns. CH46: More 1F **93**
Kensington St. L6: Liv 3A **78**
Kent Av. L21: Lith 5C **18**
Kent Cl. CH63: Brom 2B **162**
   L20: Boot 4D **35**
Kent Gro. WA7: Run 1B **166**
Kentmere Av. WA11: St. H 5C **30**
Kentmere Dr. CH61: Pens 4F **137**
Kent M. CH43: O'ton 5A **96**
Kenton Cl. L25: Gate 2B **104**
Kenton Rd. L26: Halew 5F **127**
Kent Pl. CH41: Birk 3D **97**
Kent Rd. CH44: Wall 3A **74**
   WA9: St. H 3C **66**
Kents Bank L12: W Der 2C **58**
Kent St. CH43: O'ton 5A **96**
   L1: Liv 1D **99** (7F **5**)
                  (not continuous)
   WA8: Wid 3B **132**
Kentwell Gro. L12: W Der 4D **59**
Kenview Cl. WA8: Hale B 2A **150**
Kenwood Cl. L27: N'ley 4F **105**
Kenwright Cres. WA9: St. H 3C **66**
Kenwyn Rd. CH45: Wall 1B **74**
Kenyon Cl. L33: K'by 4F **15**
Kenyon Ct. *L8: Liv* *3F 99*
                   (off Park Rd.)
Kenyon La. L15: W'tree 4A **102**
Kenyons La. L31: Lyd, Mag 3D **7**
Kenyons La. Nth. WA11: Hay 1F **49**
Kenyons La. Sth. WA11: Hay 1F **49**
Kenyon's Lodge L31: Lyd 4E **7**
Kenyon Ter. CH43: O'ton 4B **96**
Kepler St. L21: Sea 2A **34**
Keppel St. L20: Boot 2B **54**
Kerman Cl. L12: W Der 2B **58**
Kerr Cl. L33: K'by 4E **15**
Kerr Gro. WA9: St. H 5E **47**
Kerris Cl. L17: Aig 2B **122**
Kerrysdale Cl. WA9: St. H 4D **67**
Kersey Rd. L32: K'by 5F **23**
Kersey Wlk. L32: K'by 5F **23**
Kershaw Av. L23: C'by 2F **17**
Kershaw St. WA8: Wid 3D **131**
Kerswell Cl. WA9: St. H 5D **67**
Keston Wlk. L26: Halew 1F **147**
Kestral Dene L10: Faz 2A **38**
Kestrel Av. CH49: Upton 3D **93**
Kestrel Cl. CH49: Upton 3D **93**
   WA11: St. H 2B **46**
Kestrel Gro. L26: Halew 3D **127**
Kestrel Rd. CH46: More 1C **92**
   CH60: Hes 3C **158**
Kestrels Way WA7: Pal F 4F **167**
Keswick Av. CH63: East 1C **170**
Keswick Cl. L31: Mag 5E **7**
   WA8: Wid 3C **130**
Keswick Dr. L21: Lith 5D **19**
Keswick Gdns. CH63: Brom 5C **162**
Keswick Pl. CH43: Bid 5D **73**
Keswick Rd. CH45: Wall 4F **51**
   L18: Aller 2C **124**
   WA10: St. H 3E **45**
Keswick Way L16: Child 1A **104**
Kevelioc Cl. CH63: Spit 4F **141**
Kew Gdns. Cl. WA8: Wid 5D **111**
Kew St. L5: Liv 1D **77**
Keybank Rd. L12: W Der 3A **58**
Kiddman St. L9: Walt 5F **35**
Kidstone Cl. WA9: St. H 4D **67**
Kilbuck La. WA11: Hay 1F **49**
Kilburn Av. CH62: East 4E **163**
Kilburn Gro. WA9: St. H 4E **65**
Kilburn St. L21: Lith 2B **34**
Kildale Cl. L31: Mag 5C **6**
Kildare Cl. L24: Hale 5D **149**
Kildonan Rd. L17: Aig 2D **123**

Kilgraston Gdns. L17: Aig 3E **123**
Killarney Gro. CH44: Wall 3A **74**
Killarney Rd. L13: Liv 3A **80**
Killester Rd. L25: Gate 5B **104**
Killington Way L4: Kirk 3E **55**
Kilmalcolm Cl. CH43: O'ton 5F **95**
Kilmore Cl. L9: Ain 5C **20**
Kilmory Av. L25: Wltn 2C **126**
Kiln Cl. WA10: Eccl 3C **44**
Kilncroft WA7: Brook 5B **168**
                        (not continuous)
Kiln Hey L12: W Der 1B **80**
Kiln La. WA10: Eccl, Windle 3B **44**
Kiln Rd. CH49: W'chu 1A **116**
Kilnyard Rd. L23: C'by 1D **17**
Kilrea Cl. L11: N Grn. 3F **57**
Kilrea Lodge L11: N Grn. 3F **57**
Kilrea Rd. L11: N Grn. 3E **57**
Kilsail Rd. L32: K'by 1A **40**
Kilsby Dr. WA8: Wid 2E **133**
Kilshaw Rd. WA5: B'wood 5F **69**
Kilshaw St. L6: Liv 2A **78**
                        (not continuous)
Kimberley Av. L23: C'by 2D **17**
                        WA9: St. H 4E **65**
Kimberley Cl. L8: Liv 2A **100**
Kimberley Dr. L23: C'by 1D **17**
Kimberley Rd. CH44: Wall 5B **52**
Kindale Rd. CH43: Pren 3E **117**
Kinder St. L6: Liv 3F **77**
King Arthurs Wlk. WA7: Cas 2A **168**
King Av. L20: Boot 2E **35**
King Edward Cl. L35: R'hill 2B **86**
King Edward Dr. CH62: Port S . . .1B **142**
King Edward Ind. Est. L3: Liv 3B **4**
King Edward Pde. L3: Liv . . .4B **76** (3B **4**)
King Edward Rd. L35: R'hill 2B **86**
                        WA10: St. H 2D **45**
King Edward St. L3: Liv 4B **76** (3B **4**)
Kingfield Rd. L9: Walt 3F **35**
Kingfisher Bus. Pk. L20: Boot 1C **34**
Kingfisher Cl. L27: N'ley 4F **105**
                        L33: K'by 3E **15**
                        WA7: Beech 5F **167**
Kingfisher Dr. WA11: St. H 2B **46**
Kingfisher Gro. L12: W Der 2F **59**
Kingfisher Ho. L13: Liv 5A **80**
Kingfisher Way CH49: Upton 3D **93**
King George V Sports Complex . .2F **83**
King George Dr. CH44: Wall 5C **52**
King George Rd. WA11: Hay 1F **49**
King George's Dr. CH62: Port S . .1B **142**
King George's Way CH43: Bid 2E **95**
Kingham Cl. L25: Wltn 2C **126**
                        WA8: Wid 3D **133**
Kingham M. L25: Wltn 2C **126**
King James Ct. WA7: Pal F 4E **167**
Kinglake Rd. CH44: Wall 1D **75**
Kinglake St. L7: Liv 5A **78**
Kinglass Rd. CH63: Spit 4B **142**
King's Av. CH47: Meols 3D **91**
Kingsbrook Way CH63: High B 4D **119**
King's Brow CH63: High B 1D **141**
Kingsbury CH48: W Kir 4D **113**
Kingsbury Rd. WA8: Wid 5D **111**
King's Bus. Pk. L34: Prsct 1A **84**
Kings Cl. CH63: High B 5D **119**
                        L17: Aig 1C **122**
Kings Ct. CH47: Hoy 4A **90**
                        CH63: High B 1D **141**
                        L21: Sea 1F **33**
                        WA7: Mnr P 3D **155**
Kingscourt Rd. L12: W Der 1C **80**
Kingsdale Av. CH42: Tran 2D **119**
                        L35: R'hill 3D **87**
Kingsdale Rd. L18: Moss H 4C **102**
Kings Dock St. L1: Liv 2D **99**
Kingsdown Rd. L11: N Grn. 2A **58**
Kingsdown St. CH41: Tran 5E **97**
Kings Dr. CH48: Caldy 2C **134**
                        CH61: Pens 2F **137**
                        L25: Gate 5C **104**
                        L25: Wltn 2B **126**
King's Dr. Nth. CH48: W Kir 5E **113**
Kingsfield Rd. L31: Mag 3C **12**

King's Gap, The CH47: Hoy 4A **90**
Kingshead Cl. WA7: Cas 5A **154**
Kingsheath Av. L14: K Ash 2E **81**
Kingsland Cres. L11: N Grn. 5E **37**
Kingsland Rd. CH42: Tran 5C **96**
                        L11: N Grn. 5D **37**
King's La. CH63: High B 5D **119**
Kingsley Av. CH62: East 2E **171**
Kingsley Cl. CH61: Pens 4A **138**
                        L31: Lyd 5E **7**
Kingsley Cres. WA7: Run 1A **166**
Kingsley Rd. CH44: Wall 3B **74**
                        L8: Liv 2A **100**
                        WA7: Run 1A **166**
                        WA10: St. H 2D **45**
Kingsley St. CH41: Birk 1A **96**
Kingsmead Dr. L25: Hunts X 5B **126**
Kingsmead Gro. CH43: O'ton 4F **95**
Kings Mdw. WA7: Nort 2C **168**
Kingsmead Rd. CH43: O'ton 4F **95**
                        CH46: More 4F **71**
Kingsmead Rd. Nth. CH43: O'ton . .4F **95**
Kingsmead Rd. Sth. CH43: O'ton . .4F **95**
Kings Mt. CH43: O'ton 5B **96**
Kingsnorth L35: Whis 4F **85**
Kings Pde. CH45: Wall, New B 3D **51**
                        L3: Liv 1C **98**
Kings Pk. L21: Sea 1F **33**
Kings Rd. CH63: High B 4D **119**
                        L20: Boot 1C **54**
                        L23: C'by 1D **17**
                        WA10: St. H 1C **64**
Kings Sq. CH41: Birk 3E **97**
Kings Ter. L20: Boot 2C **54**
Kingsthorne Pk. L25: Hunts X 1C **146**
Kingsthorne Rd. L25: Hunts X 1C **146**
Kingston Cl. CH46: More 1E **93**
                        L12: W Der 1E **81**
                        WA7: Run 5E **153**
Kingsville Rd. CH63: High B 2E **141**
Kings Wlk. CH42: R Ferr 5A **97**
                        CH48: W Kir 4C **112**
Kingsway CH44: Wall 3F **75**
                        CH45: Wall 5A **52**
                        CH60: Hes 4C **158**
                        CH63: High B 5D **119**
                        L3: Liv 3C **76** (1C **4**)
                        L22: Water 3E **17**
                        L34: Prsct 1D **85**
                        L35: Prsct 1D **85**
                        L36: Huy, Roby 2D **83**
                        WA6: Frod 5B **172**
                        WA8: Wid 5A **132**
                        WA11: St. H 5A **30**
Kingsway Ct. L1: Liv 2E **99**
                        (off Raffles St.)
                        L3: Liv 2D **77**
Kingsway Ho. WA8: Wid 5A **132**
Kingsway Leisure Cen. 4A **132**
Kingsway Pde. L36: Huy 2C **84**
Kingsway Pk. L3: Liv 2D **77** (1F **5**)
Kingsway Tunnel App.
                        CH44: Wall 2E **73**
Kingswell Cl. L7: Liv 1B **100**
Kings Wharf CH41: Birk 5E **75**
Kingswood Av. L9: Ain 1B **36**
                        L22: Water 3F **17**
Kingswood Blvd. CH63: High B . . .4E **119**
Kingswood Cl. L33: K'by 1F **23**
Kingswood Dr. L23: C'by 2D **17**
Kingswood Rd. CH44: Wall 1C **74**
Kington Rd. CH48: W Kir 3A **112**
Kinley Gdns. L20: Boot 3E **35**
Kinloch Cl. L26: Halew 5F **127**
Kinloss Rd. CH49: Grea 1C **114**
Kinmel Cl. CH41: Birk 2D **97**
                        L4: Walt 2D **57**
Kinmel St. L8: Liv 4A **100**
                        WA9: St. H 3C **66**

Kinnaird Rd. CH45: Wall 5A **52**
Kinnaird St. L8: Liv 1A **122**
Kinnerton Cl. CH46: More 1B **92**
Kinnock Pk. WA5: B'wood 5E **69**
Kinross Rd. CH45: Wall 5D **51**
                        L10: Faz 1E **37**
                        L22: Water 5E **17**
Kinsman Ho. L19: Gras 5F **123**
Kintore Cl. CH63: East 1C **170**
Kintore Rd. L19: Gras 5B **124**
Kipling Av. CH42: R Ferr 3F **119**
                        L36: Huy 5A **84**
Kipling Cres. WA8: Wid 3F **131**
Kipling Gro. WA9: Sut M 3A **88**
Kipling St. L20: Boot 2A **34**
Kirby Cl. CH48: W Kir 5C **112**
Kirby Mt. CH48: W Kir 1C **134**
Kirby Pk. CH48: W Kir 5C **112**
Kirby Pk. Mans. CH48: W Kir 5B **112**
Kirby Rd. L20: Boot 2D **35**
Kirkbride Cl. L27: N'ley 5A **106**
Kirkbride Lawn L27: N'ley 5A **106**
Kirkbride Wlk. L27: N'ley 5A **106**
                        (off Kirkbride Clo.)
Kirkburn Cl. L8: Liv 5F **99**
KIRKBY 3E **23**
Kirkby Bank Rd. L33: Know I 3B **24**
KIRKBY PARK 2C **22**
Kirkby Row L32: K'by 2C **22**
Kirkby Station (Rail) 2C **22**
Kirk Cotts. CH45: Wall 4B **52**
KIRKDALE 3E **55**
Kirkdale Rd. L5: Kirk 5D **55**
Kirkdale Station (Rail) 2D **55**
Kirkdale Va. L4: Walt 4E **55**
Kirket Cl. CH63: Beb 3A **142**
Kirket La. CH63: Beb 3F **141**
Kirkfield Gro. CH42: R Ferr 3A **120**
Kirkham Rd. WA8: Wid 2C **132**
Kirkland Av. CH42: Tran 2D **119**
Kirkland Cl. L9: Walt 1F **35**
Kirkland Rd. CH45: New B 3C **52**
Kirklands, The CH48: W Kir 5C **112**
Kirkland St. WA10: St. H 4E **45**
Kirkmaiden Rd. L19: Aller 4B **124**
Kirkman Fold L35: R'hill 3B **86**
Kirkmore Rd. L18: Moss H 2A **124**
Kirkmount CH49: Upton 4A **94**
Kirk Rd. L21: Lith 2C **34**
Kirkside Cl. L12: Crox 5D **39**
Kirkstead Wlk. L31: Mell 2B **22**
Kirkstone Av. WA11: St. H 5C **30**
Kirkstone Cres. WA7: Beech 1A **174**
Kirkstone Rd. Nth. L21: Lith 4C **18**
Kirkstone Rd. Sth. L21: Lith 5D **19**
Kirkstone Rd. W. L21: Ford 3B **18**
Kirkston Rd. Nth. L21: Ford 3C **18**
Kirk St. L5: Liv 5E **55**
Kirkway CH45: Wall 4B **52**
                        CH49: Grea 5E **93**
                        CH49: Upton 4F **93**
                        CH63: High B 5D **119**
Kitchener Dr. L9: Walt 2F **35**
Kitchener St. WA10: St. H 4D **45**
Kitchen St. L1: Liv 2D **99**
Kitling Rd. L34: Know 3C **40**
Kiverley Cl. L18: Aller 1E **125**
Knap, The CH60: Hes 4A **158**
Knaresborough Rd. CH44: Wall 4F **73**
Knebworth Cl. L12: W Der 4D **59**
Knighton Rd. L4: Walt 2D **57**
Knight Rd. WA5: B'wood 5F **69**
Knightsbridge Cl. WA8: Wid 5D **111**
Knightsbridge Ct. CH43: Noct 1D **117**
Knightsbridge Wlk. L33: K'by 3D **15**
Knights Grange WA9: St. H 4C **46**
Knight St. L1: Liv 1E **99** (7G **5**)
Knightsway L22: Water 3F **17**
Knightswood Ct. L18: Aller 4C **124**
Knoclaid Rd. L13: Liv 4E **57**
Knoll, The CH43: O'ton 1A **118**
                        WA7: Pal F 3F **167**
Knotty M. L25: Wltn 1C **126**
Knowe, The CH64: Will 3A **170**
Knowle Cl. L12: W Der 1C **58**

Knowles, The. L23: Blun 2B 16
Knowles Ho. Av. WA10: Eccl 5F 43
Knowles St. CH41: Birk 2C 96
   WA8: Wid .2C 132
Knowl Hey Rd. L26: Halew 1A 148
KNOWSLEY 5D 41
Knowsley Bus. Pk. L34: Know 2B 40
Knowsley Cl. CH42: R Ferr 3A 120
Knowsley Ct. CH42: R Ferr 3A 120
Knowsley Ent. Workshops
   L33: Know I 4B 24
Knowsley Expressway
   L35: Tar G .3D 107
   WA8: Wid .2E 129
Knowsley Hgts. L36: Huy 1E 83
Knowsley Ind. Pk. L33: Know I 3B 24
Knowsley La.
   L34: Know, Know P 2C 60
   L36: Huy 3C 60
Knowsley Outdoor Educational Cen.
   . . . . .1F 61
KNOWSLEY PARK 3F 41
Knowsley Pk. La. L34: Prsct 4C 62
Knowsley Rd. CH42: R Ferr 3A 120
   CH45: Wall 5A 52
   L19: Gras .1A 144
   L20: Boot .3A 34
   L35: R'hill .4D 87
   WA10: St. H 5C 44
Knowsley Road Stadium 5C 44
Knowsley Safari Pk. 3C 62
Knowsley St. L4: Walt 1F 55
Knox Cl. CH62: Port S 1B 142
Knox St. CH41: Birk 3F 97
Knutsford Cl. WA10: Eccl 1B 64
Knutsford Grn. CH46: More 5F 71
Knutsford Rd. CH46: More 5E 71
Knutsford Wlk. L31: Lyd 3D 7
Kramar Wlk. L33: K'by 3F 23
Kremlin Dr. L13: Liv 1F 79
Kylemore Av. L18: Moss H 1F 123
Kylemore Cl. CH61: Pens 4E 137
Kylemore Ct. L26: Halew 5E 127
Kylemore Dr. CH61: Pens 4E 137
Kylemore Rd. CH43: O'ton 5A 96
   L26: Halew 5E 127
Kylemore Way CH61: Pens 4E 137
Kynance Rd. L11: Crox 3D 39

L

Laburnum Av. L36: Huy 1E 105
   WA11: St. H 1D 47
Laburnum Ct. L8: Liv 5A 100
             (off Weller Way)
Laburnum Cres. L32: K'by 2D 23
Laburnum Gro. CH61: Irby 1D 137
   L15: W'tree 1A 102
   L31: Mag .1E 13
   WA7: Run 2B 166
Laburnum Pl. L20: Boot 5D 35
Laburnum Rd. CH43: O'ton 5B 96
   CH45: New B 4B 52
   L7: Liv 3D 79
Lace St. L3: Liv 3D 77 (3E 4)
Lacey Ct. WA8: Wid 5A 132
Lacey Rd. L34: Prsct 5E 63
Lacey St. WA8: Wid 5A 132
   WA10: St. H 3D 65
Laddock Cl. L4: Walt 4C 56
Ladies Wlk. WA8: Bold H 4F 89
   WA9: Bold 4F 89
Lad La. L3: Liv 4B 76 (3B 4)
Ladybower Cl. CH49: Upton 3E 93
   L7: Liv 1B 100
Lady Chapel Cl. L1: Liv 2E 99
Ladyewood Rd. CH44: Wall 3C 74
Ladyfield CH43: Bid 2C 94
Ladyfields L12: W Der 1B 80
Lady Lever Art Gallery 1B 142
Lady Mountford Ho.
   L18: Moss H 1F 123
Ladypool L24: Hale 5C 148
Lady Richeld Cl. WA7: Nort 4D 155

Ladysmith Rd. L10: Faz 1F 37
LAFFAK 1D 47
Laffak Rd. WA11: St. H 5C 30
LA Fitness .1A 124
Lagan Ho. CH46: Leas 2E 71
Laggan St. L7: Liv 4B 78
Lagrange Arc. WA10: St. H 5A 46
Laird Cl. CH41: Birk 1F 95
Lairdside Technical Pk.
   . . . . .5F 97
Lairds Pl. L3: Liv 2D 77
Laithwaite Cl. WA9: Sut M 3B 88
Lake Ent. Pk. CH62: Brom 1E 143
Lakeland Cl. L1: Liv 1D 99 (7E 4)
Lakemoor Cl. WA9: St. H 4D 67
Lakenheath Rd. L26: Halew 1E 147
Lake Pl. CH47: Hoy 4B 90
Lake Rd. CH47: Hoy 4B 90
   L15: W'tree 2A 102
Lakeside CH47: Hoy 4A 130
Lakeside Cl. CH45: New B 3C 52
Lakeside Lawn L27: N'ley 5A 106
Lakeside Vw. L22: Water 5D 17
Lakes Rd. L9: Ain 1D 37
Lake St. L4: Walt 4A 56
Lake Vw. L35: Whis 1E 107
Laleston Cl. WA8: Wid 4E 131
Lambert St. L3: Liv 4E 77 (3H 5)
            (Kempston St.)
   L3: Liv 3H 5
            (Lambert Way)
Lambert Way L3: Liv 4E 77 (3H 5)
Lambeth Rd. L4: Kirk 4D 55
   L5: Kirk 4D 55
Lambeth Wlk. L4: Kirk 4D 55
Lambourn Av. WA8: Cron 4C 108
Lambourne Gro. WA9: St. H 5A 48
Lambourne Rd. L4: Walt 2D 57
Lambrigg Row L5: Liv 4F 55
Lambshear La. L31: Lyd 3C 6
Lambsickle Cl. WA7: West 4F 165
Lambsickle La.
   WA7: Run, West 4F 165
            (not continuous)
Lambton Rd. L17: Aig 1A 122
Lammermoor Rd. L18: Moss H 2A 124
Lampeter Rd. L6: Liv 5C 56
Lamport Cl. WA8: Wid 1E 133
Lamport St. L8: Liv 3E 99
Lanark Cl. WA10: St. H 1F 65
Lancashire Gdns. WA10: St. H 1F 65
Lancaster Av. L45: Wall 1B 74
   L17: Liv 3C 100
   L23: C'by .2D 17
   L35: Whis .3D 85
   WA7: Run 2E 165
   WA8: Wid .2A 130
Lancaster Cl. CH62: Port S 1B 142
   L5: Kirk 5D 55
   L31: Mag .1F 13
   WA12: New W 4F 49
Lancaster Rd. L36: Huy 2A 84
   WA8: Wid .1A 132
Lancaster St. L5: Kirk 5D 55
   L9: Walt 5F 35
Lancaster Wlk. L5: Kirk 5D 55
   L36: Huy .2A 84
Lance Cl. L5: Liv 1F 77
Lancefield Rd. L9: Walt 3F 35
Lance Gro. L15: W'tree 2A 102
Lance La. L15: W'tree 2A 102
Lancelots Hey L3: Liv 4B 76 (4B 4)
Lancelyn Ct. CH63: Spit 4A 142
Lancelyn Pct. CH63: Spit 4A 142
            (off Spital Rd.)
Lancelyn Ter. CH63: Beb 3F 141
Lancer Cl. WA7: Ast 4E 153
Lancing Cl. L25: Hunts X, Wltn 3D 127
            (not continuous)
Lancing Dr. L10: Ain 3D 21
Lancing Rd. L25: Hunts X 3D 127
Lancing Way L25: Hunts X 3D 127
Lancots La. WA9: St. H 3D 67
Land End L31: Mag 1C 14

Lander Rd. L21: Lith 2B 34
Landford Av. L9: Faz 4E 37
Landford Pl. L9: Faz 4E 37
LANDICAN .4C 116
Landican Cemetery & Crematorium
   . . . . .4B 116
Landican La. CH49: W'chu 3C 116
   CH63: Store 1F 139
Landican Rd. CH49: W'chu 5B 116
Landmark, The L5: Liv 1E 77
Landor Cl. L5: Liv 1C 76
Landseer Rd. L5: Liv 1F 77
Lanfranc Cl. L16: Child 1E 103
Lanfranc Way L16: Child 1E 103
Langbar L35: Whis 4E 85
Langdale Av. CH61: Pens 3F 137
Langdale Cl. L32: K'by 4F 23
   WA8: Wid .4C 130
Langdale Dr. L31: Mag 5E 7
Langdale Gro. WA11: St. H 1B 46
Langdale Rd. CH45: Wall 4F 51
   CH63: Beb 3E 141
   L15: W'tree 3E 101
   WA7: Run 5B 152
Langdale Way WA6: Frod 4C 172
Langfield Gro. CH62: Brom 5D 163
Langford L24: Hale 5C 148
Langford Rd. L19: Aig 4F 123
Langham Av. L17: Aig 1C 122
Langham Cl. L4: Walt 3F 55
Langham St. L4: Walt 3F 55
Langham St. Ind. Est. L4: Walt 3F 55
Langholme Hgts. L11: N Grn 4F 37
Langland Cl. L4: Walt 3D 57
Lang La. CH48: W Kir 3B 112
Lang La. Sth. CH48: W Kir 4C 112
Langley Cl. CH63: Spit 5A 142
   L12: Crox .5F 39
Langley Rd. Shop. Cen.
   L12: Crox .5F 39
Langley Rd. CH63: Spit 5A 142
Langley St. L8: Liv 3E 99
Langrove St. L5: Liv 4F 55
Langsdale St. L3: Liv 3E 77 (2H 5)
            (not continuous)
Langshaw Lea L27: N'ley 5F 105
Langstone Av. CH49: Grea 2C 114
Langton Cl. WA8: Wid 1B 130
Langton Rd. L15: W'tree 2D 101
   L33: K'by .5F 15
Langtree Cl. WA9: St. H 5C 46
Langtry Cl. L4: Kirk 2D 55
Langtry Rd. L4: Kirk 3D 55
Lansbury Av. WA9: St. H 1E 67
Lansbury Rd. L36: Huy 4A 84
Lansdown L12: W Der 5A 58
Lansdowne Cl. CH41: Birk 1A 96
Lansdowne Ct. CH43: Bid 1F 95
Lansdowne Pl. CH43: Bid 1F 95
   L5: Liv 5F 55
Lansdowne Rd. CH41: Birk 1F 95
   CH43: Bid 1F 95
   CH45: Wall 4F 51
Lansdowne Way L36: Huy 4E 83
Lanville Rd. L19: Aig 3A 124
Lanyork Rd. L3: Liv 3B 76 (2B 4)
Lapford Cres. L33: K'by 1A 24
Lapford Wlk. L33: K'by 1A 24
Lapwing Cl. L12: W Der 2F 59
Lapwing Gro. WA7: Pal F 4A 168
Lapwing La. WA4: Moore 1F 155
Lapwing Ri. CH60: Hes 4F 157
Lapworth Cl. CH46: More 1B 92
Lapworth St. L5: Kirk 5D 55
Larch Av. WA8: Wid 2B 132
Larch Cl. L19: Gras 5F 123
   WA7: Run 3C 166
Larch Ct. L8: Liv 5A 100
            (off Weller Way)
Larchdale Gro. L9: Walt 4A 36
Larchfield Rd. L23: Thorn 5B 10
Larch Gro. CH43: Bid 1E 95
   L15: W'tree 5A 80

Larch Lea L6: Liv 1B 78
(not continuous)
Larch Rd. CH42: Tran 4C 96
L36: Roby 4C 82
WA7: Run 3C 166
WA11: Hay 1E 49
Larchwood Av. L18: Mag 3C 12
Larchwood Cl. CH61: Pens 4F 137
L25: Gate 4B 104
Larchwood Dr. CH63: High B . . .5E 119
Larcombe Av. L49: Upton 4F 93
Larkfield Cl. L17: Aig 2C 122
Larkfield Ct. WA11: St. H 5F 29
Larkfield Gro. L17: Aig 2C 122
Larkfield Rd. L17: Aig 2C 122
Larkfield Vw. L15: W'tree 1E 101
Larkhill Av. CH49: Upton 2A 94
Larkhill Cl. L13: Liv 4E 57
Larkhill La. L13: Liv 4E 57
Larkhill Pl. L13: Liv 4E 57
Larkhill Vw. L13: Liv 4F 57
Larkhill Way CH49: Upton 2A 94
Larkin Ct. CH42: New F 5A 120
Lark La. L17: Aig 1B 122
Larkspur Cl. WA7: Beech 1F 173
Larkspur Ct. L31: Mell 2A 22
Larksway CH60: Hes 2B 158
Lark Way L17: Aig 1B 122
Larne Way WA8: Wid 1E 131
Larton Farm Cl. CH48: W Kir 4E 113
Larton Dr. CH48: W Kir 3E 113
Lartonwood CH48: W Kir 3E 113
Lascelles Rd. L19: Aller 5D 125
Lascelles St. WA9: St. H 5C 46
Latchford Rd. CH60: Hes 4B 158
Late Moffatt Rd. W. L9: Ain 1B 36
Latham Av. WA7: Run 5B 152
Latham St. L5: Kirk 5D 55
(not continuous)
WA9: St. H 4D 47
Latham Way CH63: Spit 5B 142
Lathbury La. L17: Aig 4E 101
Lathom Av. CH44: Wall 2B 74
L21: Sea 2F 33
Lathom Cl. L21: Sea 2F 33
Lathom Dr. L31: Mag 4E 7
Lathom Rd. L20: Boot 3C 34
L36: Huy 3E 83
Lathum Cl. L35: Prsct 1E 85
Latimer St. L5: Liv 5D 55
Latrigg Rd. L17: Aig 2E 123
Lauder Cl. L33: K'by 4D 15
Launceston Cl. WA7: Brook 4C 168
Laund, The CH45: Wall 1F 73
Laurel Av. CH60: Hes 1F 157
CH63: High B 3E 141
Laurel Bank WA8: Wid 1A 132
Laurelbanks CH60: Hes 1E 157
Laurel Ct. L7: Liv 3D 79
(off Laurel Rd.)
WA11: St. H 1B 46
Laurel Dr. CH64: Will 4B 170
WA10: Eccl 4F 43
Laurel Gro. L8: Liv 3C 100
L22: Water 3D 17
L36: Huy 1E 105
Laurelhurst Av. CH61: Pens 3A 138
Laurel Rd. CH42: Tran 5D 97
L7: Liv 3D 79
L34: Prsct 5E 63
WA10: St. H 1D 65
WA11: Hay 3F 47
Laurels, The CH46: Leas 3E 71
Laurence Deacon Ct. CH41: Birk . .2C 96
Lauren Cl. L36: Huy 4B 84
Lauriston Rd. L4: Walt 2C 56
Laurus Cl. L27: N'ley 4F 105
Lavan Cl. L6: Liv 3A 78
Lavan St. L6: Liv 3A 78
WA9: St. H 4E 65
Lavender Cl. WA7: Run 1C 166
Lavender Cres. L34: Prsct 5E 63
Lavender Gdns. L23: Thorn 8B 10
WA9: Bold 4A 68
Lavender Way L9: Walt 4B 36

Lavrock Bank L8: Liv 5E 99
Lawford Dr. CH60: Hes 2C 158
Lawler Gro. L34: Prsct 4E 63
Lawler St. L21: Lith 2B 34
Lawnhurst Gro. L17: Aig 4E 123
Lawns, The CH43: Bid 2D 95
Lawns Av. CH63: Raby M 4B 162
Lawnside CH42: R Ferr 3F 119
Lawrence Cl. L19: Gras 5A 124
Lawrence Ct. CH42: R Ferr 4A 120
Lawrence Gro. L15: W'tree 2E 101
Lawrence Rd. L15: W'tree 2D 101
WA10: Windle 2C 44
Lawrenson St. WA10: St. H 5E 45
Lawson Wlk. L12: Crox 5D 39
Lawton Cl. L20: Boot 3E 35
Lawton Rd. L22: Water 3D 17
L35: R'hill 4D 87
L36: Roby 4C 82
Laxey St. L1: Liv 5D 77 (6F 5)
Laxey St. L8: Liv 3E 99
Laxton Rd. L25: Hunts X 5C 126
Layford Cl. L36: Huy 5D 61
Layford Rd. L36: Huy 1D 83
Layton Av. CH43: Pren 2F 117
Layton Cl. L25: Wltn 2C 126
Layton Rd. L25: Wltn 2C 126
Leach Cft. L28: Stock V 4A 60
Leach La. WA9: Sut L 2D 89
Leach St. WA10: St. H 4F 45
Leach Way CH61: Irby 1C 136
Lea Cl. CH43: Noct 5E 95
Lea Cross Gro. WA8: Wid 1C 130
Leadenhall Cl. L5: Liv 5F 55
Leafield Cl. CH61: Irby 1F 137
Leafield Rd. L25: Hunts X 1B 146
Leagate L10: Faz 5F 21
LEA GREEN 1F 87
Lea Green Bus. Pk. WA9: St. H . . .2F 87
Lea Grn. Ind. Est. WA9: St. H 3A 88
Lea Grn. Rd. WA9: St. H 3F 87
Lea Green Station (Rail) 1B 88
Leamington Gdns. CH49: W'chu . .5B 94
Leamington Rd. L11: N Grn. 1D 57
Leander Way L24: Speke 3B 146
Lea Rd. CH44: Wall 1C 74
Leas, The CH45: Wall 4E 51
CH61: Thing 1B 138
Leaside WA7: Run 1D 167
LEASOWE .2B 72
Leasowe Av. CH45: Wall 5E 51
Leasowe Gdns. CH46: Leas 3E 71
Leasowe Recreation Cen. 3A 72
Leasowe Rd. CH44: Wall 2A 72
CH45: Wall 2A 72
CH46: Leas 3D 71
L9: Ain 1B 36
Leasowe Station (Rail) 4F 71
Leas Pk. CH47: Hoy 2A 112
Leatherbarrows La.
L31: Mag, Mell 3F 13
Leather La. L2: Liv 4C 76 (4D 4)
Leather's La. L26: Halew 1F 147
Leathwood L31: Mag 1E 13
Leaway CH49: Grea 5D 93
Leawood Gro. CH46: More 1F 93
LEC Complex L15: W'tree 1D 101
Leckwith Rd. L30: N'ton 3B 20
Leda Gro. L17: Aig 5C 100
(off Hadassah Gro.)
Ledbury Cl. CH43: O'ton 2E 117
L12: Crox 4F 39
WA10: Eccl 5B 44
Ledger Rd. WA11: Hay 3A 48
Ledsham Cl. CH43: Noct 5E 95
Ledsham Rd. L32: K'by 3C 22
Ledsham Wlk. L32: K'by 3C 22
Ledson Pk. L33: K'by 4F 15
Ledsons Gro. L31: Mell 2A 22
Ledston Cl. WA7: Wind H 1D 169
Leece St. L1: Liv 1E 99 (7G 5)
Lee Cl. L35: R'hill 5G 87
Leecourt Cl. L12: W Der 1D 81
Leeds St. L3: Liv 3B 76 (2B 4)

Lee Hall Rd. L25: Gate 4C 104
Lee Manor Sports Cen. 4D 105
Leeming Cl. L19: Gars 2C 144
Lee Pk. Av. L25: Gate 4C 104
Lee Rd. CH47: Hoy 4C 90
Lees Av. CH42: R Ferr 2F 119
Leeside Av. L32: K'by 5E 23
Leeside Cl. L32: K'by 4F 23
Lees Rd. L33: Know I 4B 24
Lees St. WA9: St. H 3E 67
Leeswood L22: Water 4E 17
Leeswood Rd. CH49: W'chu 1A 116
Leeward Dr. L24: Speke 3A 146
Legh Rd. CH62: New F 5B 120
WA11: Hay 2A 48
Legh St. WA12: New W 5F 49
Legion La. CH62: Brom 1D 163
Legion Rd. WA10: St. H 3D 65
Leicester Av. L22: Water 2D 17
Leicester Rd. L20: Boot 4D 35
Leicester St. WA9: St. H 3D 65
Leigh Av. WA8: Wid 3F 131
Leigh Bri. Way L5: Liv 1C 76
Leigh Grn. Cl. WA8: Wid 4C 130
Leigh Pl. L1: Liv 5D 77 (5F 5)
Leigh Rd. CH48: W Kir 3B 112
Leighs Hey Cres. L32: K'by 4F 23
Leigh St. L1: Liv 5D 77 (5E 4)
(not continuous)
L7: Liv 5C 78
Leighton Av. CH47: Meols 3E 91
L31: Mag 5D 7
Leighton Rd. CH41: Tran 5E 97
Leighton St. L4: Kirk 2E 55
Leinster Gdns. WA7: Run 4F 151
Leinster Rd. L13: Liv 3B 80
Leinster St. WA7: Run 4F 151
Leison St. L4: Kirk 4D 55
(not continuous)
Leiston Cl. CH61: Irby 5E 115
Lemon Cl. L7: Liv 5C 78
Lemon Gro. L8: Liv 3C 100
Lemon St. L5: Kirk 5D 55
Lemon Tree Wlk. WA10: St. H 2D 65
Lenfield Dr. WA11: Hay 2F 47
Lenham Way L24: Speke 3B 146
Lennox Av. CH45: New B 4B 52
Lennox La. CH43: Bid 5C 72
Lenthall St. L4: Walt 1F 55
Lenton Rd. L25: Gate 4C 104
Lentworth Dr. L19: Aig 5F 123
Leo Casino 2D 99
Leo Cl. L14: K Ash 2F 81
Leominster Rd. CH44: Wall 2B 74
Leonard Cheshire Dr. L30: N'ton . .2F 19
Leonard Ho. CH41: Birk 5F 75
Leonards Cl. L36: Huy 5D 61
Leonard St. WA7: West P 3D 165
WA9: St. H 4F 67
Leonora St. L8: Liv 5A 100
Leopold Gro. WA9: Sut L 1C 88
Leopold Rd. L7: Liv 4B 78
(not continuous)
L22: Water 3C 16
Leopold St. CH44: Wall 3E 75
Leslie Av. CH49: Grea 1D 115
Leslie Rd. WA10: St. H 3C 64
Lesseps Rd. L8: Liv 2C 100
Lessingham Rd. WA8: Wid 1F 131
Lester Cl. L4: Kirk 4E 55
Lester Dr. CH61: Irby 5C 114
WA10: Eccl 3A 44
Lester Gro. L36: Huy 2F 83
Lestock St. L8: Liv 2E 99
Leta St. L4: Walt 2F 55
(not continuous)
Letchworth St. L6: Liv 1B 78
Lethbridge Cl. L5: Kirk 5C 54
Letitia St. L8: Liv 4F 99
Letterstone Cl. L6: Liv 2F 77
Letterstone Wlk. L6: Liv 2F 77
Levens Hey CH46: More 1D 93
Leven St. L4: Kirk 3E 55
Levens Way WA8: Wid 4C 130

Lever CH44: Wall 4E 75
Lever C'way.
 CH63: High B, Store 2A 140
Leveret Rd. L24: Speke 4A 148
Leverhulme Ct. CH63: Beb 3A 142
Lever St. WA9: Clock F 3D 89
Lever Ter. CH42: Tran 1E 119
Leveson Rd. L13: Liv 5B 80
Lewis Cres. WA8: Wid 5A 132
Lewis Gro. WA8: Wid 3D 131
Lewisham Rd. CH62: Port S 1C 142
 L11: N Grn. 1F 57
Lewis St. WA10: St. H 4E 45
Lewis Wlk. L33: K'by 4E 15
Lexham Rd. L14: K Ash 3B 80
Lexington Way L33: K'by 3E 15
Leybourne Cl. L25: Gate 3A 104
Leybourne Grn. L25: Gate 3A 104
Leybourne Gro. L25: Gate 4A 104
Leybourne Rd. L25: Gate 3A 104
Leyburn Cl. L32: K'by 1E 39
 (not continuous)
Leyburn Rd. CH45: Wall 5F 51
Ley Cl. WA9: Clock F 2C 88
Leyfield Cl. L12: W Der 5D 59
Leyfield Ct. L12: W Der 5D 59
Leyfield Rd. L12: W Der 5C 58
Leyfield Wlk. L12: W Der 5D 59
Leyland Gro. WA11: Hay 2B 48
Leyland St. L34: Prsct 5D 63
Leyton Cl. WA7: Run 4B 166
Liberton Ct. L5: Liv 5F 55
Liberty St. L15: W'tree 2E 101
Libra Cl. L14: K Ash 1A 82
Library St. WA10: St. H 5A 46
Librex Rd. L20: Boot 2C 34
Lichfield Av. L22: Water 2D 17
Lichfield Cl. L30: N'ton 4A 20
Lichfield Rd. L15: W'tree 3A 102
 L26: Halew 1E 147
Lichfield St. CH45: New B 4C 52
Lickers La. L35: Whis 4D 85
Liddell Av. L31: Mell 1A 22
Liddell Ct. CH45: Wall 1D 73
Liddell Rd. L12: W Der 4F 57
Lidderdale Rd. L15: W'tree 3E 101
Lidgate Cl. L33: K'by 5F 15
Lifestyles Millennium 4E 5
Liffey Ct. L3: Liv 3J 5
Liffey St. L8: Liv 2B 100
Lifton Rd. L33: K'by 3F 23
Lightbody St. L5: Liv 1B 76
Lightburn St. WA7: Run 1F 165
Lightfoot Cl. CH60: Hes 3B 158
Lightfoot La. CH60: Hes 3B 158
Lighthouse Rd. CH47: Hoy 5B 90
Lightwood Dr. L7: Liv 1C 100
Lightwood St. L7: Liv 1C 100
Lilac Av. WA8: Wid 2B 132
Lilac Cres. WA7: Run 2C 166
Lilac Gro. L36: Huy 1D 105
 WA11: Hay 3F 47
 WN5: Bil 1D 31
Lilford Av. L9: Walt 2F 35
Lilley Rd. L7: Liv 3D 79
Lillian Rd. L4: Walt 5B 56
Lillie Cl. CH43: Bid 1C 94
Lillyfield CH60: Hes 4F 157
Lilly Grn. L4: Walt 2B 56
Lilly Gro. L4: Walt 2B 56
 (not continuous)
Lilly Va. L7: Liv 3D 79
Lily Gro. L7: Liv 5B 78
Lily Rd. L21: Lith 2B 34
Limbo Cl. CH49: Grea 4D 115
 CH61: Irby 4E 115
Lime Av. CH63: High B 3D 141
 WA6: Frod 5C 172
 WA8: Wid 2B 132
Lime Cl. L33: Liv 2A 80
Limedale Rd. L18: Moss H 4A 102
Lime Gro. L8: Liv 3B 100
 L21: Sea 2A 34
 WA7: Run 2C 166
Limehurst Gro. CH62: Brom 4D 163

Limekiln Ct. L5: Liv 1D 77
Limekiln La. CH44: Wall 4A 74
 L3: Liv 2D 77
 L5: Liv 2D 77 (1E 5)
Limekiln Row WA7: Cas 2A 168
Limerick Cl. WA8: Wid 1E 131
Limes, The CH49: Upton 4F 93
Lime St. L1: Liv 4D 77 (4F 5)
Lime St. Chambers L1: Liv 4G 5
Lime Street Staion (Rail) . .4E 77 (4G 5)
Lime Tree Cl. L9: Walt 4B 36
Lime Tree Gro. CH60: Hes 2C 158
Lime Va. Rd. WN5: Bil 2C 30
Linacre Ct. L20: Boot 1C 54
Linacre La. L20: Boot 3C 34
 WA8: Wid 4E 109
Linacre Rd. L21: Lith 1B 34
Lincoln Cl. L6: Liv 2B 78
 L36: Huy 3B 84
 WA7: Run 4C 166
Lincoln Cres. WA11: St. H 2B 46
Lincoln Dr. CH45: Wall 5C 52
 L10: Ain 2D 21
Lincoln Gdns. CH41: Birk 5A 74
Lincoln Grn. L31: Mag 2B 12
Lincoln Ho. WA10: St. H 4A 46
Lincoln Rd. WA10: St. H 1D 65
Lincoln Sq. WA8: Wid 2B 132
Lincoln St. CH41: Birk 5A 74
 L19: Gars 3C 144
Lincoln Way L35: R'hill 5D 87
 L36: Huy 3B 84
Lincombe Rd. L36: Huy 2B 82
Lindale Cl. CH46: More 5A 72
Lindale Dr. WA9: Clock F 2C 88
Lindale Rd. L7: Liv 3E 79
Lindby Cl. L32: K'by 5A 24
Lindby Rd. L32: K'by 5A 24
Linden Av. L23: Blun 1C 16
 L30: N'ton 3F 19
Linden Ct. WA8: Wid 5F 109
Linden Dr. CH43: Pren 3E 117
 L36: Huy 5E 83
Linden Gro. CH45: Wall 4B 52
 WN5: Bil 2C 30
Linden Rd. L27: N'ley 4E 105
Lindens, The CH43: O'ton 4C 96
 L31: Mag 3C 12
Linden Way WA8: Wid 5F 109
 WA10: Eccl 4B 44
Lindenwood L32: K'by 5F 23
Lindeth Av. CH44: Wall 3B 74
Lindfield Cl. L8: Liv 5E 99
Lindisfarne Av. WA8: Wid 3F 109
Lindisfarne Dr. L12: Crox 5F 39
Lindley Cl. L7: Liv 1C 100
Lindley St. L7: Liv 1C 100
Lindrick Cl. L35: R'hill 2A 86
Lindsay Rd. L4: Walt 3D 57
Lindsay St. WA9: Clock F 3D 89
Lind St. L4: Walt 2F 55
Lindwall Cl. CH43: Bid 5C 72
Linear Pk. CH46: More 5C 70
Lineside Cl. L25: Gate 4B 104
Linford Gro. WA11: St. H 3C 46
Lingdale Av. CH43: C'ton 3F 95
Lingdale Ct. CH43: C'ton 2F 95
 CH48: W Kir 4A 112
Lingdale Rd. CH43: C'ton 2F 95
 CH48: W Kir 3A 112
Lingdale Rd. Nth. CH41: Birk 2F 95
Lingfield Cl. L30: N'ton 4A 20
 L36: Roby 5C 82
Lingfield Gro. L14: B Grn 4C 80
Lingfield Rd. L14: B Grn 4C 80
 WA7: Run 1E 165
Lingford Cl. L27: N'ley 5F 105
Lingham Cl. CH46: More 5D 71
Lingham La. CH46: More 3C 70
 (not continuous)
Lingholme Rd. WA10: St. H 4E 45
Lingmell Av. WA11: St. H 4B 30
Lingmell Rd. L12: W Der 3B 58
Ling St. L7: Liv 4B 78
Lingtree Rd. L32: K'by 3B 22

Lingwell Av. WA8: Wid 2D 131
Linhope Way L17: Aig 1B 122
Link Av. L23: Thorn 5A 10
Link Rd. L36: Huy 5B 84
 WA11: St. H 1E 47
Linkfield Cl. L27: N'ley 3C 104
Link Rd. L36: Huy 5B 84
Links, The L43: O'ton 4F 95
Links Cl. CH45: Wall 4F 51
 CH63: Raby M 4B 162
Links Hey Rd. CH48: Caldy 3E 135
Linkside CH63: High B 5D 119
Linkside Ct. L23: Blun 5A 8
Linkside Rd. L25: Wltn 3C 126
Links Rd. L32: K'by 4A 24
Linkstor Rd. L25: Wltn 1F 125
Links Vw. CH43: O'ton 4E 95
 CH45: Wall 3F 51
Linksview L25: Wltn 2F 125
Linksway CH45: Wall 4F 51
Linkway WA7: Run 2C 166
 WA10: Windle 2B 44
Linkway E. WA9: St. H 1B 66
Linkway W. WA9: St. H 5F 45
 WA10: St. H 5F 45
Linner Rd. L24: Speke 5C 146
Linnet Cl. L17: Aig 4C 100
Linnet Ho. L17: Aig 4B 100
Linnet La. L17: Aig 4B 100
Linnets Pk. WA7: Run 4B 152
Linnets Way CH60: Hes 2E 157
Linnet Way L33: K'by 3E 15
Linslade Cl. L33: K'by 1F 23
Linslade Cres. L33: K'by 1F 23
Linton Pl. L32: K'by 3B 22
Linton St. L4: Walt 2F 55
Linum Gdns. WA9: Bold 4B 68
Linville Av. L23: Blun 1B 16
Linwood Cl. WA7: Brook 5C 168
Linwood Gro. L35: Whis 4E 85
Linwood Rd. CH42: Tran 1E 119
Lionel St. WA9: St. H 4F 67
Lions Cl. CH43: C'ton 3F 95
Lipton Cl. L20: Boot 1B 54
Lisburn La. L13: Liv 5E 57
 (Delamain Rd.)
 L13: Liv 4E 57
 (Malleson Rd.)
Lisburn Rd. L17: Aig 2D 123
LISCARD 1B 74
Liscard Cres. CH44: Wall 1B 74
Liscard Gro. CH44: Wall 2A 74
Liscard Ho. CH44: Wall 2B 74
Liscard Rd. CH44: Wall 2B 74
 L15: W'tree 2D 101
Liscard Village CH45: Wall 1B 74
Liscard Way CH44: Wall 2B 74
Liskeard Cl. WA7: Brook 4B 168
Lisleholme Cl. L12: W Der 5C 58
Lisleholme Cres. L12: W Der 5C 58
Lisleholme Rd. L12: W Der 5C 58
Lismore Ct. L23: Blun 1C 16
Lismore Rd. L18: Moss H 2A 124
Lister Cres. L7: Liv 4C 78
Lister Dr. CH46: Leas 4A 72
 L13: Liv 2E 79
Lister Rd. L7: Liv 3C 78
 WA7: Ast 4C 152
Liston St. L4: Walt 1F 55
Litcham Cl. CH49: Upton 2B 94
Litchborough Gro. L35: Whis 5A 64
LITHERLAND 5B 18
Litherland Av. CH46: More 5D 71
Litherland Cres. WA11: St. H 1C 46
Litherland Ho. L20: Boot 4D 35
Litherland Pk. L21: Lith 5B 18
Litherland Rd. L20: Boot 2C 34
Lithou Cl. L5: Liv 1C 76
Little Acre L31: Mag 2E 13
Lit. Barn Hey L30: N'ton 5D 11
LITTLE BONGS 2D 81
Lit. Bongs L14: K Ash 2D 81
Littlebourne WA7: Murd 3E 169
Littlebrook La. L32: K'by 5D 23
Lit. Canning St. L8: Liv 2F 99
Lit. Catharine St. L8: Liv 2F 99

Littlecote Cl. WA9: Clock F 2C 88
Little Ct. L3: Liv 2C 76
Little Cft. L35: Whis 3D 85
LITTLE CROSBY 3D 9
Lit. Crosby Rd. L23: C'by, Lit C 2D 9
Littledale L14: K Ash 3D 81
Littledale Rd. CH44: Wall 3D 75
Lit. Delph WA11: Hay 1C 48
Littlegate WA7: Run 2E 167
Lit. Hardman St.
    L1: Liv 1E 99 (7H 5)
Lit. Heath Rd. L24: Speke 5E 147
Lit. Heyes St. L5: Liv 5A 56
Lit. Howard St. L1: Liv 2B 76 (1B 4)
Lit. Huskisson St. L8: Liv 2F 99
Littlemore Cl. CH49: Upton 4D 93
Lit. Moss Hey L28: Stock V 4B 60
Lit. Parkfield Rd. L17: Aig 5B 100
Littler Rd. WA11: Hay 3F 47
Lit. St Bride St. L8: Liv 1F 99
Littlestone Cl. WA8: Wid 5A 110
Lit. Storeton La. CH63: Store 1A 140
Little St. WA9: St. H 2E 67
Littleton Cl. CH43: Noct 5E 95
Littlewood Cl. L35: Whis 3E 85
Lit. Woolton St. L7: Liv 5F 77
Littondale Av. L35: R'hill 4D 87
Liver Ind. Est. L9: Ain 4C 36
Livermore Ct. L8: Liv 3C 100
LIVERPOOL 4C 76 (3D 4)
Liverpool Cathedral Church of Christ
    . . . . .2E 99
Liverpool College Sports Cen. . . .5F 101
Liverpool Empire Theatre
    . . . . .4D 77 (4G 5)
Liverpool FC (Anfield) 4A 56
Liverpool Institute for Performing Arts
    . . . . .7H 5
    . . . . (off Mount St.)
Liverpool Intermodal Freeport Terminal
    L20: Boot 4A 34
LIVERPOOL JOHN LENNON AIRPORT
    . . . . .5C 146
Liverpool Metropolitan Cathedral
    . . . . .5F 77 (5J 5)
Liverpool Mus. 4D 77 (3F 5)
Liverpool Parish Church . .4B 76 (5B 4)
Liverpool Pl. WA8: Wid 3C 130
Liverpool Playhouse 5D 77 (5F 5)
Liverpool Rd. L23: C'by 5D 9
    L31: Lyd 4C 6
    L34: Prsct 5B 62
    L36: Huy 2B 82
    WA8: Wid 3B 130
    WA10: St. H 5F 45
    WA11: Hay 1A 48
Liverpool Rd. Nth. L31: Mag 4C 6
Liverpool Rd. Sth. L31: Mag 1C 12
Liverpool Sailing Club 5E 145
Liverpool St. WA10: St. H 5F 45
Liverpool Tennis Cen. 2E 101
Liverpool Watersports Cen. 3C 98
Liverpool Way, The L33: K'by 4A 24
Liversidge Rd. CH42: Tran 5D 97
Liver St. L1: Liv 1C 98 (7D 4)
Livingston Av. L17: Aig 5C 100
Livingston Ct. L17: Aig 5C 100
Livingston Dr. L17: Aig 1C 122
Livingston Dr. Nth. L17: Aig 1C 122
Livingston Dr. Sth. L17: Aig 1C 122
Livingston Gdns. CH41: Birk 2C 96
Livingstone Rd. CH46: Leas 2A 72
Livingstone St. CH41: Birk 2C 96
Livingwell Health Club 5A 46
Llanrwst Cl. L8: Liv 4E 99
Lloyd Cl. CH41: Birk 2B 96
Lloyd Cl. L6: Liv 2F 77
Lloyd Cres. WA12: New W 5F 49
Lloyd Dr. CH49: Grea 1C 114
Lloyd Rd. L34: Prsct 4E 63
Lloyd St. WA11: Hay 2F 47
Lobelia Av. L9: Walt 4F 35
Lobelia Gro. WA7: Beech 1F 173
Local Cen. WA7: Cas 5A 154
Lochinvar St. L9: Walt 5F 35

Lochmore Rd. L18: Moss H 3A 124
Lochryan Rd. L19: Aller 4B 124
Loch St. WA7: Run 4A 152
    (not continuous)
Lockerby Rd. L7: Liv 3D 79
Locker Pk. CH49: Grea 5C 92
Locke St. L19: Gars 3C 144
Lockett Rd. WA8: Wid 1A 132
Lockfields Vw. L3: Liv 1C 76
Lockgate E. WA7: Wind H 5C 154
Lockgate W. WA7: Wind H 5B 154
Lockington Cl. L8: Liv 5F 99
Lock St. WA9: St. H 3C 46
Lockton Rd. L34: Know 3B 40
Lockwood Vw. WA7: Pres B 5F 169
Loddon Cl. CH49: Upton 2B 94
Lodge La. CH62: Port S 1B 142
    L8: Liv 2B 100
    WA7: Halt 2E 167
    WA8: Cron 5A 108
Lodge Rd. WA8: Wid 4B 130
Lodge Works L33: Know I 2C 24
Lodwick St. L20: Kirk 2B 54
Lofthouse Ga. WA8: Wid 1F 131
Logan Rd. CH41: Birk 5B 74
Logfield Dr. L19: Gars 2D 145
Lognor Rd. L32: K'by 3C 22
Lognor Wlk. L32: K'by 3C 22
Logwood Rd. L36: Huy 1A 106
Lois Ct. CH45: Wall 5C 52
Lombard Rd. CH46: More 4F 71
Lombardy Av. CH49: Grea 2B 114
Lomond Gro. CH46: More 1F 93
Lomond Rd. L7: Liv 4E 79
Londonderry Rd. L13: Liv 4D 57
London Rd. L3: Liv 4E 77 (4G 5)
    (not continuous)
    WA6: Frod 5B 172
Longacre CH45: Wall 1D 73
Long Acres CH49: Grea 4D 93
Long Av. L9: Ain 2B 36
Longbenton Way WA7: Mnr P 3B 154
Longborough Rd. L34: Know 5C 40
Longcroft Av. L19: Aller 5D 125
Longcroft Sq. L19: Aller 5D 125
Longdale La. L29: Seft 3D 11
Longdown Rd. L10: Faz 2A 38
Longfellow Cl. L32: K'by 5D 23
Longfellow Dr. CH62: New F 5A 120
Longfellow St. L8: Liv 2B 100
    (not continuous)
    L20: Boot 3A 34
Longfield Av. L23: C'by 4E 9
Longfield Cl. CH49: Grea 5D 93
Longfield Pk. WA9: Clock F 2D 89
Longfield Rd. L21: Lith 2B 34
Longfield Wlk. L23: C'by 4E 9
Longfold L31: Mag 1E 13
Longford Dr. WA8: Wid 2E 131
Longford St. L8: Liv 1A 122
Long Hey L35: Whis 4D 85
Long Hey Rd. CH48: Caldy 2E 135
Longland Dr. CH45: Wall 5B 52
Long La. L9: Ain 2B 36
    L15: W'tree 1E 101
    L19: Gars 5C 124
    L29: Thorn 2A 10
Long Mdw. CH60: Hes 4F 157
    WA10: Eccl 4B 44
Longmeadow Rd. L34: Know 4D 41
Longmoor Cl. L10: Faz 1E 37
Longmoor Gro. L9: Ain 2B 36
Longmoor La. L9: Ain 2B 36
    L10: Faz 2B 36
Long Moss L30: N'ton 3C 18
Longreach Rd. L14: K Ash 2F 81
Longridge Av. CH49: Upton 3E 93
    WA11: St. H 3D 47
Longridge Wlk. L4: Kirk 3E 55
Long Spinney WA7: Nort 2C 168
Longstone Wlk. L7: Liv 1B 100
Longton La. L35: R'hill 1A 86
LONGVIEW 1F 83
Long Vw. Av. L35: R'hill 2A 86
Longview Av. CH45: Wall 1A 74

Longview Cres. L36: Huy 3F 83
Longview Dr. L36: Huy 2F 83
Longview La. L36: Huy 1F 83
Long Vw. Rd. L35: R'hill 2A 86
Longview Rd. L36: Huy 2F 83
Longville St. L8: Liv 4F 99
Longwood Cl. WA11: R'ford 4B 28
Longworth Way L25: Wltn 1A 126
Lonie Gro. WA10: St. H 3C 64
Lonsborough Rd. CH44: Wall 3C 74
Lonsdale Av. CH45: Wall 5A 52
    WA10: St. H 4B 64
Lonsdale Cl. L21: Ford 3B 18
    WA8: Wid 3C 130
Lonsdale M. L21: Ford 3B 18
Lonsdale Rd. L21: Ford 3B 18
    L26: Halew 1E 147
Lonsdale Vs. CH45: Wall 5A 52
Looe Cl. WA8: Wid 2E 131
Looe Rd. L11: Crox 3D 39
Loomsway CH61: Irby 1D 137
Loraine St. L5: Liv 5F 55
Lordens Cl. L14: K Ash 1A 82
Lordens Rd. L14: K Ash 1A 82
Lord Nelson St. L1: Liv 4D 77 (4G 5)
    L3: Liv 4D 77 (4G 5)
Lords Av. CH43: Bid 1C 94
Lord St. CH41: Birk 2E 97
    L2: Liv 5C 76 (5D 4)
    L19: Gars 2C 144
    WA7: Run 4F 151
    WA10: St. H 3F 45
    (not continuous)
Loreburn Rd. L15: W'tree 3A 102
Lorenzo Dr. L11: N Grn. 2E 57
Loretto Dr. CH49: Upton 3A 94
Lorford St. CH44: Wall 1F 73
Lorn Ct. CH41: Birk 3E 97
Lorne Ct. CH43: O'ton 5B 96
Lorne Rd. CH43: O'ton 5A 96
    L22: Water 4D 17
Lorne St. L7: Liv 3E 79
Lorn St. CH41: Birk 3E 97
Lorton Av. WA11: St. H 4A 30
Lorton St. L8: Liv 2B 100
Lostock Cl. WN5: Bil 1E 31
Lothair Rd. L4: Walt 4A 56
Lothian St. L8: Liv 3A 100
Lotus Gdns. WA9: Bold 4A 68
Loudon Gro. L8: Liv 3A 100
Lough Grn. CH63: Spit 5A 142
Loughlin Dr. L33: K'by 5F 15
Loughrigg Av. WA11: St. H 4B 30
Louis Braille Cl. L30: N'ton 1F 19
Louis Pasteur Av. L30: N'ton 1F 19
Lovelace Rd. L19: Gras 5B 124
Love La. CH44: Wall 3A 74
    L3: Liv 2B 76 (1B 4)
Lovel Rd. L24: Speke 5D 147
Lovel Ter. WA8: Hale B 2B 150
Lovel Way L24: Speke 4D 147
Lovett Dr. L35: Prsct 1E 85
Lowden Av. L21: Lith 3B 18
Lowell St. L4: Walt 2F 55
Lwr. Appleton Rd. WA8: Wid 3B 132
Lwr. Bank Vw. L20: Kirk 2B 54
LOWER BEBINGTON 2A 142
Lwr. Breck Rd. L6: Liv 5B 56
Lwr. Castle St. L2: Liv 5C 76 (5C 4)
Lwr. Church St. WA8: Wid 2A 152
Lower Cl. L26: Halew 4A 128
Lwr. Farm Rd. L25: Gate 2F 103
Lwr. Flaybrick Rd. CH43: Bid 1E 95
Lwr. Gill St. L3: Liv 4E 77 (4J 5)
Lower Grn. CH49: W'chu 1A 116
Lower Hey L23: Thorn 5B 10
Lwr. House La. L11: N Grn. 4F 37
    WA8: Wid 5F 131
Lower La. L9: Faz 1E 37
Lwr. Mersey Vw. L20: Kirk 2B 54
Lwr. Milk St. L3: Liv 4C 76 (3D 4)
Lower Rd. CH62: Port S 1B 142
    L26: Halew 4B 128
    WA8: Hale B 4B 128
Lwr. Sandfield L25: Gate 5B 104

Lowerson Cres. L11: N Grn. 3E 57
Lowerson Rd. L11: N Grn. 3E 57
Lwr. Thingwall La.
  CH61: Thing 1C 138
Lowe St. WA10: St. H 4F 45
Lowe St. Sth. WA10: St. H 5F 45
Loweswater Cres. WA11: Hay 2A 48
Loweswater Way L33: K'by 1D 23
Lowfield La. WA9: St. H 1E 87
Lowfield La. WA9: St. H 5F 65
Lowfield Rd. L14: K Ash 3C 80
Lowfields Av. CH62: East 2D 171
Lowfields Cl. CH62: East 2E 171
Low Hill L6: Liv 3A 78
Lowlands Rd. WA7: Run 5F 151
Lowndes Rd. L6: Liv 5D 57
Lowry Bank CH44: Wall 3E 75
Lowry Cl. L33: K'by 4E 15
Lowther Av. L10: Ain 3D 21
  L31: Mag 5E 7
Lowther Cres. WA10: St. H 3B 64
Lowther Dr. L35: R'hill 3B 86
Lowther St. L8: Liv 2A 100
Low Wood Gro. CH61: Barn 3C 138
Lowwood Gro. CH41: Birk 4D 97
Lowwood Rd. CH41: Birk 4D 97
Low Wood St. L6: Liv 3A 78
Loxdale Cl. L8: Liv 5F 99
Loxwood Cl. L25: Gate 2B 104
Loyola Hey L35: R'hill 1E 109
Lucania St. L19: Gars 2C 144
Lucan Rd. L17: Aig 2D 123
Lucerne Rd. CH44: Wall 4D 75
Lucerne St. L17: Aig 1C 122
Lucius Cl. L9: Walt 1F 35
Lucknow St. L17: Aig 5C 100
Ludlow Ct. CH48: W Kir 5B 112
Ludlow Cres. WA7: Run 2B 166
Ludlow Dr. CH48: W Kir 5B 112
Ludlow Gro. CH62: Brom 1D 163
Ludlow St. L4: Walt 2E 55
Ludwig Rd. L4: Walt 5B 56
Lugard Rd. L17: Aig 2E 123
LUGSDALE 5C 132
Lugsdale Rd. WA8: Wid 5B 132
Lugsmore La. WA10: St. H 2C 64
Luke St. CH44: Wall 4E 75
  L8: Liv .3F 99
Lulworth Av. L22: Water 3C 16
Lulworth Rd. L25: Gate 4C 104
Lumber La. WA5: B'wood 3E 69
Lumina CH62: Brom 5E 143
Lumley Rd. CH44: Wall 3D 75
Lumley St. L19: Gars 5B 124
Lumley Wlk. L24: Hale 5E 149
Lunar Dr. L30: N'ton 5F 11
Lunar Rd. L9: Ain 2B 36
Lune Av. L31: Mag 5E 7
Lunesdale Av. L9: Ain 1B 36
Lune St. L23: C'by 1E 17
Luneway WA8: Wid 3C 130
Lunsford Rd. L14: K Ash 2F 81
LUNT 2D 11
Lunt Av. L30: N'ton 3A 20
  L35: Whis 3E 85
Lunt La. L29: Seft 2D 11
Lunt Rd. L20: Boot 2C 34
  L29: Seft, Thorn 1C 10
LUNTS HEATH 5B 110
Lunt's Heath Rd. WA8: Wid 4A 110
Lupin Dr. WA11: Hay 2F 49
Lupton Dr. L23: C'by 1A 18
Luscombe Cl. L26: Halew 4A 128
Lusitania Rd. L4: Walt 1A 56
Luther Gro. WA9: St. H 1B 68
Luton Gro. L4: Walt 4B 56
Luton St. L5: Kirk 5B 54
  WA8: Wid 5A 132
Lutyens Cl. L4: Walt 3F 55
Luxmore Rd. L4: Walt 2A 56
Lycett Rd. CH44: Wall 1E 73
  L4: Walt 4B 56
Lyceum Pl. L1: Liv 6F 5
Lyceum Rd. L1: Liv 6F 5
Lycroft Cl. WA7: Run 4B 166

Lydbrook Cl. CH42: R Ferr 1F 119
Lydbury Cres. L32: K'by 5F 23
Lydford Rd. L12: W Der 3B 58
Lydia Ann St. L1: Liv 1D 99 (7E 5)
LYDIATE 2B 6
Lydiate, The CH60: Hes 3F 157
Lydiate La. L23: Thorn 4B 10
  L25: Wltn 2C 126
  L26: Halew 2C 126
  L29: Seft 4B 10
  WA7: West P 3D 165
Lydiate Pk. L23: Thorn 4B 10
Lydiate Rd. L20: Boot 3C 34
Lydia Wlk. L10: Faz 1B 38
Lydieth Lea L27: N'ley 3E 105
Lydney Rd. L36: Huy 2B 82
Lyelake Cl. L32: K'by 4F 23
Lyelake La. L32: K'by 4F 23
Lyle St. L5: Liv 1C 76
Lyme Cl. L36: Huy 5E 61
Lyme Cross Rd. L36: Huy 5E 61
Lyme Gro. L36: Huy 1F 83
Lyme St. WA11: Hay 2E 49
  WA12: New W 4E 49
Lyme Tree Ct. WA8: Cron 3C 108
Lymewood Cl. WA11: Hay 1D 49
Lymington Gro. L30: N'ton 2F 19
Lymington Rd. CH44: Wall 2F 73
Lymm Rd. CH43: Bid 2C 94
Lynas Gdns. L19: Gras 4B 124
Lynas St. CH41: Birk 1D 97
Lyncot Rd. L9: Ain 5B 20
Lyncroft Rd. CH44: Wall 4C 74
Lyndale WA7: Run 2C 166
Lyndale Av. CH62: East 1F 163
Lyndene Rd. L25: Gate 3A 104
Lyndhurst CH48: W Kir 3A 112
  L31: Mag 1D 13
Lyndhurst Av. CH61: Pens 4A 138
  L18: Moss H 1F 123
Lyndhurst Cl. CH61: Thing 2A 138
Lyndhurst Rd. CH45: Wall 5F 51
  CH47: Meols 2F 91
  CH61: Irby 2A 138
  L18: Moss H 5F 101
  L23: C'by 1A 18
Lyndhurst Way L36: Huy 4E 83
Lyndon Dr. L18: Moss H 5B 102
Lyndon Gro. WA7: Run 2B 166
Lyndor Cl. L25: Wltn 3B 126
Lyndor Rd. L25: Wltn 3B 126
Lyneham L35: Whis 4F 85
Lynholme Rd. L4: Walt 4B 56
Lynmouth Rd. L17: Aig 4E 123
Lynnbank CH43: O'ton 5B 96
Lynnbank Rd. L18: Moss H 4D 103
Lynn Cl. WA7: Run 3C 166
  WA10: St. H 4C 44
Lynscot Pl. L16: Child 1D 103
Lynsted Rd. L14: K Ash 3F 81
Lynton Cl. CH60: Hes 4B 158
  L19: Aller 4B 124
Lynton Ct. L23: Blun 1B 16
Lynton Cres. WA8: Wid 2E 131
Lynton Dr. CH63: Beb 4A 142
Lynton Grn. L25: Wltn 5F 103
Lynton Gro. WA9: Sut L 1C 88
Lynton Rd. CH45: Wall 5E 51
  L36: Huy 3B 84
Lynton Way WA10: Windle 2B 44
Lynwood Av. CH44: Wall 3A 74
Lynwood Dr. CH61: Irby 1E 137
Lynwood Gdns. L9: Walt 3F 35
Lynwood Rd. L9: Walt 3F 35
Lynxway, The L12: W Der 2D 81
Lyon Cl. WA10: St. H 5F 45
Lyon Rd. L4: Walt 5B 56
Lyons Cl. CH46: More 5E 71
Lyons Pl. L25: Hunts X 4D 127
Lyons Rd. CH46: More 5E 71
Lyon St. L19: Gars 3C 144
  WA10: St. H 5E 45
Lyra Rd. L22: Water 4D 17
Lyster Rd. L20: Boot 5A 34

M

Mab La. L12: W Der 3F 59
MacAlpine Cl. CH49: Upton 3A 94
Macbeth St. L20: Kirk 2C 54
McBride St. L19: Gars 1C 144
McClellan Pl. WA8: Wid 3B 132
McCormack Av. WA9: St. H 4E 47
McCulloch St. WA9: St. H 5C 46
Macdermott Rd. WA8: Wid 2F 151
MacDona Dr. CH48: W Kir 1B 134
Macdonald Av. WA11: St. H 3E 47
Macdonald Dr. CH49: Grea 1D 115
Macdonald Rd. CH46: More 1C 92
MacDonald St. L15: W'tree 1E 101
Mace Rd. L11: Crox 5C 38
McFarlane Av. WA10: St. H 4C 44
Macfarren St. L13: Liv 3A 80
McGough Cl. WA9: Sut M 3A 88
McGregor St. L5: Liv 1E 77
MacKenzie Rd. CH46: Leas 3B 72
McKeown Cl. L5: Liv 1D 77
Mackets Cl. L25: Wltn 3C 126
Macket's La. L25: Wltn 2C 126
Mack Gro. L30: N'ton 3D 19
McKinley Way WA8: Wid 1F 131
McMinnis Av. WA9: St. H 1A 68
McNair Hall L18: Moss H 1F 123
MacQueen St. L13: Liv 4A 80
McVinnie Rd. L35: Prsct 5F 63
Maddock Rd. CH44: Wall 1D 75
Maddocks St. L13: Liv 4A 80
Maddock St. CH41: Birk 1C 96
Maddrell St. L3: Liv 2B 76
Madeira Dr. L25: Gate 3B 104
Madelaine St. L8: Liv 3A 100
Madeleine McKenna Ct.
  WA8: Wid 1B 130
Madeley Cl. CH48: W Kir 5B 112
Madeley Dr. CH48: W Kir 5B 112
Madeley St. L6: Liv 2C 78
Madison Sq. L1: Liv 1D 99
Madryn Av. L33: K'by 3A 24
Madryn St. L8: Liv 4A 100
Maelor Cl. CH63: Brom 4C 162
Mafeking Cl. L15: W'tree 1F 101
Magazine Av. CH45: New B 4B 52
Magazine Brow CH45: New B 4C 52
Magazine La. CH45: New B 4B 52
  CH62: Brom 3E 143
Magazine Rd. CH62: Brom 4D 143
Magazines Prom.
  CH45: New B 3C 52
Magazine Wlk. CH62: Brom 4D 143
Magdala St. L8: Liv 2B 100
Magdalen Ho. L20: Boot 1C 54
Magdalen Sq. L30: N'ton 1F 19
MAGHULL .5C 6
Maghull La. L31: Mag 1B 14
Maghull Smallholdings Est.
  L31: Mag 4F 7
Maghull Station (Rail) 3E 13
Magnolia Cl. L26: Halew 2D 127
  WA11: Hay 3F 47
Magnolia Dr. WA7: Beech 1F 173
Magnolia Wlk. CH49: Grea 2C 114
Magnum Cl. L5: Liv 1F 77
Magnus Cl. L13: Liv 1F 79
Maguire Av. L20: Boot 4E 35
Mahon Av. L20: Boot 2D 35
Mahon Ct. L8: Liv 2F 99
Maiden La. L13: Liv 4D 57
Maidford Rd. L14: K Ash 1E 81
Maidstone Cl. L25: Hunts X 4C 126
Maidstone Dr. L12: W Der 1F 81

Main Av. WA10: St. H 3C 64
Main Cl. WA11: Hay 2A 48
Main Dr. L35: Whis 5D 85
Main Front L35: Whis 5E 85
Main Rd. CH62: Port S 3B 142
Mainside Rd. L32: K'by 4F 23
Main St. WA6: Frod 5A 172
   WA7: Halt 1F 167
   WN5: Bil 1D 31
Maintree Cres. L24: Speke 3A 148
Mainwaring Rd. CH44: Wall 3D 75
   CH62: Brom 2D 163
Maitland Cl. L8: Liv 2B 100
Maitland Rd. CH45: New B 3C 52
Maitland St. L8: Liv 2B 100
Major Cross St. WA8: Wid 5A 132
Major St. L5: Kirk 5D 55
Makin St. L4: Walt 1F 55
Malahide Ct. WA8: Wid 1D 131
Malcolm Cres. CH63: Brom 4C 162
Malcolm Gro. L20: Kirk 2D 55
Malcolm Pl. L15: W'tree 5F 79
Malcolm St. WA7: Run 5B 152
Malden Rd. L6: Liv 3B 78
Maldon Cl. L26: Halew 1F 147
Maldwyn Rd. CH44: Wall 1B 74
Maley Cl. L8: Liv 5A 100
Malhamdale Av. L35: R'hill 4D 87
Malin Cl. L24: Hale 5D 149
Mall, The L17: Aig 1A 78
Mallaby St. CH41: Birk 1A 96
Mallard Cl. L12: Crox 5F 39
   L26: Halew 3E 127
   WA7: Beech 5F 167
Mallard Gdns. WA9: St. H 5E 65
Mallard Ho. L31: Lyd 3B 6
Mallard Way CH46: More 5C 70
   WA11: St. H 2B 46
Malleson Rd. L13: Liv 4E 57
Mallins Cl. L8: Liv 5A 100
Mallory Av. L31: Lyd 3B 6
Mallory Gro. WA11: St. H 2D 47
Mallory Rd. CH42: Tran 2C 118
Mallowdale Cl. CH62: East 5E 163
Mallow Rd. L6: Liv 3C 78
Mallow Way L36: Huy 1F 105
Malmesbury Cl. CH49: Grea 5C 92
Malmesbury Pk. WA7: Nort 5D 155
Malmesbury Rd. L11: N Grn. 2D 57
Malpas Av. CH43: Pren 2A 118
Malpas Dr. CH63: High B 5E 119
Malpas Gro. CH45: Wall 5A 52
Malpas Rd. CH45: Wall 5F 51
   L11: Crox 3D 39
   WA7: Run 3B 166
Malta Cl. L36: Huy 3D 83
Malta St. L8: Liv 4F 99
Malta Wlk. L8: Liv 4F 99
Malt Ho. Ct. WA10: Windle 2C 44
Malton Cl. WA8: Cron 4C 108
Malton Rd. L25: Wltn 3B 126
Malt St. L7: Liv 1B 100
Malvern Av. L14: B Grn 4F 81
Malvern Cl. L32: K'by 1C 22
Malvern Cres. L14: B Grn 4F 81
Malvern Gro. CH42: Tran 2D 119
   L10: Ain 3C 20
Malvern Rd. CH45: Wall 1D 73
   L6: Liv 3C 78
   L20: Boot 3C 34
   WA9: St. H 5F 47
Malwood St. L8: Liv 5F 99
Manchester Rd. L34: Prsct 5C 62
Mandela Ct. L8: Liv 4B 100
Manderston Dr. L12: W Der 4D 59
Mandeville St. L4: Walt 1F 55
Manesty's La. L1: Liv 5D 77 (6E 4)
Manfred St. L6: Liv 4F 77
Manica Cres. L10: Faz 1F 37
Manion Av. L31: Lyd 2B 6
Manion Cl. L31: Lyd 2B 6
Manley Cl. CH43: O'ton 1F 117
Manley Pl. WA9: St. H 4E 65
Manley Rd. L22: Water 3C 16
   L36: Huy 1A 106

Mannering Ct. L17: Aig 5C 100
Mannering Rd. L17: Aig 5B 100
Manners La. CH60: Hes 4E 157
Manningham Rd. L4: Walt 5B 56
Manning St. WA10: St. H 5F 45
Mannington Cl. CH47: Meols 3E 91
Mann Island L3: Liv 5B 76 (6B 4)
Mann St. L8: Liv 3D 99
Manor Av. L23: C'by 5D 9
   L35: R'hill 4C 86
   WA12: New W 4F 49
Manorbier Cres. L9: Walt 5A 36
Manor Cl. L20: Boot 1E 55
Manor Complex L33: Know I 3B 24
Manor Ct. CH49: Grea 1C 114
   CH61: Irby 2D 137
   WA9: Sut L 2D 89
Manor Cres. L25: Wltn 3B 126
Manor Dr. CH49: Upton 2F 93
   L23: C'by 5D 9
   L30: N'ton 2B 20
Manor Farm Ct. WA6: Frod 4C 172
Mnr. Farm M. WA7: Mnr P 3D 155
Mnr. Farm Rd. L36: Huy 5F 83
   WA7: Mnr P 3D 155
Manor Fell WA7: Pal F 3B 168
MANOR GREEN 2C 94
Manor Gro. L32: K'by 3B 22
Manor Hill CH43: C'ton, O'ton 3A 96
Manor Ho. L17: Aig 1B 122
Manor Ho., The CH49: Upton 2F 93
Manor Ho. Cl. L31: Mag 1C 12
   WA11: St. H 4A 30
Manor Ho. Flats CH62: Brom 1D 163
Manor La. CH42: R Ferr 2A 120
   CH45: Wall 1C 74
Manor M. CH45: Wall 1C 74
MANOR PARK 3C 154
Manor Pk. Av. WA7: Mnr P 3C 154
Manor Park Bus. Pk.
   WA7: Mnr P 3B 154
Manor Pk. Cl. CH61: Thing 1A 138
Manor Pk. Dr. WA7: Mnr P 3C 154
Manor Pl. CH62: Brom 2D 143
   WA8: Wid 3B 130
Manor Rd. CH44: Wall 1B 74
   CH45: Wall 1B 74
   CH47: Hoy 3C 90
   CH61: Irby 1D 137
   CH62: East 4D 163
   CH63: Thorn H 1F 159
   L23: Blun, C'by 4C 8
   L25: Wltn 3B 126
   WA6: Frod 4C 172
   WA7: Run 5D 153
   WA8: Wid 3B 130
   WA11: Hay 1F 49
Manor Road Station (Rail) 4C 90
Manorside Cl. CH49: Upton 3F 93
Manor St. WA9: St. H 1C 66
Manor Vw. L12: W Der 2F 59
Manor Way CH43: Bid 2C 94
   L25: Wltn 3B 126
Manorwood Dr. L35: Whis 4E 85
Mansell Cl. WA8: Wid 4B 110
Mansell Dr. L26: Halew 1E 147
Mansell Rd. L6: Liv 3B 78
Mansfield St. L3: Liv 3E 77 (2G 5)
Mansion Dr. L11: Crox 4B 38
Mansion House 5D 103
Manton Rd. L6: Liv 3C 78
Manvers Rd. L16: Child 1E 103
Manville Rd. CH45: New B 4B 52
Manville St. WA9: St. H 2C 66
Maori Dr. WA6: Frod 5A 172
Maple Av. WA7: Run 2C 166
   WA7: Sut W 1A 174
   WA8: Wid 3B 132
   WA11: Hay 1B 48
Maple Cl. L12: Crox 5D 39
   L21: Sea 2A 34
   L35: Whis 5C 84
Maple Ct. L34: Know 4D 41
Maple Cres. L36: Roby 4D 83
Mapledale Rd. L18: Moss H 4A 102

Maple Gro. CH62: Brom 2C 162
   L8: Liv 3C 100
   L35: Prsct 1E 85
   WA10: St. H 5C 44
Maples Ct. CH43: O'ton 1A 118
Maple St. CH41: Birk 4D 97
Mapleton Cl. CH43: Pren 3E 117
Mapleton Dr. WA7: Sut W 2F 173
Maple Tree Gro.
   CH60: Hes 1C 158
Maplewood L32: K'by 5F 23
Maplewood Cl. L27: N'ley 4E 105
   WA8: Wid 5A 130
Maplewood Gro. CH43: Bid 1E 95
Marathon Cl. L6: Liv 2F 77
Marble Cl. L20: Boot 1C 54
Marbury Rd. L32: K'by 3C 22
Marc Av. L31: Mell 1B 22
Marcham Way L11: N Grn. 2B 58
Marchfield Rd. L9: Walt 3F 35
March Rd. L6: Liv 1D 79
Marchwood Way L25: Gate 2A 104
Marcien Way WA8: Wid 1F 131
Marcot Rd. L6: Liv 2D 79
Marcus Ct. L36: Huy 2A 84
Marcus St. CH41: Birk 2D 97
Mardale Av. WA11: St. H 5B 30
Mardale Cl. L27: N'ley 5A 106
Mardale Lawn L27: N'ley 1A 128
Mardale Rd. L36: Huy 1C 82
Mardale Wlk. L27: N'ley 5A 106
   L36: Huy 1C 82
Mareth Cl. L18: Moss H 2A 124
Marford Rd. L12: W Der 4B 58
Marfords Av. CH63: Brom 3C 162
Margaret Av. L20: Boot 2C 34
   WA9: St. H 4C 66
Margaret Ct. WA8: Wid 5B 132
   WA10: St. H 2D 65
Margaret Rd. L4: Walt 1E 55
   L23: Blun 5A 8
Margaret St. L6: Liv 2A 78
   WA9: Clock F 3E 89
Margery Rd. WA10: St. H 2C 64
Marian Av. WA12: New W 5F 49
Marian Cl. L35: R'hill 4C 86
Marian Cl., The L30: N'ton 1E 19
Marian Dr. CH46: More 1E 93
   L35: R'hill 4B 86
Marian Rd. WA11: Hay 1E 49
Marian Sq. L30: N'ton 2F 19
Marian Way, The L30: N'ton 1E 19
Maria Rd. L9: Walt 5F 35
Marie Curie Av. L30: N'ton 1F 19
   (not continuous)
Marigold Way WA9: Bold 4A 68
Marina Av. L21: Lith 1B 34
   WA9: St. H 4C 66
Marina Cres. L30: N'ton 4A 20
   L36: Huy 5D 83
Marina Gro. WA7: Run 5B 152
Marina La. WA7: Murd 3E 169
   (not continuous)
Marina Village WA7: Pres B 3E 169
Marine Cres. L22: Water 4D 17
Marine Dr. CH60: Hes 3D 157
Marine Pk. CH48: W Kir 2B 112
Marine Pk. Mans.
   CH45: New B 2B 52
Marine Prom. CH45: New B 2B 52
Mariner Cl. WA7: Murd 4D 169
Marine Rd. CH47: Hoy 4A 90
Mariners Pde. L1: Liv 5C 76 (6D 4)
    (off Cunard Av.)
Mariners Pk. CH44: Wall 1D 75
    (off Cunard Av.)
Mariners Rd. CH45: New B 4C 52
   L23: Blun 3B 16
Mariners Way L20: Boot 4C 34
Mariners Wharf L3: Liv 3C 98
Marine Ter. CH45: Wall 4C 52
   L22: Water 5D 17
Marion Dr. WA7: West 4F 165
Marion Gro. L18: Moss H 2B 124
Marion Rd. L20: Boot 2D 35
Marion St. CH41: Birk 3E 97

Maritime Ct. CH49: W'chu 3B 116
 L12: W Der 3A 58
 L30: N'ton 5F 11
Maritime Enterprise Pk.
 L20: Boot 4B 34
Maritime Grange CH44: Wall 4E 75
Maritime Gro. CH43: O'ton 4B 96
Maritime Lodge L5: Liv 5F 55
  (off Towson St.)
Maritime Pk. CH43: O'ton 4C 96
Maritime Pl. L3: Liv 3E 77 (2H 5)
Maritime Vw. CH42: Tran 1D 119
Maritime Way L1: Liv 1D 99 (7E 4)
Marius Cl. L4: Walt 3F 55
Market Hall WA7: Run 4A 152
  (off Alcock St.)
Market Pl. L34: Prsct 5D 63
 WA8: Wid 5A 132
Market Pl. Sth. CH41: Birk 3E 97
Market Sq. L1: Liv 5F 5
 L32: K'by 3E 23
Market St. CH41: Birk 3E 97
 CH47: Hoy 5B 90
 WA8: Wid 5A 132
 WA10: St. H 5A 46
 WA12: New W 4F 49
Market Way L1: Liv 5F 5
Markfield Cres. L25: Wltn 3C 126
 WA11: St. H 3C 46
Markfield Rd. L20: Boot 3B 34
Markham Gro. CH43: Bid 1F 95
Mark Rake CH62: Brom 1D 163
Mark St. CH44: Wall 4E 75
 L5: Liv 4E 55
Marksway CH61: Pens 3A 138
Marlborough Av. L30: N'ton 3A 20
 L31: Lyd 4D 7
Marlborough Ct. L17: Aig 2D 123
Marlborough Cres. WA8: Wid 4A 110
Marlborough Gro. CH43: O'ton . . .5B 96
Marlborough Pl. L3: Liv . . .3C 76 (2D 4)
Marlborough Rd. CH45: New B . . .4B 52
 L13: Liv 5D 57
 L22: Water 5E 17
 L23: C'by 2D 17
 L34: Prsct 4E 63
Marlborough St. L3: Liv . . .3C 76 (2D 4)
Marlbrook Rd. L25: Gate 3B 104
Marlcroft Dr. L17: Aig 4E 123
 L19: Aig 4E 123
Marldon Av. L23: C'by 3E 17
Marldon Rd. L12: W Der 3A 58
Marled Hey L28: Stock V 3A 60
Marley Cl. L35: R'hill 5E 87
Marlfield La. CH61: Pens 3A 138
Marlfield Rd. L12: W Der 5B 58
Marline Av. CH63: Brom 3C 162
Marling Pk. WA8: Wid 3B 130
Marlowe Cl. L19: Gars 2C 144
 WA8: Wid 3F 131
Marlowe Dr. L12: W Der 5F 57
Marlowe Rd. CH44: Wall 2A 74
 L33: Know I 2C 24
Marl Rd. L30: N'ton 2B 20
 L33: Know I 2C 24
Marlsford St. L6: Liv 3C 78
Marlston Av. CH61: Irby 2F 137
Marlwood Av. CH45: Wall 1E 73
Marmaduke St. L7: Liv 5B 78
Marmion Av. L20: Boot 1E 35
Marmion Rd. CH47: Hoy 4B 90
 L17: Aig 5B 100
Marmonde St. L4: Kirk 3E 55
Marnwood Rd. L32: K'by 4C 22
Marnwood Wlk. L32: K'by 4C 22
Marple Cl. CH43: O'ton 1E 117
Marquis Ho. CH62: New F 4B 120
Marquis St. CH41: Tran 5E 97
 CH62: New F 4B 120
 L3: Liv 4E 77 (4H 5)
Marram Ct. CH46: More 5A 72
Marsden Av. WA10: St. H 4C 44
Marsden Cl. CH44: Wall 1D 75
Marsden Ct. WA8: Wid 5E 109
Marsden St. L26: Halew 1F 147

Marsden St. L6: Liv 3A 78
Marsden Way L6: Liv 3A 78
MARSH, THE 2E 151
Marshall Av. WA9: St. H 3C 66
Marshall Cl. L33: K'by 5F 15
Marshall Pl. L3: Liv 2C 76 (1D 4)
Marshall's Cl. L31: Lyd 3C 6
MARSHALL'S CROSS 5A 66
Marshall's Cross Rd. WA9: St. H . .5B 66
Marshall St. CH41: Birk 1C 96
Marsham Cl. CH49: Upton 3A 94
Marsham Rd. L25: Gate 4C 104
Marsh Av. L20: Boot 2E 35
Marshfield Cl. L36: Huy 3F 83
Marshfield Ct. CH46: Leas 3E 71
Marshfield Rd. L11: N Grn. 2B 58
Marshgate WA8: Wid 5B 130
Marshgate Pl. WA6: Frod 3C 172
Marshgate Rd. L12: W Der 1B 58
MARSH GREEN 5A 172
Marsh Hall Pad WA8: Wid 5B 110
Marsh Hall Rd. WA8: Wid 5B 110
Marshlands Rd. CH45: Wall 5E 51
Marsh La. CH63: High B 5C 118
 L20: Boot 4A 34
 WA6: Frod 5A 172
 WA7: Ast 4F 153
Marshside Cl. L8: Liv 4F 99
Marsh St. L20: Kirk 2D 55
 WA8: Wid 1A 152
 WA9: St. H 4C 46
Marsland Gro. WA9: St. H 3E 67
Marston Cl. CH43: O'ton 1F 117
 CH62: East 2E 171
Marston Cres. L38: High 1A 8
Marten Av. CH63: Brom 3C 162
Martensen St. L7: Liv 5B 78
Martin Av. WA10: St. H 2F 45
Martin Cl. CH61: Irby 1C 136
 L18: Moss H 3A 124
 L35: R'hill 2A 86
 WA7: Pal F 3A 168
Martindale Gro. WA7: Beech 5E 167
Martindale Rd. CH62: Brom 1E 163
 L18: Moss H 4D 103
 WA11: St. H 3B 30
Martine Cl. L31: Mell 1B 22
Martin Gro. L35: Prsct 1E 85
Martinhall Rd. L9: Faz 4F 37
Martin Rd. L18: Moss H 3A 124
 WA6: Frod 5B 172
Martin's La. CH44: Wall 2C 74
Martland Av. L10: Ain 2E 21
Martland Rd. L25: Gate 5C 104
Martlesham Cres. CH49: Grea . . .1B 114
Martlett Rd. L12: W Der 1D 81
Martock L35: Whis 4F 85
Marton Cl. L24: Speke 5D 147
Marton Grn. L24: Speke 5D 147
Marton Rd. L36: Huy 5E 61
Marvin St. L6: Liv 3A 78
Marwood Towers L5: Liv 5D 55
Maryborne L3: Liv 3C 76 (3D 4)
Maryhill Rd. WA7: Run 2A 166
Maryland Ho. L20: Boot 5C 34
  (off Georgia Cl.)
Maryland La. CH46: More 5E 71
Maryland St. L1: Liv 1E 99 (7H 5)
  (not continuous)
Marylebone Av. WA9: St. H 5F 65
Mary Rd. L20: Boot 2D 35
Mary St. WA8: Wid 5D 133
 WA9: Clock F 3E 89
Maryton Grange L18: Aller 2D 125
Maryville Rd. L34: Prsct 5E 63
Marywell Cl. WA9: St. H 4D 67
Marzhan Way WA8: Wid 3C 132
Masefield Av. WA8: Wid 4F 131
Masefield Cl. CH62: New F 5A 120
Masefield Cres. L30: Boot 5D 19
Masefield Gro. L16: Child 1E 103
 WA10: St. H 3D 45
Masefield Pl. L30: Boot 5D 19
Masefield Rd. L23: Thorn 4C 10
Maskell Rd. L13: Liv 3F 79

Mason Av. WA8: Wid 5A 110
Mason St. CH45: New B 3B 52
 L7: Liv 5A 78
 L22: Water 4D 17
 L25: Wltn 2A 126
 WA7: Run 4C 152
Masseyfield Rd. WA7: Brook 5A 168
Massey Pk. CH45: Wall 1A 74
Massey St. CH41: Birk 1D 97
 WA9: St. H 3C 66
Master's Way L19: Gars 3D 145
Matchwood Cl. L19: Gars 2D 145
Matchworks, The L19: Gars 2E 145
Mather Av. L18: Moss H 5B 102
 L19: Aller 3C 124
 WA7: West P 3D 165
 WA9: St. H 5E 47
Mather Ct. CH43: O'ton 4B 96
Mather Rd. CH43: O'ton 4B 96
Mathew St. L2: Liv 5C 76 (5D 4)
Mathieson Rd. WA8: Wid 2E 151
Matlock Av. L9: Walt 2A 36
Matterdale Cl. WA6: Frod 5D 173
Matthew Cl. CH44: Wall 4E 75
Matthew St. CH44: Wall 4E 75
Maud Roberts Ct. L21: Lith 5A 18
Maud St. L8: Liv 3F 99
Maunders Ct. L23: C'by 5A 10
Maureen Wlk. L10: Faz 1B 38
Mauretania Rd. L4: Walt 1A 56
Maurice Jones Ct. CH46: More . . .5E 71
Mavis Dr. CH49: W'chu 1A 116
Max Rd. L14: K Ash 1F 81
Maxton Rd. L6: Liv 3C 78
Maxwell Cl. CH49: Upton 3A 94
Maxwell Pl. L13: Liv 5F 57
Maxwell Rd. L13: Liv 5F 57
Maxwell St. WA10: St. H 5E 45
May Av. CH44: Wall 3D 75
Maybank Gro. L17: Aig 3F 123
Maybank Rd. CH42: Tran 5D 97
Maybury Way L17: Aig 2C 122
May Cl. L21: Lith 2B 34
Mayer Av. CH63: Beb 3F 141
Mayew Rd. CH61: Irby 1F 137
Mayfair Av. L14: B Grn 3F 81
 L23: C'by 5E 9
Mayfair Cl. L6: Liv 2B 78
 L38: High 1A 8
Mayfair Gro. WA8: Wid 3D 131
Mayfayre Av. L31: Lyd 2C 6
Mayfield Av. WA8: Wid 3B 130
 WA9: St. H 3E 65
Mayfield Cl. L12: W Der 5C 58
Mayfield Ct. WA8: Wid 2A 132
Mayfield Gdns. L19: Gras 5F 123
Mayfield Rd. CH45: Wall 1F 73
 CH63: Beb 4A 142
 L19: Gras 5A 124
Mayfields Ho. CH62: New F 5B 120
Mayfields Nth. CH62: New F 5B 120
Mayfields Sth. CH62: New F 5B 120
Mayflower Av. L24: Speke 1A 146
Mayflower Rd. L24: Speke 1A 146
Mayford Cl. L25: Gate 3B 104
May Pl. L3: Liv 5E 77 (6H 5)
 L13: Liv 4A 80
Maypole Ct. L30: N'ton 5D 11
 L34: Know 3C 40
Mayport Cl. L5: Liv 5F 55
Mayroyd Rd. CH60: Hes 2A 158
May St. L3: Liv 5E 77 (6H 5)
 L20: Boot 3C 34
Maytree Cl. L27: N'ley 3C 104
Mayville Rd. L18: Moss H 4A 102
Mazenod Ct. L3: Liv 3C 76 (2E 4)
Mazzini Cl. L5: Liv 1E 77
Mead Av. L21: Lith 5C 18
Meade Cl. L35: R'hill 5D 87
Meade Rd. L13: Liv 5E 57
Meadfoot Rd. CH46: More 5D 71
Meadow, The CH49: W'chu 2B 116
  (not continuous)
Meadow Av. WA9: Clock F 3D 89

Meadow Bank L31: K'by 1B 22
L31: Mag 5B 6
Meadowbank Cl. L12: W Der 1E 81
Meadowbarn Cl. L32: K'by 4E 23
Mdw. Brook Cl. L12: Faz 1B 38
Meadowbrook Rd. CH46: More 2D 93
Meadow Cl. WA8: Wid 1D 131
WA12: New W 5F 49
Meadow Ct. L11: N Grn. 5B 38
L25: Wltn 1B 126
Meadow Cres. CH49: W'chu 2B 116
Meadowcroft CH60: Hes 1C 158
WA7: Cas 2A 168
WA9: St. H 5C 66
Meadowcroft Pk. L12: W Der 2D 81
Meadowcroft Rd. CH47: Meols 2E 91
Meadow Dr. L36: Huy 1F 105
Meadowfield Cl. CH42: R Ferr 2F 119
L9: Walt 1A 36
Meadowgate CH48: Caldy 4D 135
Meadow Hey L20: Boot 3A 34
Mdw. Hey Cl. L25: Wltn 1B 126
Meadow La. CH42: R Ferr 2F 119
L12: W Der 2B 58
L31: Mag 1E 13
WA9: St. H 1F 67
Mdw. Oak Dr. L25: Gate 4A 104
Meadow Pk. CH42: R Ferr 2F 119
Meadow Cl. CH48: W Kir 3F 113
Meadow Row WA7: Cas 1A 168
Meadows, The L31: Mag 1D 13
L35: R'hill 3C 86
Meadowside CH46: Leas 2B 72
WA6: Frod 5A 172
Meadowside Dr. L33: K'by 5F 15
Meadowside Rd. CH62: Brom 3D 163
Meadow St. CH45: New B 3A 52
Meadow Vw. L21: Ford 2B 18
Meadow Wlk. CH61: Pens 4E 137
WA7: Pal F 3F 167
(off Halton Lea Shop. Cen.)
Meadow Way L12: W Der 2B 58
Meads, The L34: Ecc P 4A 64
Meadway CH45: Wall 1A 74
CH49: Upton 3B 94
CH60: Hes 4F 157
CH62: Spit 5C 142
L15: W'tree 1C 102
L30: N'ton 3F 19
L31: Mag 3B 12
L35: Whis 2F 85
WA7: Run 1E 167
WA8: Wid 3A 130
Meander, The L12: W Der 2E 59
Measham Cl. WA11: St. H 3C 46
Measham Way L12: Crox 4E 39
Mecca Bingo
Birkenhead 3D 97
Knotty Ash 2E 81
Liverpool 4F 99
Netherton 2A 20
Norris Green 2E 57
St Helens 4F 45
Medbourne Cres. L32: K'by 5F 23
Meddowcroft Rd. CH45: Wall 5F 51
Medea Cl. L5: Liv 5E 55
Medlock St. L4: Kirk 3E 55
(not continuous)
Medway L20: Boot 5C 34
Medway Rd. CH42: R Ferr 2F 119
Megabowl
Netherton 2F 19
Melbourne Cl. L24: Speke 3B 146
Melbourne St. CH45: New B 3A 52
WA9: St. H 4E 65
Melbreck Rd. L18: Aller 3B 124
Melbury Rd. L14: K Ash 5B 60
Melda Cl. L6: Liv 3F 77
Meldon Cl. L12: W Der 1C 58
Meldrum Rd. L15: W'tree 3B 102
Melford Dr. CH43: Pren 3E 117
WA7: Run 1C 166
Melford Gro. L6: Liv 5C 56
Meliden Gdns. WA9: St. H 4F 67
Melksham Dr. CH61: Irby 5D 115

MELLING 5F 13
Melling Av. L9: Ain 1B 36
Melling Dr. L32: K'by 2E 23
Melling La. L31: Mag 3E 13
MELLING MOUNT 3C 14
Melling Rd. CH45: New B 4C 52
L9: Ain 5B 20
L20: Boot 3C 34
Melling Way L32: K'by 2E 23
Melloncroft Dr. CH48: Caldy 1C 134
Melloncroft Dr. W. CH48: Caldy 2C 134
Mellor Cl. L35: Tar G 2A 106
WA7: Wind H 2D 169
Mellor Rd. CH42: Tran 2C 118
Melly Rd. L17: Aig 1B 122
Melrose CH46: More 1A 94
Melrose Av. CH47: Hoy 4B 90
L23: C'by 2E 17
WA5: B'wood 4F 69
WA10: Eccl 3B 44
Melrose Gdns. CH43: Pren 3F 117
Melrose Pk. L22: Water 5E 17
(off Melrose Rd.)
Melrose Rd. L4: Kirk 3D 55
L22: Water 5E 17
L33: K'by 4D 15
Melton Cl. CH49: Upton 4E 93
Melton Rd. WA7: Run 3B 166
Melverley Rd. L32: K'by 3B 22
Melville Av. CH42: R Ferr 3A 120
Melville Cl. WA8: Wid 3D 133
(not continuous)
WA10: St. H 4D 45
Melville Gro. L8: Liv 2A 100
Melville Pl. L7: Liv 1A 100
Melville Rd. CH63: High B 2E 141
L20: Boot 1C 34
Melville St. L8: Liv 4F 99
Melwood Dr. L12: W Der 4C 58
Melwood (Liverpool FC Training Ground)
. . . . .4C 58
Menai M. L34: Prsct 5E 63
Menai Av. L20: Boot 2D 35
Menai St. CH41: Birk 3C 96
Mendell Cl. CH62: Brom 2E 163
Mendip Cl. CH42: Tran 3C 118
L26: Halew 5E 127
Mendip Gro. WA9: St. H 5F 47
Mendip Rd. CH42: Tran 3C 118
L15: W'tree 3A 102
Mendips
(Childhood home of John Lennon)
. . . . .1E 125
Menlo Av. CH61: Irby 1F 137
Menlo Cl. CH43: O'ton 5F 95
Menlove Av. L18: Moss H 4A 102
L25: Wltn 4B 102
Menlove Cres. Nth.
L18: Moss H 4B 102
Menlove Gdns. Nth.
L18: Moss H 4B 102
Menlove Gdns. Sth.
L18: Moss H 4B 102
Menlove Gdns. W.
L18: Moss H 4B 102
Menlove Mans. L18: Moss H 3C 102
Menstone Rd. L13: Liv 2F 79
Mentmore Cres. L11: N Grn. 2B 58
Mentmore Rd. L18: Moss H 2F 123
MEOLS 3E 91
Meol's Cl. L24: Hale 5E 149
Meols Ct. CH47: Hoy 5A 90
Meols Dr. CH47: Hoy 2A 112
CH48: W Kir 2A 112
Meols Pde. CH47: Meols 3C 90
Meols Station (Rail) 3E 91
Mercer Av. L32: K'by 3C 22
Mercer Ct. L12: W Der 5E 59
L20: Boot 5C 34
(off Clairville Clo.)
Mercer Dr. L4: Kirk 4E 55
Mercer Hgts. L32: K'by 4C 22
Mercer Rd. CH43: Bid 1E 95
WA11: Hay 2C 48
Mercer St. L19: Gars 2C 144
WA5: B'wood 5E 69

Merchant Cl. L30: N'ton 5B 20
Merchants Ho. L1: Liv 6D 4
Mercury Ct. L3: Liv 4C 76 (3C 4)
Mere Bank CH63: Raby M 4B 162
Mere Bank L17: Aig 4E 101
Merebank CH43: O'ton 5E 95
Merebrook Gro. L33: K'by 5F 15
Merecliff L28: Stock V 3C 60
Merecroft Av. CH44: Wall 4C 74
Meredale Rd. L18: Moss H 5A 102
Mere Farm Gro. CH43: O'ton 5F 95
Mere Farm Rd. CH43: O'ton 5F 95
Mere Grn. L4: Walt 2A 56
Mere Gro. WA11: St. H 4B 30
Mereheath CH46: Leas 3E 71
Mereheath Gdns. CH46: Leas 3E 71
(off Mereheath)
Mere Hey WA10: Eccl 5A 44
Mereland Way WA9: St. H 1F 67
Mere La. CH45: Wall 4E 51
CH60: Hes 5E 137
L5: Liv 5F 55
Mere Pk. L23: Blun 1D 17
Mere Pk. Rd. CH49: Grea 1C 114
Meres Rd. L9: Ain 1E 37
Merevale Cl. WA7: Beech 4E 167
Mereview Cres. L12: Crox 5D 39
Merewood L32: K'by 5F 23
Mereworth CH48: Caldy 3D 135
Meribel Cl. L23: C'by 5A 10
Merebank Av. CH63: Spit 1A 162
Meriden Av. CH63: Spit 1A 162
Meriden Cl. WA11: St. H 2D 47
Meriden Rd. L25: Gate 3B 104
Merlin Av. CH49: Upton 3D 93
Merlin Cl. CH49: Upton 3D 93
WA7: Cas 1A 168
WA11: St. H 2B 46
Merlin Ct. L26: Halew 3D 127
Merlin St. L8: Liv 3F 99
Merrills La. CH49: Upton 4B 94
Merrilocks Grn. L23: Blun 5A 8
Merrilocks Rd. L23: Blun 5A 8
Merrilox Av. L31: Lyd 4D 7
Merrion Cl. L25: Wltn 1F 125
Merritt Av. CH41: Birk 1B 96
Merrivale Rd. L25: Wltn 2C 126
Merrydale Dr. L11: Crox 5C 38
Mersey Av. L19: Aig 4F 123
L31: Mag 5F 7
Merseybank Ho. CH62: New F 4B 120
(off New Ferry Rd.)
Merseybank Rd. CH62: New F 4B 120
Mersey Cotts. L19: Gars 2D 145
Mersey Ct. CH44: Wall 4E 75
(off Borough Rd. E.)
L23: C'by 2C 16
Mersey Ho. L20: Boot 4B 34
Mersey Indoor Karting Cen. 1E 101
Mersey La. Sth. CH42: R Ferr 2A 120
Mersey Mt. CH42: Tran 1E 119
Mersey Rd. CH42: R Ferr 2A 120
L17: Aig 4E 123
L23: Blun 2C 16
WA7: Run 4A 152
WA8: Wid 3A 152
Merseyside Ho. L1: Liv 5C 76 (5D 4)
Merseyside Maritime Mus.
. . . . .1B 98 (7C 4)
Merseyside Youth Challenge Trust
. . . . .3F 125
Mersey St. CH44: Wall 4E 75
WA9: St. H 5A 48
Mersey Tunnel Toll L3: Liv . . .3A 76 (1A 4)
(not continuous)
Mersey Vw. CH63: High B 1D 141
L19: Gars 1C 144
L22: Water 3C 16
WA7: West 4F 165
WA7: West P 2D 165
WA8: Wid 3A 152
Mersey Vw. Cotts. WA7: West 4F 165
Mersey Vw. Rd. WA8: Hale B 3B 150
Mersham Ct. WA8: Wid 5F 109
Merstone Cl. L26: Halew 5F 127

Merthyr Gro. L16: Child	.5E 81
Merton Bank Rd. WA9: St. H	.3C 46
Merton Cl. L36: Huy	.4B 82
Merton Cres. L36: Huy	.4B 82
Merton Dr. CH49: W'chu	.1A 116
L36: Huy	.4A 82
Merton Gro. L20: Boot	.5C 34
L23: Blun	.2C 16
Merton Ho. L20: Boot	.5C 34
Merton Pl. CH43: O'ton	.3C 96
Merton Rd. CH45: Wall	.1A 74
L20: Boot	.5C 34
Merton St. WA9: St. H	.3C 46
Merton Towers L20: Boot	.5D 35
Mesham Cl. CH49: Upton	.4E 93
Metcalf Cl. L33: K'by	.4D 15
Methuen St. CH41: Birk	.1A 96
L15: W'tree	.1E 101
Mevagissey Rd. WA7: Brook	.5C 168
Mews, The L17: Aig	.3F 123
L23: C'by	.1E 17
L28: Stock V	.4C 60
WA5: B'wood	.5E 69
Mews Ct. CH64: Will	.5A 170
Meyrick Ct. WA12: New W	.5F 49
Meyrick Rd. L11: N Grn.	.1E 57
Micawber Cl. L8: Liv	.4F 99
Michael Dragonette Ct. L3: Liv	.2C 76
Michigan Cl. L27: N'ley	.4E 105
Mickfield Rd. L15: W'tree	.3F 101
Micklegate WA7: Murd	.3D 169
MICKLEHEAD GREEN	.3A 88
Middlefield Rd. L18: Aller	.1E 125
Middleham Cl. L32: K'by	.4C 22
Middlehey Av. L34: Know	.4D 41
Middlehurst Av. WA10: St. H	.4F 45
Middlehurst Cl. L34: Ecc P	.4A 64
Middlemass Way L27: N'ley	.4E 105
Middle Rd. CH62: Port S	.1B 142
L24: Halew	.2F 147
(not continuous)	
Middlesex Rd. L20: Boot	.4D 35
Middleton Ct. L24: Speke	.5E 147
Middleton Rd. L7: Liv	.4E 79
L22: Water	.3F 17
Middle Way L11: Crox	.4D 39
Middlewood L32: K'by	.5F 23
Midghall St. L3: Liv	.3C 76 (2D 4)
Midhurst Rd. L12: Crox	.5E 39
Midland St. CH43: O'ton	.4C 96
WA8: Wid	.3B 132
Midland Ter. L22: Water	.4D 17
Midlothian Dr. L23: Blun	.1C 16
Midway Rd. L36: Huy	.2E 83
Midwood St. WA8: Wid	.4B 132
Milbrook Cres. L32: K'by	.2E 23
Milbrook Dr. L32: K'by	.2E 23
Milbrook Wlk. L32: K'by	.2E 23
Mildenhall Rd. L25: Gate	.3A 104
Mildenhall Way L25: Gate	.2A 104
Mildmay Rd. L11: N Grn.	.1E 57
L20: Boot	.3B 34
Mile End L15: Liv	.2D 77
Miles Cl. CH49: Grea	.2C 114
Miles La. CH49: Grea	.2C 114
Miles St. L8: Liv	.4A 100
Milestone Hey L28: Stock V	.3B 60
Milford Dr. L12: Crox	.5E 39
Milford St. L5: Kirk	.5B 54
Milk St. WA10: St. H	.5A 46
Millachip Ct. L6: Liv	.1B 78
Milland Cl. L11: Crox	.5C 38
Millar Cres. WA8: Wid	.5A 132
Mill Bank L13: Liv	.5F 57
Millbank Cotts. L31: Mag	.4E 7
WA6: Frod	.5A 172
Millbank Ct. L9: Ain	.5D 21
WA6: Frod	.5A 172
Millbank La. L31: Augh, Mag	.4F 7
Mill Bank Rd. CH44: Wall	.3A 74
Millbeck Cl. L33: K'by	.1E 23
Millbeck Gro. WA11: St. H	.3B 30
Millbrook Bus. Pk. WA11: R'ford	.2C 28
Millbrook Ct. L34: Know	.3C 40
Millbrook La. WA10: Eccl	.4B 44

Millbrook Rd. CH41: Birk	.4B 74
Mill Brow CH63: High B	.1D 141
WA8: Wid	.2C 132
WA9: Sut L	.1D 89
WA10: Eccl	.4B 44
Mill Brow CH9: Sut L	.1D 89
Millburn Hgts. L5: Liv	.1E 77
Millbutt Cl. CH63: High B	.1D 141
Mill Ct. CH42: Tran	.5D 97
L23: C'by	.4E 9
Millcott L23: C'by	.5A 10
Millcroft L23: C'by	.5A 10
Millcroft Pk. CH49: Grea	.1B 114
Millcroft Rd. L25: Wltn	.3C 126
Millennium Rd. L8: Liv	.3A 100
Miller Av. L23: C'by	.5D 9
Millers Bri. L20: Boot	.1B 54
Millers Bri. Ind. Est. L20: Boot	.1B 54
Millers Cl. CH46: More	.1B 92
Millerscroft L32: K'by	.2C 22
Millersdale WA9: Clock F	.2C 88
Millersdale Av. L9: Ain	.1B 36
Millersdale Cl. CH62: East	.5F 163
Millersdale Gro. WA7: Beech	.4D 167
Millersdale Rd. L18: Moss H	.5A 102
Millers Fold WA10: Eccl	.4B 44
Millers Way CH46: More	.1C 92
Millfield Cl. CH63: High B	.2D 141
L13: W Der	.1A 80
Millfield La. WA11: Hay	.1F 49
Millfield Rd. WA8: Wid	.2C 132
Millfields WA10: Eccl	.5A 44
Mill Grn. CH64: Will	.5A 170
Millgreen Cl. L12: Crox	.5E 39
Mill Grn. La. WA8: Wid	.4D 111
Mill Gro. L21: Lith	.5B 18
Mill Hey L35: R'hill	.5E 87
Mill Hey Rd. CH48: Caldy	.3D 135
Mill Hill CH43: O'ton	.1A 118
Mill Hill Rd. CH61: Irby	.4C 114
Millhouse CH46: More	.5B 70
Millhouse Cl. L12: W Der	.5A 58
Millhouse La. CH46: More	.5B 70
Millington Cl. CH43: Pren	.3E 117
WA7: Sut W	.1F 173
WA8: Wid	.4F 131
Mill La. CH44: Wall	.3A 74
CH49: Grea	.1C 114
CH60: Hes	.2B 158
CH64: Will	.4A 170
L3: Liv	.4D 77 (3F 5)
L12: W Der	.5A 58
L13: Liv	.4A 80
L15: W'tree	.4A 80
L20: Boot	.5D 35
L32: K'by	.2C 22
L34: Know	.3D 41
L35: R'hill	.4C 86
WA6: Frod	.3D 173
WA8: Cron	.4D 109
WA8: Wid, Bold H	.5C 110
WA9: Sut L	.1C 88
WA11: R'ford	.2B 28
Millom Av. L35: R'hill	.2B 86
Millom Gro. L12: W Der	.2C 58
WA10: St. H	.3C 64
Mill Pk. Dr. CH62: East	.2E 171
Mill Rd. CH61: Thing	.1B 138
CH62: Brom	.4D 143
CH63: High B	.5D 119
L6: Liv	.2F 77
(not continuous)	
Mill Spring Ct. L20: Boot	.5D 35
Mill Sq. L10: Ain	.3E 21
Millstead Rd. L15: W'tree	.1A 102
Millstead Wlk. L15: W'tree	.1A 102
Mill Stile L25: Wltn	.2F 125
Mill St. CH42: Tran	.5D 97
L8: Liv	.3E 99
L25: Wltn	.2A 126
L34: Prsct	.5D 63
L35: R'hill	.4F 45
Mill Ter. CH63: High B	.2D 141
Millthwaite Ct. CH44: Wall	.2F 73
Millthwaite Rd. CH44: Wall	.2F 73

Millvale St. L6: Liv	.3B 78
Mill Vw. L8: Liv	.4E 99
L32: K'by	.1C 22
Mill Vw. Dr. CH63: High B	.1C 140
Millway Rd. L24: Speke	.3A 148
Millwood CH63: High B	.1D 141
WA7: Nort	.1C 168
Millwood Av. WA10: Eccl	.5F 43
Millwood Cl. L24: Speke	.3A 148
Millwood Est. L24: Speke	.4A 148
Millwood Gdns. L35: Whis	.4E 83
Millwood Rd. L24: Speke	.3E 147
MILL YARD	.2D 81
Mill Yd. CH61: Thing	.1B 138
Milman Cl. CH49: Upton	.5F 93
Milman Cl. L25: Wltn	.1E 125
Milman Rd. L4: Walt	.2F 55
Milner Cop CH60: Hes	.2A 158
Milne Rd. L13: Liv	.3E 57
Milner Rd. CH60: Hes	.2A 158
L17: Aig	.3E 123
Milner St. CH41: Birk	.1A 96
Milnthorpe Cl. L4: Kirk	.3E 55
Milnthorpe Rd. WA5: B'wood	.5E 69
Milnthorpe St. L19: Gars	.1C 144
Milroy St. L7: Liv	.5B 78
Milton Av. L14: B Grn	.4F 81
L35: Whis	.3E 85
WA8: Wid	.4F 131
Milton Cl. L35: Whis	.3E 85
Milton Cres. CH60: Hes	.1A 158
Milton Gro. CH61: Thing	.1B 138
Milton Pavement CH41: Birk	.3D 97
CH44: Wall	.4D 75
CH48: W Kir	.3A 112
L4: Walt	.1E 55
L7: Liv	.4E 79
L22: Water	.3E 17
WA8: Wid	.4F 131
Milton Rd. E. CH42: Tran	.5D 97
Milton St. L20: Boot	.4B 34
WA8: Wid	.2A 152
WA9: Sut M	.4A 88
Milton Way L31: Mag	.5B 6
Milverney Way WA9: St. H	.1A 66
Milverton St. L7: Liv	.5A 78
Mimosa Rd. L15: W'tree	.2A 102
Mindale Rd. L15: W'tree	.1F 101
Minehead Gro. WA9: Sut L	.1D 89
Minehead Rd. L17: Aig	.3E 123
Miners Way L24: Speke	.4A 148
WA8: Wid	.5A 132
Mines Av. L17: Aig	.5F 123
L34: Prsct	.5E 63
Mine Way WA11: Hay	.1F 49
Minshull St. L7: Liv	.5A 78
Minstead Av. L33: K'by	.3F 23
Minster Ct. L7: Liv	.1A 100
WA7: Run	.2E 165
Minton Cl. L7: Liv	.4B 78
Minton Cl. L12: Crox	.5F 39
Minton Way WA8: Wid	.4B 110
Mintor Rd. L33: K'by	.3A 24
Minto St. L7: Liv	.4B 78
Minver Rd. L12: W Der	.4D 59
Miranda Av. CH63: High B	.5E 119
Miranda Pl. L20: Kirk	.2D 55
Miranda Rd. L20: Boot	.1D 55
Mirfield Cl. L26: Halew	.1F 147
Mirfield St. L6: Liv	.3B 78
Miriam Pl. CH41: Birk	.1F 95
Miriam Rd. L4: Walt	.5A 56
Miskelly St. L20: Kirk	.3C 54
Missouri Rd. L13: Liv	.4D 57
Mistle Thrush Way L12: Crox	.4F 39
Miston St. L20: Kirk	.3C 54
Misty Cl. WA8: Wid	.2C 130
Mitchell Av. WA5: B'wood	.5E 69
Mitchell Cres. L21: Lith	.5B 18
Mitchell Pl. L1: Liv	.5G 5
Mitchell Rd. L34: Prsct	.5C 62
WA10: St. H	.2C 64
WN5: Bil	.1E 31
Mithril Cl. WA8: Wid	.1E 133

Mitre Cl. L35: Whis 5D **85**
Mitylene St. L5: Liv 5E **55**
Mobberley Way CH63: Spit 4A **142**
Mockbeggar Dr. CH45: Wall 4E **51**
Mockbeggar Wharf CH45: Wall . . .4E **51**
Modred St. L8: Liv 4F **99**
Moel Famau Vw. L17: Aig 2B **122**
Moffatdale Rd. L4: Walt 3C **56**
Moffatt Rd. L9: Ain 1B **36**
Moira Sephton Ct. CH43: Noct . . .5D **95**
Moira St. L6: Liv 4F **77**
Molesworth Gro. L16: Child 5E **81**
Molineux Av. L14: B Grn 5D **81**
Molland Cl. L12: W Der 3D **59**
Mollington Av. L11: N Grn 1F **57**
Mollington Link CH41: Birk 4E **97**
Mollington Rd. CH44: Wall 3C **74**
L32: K'by 3C **22**
Mollington St. CH41: Birk 4E **97**
Molly's La. L33: Know 1D **41**
Molton Rd. L16: Child 1C **102**
Molyneux Cl. CH49: Upton 4F **93**
L35: Prsct 2D **85**
L36: Huy 4F **83**
Molyneux Ct. L11: N Grn 5B **38**
L14: B Grn 4D **81**
Molyneux Dr. CH45: New B 3B **52**
L35: Prsct 2D **85**
Molyneux Rd. L6: Liv 3B **78**
L18: Moss H 5F **101**
L22: Water 3E **17**
L31: Mag 3F **13**
Molyneux Way L10: Ain 2C **20**
Monaghan Cl. L9: Walt 1A **36**
Monash Cl. L33: K'by 4E **15**
Monash Rd. L11: N Grn 3E **57**
Monastery La. WA9: St. H 4D **67**
Monastery Rd. L6: Liv 5C **56**
WA9: St. H 4E **67**
Mona St. CH41: Birk 2F **95**
L20: Boot 2D **35**
WA10: St. H 5D **45**
Mond Rd. L10: Faz 1F **37**
WA8: Wid 4A **132**
Monfa Rd. L20: Boot 2C **34**
Monica Dr. WA8: Wid 4A **110**
Monica Rd. L25: Wltn 3B **126**
Monkfield Way L19: Gars 3D **145**
Monk Rd. CH44: Wall 1B **74**
Monksdown Rd. L11: N Grn 2A **58**
Monks Ferry CH41: Birk 3F **97**
Monksferry Wlk. L19: Gras 5F **123**
Monk St. CH41: Birk 3F **97**
L5: Liv 5F **55**
Monks Way CH48: W Kir 4C **112**
CH63: Beb 3F **141**
L25: Wltn 2B **126**
WA7: Pres B 5E **169**
Monkswell Dr. L15: W'tree 1A **102**
Monkswell St. L8: Liv 1A **122**
Monmouth Dr. L10: Ain 4F **21**
Monmouth Gro. WA9: St. H 1D **67**
Monmouth Rd. CH44: Wall 2F **73**
Monro Cl. L8: Liv 5F **99**
Monro St. L8: Liv 5F **99**
Mons Sq. L20: Boot 5C **34**
Montague Rd. L13: Liv 4A **80**
WA8: Wid 1A **150**
Montclair Dr. L18: Moss H 3B **102**
Monterey Rd. L13: Liv 4B **80**
Montfort Dr. L19: Gras 5A **124**
Montgomery Cl. L35: Whis 4D **85**
Montgomery Hill
CH48: Caldy, Frank 1F **135**
Montgomery Rd. L9: Walt 1A **36**
L36: Huy 2D **83**
WA8: Wid 4D **131**
Montgomery Way L6: Liv 2B **78**
Montpelier Av. WA7: West 4F **165**
Montpelier Dr. L8: Liv 5F **99**
Montpellier Cres. CH45: New B . . .3A **52**
Montpellier Ho. CH45: New B 3A **52**
Montreal Cl. L27: N'ley 4E **105**
Montrose Av. CH44: Wall 5E **75**
Montrose Bus. Pk. L7: Liv 4E **79**

Montrose Ct. CH47: Hoy 5B **90**
L12: W Der 4F **59**
Montrose Pl. L26: Halew 1F **147**
Montrose Rd. L13: Liv 5D **57**
Montrose Way L13: Liv 4F **79**
Montrovia Cres. L10: Faz 1F **37**
Monument Pl. L3: Liv 4E **77** (4H **5**)
Monville Rd. L9: Ain 1C **36**
Moorbridge Cl. L30: N'ton 1A **20**
Moor Cl. L23: C'by 5F **9**
Moor Coppice L23: C'by 5F **9**
Moor Ct. L10: Faz 1A **38**
Moorcroft Rd. CH45: Wall 1D **73**
L18: Aller 3C **124**
(not continuous)
Moor Dr. L23: C'by 5E **9**
Moore Av. CH42: R Ferr 2E **119**
WA9: St. H 5A **48**
Moore Cl. WA8: Wid 2D **133**
Moore Dr. WA11: Hay 1F **49**
Moore's Ho. L4: Walt 1F **55**
Moore St. L20: Boot 3B **34**
Mooreway L35: R'hill 5E **87**
Moorfield L33: K'by 5F **15**
Moorfield Cen. L33: K'by 4F **15**
Moorfield Rd. L23: C'by 5A **10**
WA8: Wid 5D **111**
WA10: St. H 3C **44**
Moorfields L2: Liv 4C **76** (4D **4**)
Moorfields CH43: Noct 5D **95**
Moorfields Station (Rail) . .4C **76** (4D **4**)
Moorfoot Rd. WA9: St. H 5F **47**
Moorfoot Rd. Ind. Est.
WA9: St. H 4F **47**
Moorfoot Way L33: K'by 4D **15**
Moorgate Av. L23: C'by 2F **17**
Moorgate La. L23: C'by 5A **24**
Moorgate Point L33: Know I 1A **40**
Moorgate Rd. L33: K'by 2F **39**
Moorgate Rd. Sth. L34: Know 2F **39**
Moorgate St. L7: Liv 5B **78**
Moorhead Cl. L21: Lith 1A **34**
Moorhey Rd. L31: Mag 4C **12**
Moor Ho. L23: C'by 5F **9**
Mooring Cl. WA7: Murd 4D **169**
Moorings, The CH41: Birk 4D **97**
CH60: Hes 2C **156**
L31: Lyd 3B **6**
Moorland Av. L23: C'by 5E **9**
Moorland Cl. CH60: Hes 3A **158**
Moorland Dr. WA7: Murd 3B **169**
Moorland Pk. CH60: Hes 3A **158**
Moorland Rd. CH42: Tran 1E **119**
L31: Mag 4C **12**
Moorlands Rd. L23: Thorn 4B **10**
Moor La. CH60: Hes 2A **158**
L4: Walt 5F **35**
L10: Faz 5B **22**
L23: C'by 5E **9**
L23: C'by, Thorn 5E **9**
L29: Seft 2D **11**
L32: K'by 5B **22**
L38: Ince B 1F **9**
WA6: Frod 5B **172**
WA8: Wid 5F **131**
(not continuous)
Moor La. Bus. Cen. WA8: Wid . . .5A **132**
Moor La. Sth. WA8: Wid 5F **131**
MOOR PARK 1F **17**
Moor Pl. L3: Liv 4E **77** (4H **5**)
Moorside Cl. L23: C'by 1F **17**
Moorside Ct. WA8: Wid 5F **131**
Moorside Rd. L23: C'by 1F **17**
Moor St. L2: Liv 5C **76** (5C **4**)
Moorway CH60: Hes 2B **158**
Moorwood Cres. WA9: Clock F . . .2C **88**
Moray Cl. WA9: St. H 3E **45**
Morcott La. L24: Hale 5D **149**
Morcroft Rd. L36: Huy 1E **83**
Morden St. L6: Liv 2C **78**
Morecambe St. L6: Liv 1C **78**
Morecroft Rd. CH42: R Ferr 2A **120**
Morella Rd. L4: Walt 3C **56**
Morello Cl. WA10: St. H 3F **45**

Morello Dr. CH63: Spit 5B **142**
Moresby Cl. WA7: Murd 3E **169**
Moret Cl. L23: C'by 5A **10**
MORETON 1E **93**
Moreton Av. WA9: Clock F 2C **88**
MORETON COMMON 2D **71**
Moreton Gro. CH45: Wall 5E **51**
Moreton Rd. CH49: Upton 2F **93**
Moreton Station (Rail) 4E **71**
Moreton Ter. WA6: Frod 5A **172**
Morgan M. L30: N'ton 2D **19**
Morgan St. WA9: St. H 1D **67**
Morland Av. CH62: Brom 4D **163**
Morland Ct. CH41: Birk 1B **96**
Morley Ct. L14: K Ash 2E **81**
Morley Rd. CH44: Wall 3A **74**
WA7: Run 1A **166**
Morley St. L4: Walt 4E **55**
WA10: St. H 3F **45**
(not continuous)
Morley Way WA10: St. H 4F **45**
Morningside L23: C'by 2F **17**
Morningside Pl. L11: N Grn 2F **57**
Morningside Rd. L11: N Grn 2E **57**
Morningside Vw. L11: N Grn 3F **57**
Morningside Way L11: N Grn 3F **57**
Mornington Av. L23: C'by 3E **17**
Mornington Rd. CH45: New B 4B **52**
Mornington St. L8: Liv 4E **99**
Morpeth Cl. CH46: More 1B **92**
Morpeth Rd. CH47: Hoy 1A **112**
Morpeth St. L8: Liv 2F **99**
Morpeth Wharf CH41: Birk 1E **97**
Morris Cl. WA11: Hay 3F **47**
Morris Ct. CH43: O'ton 4F **95**
Morrissey Cl. WA10: St. H 4D **45**
Morris St. WA9: St. H 2E **67**
Morston Av. L32: K'by 5E **23**
Morston Cres. L32: K'by 5E **23**
Morston Wlk. L32: K'by 5E **23**
Mortar Mill Quay CH41: Birk 5D **75**
Mortimer St. CH41: Birk 2F **97**
Mortlake Cl. WA8: Wid 1C **130**
Morton Ho. L18: Moss H 1F **123**
Morton Rd. WA7: Nort 2D **169**
Morton St. L8: Liv 4F **99**
(not continuous)
Mortuary Rd. CH45: Wall 5B **52**
Morvah Cl. L12: W Der 1C **58**
Morval Cres. L4: Walt 1E **55**
WA7: Run 1D **167**
Moscow Dr. L13: Liv 1F **79**
Mosedale Av. WA11: St. H 4B **30**
Mosedale Gro. WA7: Beech 5E **167**
Mosedale Rd. CH62: Brom 5E **143**
L9: Walt 3A **36**
Moseley Av. CH45: Wall 2A **74**
Moseley Rd. CH63: Spit 1A **162**
Moses St. L8: Liv 5F **99**
MOSS BANK
St Helens 4A **30**
Widnes 5D **133**
Moss Bank Pk. L21: Lith 5A **18**
Moss Bank Rd. WA8: Wid 5D **133**
WA11: St. H 5F **29**
Mossborough Hall La.
WA11: R'ford 3B **26**
Mossborough Rd.
WA11: R'ford 3D **27**
Mossbrow Rd. L36: Huy 1E **83**
Moss Cl. CH64: Will 5A **170**
Mosscraig L28: Stock V 4C **60**
Mosscroft Cl. L36: Huy 2A **84**
Mossdale Dr. L35: R'hill 3D **87**
Mossdale Rd. L33: K'by 5F **15**
Mossdene Rd. CH44: Wall 2F **73**
Moss End Way L33: Know I 2D **25**
Mossfield Rd. L9: Walt 2F **35**
Moss Ga. Gro. L14: K Ash 3A **82**
Moss Ga. Rd. L14: K Ash 3A **82**
Moss Grn. Way WA9: St. H 2A **68**
Moss Gro. CH42: Tran 2B **118**
L8: Liv 3B **100**
Mosshill Cl. L31: Mag 4C **6**
Mosslands WA10: Eccl 4A **44**

Mosslands Dr. CH44: Wall 1E 73
  CH45: Wall 1E 73
Moss La. CH42: Tran 2B 118
  L9: Walt 2E 35
  L20: Boot 2E 35
  L21: Lith 5B 18
  L23: Lit C 1C 8
  L31: Lyd 2B 6
  L31: Mag 5E 7
  L33: K'by 2B 24
  L33: Sim 2F 15
  L38: High 1C 8
  WA9: St. H 2A 68
  WA11: Crank 1E 29
  WA11: Windle 5F 27
Mosslawn Rd. L32: K'by 4A 24
Mosslea Pk. L18: Moss H 5F 101
Mossley Av. CH62: Brom 2D 163
  L18: Moss H 4E 101
Mossley Ct. L18: Moss H 1F 123
MOSSLEY HILL 1A 124
Mossley Hill Dr. L17: Aig 4D 101
  (not continuous)
Mossley Hill Rd. L18: Moss H 2F 123
  L19: Aig 2F 123
Mossley Rd. CH42: Tran 1E 119
Mossley Hill Station (Rail) 1A 124
MOSS NOOK 2F 67
Moss Nook La. L31: Mag 2A 14
  WA11: R'ford 1F 27
  (not continuous)
Moss Pits Cl. L10: Faz 1E 37
Moss Pits La. L10: Faz 1E 37
  L15: W'tree 3B 102
MOSS SIDE
  Liverpool 5E 7
  Warrington 1E 155
Moss Side L14: K Ash 3A 82
Moss Side La. WA4: Moore 1E 155
Moss St. L6: Liv 4F 77 (3J 5)
  L19: Gars 1C 144
  L34: Prsct 4D 63
  WA8: Wid 5D 133
Moss Vw. L21: Lith 5C 18
  L31: Mag 1F 13
Mossville Cl. L18: Moss H 2A 124
Mossville Rd. L18: Moss H 2A 124
Moss Way L11: Crox 3C 38
Mossy Bank Rd. CH44: Wall 2D 75
Mostyn Av. CH48: W Kir 5B 112
  CH60: Hes 2D 157
  L10: Ain 2C 20
  L19: Aller 4D 125
Mostyn Cl. L4: Kirk 4E 55
Mostyn St. CH44: Wall 3B 74
Motherwell Cl. WA8: Wid 1E 131
Mottershead Cl. WA8: Wid 4A 132
Mottershead Rd. WA8: Wid 4A 132
Mottram Cl. L33: K'by 3F 23
Moughland La. WA7: Run 1F 165
Mould St. L5: Liv 5D 55
Mounsey Rd. CH42: Tran 4D 97
Mount, The CH44: Wall 2C 74
  CH60: Hes 2F 157
  CH63: Beb 2A 142
Mount Av. CH60: Hes 2F 157
  CH63: High B 5D 119
  L20: Boot 1D 35
Mount Cl. L32: K'by 1C 22
Mount Ct. CH45: New B 3A 52
Mount Cres. L32: K'by 1B 22
Mount Dr. CH63: High B 5D 119
Mount Gro. CH41: Birk 4C 96
Mount Gro. Pl. CH41: Birk 4C 96
Mt. Haven Cl. CH49: Upton 4A 94
Mount Merrion L25: Gate 5A 104
Mount Olive CH43: O'ton 1A 96
Mount Pk. CH63: High B 5D 119
  L25: Wltn 1A 126
Mount Pk. Ct. L25: Wltn 1A 126
Mount Pleasant CH43: O'ton 1B 118
  L3: Liv 5E 77 (6G 5)
  L22: Water 4D 17
  WA8: Wid 2B 132

Mt. Pleasant Av. WA9: St. H 1A 68
Mount Pleasant Rd.
  CH45: New B, Wall 5A 52
Mount Rd. CH42: Tran 3C 118
  CH45: Wall 3A 52
  CH48: W Kir 5C 112
  CH49: Upton 4A 94
  CH63: High B, Spit 4C 118
  L32: K'by 2B 22
  (not continuous)
  WA7: Halt 1F 167
Mount St. L1: Liv 1E 99 (7H 5)
  L22: Water 4D 17
  L25: Wltn 2A 126
  WA8: Wid 2B 132
Mount Vernon L7: Liv 5A 78
Mt. Vernon Grn. L7: Liv 4A 78
Mt. Vernon Rd. L7: Liv 4A 78
Mt. Vernon St. L7: Liv 4F 77
Mt. Vernon Vw. L7: Liv 4A 78
Mountview Cl. L8: Liv 4A 100
Mountway CH63: High B 5D 119
Mt. Wood Rd. CH42: Tran 4C 118
Mowbray Av. WA11: St. H 3C 46
Mowbray Ct. L20: Kirk 2C 54
Mowbray Gro. L13: Liv 5A 80
Mowcroft La. WA5: Cuerd 1F 133
Moxon St. WA10: St. H 1C 64
Moyles Cl. WA8: Wid 1D 131
Moyles Cl. WA8: Wid 2D 131
  (off Moyles Clo.)
Mozart Cl. L8: Liv 3B 100
Muirfield Cl. L12: W Der 5E 59
Muirfield Rd. L36: Roby 5C 82
Muirhead Av. L6: Liv 2C 78
  L13: Liv, W Der 5E 57
Muirhead Av. E.
  L11: W Der 3A 58
Mulberry Av. WA10: St. H 5C 44
Mulberry Cl. L33: K'by 4F 15
Mulberry Ct. L7: Liv 7J 5
Mulberry Gro. CH44: Wall 3D 75
Mulberry Pl. L7: Liv 1F 99 (7J 5)
Mulberry Rd. CH42: R Ferr 2D 97
Mulberry St. L7: Liv 1F 99 (7J 5)
  (not continuous)
Mulcrow Cl. WA9: St. H 4D 47
Mulgrave St. L8: Liv 2A 100
Mulliner St. L7: Liv 2C 100
Mullion Cl. L26: Halew 3E 127
  WA7: Brook 4B 168
Mullion Rd. L11: Crox 3C 38
Mullion Wlk. L11: Crox 3C 38
Mullrea Cl. L27: N'ley 3C 104
Mullwood Cl. L12: Crox 5F 39
Mulveton Rd. CH63: Spit 4F 141
Mumfords Gro. CH47: Meols 2E 91
Mumfords La. CH47: Meols 2D 91
Muncaster Cl. CH62: Brom 1D 163
Munster Rd. L13: Liv 3B 80
Murat Gro. L22: Water 4C 16
Murat St. L22: Water 4C 16
Murcote Rd. L14: K Ash 1F 81
MURDISHAW 4D 169
Murdishaw Av.
  WA7: Brook, Murd 5C 168
Murdock Way L10: Faz 1B 38
Muriel St. L4: Walt 3F 55
Murphy Gro. WA9: St. H 4E 47
Murrayfield Dr. CH46: Leas 2F 71
Murrayfield Rd. L25: Gate 3A 104
Murrayfield Wlk. L25: Gate 3A 104
Murray Gro. CH48: W Kir 3A 112
Mus. of Liverpool Life 5B 76 (7B 4)
Musker Dr. L30: N'ton 2C 18
Musker Gdns. L23: C'by 2F 17
Musker St. L23: C'by 2F 17
Muspratt Rd. L21: Sea 2A 34
Muttocks Rake L30: N'ton 5D 11
Myers Av. L35: Whis 1A 86
Myerscough Av. L20: Boot 3E 35
Myers Cl. L23: C'by 3F 17
  (off Myers Rd. E.)
Myers Rd. E. L23: C'by 2E 17
Myers Rd. W. L23: C'by 2D 17

Mynsule Rd. CH63: Spit 4F 141
Myrtle Av. WA11: Hay 1B 48
Myrtle Ct. L8: Liv 1A 100
Myrtle Gro. CH44: Wall 3D 75
  L22: Water 3D 17
  WA8: Wid 4D 131
  WN5: Bil 1D 31
Myrtle Pde. L7: Liv 1F 99
Myrtle St. L7: Liv 1F 99 (7J 5)

N

Naburn Gro. CH46: More 2E 93
Nairn Cl. CH63: East 1D 171
Nansen Gro. L4: Walt 2A 56
Nant Pk. Ct. CH45: New B 3C 52
Nantwich Cl. CH49: W'chu 2A 116
Napier Cl. WA10: St. H 5E 45
Napier Dr. CH46: More 1F 93
Napier Rd. CH62: New F 4B 120
Napier St. L20: Boot 2B 54
  WA10: St. H 5E 45
Naples Rd. CH44: Wall 3C 75
Napps Cl. L25: Gate 2F 103
Napps Wlk. L25: Gate 2F 103
  (off Napps Clo.)
Napps Way CH61: Hes 5A 138
  L25: Gate 1F 103
Naseby Cl. CH43: Noct 5C 94
Naseby St. L4: Walt 1F 55
Natal Rd. L9: Ain 2B 36
Nathan Dr. WA11: Hay 2E 49
Nathan Gro. L33: K'by 1F 23
National Wildflower Cen. 1F 103
Naughton Lea WA8: Wid 1D 131
Naughton Rd. WA8: Wid 4A 132
Navigation Cl. L30: N'ton 1A 20
  WA7: Murd 4D 169
Navigation Wharf L3: Liv 3D 99
Naylor Rd. CH43: Bid 1E 95
  WA8: Wid 3D 133
Naylorsfield Dr. L27: N'ley 2C 104
Naylor's Rd. L27: N'ley 2D 105
Naylor St. L3: Liv 3C 76 (2D 4)
Nazeby Av. L23: C'by 2F 17
Neale Dr. CH49: Grea 1E 115
Neasham Cl. L26: Halew 4F 127
Nedens Gro. L31: Lyd 4C 6
Nedens La. L31: Lyd 4C 6
Needham Cl. WA7: Run 5D 153
Needham Cres. CH43: Noct 5D 95
Needham Rd. L7: Liv 4C 78
Needwood Dr. CH63: Beb 4F 141
Neills Rd. WA9: Bold 5B 68
Neilson Dr. L17: Aig 1B 122
Neilson St. L17: Aig 1B 122
Neil St. WA8: Wid 2B 132
Nell's La. L39: Augh 2F 7
Nelson Av. L35: Whis 4E 85
Nelson Cl. CH42: R Ferr 3A 120
  CH45: New B 2B 52
Nelson Dr. CH61: Pens 3E 137
  WA7: West 4F 165
Nelson Memorial 4C 4
  (off Exchange Pas. W.)
Nelson Pl. L35: Whis 4E 85
Nelson Rd. CH42: R Ferr 3A 120
  L7: Liv 5B 78
  L21: Lith 1B 34
Nelson's Cft. CH63: Beb 4A 142
Nelson St. CH45: New B 4C 52
  L1: Liv 2D 99
  L15: W'tree 2E 101
  L20: Boot 1B 54
  WA7: Run 4A 152
  WA8: Wid 4A 152
  WA9: St. H 4D 67
  WA12: New W 5F 49
  (not continuous)
Nelville Rd. L9: Ain 1C 36
Neptune Cl. WA7: Murd 3D 169
Neptune St. CH41: Birk 1D 97
Neptune Theatre 5D 77 (6F 5)
Ness Gro. L32: K'by 3C 22

Neston Av. WA9: Clock F 2B 88
Neston Rd. CH63: Thorn H 5F 159
  CH64: Nest 5F 159
  CH64: Will 5A 170
Neston St. L4: Walt 2F 55
Netherby St. L8: Liv 1F 121
Netherfield WA8: Wid 4D 131
Netherfield Cl. CH43: Noct 5C 94
Netherfield Nth. L5: Liv 5E 55
Netherfield Sth. L5: Liv 2E 77
NETHERLEY 4E 105
Netherley Rd. L27: N'ley 4F 105
  L35: Tar G 4F 105
  WA8: Wid 4F 105
NETHERTON 2F 19
Netherton Activity Cen. 1E 19
Netherton Dr. WA6: Frod 5A 172
Netherton Grange L30: N'ton 2B 20
Netherton Grn. L30: N'ton 5F 11
Netherton Ind. Est.
  L30: N'ton 4F 19
Netherton La. L30: N'ton 5E 11
                (not continuous)
Netherton Pk. Rd. L21: Lith 5D 19
Netherton Rd. CH46: More 1E 93
  L18: Moss H 3F 123
  L20: Boot 2D 35
Netherton Way
  L30: Boot, N'ton 4E 19
                (not continuous)
Netherwood Rd. L11: N Grn. 1E 57
Netley St. L4: Kirk 3E 55
Nettlestead Rd. L11: N Grn. 3A 58
Neva Av. CH46: More 1D 93
Neville Av. WA9: St. H 1B 68
Neville Cl. CH43: Noct 5C 94
Neville Dr. CH44: Wall 2A 74
  CH62: Brom 3E 163
  L22: Water 4E 17
Neville St. WA12: New W 4F 49
Nevin St. L6: Liv 3A 78
Nevison St. L7: Liv 5B 78
Nevitte Cl. L28: Stock V 3A 60
New Acres Cl. CH43: Bid 1C 94
New Albert Ter. WA7: Run 4B 152
                (off Bold St.)
Newark Cl. CH43: Noct 5C 94
  L30: N'ton 5B 12
  L36: Huy 5D 61
Newark St. L4: Walt 2E 55
New Bank Pl. WA8: Wid 3B 130
New Bank Rd. WA8: Wid 3B 130
New Barnet WA8: Wid 5F 109
New Bird St. L1: Liv 2D 99
Newbold Cres. CH48: W Kir 3E 113
Newbold Gro. L12: Crox 1F 59
Newborough Av. L18: Moss H 4F 101
  L23: C'by 1A 18
NEW BOSTON 1E 49
Newbridge Cl. CH49: W'chu 1B 116
  WA7: Brook 4C 168
NEW BRIGHTON 2B 52
New Brighton Station (Rail) 3A 52
Newburgh Cl. WA7: Wind H 1D 169
Newburn CH43: O'ton 4B 96
Newburns La. CH43: O'ton 1B 118
Newburn St. L4: Walt 1F 55
Newbury Cl. L36: Roby 5D 83
  WA8: Wid 5A 110
Newbury Way CH46: Leas 3F 71
  L12: W Der 1E 81
Newby Av. L35: R'hill 2A 86
Newby Dr. L36: Huy 3C 82
Newby Gro. L12: W Der 1C 58
Newby Pl. WA11: St. H 5A 30
Newby St. L4: Walt 3F 55
Newcastle Rd. L15: W'tree 3A 102
New Chester Rd.
  CH41: Birk, Tran 4F 97
  CH42: R Ferr 1F 119
  CH62: Brom, East, Port S 2C 142
  CH62: New F 3A 120
  CH66: Hoot 3F 171
Newcombe St. L6: Liv 1B 78
Newcroft Rd. L25: Wltn 5F 103

New Cross St. L34: Prsct 4D 63
  WA10: St. H 4F 45
                (Duke St.)
  WA10: St. H 5F 45
            (Westfield St.)
New Cut La. L33: Know 1A 42
  WA11: R'ford 3B 26
Newdales Cl. CH43: Bid 1C 94
Newdown Rd. L11: Crox 3C 38
Newdown Wlk. L11: Crox 3D 39
Newell Rd. CH44: Wall 1B 74
Newenham Cres. L14: K Ash 2E 81
NEW FERRY 5B 120
New Ferry By-Pass
  CH62: New F, Port S 4B 120
New Ferry Rd. CH62: New F 5B 120
Newfield Cl. L23: Thorn 4C 10
Newfields WA10: St. H 4C 44
Newfort Way L20: Boot 2A 34
New Glade Hill WA11: St. H 2E 47
New Grey Rock Cl. L6: Liv 2B 78
New Hall L10: Faz 5F 21
New Hall La. CH47: Hoy 5B 90
  L11: N Grn. 3E 57
New Hall Manor CH64: Nest 4E 159
New Hall Pl. L3: Liv 4B 76 (4B 4)
Newhall St. L1: Liv 2D 99
Newhall Swimming Pool 5F 21
Newhaven Rd. CH45: New B 4C 52
New Hawthorne Gdns.
  L18: Moss H 1E 123
New Hedley Gro. L5: Liv 1C 76
New Henderson St. L8: Liv 3E 99
New Hey L12: W Der 1A 80
New Hey Rd. CH49: W'chu 5B 94
New Heys Dr. L18: Aller 3D 125
Newholme Cl. L12: Crox 5E 39
Newhope Rd. CH41: Birk 2C 96
Newhouse Rd. L15: W'tree 2D 101
New Hutte La. L26: Halew 1F 147
Newick Rd. L32: K'by 4C 22
Newington L1: Liv 5D 77 (6G 5)
Newington Way WA8: Wid 1F 131
New Islington L3: Liv 3E 77 (3G 5)
Newland Cl. WA8: Wid 1C 130
Newland Dr. L17: Aig 1C 122
Newland Dr. CH44: Wall 2A 74
Newlands Rd. CH63: Beb 3B 142
  WA11: St. H 1C 46
Newling St. CH41: Birk 2C 96
Newlyn Av. L21: Lith 4A 18
  L31: Mag 1E 13
Newlyn Cl. CH47: Meols 2E 91
  WA7: Brook 4B 168
Newlyn Gro. WA11: St. H 1D 47
Newlyn Rd. CH47: Meols 2E 91
  L11: Crox 3C 38
Newlyn Wlk. L11: Crox 3D 39
Newman St. L4: Kirk 3D 55
New Mkt. Cl. L21: Lith 1B 34
Newmarket Gdns. WA9: St. H 5C 64
New Mkt. Hall WA7: Run 4A 152
             (off Church St.)
New Mersey Shop. Pk.
  L24: Speke 2F 145
New Mill Stile L25: Wltn 1A 126
Newmoore La. WA7: Nort 4E 155
Newmorn Ct. L17: Aig 2C 122
New Palace Amusement Pk. 2B 52
Newport Av. CH45: Wall 4F 51
Newport Cl. CH43: Noct 5C 94
Newport Ct. L5: Liv 5C 54
New Quay L3: Liv 4B 76 (4B 4)
Newquay Cl. WA7: Brook 4C 168
New Quay Ter. L3: Liv 4B 76 (4B 4)
New Red Rock Vw. L6: Liv 2B 78
New Rd. L13: Liv 1D 79
  L34: Ecc P 4E 63
New St. CH47: Hoy 4C 90
New St. Ct. L13: Liv 1E 79
Newsham Cl. WA8: Wid 5B 108
Newsham Dr. L6: Liv 2C 78
                (not continuous)
Newsham Rd. L36: Huy 1B 106
Newsham St. L5: Liv 1D 77
Newstead Av. L23: Blun 2B 16

Newstead Rd. L8: Liv 2B 100
  WA8: Wid 1F 149
Newstet Rd. L33: Know I 3B 24
New St. CH44: Wall 4E 75
  WA7: Run 5A 152
  WA8: Wid 4B 132
  WA9: Sut L 1C 88
NEWTON 4E 113
Newton Cl. L12: W Der 3B 58
NEWTON COMMON 5E 49
Newton Ct. L13: W'tree 5E 79
Newton Cross La. CH48: W Kir 4E 113
Newton Dr. CH48: W Kir 4E 113
Newton Pk. Rd. CH48: W Kir 4E 113
Newton Rd. CH44: Wall 2A 74
  CH47: Hoy 4C 90
  L13: Liv 3E 79
  WA9: St. H 5A 48
Newton St. CH41: Birk 2C 96
Newton Wlk. L20: Boot 4B 34
Newton Way CH49: Upton 4F 93
  L3: Liv 5F 77 (5J 5)
NEWTOWN 4D 173
Newtown Gdns. L32: K'by 3E 23
New Way L14: K Ash 1A 82
New Way Bus. Cen. CH44: Wall 4D 75
Nicander Rd. L18: Moss H 4F 101
Nicholas Rd. L23: Blun 1B 16
  WA8: Wid 4C 130
Nicholas St. L3: Liv 3D 77 (1E 5)
Nicholl Rd. WA10: Eccl 2A 44
Nicholls Dr. CH61: Pens 4F 137
Nichol's Gro. L18: Aller 2C 124
Nicholson St. L5: Liv 5E 55
  WA9: St. H 4E 47
Nickleby Cl. L8: Liv 4F 99
Nickleford Hall Dr. WA8: Wid 3F 109
Nicola Cl. CH45: Wall 5C 52
Nidderdale Av. L35: R'hill 3D 87
Nigel Rd. CH60: Hes 2C 158
Nigel Wlk. WA7: Cas 5A 154
Nightingale Cl. L27: N'ley 4F 105
  L32: K'by 2B 22
  L33: Beech 5F 167
Nightingale Rd. L12: Crox 5F 39
Nimrod St. L4: Walt 2F 55
Ninth Av. L9: Ain 1D 37
Nithsdale Rd. L15: W'tree 3E 101
Nixon St. L4: Walt 1F 55
NOCTORUM 5D 95
Noctorum Av. CH43: Noct 4C 94
Noctorum Dell CH43: Noct 5D 95
Noctorum La. CH43: Noct, O'ton . . .3D 95
Noctorum Rd. CH43: Noct 4D 95
Noctorum Way CH43: Noct 5D 95
Noel St. L8: Liv 2B 100
Nook, The CH43: O'ton 4B 96
  CH48: Frank 2B 114
  L25: Gate 1B 126
  WA10: Windle 2B 44
Nook La. WA9: St. H 2F 67
Nook Ri. L15: W'tree 1B 102
Noonan Cl. L9: Walt 4F 35
Norbreck Av. L14: B Grn 4E 81
Norbury Av. CH63: High B 2E 141
  L18: Moss H 4F 101
Norbury Cl. CH63: High B 2F 141
  L32: K'by 3D 23
  WA8: Wid 3D 133
Norbury Fold L35: R'hill 5E 87
Norbury Rd. L32: K'by 3D 23
Norbury Wlk. L32: K'by 3D 23
Norcliffe Rd. L35: R'hill 2B 86
Norcott Dr. WA5: B'wood 5F 69
Norfolk Cl. CH43: Noct 5C 94
  L20: Boot 4D 35
Norfolk Dr. CH48: W Kir 5C 112
Norfolk Pl. L21: Sea 1A 34
  WA8: Wid 4C 130
Norfolk Rd. L31: Mag 3C 12
  WA10: St. H 2D 65
Norfolk St. L1: Liv 2D 99
  WA7: Run 4B 152
Norgate St. L4: Walt 4F 55

Norgrove Cl. WA7: Murd 2D **169**
Norlands Ct. CH42: R Ferr 3E **119**
Norland's La. L35: R'hill 1E **109**
  WA8: Cron 1E **109**
  WA8: Wid 3F **109**
Norlands Pk. WA8: Wid 3F **109**
Norland St. WA8: Wid 3D **133**
Norleane Cres. WA7: Run 2B **166**
Norley Av. CH62: East 2E **171**
Norley Dr. WA10: Eccl 5A **44**
Norley Rd. WA11: Hay 1F **49**
Norley Pl. L26: Halew 1E **147**
Norman Av. WA11: Hay 1F **49**
Normandale Rd. L4: Walt 2D **57**
Normandy Rd. L36: Huy 3D **83**
Norman Rd. CH44: Wall 4E **75**
  L20: Boot 1C **34**
  L23: C'by 2D **17**
  WA7: Nort 1A **166**
Norman Salisbury Ct.
  WA10: St H 4F **45**
Normans Rd. WA9: St. H 4F **67**
Normanston Cl. CH43: O'ton 5B **96**
Normanston Rd.
  CH43: O'ton 5B **96**
Norman St. CH41: Birk 1F **95**
  L3: Liv 4F **77** (3J **5**)
Normanton Av. L17: Aig 1C **122**
Norma Rd. L22: Water 4E **17**
Normington Cl. L31: Lyd 3C **6**
Norris Cl. CH43: Noct 5C **94**
NORRIS GREEN 1F **57**
Norris Grn. Cres. L11: N Grn. 2F **57**
Norris Grn. Rd. L12: W Der 5B **58**
Norris Grn. Way L11: N Grn. 2A **58**
Norris Rd. L34: Prsct 5C **62**
Norseman Cl. L12: W Der 3B **58**
Nth. Atlantic Cl. L36: Huy 2D **83**
North Av. L10: Ain 3E **21**
  L24: Speke 1A **146**
Nth. Barcombe Rd. L16: Child 2D **103**
Northbrook Cl. L8: Liv 2A **100**
Northbrooke Way CH49: W'chu . .1A **116**
Northbrook Rd. CH44: Wall 3D **75**
Northbrook St. L8: Liv 2A **100**
  (Granby St.)
  L8: Liv 2F **99**
  (Park Way)
Nth. Cantril Av. L12: W Der 3E **59**
  (not continuous)
Nth. Cheshire Trad. Est.
  CH43: Pren 4E **117**
North Cl. CH62: Brom 5C **142**
Northcote Cl. L5: Liv 2F **77**
Northcote Rd. CH45: Wall 5D **51**
  L9: Walt 5F **35**
Northdale Rd. L15: W'tree 1F **101**
North Dingle L4: Kirk 3D **55**
North Dr. CH45: Wall 3F **51**
  CH60: Hes 3A **158**
  L12: W Der 1A **80**
  L15: W'tree 1F **101**
NORTH END 1E **127**
North End La. L26: Halew 1E **127**
Northern La. WA8: Wid 1A **130**
Northern Perimeter Rd.
  L30: N'ton 5E **11**
Northern Rd. L24: Speke 3E **147**
Northern Rd., The L23: C'by 5E **9**
Northfield Cl. L33: K'by 1A **24**
  WA9: Clock F 3D **89**
Northfield Rd. L9: Walt 2E **35**
  L20: Boot 2E **35**
NORTH FLORIDA 1D **49**
Nth. Florida Rd. WA11: Hay 1D **49**
North Front L35: Whis 5E **85**
Northgate Rd. L13: Liv 1F **79**
North Gro. L18: Aller 3C **124**
Nth. Hill St. L8: Liv 4F **99**
Nth. John St. L2: Liv 4C **76** (4D **4**)
  WA10: St. H 5F **45**
Nth. Linkside Rd. L25: Wltn 3C **126**
North Mnr. Way L25: Wltn 3C **126**
North Meade L31: Mag 5B **6**
Northmead Rd. L19: Aller 5E **125**

Nth. Mersey Bus. Cen.
  L33: Know I 1C **24**
Nth. Mossley Hill Rd.
  L18: Moss H 5F **101**
North Mt. Rd. L32: K'by 1B **22**
Northop Rd. CH45: Wall 5F **51**
North Pde. CH47: Hoy 4A **90**
  L24: Speke 4E **147**
  L32: K'by 3E **23**
North Pk. Ct. CH44: Wall 3E **75**
North Pk. Rd. L32: K'by 1B **22**
Nth. Parkside Wlk. L12: W Der 3A **58**
Nth. Perimeter Rd. L33: Know I . . .1C **24**
Northridge Rd. CH61: Pens 2A **138**
North Rd. CH42: Tran 1C **118**
  CH48: W Kir 4A **112**
  L14: B Grn 4C **80**
  L19: Gras 5F **123**
  L24: Halew 2E **147**
  WA10: St. H 3F **45**
  WA11: Hay 2E **49**
Nth. Sudley Rd. L17: Aig 2E **123**
North Ter. CH47: Meols 2E **91**
Northumberland Gro. L8: Liv 4D **99**
Northumberland St. L8: Liv 4D **99**
Northumberland Ter. L5: Liv 5E **55**
Northumberland Way
  L30: N'ton 2C **18**
North Vw. L7: Liv 5A **78**
  L36: Huy 4A **84**
Nth. Wallasey App. CH45: Wall . . .1C **72**
Northway CH60: Hes 1D **159**
  L15: W'tree 5B **80**
  L31: Augh, Mag, Lyd 3C **12**
  (not continuous)
  L39: Augh 2E **7**
  WA7: Pal F 2F **167**
  WA8: Wid 3D **131**
Northways CH62: Brom 4D **143**
Northwich Cl. L23: Thorn 4B **10**
Northwich Rd. WA4: Dutt 1F **175**
  WA7: Brook 5B **168**
  WA7: Dutt, Pres B 1D **175**
Nth. William St. CH44: Wall 4E **75**
North Wirral Coastal Pk. 2D **73**
NORTHWOOD 3F **23**
Northwood Rd. CH43: Pren 2F **117**
  L36: Huy 2F **83**
  WA7: Run 5E **153**
NORTON 2D **169**
Norton Dr. CH61: Irby 5C **114**
Norton Ga. WA7: Nort 2C **168**
Norton Gro. L31: Mag 4D **13**
  WA9: St. H 4D **65**
Norton Hill WA7: Wind H 1C **168**
Norton La. WA7: Halt, Nort 2A **168**
  (not continuous)
Norton Priory 4B **154**
Norton Priory Gardens 4B **154**
Norton Rd. CH48: W Kir 3A **112**
Norton Sta. Rd.
Norton St. L3: Liv 4E **77** (3G **5**)
  L20: Boot 3B **34**
Norton Vw. WA7: Halt 2A **168**
Norton Village WA7: Nort 2C **168**
Nortonwood La. WA7: Wind H 2C **168**
Norville Rd. L14: B Grn 4C **80**
Norwich Dr. CH49: Upton 2A **94**
Norwich Rd. L15: W'tree 3A **102**
Norwich Way L32: K'by 3E **23**
Norwood Av. L21: Lith 4B **18**
Norwood Cl. CH49: Grea 1D **115**
Norwood Gro. L6: Liv 2B **78**
Norwood Rd. CH44: Wall 4B **74**
  CH49: Grea 5E **93**
Norwyn Rd. L11: N Grn. 1E **57**
Nottingham Cl. L35: R'hill 1C **86**
Nottingham Rd. L36: Roby 5C **82**
Nowshera Av. CH61: Pens 2F **137**
Nuffield Cl. CH49: Upton 5F **93**
Nun Cl. CH43: O'ton 1B **118**
Nunn St. WA9: St. H 5D **47**

Nunsford Cl. L21: Lith 3D **19**
Nunthorpe Rd. L34: Know 3B **40**
Nurse Rd. CH61: Thing 1B **138**
Nursery Cl. CH43: O'ton 1B **118**
  L25: Hunts X 4C **126**
  WA8: Wid 1D **133**
Nursery La. L19: Gars 5C **124**
Nursery Rd. L31: Lyd 3C **6**
  WA11: Hay 4D **65**
Nursery St. L5: Liv 5D **55**
NUTGROVE 5C **64**
Nutgrove Av. WA9: St. H 4D **65**
Nutgrove Hall Dr. WA9: St. H 4D **65**
Nutgrove Rd. WA9: St. H 5C **64**
Nut St. WA9: St. H 4D **65**
Nuttall St. L7: Liv 5B **78**
Nyland Rd. L36: Huy 1D **83**

O

Oak Av. CH49: Upton 3D **93**
  L9: Ain 2B **36**
  WA11: Hay 1E **49**
Oak Bank CH41: Birk 4C **96**
  CH63: Beb 2A **142**
Oakbank Rd. L18: Moss H 4E **101**
Oakbank St. CH44: Wall 3C **74**
Oakbourne Cl. L17: Aig 2C **122**
Oak Cl. CH46: More 2D **93**
  L12: W Der 2F **59**
  L35: Whis 3E **85**
Oak Ct. L8: Liv 5A **100**
  (off Weller Way)
Oakcross Gdns. L25: Wltn 2C **126**
Oakdale Av. CH44: Wall 4D **75**
Oakdale Cl. L32: K'by 4B **22**
Oakdale Dr. CH49: Grea 2C **114**
Oakdale Rd. CH44: Wall 4D **75**
  L18: Moss H 4A **102**
  L22: Water 3D **17**
Oakdene Cl. CH62: Brom 5D **163**
Oakdene Ct. L35: R'hill 4C **86**
Oakdene Rd. CH42: Tran 1C **118**
  L4: Walt 4B **56**
Oak Dr. WA7: Run 3C **166**
Oakenholt Rd. CH46: More 5E **71**
Oakes St. L3: Liv 4F **77** (4J **5**)
Oakfield L4: Walt 5B **56**
Oakfield Av. L25: Gate 5A **104**
Oakfield Cl. WA9: St. H 4D **65**
Oakfield Dr. L36: Huy 1F **105**
  WA8: Wid 4A **130**
Oakfield Gro. L36: Huy 5F **83**
Oakfield Rd. CH62: Brom 2C **162**
  CH66: Chil T 5E **171**
  L4: Walt 5A **56**
  L38: High 1A **8**
Oakfield Ter. CH66: Chil T 5E **171**
Oakgate Cl. L11: N Grn. 5B **38**
Oakham Dr. CH46: More 5B **70**
  L10: Ain 4F **21**
Oakham St. L8: Liv 3D **99**
Oakhill Av. WA9: Clock F 2C **88**
Oakhill Cl. L12: Crox 5D **39**
  L31: Mag 5D **7**
Oakhill Cottage La. L31: Lyd 3D **7**
Oakhill Dr. L31: Lyd 3D **7**
OAK HILL PARK 4B **80**
Oakhill Pk. L13: Liv 4B **80**
Oakhill Rd. L13: Liv 4B **80**
  L31: Mag 5D **7**
Oakhouse Pk. L9: Walt 5F **35**
Oakhurst Cl. L25: Gate 4B **104**
Oakland Cl. L21: Lith 2C **34**
Oakland Dr. CH49: Upton 3A **94**
Oakland Rd. L19: Aig 4F **123**
Oaklands CH62: Brom 4D **163**
  L35: R'hill 4C **86**
Oaklands Av. L23: C'by 4D **9**
Oaklands Bus. Cen.
  CH66: Hoot 3E **171**
Oaklands Ct. WA9: Clock F 2C **88**
Oaklands Dr. CH61: Hes 1A **158**
  CH63: Beb 1F **141**
Oaklands Ter. CH61: Hes 1A **158**

Oakland St. WA8: Wid 3A 152
Oakland Va. CH45: New B 3C 52
Oak La. L12: W Der 2B 58
Oakleaf M. CH43: Noct 4D 95
Oaklea Rd. CH61: Irby 1F 137
Oaklee Gro. L33: K'by 1A 24
Oak Leigh L13: Liv 1E 79
Oakleigh Gro.
  CH63: Beb 1F 141
Oakley Cl. L12: Crox 5E 39
Oak Mdws. L35: R'hill 5E 87
Oakmere Cl. CH46: Leas 3E 71
  L9: Walt 1A 36
Oakmere Dr. CH49: Grea 5C 92
Oakmere St. WA7: Run 5A 152
Oakridge Cl. CH62: Spit 5C 142
Oakridge Rd. CH62: Spit 5C 142
Oak Rd. CH63: High B 5F 119
  CH66: Hoot 4E 171
  L35: Whis 3E 85
  L36: Huy 5D 83
Oaks, The CH62: Brom 2C 162
  L12: Crox 5F 39
  WA9: Sut L 2D 89
Oaks Cl. WA9: Clock F 3D 89
Oaks La. CH61: Pens 3A 138
Oaksmeade Cl. L12: Crox 1F 59
Oaks Pl. WA8: Wid 5A 132
Oakston Av. L35: R'hill 4D 87
Oak St. L20: Boot 4C 34
  WA9: St. H 3E 67
Oaksway CH60: Hes 4B 158
Oak Ter. L7: Liv 4C 78
Oakthorn Gro. WA11: Hay 2C 48
Oaktree Pl. CH42: R Ferr 1F 119
Oaktree Rd. WA10: Eccl 3A 44
Oak Va. L13: Liv 4B 80
OAK VALE PARK 4B 80
Oak Vw. L24: Speke 4A 148
Oakwood Cl. L25: Gate 4B 104
Oakwood Dr. CH43: Bid 1E 95
  L36: Huy 5F 83
Oakwood Pk. CH62: Brom 5D 163
Oakwood Rd. L26: Halew 5E 127
Oakworth Cl. L33: K'by 1E 23
Oakworth Dr. CH62: New F 5C 120
  L35: Tar G 2A 106
Oarside Dr. CH45: Wall 5A 52
Oatfield La. L21: Ford 3B 18
Oatlands, The CH48: W Kir 5C 112
Oatlands Rd. L32: K'by 3C 22
Oban Dr. CH60: Hes 2A 158
Oban Rd. L4: Walt 5B 56
Oberon St. L20: Kirk 2C 54
O'Brien Gro. WA9: St. H 4E 47
Observatory Rd. CH43: Bid 1E 95
Oceanic Rd. L13: Liv 4F 79
Ocean Pk. CH44: Wall 5D 75
Ocean Rd. L21: Lith 1B 34
O'Connell Cl. WA11: Hay 2C 48
O'Connell Rd. L3: Liv 2D 77
O'Connor Gro. L33: K'by 4E 15
Octavia Cl. L36: Huy 5F 83
Octavia Hill Rd. L21: Ford 4C 18
Oddfellows Arms Yd. L25: Wltn . . .2A 126
  (off Allerton Rd.)
Odeon Cinema
  Bromborough 4E 143
  Liverpool 4E 77 (4G 5)
  Mossley Hill 5B 102
  Netherton 2F 19
Odsey St. L7: Liv 4C 78
Odyssey Cen. CH41: Birk 1C 96
Ogden Cl. L13: W Der 3F 57
Ogle Cl. L35: Prsct 1E 85
Oglet La. L24: Speke 5C 146
Oil St. L3: Liv 2B 76 (1A 4)
O'Keefe Rd. WA9: St. H 4C 46
Okehampton Rd. L16: Child 1D 103
Okell Dr. L26: Halew 2D 127
Okell St. WA7: Run 5A 152
Old Albert Ter. WA7: Run 4B 152
  (off Thomas St.)
Old Barn La. CH64: Will 5A 170

Old Barn Rd. CH44: Wall 3A 74
  L4: Walt 5B 56
Old Bidston Rd. CH41: Birk 1B 96
OLD BOSTON 1F 49
Oldbridge Rd. L24: Speke 5F 147
Old Chester Rd. CH41: Tran 5E 97
  CH42: R Ferr, Tran 3F 119
  CH63: Beb, High B 5A 120
Old Church Cl. L9: Ain 1B 36
Old Church Yd. L2: Liv 4B 76 (5C 4)
Old Clatterbridge Rd.
  CH63: Spit 5E 141
Old Coach Rd. WA7: Run 4F 151
Old College Pl. L7: Liv 5C 78
Old Colliery Rd. L35: Whis 3D 85
Old Court Ho. Rd. CH62: Brom . . .2D 143
Old Dover Rd. L36: Roby 5C 82
Old Eccleston La. WA10: St. H . . .5C 44
Old Farm Cl. CH64: Will 5A 170
Old Farm Rd. L23: C'by 5F 9
  L32: K'by 2F 39
Old Field L35: Whis 2F 85
Oldfield Cl. CH60: Hes 5E 137
Oldfield Cotts. CH60: Hes 5D 137
Oldfield Dr. CH60: Hes 1D 157
Oldfield Farm La. CH60: Hes 5D 137
Oldfield Gdns. CH60: Hes 1D 157
Oldfield La. CH48: W Kir 5A 92
Oldfield Rd. CH45: Wall 5F 51
  CH60: Hes 5D 137
  L19: Aig 4A 124
Oldfield Way CH60: Hes 5D 137
Oldgate WA8: Wid 5C 130
Old Gorsey La. CH44: Wall 4B 74
Old Greasby Rd. CH49: Upton 4F 93
Old Hall Cl. L31: Mag 3D 13
Old Hall La. L32: K'by 3D 23
Old Hall Rd. CH62: Brom 1E 163
  L31: Mag 3D 13
Old Hall St. L3: Liv 4B 76 (3B 4)
  L31: Mag 5E 77 (6H 5)
Oldham St. L1: Liv 5E 77 (7G 5)
Old Haymarket L1: Liv 4D 77 (4E 5)
  (not continuous)
Old Higher Rd. WA8: Hale B 2D 149
Old Hutte La. L24: Halew 2A 148
  L26: Halew 2A 148
Old Kennel Cl. L12: W Der 3F 59
Old La. CH60: Hes 2D 159
  L31: Lyd 3E 7
  L34: Ecc P 4F 63
  L35: R'hill 3B 86
Old Leeds St. L3: Liv 4B 76 (3B 4)
Old Lodge Cl. L12: W Der 3B 58
Old Maryland La. CH46: More 5E 71
Old Mdw. L34: Know 4D 41
Old Mdw. Rd. CH61: Pens 4E 137
Old Mill Av. WA9: Sut L 1D 89
Old Mill Cl. CH60: Hes 3B 158
  L15: W'tree 1A 102
Old Mill La. L15: W'tree 1A 102
  L34: Know P 4E 41
Old Nook La. WA11: St. H 2E 47
Old Orchard L35: Whis 5E 85
Old Post Office Pl. L1: Liv 6E 5
Old Pump La. CH49: Grea 1C 114
Old Quarry, The L25: Wltn 2A 126
Old Quay St. WA7: Run 4B 152
Old Racecourse, The
  WA12: New W 5E 49
Old Racecourse Rd. L31: Mag 2B 12
Old Rectory Grn. L29: Seft 3E 11
  L39: Augh 1F 7
Old Riding L14: K Ash 1F 81
Old Roan Station (Rail) 2B 20
Old Ropery L2: Liv 5C 76 (5C 4)
Old Rough La. L33: K'by 2E 23
Old School Way CH41: Birk 2E 95
Old Stable Yd. L7: Liv 5A 78
OLD SWAN 3F 79
Old Thomas La. L14: B Grn 5D 81
Old Upton La. WA8: Wid 5E 109
Old Vicarage Rd. CH64: Will 5A 170
Old Whint Rd. WA11: Hay 2A 48

Old Wood Rd. CH61: Pens 3F 137
Oleander Dr. WA10: St. H 4C 44
Olga Rd. WA9: St. H 4C 66
Olinda St. CH62: New F 5B 120
Olive Cl. L31: Mell 3A 22
Olive Cres. CH41: Tran 5E 97
Olivedale Rd. L18: Moss H 4F 101
Olive Gro. L15: W'tree 5A 80
  L30: N'ton 4A 20
  L36: Roby 4D 83
Olive La. L15: W'tree 5A 80
Olive Mt. L15: W'tree 5E 97
Olive Mt. Heights L15: W'tree 1A 102
Olive Mt. Rd. L15: W'tree 1A 102
Olive Mt. Vs. L15: W'tree 5A 80
Olive Mt. Wlk. L15: W'tree 1A 102
Oliver La. CH41: Birk 3E 97
Oliver Lyme Ho. L34: Prsct 5E 63
Oliver Lyme Rd. L34: Prsct 5E 63
Olive Rd. L22: Water 5E 17
Oliver St. WA10: St. H 2C 64
Oliver St. CH41: Birk 3D 97
Oliver St. E. CH41: Birk 3E 97
Olivetree Rd. L15: W'tree 5B 80
Olive Va. L15: W'tree 1F 101
Olivia Cl. CH43: Noct 5C 94
Olivia M. CH43: Noct 5C 94
Olivia St. L20: Boot 2D 55
Olivia Way L36: Huy 4B 84
Ollerton Cl. CH43: Noct 5C 94
Ollerton Pk. WA5: B'wood 4E 69
Ollery Grn. L30: N'ton 1B 20
Ollier St. WA8: Wid 5A 132
Olney St. L4: Walt 1F 55
Olton St. L15: W'tree 1E 101
Olympia St. L6: Liv 3A 78
Olympic Way L30: N'ton 5B 20
O' Neill St. L20: Boot 4B 34
  (not continuous)
Onslow Rd. CH45: New B 3B 52
  CH62: New F 3B 120
  L6: Liv 3C 78
Ontario Cl. L27: N'ley 4E 105
Opal Cl. L6: Liv 2B 78
  L21: Lith 5C 18
Open Eye Gallery 5D 77 (6F 5)
Openfields Cl. L26: Halew 2E 127
Oppenheim Av. WA10: St. H 3C 64
Orange Gro. L8: Liv 3B 100
Orange Tree Cl. L28: Stock V 3B 60
Oran Way L36: Huy 3D 83
Orb Cl. L11: Crox 4C 38
Orb Wlk. L11: Crox 5C 38
Orchard, The CH45: Wall 4A 52
  L17: Aig 3F 123
  L35: R'hill 1C 86
  L36: Huy 4E 83
Orchard Av. L14: B Grn 5D 81
Orchard Cl. L34: Ecc P 4A 64
  L35: Whis 5E 85
  WA11: St. H 1D 47
Orchard Cl. CH41: Tran 1F 119
  L31: Mag 1E 13
  WA6: Frod 5A 172
Orchard Dale L23: C'by 1F 17
Orchard Dene L35: R'hill 3C 86
Orchard Gdns. L35: Whis 1E 107
Orchard Grange CH46: More 2C 92
Orchard Hey L30: N'ton 1B 20
  L31: Mag 2E 13
  WA10: Eccl 5A 44
Orchard Rd. CH46: More 5E 71
Orchard Wlk. WA7: Pal F 3F 167
  (off Halton Lea Shop. Cen.)
Orchard Way CH63: High B 1D 141
  WA8: Wid 1A 130
Orchid Gro. L17: Aig 1F 121
Orchid Way WA9: Bold 4B 68
O'Reilly Ct. L3: Liv 2C 76
Orford Cl. L24: Hale 5D 149
Orford St. L15: W'tree 1F 101
Oriel Cl. L2: Liv 5B 76 (5C 4)
  L10: Ain 2D 21
Oriel Cres. L20: Kirk 2C 54
Oriel Dr. L10: Ain 2C 20

Oriel Lodge. L20: Boot 1C 54
Oriel Rd. CH42: Tran 1E 119
  L20: Boot 5B 34
  L20: Kirk 2C 54
Oriel St. L3: Liv 3C 76 (1D 4)
Orient Dr. L25: Wltn 1B 126
Origen Rd. L16: Child 5D 81
Oriole Cl. WA10: St. H 4B 64
Orith Av. WA10: Eccl 5F 43
Orkney Cl. WA8: Wid 1E 133
  WA11: St. H 1D 47
Orlando Cl. CH43: Noct 5C 94
Orlando St. L20: Boot 2C 54
Orleans Rd. L13: Liv 3A 80
Ormande St. WA9: St. H 2B 66
Ormesby Gdns. WA9: St. H 5E 65
Ormesby Gro. CH63: Raby M 4B 162
Ormiston Rd. CH45: New B 4B 52
Ormond Cl. WA8: Wid 2C 130
Ormonde Av. L31: Mag 3C 12
Ormonde Cres. L33: K'by 3A 24
Ormonde Dr. L31: Mag 2C 12
Ormond M. CH43: Noct 5C 94
Ormond St. CH45: Wall 1B 74
  L3: Liv 4C 76 (4C 4)
Ormond Way CH43: Noct 5C 94
Ormsby St. L15: W'tree 2E 101
Ormside Gro. WA9: St. H 4D 67
Ormskirk Rd. L9: Ain 5B 20
  L10: Ain, N'ton 5B 20
  L30: N'ton 5B 20
  L34: Know 2D 41
Ormskirk St. WA10: St. H 4F 45
Orphan Dr. L6: Liv 1D 79
  (not continuous)
Orphan St. L7: Liv 1A 100
ORRELL .2D 35
Orrell Hey L20: Boot 1D 35
Orrell La. L9: Walt 1E 35
  L20: Boot 1E 35
Orrell Lodge L20: Boot 2E 35
Orrell Mt. L20: Boot 1C 34
Orrell Mt. Ind. Est. L21: Lith 1C 34
ORRELL PARK 2A 36
Orrell Park Station (Rail) 2A 36
Orrell Rd. CH45: New B 4C 52
  L20: Boot 5C 18
  L21: Lith 5C 18
Orrell St. WA9: St. H 4C 46
Orret's Mdw. Rd.
  CH49: W'chu 1B 116
Orrysdale Rd. CH48: W Kir 3A 112
Orry St. L5: Liv 1D 77
Orsett Rd. L32: K'by 5F 23
Orston Cres. CH63: Spit 5A 142
Ortega Cl. CH62: New F 5C 120
Orthes St. L3: Liv 5F 77 (6J 5)
Orton Rd. L16: Child 1C 102
Orville St. WA9: St. H 4E 67
Orwell Cl. WA9: Sut M 3A 88
Orwell Rd. L4: Kirk 3D 55
Osbert Rd. L23: Blun 1B 16
Osborne Av. CH45: New B 4B 52
Osborne Gro. CH45: New B 5B 52
  L34: Prsct 1A 84
Osborne Rd. CH43: O'ton 4B 96
  CH45: New B 4C 52
  L13: Liv 5E 57
  L21: Lith 4C 18
  (not continuous)
  WA10: Eccl 3A 44
Osborne Va. CH45: New B 4B 52
Osborne Wood L17: Aig 3C 122
Osbourne Cl. CH62: Brom 3E 163
Osbourne Ct. WA10: St. H 3C 64
Osmaston Rd. CH42: Tran 2A 118
Osprey Cl. L27: N'ley 4F 105
  WA7: Beech 5F 167
Ossett Cl. CH43: Noct 5C 94
  WA7: Nort 2D 169
Osterley Gdns. L9: Walt 2F 35
O'Sullivan Cres. WA11: St. H 3E 47
Oswald Cl. L33: K'by 4E 15
Oteley Av. CH62: Brom 2D 163
Othello Cl. L20: Kirk 2C 54

Otterburn Cl. CH46: More 1B 92
OTTERSPOOL 3C 122
Otterspool Dr. L17: Aig 4D 123
Otterspool Rd. L17: Aig 3D 123
Otterton Rd. L11: Crox 3C 38
Ottley St. L6: Liv 3C 78
Otway St. L19: Gars 3C 144
Oulton Cl. CH43: O'ton 1E 117
  L31: Lyd 3B 6
Oulton Gdns. WA9: St. H 5E 65
Oulton La. L36: Roby 1D 105
Oulton Rd. L16: Child 3D 103
Oulton Way CH43: O'ton 2E 117
Oundle Dr. L10: Ain 2C 20
Oundle Pl. L25: Hunts X 5B 126
Oundle Rd. CH46: More 5E 71
Outer Central Rd.
  L24: Halew 2E 147
Outer Forum L11: N Grn 1E 57
Out La. L25: Wltn 2A 126
Outlet La. L31: Bic, Mell 1D 15
  L39: Bic 1F 15
Oval, The 5F 119
Oval, The CH45: Wall 5F 51
Overbrook La. L34: Know 3B 40
Overbury St. L7: Liv 1B 100
Overchurch Rd.
  CH49: Upton 3E 93
Overdale Av. CH61: Barn 2D 139
Overdale Rd. CH64: Will 4A 170
Overdene Wlk. L32: K'by 4F 23
Overgreen Gro.
  CH46: More 5D 71
Overton Av. L21: Lith 4B 18
Overton Cl. CH43: O'ton 1F 117
  L32: K'by 4D 23
Overton Rd. CH44: Wall 2B 74
Overton St. L13: Liv 5B 78
Overton Way CH43: O'ton 1F 117
Ovington Cl. WA7: Sut W 1F 173
Ovolo Rd. L13: Liv 2A 80
Owdale Rd. L9: Walt 4A 36
Owen Av. WA10: St. H 2D 65
Owen Dr. L24: Speke 4B 146
Owen Rd. L4: Kirk 3D 55
  L33: Know I 1C 40
  L35: R'hill 4C 86
Owen St. WA10: St. H 2C 64
Oxborough Cl. WA8: Wid 1F 131
Oxbow Rd. L12: W Der 3E 59
Oxendale Cl. L8: Liv 2B 100
Oxenholme Cres.
  L11: N Grn 2A 58
Oxford Av. L20: Boot 5D 35
  L21: Lith 5B 18
Oxford Cl. L17: Aig 2C 122
Oxford Ct. L22: Water 3C 16
Oxford Dr. CH63: Thorn H 4F 159
  L22: Water 3C 16
  L26: Halew 4F 127
Oxford Ho. L20: Boot 5E 35
  (off Fernhill Rd.)
Oxford Rd. CH44: Wall 2C 74
  L9: Ain 5B 20
  L20: Boot 5D 35
  L22: Water 3C 16
  L36: Huy 2A 84
  WA7: Run 1A 166
Oxford St. L7: Liv 5F 77 (6J 5)
  (not continuous)
  WA8: Wid 5B 132
  WA10: St. H 1F 45
  (Cooper St.)
  WA10: St. H 1F 45
  (Rutland St.)
Oxford St. E. L7: Liv 5A 78
Oxheys WA7: Nort 2C 168
Ox La. L35: Tar G 2C 106
Oxley Av. CH46: Leas 3B 72
Oxley St. WA9: St. H 4D 67
Oxmoor Cl. WA7: Brook 5A 168
OXTON 5F 95
Oxton Cl. L17: Aig 2C 122
  L32: K'by 5B 22
  WA8: Wid 5C 108

Oxton Rd. CH41: Birk 4C 96
  CH43: O'ton 4C 96
  CH44: Wall 3B 74
Oxton St. L4: Walt 3F 55

P

Pacific Rd. CH41: Birk 2F 97
  L20: Boot 5B 34
  (Atlantic Rd.)
  L20: Boot 4B 34
  (Sea Vw. Rd.)
Packenham Rd. L13: Liv 5F 57
Padbury St. L8: Liv 4A 100
Paddington L7: Liv 5A 78
  (not continuous)
Paddock, The CH46: More 2C 92
  CH49: Upton 4B 94
  CH60: Hes 2C 158
  L25: Gate 5B 104
  L32: K'by 1D 39
  L34: Ecc P 4A 64
Paddock Cl. L23: Blun 4B 8
Paddock Gro. WA9: Clock F 3D 89
Paddock Ri. WA7: Beech 1E 173
Paddock Rd. L34: Prsct 5A 62
Padeswood Cl. WA9: St. H 5C 66
Padstow Cl. L26: Halew 3E 127
Padstow Dr. WA10: Windle 2B 44
Padstow Rd. CH49: Grea 1C 114
  L16: Child 1D 103
Padstow Sq. WA7: Brook 5B 168
Pagebank Rd. L14: K Ash 3A 82
Pagefield Rd. L15: W'tree 3F 101
Page Grn. L36: Huy 3C 82
Page La. WA8: Wid 3C 132
PAGE MOSS 4B 82
Page Moss Av. L36: Huy 2B 82
Page Moss La. L14: K Ash 3A 82
Page Moss Pde. L36: Huy 2B 82
Page Wlk. L3: Liv 3E 77 (2H 5)
  (not continuous)
Pagewood Cl. CH43: Noct 5D 95
Paignton Cl. L36: Huy 3B 84
Paignton Rd. CH45: Wall 5F 51
  L16: Child 1D 103
Paisley Av. CH62: East 1E 171
  WA11: St. H 1D 47
Paisley Ct. L14: K Ash 2F 81
Paisley St. L3: Liv 3B 76 (2A 4)
PALACE FIELDS 4A 168
Palacefields Av. WA7: Pal F 4F 167
Palace Rd. L9: Ain 2A 36
Palatine, The L20: Boot 5C 34
Palatine Arc. WA10: St. H 5A 46
Palatine Rd. CH44: Wall 4D 75
  CH62: Brom 1C 162
Palermo Cl. CH44: Wall 4D 75
Paley Cl. L4: Walt 4F 55
Palladio Rd. L13: Liv 2A 80
Pall Mall L3: Liv 3B 76 (1C 4)
Pall Mall Cen. L3: Liv 3B 76 (2C 4)
Palm Cl. L9: Walt 5C 36
Palm Ct. L8: Liv 5A 100
  (off Weller Way)
Palmer Cl. CH43: Noct 1D 117
  WA10: St. H 4F 45
Palmerston Av. L21: Lith 1A 34
Palmerston Cl. L18: Moss H 1F 123
Palmerston Ct. L18: Moss H 1F 123
Palmerston Dr. L21: Lith 1B 34
  L25: Hunts X 5D 127
Palmerston Rd. CH44: Wall 2F 73
  L18: Moss H 1F 123
  L19: Gars 1C 144
Palmerston St. CH42: R Ferr 2F 119
Palm Gro. CH43: O'ton 3B 96
  L25: Wltn 3B 126
Palm Hill CH43: O'ton 5B 96
Palmwood Av. L35: R'hill 4D 87
Palmwood Cl. CH43: Pren 3E 117
Paltridge Way CH61: Pens 3F 137
Pamela Cl. L10: Faz 1B 38
Pampas Gro. L9: Walt 4B 36

Pankhurst Rd. L21: Ford 3C 18
Pansy St. L5: Kirk 4D 55
Panton Way L10: Faz 2B 38
Parade, The L15: W'tree 5B 80
L26: Halew 5E 127
Parade Cres. L24: Speke 5E 147
Parade St. WA10: St. H 4A 46
Paradise Gdns. L15: W'tree 2F 101
Paradise La. L35: Whis 4D 85
Paradise St.
    L1: Liv 1C 98 (6E 4)
Paragon Cl. WA8: Wid 4B 110
Parbold Av. WA11: St. H 3D 47
Parbold Cl. WA8: Wid 4D 131
Parbrook Cl. L36: Huy 5D 61
Parbrook Rd. L36: Huy 5D 61
Parc Play & Resource Cen. 4A 24
Parish M. L14: K Ash 2E 81
Park, The L36: Huy 5E 83
Park Av. CH44: Wall 3D 75
    L9: Ain 1C 36
    L18: Moss H 1E 123
    L23: C'by 5E 9
    L31: Lyd 4D 7
    L34: Ecc P 4F 63
    L35: R'hill 2C 86
    WA8: Wid 2B 132
    WA11: Hay 2A 48
Parkbourne Dr. L31: Mag 5F 7
Parkbourn Sq. L31: Mag 5F 7
Parkbridge Rd. CH42: Tran 1C 118
Pk. Brow Dr. L32: K'by 5F 23
Parkbury Cl. L30: O'ton 1A 118
Park Cl. CH41: Birk 3C 96
    L32: K'by 1B 22
            (not continuous)
Park Ct. CH48: W Kir 4A 112
    L22: Water 5E 17
    L32: K'by 2C 22
    WA6: Frod 5A 172
    WA7: Run 2A 166
    WA9: St. H 3B 66
Parkdale CH48: Caldy 3D 135
Parkdale Av. L9: Walt 1A 36
Park Dr. CH41: Birk 2B 96
    CH43: C'ton 2A 96
    L23: Blun 5A 8
    L23: Thorn 3A 10
Parkend Rd. CH42: Tran 1C 118
Parker Av. L21: Sea 1F 33
Parker Cl. L30: N'ton 4B 20
Parkers Ct. WA7: Pal F 4E 167
Parker St. L1: Liv 5D 77 (5F 5)
    WA7: Run 4B 152
Parkfield Av. CH41: Birk 3D 97
    L30: N'ton 5A 20
Parkfield Dr. CH44: Wall 2B 74
Parkfield Gro. L31: Mag 1C 12
Parkfield Pl. CH41: Birk 3D 97
Parkfield Rd. CH63: Beb 4A 142
    L17: Aig 5B 100
    L22: Water 3E 17
Parkgate Cl. L17: Aig 3E 123
Parkgate La. CH64: Nest 5A 159
Parkgate Way WA7: Murd 4C 168
Park Gro. CH41: Birk 4D 97
Pk. Hill Ct. L8: Liv 5F 99
Park Hill Rd. L8: Liv 5F 99
Parkhill Rd. CH42: Tran 1C 118
Parkholme L22: Water 4E 17
Parkhurst Rd. CH42: Tran 2C 118
    L11: N Grn. 2F 57
Parkinson Rd. L9: Walt 4A 36
Parkland Cl. L8: Liv 4F 99
Parkland Ct. CH43: Bid 1C 94
Parklands L34: Know 5D 41
    WA8: Wid 1C 130
Parklands Ct. CH49: W'chu 2A 116
            (off Childwall Grn.)
Parklands Dr. CH60: Hes 4B 158
Parklands Way L22: Water 4E 17
Park La. CH47: Meols 5A 70
    L1: Liv 1C 98 (7D 4)
    L20: Boot 1E 35
    L30: N'ton 3F 19

Park La. L31: Mag . . . . . . .4F 7 & 1A 14
    WA6: Frod 5B 172
Park La. W. L30: N'ton 2F 19
Park Pl. L8: Liv 3E 99
    L20: Boot 5C 34
Park Rd. CH42: Tran 1E 119
    CH44: Wall 2C 74
    CH47: Meols 2E 91
    CH48: W Kir 4A 112
    CH60: Hes 1B 158
    CH62: East 4F 163
    CH62: Port S 2B 142
    CH64: Will 5B 170
    L8: Liv 4F 99
    L22: Water 4E 17
    L32: K'by 2B 22
            (not continuous)
    L34: Prsct 4C 62
    WA7: Run 2F 165
    WA8: Wid 3B 132
    WA9: St. H 4C 46
    WA11: St. H 5C 46
Park Rd. E. CH41: Birk 3C 96
Park Rd. Nth. CH41: Birk 2F 95
Park Rd. Sth. CH43: C'ton 3B 96
Park Road Sports Cen. 4F 99
Park Rd. W. CH43: C'ton 2F 95
Parkside CH44: Wall 3C 74
    L20: Boot 4C 34
Parkside Av. WA9: Sut M 3B 88
Parkside Cl. CH63: Beb 1A 142
    L27: N'ley 5E 105
Parkside Ct. WA8: Wid 2A 132
Parkside Dr. L12: W Der 3A 58
Parkside Mans. L36: Huy 4B 84
Parkside Rd. CH42: Tran 1E 119
    CH63: Beb 1A 142
Parkside St. L6: Liv 3F 77
Parkstile La. L11: Crox 4C 38
Parkstone Rd. CH42: Tran 1C 118
Park St. CH41: Birk 3D 97
            (not continuous)
    CH44: Wall 2C 74
    L8: Liv 4D 99
    L20: Boot 5C 34
    WA9: St. H 4C 46
Park Ter. L22: Water 5E 17
Parkvale Av. CH43: Pren 4E 117
Pk. Vale Rd. L9: Walt 2A 36
Park Vw. CH62: Brom 2C 162
    L6: Liv 1D 79
    L22: Water 3D 17
    L23: Thorn 3B 10
    L36: Huy 2C 82
Parkview L9: Walt 4A 36
Parkview Cl. CH41: Birk 2C 96
Parkview Ct. CH60: Hes 2F 157
Parkview Dr. L27: N'ley 5E 105
Park Vw. Flats L21: Sea 5A 18
Parkview Rd. L11: Crox 2D 39
Pk. Wall Rd. L29: Thorn 1A 10
    L38: Ince B, Thorn 1B 10
Park Way L8: Liv 2F 99
            (not continuous)
    L36: Huy 4D 61
Parkway CH45: Wall 4E 51
    CH47: Meols 3E 91
    CH61: Irby 5F 115
    L23: C'by 3F 17
    L30: N'ton 5F 11
Parkway Cl. CH61: Irby 5F 115
Parkway E. L32: K'by 2B 22
Parkway W. L32: K'by 2B 22
Park W. CH60: Hes 3D 157
Parkwood Cl. CH62: Brom 1D 163
Parkwood Rd. L25: Wltn 5A 104
    L35: Whis 4E 85
Parlane St. WA9: St. H 4C 46
            (not continuous)
Parle Ct. L6: Liv 1B 78
Parliament Bus. Pk.
    L8: Liv 2B 100
Parliament Cl. L1: Liv 2E 99
Parliament Pl. L8: Liv 2F 99

Parliament St. L8: Liv 2D 99
    WA9: St. H 4D 65
Parlington Cl. WA8: Wid 5C 130
Parlow Rd. L11: N Grn. 3E 57
Parnell Rd. CH63: Spit 4A 142
PARR 5D 47
Parr Community Swimming Pool 5C 46
Parren Av. L35: Whis 5C 84
Parr Gro. CH49: Grea 5C 92
    WA11: Hay 2A 48
Parr Ind. Est. WA9: St. H 1E 67
Parr Mt. Ct. WA9: St. H 5C 46
Parr Mt. St. WA9: St. H 5C 46
Parrs Cnr. Trad. Est. L20: Boot 4C 34
            (off Stanley Rd.)
Parr's Rd. CH43: O'ton 1B 118
PARR STOCKS 1D 67
Parr Stocks Rd. WA9: St. H 5D 47
Part St. L1: Liv 1D 99 (7F 5)
    WA8: Wid 3C 132
    WA9: St. H 5B 46
    WA10: St. H 5B 46
Parry's La. WA7: Run 1A 166
Parry St. CH44: Wall 4D 75
Parsonage Rd. WA8: Wid 3A 152
Parthenon Dr. L11: N Grn. 5D 37
Partington Av. L20: Boot 4E 35
Parton St. L6: Liv 3C 78
Partridge Cl. L12: Crox 5F 39
Partridge Rd. L23: Blun 1B 16
    L32: K'by 2B 22
Passway WA11: St. H 5C 30
Pasture Av. CH46: More 4E 71
Pasture Cl. L25: Wltn 3B 126
    WA9: Clock F 2C 88
Pasture Cres. CH46: More 5E 71
Pasture La. WA11: R'ford 1A 28
Pasture La. Bus. Cen.
    WA11: R'ford 1A 28
Pasture Rd. CH46: More 3D 71
Pastures, The CH48: W Kir 4F 113
    WA9: Bold 4A 68
Pateley Cl. L32: K'by 4C 22
Pateley Wlk. L24: Speke 3F 147
Paterson St. CH41: Birk 3C 96
Patmos Cl. L5: Liv 5E 55
Paton Cl. CH48: W Kir 3D 113
Patricia Av. CH41: Birk 5F 73
Patricia Ct. WA10: St. H 4F 45
Patricia Gro. L20: Boot 2D 35
Patrick Av. L20: Boot 1D 35
Pattens Cl. L30: N'ton 1D 19
Patten St. CH41: Birk 1A 96
Patten's Wlk. L34: Know P 3D 41
Patterdale Cres. L31: Mag 5E 7
Patterdale Dr. WA10: St. H 3B 64
Patterdale Rd. CH63: Beb 4F 141
    L15: W'tree 3E 101
Pauldings La. L21: Lith 5A 18
Pauline Wlk. L10: Faz 1B 38
Paul McCartney Way L6: Liv 3B 78
Paul Orr Ct. L3: Liv 2C 76
Paulsfield Dr. CH46: More 2E 93
Paul St. L3: Liv 3C 76 (1D 4)
Paulton Cl. L8: Liv 5F 99
Paverley Bank L27: N'ley 3D 105
Pavilion Cl. L8: Liv 2B 100
Pavilion Ct. WA12: New W 5F 49
Pavilion Sports Cen. 5A 58
Paxton Rd. L36: Huy 2E 83
Peacehaven Cl. L16: Child 1F 103
Peach Gro. L31: Mell 1B 22
    WA11: Hay 1E 49
Peach St. L7: Liv 5F 77
Peach Tree Cl. L24: Hale 5E 149
Pearce Cl. L25: Wltn 3F 103
Pear Gro. L6: Liv 3B 78
Pearl Way L6: Liv 2B 78
Pearson Dr. L20: Boot 1E 35
Pearson Rd. CH42: Tran 5E 97
Pearson St. L15: W'tree 2F 101
Pear Tree Av. L12: W Der 2F 59
    WA7: Run 3C 166
Pear Tree Cl. CH60: Hes 1C 158
    L24: Hale 5E 149

Peartree Cl. WA6: Frod 4D 173
Pear Tree Rd. L36: Huy 1E 105
Peasefield Rd. L14: K Ash 2A 82
PEASLEY CROSS 2C 66
Peasley Cross La. WA9: St. H 5B 46
Peatwood Av. L32: K'by 1F 39
Peckers Hill Rd. WA9: St. H 4E 67
Peckfield Cl. WA7: Brook 5A 168
Peckforton Cl. L13: Liv 5E 57
Peckforton Dr. WA7: Sut W 1F 173
Peckmill Grn. L27: N'ley 5F 105
Pecksniff Cl. L8: Liv 4F 99
Peebles Av. WA11: St. H 1D 47
Peebles Cl. L33: K'by 4D 15
Peel Av. CH42: Tran 1F 119
Peel Cl. L35: Whis 3E 85
Peel Cott. L31: Mag 5B 6
Peel Ho. La. WA8: Wid 1B 132
Peel Pl. L8: Liv 2F 99
　　　　WA10: St. H 3A 46
Peel Rd. L20: Boot 3A 34
Peel St. L8: Liv 5A 100
　　　　WA7: Run 4F 151
Peel Wlk. L31: Mag 5B 6
Peet Av. WA10: St. H 4C 44
Peet St. L7: Liv 5B 78
Pelham Gro. L17: Aig 5C 100
Pelham Rd. CH44: Wall 3A 74
Pemberton Cl. CH64: Will 5A 170
Pemberton Rd. CH49: W'chu 1B 116
　　　　L13: Liv 3A 80
Pemberton St. WA10: St. H 5E 45
Pembroke Av. CH46: More 2E 93
Pembroke Cl. WA10: St. H 1E 65
Pembroke Ct. CH41: Tran 5E 97
　　　　WA7: Mnr P 2C 154
Pembroke Gdns. L3: Liv 4F 77 (4J 5)
　　　　L20: Boot 5C 78
Pembroke Ho. L6: Liv 2C 78
Pembroke Pl. L3: Liv 4E 77 (4J 5)
　　　　L20: Boot 5C 34
Pembroke St. L3: Liv 4F 77 (5J 5)
Pembury Cl. L12: Crox 5E 39
Penare WA7: Brook 5C 168
Penarth Cl. L7: Liv 1B 100
Penbrey Way L25: Hunts X 4D 127
Pencombe Rd. L36: Huy 2B 82
Penda Dr. L33: K'by 4E 15
Pendennis Rd. CH44: Wall 3C 74
Pendennis St. L6: Liv 1C 78
Pendine Cl. L6: Liv 2C 78
Pendle Av. WA11: St. H 3D 47
Pendlebury St. WA9: Clock F 2C 88
Pendle Cl. CH49: Upton 3E 93
Pendle Dr. L21: Ford 1C 18
Pendleton Grn. L26: Halew 5E 127
　　　　　　　　(not continuous)
Pendleton Rd. L4: Walt 1A 56
Pendle Vw. L21: Ford 1C 18
Pendle Vs. L21: Ford 2C 18
Penfold L31: Mag 1E 13
Penfold Cl. L18: Moss H 4D 103
Penfolds WA7: Run 1D 167
Pengwern Gro. L15: W'tree 1D 101
Pengwern St. L8: Liv 4A 100
Pengwern Ter. CH45: New B 4C 52
Penhale Cl. L17: Aig 2B 122
Peninsula Cl. CH45: Wall 3E 51
Penketh Ct. WA7: Run 4B 152
Penketh Grn. L24: Speke 3E 147
Penketh's La. WA7: Run 4A 152
Penkett Cl. CH45: Wall 5C 52
Penkett Gdns. CH45: Wall 5C 52
Penkett Gro. CH45: Wall 5C 52
Penkett Rd. CH45: Wall 5B 52
Penkford La. WA5: C Grn 2D 69
Penkford St. WA12: New W 5E 49
Penlake Ind. Est. WA9: St. H 4E 67
Penlake La. WA9: St. H 4F 67
Penley Cres. L32: K'by 3B 22
Penlinken Dr. L6: Liv 2B 78
Penmann Cl. L26: Halew 4F 127
Penmann Cres. L26: Halew 4F 127
Penmon Dr. CH61: Pens 4F 137
Pennant Av. L12: W Der 2C 58
Pennard Av. L36: Huy 5D 61

Pennine Cl. WA9: St. H 5E 47
Pennine Dr. WA9: St. H 5F 47
Pennine Rd. CH42: Tran 3C 118
　　　　CH44: Wall 2F 73
Pennine Way L32: K'by 1C 22
Pennington Av. L20: Boot 1E 35
Pennington Cl. WA6: Frod 3D 173
Pennington Gdns. L34: Prsct 5D 63
Pennington La. WA5: C Grn 5B 48
　　　　WA9: St. H 5B 48
Pennington Rd. L21: Lith 2C 34
Pennington St. L4: Walt 1F 55
Penn La. WA7: Run 5F 151
Pennsylvania Rd. L13: Liv 4D 57
Pennyford Dr. L18: Moss H 1E 123
Penny La. L18: Moss H 5F 101
　　　　WA5: C Grn 3D 69
　　　　WA8: Coron 2F 107
　　　　WA11: Hay 1F 49
Penny La. Neighbourhood Cen.
　　　　L15: W'tree 3F 101
Pennystone Cl. CH49: Upton 3D 93
Pennywood Dr. L35: Whis 4E 85
Penpoll Ind. Est. L20: Boot 2C 34
Penrhos Rd. CH47: Hoy 5A 90
Penrhyd Rd. CH61: Irby 2D 137
Penrhyn Av. CH61: Thing 1A 138
　　　　L21: Lith 1B 34
Penrhyn Cres. WA7: Run 3A 166
Penrhyn Rd. L34: Know 3B 40
Penrhyn St. L5: Liv 1D 77
Penrith Cl. WA6: Frod 4D 173
Penrith Cres. L31: Mag 5E 7
Penrith Rd. WA10: St. H 3B 64
Penrith St. CH41: Birk 4C 96
Penrose Av. E. L14: B Grn 4E 81
Penrose Av. W. L14: B Grn 4E 81
Penrose St. L5: Liv 5E 55
Penryn Av. WA11: St. H 1D 47
Pensall Dr. CH61: Hes 5F 137
Pensarn Rd. L13: Liv 4F 79
PENSBY 3A 138
Pensby Cl. CH61: Thing 2A 138
Pensby Hall La. CH61: Hes 5F 137
Pensby Rd. CH60: Hes 2F 157
　　　　CH61: Pens, Thing 2A 138
Pensby St. CH41: Birk 1E 96
Penshaw Ct. WA7: Pal F 3E 167
Pentire Av. WA10: Windle 2B 44
Pentire Cl. L10: Faz 2B 38
Pentland Av. L4: Walt 2A 56
　　　　WA9: St. H 5F 47
Pentland Rd. L33: K'by 1A 24
Penuel Rd. L4: Walt 1F 55
Penvalley Cres. L6: Liv 2C 78
Peony Gdns. WA9: Bold 4B 68
Peover St. L3: Liv 3D 77 (1F 5)
Peploe Rd. L4: Walt 1D 57
Peplow Rd. L32: K'by 3B 22
Pepper St. L24: Hale 5D 149
Pera Cl. L6: Liv 3A 78
Percival Cl. WA7: Run 1D 165
Percival La. WA7: Run 1D 165
Percival Way WA10: St. H 3C 44
Percy Rd. CH44: Wall 4D 75
Percy St. L8: Liv 2F 99
　　　　L20: Boot 3B 34
　　　　WA9: St. H 4F 67
Peregrine Way L26: Halew 3E 127
Perimeter Rd. L33: Know I 5D 25
Perriam Rd. L19: Aller 4D 125
Perrin Av. WA7: Run 2E 165
Perrin Rd. CH45: Wall 1E 73
Perrins Rd. WA5: B'wood 5F 69
Perrygate Cl. L7: Liv 1B 100
Perry St. L8: Liv 3D 99
　　　　WA7: Run 5B 152
Pershore Ho. CH42: Tran 3B 118
Pershore Rd. L32: K'by 5E 23
Perth Av. WA9: St. H 4E 65
Perth Cl. L33: K'by 4D 15
Perth St. L6: Liv 3A 78
Peterborough Dr. L30: N'ton 1E 19
Peterborough Rd. L15: W'tree . .3A 102
Peterlee Cl. WA9: St. H 4F 65

Peterlee Way L30: N'ton 4A 20
Peter Lloyd Leisure Cen. 1E 79
Peter Mahon Way L20: Boot 4B 34
Peter Price's La. CH63: High B . . .3E 141
Peter Rd. L4: Walt 1E 55
　　　　　　　　(not continuous)
Petersfield Cl. L30: N'ton 4A 20
Petersgate WA7: Murd 3D 169
Peter's La. L1: Liv 5D 77 (6E 4)
Peter St. CH44: Wall 4E 75
　　　　L1: Liv 4D 77 (4E 4)
　　　　WA10: St. H 4E 45
Peterwood CH42: R Ferr 3A 120
Petham Ct. WA8: Wid 5E 109
Petherick Rd. L11: Crox 3C 38
Petra Ct. L4: Walt 4C 56
Petton St. L5: Liv 5F 55
Petunia Cl. L14: K Ash 2A 82
　　　　WA9: Bold 4A 68
Petworth Cl. L24: Speke 3B 146
Peveril St. L9: Walt 5F 35
Pex Hill Country Pk. 3E 109
Pex Hill Ct. WA8: Wid 4E 109
Pharmacy Rd. L24: Speke 3C 146
Pheasant Fld. L24: Hale 5C 148
Pheasant Gro. L26: Halew 3E 127
Philbeach Rd. L4: Walt 1D 57
　　　　L11: N Grn 1D 57
Philharmonic Cl. L7: Liv 7J 5
Philharmonic Hall 1F 99 (7J 5)
Philip Gro. WA9: St. H 4C 66
Philip Leverhulme Lodge
　　　　CH62: Port S 1B 142
Philip Rd. WA8: Wid 4B 130
Phillimore Rd. L6: Liv 3C 78
Phillip Gro. L12: W Der 1E 81
Phillips Cl. L23: Thorn 4B 10
Phillips St. L3: Liv 3C 76 (2D 4)
Phillips Way CH60: Hes 2E 157
Phipps' La. WA5: B'wood 3E 69
Phoenix Dr. L14: K Ash 2A 82
Physics Rd. L24: Speke 2C 146
Phythian Cl. L6: Liv 3A 78
Phythian St. L6: Liv 3A 78
　　　　WA5: Hay 2F 47
Picadilly WN5: Bil 1E 31
Pickerill Rd. CH49: Grea 1D 115
Pickering Rake L30: N'ton 5D 11
Pickering Rd. CH45: New B 3B 52
Pickerings Cl. WA7: Run 4C 166
Pickerings Pasture Local Nature Reserve
　　　　　　　　. . . . . .4B 150
Pickerings Pasture Local Nature Reserve
　　　　Vis. Cen. 3B 150
Pickerings Rd. WA8: Hale B 2B 150
Pickering St. L6: Liv 1A 78
Pickmere Dr. CH62: East 2F 171
　　　　　　　　(not continuous)
Pickop St. L3: Liv 3C 76 (2D 4)
　　　　WA7: Brook 5C 168
Pickwick St. L8: Liv 3F 99
Pickworth Way L31: Mell 3B 22
Picow Farm Rd.
　　　　WA7: Run, West P 1F 165
Picow St. WA7: Run 5A 152
Picton Av. WA7: Run 1B 166
Picton Cl. CH43: O'ton 5F 95
　　　　CH62: East 2D 171
Picton Cres. L15: W'tree 1E 101
Picton Gro. L15: W'tree 1D 101
Picton Hall .4D 77
　　　　　　　　(off Cuerden St.)
Picton Rd. L15: W'tree 1D 101
　　　　L22: Water 4D 17
Picton Sports Cen. 2E 101
Piele Rd. WA11: Hay 1D 49
Pighue La. L7: Liv 5E 79
　　　　L13: Liv 5E 79
Pigot St. WA10: St. H 5E 45
Pike Ho. Rd. WA10: Eccl 3A 44
Pike Pl. WA10: Eccl 4B 44
Pikes Bri. Fold WA10: Eccl 4A 44
Pikes Hey Rd. CH48: Caldy 2F 135
Pilch Bank Rd. L14: K Ash 2E 81

Pilch La. L14: K Ash 2E **81**
Pilch La. E. L36: Huy 4A **82**
Pilgrim St. CH41: Birk 3F **97**
  L1: Liv 1E **99** (7H 5)
Pilgrims Way WA7: Nort 4D **155**
Pilkington Glass Mus. 1D 65
Pilling La. L31: Lyd 2A 6
Pilot Gro. L15: W'tree 1D **101**
Pimblett Rd. WA11: Hay 1E **49**
Pimbley Gro. E. L31: Mag 4C **12**
Pimbley Gro. W. L31: Mag 4C **12**
Pimhill Cl. L8: Liv 3A **100**
Pimlico Rd. WA7: Run 5E **151**
Pincroft Way L4: Kirk 4D **55**
Pine Av. CH63: Beb 4F **141**
  WA8: Wid 2B **132**
  WA10: St. H 2F **45**
Pine Cl. L32: K'by 2C **22**
  L35: Whis 3E **85**
  L36: Huy 2D **83**
  WA11: Hay 2C **48**
Pine Ct. CH41: Birk 3D **97**
  L8: Liv 5A **100**
  (off Byles St.)
Pinedale Cl. CH43: Noct 5D **95**
Pine Gro. L20: Boot 4D **35**
  L22: Water 3D **17**
Pinehurst Av. L4: Walt 4B **56**
  L22: Water 2C **16**
Pinehurst Rd. L4: Walt 4B **56**
Pinellas WA7: Run 4B **152**
Pine Lodge L4: Walt 3C **56**
Pine M. L1: Liv 2E **99**
Pinemore Rd. L18: Moss H 2A **124**
Pineridge Cl. CH62: Spit 5C **142**
Pine Rd. CH60: Hes 1C **158**
  WA7: Run 3C **166**
Pines, The CH63: Spit 4B **142**
  L12: Crox 4F **39**
Pinetop Cl. L6: Liv 2B **78**
Pine Tree Av. CH43: Noct 5C **94**
Pine Tree Cl. CH46: More 1F **93**
Pinetree Cl. L30: N'ton 2F **19**
Pinetree Ct. CH44: Wall 1F **93**
Pinetree Dr. CH48: W Kir 5D **113**
Pinetree Gro. CH46: More 1F **93**
Pinetree Rd. L36: Huy 5D **83**
Pine Vw. Dr. CH61: Hes 5A **138**
Pine Walk Ridge CH42: Tran 4C **118**
Pine Walks CH42: Tran 3B **118**
  CH48: W Kir 5D **113**
Pine Way CH60: Hes 5E **137**
Pinewood Av. L12: Crox 5D **39**
Pinewood Cl. L27: N'ley 3E **105**
Pinewood Dr. CH60: Hes 2B **158**
Pinewood Gdns. L33: K'by 5E **15**
Pinewood Rd. L33: B'wood 4F **69**
Pinfold Cl. L30: N'ton 5E **11**
Pinfold Ct. CH48: W Kir 2A **112**
  L23: C'by 5D **9**
Pinfold Cres. L32: K'by 5A **24**
Pinfold Dr. WA10: Eccl 4A **44**
Pinfold La. CH48: W Kir 2A **112**
  L34: Know 5B **40**
Pinfold Rd. L25: Hunts X 5C **126**
Pingwood La. L33: K'by 4F **15**
Pinmill Brow WA6: Frod 5B **172**
Pinners Fold WA7: Nort 2C **168**
Pinnington Pl. L36: Huy 4D **83**
Pinnington Rd. L35: Whis 3E **85**
Pintail Cl. WA11: St. H 2B **46**
Pipers, The CH60: Hes 1D **157**
Piper's Cl. CH60: Hes 2D **157**
Piper's End CH60: Hes 2D **157**
Pipers La. CH60: Hes 5C **136**
  (not continuous)
Pipistrelle Ri. CH43: Noct 5E **95**
Pipit Cl. L26: Halew 2E **127**
Pippits Row WA7: Beech 1E **173**
Pirrie Rd. L9: Ain 5D **37**
Pitch Cl. CH49: Grea 5D **93**
Pit La. WA8: Wid 5A **110**
Pit Pl. L25: Wltn 2A **126**
Pitsmead Rd. L32: K'by 4E **23**
Pitts Heath La. WA7: Nort 4D **155**

Pitt St. L1: Liv 1D **99**
  WA8: Wid 2A **152**
  WA9: St. H 5C **46**
Pitville Av. L18: Moss H 1A **124**
Pitville Cl. L18: Moss H 2A **124**
Pitville Gro. L18: Moss H 5A **102**
Pitville Rd. L18: Moss H 1A **124**
Pitville Ter. WA8: Wid 5C **130**
Plaistow Ct. WA7: Pal F 3E **167**
Plane Cl. L9: Walt 5B **36**
Plane Tree Gro. WA11: Hay 1F **49**
Plane Tree Rd. CH63: High B 3E **141**
Planetree Rd. L12: W Der 4E **59**
Plantation Bus. Pk.
  CH62: Brom 5F **143**
Plantation Cl. WA7: Cas 1A **168**
Plantation Rd. CH62: Brom 1F **163**
Planters, The CH49: Grea 5C **92**
  L30: N'ton 1B **20**
Platt Gro. CH42: R Ferr 4A **120**
Platts St. WA11: Hay 2A **48**
Plattsville Rd. L18: Moss H 4A **102**
Playfield Rd. L12: W Der 4F **59**
Playfield Wlk. L12: W Der 4F **59**
Pleasant Hill St. L8: Liv 3D **99**
Pleasant St. CH45: New B 4B **52**
  L3: Liv 5E **77** (6H **5**)
  L20: Boot 1B **54**
Pleasant Vw. L20: Boot 1B **54**
Pleasington Cl. CH43: Noct 5E **95**
Pleasington Dr. CH43: Noct 5E **95**
Plemont Rd. L13: Liv 1F **79**
Plimsoll St. L7: Liv 5B **78**
Ploughboy Cl. WA12: New W 4E **49**
Plover Dr. WA7: Nort 2D **169**
Pluckington Rd. L36: Huy 3B **84**
Plumbers Way L36: Huy 4F **83**
Plumer St. CH41: Birk 1A **96**
  L15: W'tree 2E **101**
Plumley Gdns. WA8: Wid 2A **130**
Plumpstons La. WA6: Frod 4B **172**
Plumpton St. L6: Liv 2F **77**
Plum Tree Cl. L28: Stock V 3B **60**
  L35: Ecc P 5A **64**
Plymouth Cl. WA7: Murd 4E **169**
Plymyard Av. CH62: Brom 4C **162**
Plymyard Cl. CH62: Brom 5D **163**
Plymyard Copse CH62: Brom 5D **163**
Pochard Ri. WA7: Nort 2D **169**
POCKET NOOK 5C **46**
Pocket Nook St. WA9: St. H 4B **46**
Poets Cnr. CH62: Port S 2B **142**
Poets Grn. L35: Whis 3F **85**
  (not continuous)
Poleacre Dr. WA8: Wid 2D **131**
Pollard Av. WA6: Frod 5D **173**
Pollard Rd. L15: W'tree 5A **80**
POLL HILL 5F **137**
Poll Hill Rd. CH60: Hes 1F **157**
Pollitt Cres. WA9: Clock F 2C **88**
Pollitt Sq. CH62: New F 4C **120**
Pollitt St. WA9: Clock F 3C **88**
Polperro Cl. L11: Crox 3D **39**
Pomfret St. L8: Liv 3F **99**
Pomona St. L3: Liv 5E **77** (6H **5**)
Pond Cl. L6: Liv 2C **78**
Pond Grn. Way WA9: St. H 2F **67**
Pond Vw. Cl. CH60: Hes 2C **158**
Pond Wlk. WA9: St. H 2A **68**
Pondwater Cl. L32: K'by 4E **23**
Ponsonby Rd. CH45: Wall 1E **73**
Ponsonby St. L8: Liv 2A **100**
Pool Bank CH62: Port S 5B **120**
Poolbank Rd. CH62: New F 5B **120**
Pool End WA9: St. H 1F **67**
Poole Rd. CH44: Wall 1D **75**
Poole Wlk. L8: Liv 5A **100**
Pool Hey L28: Stock V 3B **60**
  (not continuous)
Pool Hollow WA7: Run 1B **166**
Pool La. CH49: W'chu 2A **116**
  CH62: Brom 2C **142**
  WA7: Run 4B **152**

Poolside Rd. WA7: Run 1B **166**
Pool St. CH41: Birk 2D **97**
  WA8: Wid 5B **132**
Poolwood Rd. CH49: W'chu 5B **94**
Pope St. L20: Boot 3A **34**
Poplar Av. CH49: Upton 4F **93**
  L23: C'by 5F **9**
  WA7: Run 3C **166**
  WA10: Eccl 4A **44**
Poplar Bank L36: Huy 4E **83**
Poplar Cl. WA7: Run 3C **166**
Poplar Ct. L8: Liv 5A **100**
  (off Weller Way)
Poplar Dr. CH63: Beb 3A **142**
  L5: Liv 1A **78**
  L32: K'by 2C **22**
Poplar Farm Cl. CH46: More 3C **92**
Poplar Gro. CH42: Tran 5D **97**
  L21: Sea 2F **33**
  L35: Prsct 1E **85**
  WA10: St. H 5C **44**
  WA11: Hay 2C **48**
Poplar Rd. CH43: O'ton 5B **96**
  L25: Wltn 1F **125**
  WA11: Hay 2C **48**
Poplar Ter. CH45: New B 4B **52**
Poplar Way L4: Kirk 3D **55**
Poppleford Cl. L25: Gate 4C **104**
Poppy Cl. CH46: More 4A **72**
Poppy Rd. L23: Thorn 4B **10**
Porchester Rd. L11: N Grn. 2F **57**
Porchfield Cl. L11: N Grn. 5B **38**
Porlock Av. L16: Child 4E **103**
  WA9: Sut L 1C **88**
Porlock Cl. CH60: Hes 4B **158**
Portal M. CH61: Pens 4F **137**
Portal Rd. CH61: Pens 4F **137**
Portal Way L11: Crox 1C **38**
Portbury Cl. CH62: Port S 1B **142**
Portbury Wlk. CH62: Port S 1B **142**
Portbury Way CH62: Port S 1C **142**
Port C'way. CH62: Brom 3C **142**
Portelet Rd. L13: Liv 2F **79**
Porter Cl. L35: R'hill 5E **87**
Porter St. L3: Liv 2B **76**
  WA7: Run 5C **152**
Portgate Cl. L12: W Der 1C **58**
Porthcawl Cl. WA8: Wid 1C **130**
Porthleven Rd. WA7: Brook 5B **168**
Portia Av. CH63: High B 5E **119**
Portia Gdns. CH63: High B 5E **119**
Portia St. L20: Kirk 2C **54**
PORTICO 4B **64**
Portico Av. L35: Ecc P 5A **64**
Portico Ct. L35: Ecc P 5A **64**
Portico La. L34: Ecc P 5A **64**
  L35: Prsct, Ecc P 5F **63**
Portland Av. L22: Water 3C **16**
Portland Ct. CH45: New B 2A **52**
Portland Gdns. L5: Liv 2C **76**
Portland Ga. CH62: Port S 1C **142**
Portland Pl. L5: Liv 2E **77**
Portland St. CH41: Birk 1A **96**
  CH45: New B 2A **52**
  L5: Liv 2C **76**
  WA7: Run 4F **151**
  WA12: New W 4F **49**
Portland Way WA9: St. H 2F **67**
Portlemouth Rd. L11: Crox 3C **38**
Portloe Av. L26: Halew 3F **127**
Portman Rd. L15: W'tree 2D **101**
Porto Hey Rd. CH61: Irby 2D **137**
Porton Rd. L32: K'by 4C **22**
Portreath Way WA10: Windle 2B **44**
Portree Av. CH63: East 5D **163**
Portrush Cl. L9: Walt 4F **35**
Portrush St. L13: Liv 5E **57**
Portside WA7: Pres B 3E **169**
Portsmouth Pl. WA7: Murd 4E **169**
PORT SUNLIGHT 2B **142**
Port Sunlight Heritage Cen. 2B **142**
Port Sunlight Station (Rail) 2B **142**
Portway L25: Hunts X 5C **126**
Portwood Cl. L7: Liv 1B **100**

Post Office La.—Quarrybank Workshops

Post Office La. WA7: West P 3D 165
Potters La. L18: Moss H 4C 102
   WA8: Hale B 2F 149
Pottery CI. L35: Whis 3C 84
Pottery Flds. L34: Prsct 5E 63
Pottery La. L35: Whis 3B 84
   L36: Huy 3B 84
Poulsom Dr. L30: N'ton 3C 18
Poulter Ct. L9: Ain 1B 36
POULTON
   Wallasey 3B 74
   Wirral 1A 162
Poulton Bri. Rd. CH41: Birk 4A 74
Poulton CI. L26: Halew 1D 147
Poulton Dr. WA8: Wid 4C 130
Poulton Grn. CI. CH63: Spit 5F 141
Poulton Hall Rd.
   CH44: Wall 3A 74
   CH63: Raby M 3A 162
Poulton Rd. CH44: Wall 3A 74
   CH63: Spit 4A 142
Poulton Royd Dr. CH63: Spit 5F 141
Poulton Va. CH44: Wall 4A 74
Poverty La. L31: Mag 2E 13
Powell Dr. WN5: Bil 2D 31
Powell St. L5: St. H 4E 67
Powerhouse L8: Liv 2B 100
               (off Commerce Way)
Powerleague Liverpool 4E 55
Power Rd. CH42: R Ferr 4A 120
   CH62: Brom 1F 163
Powis St. L8: Liv 4A 100
Pownall Sq. L3: Liv 4C 76 (3D 4)
Pownall St. L1: Liv 1C 98 (7D 4)
Poynter St. WA9: St. H 4E 65
Pratt Rd. L34: Prsct 5C 62
Precincts, The L23: C'by 1E 17
Preece CI. WA8: Wid 3C 38
            (not continuous)
Preesall Way L11: Crox 1F 37
Premier St. L5: Liv 1F 77
Prentice Rd. CH42: R Ferr 3E 119
PRENTON .4F 117
Prenton Av. WA9: Clock F 2B 88
Prenton Dell Av. CH43: Pren 4A 118
Prenton Dell Rd. CH43: Pren 3E 117
Prenton Farm Rd. CH43: Pren 4A 118
Prenton Grn. L24: Speke 4E 147
Prenton Hall Rd. CH43: Pren 3F 117
Prenton La. CH42: Tran 3B 118
Prenton Pk. .2C 118
Prenton Pk. Rd. CH42: Tran 1C 118
Prenton Rd. E. CH42: Tran 2C 118
Prenton Rd. W. CH42: Tran 2B 118
Prenton Village Rd.
   CH43: Pren 3F 117
Prenton Way CH43: Pren 3E 117
Prentonwood Ct. CH42: Tran 3C 118
PRESCOT 5D 63
Prescot By-Pass L34: Prsct 5B 62
Prescot Cables AFC 4D 63
Prescot Cen. L34: Prsct 5D 63
Prescot Dr. L6: Liv 3D 79
Prescot Leisure Cen. 1E 85
Prescot Mus. of Clock & Watchmaking
   . . . . .5C 62
Prescot Rd. L7: Liv 3C 78
   L13: Liv .3A 80
   L31: Mag, Mell 1C 22
   WA8: Cron 5F 107
   WA8: Wid 1D 131
   WA10: St. H 3A 64
Prescot Station (Rail) 1E 85
Prescot St. CH45: New B 3A 52
   L7: Liv 4F 77 (3J 5)
Prescot Trade Cen. L34: Prsct 5E 63
Preseland Rd. L23: C'by 2E 17
Prestbury Av. CH43: O'ton 2E 117
Prestbury CI. CH43: O'ton 2E 117
   WA8: Wid 4E 131
Prestbury Dr. WA10: Eccl 1B 64
Prestbury Rd. L11: N Grn. 4F 37
Preston Av. L34: Prsct 1C 84
PRESTON BROOK 4F 169
Preston Gro. L6: Liv 1C 78

PRESTON ON THE HILL 4F 169
Preston St. L1: Liv 4D 77 (4E 4)
   WA9: Sut M 4A 88
Preston Way L21: Sea 1A 18
Prestwick CI. WA8: Wid 1F 131
Prestwick Dr. L23: Blun 4C 8
Prestwood Cres. L14: K Ash 2F 81
Prestwood Rd. L14: K Ash 2F 81
Pretoria Rd. L9: Ain 2B 36
Price Gro. WA9: St. H 1A 68
Price's La. CH43: O'ton 5B 96
Price St. CH41: Birk 1B 96
   L1: Liv 1C 98 (7E 4)
Price St. Bus. Cen.
   CH41: Birk 1C 96
Primary Av. L30: N'ton 1B 20
Primrose CI. WA7: Cas 1A 168
   WA8: Wid 3E 131
Primrose Ct. CH45: New B 3B 52
Primrose Dr. L36: Huy 1E 83
Primrose Gro. CH44: Wall 4E 75
   WA11: Hay 1E 49
Primrose Hill CH62: Port S 1A 142
   L3: Liv 4D 77 (3E 4)
Primrose Rd. CH41: Birk 2F 95
   L18: Moss H 4C 102
Primrose St. L4: Kirk 3D 55
Primula CI. WA9: Bold 4A 68
Primula Dr. L9: Walt 4B 36
Prince Albert Ct. WA9: St. H 3F 67
Prince Albert M. L1: Liv 2D 99
Prince Alfred Rd. L15: W'tree 2F 101
Prince Andrew's Gro.
   WA10: Windle 2C 44
Prince Edward St.
   CH41: Birk 2C 96
Prince Edwin St. L5: Liv 2E 77
Princes Av. CH48: W Kir 4B 112
   CH62: East 4E 163
   L8: Liv .2F 99
   L23: C'by 1D 17
Princes Blvd. CH63: High B 4D 119
Prince's CI. WA7: Cas 1F 167
Princes Ct. L8: Liv 3B 100
Princes Gdns. L3: Liv 3C 76 (2C 4)
            (not continuous)
Princes Ga. E. L8: Liv 3B 100
Princes Ga. W. L8: Liv 3A 100
Princes Pde. L3: Liv 4A 76 (3A 4)
PRINCES PARK 3B 100
Princes Pk. Mans. L8: Liv 4B 100
Princes Pavement CH41: Birk 3E 97
Princes PI. CH41: Tran 5E 97
   WA8: Wid 3E 131
Princes Rd. L8: Liv 2F 99
   WA10: St. H 2C 64
Princess Av. WA10: St. H 3E 45
   WA11: Hay 1F 49
Princess Dr. L12: W Der 3E 59
   L14: K Ash 3E 59
Princess Rd. CH45: New B 4B 52
Princess St. WA7: Run 4A 152
Princess Ter. CH43: O'ton 4C 96
Princes St. L2: Liv 4C 76 (4D 4)
   L20: Boot 2B 54
   WA8: Wid 4A 132
Princess Way L21: Sea 2F 33
Prince St. L22: Water 5E 17
Princes Way WA11: St. H 5A 30
Princesway CH45: Wall 5A 52
Princeway WA7: Frod 5B 172
Prince William St. L8: Liv 3E 99
Priors CI. L25: Wltn 2B 126
Priorsfield CH46: More 1E 93
Priorsfield Rd. L25: Wltn 2B 126
Prior St. L20: Boot 2A 34
Priory, The L35: R'hill 3C 86
Priory CI. CH63: Beb 4A 142
   L17: Aig 2B 122
   L35: Whis 5C 84
   WA7: Halt 1A 168
Priory Ct. L36: Huy 4D 83
   WA7: Pres B 5E 169
Priory Farm CI. L19: Gras 5A 124
Priory Gdns. WA10: St. H 1F 45

Priory M. CH41: Birk 3F 97
Priory Rd. CH44: Wall 3E 75
   CH48: W Kir 4C 112
   L4: Walt .3A 56
   WA7: Wind H 5C 154
Priory St. CH41: Birk 3F 97
   L19: Gars 3D 145
Priory Way L25: Wltn 2B 126
Priory Wharf CH41: Birk 3F 97
Pritchard Av. L21: Sea 1F 33
Pritt St. L3: Liv 3E 77 (1G 5)
Private Dr. CH61: Barn 2D 139
Prizett Rd. L19: Gras 5B 124
Probyn Rd. CH45: Wall 1E 73
Procter Rd. CH42: R Ferr 3A 120
Proctor Ct. L30: N'ton 1D 19
Proctor Rd. CH47: Hoy 5C 90
Proctors CI. WA8: Wid 2C 132
Progress PI. L1: Liv 4D 4
Promenade CH47: Meols 3B 90
Promenade, The L17: Aig 3B 122
   L19: Aig 5E 123
Promenade Gdns. L17: Aig 1F 121
Prophet Wlk. L8: Liv 4E 99
Prospect Ct. L6: Liv 2D 79
Prospect Point L6: Liv 4F 77
Prospect Rd. CH42: Tran 3B 118
   WA9: St. H 4D 47
Prospect Row WA7: West 3F 165
Prospect St. L6: Liv 4F 77
Prospect Va. CH45: Wall 1F 73
   L6: Liv .2D 79
Prospect Way L30: N'ton 2B 20
Providence Cres. L8: Liv 3E 99
Provident St. WA9: St. H 5A 48
Province PI. L20: Boot 2D 35
Province Rd. L20: Boot 2D 35
Prussia St. L3: Liv 4B 76 (3C 4)
              (Old Hall St.)
   L3: Liv 4C 76 (3C 4)
                 (Pall Mall)
Public Hall St. WA7: Run 4A 152
Pudsey St. L1: Liv 4E 77 (4G 5)
Pugin St. L4: Walt 4E 55
Pulford Av. CH43: Pren 2A 118
Pulford CI. WA7: Beech 4E 167
Pulford Rd. CH63: Beb 2F 141
Pulford St. L4: Walt 4F 55
Pullman CI. CH60: Hes 2D 159
Pumpfields Rd. L3: Liv 3C 76 (1C 4)
Pump La. CH49: Grea 4B 92
   WA7: Halt 2F 167
Punnell's La. L31: Lyd 2A 6
Purbeck Dr. CH61: Irby 5D 115
Purley Gro. L18: Moss H 2A 124
Purley Rd. L22: Water 3C 16
Purser Gro. L15: W'tree 1D 101
Putney St. WA7: Pal F 3E 167
Pye Rd. CH60: Hes 2A 158
Pyes Gdns. WA11: St. H 1B 46
Pyes La. L36: Huy 4C 60
Pye St. L15: W'tree 2F 101
PYGON'S HILL 1D 7
Pygon's Hill La. L31: Lyd 1D 7
Pym St. L4: Walt 1F 55
Pyramids Shop. Cen., The
   CH41: Birk 3D 97

Q

Quadrangle, The
   L18: Moss H 5B 102
Quadrant, The CH47: Hoy 5B 90
              (off Station Rd.)
Quadrant CI. WA7: Murd 5D 169
Quaker La. CH60: Hes 1F 157
Quakers All. L2: Liv 4D 4
Quakers Mdw. L34: Know 4D 41
Quarry Av. CH63: Beb 3F 141
Quarry Bank CH41: Birk 4D 97
   L33: K'by 2F 23
Quarrybank St. CH41: Birk 4C 96
Quarrybank Workshops
   CH41: Birk 4C 96

Quarry Cl. CH61: Hes 5F 137
  L13: Liv 1F 79
  L33: K'by 2F 23
  WA7: Run 1D 167
Quarry Ct. WA8: Wid 3C 130
Quarry Dale L33: K'by 2F 23
Quarry Grn. L33: K'by 2F 23
Quarry Grn. Flats
  L33: K'by 2F 23
Quarry Hey L33: K'by 2F 23
Quarry La. CH61: Thing 1B 138
Quarry Pk. L35: R'hill 5D 87
Quarry Pl. L25: Wltn 2F 125
Quarry Rd. L13: Liv 1F 79
  L20: Boot 1D 55
  L23: Thorn 4A 10
Quarry Rd. E. CH60: Hes 1E 157
  CH61: Hes 1E 157
  CH63: Beb 3A 142
Quarry Rd. W. CH60: Hes 1E 157
Quarryside Dr. L33: K'by 2A 24
Quarry St. L25: Wltn 1F 125
Quarry St. Sth. L25: Wltn 2A 126
Quartz Way L21: Lith 5C 18
Quay, The WA6: Frod 3D 173
Quayle Cl. WA11: Hay 2B 48
Quay Pl. WA7: Murd 3E 169
Quay Side WA6: Frod 3D 173
Quebec Quay L3: Liv 3C 98
Queen Anne Pde.
  L3: Liv 4B 76 (4B 4)
Queen Anne St. L3: Liv 3E 77 (2G 5)
Queen Av. L2: Liv 4C 76 (5D 4)
Queen Av. Shop. Arc. L2: Liv 5C 4
Queen Elizabeth Ct.
  L21: Lith 5A 18
Queen Mary's Dr.
  CH62: Port S 1B 142
Queen's Av. CH47: Meols 3D 91
  WA8: Wid 4B 130
Queensbury CH48: W Kir 3D 113
Queensbury Av. CH62: Brom 1E 163
Queensbury St. L8: Liv 4F 99
Queensbury Way WA8: Wid 1D 131
Queens Cl. L19: Gars 1C 144
  WA7: Run 1F 165
Queens Ct. L6: Liv 1A 78
  L15: W'tree 5C 80
Queenscourt Rd. L12: W Der 1C 80
Queensdale Rd.
  L18: Moss H 4A 102
Queens Dock Commercial Cen.
  L1: Liv 2D 99
Queens Dr. CH43: Pren 3A 118
  CH60: Hes 2E 157
  WA10: Windle 2C 44
Queens Dr. Mossley Hill
  L18: Moss H 5E 101
Queens Dr. Stoneycroft
  L12: W Der 2B 80
  L13: Liv 1A 80
Queens Dr. Walton L4: Walt 1A 56
Queens Dr. Wavertree
  L15: W'tree 5C 80
Queens Dr. W. Derby
  L13: W Der 3E 57
Queensland Av. WA9: St H 4E 65
Queensland Pl. WA9: St H 4E 65
Queensland St. L7: Liv 5A 78
Queens M. L6: Liv 1A 78
Queens Pk. Community Leisure Cen.
  . . . . .4E 45
Queens Pl. CH41: Tran 5E 97
Queen Sq. L1: Liv 4D 77 (4E 5)
  (not continuous)
Queens Rd. CH42: R Ferr 3F 119
  CH44: Wall 2E 75
  CH47: Hoy 4A 90
  L6: Liv 1A 78
  L20: Boot 1C 54
  L23: C'by 1E 17
  L34: Prsct 5E 63
  WA7: Run 1F 165
  WA10: St H 2C 64
  WA11: Hay 1F 49

Queen St. CH41: Tran 5E 97
  CH45: Wall 1B 74
  L19: Gars 2C 144
  L22: Water 5D 17
  WA7: Run 4A 152
  WA10: St. H 3F 45
Queens Wlk. L1: Liv 2E 99
Queensway CH41: Birk 1A 98 (7A 4)
  CH45: Wall 5A 52
  CH60: Hes 4D 158
  L3: Liv 1A 98 (7A 4)
  L22: Water 3F 17
  WA6: Frod 5B 172
  WA7: Run 4F 151
  WA8: Wid 4F 151
  WA11: St. H 5A 30
Queensway Trad. Est.
  WA8: Wid 2F 151
Queens Wharf L3: Liv 2C 98
Queenswood Av. CH63: High B 4E 119
Quernmore Rd. L33: K'by 2A 24
Quernmore Wlk. L33: K'by 2A 24
Quickswood Cl. L25: Wltn 4F 103
Quickswood Dr. L25: Wltn 4F 103
Quickswood Grn. L25: Wltn 4F 103
Quickthorn Cres. L28: Stock V 4B 60
Quigley Av. L30: N'ton 4A 20
Quigley St. CH41: Tran 5E 97
Queensway CH49: Upton 4A 94
Quinn St. WA8: Wid 5B 132
Quintbridge Cl. L26: Halew 4E 127
Quorn St. L7: Liv 4B 78

R

RABY 5C 160
Raby Av. CH63: Raby M 4B 162
Raby Cl. CH60: Hes 3F 157
  CH63: Raby M 3A 162
  WA8: Wid 2D 133
Raby Dell CH63: Raby M 4B 162
Raby Dr. CH46: More 2D 93
  CH63: Raby M 3A 162
Raby Gro. CH63: High B 4D 119
Raby Hall Rd. CH63: Raby M 5E 161
RABY MERE 3A 162
Raby Mere Rd.
  CH63: Raby, Raby M 5C 160
  (not continuous)
Raby Rd. CH63: Thorn H 4B 160
Racecourse Retail Pk.
  L9: Ain 3B 20
Rachel St. L5: Liv 2D 77
Radburn Cl. L23: Thorn 5B 10
Radburn Rd. L23: Thorn 5B 10
Radford Av. CH63: Spit 5B 142
Radford Cl. WA8: Wid 5C 130
Radley Dr. CH63: Thorn H 4F 159
  L10: Ain 2C 20
Radley Rd. CH44: Wall 1F 73
Radleys Ct. L8: Liv 3F 99
Radley St. WA9: St. H 4E 65
Radmore Rd. L14: K Ash 3C 80
Radnor Av. CH60: Hes 1F 157
Radnor Cl. L26: Halew 1D 147
Radnor Dr. CH45: Wall 5C 52
  L20: Boot 4E 35
  WA8: Wid 2C 130
Radnor Pl. CH43: O'ton 3C 96
  L6: Liv 1D 79
Radnor Rd. L32: K'by 2E 39
Radstock Gro. WA9: Sut L 1D 89
Radstock Rd. CH44: Wall 1E 73
  L6: Liv 3C 78
Radstock Wlk. L26: Halew 1F 147
Radway Rd. L36: Huy 1F 83
Raeburn Av. CH48: W Kir 3C 112
  CH62: East 4D 163
Raffles Rd. CH42: Tran 4C 96
Raffles St. L1: Liv 2E 99
Rafter Av. L20: Boot 1E 35
Raglan St. L19: Gars 2C 144
Raglan Wlk. L19: Gars 2C 144
Railbrook Hey L13: Liv 5A 80

Railside Ct. L5: Liv 1C 76
Railton Av. L35: R'hill 4D 87
Railton Cl. L35: R'hill 5D 87
Railton Rd. L11: N Grn. 1E 57
Railway Cotts. CH66: Hoot 4D 171
  L25: Hunts X 5C 126
Railway Rd. CH42: R Ferr 2F 119
  (not continuous)
Railway St. L19: Gars 2C 144
  WA10: St. H 4B 46
Railway Ter. WA9: St. H 4E 67
Railway Vw. L32: K'by 2C 22
  WA5: C Grn 2D 69
Railyard, The L7: Liv 1A 100
  (off Crown Station Pl.)
Rainbow Cl. WA8: Wid 1C 130
Rainbow Dr. L26: Halew 4E 127
  L31: Mell 1B 22
Raines Cl. CH49: Grea 5E 93
Rainford Art Gallery 5A 46
Rainford Av. L20: Boot 2E 35
Rainford By-Pass WA11: R'ford 1F 27
Rainford Gdns. L2: Liv 5C 76 (5E 4)
Rainford Hall Cotts.
  WA11: Crank 3E 29
Rainford Ind. Est. WA11: R'ford 1B 28
Rainford Rd.
  WA10: St. H, Windle 1C 44
  WA11: Windle 1C 44
  WN5: Bil 1B 30
Rainford Sq. L2: Liv 5C 76 (5D 4)
Rainford Trials Exhibition 3C 86
Rainham Cl. L19: Aller 4C 124
RAINHILL 3C 86
Rainhill Rd. L35: R'hill 3C 86
  WA9: St. H 5C 64
Rainhill Station (Rail) 3C 86
RAINHILL STOOPS 5E 87
Rake, The CH62: Brom 2C 162
Rake Cl. CH49: Upton 5A 94
Rake Hey CH46: More 1B 92
Rake Hey Cl. CH46: More 1C 92
Rake La. CH45: Wall 1B 74
  CH49: Upton 5A 94
Rake M. CH49: Upton 5A 94
Rakersfield Ct. CH45: New B 3C 52
Rakersfield Rd. CH45: New B 3C 52
Rakes La. L23: Thorn 4C 10
  L29: Thorn 4C 10
Raleigh Av. L35: Whis 4D 85
Raleigh Rd. CH46: Leas 2A 72
Raleigh St. L20: Boot 2B 54
Rame Cl. L10: Faz 2B 38
Ramford St. WA9: St. H 1D 67
Ramilies Rd. L18: Moss H 4F 101
Ramleh Pk. L23: Blun 2B 16
Rampit Cl. WA11: Hay 1F 49
Ramsbrook Cl. L24: Speke 3C 146
Ramsbrook La. L24: Hale 3C 148
  WA8: Hale B 2C 148
Ramsbrook Rd. L24: Speke 3C 146
Ramsey Cl. L19: Aller 4D 125
  L35: Whis 3E 85
  WA8: Wid 1E 133
Ramsey Ct. CH48: W Kir 5B 112
Ramsey Rd. L19: Aller 4D 125
Ramsfield Rd. L24: Speke 3A 148
Ramsons Cl. L26: Halew 3E 127
Randall Dr. L30: N'ton 2C 18
Randle Cl. CH63: Spit 5F 141
Randle Hgts. L11: Crox 3E 39
Randles Rd. L34: Know 3A 40
Randolph St. L4: Walt 4F 55
Randon Gro. WA10: St. H 4F 45
Ranelagh Av. L21: Lith 5A 18
Ranelagh Dr. Nth. L19: Gras 4A 124
Ranelagh Dr. Sth. L19: Gras 4A 124
Ranelagh Pl. L3: Liv 5E 77 (5G 5)
Ranelagh St. L1: Liv 5D 77 (6F 5)
Ranfurly Rd. L19: Gras 5B 124
Rangemore Rd. L18: Moss H 3F 123
Rankin Hall L18: Moss H 2E 123
Rankin St. CH44: Wall 4A 74
Ranworth Cl. L11: N Grn. 5E 37
Ranworth Gdns. WA9: St. H 5D 65

Ranworth Pl.—Richardson Rd.

Ranworth Pl. L11: N Grn. 5E **37**
Ranworth Sq. L11: N Grn. 5E **37**
Ranworth Way L11: N Grn. 5F **37**
Rappart Rd. CH44: Wall 3D **75**
Rashid Mufti Ct. L8: Liv 3A **100**
Ratcliffe Pl. L35: R'hill 2B **86**
Rathbone Hall L17: Aig 5E **101**
Rathbone Rd. L13: W'tree 1F **101**
L15: W'tree 1F **101**
Rathlin Cl. WA8: Wid 1E **133**
Rathmore Av. L18: Moss H 1A **124**
Rathmore Cl. CH43: O'ton 1A **118**
Rathmore Dr. CH43: O'ton 5A **96**
Rathmore Rd. CH43: O'ton 5A **96**
Raven Cl. L6: Liv 3A **78**
Ravendale Cl. CH43: Noct 5D **95**
Ravenfield Cl. L26: Halew 4E **127**
Ravenfield Dr. WA8: Wid 1C **130**
Ravenglass Av. L31: Mag 5D **7**
RAVENHEAD 1E **65**
Ravenhead Av. L32: K'by 1E **39**
Ravenhead Retail Pk.
WA9: St. H 2A **66**
Ravenhead Rd. WA10: St. H 2E **65**
Ravenhill Cres. CH46: Leas 2F **71**
Ravenhurst Way L35: Whis 5D **85**
Ravenna Rd. L19: Aller 4D **125**
Ravens Ct. L26: Halew 5F **127**
Ravenscroft Rd. CH43: O'ton 4C **96**
Ravensthorpe Grn. L11: N Grn. 5F **37**
Ravenstone Cl. CH49: Upton 2E **93**
Ravenstone Dr. WA9: St. H 4C **66**
Ravenstone Rd. L19: Aller 4B **124**
Ravenswood Av. CH42: R Ferr 4F **119**
Ravenswood Rd. CH61: Hes 5A **138**
L13: Liv 3A **80**
Raven Way L20: Boot 5C **34**
Rawcliffe Cl. WA8: Wid 5F **109**
Rawcliffe Rd. CH42: Tran 4D **97**
L9: Walt 4F **35**
Rawdon Cl. WA7: Pal F 3A **168**
Rawlinson Cres. L26: Halew 4B **128**
Rawlinson Rd. L13: Liv 3F **79**
Rawlins St. L7: Liv 3D **79**
Rawson Cl. L21: Sea 1F **33**
Rawson Rd. L21: Sea 5F **17**
(not continuous)
Raydale Cl. L9: Walt 5A **36**
Raymond Av. L30: N'ton 4A **20**
Raymond Pl. L5: Liv 2D **77**
Raymond Rd. CH44: Wall 3C **74**
Raynham Rd. L13: Liv 4F **79**
Reade Cl. CH63: Spit 1A **162**
Reading Cl. L5: Kirk 4D **55**
Reading St. L5: Kirk 4D **55**
Reads Ct. L9: Walt 1F **35**
Reapers Way L30: N'ton 1A **20**
Rear Comn. Pas. L6: Liv 3D **79**
Reay Ct. CH44: Wall 3E **75**
Reay St. WA8: Wid 2C **132**
Rebecca Gdns. WA9: St. H 4C **66**
Recreation St. WA9: St. H 5C **46**
Rector Rd. L6: Liv 4C **56**
Rectory Cl. CH42: Tran 5D **97**
CH60: Hes 3F **157**
Rectory Dr. L26: Halew 3F **127**
Rectory Gdns. WA9: St. H 5C **66**
Rectory La. CH60: Hes 3E **157**
Rectory Rd. CH48: W Kir 5B **112**
Redacre Cl. WA4: Dutt 2F **175**
Redbourn Av. L26: Halew 1F **147**
Redbourne Dr. WA8: Wid 5B **108**
Redbourn St. L6: Liv 5C **56**
Redbrook Cl. CH62: Brom 4D **163**
Redbrook St. L6: Liv 5B **56**
Red Brow La. WA4: Dares 2E **169**
WA7: Murd 2E **169**
Redbrow Way L33: K'by 1E **23**
Redburn Cl. L8: Liv 5A **100**
Redcap Cl. CH45: Wall 3E **51**
Redcar Dr. CH62: East 5D **163**
Redcar M. L6: Liv 5B **56**
Redcar Rd. CH45: Wall 5D **51**
Redcar St. L6: Liv 5B **56**
Red Cat La. WA11: Crank 1E **29**
Redcote Ct. CH48: W Kir 5A **112**
Redcroft CH49: Grea 1C **114**
Red Cross St. L1: Liv 5C **76** (6C **4**)
Red Cut La. L33: Know 5E **25**
Redditch Cl. CH49: Grea 5C **92**
Redfern St. L20: Kirk 3C **54**
Redfield Cl. CH44: Wall 2D **75**
Redford Cl. CH49: Grea 5C **92**
Redford St. L6: Liv 5C **56**
Redgate Av. L23: C'by 1A **18**
Redgate Dr. WA9: St. H 5D **47**
Redgrave St. L7: Liv 4C **78**
Redhill Av. L32: K'by 5F **23**
Red Hill Rd. CH63: Store 2B **140**
Redhouse Bank CH48: W Kir 3A **112**
Redhouse La. CH48: W Kir 3A **112**
Redington Rd. L19: Aller 4D **125**
Redland Rd. L9: Ain 5B **20**
Red La. WA6: Frod 5C **172**
Red Lion Cl. L31: Mag 1C **12**
Red Lomes L30: N'ton 5D **11**
Redmain Way L12: Crox 1F **59**
Redmere Dr. CH60: Hes 2D **159**
Redmires Cl. L7: Liv 1B **100**
Redmont St. CH41: Tran 5E **97**
Redmoor Cres. L33: K'by 5E **15**
Redpoll Gro. L26: Halew 2E **127**
Red Rock St. L6: Liv 2B **78**
Red Rum Cl. L9: Ain 5D **21**
Redruth Av. WA11: St. H 1D **47**
Redruth Cl. WA7: Brook 4C **168**
Redruth Rd. L11: Crox 3D **39**
Redstone Cl. CH47: Meols 3D **91**
Redstone Dr. CH60: Hes 1C **156**
Redstone Pk. CH45: Wall 3F **51**
Redstone Ri. CH43: Noct 3D **95**
Redtail Cl. WA7: Run 4F **151**
Redvers Av. CH66: Hoot 3F **171**
Redvers Dr. L9: Walt 2F **35**
Redwald Cl. L33: K'by 4F **15**
Redwing La. L25: Gate 4F **103**
Redwing Way L26: Halew 2D **127**
Redwood Av. L31: Lyd 4C **6**
Redwood Cl. CH43: O'ton 2F **117**
L25: Gate 4B **104**
Redwood Ct. *L8: Liv 5A 100*
(off Byles St.)
Redwood Dr. WA11: Hay 3F **47**
Redwood Gro. L20: Boot 4C **34**
Redwood Rd. L25: Gate 4B **104**
Redwood Way L33: K'by 4E **15**
Reedale Cl. L18: Moss H 5A **102**
Reedale Rd. L18: Moss H 5A **102**
Reeds Av. E. CH46: Leas 3F **71**
Reeds Av. W. CH46: Leas 3F **71**
Reeds La. CH46: Leas, More 2F **71**
WA11: R'ford 1E **27**
Reeds Rd. L36: Huy 2E **83**
Reedville CH43: O'ton 4B **96**
Reedville Gro. CH46: Leas 4F **71**
Reedville Rd. CH63: Beb 2F **141**
Reeves Av. L20: Boot 3E **35**
Reeves St. WA9: St. H 5E **47**
Reflection Ct. WA10: St. H 5F **45**
Regal Cres. WA8: Wid 4B **130**
Regal Dr. WA10: Windle 3C **44**
Regal Rd. L11: Crox 5C **38**
Regal Twr. L11: Crox 5C **38**
Regal Wlk. L4: Walt 4E **55**
Regency Pk. WA8: Wid 1E **131**
Regent Av. L14: B Grn 4E **81**
L30: N'ton 2F **19**
WA11: Hay 1B **48**
Regent Pk. L36: Huy 1E **83**
Regent Rd. CH45: Wall 5D **51**
L3: Liv .1B **76**
L5: Liv, Kirk 1B **76**
L20: Boot, Kirk 3F **33**
L23: C'by 1D **17**
WA8: Wid 3B **132**
Regents Cl. CH61: Thing 2B **138**
Regents Rd. WA10: St. H 1C **64**
Regent St. L3: Liv 2B **76**
WA7: Run 4A **152**
WA12: New W 5F **49**
Regents Way CH63: High B 4D **119**
Regina Av. L22: Water 3C **16**
Reginald Rd. WA9: St. H 5E **67**
Reginald Rd. Ind. Est.
WA9: St. H 5F **67**
Regina Rd. L9: Walt 2A **36**
Reigate Cl. L25: Wltn 1C **126**
Rembury Pl. WA4: Dutt 2F **175**
Renaissance Way L24: Halew 2D **147**
Rendal Cl. L5: Liv 1A **78**
Rendcombe Grn. L11: N Grn. 5F **37**
Rendelsham Cl. CH49: Upton 4E **93**
Rendel St. CH41: Birk 2D **97**
Renfrew Av. CH62: East 5E **163**
WA11: St. H 1D **47**
Renfrew St. L7: Liv 4A **78**
Rennell Rd. L14: K Ash 3C **80**
Rennie Av. WA10: St. H 4C **44**
Renown Way L24: Speke 1A **146**
Renshaw St. L1: Liv 5E **77** (6G **5**)
Renton Av. WA7: Run 5D **153**
Renville Rd. L14: B Grn 4C **80**
Renwick Av. L35: R'hill 2A **86**
Renwick Rd. L9: Walt 3A **36**
Repton Gro. L10: Ain 3C **20**
Repton Rd. L16: Child 1C **102**
Reservoir Rd. CH42: Tran 3B **118**
L25: Wltn 1F **125**
Reservoir Rd. Nth. CH42: Tran . . .3B **118**
Reservoir St. L6: Liv 2A **78**
WA9: St. H 4C **64**
Rest Hill Rd. CH63: Store 2B **140**
Retford Rd. L33: K'by 3F **23**
Retford Wlk. L33: K'by 3F **23**
Reva Rd. L14: B Grn 3E **81**
Revesby Cl. WA8: Wid 2D **131**
Rex Cohen Ct. L17: Aig 4E **101**
Rexmore Rd. L18: Moss H 2A **124**
Rexmore Way L15: W'tree 2E **101**
Reynolds Av. WA9: St. H 1B **68**
Reynolds Cl. L6: Liv 2A **78**
Reynolds Way L25: Wltn 2A **126**
Rhiwlas St. L8: Liv 4A **100**
Rhodesia Rd. L9: Ain 2B **36**
Rhodesway CH60: Hes 3B **158**
Rhona Cl. CH63: East 1C **170**
Rhosesmor Cl. L32: K'by 1F **39**
Rhosesmor Rd. L32: K'by 2F **39**
Rhuddlan Cl. L13: Liv 4F **79**
Rhyl St. L8: Liv 4E **99**
WA8: Wid 5F **131**
Rialto Cl. L8: Liv 2F **99**
Ribble Av. L31: Mag 5E **7**
L35: R'hill 3C **86**
Ribble Cl. WA8: Wid 1F **133**
Ribble Cres. WN5: Bil 2C **30**
Ribbledale Rd. L18: Moss H 5A **102**
Ribble Ho. L25: Gate 1C **126**
Ribble Rd. L25: Gate 1C **126**
Ribbler's Ct. L32: K'by 2F **39**
Ribbler's La. L32: K'by 1D **39**
L34: Know 2F **39**
Ribblesdale Av. L9: Ain 1B **36**
Ribblesdale Cl. CH62: East 5F **163**
Ribble St. CH41: Birk 5F **73**
Ribchester Way L35: Tar G 2A **106**
Rice Hey Rd. CH44: Wall 1C **74**
Rice La. CH44: Wall 1C **74**
(not continuous)
L9: Walt 5F **35**
Rice Lane City Farm 4F **35**
Rice Lane Station (Rail) 3A **36**
Rice St. L1: Liv 1E **99** (7H **5**)
Richard Allen Way L5: Liv 2E **77**
Richard Chubb Dr. CH44: Wall 5D **53**
Richard Cl. WA7: Cas 1A **168**
Richard Gro. L12: W Der 1E **81**
Richard Hesketh Dr. L32: K'by 3C **22**
Richard Kelly Cl. L4: Walt 3D **57**
Richard Kelly Dr. L4: Walt 1D **57**
Richard Kelly Pl. L4: Walt 3D **57**
Richard Martin Rd. L21: Ford 4C **18**
Richard Rd. L23: Blun 4A **8**
Richards Gro. WA9: St. H 4E **47**
Richardson Rd. CH42: R Ferr 3E **119**

Richardson St.—Rockwell Rd.

Richardson St. L7: Liv 2C **100**
Richland Rd. L13: Liv 1F **79**
Richmond Av. L21: Lith 5A **18**
WA7: Run 5E **153**
WA11: Hay 1B **48**
Richmond Cl. CH63: Beb 1F **141**
L38: High 1A **8**
WA10: Eccl 4A **44**
Richmond Ct. L5: Liv 1A **78**
L21: Lith 1B **34**
Richmond Cres. L30: N'ton 2F **19**
Richmond Gro. L31: Lyd 4E **7**
Richmond Ho.
L3: Liv 4B **76** (4B **4**)
Richmond Pde. L3: Liv 4B **4**
Richmond Pk. L6: Liv 5B **56**
Richmond Rd. CH63: Beb 1F **141**
L23: C'by 5E **9**
Richmond Row L3: Liv 3E **77** (1G **5**)
Richmond St. CH45: New B 2B **52**
L1: Liv 5D **77** (5E **5**)
WA8: Wid 3C **132**
Richmond Ter. L6: Liv 1A **78**
Richmond Way CH61: Hes 5F **137**
CH61: Thing 1A **138**
L35: Tar G 2A **106**
Rich Vw. CH43: O'ton 1B **118**
Rickaby Cl. CH63: Brom 2C **162**
Rickman St. L4: Kirk 3D **55**
Rickman Way L36: Huy 1F **105**
Ridding La. WA7: Brook 5B **168**
Riddock Rd. L21: Lith 3B **34**
Ridge, The CH60: Hes 5D **137**
Ridgefield Rd. CH61: Pens 2F **137**
Ridgemere Rd. CH61: Pens 2F **137**
Ridgetor Rd. L25: Wltn 1F **125**
Ridgeview Rd. CH43: Noct 4D **95**
Ridgeway, The CH47: Meols 4E **91**
CH60: Hes 3B **158**
CH63: High B 4D **119**
L25: Wltn 1A **126**
WA7: Murd 4D **169**
WA8: Cron 3C **108**
Ridgeway Dr. L31: Lyd 3D **7**
Ridgewell Cl. L21: Lith 1A **34**
Ridgewood Dr. CH61: Pens 3F **137**
WA9: St. H 5C **66**
Ridgewood Way L9: Walt 1A **36**
Ridgmont Av. L11: N Grn. 1F **57**
Riding Cl. WA9: Clock F 2C **88**
Ridingfold L26: Halew 2D **127**
Riding Hill Rd. L34: Know 1D **61**
Riding Hill Wlk. L34: Know 1D **61**
Ridings, The CH43: Noct 4D **95**
Ridings Hey CH43: Noct 5D **95**
Riding St. L3: Liv 4E **77** (4J **5**)
Ridley Gro. CH48: W Kir 3A **112**
Ridley La. L31: Mag 1D **13**
Ridley Rd. L6: Liv 3C **78**
Ridley St. CH43: O'ton 4C **96**
Ridsdale WA8: Wid 4C **130**
Ridsdale Lawn L27: N'ley 1A **128**
Riesling Dr. L33: K'by 5D **15**
Rigby Dr. CH49: Grea 2D **115**
Rigby Rd. L31: Mag 4B **6**
Rigby St. L3: Liv 4B **76** (3B **4**)
WA10: St. H 4F **45**
Rigby St. Sth. WA10: St. H 5F **45**
Riley Av. L20: Boot 3D **35**
Riley Dr. WA7: Run 2A **166**
Rimmer Av. L16: Child 5A **82**
Rimmerbrook Rd. L25: Gate 2B **104**
Rimmer Cl. L21: Lith 1B **34**
Rimmer Gro. WA9: St. H 5E **47**
Rimmer St. L3: Liv 4E **77** (3H **5**)
Rimmington Rd. L17: Aig 2E **123**
Rimrose Bus. Pk. L20: Boot 4A **34**
Rimrose Rd. L20: Boot 3A **34**
Rimrose Valley Country Pk. 2A **18**
Rimrose Valley Rd. L23: C'by 2A **18**
Rimsdale Cl. L17: Aig 5E **123**
Rindlebrook La. L34: Prsct 1C **84**
Ringcroft Rd. L13: Liv 3B **80**
Ringo Starr Dr. L6: Liv 3B **78**
Ringsfield Rd. L24: Speke 4A **148**
Ringway Rd. L25: Gate 5C **104**
WA7: Run 5D **153**
Ringways CH62: Brom 4D **143**
Ringwood CH43: O'ton 1A **118**
Ringwood Av. L14: B Grn 4F **81**
Rio Ct. L34: Prsct 4D **63**
Ripley Av. L21: Lith 4B **18**
Ripley Cl. L31: Mag 1E **13**
Ripon Cl. L30: N'ton 4F **19**
L36: Huy 3A **84**
Ripon Rd. CH45: Wall 5E **51**
Ripon Row WA7: Run 3D **167**
Ripon St. CH41: Tran 5E **97**
L4: Walt 2F **55**
Risbury Rd. L11: N Grn. 1F **57**
Rishton Cl. L5: Liv 1F **77**
Rishton St. L5: Liv 1A **78**
Ritchie Av. L9: Ain 2C **36**
Ritherup La. L35: R'hill 2C **86**
Ritson St. L8: Liv 3B **100**
Rivacre Rd. CH62: East 5F **163**
Riva La. CH60: Hes 5E **137**
River Avon St. L8: Liv 2B **100**
Riverbank Cl. CH60: Hes 4F **157**
Riverbank Rd.
CH60: Hes 4F **157**
CH62: Brom 4E **143**
L19: Gras 5A **124**
River Gro. CH62: New F 4B **120**
Riverpark Gdns. *L8: Liv* *3E 99*
(off Hyslop St.)
Riversdale WA6: Frod 4C **172**
Riversdale Cl. L33: K'by 1E **23**
Riversdale Ct. L19: Aig 4F **123**
Riversdale M. L19: Aig 4F **123**
Riversdale Rd.
CH44: Wall 2D **75**
CH48: W Kir 4A **112**
L19: Aig 5E **123**
L21: Sea 1F **33**
WA7: Halt 1E **167**
Riverside CH48: W Kir 1B **134**
CH62: Port S 2B **142**
L12: W Der 2E **59**
Riverside Bowl 2B **52**
Riverside Cl. L20: Boot 3A **34**
Riverside Ct. CH62: New F 4B **120**
Riverside Dr. L3: Liv 1E **121**
L17: Aig 2A **122**
Riverside Gro. WA9: St. H 4D **67**
Riverside Ho. CH41: Birk 5F **75**
Riverside Vw. L17: Aig 3C **122**
Riverside Wlk. L3: Liv 1B **98** (7B **4**)
Riverslea Rd. L23: Blun 3B **16**
River Vw. CH62: New F 4C **120**
L22: Water 3C **16**
Riverview Gdns. CH42: R Ferr 2F **119**
River Vw. Residential Cvn. Pk.
WA8: Wid 4C **132**
Riverview Rd. CH44: Wall 3E **75**
CH62: Brom 5F **143**
Riverview Wlk. L8: Liv 5F **99**
River Wlk. *WA7: Pal F* *3F 167*
(off Halton Lea Shop. Cen.)
River Way L25: Gate 1C **126**
Riverwood Rd. CH62: Brom 1F **163**
Riviera Dr. CH42: R Ferr 3D **119**
L11: Crox 4C **38**
Rivington Av. CH43: Noct 5E **95**
WA10: St. H 2E **45**
Rivington Rd. CH44: Wall 3C **74**
WA7: Pres B 2E **175**
WA10: St. H 5D **45**
Rivington St. WA10: St. H 1D **65**
Roadwater Cl. L25: Gate 2B **104**
Robarts Rd. L4: Walt 5A **56**
ROBBINS BRIDGE 2E **7**
Robeck Rd. L13: Liv 5B **80**
Robert Dr. CH49: Grea 1E **115**
Robert Gro. L12: W Der 1E **81**
Roberts Av. WA11: Hay 3F **47**
Roberts Ct. WA7: Pal F 4F **167**
Roberts Dr. L20: Boot 1E **35**
Robertson St. L8: Liv 4E **99**
Roberts St. L3: Liv 3B **76** (2A **4**)
Robert St. CH41: Birk 2D **97**
WA7: Run 5C **152**
WA8: Wid 3B **132**
Robina Rd. WA9: St. H 3D **67**
Robin Cl. WA7: Murd 3D **169**
Robins La. WA9: St. H 3C **66**
Robinson M. *CH41: Birk* *3F 97*
(off Gertrude St.)
Robinson Pl. WA9: St. H 5C **46**
Robinson Rd. L21: Lith 4C **18**
Robinson St. WA9: St. H 5D **47**
Robin Way CH49: W'chu 2B **116**
Robsart St. L5: Liv 1E **77**
Robson St. L5: Liv 4F **55**
L13: Liv 5F **79**
ROBY 4C **82**
Roby Cl. L35: R'hill 2C **86**
Roby Ct. L36: Roby 5D **83**
Roby Mt. Av. L36: Roby 4D **83**
Roby Rd. L14: B Grn 5F **81**
L36: Roby 4B **82**
(not continuous)
Roby Station (Rail) 4C **82**
Roby St. L15: W'tree 2E **101**
L20: Boot 4C **34**
WA10: St. H 2D **65**
Roby Well Way WN5: Bil 1D **31**
Rocastle Cl. L6: Liv 3A **78**
Rochester Av. L30: N'ton 4F **19**
Rochester Gdns.
WA10: St. H 2D **65**
Rochester Rd. CH42: R Ferr 2F **119**
Rock Av. CH60: Hes 1F **157**
Rock Bank CH49: Upton 4A **94**
Rockbank Rd. L13: Liv 1E **79**
Rockbourne Av. L25: Wltn 4F **103**
Rockbourne Grn. L25: Wltn 4F **103**
Rockbourne Way L25: Wltn 4F **103**
Rock Cl. CH42: R Ferr 2F **119**
Rock Dr. WA6: Frod 4C **172**
Rocket Trad. Cen.
L14: B Grn 5C **80**
ROCK FERRY 2F **119**
Rock Ferry By-Pass
CH42: R Ferr 1A **120**
Rock Ferry Station (Rail) 2F **119**
Rockfield Cl. WA8: Wid 2D **131**
Rockfield Gdns. L31: Mag 5C **6**
Rockfield Rd. L4: Walt 4F **55**
Rockford Av. L32: K'by 1E **39**
Rockford Cl. L32: K'by 1E **39**
Rockford Wlk. L32: K'by 1E **39**
Rock Gro. L13: Liv 3F **79**
Rockhill Rd. L25: Wltn 2B **126**
Rockhouse St. L6: Liv 1C **78**
Rockingham Ct. L33: K'by 1F **23**
Rockland Rd. CH45: Wall 4F **51**
L22: Water 3E **17**
Rocklands Av. CH63: Beb 5A **120**
Rocklands La. CH63: Thorn H 3C **160**
Rock La. L31: Mell 4F **13**
WA8: Wid 5F **109**
Rock La. E. CH42: R Ferr 3A **120**
(not continuous)
Rock La. W. CH42: R Ferr 3F **119**
Rockley St. L4: Kirk 3E **55**
(not continuous)
Rockmount Cl. L25: Wltn 1F **125**
Rock Mt. Pk. L25: Wltn 1F **125**
Rockmount Rd. L17: Aig 3F **123**
Rock Pk. CH42: R Ferr 2A **120**
(not continuous)
Rock Pk. Rd. CH42: R Ferr 3B **120**
Rockpoint Av. CH45: New B 4C **52**
Rock Retail Pk. CH41: Birk 4E **97**
Rocksavage Way WA7: Run 5A **166**
Rockside Rd. L18: Moss H 2A **124**
Rock St. L13: Liv 3A **80**
WA10: St. H 3C **64**
Rock Vw. L5: Liv 5E **55**
L31: Mell 1A **22**
Rockville Rd. L14: B Grn 5C **80**
Rockville St. CH42: R Ferr 2F **119**
Rockwell Cl. L12: W Der 3D **59**
Rockwell Rd. L12: W Der 3D **59**

Rockybank Rd. CH42: Tran 1D 119
Rocky La. CH60: Hes 2F 157
  L6: Liv 1C 78
  L16: Child 1C 102
Rocky La. Sth. CH60: Hes 2A 158
Roderick Rd. L4: Walt 1A 56
Roderick St. L3: Liv 3E 77 (2H 5)
Rodgers Cl. WA6: Frod 4B 172
Rodick St. L25: Wltn 2F 125
Rodmell Rd. L9: Ain 2B 36
Rodney St. CH41: Birk 4D 97
  L1: Liv 1E 99 (7H 5)
  WA10: St. H 5E 45
Roe All. L1: Liv 5D 77 (6F 5)
Roedean Cl. L25: Wltn 3B 126
  L31: Mag 5D 7
Roehampton Dr. L23: Blun 4C 8
  WA7: Pal F 3E 167
Roemarsh Cl. L12: W Der 1B 58
Roemarsh Ct. WA7: Pal F 4E 167
Roe St. L1: Liv 5F 5
Roften Works Ind. Est.
  CH66: Hoot 5D 171
Roger Arden Ct. L20: Boot 4D 35
Rogers Av. L20: Boot 3E 35
Rogersons Grn. L26: Halew 2E 127
Rokeby Cl. L3: Liv 2E 77 (1H 5)
Rokeby Ct. WA7: Mnr P 2D 155
Rokeby St. L3: Liv 3E 77 (1H 5)
Roker Av. CH44: Wall 3A 74
Rokesmith Av. L7: Liv 1C 100
Roklis Ct. CH49: Upton 5A 94
Roland Av. CH63: High B 1D 141
  WA7: Run 1F 165
  WA11: St. H 1C 46
Rolands Wlk. WA7: Cas 5F 153
Rolesby Gdns. WA9: St. H 5E 65
Roleton Cl. L30: N'ton 1B 20
Rolleston Dr. CH45: Wall 4F 51
  CH63: Beb 3A 142
Rolling Mill La. WA9: St. H 3F 67
Rollo St. L4: Kirk 4D 55
Roman Cl. WA7: Cas 5E 153
Roman Rd. CH43: Pren 4A 118
  CH47: Meols 2D 91
  CH63: Store 5A 118
Rome Cl. L36: Huy 3D 83
Romer Rd. L6: Liv 3C 78
Romford Way L26: Halew 1F 147
  (not continuous)
Romilly St. L6: Liv 3A 78
Romley St. L4: Walt 1F 55
Romney Cl. WA8: Wid 2E 133
Romulus St. L7: Liv 4D 79
Ronald Cl. L22: Water 4F 17
Ronald Rd. L22: Water 4F 17
Ronald Ross Av. L30: N'ton 2F 19
Ronaldshay WA8: Wid 2E 133
Ronald St. L13: Liv 3F 79
Ronaldsway CH49: Upton 3F 93
  CH60: Hes 4F 157
  L10: Faz 1A 38
  L23: Thorn 4A 10
  L26: Halew 4A 128
Ronan Cl. L20: Boot 4A 34
Ronan Rd. WA8: Wid 2D 151
Rookery Dr. L19: Aig 4F 123
Rookery La. WA11: R'ford 1A 28
Rookley Cl. L27: N'ley 5F 105
Rooks Way CH60: Hes 2E 157
Rooley, The L36: Huy 5D 83
Roosevelt Dr. L9: Ain 5B 20
Roper's Bri. Cl. L35: Whis 3D 85
Roper St. L8: Liv 4F 99
  WA9: St. H 4C 46
Ropewalks Sq. L1: Liv 7G 5
Rosalind Av. CH63: High B 5E 119
Rosalind Way L20: Kirk 2D 55
Rosam Ct. WA7: Pal F 4E 167
Rosclare Dr. CH45: Wall 5F 51
Roscoe & Gladstone Hall
  L17: Aig 5E 101
Roscoe Cl. L35: Tar G 2A 106
Roscoe Cres. WA7: West P 3E 165

Roscoe La. L1: Liv 1E 99 (7G 5)
Roscoe Pl. L1: Liv 5E 77 (7G 5)
Roscoe St. L1: Liv 1E 99 (7H 5)
  WA10: St. H 1D 65
Roscommon St. L5: Liv 2E 77
  (not continuous)
Roscommon Way
  WA8: Wid 1E 131
Roscote, The CH60: Hes 3F 157
Roscote Cl. CH60: Hes 3F 157
Roseacre CH48: W Kir 3A 112
Roseate Cl. CH45: Wall 3E 51
Rose Av. L20: Boot 1C 34
  WA9: St. H 4C 66
  WA11: Hay 2E 49
Rose Bank Rd. L16: Child 2D 103
Rosebank Rd. L36: Huy 5C 60
Rosebank Way L36: Huy 1C 82
Rosebery Av. CH44: Wall 2C 74
  L22: Water 3C 16
Rosebery Gro. CH42: Tran 2B 118
Rosebery Rd. WA10: St. H 3D 45
Rosebery St. L8: Liv 2A 100
Rosebourne Cl. L17: Aig 2B 122
Rose Brae L18: Moss H 5A 102
  CH60: Hes 1A 158
Rose Brow L25: Witn 5A 104
Rose Cl. L26: Halew 5A 128
  WA7: Murd 5D 169
Rose Ct. CH41: Birk 3D 97
  L15: W'tree 2E 101
Rose Cres. WA8: Wid 5F 131
Rosecroft CH62: Brom 4C 162
Rosecroft Ct. CH47: Hoy 5A 90
Rosedale Av. L23: C'by 1E 17
Rosedale Cl. L9: Walt 4B 36
Rosedale Rd. CH42: Tran 1E 119
  L18: Moss H 4A 102
Rose Dr. WA11: R'ford 1A 28
Rosefield Av. CH63: High B 5E 119
Rosefield Rd. L25: Witn 3C 126
Rosegarth Grn. L13: Liv 2B 80
Roseheath Dr. L26: Halew 5F 127
Rose Hill L3: Liv 3D 77 (1F 5)
Rosehill Av. WA9: Bold 5B 68
Rosehill Ct. L25: Witn 5A 104
Roseland Cl. L31: Lyd 3B 6
Roselands Ct. CH42: R Ferr 3E 119
Rose La. L18: Moss H 1F 123
Rose Lea Cl. WA8: Wid 5A 110
Roselee Cl. CH42: R Ferr 3A 120
Rosemary Av. WA7: Beech 1F 173
Rosemary Cl. CH43: Bid 1E 95
  L7: Liv 1A 100
Rosemead Av. CH61: Pens 3F 137
Rosemont Rd. L17: Aig 2E 123
Rosemoor Dr. L23: C'by 5A 10
Rose Mt. CH43: O'ton 1B 118
Rosemount Cl. CH43: O'ton 1A 118
Rose Mt. Dr. CH45: Wall 5A 52
Rose Pl. CH42: Tran 5D 97
  L3: Liv 3D 77 (1F 5)
  (not continuous)
  WA11: R'ford 1A 28
Roseside Dr. L27: N'ley 4F 105
Rose St. L1: Liv 4F 5
  L25: Witn 2F 125
  WA8: Wid 5F 131
Rose Ter. L18: Moss H 5A 102
Rose Va. L5: Liv 1E 77
  (Gt. Homer St., not continuous)
  L5: Liv .1E 77
  (Netherfield Rd. N.)
Rose Vw. Av. WA8: Wid 2A 132
Rose Vs. L15: W'tree 2F 101
Rosewarne Cl. L17: Aig 2D 123
Rosewood Cl. L27: N'ley 4E 105
  L28: Stock V 4B 60
  WA8: Wid 4B 130
Rosewood Dr. CH46: More 1B 92
Rosewood Farm Ct. WA8: Wid 4E 109
Rosewood Gdns. L11: N Grn. 2B 58
Roseworth Av. L9: Walt 1A 36
Roskell Rd. L25: Hunts X 5C 126

Roslin Rd. CH43: O'ton 5B 96
  CH61: Irby 1D 137
Roslyn St. CH42: Tran 1F 119
Rossall Av. L10: Ain 2D 21
Rossall Cl. L24: Hale 5E 149
Rossall Ct. CH46: Leas 4F 71
Rossall Rd. CH46: More 5F 71
  L13: Liv 4B 80
  WA8: Wid 2D 133
Ross Av. CH46: Leas 2C 72
Ross Cl. L34: Know 5D 41
Rossendale Cl. CH43: Noct 5D 95
Rossett Av. L17: Liv 3D 101
Rossett Rd. L23: C'by 2C 16
Rossett St. L6: Liv 1C 78
Rossini St. L21: Sea 2A 34
Rosslyn Av. L31: Mag 2B 12
Rosslyn Cres. CH46: More 1E 93
Rosslyn Dr. CH46: More 1E 93
Rosslyn Pk. CH46: More 2E 93
Rosslyn St. L17: Aig 1B 122
Rossmore Gdns. L4: Walt 3B 56
Ross St. WA8: Wid 3B 132
Ross Tower Ct. CH45: New B 3C 52
Rostherne Av. CH44: Wall 3A 74
Rostherne Cres. WA8: Wid 2D 131
Rosthwaite Gro. WA11: St. H 4B 30
Rosthwaite Rd. L12: W Der 5B 58
Roswell Ct. L28: Stock V 5B 60
Rothbury Cl. CH46: More 1C 92
  WA7: Beech 4E 167
Rothbury Ct. WA9: Sut M 4B 88
Rothbury Rd. L14: K Ash 5F 59
Rotherham Cl. L36: Huy 2E 83
Rotherwood CH43: Noct 4D 95
Rotherwood Cl. CH63: High B 1D 141
Rothesay Cl. WA7: Cas 5F 153
  WA11: St. H 1E 47
Rothesay Ct. CH63: Beb 3F 141
Rothesay Dr. CH62: East 1E 171
  L23: C'by 2E 17
Rothesay Gdns. CH43: Pren 3F 117
Rothsay Cl. L5: Liv 2E 77
Rothwells La. L23: Thorn 3B 10
Rothwell St. L6: Liv 2A 78
Rotunda St. L5: Liv 1D 77
Roughdale Av. L32: K'by 1F 39
  WA9: Sut M 2B 88
Roughdale Cl. L32: K'by 1F 39
Roughsedge Ho. L28: Stock V 3B 60
Roughwood Dr. L33: K'by 2F 23
Roundabout, The WA8: Cron 3D 109
Round Hey L28: Stock V 3A 60
Round Meade, The L31: Mag 5B 6
Roundwood Dr. WA9: St. H 2B 66
Routledge St. WA8: Wid 3B 132
Rowan Av. L12: W Der 2F 59
Rowan Cl. WA7: Run 3C 166
  WA11: Hay 3F 47
  WA11: St. H 1D 47
Rowan Ct. CH49: Grea 2B 114
  CH63: High B 1D 141
  L17: Aig 2E 123
Rowan Dr. L32: K'by 2C 22
Rowan Gro. CH63: High B 3E 141
  L36: Huy 1D 105
Rowan Tree Cl. CH49: Grea 1C 114
Rowena Cl. L23: C'by 5F 9
Rowlings Way L32: K'by 5F 23
Rowsley Gro. L9: Ain 1B 36
Rowson St. CH45: New B 2B 52
  L34: Prsct 4D 63
Rowthorn Cl. WA8: Wid 4E 131
Rowton Cl. CH43: O'ton 1F 117
Roxborough Av. WA5: B'wood 5F 69
Roxborough Wlk. L25: Wltn 1C 126
Roxburgh Av. CH42: Tran 2D 119
  L17: Aig 1C 122
Roxburgh St. L4: Kirk 1E 55
  L20: Boot 1E 55
Royal, The CH47: Hoy 5A 90
Royal Av. WA8: Wid 3B 130
Royal Court Theatre 4D 77 (4F 5)
Royal Cft. L12: W Der 2B 80
Royal Gro. WA10: St. H 2D 65

Royal Liverpool Golf Course 1A 112
Royal Mail St. L3: Liv 5E 77 (5G 5)
Royal Pl. WA8: Wid 4B 130
Royal Quay L3: Liv 1C 98
Royal Standard Way
    CH42: Tran 1F 119
Royal St. L4: Walt 4E 55
Royden Av. CH44: Wall 1D 75
    WA7: Run 2F 165
Royden Ct. CH49: Upton 3E 93
    WN5: Bil 1E 31
Royden Way L3: Liv 1E 121
Roysten Gdns. WA9: St. H 1D 67
Royston Av. CH44: Wall 2D 75
Royston St. L7: Liv 5B 78
Royton Cl. L26: Halew 1F 147
Royton Rd. L22: Water 3F 17
Rubbing Stone CH48: Caldy 3D 135
Ruby St. L8: Liv 1F 121
    (not continuous)
Rudd Av. WA9: St. H 1A 68
Rudd St. CH47: Hoy 4B 90
Rudgate L35: Whis 4E 85
Rudgrave M. CH44: Wall 1D 75
Rudgrave Pl. CH44: Wall 1D 75
Rudgrave Sq. CH44: Wall 1D 75
Rudheath La. WA7: Nort 4D 155
Rudley Wlk. L24: Speke 5F 147
Rudston Rd. L16: Child 1C 102
Rudyard Cl. L14: K Ash 3C 80
Rudyard Rd. L14: K Ash 3C 80
Rufford Av. L31: Mag 4E 7
Rufford Cl. L10: Faz 5F 21
    L35: Prsct 1F 85
    WA8: Wid 2C 130
Rufford Rd. CH44: Wall 3B 74
    L6: Liv 3C 78
    L20: Boot 3C 34
Rufford Wlk. WA11: St. H 2E 47
Rugby Dr. L10: Ain 4E 21
Rugby Rd. CH44: Wall 1F 73
    L9: Ain 5B 20
Ruislip Cl. L25: Wltn 2C 126
Rullerton Rd. CH44: Wall 2A 74
Rumford Pl. L3: Liv 4B 76 (4B 4)
Rumford St. L2: Liv 4C 76 (4C 4)
Rumney Pl. L4: Kirk 3D 55
    (not continuous)
Rumney Rd. L4: Kirk 3E 55
Rumney Rd. W. L4: Kirk 3D 55
RUNCORN 4A 152
Runcorn Dock Rd. WA7: Run 5E 151
Runcorn East Station (Rail) 3D 169
Runcorn Hill Local Nature Reserve
    . . . . .2F 165
Runcorn Hill Local Nature Reserve
    Vis. Cen. 2F 165
Runcorn Rd.
    WA4: Dares, Moore, H Walt
    . . . . .3F 155
Runcorn Ski & Snowboard Cen.
    . . . . .3B 168
Runcorn Spur Rd. WA7: Run 5B 152
Runcorn Station (Rail) 5F 151
Runcorn Swimming Pool 4B 152
    (off Bridge St.)
Rundle Rd. L17: Aig 2E 123
Rundle St. CH41: Birk 1A 96
Runic St. L13: Liv 4F 79
Runnell, The CH64: Nest 5E 159
Runnell's La. L23: Thorn 5C 10
Runnymead Wlk. WA8: Wid 2C 132
    (off William St.)
Runnymede L36: Huy 2D 83
Runnymede Cl. L25: Wltn 5A 104
Runnymede Ct. WA8: Wid 3C 132
    (off William St.)
Runnymede Dr. WA11: Hay 2A 48
Runnymede Gdns. WA8: Wid 3C 132
    (off Cliffe St.)
Runton Rd. L25: Gate 4C 104
Rupert Dr. L6: Liv 3A 78
Rupert Rd. L36: Huy 3C 82
Rupert Row WA7: Cas 2A 168
Ruscar Cl. L26: Halew 2E 127

Ruscombe Rd. L14: K Ash 1F 81
Rushden Rd. L32: K'by 4A 24
Rushey Hey Rd. L32: K'by 3E 23
Rushfield Cres. WA7: Brook 5B 168
Rushlake Ct. WA43: Bid 2C 94
Rushlake Dr. L27: N'ley 4D 105
Rushmere Rd. L11: N Grn. 1F 57
Rushmore Dr. WA8: Wid 1F 131
Rusholme Cl. L26: Halew 1A 148
Rushton Cl. WA5: B'wood 4F 69
    WA8: Wid 1F 131
Rushton Pl. L25: Wltn 2A 126
Rushton's Wlk. L30: N'ton 1D 19
Rusty Vw. WA12: New W 4F 49
Ruskin Av. CH42: R Ferr 3F 119
    CH44: Wall 3A 74
Ruskin Cl. L20: Boot 5C 34
Ruskin Dr. WA10: St. H 4D 45
Ruskin Leisure Cen. 4D 45
Ruskin St. L4: Kirk 2E 55
Ruskin Way CH43: Noct 1D 117
    L36: Huy 5D 83
Rusland Av. CH61: Pens 3F 137
Rusland Rd. L32: K'by 5E 23
Russell Ct. WA8: Wid 5B 110
Russell Pl. L3: Liv 5E 77 (5H 5)
    L19: Gars 1C 144
Russell Rd. CH42: R Ferr 1F 119
    (not continuous)
    CH44: Wall 1E 73
    L18: Moss H 4F 101
    L19: Gars 1C 144
    L36: Huy 4B 84
    WA7: Run 1E 165
Russell St. CH41: Birk 2E 97
    L3: Liv 4E 77 (4H 5)
    WA10: St. H 3F 45
Russet Cl. L27: N'ley 4E 105
Russian Av. L13: Liv 1F 79
Russian Dr. L13: Liv 1F 79
Rutherford Cl. L13: W'tree 5E 79
Rutherford Rd. L18: Moss H 3A 102
    L31: Mag 3E 13
    WA10: Windle 2C 44
Rutherglen Av. L23: Crosb 3F 17
Ruth Evans Ct. L35: R'hill 2A 86
Ruthven Cl. L21: Lith 1A 34
    (off Ruthven Rd.)
Ruthven Rd. L13: Liv 5B 80
    L21: Lith 1A 34
Rutland Av. L17: Liv 3D 101
    L26: Halew 4F 127
Rutland Cl. L5: Liv 1F 77
Rutland Ho. L17: Aig 4D 101
    L23: Blun 2B 16
Rutland St. L20: Boot 4D 35
    WA7: Run 4F 151
    WA10: St. H 3F 45
Rutland Way L36: Huy 3B 84
Rutter St. L8: Liv 4E 99
Rycot Rd. L24: Speke 3B 146
Rycroft Rd. CH44: Wall 3C 74
    CH47: Meols 3E 91
    L10: Faz 1E 37
Rydal Av. CH43: Noct 4C 94
    L23: C'by 3F 17
    L34: Prsct 5F 63
Rydal Bank CH44: Wall 2C 74
    CH63: Beb 5A 120
Rydal Cl. CH61: Pens 3A 138
    L10: Ain 3F 21
    L33: K'by 1D 23
Rydal Gro. WA7: Run 2B 166
    WA11: St. H 1A 46
Rydal Rd. L36: Huy 5E 83
Rydal St. L5: Liv 5A 56
Rydal Way WA8: Wid 3C 130
Rydecroft L25: Wltn 2F 125
Ryder Cl. L35: R'hill 2A 86
Ryder Rd. WA8: Wid 5B 110
Rye Cl. WA9: Clock F 2C 88
Ryecote L32: K'by 1E 39
Rye Ct. L12: W Der 5E 59
Rye Cft. L21: Ford 2B 18
Ryecroft Rd. CH60: Hes 3C 158

Ryedale Cl. L8: Liv 2B 100
Ryefield La. L21: Ford 2B 18
Ryegate Rd. L19: Gras 4B 124
Rye Gro. L12: W Der 5E 59
Rye Hey Rd. L32: K'by 3E 23
Ryland Pk. CH61: Thing 2A 138
Rylands Hey CH49: Grea 5D 93
Rylands St. WA8: Wid 4B 132
Ryleys Gdns. L2: Liv 4C 76 (4D 4)
Rymer Gro. L4: Walt 2A 56

S

Sabre Cl. WA7: Murd 3D 169
Sackville Rd. WA10: Windle 2C 44
Saddle Cl. L9: Ain 5D 21
Saddlers Ri. WA7: Nort 2C 168
Saddlestone Gro. L8: Liv 4E 99
Sadler's La. WA11: Windle 1E 43
Sadler St. WA8: Wid 3C 132
Saffron Gdns. WA9: St. H 1D 67
Saffron M. L23: Thorn 4B 10
Saffron Rd. L4: Kirk 3D 55
    L36: Huy 4E 83
St Aidan's Ct. CH43: C'ton 3F 95
St Aidan's Gro. L36: Huy 4C 60
St Aidans Ter. CH43: C'ton 3F 95
    L5: Kirk 5D 55
    (off Latham St.)
St Aidan's Way L30: N'ton 2E 19
St Albans L6: Liv 1A 78
St Albans Cl. WA11: Hay 1F 49
St Albans Ct. L5: Liv 1C 76
St Albans Rd. CH43: C'ton 2A 96
    CH44: Wall 2B 74
    L20: Boot 5C 34
St Alban's Sq. L20: Boot 1C 54
St Alexander Cl. L20: Kirk 2D 55
St Ambrose Cft. L30: N'ton 1E 19
St Ambrose Gro. L4: Walt 5B 56
St Ambrose Rd. WA8: Wid 3C 132
St Ambrose Way L5: Liv 2E 77
St Andrew Rd. L4: Walt 5B 56
St Andrews Av. L12: W Der 5E 59
St Andrews Cl. CH43: Noct 3D 95
    L22: Water 5E 17
St Andrews Dr. L23: Blun 4B 8
    L36: Huy 4C 60
St Andrews Gdns.
    L3: Liv 4E 77 (4H 5)
St Andrews Gro. L30: N'ton 2C 18
    WA11: St. H 2B 46
St Andrews Pl. L17: Aig 1C 122
St Andrews Rd. CH43: O'ton 3B 96
    CH63: Beb 3A 142
    L20: Boot 2C 34
    L23: Blun 4B 8
St Andrew St. L3: Liv 5E 77 (5H 5)
St Andrews Vw. L33: K'by 4E 15
St Annes Cl. CH41: Birk 2D 97
St Annes Cotts. L14: K Ash 2C 80
St Annes Ct. L3: Liv 1G 5
    L13: Liv 3F 79
    L17: Aig 3E 123
St Annes Gdns. L17: Aig 3E 123
St Annes Gro. CH41: Birk 1C 96
    L17: Aig 3E 123
St Anne's Ho. L20: Boot 1C 54
St Annes Pl. CH41: Birk 1C 96
St Annes Rd. L17: Aig 3E 123
    L36: Huy 5E 83
    WA8: Wid 2B 132
St Annes Ter. CH41: Birk 2C 96
St Anne St. CH41: Birk 1C 96
    (not continuous)
    L3: Liv 3D 77 (1G 5)
St Ann's Rd. CH41: Birk 2D 97
St Ann Pl. L35: R'hill 2C 86
ST ANNS 1D 65
St Ann's Rd. WA10: St. H 5C 44
St Anthony's Cl. L36: Huy 4C 60
St Anthony's Gro. L30: N'ton 2D 19
St Anthony's Rd. L23: Blun 5B 8
St Anthony's Shop. Cen. L5: Liv . . .1D 77

St Asaph Gro. L30: N'ton 4F **19**
St Augustine St. L5: Liv 1D **77**
St Augustine's Way L30: N'ton . . .1D **19**
St Austell Cl. CH46: More 5B **70**
   WA7: Brook 4B **168**
St Austells Rd. L4: Walt 1E **55**
St Bartholomew Rd.
   L3: Liv 3C **76** (1E **4**)
St Bartholomews Cl. L36: Huy 3C **82**
St Benedict's Gro. L36: Huy 4C **60**
St Benet's Way L30: N'ton 2E **19**
St Bernards Cl. L8: Liv 2A **100**
   L30: N'ton 2D **19**
St Bernard's Dr. L30: N'ton 2D **19**
St Brendan's Cl. L36: Huy 4C **60**
St Bride's Rd. CH44: Wall 1D **75**
St Bride St. L8: Liv 1F **99**
St Bridget's Gro. L30: N'ton 2D **19**
St Bridget's La. CH48: W Kir 5B **112**
St Brigids Cres. L5: Liv 1C **76**
St Catherine's Cl. L36: Huy 5E **83**
St Catherines Gdns. CH42: Tran . .5D **97**
St Catherine's Rd. L20: Boot 5C **34**
St Chad's Dr. L32: K'by 3E **23**
St Chads Pde. L32: K'by 3E **23**
St Christoper's Dr. L36: Huy 4C **60**
St Christopher's Av. L30: N'ton . . .1D **19**
St Clare Rd. L15: W'tree 2E **101**
St Columbas Cl. CH44: Wall 1D **75**
St Cuthberts Cl. L12: Crox 5E **39**
St Cyrils Cl. L27: N'ley 3C **104**
St Cyril's Ct. L27: N'ley 2C **104**
St Damian's Cft. L30: N'ton 2E **19**
St David Rd. CH43: C'ton 3A **96**
   CH62: East 4F **163**
St David's Cl. L35: R'hill 2C **86**
St David's Gro. L30: N'ton 3D **19**
St Davids La. CH43: Noct 4D **95**
St Davids Rd. L4: Walt 5B **56**
   L14: K Ash 1B **82**
St Domingo Gro. L5: Liv 5F **55**
St Domingo Rd. L5: Liv 4E **55**
St Domingo Va. L5: Liv 5F **55**
St Dunstan's Gro. L30: N'ton 2D **19**
St Edmond's Rd. L20: Boot 1C **54**
St Edmund's Rd. CH63: Beb 2F **141**
St Edwards Cl. CH41: Birk 1B **96**
St Elmo Rd. CH44: Wall 1D **75**
St Gabriel's Av. L36: Huy 4A **84**
St George's Av. CH42: Tran 2D **119**
   WA10: Windle 3C **44**
St Georges Ct. CH45: Wall 1E **73**
   L31: Mag 2D **13**
   WA8: Wid 4D **131**
St George's Gro. CH46: More 1D **93**
   L30: N'ton 3D **19**
St George's Hgts. L5: Liv 1E **77**
St George's Hill L5: Liv 1E **77**
St George's M. CH45: New B 3B **52**
St George's Pk. CH45: New B 3B **52**
St George's Pl. L1: Liv 4D **77** (4F **5**)
St Georges Rd. CH45: Wall 5E **51**
   L36: Huy 1E **83**
   WA10: St. H 1D **65**
St George's Way
   CH63: Thorn H 3A **160**
   L1: Liv .5F **5**
St Gerald's Cl. L5: Liv 5D **55**
St Gregory's Cft. L30: N'ton 1E **19**
ST HELENS 5A **46**
St Helens Central Station (Rail) . .5B **46**
St Helens Cl. CH43: C'ton 3B **96**
St Helens Club Figure & Fitness
   . . . . .1E **87**
St Helens Crematorium
   WA10: Windle 1C **44**
St Helens Junction Station (Rail)
   . . . . .4F **67**
St Helens Linkway L35: R'hill 3F **87**
   WA9: St. H 1A **66**
St Helens Martial Arts & Fitness Studio
   . . . . .4A **46**
               (off Tolver St.)
St Helens Mus. & Art Gallery 4A **46**
St Helens Retail Pk. WA9: St. H . . .5B **46**

St Helens RLFC 5C **44**
St Helens Rd. L34: Prsct, Ecc P . . .4D **63**
   WA11: R'ford 3B **28**
St Helens Theatre Royal 4A **46**
St Hilary Brow CH44: Wall 2F **73**
St Hilary Dr. CH45: Wall 1F **73**
St Hilda's Dr. WA6: Frod 4C **172**
St Hilda St. L4: Walt 3E **55**
St Hugh's Cl. CH43: C'ton 3B **96**
St Hugh's Ho. L20: Boot 5C **34**
St Ives Cl. CH43: C'ton 3A **96**
St Ives Gro. L13: Liv 3F **79**
St Ives Rd. CH43: C'ton 3A **96**
St Ives Way L26: Halew 4F **127**
St James Cl. CH49: Grea 5D **93**
   L12: W Der 5A **58**
   WA6: Frod 4B **172**
St James Ct. CH45: New B 3B **52**
St James Dr. L20: Boot 4B **34**
St James M. L20: Boot 4B **34**
St James Mt. L35: R'hill 4C **86**
St James Pl. L8: Liv 2E **99**
St James Rd. CH41: Birk 1F **95**
   CH45: New B 3B **52**
   L1: Liv .2E **99**
   L34: Prsct 5E **63**
   L35: R'hill 4C **86**
   L36: Huy 5E **83**
St James St. L1: Liv 2D **99**
St James Way L30: N'ton 1D **19**
St Jerome's Way L30: N'ton 1E **19**
St Johns Av. L9: Walt 3A **36**
St Johns Brow WA7: Run 4B **152**
St John's Cen. L1: Liv 5D **77** (5F **5**)
St John's Cl. CH47: Meols 3D **91**
St John's Ct. L22: Water 4D **17**
St John's Ho. L20: Boot 5D **35**
St John's La. L1: Liv 4D **77** (4F **5**)
St John's Pavement CH41: Birk . . .3D **97**
St John's Pl. L22: Water 4D **17**
St John's Rd. CH45: Wall 1E **73**
   CH62: East 5F **163**
   L20: Boot 1B **54**
   L20: Kirk 3C **54**
   L22: Water 4D **17**
   L36: Huy 5F **83**
St John's Sq. CH41: Birk 3D **97**
   L1: Liv .5F **5**
St John's Ter. L20: Boot 1B **54**
St John St. CH41: Birk 3D **97**
   WA7: Run 4B **152**
   WA10: St. H 3D **65**
   WA12: New W 5F **49**
St Johns Vs. WA8: Wid 2D **131**
St Johns Way L1: Liv 5D **77** (5F **5**)
St Josephs Cl. L36: Huy 4C **60**
   WA9: St. H 2C **68**
St Josephs Cres. L3: Liv 3D **77** (2G **5**)
St Jude's Cl. L36: Huy 4C **60**
St Kevin's Dr. L33: K'by 1E **23**
St Kilda's Rd. CH46: More 2E **93**
St Laurence Cl. CH41: Birk 2D **97**
St Laurence Dr. CH41: Birk 2D **97**
St Laurence Gro. L32: K'by 5F **23**
St Lawrence Cl. L8: Liv 5A **100**
St Lawrence Rd. WA6: Frod 5B **172**
St Leonard's Cl. L30: N'ton 1D **19**
St Lucia Rd. CH44: Wall 1D **75**
St Lukes Cl. L14: K Ash 5F **59**
St Luke's Cl. L4: Walt 1A **56**
St Luke's Cres. WA8: Wid 5B **110**
St Luke's Gro. L30: N'ton 1D **19**
St Lukes Pl. L1: Liv 1E **99** (7G **5**)
St Luke's Rd. L23: C'by 1D **17**
   WA10: St. H 5D **45**
St Luke's Way L36: Huy 4C **60**
   WA6: Frod 4B **172**
St Margaret's Gro. L30: N'ton 2C **18**
St Margaret's Rd. CH47: Hoy 5A **90**
St Marks Ct. CH43: C'ton 4B **96**
St Mark's Gro. L30: N'ton 1C **18**
St Mark's St. WA11: Hay 2A **48**
St Martins Gro. L32: K'by 1F **39**
St Martin's Ho. L20: Boot 5C **34**

St Martin's La. WA7: Murd 3D **169**
St Martin's Mkt. L5: Liv 1E **77**
St Martins M. L5: Liv 2E **77**
St Mary's Arc. WA10: St. H 5A **46**
               (off St Mary's Mkt.)
St Mary's Av. CH44: Wall 2B **74**
   L4: Walt 1A **56**
   WN5: Bil 1C **30**
St Mary's Cl. L13: Liv 5F **79**
   L20: Boot 5B **34**
   L24: Hale 5D **149**
St Marys Ct. CH49: Upton 5A **94**
   L25: Wltn 2A **126**
St Mary's Ga. CH41: Birk 3F **97**
St Mary's Gro. L4: Walt 1A **56**
   L30: N'ton 2C **18**
St Mary's La. L4: Walt 1A **56**
St Mary's Mkt. WA10: St. H 5A **46**
St Mary's Pl. L4: Walt 1A **56**
St Marys Rd. L19: Gars, Gras 5A **124**
   L22: Water 4F **17**
   L36: Huy 4E **83**
   WA7: Halt 1F **167**
   WA8: Wid 3A **152**
St Mary's St. CH44: Wall 2B **74**
   L25: Wltn 2A **126**
St Mathews Cl. L4: Walt 1D **57**
   L36: Huy 3F **83**
St Matthew's Av. L21: Lith 5C **18**
St Matthews Gro. WA10: St. H 3C **64**
St Mawes Cl. WA8: Wid 2E **131**
St Mawes Way WA10: Windle 2B **44**
St Michael Rd. L39: Augh 1F **7**
St Michael's Chu. Rd. L17: Aig . . .1B **122**
St Michaels Cl. L17: Aig 2C **122**
   WA8: Wid 5C **130**
St Michaels Cl. L36: Huy 3E **83**
St Michaels Gro. CH46: More 1D **93**
   L6: Liv .2B **78**
   L30: N'ton 2C **18**
St Michael's Hall L17: Aig 2B **122**
ST MICHAEL'S HAMLET 2B **122**
St Michaels Ind. Est.
   WA8: Wid 5C **130**
St Michaels Pk. CH62: Port S 1B **142**
St Michaels Rd. L17: Aig 2B **122**
   L23: Blun, C'by 5B **8**
   WA8: Wid 5C **130**
   WA9: St. H 3A **88**
St Michael's Station (Rail) 2B **122**
St Monica's Dr. L30: N'ton 1D **19**
St Nicholas' Dr. L30: N'ton 1D **19**
St Nicholas Gro. WA9: St. H 4D **67**
St Nicholas Pl. L3: Liv 5B **76** (5A **4**)
              (not continuous)
St Nicholas Rd. CH45: Wall 1D **73**
   L35: Whis 5D **85**
St Oswald's Av. CH43: Bid 1C **94**
St Oswald's Cl. L30: N'ton 2F **19**
St Oswald's La. L30: N'ton 2F **19**
St Oswald's M. CH43: Bid 5C **72**
St Oswald's St. L13: Liv 4A **80**
St Paschal Baylon Blvd.
   L16: Child 1F **103**
St Patrick's Cl. L33: K'by 5E **15**
St Patrick's Dr. L30: N'ton 1D **19**
St Paul's Av. CH44: Wall 4E **75**
St Pauls Cl. CH42: R Ferr 2E **119**
   L33: K'by 5D **15**
St Pauls Pl. L20: Boot 1D **55**
St Paul's Rd. CH42: R Ferr 2F **119**
             (not continuous)
   CH44: Wall 4D **75**
   WA8: Wid 5A **132**
St Paul's Sq. L3: Liv 4B **76** (3C **4**)
St Paul St. WA10: St. H 5E **45**
St Paul's Vs. CH42: R Ferr 2E **119**
St Peters Cl. CH60: Hes 3F **157**
   L33: K'by 5D **15**
St Peter's Ct. CH42: R Ferr 3A **120**
   L17: Aig 5B **100**
St Peter's Ho. L20: Boot 1D **55**
St Peter's M. CH42: R Ferr 3A **120**
St Peter's Rd. CH42: R Ferr 3A **120**
   L9: Ain .2C **36**

St Peters Row L31: Mag 4D 13
St Peter's Sq. L1: Liv 7G 5
St Peter's Way CH43: Noct 5C 94
St Philip's Av. L21: Lith 5C 18
St Richards Cl. L20: Kirk 2D 55
St Seiriol Gro. CH43: C'ton 3A 96
St Stephens Cl. CH60: Hes 4C 158
L25: Gate 4C 104
St Stephen's Ct. CH42: Tran 3B 118
St Stephen's Gro. L30: N'ton 2D 19
St Stephen's Pl.
L3: Liv 3D 77 (2E 5)
St Stephen's Rd. CH42: Tran 2B 118
St Teresa's Rd. WA10: St. H 4D 45
St Thomas Ct. WA8: Wid 3D 131
St Thomas's Dr. L30: N'ton 2D 19
St Vincent Rd. CH43: C'ton 3A 96
CH44: Wall 1D 75
St Vincents Cl. L12: W Der 5E 59
St Vincent St. L3: Liv 4E 77 (4H 5)
St Vincent Way L3: Liv 4E 77 (4H 5)
St Werburghs Sq. CH41: Birk 3D 97
St William Rd. L23: Thorn 5B 10
St William Way L23: Thorn 5B 10
St Winifred Rd. CH45: New B 4B 52
L35: R'hill 1B 86
Saker St. L4: Walt 4F 55
Salacre Cl. CH49: Upton 5B 94
Salacre Cres. CH49: Upton 5A 94
Salacre La. CH49: Upton 4A 94
Salacre Ter. CH49: Upton 4A 94
Salcombe Dr. L25: Hunts X 5B 126
Salem Vw. CH43: O'ton 1B 118
Salerno Dr. L36: Huy 2D 83
Saleswood Av. WA10: Eccl 5A 44
Salhouse Gdns. WA9: St. H 5D 65
Saline Cl. L14: K Ash 5A 60
Salisbury Av. CH48: W Kir 4A 112
L30: N'ton 4F 19
Salisbury Dr. CH62: New F 5B 120
Salisbury Hall L18: Moss H 2E 123
Salisbury Ho. L20: Boot 4B 34
Salisbury Pk. L16: Child 4D 103
Salisbury Rd. CH45: New B 3A 52
L5: Liv 5F 55
L15: W'tree 2D 101
L19: Gras 5A 124
L20: Boot 3B 34
Salisbury St. CH41: Birk 4D 97
L3: Liv 2E 77 (1J 5)
L34: Prsct 4D 63
WA7: Run 1A 166
WA8: Wid 4B 132
Salisbury Ter. L15: W'tree 1F 101
Salop St. L4: Walt 3F 55
Saltash Cl. L26: Halew 3E 127
WA7: Brook 4B 168
Saltburn Rd. CH45: Wall 1D 73
Saltergate Rd. L8: Liv 5A 100
Salthouse Quay L3: Liv 1C 98 (7C 4)
Saltney St. L3: Liv 1B 76
Saltpit La. L31: Mag 1E 13
Saltwood Dr. WA7: Brook 5C 168
Saltworks Cl. WA6: Frod 3D 173
Salvia Way L33: K'by 5D 15
Samaria Av. CH62: New F 5C 120
Samphire Gdns. WA9: Bold 4B 68
Samuel St. WA9: St. H 4D 65
Sanbec Gdns. WA8: Cron 4D 109
Sandalwood Mt. L4: Nort 1C 168
Sandalwood Cl. L6: Liv 1B 78
Sandalwood Dr. CH43: Noct 5D 95
Sandalwood Gdns.
WA9: St. H 4C 66
Sandbeck St. L8: Liv 1F 121
Sandbourne CH46: More 1A 94
Sandbrook Ct. CH46: More 1E 93
Sandbrook La. CH46: More 1E 93
Sandbrook Rd. L25: Gate 1A 104
Sandcliffe Rd. CH45: Wall 3E 51
Sandeman Rd. L4: Walt 3D 57
Sanderling Rd. L33: K'by 2A 24
Sanders Hey Cl. WA7: Brook 5A 168
Sandfield L36: Huy 4D 83
Sandfield Av. CH47: Meols 2D 91

Sandfield Cl. CH63: High B 1D 141
L12: W Der 1C 80
Sandfield Ct. WA6: Frod 5B 172
Sandfield Cres.
WA10: St. H 5F 45
Sandfield Hey L12: W Der 5C 58
(off Sandfield Pk. E.)
SANDFIELD PARK 1B 80
Sandfield Pk. CH60: Hes 2D 157
Sandfield Pk. E.
L12: W Der 5C 58
Sandfield Pl. L20: Boot 4B 34
Sandfield Rd. CH45: New B 4B 52
CH49: W'chu 3B 116
CH63: High B 1D 141
L20: Boot 5D 35
L25: Gate 5B 104
WA10: Eccl 3A 44
Sandfields WA6: Frod 5B 172
Sandfield Ter. CH45: New B 4B 52
Sandfield Wlk. L12: W Der 2B 80
Sandford Dr. L31: Mag 5D 7
Sandford St. CH41: Birk 2E 97
Sandforth Cl. L12: W Der 1A 80
Sandforth Ct. L12: W Der 1A 80
Sandforth Rd. L12: W Der 1A 80
Sandgate Cl. L24: Speke 3B 146
Sandham Gro. CH60: Hes 2C 158
Sandham Rd. L24: Speke 3A 148
Sandhead St. L7: Liv 1D 101
Sandhey Rd. CH47: Meols 3C 90
Sandheys Av. L22: Water 4C 16
Sandheys Cl. L4: Walt 4E 55
Sandheys Gro. L22: Water 3C 16
Sandheys Rd. CH45: New B 4B 52
Sandheys Ter. L22: Water 4C 16
Sandhills, The CH46: Leas 3E 71
Sandhills Bus. Pk. L5: Kirk 4C 54
Sandhills Ind. Est. L5: Kirk 5C 54
Sandhills La. L5: Kirk 4B 54
Sandhills Station (Rail) 4C 54
Sandhills Vw. CH45: Wall 1D 73
Sandhurst L23: Blun 1C 16
Sandhurst Cl. L21: Sea 1F 33
Sandhurst Dr. L10: Ain 3D 21
L35: R'hill 1A 86
Sandhurst Rd. L26: Halew 1A 148
L35: R'hill 1A 86
Sandhurst St. L17: Aig 1A 122
Sandhurst Way L31: Lyd 2B 6
Sandicroft Rd. L12: Crox 1F 59
Sandino St. L8: Liv 3E 99
Sandiway CH47: Meols 2D 91
CH63: Brom 4C 162
L35: Whis 4D 85
L36: Huy 5F 83
Sandiway Av. WA8: Wid 3A 130
Sandiways L31: Mag 1E 13
Sandiways Av. L30: N'ton 3A 20
Sandiways Rd. CH45: Wall 5E 51
Sandlea Pk. CH48: W Kir 4A 112
Sandlewood Gro. L33: K'by 1F 23
Sandon Cl. L35: R'hill 2B 86
Sandon Ct. L22: Water 4D 17
(off Sandon St.)
Sandon Ind. Est. L5: Kirk 5B 54
Sandon Pl. WA8: Wid 3D 133
Sandon Prom. CH44: Wall 2D 75
Sandon Rd. CH44: Wall 2D 75
Sandon St. L8: Liv 1F 99
L22: Water 4D 17
Sandon Way L5: Kirk 5B 54
Sandown Cl. WA7: Run 4B 166
Sandown Ct. L15: W'tree 1F 101
Sandown La. L15: W'tree 1F 101
SANDOWN PARK 5F 79
Sandown Pk. Rd. L10: Ain 2E 21
Sandown Rd. L15: W'tree 5F 79
L21: Sea 1F 33
Sandpiper Cl. CH49: Upton 3D 93
Sandpiper Gro. L26: Halew 3E 127
Sandpipers Ct. CH47: Hoy 4A 90
Sandridge Rd. CH45: New B 4B 52
CH61: Pens 2F 137
Sandringham Av. CH47: Meols 3C 90
L22: Water 5E 17

Sandringham Cl. CH47: Meols 3C 90
CH62: New F 5A 120
L33: K'by 5E 15
Sandringham Dr. CH45: New B 3A 52
L17: Aig 5B 100
WA9: St. H 5C 66
Sandringham M.
CH47: Meols 4C 90
Sandringham Rd. L13: Liv 5D 57
L22: Water 5E 17
L31: Mag 2C 12
WA8: Wid 5F 109
Sandrock Rd. CH45: New B 4B 52
Sands Rd. L18: Moss H 5F 101
Sandstone CH45: Wall 1C 74
Sandstone Cl. L35: R'hill 5C 86
Sandstone Dr. CH48: W Kir 4E 113
L35: Whis 1A 86
Sandstone M. WA8: Wid 5E 109
Sandstone Rd. E. L13: Liv 2F 79
Sandstone Rd. W. L13: Liv 2F 79
Sandstone Wlk. CH60: Hes 3A 158
Sandwash Cl. WA11: R'ford 1B 28
Sandway Cres. L11: N Grn 1A 58
Sandy Brow La. L33: Know 1E 41
Sandy Grn. L9: Ain 2C 36
Sandy Gro. L13: Liv 5F 57
Sandy Ho. L21: Sea 1F 33
(off Sandy Rd.)
Sandy Knowle L15: W'tree 1A 102
Sandy La. CH45: Wall 5E 51
CH48: W Kir 1B 134
CH60: Hes 1A 158
CH61: Irby 5C 114
L9: Ain 2B 36
L13: Liv 5F 57
L21: Sea 4C 16
(not continuous)
L31: Lyd 1B 6
L31: Mell 5A 14
WA7: Pres B 4E 169
WA7: West P 3D 165
WA8: Cron 4D 109
WA8: Wid 3F 111
WA11: St. H 4E 29
Sandy La. Nth. CH61: Irby 5C 114
Sandy Moor La. WA7: Nort 5D 155
Sandymoor La. WA7: Nort 4D 155
Sandymount Dr. CH45: Wall 4A 52
CH63: Beb 3F 141
Sandyville Gro. L4: Walt 3E 57
Sandyville Rd. L4: Walt 3D 57
Sandy Way CH43: O'ton 4A 96
Sankey Rd. L31: Mag 3D 13
WA11: Hay 3F 47
Sankey St. L1: Liv 1E 99
WA8: Wid 1A 152
WA9: St. H 1D 67
WA12: New W 5F 49
Sankey Valley Country Pk. 1E 47
Sankey Valley Country Pk. Vis. Cen.
. . . . .2E 47
Sankey Valley Ind. Est.
WA12: New W 1F 69
Santon Av. L13: Liv 1E 79
Sapphire Dr. L33: K'by 5E 15
Sapphire St. L13: Liv 5F 79
Sarah's Cft. L30: N'ton 2E 19
Sark Rd. L13: Liv 2F 79
Sartfield Cl. L16: Child 1E 103
Sarum St. L25: Gate 2A 104
Sarus Ct. WA7: Mnr P 3B 154
Satinwood Cres. L31: Mell 2A 22
SAUGHALL MASSIE 3C 92
Saughall Massie La.
CH49: Upton 4F 93
Saughall Massie Rd.
CH48: W Kir 3D 113
CH49: Grea, Upton 3D 113
(not continuous)
Saughall Rd. CH46: More 2C 92
Saunders Av. L35: Prsct 2D 85
Saunders La. L23: Crosb 3A 10
Saunderton Cl. WA11: Hay 1C 48

Saville Rd. L13: Liv 4B 80
    L31: L6 .4C 6
Savoylands Cl. L17: Aig 2C 122
Sawley Cl. WA7: Murd 3E 169
Sawpit La. L36: Huy 4F 83
Saxby Rd. L14: K Ash 1A 82
Saxon Cl. L6: Liv 1B 78
Saxon Ct. WA10: St. H 3E 45
Saxonia Rd. L4: Walt 1A 56
Saxon Rd. CH46: More 5F 71
    CH47: Meols 3C 90
    L23: C'by 2D 17
    WA7: Run 5C 152
Saxon Ter. WA8: Wid 3B 132
Saxon Way L33: K'by 4E 15
Saxony Rd. L7: Liv 4A 78
                        (not continuous)
Sayce St. WA8: Wid 3B 132
Scafell Cl. CH62: East 2D 171
Scafell Lawn L27: N'ley 1A 128
Scafell Rd. WA11: St. H 5A 30
Scafell Wlk. L27: N'ley 5A 106
                        (not continuous)
Scape La. L23: C'by 5E 9
Scargreen Av. L11: N Grn 5F 37
Scarisbrick Av. L21: Lith 1B 34
Scarisbrick Cl. L31: Mag 4E 7
Scarisbrick Cres. L11: N Grn 5D 37
Scarisbrick Dr. L11: N Grn 5D 37
Scarisbrick Pl. L11: N Grn 1D 57
Scarisbrick Rd. L11: N Grn 5D 37
Scarsdale Rd. L11: N Grn. 2F 57
Sceptre Cl. WA12: New W 5F 49
Sceptre Rd. L11: Crox 4C 38
Sceptre Twr. L11: Crox 5C 38
Sceptre Wlk. L11: Crox 5C 38
Scholar St. L7: Liv 2C 100
Scholes La. WA10: St. H 4B 64
Scholes Pk. WA10: St. H 4B 64
Schomberg St. L6: Liv 3A 78
School Cl. CH46: More 4F 71
    L27: N'ley 2C 104
Schoolfield Cl. CH49: W'chu 2B 116
Schoolfield Rd. CH49: W'chu 2B 116
School Hill CH60: Hes 3F 157
School La. CH43: Bid 5C 72
    CH44: Wall 1E 73
    CH45: Wall 2E 73
                        (not continuous)
    CH47: Hoy 4B 90
                        (not continuous)
    CH47: Meols 2D 91
    CH61: Thurs 1B 136
    CH62: New F 5B 120
    CH63: High B 1D 141
    CH66: Chil T 4F 171
    L1: Liv 5D 77 (6E 4)
    L10: Ain 3D 21
    L21: Lith 5B 18
    L21: Sea 1A 34
    L25: Wltn 5A 126
    L31: Mag 5F 7
    L31: Mell 5A 14
    L34: Know 2A 40
    L35: R'hill 5E 87
                        (not continuous)
    L36: Huy 4A 84
    WA7: Halt 2F 167
    WA8: Bold H 2E 111
School Pl. CH41: Birk 2D 97
School St. WA11: Hay 2F 47
School Way L24: Speke 4B 146
    WA8: Wid 1D 133
Schooner Cl. WA7: Murd 4D 169
Science Rd. L24: Speke 3C 146
Scone Cl. L11: Crox 5C 38
Score, The WA9: St. H 5A 66
Scorecross WA9: St. H 3B 66
Score La. L16: Child 5C 80
Scoresby Rd. CH46: Leas 3C 72
Scorpio Cl. L14: K Ash 1A 82
Scorton St. L6: Liv 1C 78
Scotchbarn La. L34: Prsct 5E 63
    L35: Prsct 5F 63
Scotchbarn Sports Cen. 5E 63

Scoter Rd. L33: K'by 3F 23
Scotia Av. CH62: New F 5C 120
Scotia Cl. L13: Liv 2A 80
Scotland Rd. L3: Liv 3D 77 (2F 5)
    L5: Liv .2D 77
Scott Av. L35: Whis 3F 85
    L36: Huy 5A 84
    WA8: Wid 4F 131
    WA9: Sut M 3A 88
Scott Cl. L4: Walt 4F 55
Scotts Pl. CH41: Birk 2F 95
Scotts Quays CH41: Birk 5E 75
Scott St. CH45: Wall 1B 74
    L20: Boot 3B 34
Scythes, The CH49: Grea 5C 92
    L30: N'ton 1B 20
Scythia Cl. CH62: New F 4C 120
Seabank Av. CH44: Wall 1C 74
Seabank Cotts. CH47: Meols 1F 91
Seabank Rd. CH44: Wall 3B 52
    CH45: New B 3B 52
    CH60: Hes 4E 157
Sea Brow L1: Liv 5C 76 (6C 4)
Seacole Cl. L8: Liv 3B 100
SEACOMBE 5D 75
Seacombe Prom. CH44: Wall 2E 75
                        (not continuous)
Seacombe Vw. CH44: Wall 4E 75
Seacroft Cl. L14: K Ash 5A 60
Seacroft Rd. L14: K Ash 5A 60
Seafield Av. CH60: Hes 4E 157
    L23: C'by 2E 17
Seafield Dr. CH45: Wall 4F 51
Seafield Rd. CH62: New F 4B 120
    L9: Walt 3F 35
    L20: Boot 4B 34
Seaford Cl. WA7: Wind H 1D 169
Seafore Cl. L31: Lyd 3B 6
SEAFORTH 2A 34
Seaforth & Litherland Station (Rail)
                        . . . . .1A 34
Seaforth Dr. CH46: More 2E 93
Seaforth Nature Reserve 1D 33
Seaforth Rd. L21: Sea 3A 34
Seaforth Va. Nth. L21: Sea 1A 34
Seaforth Va. W. L21: Sea 2A 34
Seagram Cl. L9: Ain 5C 20
Sea La. WA7: Run 5D 153
Sealy Cl. CH63: Spit 1A 162
Seaman Rd. L15: W'tree 2E 101
Seaport St. L8: Liv 3A 100
Sea Rd. CH45: Wall 3F 51
Seascale Av. WA10: St. H 3B 64
Seath Av. WA9: St. H 4E 47
Seathwaite Cl. L23: Blun 2B 16
Seathwaite Cres. L33: K'by 1D 23
Seaton Cl. L12: Crox 5A 40
Seaton Gro. WA9: St. H 5D 65
Seaton Pk. WA7: Nort 4E 155
Seaton Rd. CH42: Tran 5C 96
    CH45: Wall 5A 52
Sea Vw. CH47: Hoy 4B 90
Seaview Av. CH45: Wall 1A 74
    CH61: Irby 1D 137
Sea Vw. Rd. L20: Boot 4A 34
Seaview Rd. CH45: Wall 5A 52
Seaview Ter. L22: Water 4C 16
Seawood Gro. CH46: More 2D 93
Second Av. CH43: Bid 3B 94
    L9: Ain .2C 20
                        (Lower La.)
    L9: Ain .1C 36
                        (Park Av.)
    L23: C'by 1D 17
    L35: R'hill 2B 86
    WA7: Pal F 2F 167
Sedbergh Av. L10: Ain 2C 20
Sedbergh Gro. WA7: Beech 5E 167
Sedbergh Rd. CH44: Wall 1F 73
Sedburgh Gro. L36: Huy 3B 82
Sedburn Rd. L32: K'by 1A 40

Seddon Cl. WA10: Eccl 5F 43
Seddon Ct. L34: Prsct 5D 63
Seddon Rd. L19: Gars 1B 144
    WA10: St. H 2B 64
Seddon St. L1: Liv 1D 99 (7E 4)
    WA10: St. H 1F 45
Sedgefield Cl. CH46: More 1A 94
Sedgefield Rd. CH46: More 1A 94
Sedgeley Wlk. L36: Huy 1F 83
Sedgemoor Rd. L11: N Grn. 5E 37
Sedgewick Cres. WA5: B'wood 5E 69
Sedley St. L6: Liv 5B 56
Sedum Gro. L33: K'by 5D 15
Seeds La. L9: Ain 5C 20
Seeley Av. CH41: Birk 2A 96
Seel Rd. L36: Huy 4F 83
Seel St. L1: Liv 5D 77 (6F 5)
SEFTON 3F 11
Sefton Av. L21: Lith 1B 34
    WA8: Wid 1A 132
Sefton Bus. Pk. L30: N'ton 5A 20
Sefton Cl. L32: K'by 2B 22
Sefton Dr. L8: Liv 4B 100
    L10: Ain 3D 21
    L23: Thorn 3A 10
    L31: Mag 2B 12
    L32: K'by 2C 22
Sefton Fold Dr. WN5: Bil 1D 31
Sefton Fold Gdns. WN5: Bil 1D 31
Sefton Gro. L17: Aig 5C 100
Sefton Ho. L9: Ain 1B 36
Sefton La. L31: Mag 2A 12
Sefton La. Ind. Est. L31: Mag 2A 12
Sefton Mill La. L29: Seft 3F 11
Sefton Mills L29: Seft 3F 11
Sefton Moss La. L30: N'ton 2D 19
Sefton Moss Vs. L21: Lith 5B 18
SEFTON PARK 5E 101
Sefton Pk. Ct. L17: Aig 1E 123
Sefton Pk. Palm House 5D 101
Sefton Pk. Rd. L8: Liv 3B 100
Sefton Rd. CH42: R Ferr 3A 120
    CH45: New B 4B 52
    CH62: New F 4A 120
    L9: Ain .1D 37
    L9: Walt 3A 36
    L20: Boot 3D 35
    L21: Lith 5B 18
Sefton St. L8: Liv 3D 99
    L21: Lith 5B 18
                        (not continuous)
    WA12: New W 5F 49
SEFTON TOWN 1D 19
Sefton Vw. L21: Lith 5B 18
    L23: C'by 1A 18
Seiont Ho. L8: Liv 4F 99
Selborne L35: Whis 4F 85
Selborne Cl. L8: Liv 2A 100
Selborne St. L8: Liv 2F 99
Selbourne Cl. CH49: W'chu 1C 116
Selby Cl. WA7: Nort 3F 155
    WA10: St. H 1D 65
Selby Gro. L36: Huy 3B 84
Selby Rd. L9: Walt 2A 36
Selby St. CH45: Wall 1B 74
Seldon St. L6: Liv 3A 78
Selina Rd. L4: Walt 1E 55
Selkirk Av. CH62: East 1E 171
Selkirk Dr. WA10: Eccl 3B 44
Selkirk Rd. L13: Liv 4F 79
Sellar St. L4: Kirk 4E 55
Selsdon Rd. L22: Water 3C 16
Selsey Cl. L7: Liv 1B 100
Selside Lawn L27: N'ley 1A 128
Selside Rd. L27: N'ley 1A 128
Selside Wlk. L27: N'ley 1A 128
Selston Cl. CH63: Spit 5A 142
Selworthy Grn. L16: Child 3D 103
Selwyn Cl. WA8: Wid 1D 133
Selwyn St. L4: Kirk 2E 55
Senator Point L33: Know I 5C 24
Senator Rd. WA9: St. H 4D 65
Seneschal Ct. WA7: Pal F 4E 167
Sennen Cl. WA7: Brook 5B 168
Sennen Rd. L32: K'by 5F 23

Sentinel Way L30: N'ton 5B 20
September Rd. L6: Liv 1C 78
Serenade Rd. L33: K'by 4F 15
Sergrim Rd. L36: Huy 3C 82
Serpentine, The L19: Gras 4A 124
  L23: Blun 1A 16
Serpentine Nth., The L23: Blun 5A 8
Serpentine Rd. CH44: Wall 1C 74
Serpentine Sth., The L23: Blun 1B 16
Servia Rd. L21: Lith 1B 34
Servite Cl. L22: Water 3C 16
Servite Ct. L25: Wltn 3C 126
Servite Ho. L17: Aig 5B 100
Sessions Rd. L4: Kirk 3D 55
Seth Powell Way L36: Huy 5C 60
Settrington Rd. L11: N Grn. 2F 57
Seven Acre Rd. L23: Thorn 5B 10
Seven Acres La. CH61: Thing 2A 138
Sevenoaks Cl. L5: Liv 1E 77
Seventh Av. L9: Ain 1D 37
                                   (Lakes Rd.)
  L9: Ain .1D 37
                                   (Park Av.)
Severn Cl. WA8: Wid 2E 133
  WA9: Sut L 5C 66
  WN5: Bil 2D 31
Severn Rd. L33: K'by 4F 15
  L35: R'hill 3B 86
Severn St. CH41: Birk 5A 74
  L5: Liv .5F 55
Severs St. L6: Liv 2A 78
Sewell St. L34: Prsct 5D 63
  WA7: Run 5B 152
Sextant Cl. WA7: Murd 5D 169
Sexton Av. WA9: St. H 1B 68
Sexton Way L14: B Grn 4E 81
Seymoor Ct. L14: B Grn 5D 81
Seymour Ct. CH42: Tran 5E 97
  WA7: Mnr P 3C 154
Seymour Dr. L31: Lyd 4E 7
Seymour Pl. E. CH45: New B 3B 52
Seymour Pl. W. CH45: New B 3B 52
Seymour Rd. L14: B Grn 4D 81
  L21: Lith 1B 34
Seymour St. CH42: Tran 5D 97
  CH45: New B 3B 52
  L3: Liv 4E 77 (4H 5)
  L20: Boot 1B 54
  WA9: St. H 4D 67
Seymour Ter. L3: Liv 4H 5
Shacklady Rd. L33: K'by 1A 24
Shackleton Rd. CH46: Leas 2B 72
Shadwell St. L5: Liv 5B 54
Shaftesbury Rd. L23: C'by 1D 17
Shaftesbury St. L8: Liv 3E 99
Shaftesbury Ter. L13: Liv 3A 80
Shaftesbury Way WA5: B'wood 4F 69
Shaftsbury Av. L33: K'by 5E 15
Shaftway Cl. WA11: Hay 1F 49
Shakespeare Av. CH42: R Ferr 3F 119
  L32: K'by 5D 23
Shakespeare Cl. L6: Liv 2A 78
Shakespeare Rd. CH44: Wall 4D 75
  WA8: Wid 3A 132
  WA9: Sut M 4A 88
Shakespeare St. L19: Gars 2C 144
                              (not continuous)
  L20: Boot 3A 34
Shalcombe Cl. L26: Halew 5A 128
Shaldon Cl. L32: K'by 5A 24
Shaldon Gro. L32: K'by 5A 24
Shaldon Rd. L32: K'by 1A 40
Shaldon Wlk. L32: K'by 5A 24
Shalem Ct. CH63: High B 1D 141
Shalford Gro. CH48: W Kir 4D 113
Shallcross Cl. L6: Liv 2A 78
Shallcross Pl. L6: Liv 2A 78
Shallmarsh Cl. CH63: High B 2D 141
Shallmarsh Ct. CH63: High B 2D 141
Shallmarsh Rd. CH63: High B 2D 141
Shalom Ct. L17: Aig 4E 101
Shamrock Rd. CH41: Birk 2F 95
Shand St. L19: Gars 3C 144
Shanklin Rd. L15: W'tree 5F 79
Shannon Gro. WA8: Wid 2E 131

Shannon Ho. CH46: Leas 2E 71
Shannons La. L34: Know 2C 60
Shannon St. CH41: Birk 5F 73
Shard Cl. L11: Crox 3B 38
Shard St. WA9: St. H 1E 67
Sharpeville Cl. L4: Kirk 4D 55
Sharples Cres. L23: C'by 2F 17
Sharp St. WA8: Wid 4A 132
Sharwood Rd. L27: N'ley 5F 105
Shavington Av. CH43: O'ton 1F 117
Shawbury Av. CH63: High B 5D 119
Shawell Cl. WA8: Wid 2E 133
Shaw Entry L35: Whis 1F 107
Shaw Gdns. WA9: St. H 5E 65
Shaw Hill St. L1: Liv 4D 77 (4E 5)
Shaw La. CH49: Grea 2C 114
  L35: Prsct, Whis 2D 85
Shaw Rd. L24: Speke 2C 146
Shaws All. L1: Liv 1C 98
Shaws Dr. CH47: Meols 3D 91
Shaw St. CH41: Birk 4C 96
  CH47: Hoy 1C 90
  L6: Liv 2F 77 (1J 5)
  WA7: Run 5F 151
                              (not continuous)
  WA10: St. H 5B 46
  WA11: Hay 2E 49
Shawton Rd. L16: Child 1C 102
Shearman Cl. CH61: Pens 3A 138
Shearman Rd. CH61: Pens 3A 138
Shearwater Cl. L27: N'ley 5F 105
Sheehan Hgts. L5: Liv 5C 54
Sheen Rd. CH45: New B 5C 52
Sheila Wlk. L10: Faz 2B 38
Sheil Pl. L6: Liv 3C 78
Sheil Rd. L6: Liv 2C 78
Shelagh Av. WA8: Wid 3A 132
Sheldon Cl. CH63: Spit 1A 162
Sheldon Rd. L12: W Der 3D 59
Shelley Cl. L36: Huy 5F 83
Shelley Ct. L32: K'by 5D 23
Shelley Gro. L19: Gars 2C 144
Shelley Pl. L35: Whis 3F 85
Shelley Rd. WA8: Wid 3A 132
Shelley St. L20: Boot 4B 34
                              (not continuous)
  WA9: Sut M 4B 88
Shelley Way CH48: W Kir 1B 134
SHELL GREEN 3D 133
Shell Grn. Est., The WA8: Wid 4E 133
Shell Grn. Ho. WA8: Wid 4E 133
Shellingford Rd. L14: K Ash 2A 82
Shelmore Dr. L8: Liv 5E 99
Shelton Cl. L13: Liv 4F 79
  WA8: Wid 1E 133
Shelton Rd. CH45: Wall 5A 52
Shenley Cl. CH63: Beb 1F 141
Shenley Rd. L15: W'tree 1C 102
Shenstone St. L7: Liv 5B 78
Shenton Av. WA11: St. H 2D 47
Shepherd Cl. CH49: Grea 5C 92
Shepherds Fold Cl. L8: Liv 3A 100
Shepherds Row WA7: Cas 5F 153
Shepherd St. L6: Liv 4F 77
Sheppard Av. L16: Child 1A 104
Shepston Av. L4: Walt 2A 56
Shepton Rd. L36: Huy 5D 61
Sherborne Av. L25: Hunts X 4D 127
  L30: N'ton 1E 19
Sherborne Cl. WA7: Nort 4F 155
Sherborne Rd. CH44: Wall 4A 74
Sherborne Sq. L36: Huy 4E 83
Sherbourne Way WA5: B'wood 5F 69
Sherbrooke Cl. L14: K Ash 2E 81
Sherburn Cl. L9: Ain 5D 21
Sherdley Bus. Pk. WA9: St. H 2B 66
Sherdley Cl. L35: R'hill 2C 86
Sherdley Dr. WA9: St. H 4B 66
Sherdley Pk. Dr. WA9: St. H 5C 66
Sherdley Rd. WA9: St. H 5F 65
                              (not continuous)
Sherdley Rd. Cvn. Pk.
  WA9: St. H 3A 66
Sherford Cl. L27: N'ley 5F 105
Sheridan Way WA7: Nort 5D 155

Sheriff Cl. L5: Liv 2E 77
Sheringham Cl. CH49: Upton 2A 94
  WA9: St. H 5D 47
Sherlock Av. WA11: Hay 1E 49
Sherlock La. CH44: Wall 4A 74
Sherman Dr. L35: R'hill 5D 87
Sherry Ct. L17: Aig 4D 101
Sherry La. CH49: W'chu 2A 116
Sherwell Cl. L15: W'tree 5A 80
Sherwood Av. CH61: Irby 1D 137
  L23: C'by .5D 9
Sherwood Cl. L35: R'hill 1B 86
  WA8: Wid 3C 130
Sherwood Ct. L12: Crox 5F 39
  L36: Huy 4F 83
Sherwood Cres. WA5: B'wood 5E 69
Sherwood Dr. CH63: High B 5E 119
  L35: Whis 4F 85
Sherwood Gro. CH47: Meols 3F 91
Sherwood Rd. CH44: Wall 3C 74
  CH47: Meols 4F 91
  L23: C'by .5C 8
Sherwood Row L26: Halew 1E 147
Sherwood's La. L10: Faz 5F 21
Sherwyn Rd. L4: Walt 3C 56
Shetland Cl. WA8: Wid 1E 133
Shetland Dr. CH62: Brom 2E 163
Shevington Cl. WA8: Wid 1E 133
  WA9: St. H 4C 66
Shevington's La. L33: K'by 5D 15
Shevington Wlk. WA8: Wid 1E 133
Shewell Cl. CH42: Tran 5D 97
Shiel Rd. CH45: New B 4B 52
Shimmin St. L7: Liv 5A 78
Shipley Wlk. L24: Speke 3D 147
Ship St. WA6: Frod 4B 172
Shipton Cl. CH43: Pren 3E 117
  L19: Aller 3B 124
  WA8: Wid 1D 131
Shirdley Av. L32: K'by 1F 39
Shirdley Wlk. L32: K'by 1F 39
Shirebourne Av. WA11: St. H 1B 46
Shiregreen WA9: St. H 5C 66
Shires, The WA10: St. H 1E 65
Shirley Rd. L19: Aller 4C 124
Shirley St. CH44: Wall 3E 75
Shirwell Gro. WA9: Sut L 2C 88
Shobdon Cl. L12: Crox 4F 39
Shop La. L31: Mag 1C 12
Shop Rd. L34: Know 4C 40
Shore Bank CH62: New F 4C 120
Shore Dr. CH62: Port S 1C 142
Shorefields CH62: New F 4B 120
Shorefields Ho. CH62: New F 5C 120
Shorefields Village L8: Liv 1F 121
Shore La. CH48: Caldy 2C 134
Shore Rd. CH41: Birk 2E 97
  CH48: Caldy 2C 134
  L20: Boot 3F 33
Shore Road Pumping Station 2F 97
Short Cl. WA12: New W 5E 49
Shortfield Cl. CH49: Upton 5A 94
Shortfield Way CH49: Upton 5A 94
Short St. WA8: Wid 2A 152
  WA11: Hay 2E 49
  WA12: New W 5E 49
Shortwood Rd. L14: K Ash 3F 81
Shottesbrook Grn. L11: N Grn. 5F 37
Showcase Cinema 4A 38
Shrewsbury Av. L10: Ain 2C 20
  L22: Water 2D 17
Shrewsbury Cl. CH43: C'ton 3F 95
Shrewsbury Dr. CH49: Upton 3A 94
Shrewsbury Pl. L19: Gars 1C 144
Shrewsbury Rd. CH43: C'ton 2F 95
  CH44: Wall 1F 73
  CH48: W Kir 5A 112
  CH60: Hes 1A 158
  L19: Gars 1C 144
Shrewton Rd. L25: Gate 2A 104
Shropshire Cl. L30: N'ton 1A 20
Shropshire Gdns. WA10: St. H 1F 65
Sibford Rd. L12: W Der 1D 81
Siddall St. WA10: St. H 1F 45

Siddeley Dr. WA12: New W 5F 49
Siddeley St. L17: Aig 1C 122
Sidgreave St. WA10: St. H 5E 45
Sidings, The CH42: R Ferr 2F 119
   L7: Liv 1A 100
   (off Crown Station Pl.)
Sidlaw Av. WA9: St. H 5F 47
Sidmouth Cl. WA10: Windle 2C 44
Sidney Av. CH45: New B 3A 52
Sidney Ct. CH42: Tran 5E 97
Sidney Pl. L7: Liv 5A 78
Sidney Powell Av.
   L32: K'by 3C 22
Sidney Rd. CH42: Tran 5E 97
   L20: Boot 1D 55
Sidney St. CH41: Birk 2E 97
   WA10: St. H 4D 45
Sidney Ter. CH42: Tran 1E 119
Sidwell St. L19: Gars 2C 144
Sienna Cl. L17: N'ley 3C 122
Signal Works Rd. L9: Ain 5E 21
Silcroft Rd. L32: K'by 5E 23
Silkhouse Ct. L3: Liv 4C 4
Silkhouse La. L2: Liv 4C 76 (4C 4)
Silkstone Cl. L7: Liv 1B 100
   WA10: St. H 5D 45
Silkstone Cres. WA7: Pal F 3B 168
Silkstone St. WA10: St. H 5D 45
   (not continuous)
Silver Av. WA11: Hay 3A 48
Silverbeech Av. L18: Moss H 5B 102
Silverbeech Rd. CH44: Wall 3C 74
Silverbirch Gdns. CH44: Wall 1E 73
Silver Birch Way L31: Lyd 2B 6
Silverbrook Rd. L27: N'ley 2C 104
Silverburn Av. CH46: More 5E 71
Silverdale Av. L13: Liv 1E 79
Silverdale Cl. L36: Huy 1E 105
   WA6: Frod 5C 172
Silverdale Dr. L21: Lith 5D 19
Silverdale Gro. WA11: St. H 5A 30
Silverdale Rd. CH43: O'ton 5A 96
   CH63: High B 5F 119
Silverlake Cl. L9: Walt 5F 35
Silverlea Av. CH45: Wall 1A 74
Silver Leigh L17: Aig 3D 123
Silverlime Gdns. WA9: St. H 4C 64
Silverstone Dr. L36: Roby 1D 105
Silverstone Gro. L31: Lyd 2B 6
Silverton Rd. L17: Aig 4E 123
Silverwell Rd. L11: Crox 3D 39
Silverwell Wlk. L11: Crox 3D 39
Silverwing Ho. L19: Aig 5F 123
Silvester St. L5: Liv 1C 76
Simms Av. WA9: St. H 5E 47
SIMM'S CROSS 4B 132
Simm's Rd. L6: Liv 5D 57
Simnel Cl. L25: Gate 3B 104
Simon Ct. CH48: W Kir 4A 112
Simonsbridge CH48: Caldy 3D 135
Simons Cl. L35: Whis 1D 107
Simon's Cft. L30: N'ton 2C 18
Simonside WA8: Wid 2C 130
Simonstone Gro. WA9: St. H 4D 67
SIMONSWOOD 4F 15
Simonswood La. L33: K'by 4A 24
Simonswood Wlk. L33: K'by 3A 24
Simpson St. CH41: Birk 3D 97
   L1: Liv 2D 99
Sim St. L3: Liv 3E 77 (2H 5)
Sinclair Av. L35: Prsct 1F 85
   WA8: Wid 4F 131
Sinclair Cl. L35: Prsct 5F 63
Sinclair Dr. L18: Moss H 3B 102
Sinclair St. L19: Gars 2C 144
Singleton Av. CH42: Tran 1C 118
   WA11: St. H 3D 47
Singleton Dr. L34: Know 5D 41
Sirdar Cl. L7: Liv 1B 100
Sir Howard St. L8: Liv 1F 99
Sir Howard Way L8: Liv 1F 99
Sir Thomas St. L1: Liv 4C 76 (4D 4)
Siskin Grn. L25: Gate 4A 104
Sisters Way CH41: Birk 3D 97
Six Acre La. WA4: Moore 2F 155

Sixth Av. L9: Ain 1D 37
   (Lakes Rd.)
   L9: Ain 1D 37
   (Park Av.)
Skeffington L35: Whis 4E 85
Skelhorne St. L3: Liv 5D 77 (5G 5)
Skelton Cl. WA11: St. H 1A 46
Skerries Rd. L4: Walt 4A 56
Skiddaw Cl. WA7: Beech 1A 174
Skiddaw Rd. CH62: Brom 5E 143
Skipton Rd. L4: Walt 4B 56
   L36: Huy 3B 84
Skirving St. L5: Liv 5D 55
Skye Cl. WA8: Wid 1E 133
Sky Lark Ri. WA9: St. H 5A 48
Sky Pk. Ind. Est. L24: Speke 4B 146
Slag La. WA11: Hay 1B 48
   (not continuous)
Slater Pl. L1: Liv 1D 99 (7F 5)
Slater St. L1: Liv 1D 99 (7F 5)
Slatey Rd. CH43: O'ton 3B 96
Sleaford Rd. L14: K Ash 1B 82
Sleepers Hill L4: Walt 4F 55
Slessor Av. CH48: W Kir 3D 113
Slim Rd. L36: Huy 2E 83
Slingsby Dr. CH49: Upton 5A 94
Smallholdings, The L31: Mag 4F 7
Smallridge Cl. CH61: Pens 3E 137
Smallwoods M. CH60: Hes 5E 137
Smeaton St. L4: Kirk 2E 55
   (not continuous)
Smethick Wlk. L30: N'ton 1A 20
Smilie Av. CH46: More 5C 70
Smith Av. CH41: Birk 1B 96
Smithdown Gro. L7: Liv 1A 100
Smithdown La. L7: Liv 1B 100
   (Falkner St.)
   L7: Liv 5A 78
   (Paddington)
Smithdown Pl. L15: W'tree 4A 102
Smithdown Rd. L7: Liv 2B 100
   L15: W'tree 3D 101
Smith Dr. L20: Boot 3E 35
Smithfield St. L3: Liv 4C 76 (3D 4)
   WA9: St. H 1D 67
Smithford Wlk. L35: Tar G 2B 106
Smith Pl. L5: Kirk 5D 55
Smith Rd. WA8: Wid 5F 131
Smith St. L5: Kirk 4D 55
   L34: Prsct 5E 63
   WA9: St. H 4E 67
Smithy Cl. WA8: Cron 4C 108
Smithy Hey CH48: W Kir 4C 112
Smithy Hill CH63: Thorn H 4A 160
Smithy La. CH64: Will 5A 170
   L4: Walt 1F 55
   L39: Augh 1F 7
   WA8: Cron 3C 108
Smithystone Cl. L15: W'tree 2A 102
Smollett St. L6: Liv 3B 78
   L20: Boot 2A 34
Smugglers Way CH45: Wall 3E 51
Smyth Rd. WA8: Wid 0D 133
Snaefell Av. L13: Liv 1E 79
Snaefell Gro. L13: Liv 1E 79
Snave Ct. L21: Lith 2B 34
Snowberry Cl. WA8: Wid 5E 111
Snowberry Rd. L14: K Ash 5F 59
Snowden Rd. CH46: More 1C 92
Snowdon Gro. WA9: St. H 4C 66
Snowdon La. L5: Liv 1C 76
Snowdon Rd. CH42: Tran 2D 119
Snowdrop Av. CH41: Birk 1F 95
Snowdrop Cl. WA7: Beech 1F 173
Snowdrop M. L21: Lith 2B 34
Snowdrop St. L5: Kirk 4D 55
Soho Pl. L3: Liv 3E 77 (2H 5)
Soho St. L3: Liv 3E 77 (1H 5)
   (not continuous)
Solar Rd. L9: Ain 2B 36
Solly Av. CH42: R Ferr 2E 119
Solomon St. L7: Liv 4B 78
Solway Gro. WA7: Beech 5D 167
Solway St. CH41: Birk 5A 74
Solway St. E. L8: Liv 2B 100

Solway St. W. L8: Liv 2B 100
Soma Av. L21: Lith 5C 18
Somerford Ho. L23: Blun 2B 16
Somerford Rd. L14: K Ash 2F 81
Somerford Wlk. WA8: Wid 1E 133
   (off Barneston Rd.)
Somerley Cl. L12: W Der 3D 59
Somerset Pl. L6: Liv 1D 79
Somerset Rd. CH45: Wall 1E 73
   CH48: W Kir 3C 112
   CH61: Pens 3E 137
   L20: Boot 4D 35
   L22: Water 3C 16
Somerset St. WA9: St. H 1D 67
Somerton St. L15: W'tree 1E 101
Somerville Cl. CH63: Brom 4B 162
Somerville Gro. L22: Water 3D 17
Somerville Rd. L22: Water 3D 17
   WA8: Wid 4D 131
Somerville St. CH15: Liv 5E 55
Sommer Av. L12: W Der 4A 58
Sonning Av. L21: Lith 4A 18
Sonning Rd. L4: Walt 1D 57
Sorany Cl. L23: Thorn 4A 10
Sorogold St. WA9: St. H 5C 46
Sorrel Cl. CH43: Noct 4D 95
Sth. Albert Rd. L17: Aig 5B 100
Southampton Way
   WA7: Murd 4E 169
South Av. L34: Prsct 5B 62
South Bank CH43: O'ton 1B 118
   L19: Gras 5B 124
Sth. Bank Rd. L7: Liv 4D 79
Sth. Bank Ter. WA7: Run 4F 151
Sth. Barcombe Rd. L16: Child 2E 103
Sth. Boundary Rd.
   L33: Know I 5B 24
Southbourne Rd. CH45: Wall 1D 73
Southbrook Rd. L27: N'ley 3C 104
Southbrook Way L27: N'ley 3C 104
Sth. Cantril Av. L12: W Der 4F 59
Sth. Chester St. L8: Liv 3E 99
Southcroft Rd. CH45: Wall 1D 73
Southdale Rd. CH42: R Ferr 2E 119
   L15: W'tree 1F 101
SOUTHDENE 5A 24
South Dr. CH49: Upton 4A 94
   CH60: Hes 3A 158
   CH61: Irby 2C 136
   L12: W Der 1B 80
   L15: W'tree 1F 101
Southern Cres. L8: Liv 4D 99
Southern Rd. L24: Speke 5E 147
Southey Cl. WA8: Wid 4F 131
Southey Gro. L31: Mag 4D 13
Southey Rd. WA10: St. H 3C 64
Southey St. L15: W'tree 2D 101
   L20: Boot 4B 34
   (not continuous)
Sth. Ferry Quay L3: Liv 3C 98
Southfield Rd. L9: Walt 2E 35
South Front L35: Whis 1E 107
Southgate Cl. L12: Crox 5E 39
Southgate Rd. L13: Liv 3A 80
South Gro. L8: Liv 5A 100
   L18: Aller 3C 124
Sth. Hey Rd. CH61: Irby 3D 137
Sth. Highville Rd. L16: Child 3D 103
Sth. Hill Gro. CH43: O'ton 1B 118
   L8: Liv 5A 100
Sth. Hill Rd. CH43: O'ton 5B 96
   L8: Liv 1F 121
Sth. Hunter St. L1: Liv 1E 99 (7J 5)
Sth. John St. L1: Liv 5C 76 (5D 4)
   (not continuous)
   L2: Liv 5C 76 (5D 4)
   WA9: St. H 5C 46
Southlands M. WA7: Nun 1F 165
South La. WA8: Wid 4E 111
South La. Entry WA8: Wid 5F 111
Sth. Mnr. Way L25: Wltn 3C 126
South Meade L31: Mag 1B 12
Southmead Gdns. L19: Aller 5E 125
Southmead Rd. L19: Aller 5E 125
Sth. Mossley Hill Rd. L19: Aig . . .3A 124

Southney Cl. L31: Mell 3B 22
South Pde. CH48: W Kir 4A 112
  L23: C'by 2F 17
  L24: Speke 4E 147
  L32: K'by 3E 23
  WA7: West P 3D 165
Sth. Park Ct. CH44: Wall 3E 75
  L32: K'by 2C 22
South Pk. Rd. L32: K'by 2B 22
Sth. Parkside Dr. L12: W Der . . .4B 58
Sth. Parkside Wlk. L12: W Der . .3B 58
South Pk. Way L20: Boot 1D 55
Southport Rd. L20: Boot 2E 35
  L23: Thorn 3A 10
  L31: Lyd 1A 6
Southport St. WA9: St. H 5A 48
South Quay L3: Liv 1C 98
Southridge Rd. CH61: Pens . . .2A 138
South Rd. CH42: Tran 1C 118
  CH48: W Kir 5B 112
  L9: Ain 2D 37
  L14: B Grn 3C 80
  L19: Gras 1A 144
  L22: Water 5D 17
  L24: Halew 3E 147
  WA7: West P 3D 165
Sth. Sefton Bus. Cen. L20: Boot . .1B 54
South Sta. Rd. L25: Gate 4B 104
South St. L8: Liv 4A 100
  WA8: Wid 4B 132
  WA9: St. H 4D 65
Sth. Sudley Rd. L19: Aig 3F 123
South Vw. CH62: Brom 2D 143
  L22: Water 5E 17
  L36: Huy 4B 84
South Vw. Ct. L22: Water 5E 17
South Vw. Ter. WA5: Cuerd 2F 133
South Vs. CH45: New B 4B 52
Southward Rd. WA11: Hay 1F 49
Southwark Gro. L30: N'ton 4F 19
South Way L15: W'tree 1B 102
Southway WA7: Pal F 3F 167
  (not continuous)
  WA8: Wid 4D 131
Southwell Pl. L8: Liv 4E 99
Southwell St. L8: Liv 4E 99
Southwick Rd. CH42: Tran 1E 119
Sth. Wirral Retail Pk.
  CH62: Brom 4D 143
Southwood Av.
  WA7: Wind N 5C 154
Southwood Cl. L32: K'by 5A 24
Southwood Rd. L17: Aig 2B 122
Sovereign Cl. WA7: Murd 3D 169
Sovereign Hey L11: Crox 5C 38
Sovereign Pk. L11: Crox 5C 38
Sovereign Way CH44: Wall 5D 75
  L11: Crox 5C 38
Spark La. WA7: Halt 1F 167
Sparks La. CH61: Thing 1B 138
Sparling St. L1: Liv 2D 99
  (not continuous)
SPARROW HALL 4F 37
Sparrow Hall Cl. L9: Faz 4E 37
Sparrow Hall Rd. L9: Faz 4E 37
Sparrowhawk Cl.
  L26: Halew 3E 127
  WA7: Pal F 3A 168
Speakman Rd. WA10: St. H 2D 45
Speakman St. WA7: Run 4F 151
Spear St. L8: Liv 4A 100
Speedwell Cl. L36: Huy 2C 158
Speedwell Dr. CH60: Hes 2C 158
Speedwell Rd. CH41: Birk 2F 95
SPEKE .5E 147
Speke Blvd. L24: Speke 3B 146
Speke Chu. Rd. L24: Speke 4B 146
Speke Hall Av. L24: Speke 5F 145
Speke Hall Av. L24: Speke 2A 146
Speke Hall Ind. Est.
  L24: Speke 4A 146
Speke Hall Rd. L24: Speke 2A 146
  L25: Hunts X, Wltn 5A 126
Speke Ho. L24: Speke 5A 148
Spekeland Rd. L7: Liv 1C 100

Speke Rd. L19: Gars 2C 144
  (not continuous)
  L24: Speke 2D 145
  L25: Wltn 2B 126
  L26: Halew 2C 148
  WA8: Hale B 2C 148
  WA8: Wid 5F 129
Speke Town La. L24: Speke 3B 146
Spellow La. L4: Walt 3F 55
Spellow Pl. L3: Liv 4B 4
Spence Av. L20: Boot 3D 35
Spencer Av. CH46: More 5A 72
Spencer Cl. L36: Huy 1F 105
Spencer Gdns. WA9: St. H 3D 67
Spencer Pl. L20: Boot 1D 35
Spencer's La. L31: Mell 3E 21
Spencer St. L6: Liv 2F 77
Spennymoor Ct. WA7: Pal F 3E 167
Spenser Av. CH42: R Ferr 3F 119
Spenser Cl. WA8: Wid 3F 131
Spenser St. L20: Boot 4B 34
Spicer Gro. L32: K'by 3E 23
Spice St. L9: Ain 2B 36
Spike Island Vis. Cen. 2A 152
Spindle Cl. L6: Liv 2F 77
Spindrift Ct. CH48: W Kir 5A 112
Spindus Rd. L24: Speke 4A 146
Spinnaker Cl. WA7: Murd 4D 169
Spinney, The CH48: W Kir 4E 113
  CH49: Upton 3A 94
  CH60: Hes 5C 158
  CH63: Spit 4B 142
  L28: Stock V 4A 60
  L34: Prsct 4C 62
Spinney Av. WA8: Wid 3A 130
Spinney Cl. L33: Know I 5C 24
  WA9: Clock F 2C 88
Spinney Cres. L23: Blun 4B 8
Spinney Grn. WA10: Eccl 1A 64
Spinney Rd. L33: Know I 5C 24
Spinney Vw. L33: Know I 5D 25
Spinney Wlk. WA7: Cas 1A 168
Spinney Way L36: Huy 3C 82
Spire Grn. L9: Walt 2A 36
Spires, The WA10: Eccl 5A 44
SPITAL .4B 142
Spital Heyes CH63: Spit 4B 142
Spital Rd. CH62: Brom, Spit 4C 142
  CH63: Spit 4A 142
Spital Station (Rail) 4B 142
Spitfire Rd. L24: Speke 1F 145
Spofforth Rd. L7: Liv 1D 101
Spooner Av. L21: Lith 5C 18
Sprainger St. L3: Liv 2B 76
Sprakeling Pl. L20: Boot 1E 35
Spray St. WA10: St. H 4E 45
Spreyton Cl. L12: W Der 1C 58
Sprig Cl. L9: Ain 5D 21
Springbank Cl. WA7: Run 4B 166
Spring Bank Rd. L4: Walt 1B 78
Springbourne Rd. L17: Aig 2B 122
Springbrook Cl. WA10: Eccl 4A 44
Spring Cl. L33: K'by 5F 15
Spring Ct. WA7: Run 5B 152
Springdale Cl. L12: W Der 5C 58
Springdale Rd. CH46: More 5A 72
Springfield L3: Liv 3E 77 (2G 5)
  (not continuous)
Springfield Av. CH48: W Kir 4F 113
  L21: Lith 5C 18
Springfield Cl. CH49: W'chu 2C 116
  WA10: St. H 3C 64
Springfield La. WA10: Eccl 3A 44
Springfield Pk. WA11: Hay 1C 48
Springfield Rd. L39: Augh 2F 7
  WA8: Wid 4A 130
  WA10: St. H 3D 64
Springfield Sq. L4: Walt 3F 55
Springfield Way L12: W Der 3E 59
Spring Gdns. L31: Mag 2E 13
Spring Gro. L12: W Der 5C 58
Springhill Av. CH62: Brom 4D 163
Springmeadow Rd. L25: Gate . . .4A 104

Springpool WA9: St. H 4D 67
Springs Cl. L20: Boot 4D 35
Springside Cl. L36: Huy 5C 60
Spring St. CH42: Tran 1F 119
  WA8: Wid 1A 152
Spring Va. CH45: Wall 4E 51
Springvale Cl. L32: K'by 4D 23
Springville Rd. L9: Ain 1C 36
Springwell Rd. L20: Boot 1D 35
Springwood Av. L19: Aller 4D 125
  L25: Wltn 4D 125
Springwood Ct. L19: Aller 4D 125
  (off Ramsey Rd.)
Springwood Crematorium
  L25: Wltn 4F 125
Springwood Gro. L32: K'by 1F 39
Springwood Way CH62: New F . .4A 120
Spruce Cl. CH47: Aston 5D 97
Spruce Gro. L28: Stock V 4B 60
Sprucewood Cl. L6: Liv 1B 78
Spur WA7: Pal F 2D 17
Spur Cl. L11: Crox 5C 38
Spurgeon Cl. L5: Liv 1F 77
Spurling Rd. WA5: B'wood 5F 69
Spurriers La. L31: Mell 2C 14
Spurstow Cl. CH43: O'ton 1F 117
Squibb Dr. CH46: Leas 4A 72
Squires Av. WA8: Wid 3F 131
Squires Cl. WA11: Hay 2B 48
Squires St. L7: Liv 1A 100
Stable Cl. CH49: Grea 5D 93
Stables, The L23: C'by 5A 10
Stables Bus. Cen. L13: Liv 4E 57
  (off Larkhill La.)
Stables Ct. WA9: St. H 1C 66
Stackfield, The CH48: W Kir 3F 113
Stadium Rd. CH62: Brom 4E 143
Stadt Moers Pk. 4C 84
Stadt Moers Vis. Cen. 4C 84
Stafford Cl. L36: Huy 2A 84
Stafford Moreton Way L31: Mag . . .1C 12
  (not continuous)
Stafford Rd. WA10: St. H 2D 65
Staffordshire Cl. L5: Liv 5E 55
Stafford St. L3: Liv 4E 77 (3H 5)
Stag Rd. L24: Speke 1E 145
Stainburn Av. L11: N Grn. 5E 37
Stainer Cl. L14: K Ash 1F 81
Stainton Cl. L26: Halew 4E 127
  WA11: St. H 5B 30
Stairhaven Rd. L19: Aller 3B 124
Stakes, The CH46: Leas 3E 71
Stalbridge Av. L18: Moss H 4F 101
Staley Av. L23: C'by 2F 17
Staley St. L20: Boot 2C 34
Stalisfield Av. L11: N Grn. 1A 58
Stalisfield Gro. L11: N Grn. 1A 58
Stalisfield Pl. L11: N Grn. 1A 58
Stalmine Rd. L9: Walt 4A 36
Stamford Ct. L20: Boot 5D 35
Stamfordham Dr. L19: Aller 4C 124
Stamfordham Gro. L19: Aller 5D 125
Stamfordham Pl. L19: Aller 5C 124
Stamford St. L7: Liv 4C 78
Stanbury Av. CH63: Beb 1A 142
Standale Rd. L15: W'tree 1F 101
Standard Pl. CH42: R Ferr 1F 119
Standard Rd. L11: Crox 4C 38
Standedge Way L14: K Ash 5F 59
Standen Cl. WA10: St. H 4E 45
Standish Av. WN5: Bil 1E 31
Stand Farm Rd. L12: Crox 5E 39
Standish Av. WN5: Bil 1E 31
Standish Cl. WA8: Wid 4D 131
Standish St. L3: Liv 3D 77 (2E 4)
  WA10: St. H 4A 46
Stand Pk. Av. L30: N'ton 3F 19
Stand Pk. Cl. L30: N'ton 3F 19
Stand Pk. Rd. L16: Child 3D 103
Stand Pk. Way L30: N'ton 2E 19
Standring Gdns. WA10: St. H 3B 64
Stanfield Av. L5: Liv 1F 77
Stanfield Dr. CH63: Beb 4F 141
Stanford Av. CH45: New B 4B 52
Stanford Cres. L25: Hunts X 3D 127
Stangate L31: Mag 5B 6

Stanhope Dr. CH62: Brom 1D **163**
   L36: Huy 3C **82**
Stanhope St. L8: Liv 3D **99**
   (not continuous)
   WA10: St. H 3F **45**
Stanier Way L7: Liv 5C **78**
Staniforth Pl. L16: Child 5D **81**
STANLEY 4E **79**
Stanley Av. CH45: Wall 5D **51**
   CH63: High B 4B **118**
Stanley Bank Rd. WA11: Hay 1A **48**
Stanley Bungalows L34: Know 5C **40**
Stanley Cl. CH44: Wall 4E **75**
   L4: Kirk 4D **55**
   WA8: Wid 2C **132**
Stanley Ct. CH42: Tran 1F **119**
Stanley Cres. L34: Prsct 5C **62**
Stanley Gdns. L9: Walt 3F **35**
Stanley Ho. L20: Boot 4B **34**
Stanley La. CH62: East 1F **171**
STANLEY PARK 4C **18**
Stanley Pk. L21: Lith 4A **18**
Stanley Pk. Av. Nth. L4: Walt 2B **56**
   (not continuous)
Stanley Pk. Av. Sth. L4: Walt 3B **56**
Stanley Pct. L20: Boot 5C **34**
Stanley Rd. CH41: Birk 5F **73**
   CH47: Hoy 5A **90**
   CH62: New F 4A **120**
   L5: Kirk 3C **34**
   L20: Boot, Kirk 2C **34**
   L22: Water 4C **12**
   L31: Mag 3E **83**
   L36: Huy 4E **75**
Stanley St. CH44: Wall 4E **75**
   L1: Liv 4C **76** (4D **4**)
   L7: Liv 3D **79**
   L19: Gars 3C **144**
   WA7: Run 4B **152**
Stanley Ter. CH45: New B 4B **52**
   L8: Liv 2F **99**
   (off Up. Parliament St.)
   L18: Moss H 1A **124**
Stanley Theatre L7: Liv 5F **77**
   (off Mt. Pleasant)
Stanley Vs. WA7: Run 1F **165**
Stanlowe Vw. L19: Gras 5F **123**
Stanmore Pk. CH49: Grea 1B **114**
Stanmore Rd. L15: W'tree 3B **102**
   WA7: Run 5D **153**
Stanney Cl. CH62: East 2E **171**
Stannyfield Cl. L23: Thorn 4B **10**
Stannyfield Dr. L23: Thorn 4B **10**
Stansfield Av. L31: Mag 1F **13**
Stanton Av. L21: Lith 4A **18**
Stanton Cl. L30: N'ton 5D **11**
   WA11: Hay 2C **48**
Stanton Cres. L32: K'by 3C **22**
Stanton Rd. CH63: Beb 4E **141**
   L18: Moss H 4F **101**
Stanwood Cl. WA10: Eccl 5F **43**
Stanwood Gdns. L35: Whis 3E **85**
Stapehill Cl. L13: Liv 4B **80**
Stapeley Gdns. L26: Halew 1A **148**
Staplands Rd. L14: B Grn 4D **81**
Stapleford Rd. L25: Gate 3C **104**
Staplehurst Cl. L12: Crox 5E **39**
Stapleton Av. CH49: Grea 5D **93**
   L24: Speke 4D **147**
   L35: R'hill 2C **86**
Stapleton Cl. L25: Gate 2B **104**
   L35: R'hill 2C **86**
Stapleton Rd. WA6: Frod 5C **172**
Stapleton Rd. L35: R'hill 1B **86**
Stapleton Way WA8: Hale B 2B **150**
Stapley Cl. WA7: Run 1F **165**
Star Inn Cotts. WA11: R'ford 1A **28**
Starling Cl. WA7: Murd 3D **169**
Starling Gro. L12: W Der 2F **59**
Star St. L8: Liv 3E **99**
Startham Av. WN5: Bil 2D **31**
Starworth Dr. CH62: New F 5C **120**
Statham Rd. CH43: Bid 1C **94**
Station App. CH46: More 4E **71**
   CH47: Meols 3E **91**

Station Cl. L25: Hunts X 5C **126**
Station M. L32: K'by 2C **22**
Station Pas. L9: Walt 4F **35**
Station Rd. CH41: Birk 5F **73**
   CH44: Wall 2A **74**
   CH47: Hoy 5B **90**
   CH60: Hes 4F **157**
   CH61: Barn 2D **139**
   CH61: Thurs 5F **135**
   CH63: Store 2D **139**
   L25: Gate 4A **104**
   L31: Lyd 1A **6**
   L31: Mag 2E **13**
   L31: Mell 2A **22**
   L34: Prsct 5D **63**
   (not continuous)
   L35: R'hill 3C **86**
   L36: Roby 4C **82**
   WA7: Run 5F **151**
   WA7: Sut W 1B **174**
   WA8: Wid 5C **110**
   WA9: St. H 4E **67**
   WA11: Hay 2C **48**
Station St. L35: R'hill 3C **86**
Statton Rd. L13: Liv 5B **80**
Staveley Rd. L19: Gras 4B **124**
Stavert Cl. L11: N Grn 5B **38**
Staverton Pk. L32: K'by 4C **22**
Stavordale Rd.
   CH46: More 5A **72**
Steble St. L8: Liv 4F **99**
Steel Av. CH45: Wall 5C **52**
Steel Cl. L5: Liv 5C **54**
Steeple, The CH48: Caldy 3D **135**
Steeplechase Cl. L9: Ain 5C **20**
Steeple Vw. L33: K'by 5E **15**
Steers Cft. L28: Stock V 3F **59**
Steinberg Ct. L3: Liv 2C **76**
Steley Way L34: Prsct 2A **34**
Stella Pct. L21: Sea 1A **34**
Stenhills Cres. WA7: Run 5C **152**
Stephens La. L2: Liv 4C **76** (4D **4**)
Stephenson Ct. L7: Liv 5C **78**
   (off Crosfield Rd.)
Stephenson Ho. L7: Liv 1A **100**
Stephenson Rd. L13: Liv 4A **80**
Stephenson Way L13: W'tree 5E **79**
Stephen Way L35: R'hill 1B **86**
Stepney Gro. L4: Walt 2A **56**
Sterling Way L5: Kirk 5D **55**
Sterndale Cl. L7: Liv 1B **100**
Sterrix Av. L30: N'ton 3C **18**
Sterrix Grn. L21: Lith 3C **18**
Sterrix La. L21: Lith 3C **18**
   L30: N'ton 3D **19**
Steve Biko Cl. L8: Liv 2B **100**
Stevenage Cl. WA9: St. H 4F **65**
Stevenson Cres. WA10: St. H 4D **45**
Stevenson Dr. CH63: Spit 4F **141**
Stevenson St. L15: W'tree 1E **101**
Stevens Rd. CH60: Hes 3C **158**
Stevens St. WA9: St. H 3D **65**
Steventon WA7: Nort 4D **155**
Steward Cl. L35: Prsct 1F **85**
Stewards Av. WA8: Wid 4F **131**
Stewart Av. L20: Boot 4E **35**
Stewart Cl. CH61: Pens 4F **137**
Stile Hey L23: Thorn 5B **10**
Stiles Rd. L33: K'by 4F **15**
Stillington Rd. L8: Liv 5A **100**
Stirling Av. L23: C'by 2E **17**
Stirling Cres. WA9: St. H 5C **66**
Stirling La. L25: Hunts X 5D **127**
Stirling Rd. L24: Speke 4B **146**
Stirling St. CH44: Wall 4B **74**
Stockbridge La. L36: Huy 1B **82**
   (not continuous)
Stockbridge Pl. L5: Liv 5A **56**
Stockbridge St. L5: Liv 1A **78**
STOCKBRIDGE VILLAGE 3A **60**
Stockdale Cl. L3: Liv 3C **76** (2D **4**)
Stockham La. WA7: Halt 2A **168**
Stockham La.
   WA7: Brook, Pal F, Halt 2A **168**
   (not continuous)

Stockham Lodge Racquet & Health Club
   . . . . .3B **168**
Stockmoor Rd. L11: N Grn 5F **37**
Stockpit Rd. L33: Know I 3C **24**
Stocks Av. WA9: St. H 5E **47**
Stockswell Farm Ct. WA8: Wid 5E **109**
Stockswell Rd. WA8: Wid 5F **107**
Stockton Cres. L33: K'by 4D **15**
Stockton Gro. WA9: St. H 1C **66**
Stockton Wood Rd. L24: Speke 4C **146**
Stockville Rd. L18: Moss H 5E **103**
Stoddart Rd. L4: Walt 1A **56**
Stoke Cl. CH62: East 2E **171**
Stoker Way L8: Walt 3A **36**
Stokesay CH43: Noct 3D **95**
Stokes Cl. L26: Halew 3A **128**
Stokesley Av. L32: K'by 3C **22**
Stoke St. CH41: Birk 1B **96**
Stonebarn Dr. L31: Mag 4C **6**
Stone Barn La. WA7: Pal F 4F **167**
Stonebridge La. L10: Faz 2A **38**
   L11: Crox 3B **38**
Stoneby Dr. CH45: Wall 4A **52**
Stonechat Cl. L27: N'ley 5E **105**
   WA7: Beech 5F **167**
Stonecrop L18: Moss H 4E **103**
Stonecrop Cl. WA7: Beech 5F **167**
Stone Cross Dr. WA8: Wid 4E **109**
Stonecross Dr. L35: R'hill 5D **87**
Stonedale Cres. L11: Crox 4A **38**
Stonedale Pk. L11: Crox 4A **38**
Stonefield Rd. L14: K Ash 2F **81**
Stonefont Cl. L9: Walt 5A **36**
Stonegate Dr. L8: Liv 5F **99**
Stonehaven Cl. L16: Child 1F **103**
Stone Hey L35: Whis 5D **85**
Stonehey Dr. CH48: W Kir 1C **134**
Stonehey Rd. L32: K'by 5E **23**
Stone Hey Wlk. L32: K'by 5E **23**
Stonehill Av. CH63: Beb 1A **142**
   L4: Walt 5B **56**
Stonehills Ct. WA7: Run 5C **152**
Stonehills La. WA7: Run 5C **152**
Stonehill St. L4: Walt 5B **56**
Stonehouse M. L18: Aller 1D **125**
Stonehouse Rd. CH44: Wall 1E **73**
Stonelea WA7: Wind 1B **168**
Stoneleigh Gro. CH42: R Ferr 4F **119**
Stonemasons Ct. L25: Wltn 1A **126**
   (off Clay Cross Rd.)
Stoneridge Ct. CH43: Bid 1C **94**
Stone Sq. L20: Boot 3E **35**
Stone St. L3: Liv 2B **76**
   L34: Prsct 5D **63**
Stoneville Rd. L13: Liv 2A **80**
Stoneycroft L13: Liv 1A **80**
Stoneycroft Cres. L13: Liv 1A **80**
Stoney Hey Rd. CH45: New B 4A **52**
Stoneyhurst Av. L10: Ain 2C **20**
Stoney La. L35: R'hill, Whis 2F **85**
Stoney La. Ind. Est. L35: R'hill 3A **86**
Stoney Vw. L35: R'hill 3B **86**
Stonham Cl. CH49: Upton 4E **93**
Stonyfield L30: N'ton 5E **11**
Stony Holt WA7: Nort 2C **168**
Stonyhurst Cl. WA11: St. H 1B **46**
Stonyhurst Rd. L25: Wltn 3B **126**
Stopford St. L8: Liv 5F **99**
Stopgate La. L9: Ain 4D **37**
   L33: Sim 4F **15**
Store St. L20: Kirk 2D **55**
STORETON 2A **140**
STORETON BRICKFIELDS 2E **139**
Storeton Cl. CH43: O'ton 1A **118**
Storeton La. CH61: Barn 4C **138**
Storeton Rd. CH42: Tran 1B **118**
   CH43: O'ton 1B **118**
Stormont Rd. L19: Gars 5B **124**
Storrington Av. L11: N Grn 5A **38**
Storrington Heys L11: N Grn 4B **38**
Storrsdale Rd. L18: Moss H 1B **124**
Stour Av. L35: R'hill 3C **86**
Stourcliffe Rd. CH44: Wall 2A **74**
Stourport Cl. CH49: Grea 5C **92**
Stourton Rd. L32: K'by 5E **23**

Stourton St. CH44: Wall 4C 74
Stourvale Rd. L26: Halew 4F 127
Stowe Av. L13: Ain 3E 21
Stowe Cl. L25: Hunts X 5A 126
Stowell St. L7: Liv 1F 99 (7J 5)
Stowford Cl. L12: W Der 1C 58
Strada Way L3: Liv 3F 77 (2J 5)
Stradbroke Rd. L15: W'tree 3A 102
Strafford Dr. L20: Boot 4E 35
Strand, The L2: Liv 5B 76 (5C 4)
Strand Rd. CH47: Hoy 4B 90
L20: Boot 5B 34
(not continuous)
Strand Shop. Cen.
L20: Boot 4C 34
Strand St. L1: Liv 5C 76 (6C 4)
Stratford Rd. L19: Aig 4F 123
Strathallan Cl. CH60: Hes 5E 137
Strathcona Rd. CH45: Wall 5B 52
L15: W'tree 2E 101
Strathearn Rd. CH60: Hes 4F 157
Strathlorne Cl. CH42: Tran 1F 119
Strathmore Dr. L23: C'by 2E 17
Strathmore Gro. WA9: St. H 5C 66
Strathmore Rd. L6: Liv 2C 78
Stratton Cl. CH45: Wall 5C 52
L18: Aller 1E 125
WA7: Brook 4B 168
Stratton Dr. WA9: St. H 5D 65
Stratton Pk. WA8: Wid 4F 109
Stratton Rd. L32: K'by 4C 22
Stratton Wlk. L32: K'by 4C 22
Strauss Cl. L8: Liv 3B 100
Strawberry Fld. L25: Wltn 1E 125
Strawberry Rd. L11: N Grn. 1E 57
Streatham Av. L18: Moss H 4F 101
Street Hey La. CH64: Will 2B 170
Stretford Cl. L33: K'by 5E 15
Stretton Av. CH44: Wall 2A 74
WA9: St. H 5F 47
WN5: Bil 1E 31
Stretton Cl. CH43: O'ton 1E 117
CH62: East 2E 171
L12: Crox 5A 40
Stretton Way L36: Huy 5B 84
Strickland St. WA10: St. H 4B 46
Stringhey Rd. CH44: Wall 1C 74
Stroma Rd. L18: Aller 3B 124
Stroud Cl. CH49: Grea 1C 114
Stuart Av. CH46: More 5F 71
L25: Hunts X 5C 126
Stuart Cl. CH46: More 1A 94
Stuart Dr. L14: B Grn 3E 81
Stuart Gro. L20: Kirk 2D 55
Stuart Rd. CH42: Tran 1D 119
L4: Walt 1E 55
L22: Water 3E 17
L23: C'by 3F 17
L31: Mell 2B 22
WA7: Mnr P 3B 154
WA10: Windle 2C 44
Stuart Rd. Nth. L20: Boot 5E 35
Stubbs La. CH43: Noct 1E 117
Studholme St. L20: Kirk 4C 54
Studland Rd. L9: Faz 4E 37
Studley Rd. CH45: Wall 5E 51
Sturdee Rd. L13: Liv 5B 80
Sturgess St. WA12: New W 5F 49
Suburban Rd. L6: Liv 5C 56
Sudbury Cl. L27: N'ley 2D 127
Sudbury Gdns. WA9: St. H 5C 64
Sudbury Rd. L22: Water 3B 16
Sudell Av. L31: Mag 5F 7
Sudell La. L31: Lyd 1D 7
L39: Augh 1D 7
Sudley Grange L17: Aig 3E 123
Sudworth Rd. CH45: New B 4A 52
Suffield Rd. L4: Kirk 3D 55
Suffolk Pl. WA8: Wid 5C 130
Suffolk St. L1: Liv 1D 99 (7F 5)
L20: Boot 4D 35
WA7: Run 4F 151
Suffton Pk. L32: K'by 4C 22
Sugar La. L34: Know 5C 40
Sugar St. L9: Ain 3B 36

Sugnall St. L7: Liv 1F 99 (7J 5)
(not continuous)
Sulby Av. L13: Liv 1E 79
Sulgrave Cl. L16: Child 5C 80
Sullington Dr. L27: N'ley 3E 105
Sullivan Av. CH49: Upton 5F 93
Sullivans Way WA9: St. H 3B 66
Sumley Cl. WA11: St. H 3D 47
Summer Cl. WA7: Halt 1F 167
Summerfield L20: Boot 5D 143
Summerfield Av. WA10: Eccl 5F 43
Summerford Cl. CH42: Tran 1E 119
Summerhill Dr. L31: Mag 3F 13
Summer La. WA4: Pres H 4F 169
WA7: Halt 1F 167
Summer Rd. L20: Boot 3C 34
Summers Av. L20: Boot 4E 35
Summer Seat L3: Liv 2C 76 (1E 4)
L20: Boot 5A 34
Summers Rd. L3: Liv 4D 99
Summertrees Av. CH49: Grea 5D 93
Summertrees Cl. CH49: Grea 5D 93
Summerwood CH61: Irby 5D 115
Summit, The CH44: Wall 1C 74
Summit Way L25: Wltn 1F 125
Sumner Cl. L5: Liv 1C 76
L35: R'hill 5D 87
Sumner Gro. L33: K'by 5F 15
Sumner Rd. CH43: Bid 1F 95
WA11: Hay 2A 48
Sunbeam Cl. WA7: Run 4F 151
Sunbeam Rd. L13: Liv 3A 80
Sunbourne Rd. L17: Aig 2B 122
Sunbury Rd. CH44: Wall 3C 74
L4: Walt 4B 56
Sunbury St. WA10: St. H 4C 46
Suncroft Rd. CH60: Hes 3C 158
Sundale Av. L35: Prsct 5F 63
Sundene Lodge L22: Water 1E 33
Sundew Cl. L9: Walt 1F 35
Sundridge St. L8: Liv 5A 100
Sunfield Rd. CH46: More 4F 71
Sunflower Cl. WA9: Bold 4A 68
Sunlight Lodge CH62: Port S 1B 142
Sunlight St. L6: Liv 1C 78
Sunloch Cl. L9: Ain 5D 21
Sunningdale CH46: More 1A 94
Sunningdale Av. WA8: Wid 3B 130
Sunningdale Cl. L36: Roby 5C 82
WA5: B'wood 5F 69
Sunningdale Dr. CH61: Thing 2A 138
CH63: Brom 4B 162
L23: Blun 4C 8
Sunningdale Rd. CH45: Wall 3F 51
L15: W'tree 1F 101
Sunniside La. WA7: Nort 3E 155
Sunny Bank CH63: High B 1D 141
Sunnybank CH49: Upton 3F 93
Sunnybank Av. L35: Noct 5D 95
Sunny Bank Rd. L16: Child 2D 103
Sunnydale L35: R'hill 3D 87
Sunnygate Rd. L19: Gras 4A 124
Sunnymede Dr. L31: Lyd 4D 7
Sunnyside CH46: More 4D 71
L8: Liv .4A 100
Sunnyside Rd. L23: C'by 2C 16
Sunrise Cl. L19: Gras 5B 124
Sunsdale Rd. L18: Moss H 4A 102
Sunset Cl. L33: K'by 5F 15
Superior Cl. L27: N'ley 4E 105
Surby Cl. L16: Child 1E 103
Surlingham Gdns. WA9: St. H 5E 65
Surrey Av. CH49: Upton 4F 93
Surrey Dr. CH48: W Kir 1C 134
Surrey St. CH44: Wall 3A 74
L1: Liv 1D 99 (7E 5)
L20: Boot 4D 35
WA7: Run 5A 152
(not continuous)
WA9: St. H 5D 47
Susan Gro. CH46: More 1D 93
Susan St. WA8: Wid 2C 132
Susan Wlk. L35: Whis 1F 85
Sussex CH61: Pens 3E 137
L20: Boot 4D 35

Sussex Gro. WA9: St. H 1C 66
Sussex Rd. CH48: W Kir 3C 112
L31: Mag 3D 13
Sussex St. L20: Boot 4D 35
L22: Water 3C 16
WA8: Wid 3D 133
Sutcliffe St. L6: Liv 3B 78
Sutherland Ct. WA7: Run 5B 152
Sutherland Dr. CH62: East 1D 171
Sutherland Rd. L34: Prsct 5E 63
SUTTON 4F 67
Sutton C'way. WA6: Frod 3E 173
Sutton Cl. CH62: East 2E 171
Sutton Fields Golf Driving Range
. . . . .2C 174
Sutton Fold WA9: St. H 3D 67
SUTTON HEATH 4F 65
Sutton Heath Rd. WA9: St. H 5E 65
SUTTON LEACH 1D 89
Sutton Leisure Cen. 5B 66
Sutton Lodge Rd. WA9: St. H 1B 66
SUTTON MANOR 4B 88
Sutton Moss Rd. WA9: St. H 3F 67
Sutton Oak Dr. WA9: St. H 2D 67
Sutton Pk. Dr. WA9: St. H 4C 66
Sutton Quays Bus. Pk.
WA7: Sut W 2E 173
Sutton Rd. CH45: New B 4B 52
WA9: St. H 2C 66
Suttons La. WA8: Wid 5B 132
Sutton St. L13: Liv 1E 79
WA7: Run 5B 152
Suttons Way L26: Halew 3E 127
SUTTON WEAVER 2A 174
Sutton Wood Rd. L24: Speke 4D 146
Suzanne Boardman Ho. L6: Liv 1C 78
Swainson Rd. L10: Faz 1E 37
Swale Av. L35: R'hill 3C 86
Swaledale Av. L35: R'hill 3D 87
Swaledale Cl. CH62: East 5E 163
Swalegate L31: Mag 5C 6
Swallow Cl. L12: Crox 5F 39
L27: N'ley 4F 105
L33: K'by 3E 15
Swallow Rd. WA10: St. H 5D 45
Swallow Flds. L9: Faz 4E 37
Swallowhurst Cres. L11: N Grn. 1A 58
Swan Av. WA9: St. H 1A 68
Swan Cl. CH43: Pren 2F 117
Swan Cres. L15: W'tree 1A 102
Swan Hey L31: Mag 3E 13
Swan La. L39: Augh 1E 7
Swan Rd. WA12: New W 4D 49
Swan St. L13: Liv 3F 79
Swan Wlk. L31: Mag 3E 13
Sweden Gro. L22: Water 4D 17
Sweet Briar Ct. WA9: Clock F 4D 68
Sweeting St. L2: Liv 5C 76 (5D 4)
Sweet William Pl.
WA12: New W 5E 49
Swift Gro. L12: Crox 4F 39
Swift's Cl. L30: N'ton 1D 19
Swift's La. L30: N'ton 1D 19
Swift St. WA10: St. H 3A 46
Swinbrook Grn. L11: N Grn. 5F 37
Swinburne Cl. L16: Child 1F 103
Swinburne Rd. WA10: St. H 3D 45
Swindale Cl. L8: Liv 2B 100
Swinderby Dr. L31: Mell 2B 22
Swindon Cl. CH49: Grea 5C 92
L5: Kirk .4D 55
Swindon St. L5: Kirk 4D 55
Swinford Av. WA8: Wid 2E 133
Swisspine Gdns. WA9: St. H 4C 64
Swiss Rd. L6: Liv 3C 78
Switch Island L30: N'ton 5B 12
Switch Island Leisure Pk.
L30: N'ton 2A 20
Sword Cl. L11: Crox 5C 38

Sword Wlk. L11: Crox 5C **38**
Swynnerton Way WA8: Wid 4B **110**
Sybil Rd. L4: Walt 4A **56**
Sycamore Av. WA7: Upton 2D **93**
　　L23: C'by 4F **9**
　　L26: Halew 1F **147**
　　WA8: Wid 2B **132**
　　WA11: Hay 3F **47**
Sycamore Cl. WA7: Upton 2D **93**
　　L9: Walt 5C **36**
　　WA10: Eccl 4B **44**
Sycamore Ct. *L8: Liv* *5A **100***
　　　　　　　　(off Weller Way)
Sycamore Dr. WA7: Sut W 1A **174**
Sycamore Gdns. WA10: St. H 2E **45**
Sycamore Pk. L18: Aller 2D **125**
Sycamore Ri. CH49: Grea 2C **114**
Sycamore Rd. CH42: Tran 5D **97**
　　L22: Water 3E **17**
　　L36: Huy 1E **105**
　　WA7: Run 2C **166**
Sydenham Av. L17: Liv 3C **100**
Sydenham Ho. L17: Aig 4C **100**
Syder's Gro. L34: Know 5C **40**
Sydney St. L9: Ain 2A **36**
　　WA7: West P 3D **165**
Sylvan Cl. L25: Wltn 3A **126**
Sylvandale Gro. CH62: Brom 4D **143**
Sylvania Rd. L4: Walt 1A **56**
Sylvia Cl. L10: Faz 2B **38**
Syren St. L20: Kirk 3C **54**
Syston Av. WA11: St. H 2C **46**

T

Tabley Av. WA8: Wid 2C **130**
Tabley Cl. CH43: O'ton 2F **117**
Tabley Gdns. WA9: St. H 5D **65**
Tabley Rd. L15: W'tree 2D **101**
Tabley St. L1: Liv 1C **98**
Tace Cl. L8: Liv 2F **99**
Taggart Av. L16: Child 3D **103**
Tagus Cl. L8: Liv 3B **100**
Tagus St. L8: Liv 2B **100**
Tailor's La. L31: Mag 2E **13**
Talbot Av. CH63: Brim 1A **160**
Talbot Cl. WA10: St. H 4F **45**
Talbot Ct. CH43: O'ton 5A **96**
　　L36: Huy 5E **83**
Talbot Rd. CH43: O'ton 5A **96**
Talbotville Rd. L13: Liv 5B **80**
Talgarth Way L25: Gate 2A **104**
Taliesin St. L5: Liv 1D **77**
Talisman Cl. WA7: Murd 3D **169**
Talisman Way L20: Boot 4A **34**
Talland Dr. L26: Halew 3E **127**
Tallarn Rd. L32: K'by 3B **22**
Tall Trees WA9: St. H 3B **66**
Talton Rd. L15: W'tree 2D **101**
Tamar Cl. L6: Liv 2A **78**
Tamar Gro. CH46: More 1D **93**
Tamarisk Gdns. WA9: St. H 4C **64**
Tamar Rd. WA11: Hay 2C **48**
Tamerton Cl. L18: Aller 2E **125**
Tam o'Shanter Urban Farm 2E **95**
Tamworth St. L8: Liv 4E **99**
　　WA10: St. H 4E **45**
　　WA12: New W 5F **49**
Tanar Cl. CH63: Spit 4B **142**
Tanat Dr. L18: Moss H 5B **102**
Tancred Rd. CH45: Wall 1A **74**
　　L4: Walt 4F **55**
Tanhouse WA7: Halt 1E **167**
Tan Ho. La. WA5: B'wood 5F **69**
Tanhouse La. WA8: Wid 4C **132**
Tanhouse Rd. L23: Thorn 5B **10**
Tansley Cl. CH48: W Kir 4E **113**
Tanworth Gro. CH46: More 5B **70**
Tapley Pl. L13: Liv 4F **79**
Taplow St. L6: Liv 5B **56**
Tapton Way L13: W'tree 5F **79**
Tara Pk. Cvn. Site
　　L3: Liv 2B **76** (1B **4**)
TARBOCK GREEN 5C **106**

Tarbock Rd. L24: Speke 3D **147**
　　L36: Huy 5D **83**
Tarbot Hey CH46: More 1C **92**
Tarbrock Ct. L30: N'ton 5D **11**
Target Rd. CH60: Hes 2C **156**
Tariff St. L5: Liv 1C **76**
Tarleton St. L1: Liv 5D **77** (5E **5**)
Tarlton St. L35: R'hill 1A **86**
Tarnbeck WA7: Nort 2C **168**
Tarncliff L28: Stock V 3C **60**
Tarn Gro. WA11: St. H 5B **30**
Tarporley Cl. CH43: O'ton 1F **117**
Tarragon Cl. L23: Thorn 5B **10**
Tarran Dr. CH46: More 4D **71**
Tarran Rd. CH46: More 4D **71**
Tarran Way E. CH46: More 3D **71**
Tarran Way Ind. Est.
　　CH46: More 4D **71**
Tarran Way Nth. CH46: More 4D **71**
Tarran Way Sth. CH46: More 4D **71**
Tarran Way W. CH46: More 4D **71**
Tarves Wlk. L33: K'by 3F **23**
Tarvin Cl. WA7: Run 4C **166**
　　WA9: Sut M 2B **88**
Tarvin Rd. CH62: East 1F **171**
Tasker Ter. L35: R'hill 2C **86**
Tasman Gro. WA9: St. H 4E **65**
Tate Cl. WA8: Wid 1D **131**
Tate Gallery 1B **98** (7B **4**)
Tate St. L4: Walt 1E **55**
Tatlock Cl. WN5: Bil 1E **31**
Tatlock St. L5: Liv 2C **76**
　　　　　　　　(not continuous)
Tattersall Pl. L20: Boot 1B **54**
Tattersall Rd. L21: Lith 1B **34**
Tattersall Way L7: Liv 4E **79**
Tatton Rd. CH42: Tran 4D **97**
　　L9: Walt 2F **35**
Taunton Av. WA9: Sut L 1D **89**
Taunton Dr. L10: Ain 3E **21**
Taunton Rd. CH45: Wall 5E **51**
　　L36: Huy 4B **84**
Taunton St. L15: W'tree 1E **101**
Taurus Rd. L14: K Ash 2A **82**
Tavener Cl. CH63: Brom 5C **162**
Tavington Rd. L26: Halew 3A **128**
Tavistock Cl. WA5: Wall 5F **51**
Tavy Rd. L6: Liv 2A **78**
Tawd St. L4: Kirk 3E **55**
Tawny Ct. WA7: Pal F 3E **167**
Taylor Cl. WA9: St. H 3E **67**
Taylor Rd. WA11: Hay 2E **49**
Taylors Cl. L9: Walt 5E **35**
Taylors La. L9: Walt 5E **35**
　　WA5: Cuerd 2F **133**
　　　　　　　　(not continuous)
Taylors Row WA7: Run 5C **152**
Taylor St. CH41: Birk 2E **97**
　　L5: Liv 1D **77**
　　WA8: Wid 3C **132**
　　WA9: St. H 4E **67**
Taylor St. Ind. Est. L5: Liv 5D **55**
Teakwood Cl. L6: Liv 1A **78**
Teal Cl. WA11: St. H 2B **46**
Teal Gro. L26: Halew 3E **127**
Teals Way CH60: Hes 2E **157**
Teasville Rd. L18: Moss H 5E **103**
Tebay Cl. L31: Mag 5F **7**
Tebay Rd. CH62: East 2E **163**
Teck St. L7: Liv 4A **78**
Tedburn Cl. L25: Gate 5C **104**
Tedbury Cl. L32: K'by 5E **23**
Tedbury Wlk. L32: K'by 5E **23**
Tedder Sq. WA8: Wid 4D **131**
Teehey Cl. CH63: High B 1D **141**
Teehey Gdns. CH63: High B 1D **141**
Teehey La. CH63: High B 1D **141**
Tees Cl. L4: Kirk 2D **55**
Teesdale Cl. CH63: Beb 3E **141**
　　WA11: Hay 1C **48**
Teesdale Way L35: R'hill 1C **86**
Tees Pl. L4: Kirk 2D **55**
Tees St. CH41: Birk 5F **73**
　　L4: Kirk 2D **55**

Teign Cl. L6: Liv 2A **78**
Teilo St. L8: Liv 4F **99**
Telary Cl. L5: Liv 1C **76**
Telegraph Rd. L23: C'by 5E **9**
Telegraph La. CH45: Wall 1C **72**
Telegraph Rd. CH48: Caldy 2F **135**
　　CH60: Hes 4D **137**
　　CH61: Thurs 2F **135**
Telegraph Way L32: K'by 3E **23**
Telford Cl. CH43: O'ton 5B **96**
　　WA8: Wid 5D **109**
Telford Ct. L7: Liv 5B **78**
Telford Dr. WA9: St. H 4F **67**
Tempest Hey L2: Liv 4C **76** (4C **4**)
Temple Cl. L2: Liv 5C **76** (5D **4**)
Temple La. L2: Liv 4C **76** (4D **4**)
Templemore Av. L18: Moss H ...1A **124**
Templemore Rd.
　　CH43: O'ton 5A **96**
Temple Rd. CH42: Tran 2C **97**
Temple St. L2: Liv 4C **76** (4D **4**)
Templeton Cres. L12: W Der 2B **58**
Tenby Av. L21: Lith 4A **18**
Tenby Dr. CH46: More 1F **93**
　　WA7: Run 5D **153**
Tenby St. L5: Liv 5A **56**
Tennis St. WA10: St. H 3D **45**
Tennis St. Nth. WA10: St. H 3E **45**
Tennyson Av. CH42: R Ferr 3F **119**
Tennyson Rd. L36: Huy 1A **106**
　　WA8: Wid 3A **132**
Tennyson St. L20: Boot 3B **34**
　　WA9: Sut M 4A **88**
Tennyson Way L32: K'by 4D **23**
Tensing Rd. L31: Mag 1D **13**
Tenterden St. L5: Liv 2D **77**
Tenth Av. L9: Ain 1D **37**
Terence Rd. L16: Child 3D **103**
Terminus Rd. CH62: Brom 4D **143**
　　L36: Huy 1B **82**
Tern Cl. L33: K'by 3E **15**
　　WA8: Wid 5B **110**
Ternhall Rd. L9: Faz 4F **37**
Ternhall Way L9: Faz 4F **37**
Tern Way CH46: More 5B **70**
　　WA10: St. H 4A **64**
Terrace Rd. WA8: Wid 2A **152**
Terret Cft. L28: Stock V 4B **60**
Tetbury St. CH41: Birk 4C **96**
Tetchill Cl. WA7: Nort 2D **169**
Tetlow St. L4: Walt 3F **55**
Tetlow Way L4: Walt 3F **55**
Teulon Cl. L4: Walt 3F **55**
Tewit Hall Cl. L24: Speke 4C **146**
Tewit Hall Rd. L24: Speke 4C **146**
Tewkesbury Cl. L12: Crox 4F **39**
　　L25: Wltn 3C **126**
Teynham Av. L34: Know 4D **41**
Teynham Cres. L11: N Grn 1F **57**
Thackeray Cl. L8: Liv 3F **99**
Thackeray Gdns. L30: Boot 5D **19**
Thackray Rd. WA10: St. H 5C **66**
Thames Cl. L8: Liv 3B **100**
Thames St. L8: Liv 3B **100**
Thatcher's Mt. WA5: C Grn 2D **69**
THATTO HEATH 3D **65**
Thatto Heath Rd. WA9: St. H ...3D **65**
　　WA10: St. H 3D **65**
Thatto Heath Station (Rail) 3D **65**
Thermal Rd. CH62: Brom 3D **143**
Thermopylae Ct. *CH43: Noct* ..*3D **95***
　　　　　　　(off Redstone Ri.)
Thermopylae Pas. CH43: Noct ...3C **94**
　　　　　　　　(not continuous)
THINGWALL 2B **138**
Thingwall Av. L14: K Ash 4D **81**
Thingwall Dr. CH61: Irby 1A **138**
Thingwall Hall Dr.
　　L14: B Grn 4D **81**
Thingwall La. L14: K Ash 3D **81**
Thingwall Recreation Cen. 1B **138**
Thingwall Rd. CH61: Irby 1D **137**
　　L15: W'tree 2B **102**
Thingwall Rd. E.
　　CH61: Thing 1A **138**

Third Av. CH43: Bid 3B **94**
L9: Ain 1E **37**
(Meres Rd.)
L9: Ain 1D **37**
(Park Av.)
L23: C'by 1D **17**
WA7: Pal F 2F **167**
Thirlmere Av. CH43: Noct 3C **94**
L21: Lith 5D **19**
WA11: St. H 5A **30**
Thirlmere Cl. L31: Mag 5E **7**
WA6: Frod 5D **173**
Thirlmere Ct. L5: Liv 1A **78**
Thirlmere Dr. CH45: Wall 1B **74**
L21: Lith 5D **19**
Thirlmere Grn. L5: Liv 1A **78**
Thirlmere Rd. L15: W'tree 1A **78**
Thirlmere Wlk. L33: K'by 1D **23**
Thirlmere Way WA8: Wid 4C **130**
Thirlstane St. L17: Aig 1B **122**
Thirsk Cl. WA7: Run 4C **166**
Thistledown Cl. L17: Aig 1F **121**
Thistleton Av. CH41: Birk 1F **95**
Thistlewood Rd. L7: Liv 4E **79**
Thistley Hey Rd. L32: K'by 3F **23**
Thomas Cl. L19: Gars 2C **144**
Thomas Ct. WA7: Pal F 3F **167**
Thomas Dr. L14: B Grn 4C **80**
L35: Prsct 2C **84**
Thomas La. L14: B Grn, K Ash 4D **81**
L14: K Ash 2D **81**
Thomas St. CH41: Birk 4E **97**
WA7: Run 4B **152**
WA8: Wid 5A **132**
Thomaston St. L5: Liv 5E **55**
(not continuous)
Thomas Winder Ct. L5: Kirk 5D **55**
Thompson St. CH41: Tran 5E **97**
WA10: St. H 2D **65**
Thomson Rd. L21: Sea 1F **33**
(not continuous)
Thomson St. L6: Liv 2B **78**
Thorburn Cl. CH62: New F 4B **120**
Thorburn Ct. CH62: New F 3B **120**
Thorburn Cres. CH62: New F 4B **120**
Thorburn Rd. CH62: New F 4B **120**
Thorburn St. L7: Liv 5B **78**
Thorley Cl. L15: W'tree 5A **80**
Thornaby Gro. WA9: St. H 5D **65**
Thornbeck Av. L38: High 1A **8**
Thornbeck Cl. L12: Crox 5E **39**
Thornbridge Av. L21: Lith 5D **19**
Thornbrook Cl. L12: W Der 4D **59**
Thornbury Rd. L4: Walt 4C **56**
Thorncliffe Rd. CH44: Wall 3A **74**
Thorn Cl. WA7: Run 3C **166**
Thorncroft Dr. CH61: Barn 3B **138**
Thorndale Rd. L22: Water 3D **17**
Thorndyke Cl. L35: R'hill 5E **87**
Thorne La. CH44: Wall 1F **73**
Thornes Rd. L6: Liv 3B **78**
Thorness Cl. CH49: Grea 2C **114**
Thorneycroft St. CH41: Birk 1A **96**
Thornfield Hey CH63: Spit 5A **142**
Thornfield Rd. L9: Walt 3F **35**
L23: Thorn 4A **10**
Thornham Av. WA9: St. H 3C **66**
Thornham Cl. CH49: Upton 4A **94**
Thornhead La. L12: W Der 5D **59**
Thornhill Rd. L15: W'tree 2A **102**
Thornholme Cres. L11: N Grn 2F **57**
Thornhurst L32: K'by 1E **39**
Thornleigh Av. CH62: East 1F **171**
Thornley Rd. CH46: More 2C **92**
Thornridge CH46: More 1A **94**
Thorn Rd. WA7: Run 3C **166**
WA10: St. H 5C **44**
Thorns, The L31: Mag 5B **6**
Thorns Dr. CH49: Grea 2C **114**
Thornside Wlk. L25: Gate 5B **104**
Thornton WA8: Wid 4E **131**
Thornton Av. CH63: High B 4D **119**
L20: Boot 1D **35**
Thornton Comn. Rd.
CH63: Raby M, Thorn H 4B **160**

Thornton Crematorium
L23: Thorn 3C **10**
Thornton Cres. CH60: Hes 4B **158**
Thornton Gro. CH63: High B 4D **119**
L36: Huy 3C **82**
THORNTON HOUGH 4A **160**
Thornton Rd. CH45: Wall 5A **52**
CH63: High B 4C **118**
L16: Child 5E **81**
L20: Boot 3C **34**
Thornton St. CH41: Birk 1A **96**
L21: Lith 2B **34**
Thorn Tree Cl. L24: Hale 5E **149**
Thorntree Cl. L17: Aig 1F **121**
Thornwood Cl. L6: Liv 1B **78**
Thornycroft Rd. L15: W'tree 2D **101**
Thorpe Bank CH42: R Ferr 4F **119**
Thorstone Dr. CH61: Irby 5C **114**
Thorsway CH42: R Ferr 2F **119**
CH48: Caldy 1D **135**
Threadneedle Ct. WA9: St. H 3F **67**
Three Acres Cl. L25: Wltn 1E **125**
Three But La. L12: W Der 5F **57**
THREE LANES END 4B **92**
Threlfall St. L8: Liv 5A **100**
Thresher Av. CH49: Grea 5C **92**
Threshers, The L30: N'ton 1B **20**
Throne Rd. L11: Crox 5C **38**
Throne Wlk. L11: Crox 4C **38**
Thurne Way L25: Gate 3A **104**
Thurnham St. L6: Liv 1C **78**
Thursby Cl. L32: K'by 5F **23**
Thursby Cres. L32: K'by 4F **23**
Thursby Rd. CH62: Brom 5E **143**
Thursby Wlk. L32: K'by 5F **23**
THURSTASTON 2B **136**
Thurstaston Rd. CH60: Hes 1E **157**
CH61: Irby, Thurs 2B **136**
Thurston Rd. L4: Walt 5B **56**
Tibb's Cross La.
WA8: Bold H 2C **110**
Tichbourne Way L6: Liv 3F **77**
Tickle Av. WA9: St. H 5D **47**
Tideswell Cl. L7: Liv 1B **100**
Tideway CH45: Wall 3E **51**
Tilbey Dr. WA6: Frod 5A **172**
Tilbrook Dr. WA9: St. H 4D **67**
Tilbury Pl. WA7: Murd 4E **169**
Tildsley Cres. WA7: West 4F **165**
Tillotson Cl. L8: Liv 4E **99**
Tilney St. L9: Walt 2A **36**
Tilstock Av. CH62: New F 4B **120**
Tilstock Cl. L26: Halew 2A **128**
Tilstock Cres. CH43: Pren 3F **117**
Tilston Cl. L9: Faz 5D **37**
Tilston Rd. CH45: Wall 5A **52**
L9: Faz 4D **37**
L32: K'by 3C **22**
Time Pk. L35: Whis 1F **85**
Timmis Cres. WA8: Wid 3A **132**
Timon Av. L20: Boot 3E **35**
Timor Av. WA9: St. H 3E **65**
Timperley Ct. WA8: Wid 4B **132**
(off Alfred Cl.)
Timpron St. L7: Liv 1B **100**
Timway Dr. L12: W Der 3E **59**
Tinas Way CH49: Upton 4A **94**
Tinling Cl. L34: Prsct 5E **63**
Tinsley Cl. L26: Halew 2E **127**
Tinsley St. L4: Walt 5A **36**
Tintagel Cl. WA7: Brook 5C **168**
Tintagel Rd. L11: Crox 3D **39**
Tintern Dr. CH46: More 1E **93**
Tiptree Cl. L12: Crox 4F **39**
Titchfield St. L3: Liv 2C **76**
L5: Liv 2C **76**
Tithebarn Cl. CH60: Hes 3F **157**
Tithebarn Gro. L15: W'tree 2A **102**
Tithe Barn La. L32: K'by 4D **23**
Tithebarn La. L31: Mell 5F **13**
Tithebarn Rd. L23: C'by 1F **17**
L34: Know 4A **40**
Tithebarn St. L2: Liv 4C **76** (4C **4**)
Tithings, The WA7: Run 1E **167**
Tiverton Av. CH44: Wall 2A **74**

Tiverton Cl. L36: Huy 3B **84**
WA8: Wid 1C **130**
Tiverton Rd. L26: Halew 1E **147**
Tiverton St. L15: W'tree 1E **101**
Tobermory Cl. WA11: Hay 3A **48**
Tobin Cl. L5: Liv 2C **76**
Tobin St. CH44: Wall 2D **75**
Tobruk Rd. L36: Huy 2D **83**
Todd Rd. WA9: St. H 5B **46**
Toft Cl. WA8: Wid 3F **131**
Toft St. L7: Liv 4C **78**
Toftwood Av. L35: R'hill 5D **87**
Toftwood Gdns. L35: R'hill 5D **87**
(not continuous)
Tokenspire Pk. L33: Know I 1B **40**
Toleman Av. CH63: Beb 2A **142**
Tollemache Rd. CH41: Birk 2E **95**
CH43: Bid 2E **95**
Tollemache St. CH45: New B 3B **52**
Tollerton Rd. L12: W Der 5F **57**
Tolpuddle Rd. L25: Wltn 1F **125**
Tolpuddle Way L4: Kirk 3D **55**
Tolver Ho. WA10: St. H 4A **46**
Tolver St. WA10: St. H 4A **46**
Tom Mann Cl. L3: Liv 3D **77** (3F **5**)
Tommy Gent Way L31: Mag 2D **13**
Tonbridge Cl. L24: Speke 3B **146**
Tonbridge Dr. L10: Ain 2D **21**
Topaz Cl. L4: Walt 1E **55**
Topcliffe Gro. L12: Crox 5A **40**
Topgate Cl. CH60: Hes 2B **158**
Topham Dr. L9: Ain 3B **20**
Topham Ter. L9: Ain 5B **20**
Topsham Cl. L25: Gate 5C **104**
Torcross Way L25: Wltn 5C **104**
L26: Halew 3E **127**
Tordelow Cl. L6: Liv 2A **78**
Toronto Cl. L36: Huy 4D **61**
Toronto St. CH44: Wall 3E **75**
Torr Dr. CH62: East 3F **163**
Torrington Dr. CH61: Thing 1B **138**
L26: Halew 5E **127**
Torrington Gdns. CH61: Thing 5B **116**
Torrington Rd. CH44: Wall 2A **74**
L19: Gras 5B **124**
Torrisholme Rd. L9: Ain 5D **37**
Torr St. L5: Liv 5E **55**
(not continuous)
Torus Rd. L13: Liv 2A **80**
Torview L15: W'tree 3A **102**
Torwood CH43: Noct 3D **95**
Total Fitness
Netherton 1B **20**
Prenton 3D **117**
Victoria Pk. 5F **79**
Tothale Turn L27: N'ley 5F **105**
Totnes Av. L26: Halew 3F **127**
Totnes Rd. L11: Crox 3C **38**
Tourist Info. Cen.
Liverpool 1C **98** (7C **4**)
Queen Sq. 4D **77** (5F **5**)
Runcorn 4A **152**
Runcorn (Town Hall) 1B **166**
Towcester St. L21: Lith 2C **34**
Tower Gdns. L3: Liv 5B **76** (5C **4**)
TOWER HILL 5F **15**
Tower Hill CH42: Tran 1D **119**
Towerlands St. L7: Liv 5A **78**
Tower La. WA7: Nort 3C **168**
Tower Prom. CH45: New B 2C **52**
Tower Quays CH41: Birk 1E **97**
Tower Rd. CH41: Birk 1E **97**
CH42: Tran 3B **118**
(Reservoir Rd.)
CH42: Tran 1D **119**
(Stuart Rd.)
Tower Rd. Nth. CH60: Hes 5E **137**
Tower Rd. Sth. CH60: Hes 1F **157**
Towers, The CH42: Tran 2E **119**
Towers Av. L31: Mag 5C **6**
Towers Rd. L16: Child 3C **102**
Tower St. L3: Liv 4D **99**
Tower Way L25: Wltn 1A **126**
Tower Wharf CH41: Birk 1E **97**
Towneley Ct. WA8: Wid 3A **132**

TOWN END 3C 108
Townfield Cl. CH43: O'ton 1E 117
Townfield Gdns. CH63: High B . .5F 119
Townfield La. CH43: O'ton 1E 117
 CH63: Beb, High B 5F 119
 WA6: Frod 5C 172
Townfield Rd. CH48: W Kir 4B 112
 WA7: Wind H 5C 154
Town Flds. CH45: Wall 5E 51
Townfield Vw. WA7: Wind H . . .5C 154
Townfield Way CH44: Wall 2B 74
Town Hall Dr. WA7: Run 1B 166
Town La. CH63: High B 1D 141
 L24: Hale 5D 149
Townley Ct. CH47: Hoy 4B 90
 (off Marmion Rd.)
Town Mdw. La. CH46: More 5B 70
Town Rd. CH42: Tran 1D 119
Town Row L12: W Der 4B 58
Townsend Av. L11: N Grn. 5E 37
 L13: Liv 3E 57
Townsend La. L6: Liv 5C 56
 L13: Liv 5C 56
Townsend St. CH41: Birk 5E 73
 L5: Kirk 5B 54
Townsend Vw. L11: N Grn. 5E 37
 L21: Ford 3B 18
Townshend Av. CH61: Irby 2D 137
Town Sq. WA7: Pal F 3F 167
 (off Halton Lea Shop. Cen.)
Town Vw. CH43: O'ton 4C 96
Town Vw. M. CH43: O'ton 4C 96
Town Wlk. WA7: Pal F 3F 167
 (off Halton Lea Shop. Cen.)
Towson Dr. L5: Liv 5F 55
 (not continuous)
TOXTETH 4E 99
Toxteth Gro. L8: Liv 5A 100
Toxteth Sports Cen. 3F 99
Toxteth St. L8: Liv 4E 99
Tradewind Sq. L1: Liv 1D 99
TRAFALGAR 3A 142
Trafalgar Av. CH44: Wall 1D 75
Trafalgar Cl. WA8: Wid 1A 152
Trafalgar Dr. CH63: Beb 3A 142
Trafalgar Rd. CH44: Wall 1C 74
Trafalgar St. WA10: St. H 4E 45
Trafalgar Way L6: Liv 3F 77
Trafford Cres. WA7: Run 4C 166
Tramway Rd. L17: Aig 1C 122
TRANMERE 1E 119
Tranmere Rovers FC 2C 118
Trapwood Cl. WA10: Eccl 5A 44
Travanson Cl. L10: Faz 2B 38
Travers' Entry WA9: Bold 4A 68
Traverse St. WA9: St. H 5C 46
Travis Dr. L33: K'by 5F 15
Travis St. WA8: Wid 4B 132
Trawden Way L21: Ford 1C 18
Treborth St. L8: Liv 1A 24
Trecastle Rd. L33: K'by 1A 24
Treebank Cl. WA7: Run 2A 166
Treetop Ct. L6: Liv 2B 78
Treetops Dr. CH41: Birk 5D 73
Tree Vw. CH. L31: Mag 2E 13
Treforris Rd. CH45: Wall 4F 51
Trefula Pk. L12: W Der 5A 58
Trelawney Cl. L25: Gate 3B 104
Tremore Cl. L12: W Der 2B 58
Trenance Cl. WA7: Brook 5B 168
Trendeal Rd. L11: Crox 3D 39
Trent Av. L14: B Grn 3F 81
 L31: Mag 5F 7
Trent Cl. L12: Crox 5D 39
 L35: R'hill 3B 86
 WA8: Wid 5B 110
 WA9: Sut L 1C 88
Trentham Av. L18: Moss H 4F 101
Trentham Cl. WA8: Wid 5B 110
Trentham Rd. CH44: Wall 3C 74
 L32: K'by 4C 22
Trentham St. WA7: Run 4F 151
Trentham Wlk. L32: K'by 4C 22
Trent Pl. L35: R'hill 3B 86
 (not continuous)

Trent Rd. L35: R'hill 3B 86
 WN5: Bil 1C 30
Trent St. CH41: Birk 5F 73
 L5: Kirk 5C 54
Trent Way CH60: Hes 4C 158
 L21: Lith 4A 18
Tressel Dr. WA9: Sut M 3A 88
Tresserial St. L9: Walt 5F 35
Trevelyan St. L9: Walt 5F 35
Treviot Cl. L33: K'by 4D 15
Trevor Dr. L23: C'by 1F 17
Trevor Rd. L9: Walt 2A 36
Triad, The L20: Boot 4C 34
Trident Pk. WA7: Pal F 3E 167
Trimley Cl. CH49: Upton 4E 93
Tring Cl. CH49: Upton 2A 94
Trinity Cl. CH47: Hoy 4B 90
Trinity Gdns. CH47: Hoy 4B 90
 WA6: Frod 4C 172
Trinity Gro. L23: Blun 2B 16
Trinity Ho. WA6: Frod 4C 172
Trinity La. CH41: Birk 2E 97
Trinity Pl. L20: Boot 5D 35
 WA8: Wid 5B 132
Trinity Rd. CH44: Wall 1B 74
 CH47: Hoy 4B 90
 L20: Boot 1C 54
Trinity St. CH41: Birk 2C 96
 WA7: Run 4B 152
 WA9: St. H 4E 46
Trinity Wlk. L3: Liv 3E 77 (2H 5)
Trispen Cl. L26: Halew 4E 127
Trispen Rd. L11: Crox 4D 39
Trispen Wlk. L11: Crox 4D 39
Tristram's Cft. L30: N'ton 2D 19
Triumph Trad. Pk. L24: Hunts X . .1A 146
Triumph Trading Pk., The
 L24: Speke 1F 145
Triumph Way
 L24: Hunts X, Speke 1F 145
Troon Cl. CH63: Brom 5E 59
 L12: W Der 5E 59
 L33: Hay 3A 48
Trotwood Cl. L9: Ain 5D 21
Troutbeck Av. L31: Mag 5E 7
 WA12: New W 4E 49
Troutbeck Cl. CH49: W'chu 5A 168
 WA7: Beech 5A 168
Troutbeck Gro. WA11: St. H 3B 32
Troutbeck Rd. L18: Moss H 4D 103
Trouville Rd. L4: Walt 4C 36
Trowbridge St. L3: Liv 5E 77 (5H 5)
Trueman Cl. CH43: Bid 1C 94
Trueman St. L3: Liv 4D 77 (3E 4)
Truman Cl. WA8: Wid 1F 131
Truro Av. L30: N'ton 1F 19
Truro Cl. WA7: Brook 4C 168
 WA11: St. H 1D 47
Truro Rd. L15: W'tree 3A 102
Tudor Av. CH44: Wall 4E 75
 CH63: Beb 4A 142
Tudor Cl. L7: Liv 5F 77 (6J 5)
Tudor Cl. L19: Gras 5A 124
Tudor Grange CH49: Grea 1D 115
Tudor Rd. CH42: Tran 1E 119
 L23: C'by 2D 17
 L25: Hunts X 5C 126
 WA7: Mnr P 4B 154
Tudor St. Nth. L6: Liv 3B 78
Tudor St. Sth. L6: Liv 3B 78
Tudor Vw. L33: K'by 5E 15
 (not continuous)
Tudorville Rd. CH63: Beb 2F 141
Tudorway CH60: Hes 2B 158
TUE BROOK 5E 57
Tue La. WA8: Cron 3B 108
Tuffins Cnr. L27: N'ley 4D 105
Tulip Av. CH41: Birk 1F 95
Tulip Rd. L15: W'tree 2A 102
 WA11: Hay 2F 49
Tullimore Rd. L18: Moss H 3F 123
Tullis St. WA10: St. H 1E 65
Tulloch St. L6: Liv 3B 78
Tully Av. WA12: New W 5E 49
Tumilty Av. L20: Boot 4E 35

Tunnage Sq. L1: Liv 1D 99 (7F 5)
Tunnel Rd. CH41: Birk 4E 97
 L7: Liv 1B 100
Tunnel Top Nth.
 WA4: Pres H 4F 169
 WA7: Dutt, Pres B 4F 169
Tunstall Cl. CH49: Upton 4E 93
Tunstall St. L7: Liv 2C 100
Tunstalls Way WA9: Clock F 2D 89
Tupelo Cl. L12: Crox 4F 39
Tupman St. L8: Liv 4F 99
Turmar Av. CH61: Thing 1B 138
Turnacre L14: B Grn 3E 81
Turnall Rd. WA8: Wid 5B 130
Turnberry Cl. CH46: More 5B 70
 L12: W Der 5F 59
 L36: Roby 5C 82
Turnbridge Rd. L31: Mag 4C 6
Turner Av. L20: Boot 1E 35
Turner Cl. L8: Liv 1A 122
 WA8: Wid 1D 131
Turner Gro. L33: K'by 4E 15
Turner Home, The L8: Liv 5A 100
Turners Cl. WA9: Gate 1B 126
Turner St. CH41: Birk 4C 96
Turney Rd. CH44: Wall 2A 74
Turnstone Cl. L12: Crox 5E 39
Turnstone Dr. L26: Halew 3E 127
Turret Rd. CH45: Wall 5A 52
Turriff Dr. CH63: East 1C 170
Turriff Rd. L14: K Ash 2A 82
Turton Cl. L24: Hale 5D 149
Turton St. L5: Kirk 5D 55
Tuscan Cl. WA8: Wid 4B 110
Tuson Dr. WA8: Wid 5F 109
Tweed Cl. L6: Liv 2B 78
Tweed St. CH41: Birk 5A 74
Twickenham Dr. CH46: Leas 3F 71
 L36: Roby 5C 82
Twickenham St. L6: Liv 5B 56
Twigden Cl. L10: Faz 5F 21
Twig La. L31: Mag 1E 13
 L36: Huy 3C 82
Two Butt La. L35: Whis, R'hill . . .1A 86
Twomey Cl. L5: Liv 2C 76
Twyford Av. L21: Lith 4B 18
Twyford Cl. L31: Mag 1E 13
 WA8: Wid 4B 110
Twyford La. WA8: Wid 2C 110
Twyford Pl. WA9: St. H 5C 46
Twyford St. L6: Liv 5B 56
Tyberton Pl. L25: Hunts X 1C 146
Tyburn Cl. CH63: Spit 5F 141
Tyburn Rd. CH63: Spit 5F 141
Tyndall Av. L22: Water 5F 17
Tyne Cl. L4: Kirk 3E 55
 WA9: St. H 5D 65
Tynemouth Cl. L5: Liv 1A 78
Tynemouth Rd. WA7: Murd 4C 168
Tyne St. CH41: Birk 5F 73
Tynron Gro. CH43: Noct 5D 95
Tynville Rd. L9: Ain 1C 36
Tynwald Cl. L13: Liv 1F 79
Tynwald Cres. WA8: Wid 4F 109
Tynwald Hill L13: Liv 2F 79
Tynwald Pl. L13: Liv 2F 79
Tynwald Rd. CH48: W Kir 4A 112
Tyrer Gro. L34: Prsct 4E 63
Tyrers Av. L31: Lyd 2B 6
Tyrer St. CH41: Birk 5F 73
 L1: Liv 5D 77 (5F 5)

U

UGC Cinema 5F 79
Uldale Cl. L11: N Grn. 1A 58
Uldale Way L11: N Grn. 1A 58
Ullet Rd. L8: Liv 5B 100
 L17: Aig 5B 100
Ullet Wlk. L17: Aig 4D 101
Ullswater Av. CH43: Noct 3D 95
 WA11: St. H 5A 30
Ullswater Cl. L33: K'by 1D 23
Ullswater Gro. WA7: Beech 5D 167

Ullswater Ho. L17: Aig 2D **123**
Ullswater St. L5: Liv 5A **56**
Ulster Rd. L13: Liv 3B **80**
Ultonia St. L19: Gars 3C **144**
Ulverscroft CH43: O'ton 5F **95**
Ulverston Cl. L31: Mag 5E **7**
  WA11: Hay 2A **48**
Ulverston Lawn L27: N'ley 5F **105**
Umbria St. L19: Gars 3C **144**
Undercliffe Rd. L13: Liv 2A **80**
Underhill Rd. WA10: St. H 1D **65**
Underley St. L7: Liv 2C **100**
Underley Ter. CH62: New F 5B **120**
Underway, The WA7: Halt 2F **167**
Unicorn Rd. L11: Crox 4C **38**
Unicorn Way CH41: Tran 4F **97**
Union Bank La. WA8: Bold H 5B **88**
Union Cl. L2: Liv 5C **76** (5D **4**)
Union St. CH42: Tran 1E **119**
  CH44: Wall 2D **75**
  L3: Liv 4B **76** (4B **4**)
  WA7: Run 5B **152**
  WA10: St. H 3A **46**
Union Ter. CH45: New B 2B **52**
Unity Gro. L34: Know 2A **40**
Unity Theatre 7H **5**
University of Liverpool 5J **5**
University of Liverpool Art Gallery
  . . . . .5F **77**
University of Liverpool Sports Cen.
  . . . . .5F **77**
University Rd. L20: Boot 1D **55**
Upavon Av. CH49: Grea 1B **114**
Upchurch Cl. L8: Liv 5F **99**
Upland Cl. WA10: St. H 3B **64**
Upland Rd. CH49: Upton 3F **93**
  WA10: St. H 3B **64**
Uplands, The CH43: O'ton 5E **95**
  WA7: Pal F 3F **167**
Uplands Rd. CH62: Brom 1C **162**
Up. Baker St. L6: Liv 3A **78**
Up. Beau St. L5: Liv 2E **77** (1G **5**)
Up. Beckwith St. CH41: Birk 1B **96**
UPPER BIDSTON VILLAGE 5C **72**
Up. Brassey St. CH41: Birk 1F **95**
Up. Bute St. L5: Liv 2E **77** (1H **5**)
Up. Duke St. L1: Liv 1E **99** (7G **5**)
Up. Essex St. L8: Liv 4F **99**
Up. Flaybrick Rd. CH41: Birk 2E **95**
Up. Frederick St. L1: Liv 1D **99** (7E **5**)
  (not continuous)
Up. Hampton St. L8: Liv 2F **99**
Up. Harrington St. L8: Liv 3E **99**
Up. Hill St. L8: Liv 3E **99**
  (not continuous)
Up. Hope Pl. L7: Liv 1F **99** (7J **5**)
Up. Huskisson St. L8: Liv 2A **100**
Up. Mann St. L8: Liv 3E **99**
  (not continuous)
Up. Mason St. L7: Liv 5A **78**
Up. Mersey Rd. WA8: Wid 2A **152**
Up. Newington L1: Liv 5E **77** (6G **5**)
Up. Park St. L8: Liv 4F **99**
Up. Parliament St. L8: Liv 2E **99**
Up. Pitt St. L1: Liv 1D **99**
Up. Pownall St. L1: Liv 1D **99**
Up. Rice La. CH44: Wall 1C **74**
Up. Stanhope St. L8: Liv 2E **99**
  (not continuous)
Up. Warwick St. L8: Liv 3F **99**
Up. William St. L3: Liv 2B **76**
Uppingham Av. L10: Ain 3E **21**
Uppingham Rd. CH44: Wall 1F **73**
  L13: Liv 1F **79**
UPTON
  Widnes 1C **130**
  Wirral .4A **94**
Upton Barn L31: Mag 5C **6**
Upton Bridle Path WA8: Wid 5F **109**
  (not continuous)
Upton By-Pass CH49: Upton 3E **93**
Upton Cl. CH49: Upton 4F **93**
  L24: Speke 4E **147**
Upton Ct. CH49: Upton 3A **94**
Upton Grange WA8: Wid 1D **131**

Upton Grn. L24: Speke 4E **147**
Upton La. WA8: Wid 5E **109**
Upton Pk. Dr. CH49: Upton 3A **94**
Upton Rd. CH41: Birk 3D **95**
  CH43: Bid, Noct, C'ton 4C **94**
  CH46: More 1E **93**
UPTON ROCKS 1F **131**
Upton Rocks Av.
  WA8: Wid 5E **109**
Upton Rocks M. WA8: Wid 5E **109**
Upton Station (Rail) 4C **94**
Urmson Rd. CH45: Wall 1B **74**
Ursula St. L20: Boot 2D **55**
Utkinton Cl. CH43: O'ton 1F **117**
Utting Av. L4: Walt 4B **56**
Utting Av. E. L11: N Grn. 2E **57**
UVECO Bus. Cen. CH41: Birk 4A **74**
Uxbridge St. L7: Liv 1B **100**
  (not continuous)

V

Vahler Ter. WA7: Run 5C **152**
Vale Cl. L25: Wltn 2F **125**
Vale Ct. WA4: Dutt 2F **175**
Vale Dr. CH45: New B 4C **52**
Vale Gdns. L32: K'by 4A **24**
Vale Lodge L9: Walt 4F **35**
Valencia Gro. L34: Ecc P 4F **63**
Valencia Rd. L15: W'tree 1A **102**
Valentia Rd. CH47: Hoy 5A **90**
Valentine Gro. L10: Ain 4E **21**
Valentine Rd. WA12: New W 5F **49**
Valentines Bldg. L9: Ain 4C **20**
Valentines Way L9: Ain 3C **20**
Valerie Cl. L10: Faz 2B **38**
Vale Rd. L23: C'by 1D **17**
  L25: Wltn 1E **125**
Valescourt Rd. L12: W Der 1C **80**
Valeview Towers L25: Wltn 2F **125**
Valiant Cl. L12: Crox 1A **60**
Valiant Way CH41: Tran 5F **97**
Valkyrie Rd. CH45: Wall 1A **74**
Vallance Rd. L4: Walt 4C **56**
Valleybrook Gro. CH63: Spit 5B **142**
Valley Cl. L10: Ain 4F **21**
  L23: C'by 1B **18**
Valley Community Theatre 4D **105**
Valley Rd. CH41: Birk 4D **73**
  CH62: Brom 2D **163**
  L4: Walt 5A **56**
  L10: Faz 5A **22**
  L32: K'by 5A **22**
Valley Rd. Bus. Pk.
  CH41: Birk 5E **73**
Vanbrugh Cres. L4: Walt 4C **56**
Vanbrugh Rd. L4: Walt 3C **56**
Vancouver Rd. L27: N'ley 4E **105**
Vanderbilt Av. L9: Ain 5B **20**
Vanderbyl Av. CH62: Spit 5C **142**
Vandries St. L3: Liv 2B **76** (1A **4**)
Vandyke St. L8: Liv 2B **100**
Vanguard St. L5: Liv 5F **55**
Vanguard Way CH41: Tran 1F **119**
Vardon St. CH41: Birk 1C **96**
Varley Rd. L19: Aig 3A **124**
  WA9: St. H 4C **46**
Varthen St. L5: Liv 4F **55**
Vatt Way L7: Liv 5C **78**
Vaughan Av. CH45: New B 4B **52**
Vaughan St. CH41: Birk 1F **95**
Vaux Cres. L20: Boot 3D **35**
VAUXHALL 3C **76**
Vauxhall Rd. L3: Liv 3C **76** (1D **4**)
  L5: Liv 3C **76**
Vaux Pl. L20: Boot 3D **35**
Venables Cl. CH63: Spit 1B **162**
Venables Dr. CH63: Spit 5A **142**
Venice St. L5: Liv 5F **55**
Venmore St. L5: Liv 5F **55**
  (not continuous)
Ventnor Rd. L15: W'tree 1F **101**

Venture Ct. CH41: Birk 4E **97**
  (off Clifton Rd.)
Venturepoint Bus. Pk.
  L24: Speke 2C **146**
Venture Works L33: Know I 4C **24**
Verbena Cl. WA7: Beech 1F **173**
Verdala Pk. L18: Moss H 2C **124**
Verdi Av. L21: Sea 2A **34**
Verdi St. L21: Sea 2A **34**
Verdi Ter. L21: Sea 2F **33**
Vere St. L8: Liv 4E **99**
  (not continuous)
Vermont Av. L23: C'by 1D **17**
Vermont Cl. L33: K'by 3D **15**
Vermont Rd. L23: C'by 1D **17**
Vermont Way L20: Boot 4C **34**
Verney Cres. L19: Aller 4C **124**
Verney Cres. Sth. L19: Aller 4C **124**
Vernon Av. CH44: Wall 4D **75**
  CH66: Hoot 3F **171**
Vernon St. L2: Liv 4C **76** (3D **4**)
  WA9: St. H 4C **46**
Verona St. L5: Liv 5F **55**
Veronica M. WA8: Wid 3D **131**
Verulam Cl. L8: Liv 2A **100**
Verwood Cl. CH61: Irby 5D **115**
Verwood Dr. L12: Crox 5A **40**
Veryan Cl. L26: Halew 3F **127**
Vescock St. L5: Liv 1D **77**
Vesta Rd. L19: Gars 3D **145**
Vesuvius Pl. L5: Kirk 5D **55**
Vesuvius St. L5: Kirk 5D **55**
Viaduct St. WA8: Wid 3A **152**
  WA12: New W 5F **49**
Vicarage Cl. CH42: Tran 3B **118**
  L18: Moss H 2B **124**
  L24: Hale 5E **149**
Vicarage Dr. WA11: Hay 1A **48**
Vicarage Gro. CH44: Wall 1C **74**
Vicarage Lawn L25: Gate 4C **104**
Vicarage Pl. L34: Prsct 5C **62**
Vicarage Rd. WA8: Wid 5A **132**
  WA11: Hay 1A **48**
Vicar Rd. L6: Liv 4C **56**
Viceroy St. L5: Liv 5F **55**
Vickers Rd. WA8: Wid 2E **151**
Victoria Av. CH60: Hes 4A **158**
  L14: B Grn 4D **81**
  L15: W'tree 1F **101**
  L23: Blun 1C **16**
  WA8: Wid 1A **132**
  WA11: St. H 5A **30**
Victoria Cl. L17: Aig 1E **123**
Victoria Ct. L15: W'tree 1F **101**
  L17: Aig 5B **100**
Victoria Dr. CH42: R Ferr 3A **120**
  CH48: W Kir 4A **112**
  L9: Walt 2F **35**
Victoria Falls Rd. L27: N'ley 5F **105**
Victoria Flds. CH42: Tran 5C **96**
Victoria Gdns. CH43: O'ton 5B **96**
Victoria Gro. WA8: Wid 1A **132**
Victoria Hall L2: Liv 3D **4**
Victoria Ho. L34: Prsct 5D **63**
Victoria La. CH43: O'ton 5B **96**
Victoria Mt. CH43: O'ton 5B **96**
Victoria Pde. CH45: New B 2C **52**
VICTORIA PARK
  Bootle 1E **35**
  Liverpool 1F **101**
Victoria Pk.
  Birchfield Rd. 2A **132**
  City Rd. 2F **45**
Victoria Pk. Glasshouses 3A **132**
Victoria Pk. Rd. CH42: Tran 2D **119**
Victoria Pl. CH44: Wall 4E **75**
  L35: R'hill 3C **86**
Victoria Prom. WA8: Wid 3A **152**
Victoria Rd. CH42: Tran 5C **96**
  CH45: New B 3A **52**
  CH48: W Kir 5B **112**
  CH63: High B 1D **141**
  L13: Liv 5E **57**
  L17: Aig 1E **123**

Victoria Rd. L22: Water 5E **17**
 L23: C'by 1D **17**
 L36: Huy 4F **83**
 WA7: Run 5A **152**
 (not continuous)
 WA8: Wid 5A **132**
Victoria Rd. W. L23: Blun 1C **16**
Victoria Sq. WA8: Wid 5A **132**
 WA10: St. H 4A **46**
Victoria St. CH62: Port S 2B **142**
 L1: Liv 5C **76** (5D **4**)
 L2: Liv 5C **76** (5D **4**)
 L35: R'hill 3C **86**
 WA8: Wid 5B **132**
 WA10: St. H 3A **46**
Victoria Ter. L15: W'tree 3A **102**
 (off Pearson Ct., not continuous)
 L35: R'hill 3C **86**
Victoria Trad Est. L35: R'hill 3C **86**
Victoria Trad. Est. WA8: Wid . . .1A **152**
Victoria Vs. L35: R'hill 3C **86**
Victor St. L15: W'tree 1D **101**
Victory Cl. L30: Boot 5E **19**
Vienna St. L5: Liv 5F **55**
Viennese Rd. L25: Gate 3B **104**
Viewpark Cl. L16: Child 2F **103**
View Rd. L35: R'hill 1A **34**
Viking Cl. L21: Lith 1A **34**
Village, The CH63: Beb 1A **142**
Village Cl. CH45: Wall 5E **51**
 WA7: Cas 2A **168**
Village Ct. CH61: Irby 1D **137**
 L17: Aig 2C **122**
Village Courts L30: N'ton 5F **11**
Village Grn. Ct. CH43: Bid 1C **94**
Village M. CH45: Wall 5E **51**
Village Nook L10: Ain 3E **21**
Village Rd. CH43: O'ton 5A **96**
 CH48: W Kir 4C **112**
 CH60: Hes 3F **157**
 CH63: High B 1D **141**
Village Sq. CH64: Will 5A **170**
Village St. L6: Liv 2F **77**
 WA7: Nort 5D **155**
Village Way CH45: Wall 5E **51**
Villa Gloria Cl. L19: Aig 4A **124**
Villas Rd. L31: Mag 1B **14**
Villiers Ct. L34: Know 3B **40**
Villiers Cres. WA10: Eccl 3F **43**
Villiers Rd. L34: Know 2B **40**
Vincent Cl. L1: Liv 1D **99** (7F **5**)
Vincent Naughton Ct.
 CH41: Birk 4E **97**
Vincent Rd. L21: Lith 4C **18**
 L35: R'hill 2B **86**
Vincent St. CH41: Birk 3D **97**
 L13: Liv 5F **79**
 WA10: St. H 4A **46**
Vineries, The L25: Wltn 1E **125**
Vineside Rd. L12: W Der 1D **81**
Vine St. CH41: Birk 2C **96**
 L7: Liv 1F **99**
 WA7: Run 5A **152**
 WA8: Wid 5A **132**
Vine Ter. WA8: Wid 2A **130**
Vineyard St. L19: Gars 2E **145**
Vining Rd. L35: Prsct 5F **63**
Vining St. L8: Liv 3F **99**
Viola Cl. L33: K'by 5D **15**
Viola St. L20: Boot 2C **54**
Violet Rd. CH41: Birk 2F **95**
 L21: Lith 2B **34**
Violet St. WA8: Wid 5A **132**
Virgil St. L5: Liv 2D **77**
 WA10: St. H 4E **45**
Virginia Av. L31: Lyd 4C **6**
Virginia Gro. L31: Lyd 4C **6**
Virginia Rd. CH45: New B 2B **52**
Virginia St. L3: Liv 4B **76** (3B **4**)
Virgin's La. L23: Thorn 3F **9**
Viscount Cen. L24: Speke 2D **147**
Viscount Dr. L24: Hale 5E **147**
Vista Rd. WA7: Run 2A **166**
 WA11: Hay 1F **49**
 WA12: New W 4F **49**

Vista Way WA12: New W 4F **49**
Vitesse Rd. L24: Speke 1F **145**
Vittoria Cl. CH41: Birk 2D **97**
Vittoria Cl. CH41: Birk 2D **97**
Vittoria St. CH41: Birk 2C **96**
Vivian Av. CH44: Wall 4E **75**
Vixen Gro. WA8: Wid 5F **109**
Voelas St. L8: Liv 3A **100**
Vogan Av. L23: C'by 2A **18**
Volunteer St. WA6: Frod 4D **173**
 WA10: St. H 4F **45**
Vronhill Cl. L8: Liv 3A **100**
Vue Cinema 3D **97**
Vulcan Cl. CH41: Birk 1F **95**
Vulcan St. CH41: Birk 1F **95**
 L3: Liv 2B **76**
 L19: Gars 3C **144**
 L20: Boot 4A **34**
Vyner Cl. CH43: Noct 3E **95**
Vyner Ct. CH43: Noct 3E **95**
Vyner Rd. CH45: Wall 1F **73**
Vyner Rd. Nth. CH43: Bid 2D **95**
 L25: Gate 4A **104**
Vyner Rd. Sth. CH43: Bid 3D **95**
 L25: Gate 4A **104**
Vyrnwy St. L5: Liv 4F **55**

W

WADDICAR 1B **22**
Waddicar La. L31: Mell 2A **22**
Wadebridge Rd. L10: Faz 2A **38**
Wadeson Rd. L4: Walt 1D **57**
Wadham Pk. L20: Boot 1C **54**
Wadham Rd. L20: Boot 2C **54**
Wagon La. WA11: Hay 4A **48**
Waine Gro. L35: Whis 1A **86**
Waine St. WA9: St. H 4D **47**
 WA11: Hay 2F **47**
Wainwright Cl. L7: Liv 1B **100**
Wainwright Gro. L19: Gars 1B **144**
Wakefield Dr. CH46: Leas 2F **71**
Wakefield Rd. L30: N'ton 3A **20**
Wakefield St. L3: Liv 3E **77** (2G **5**)
Walby Cl. CH49: W'chu 2C **116**
Walden Rd. L14: K Ash 3C **80**
Waldgrave Pl. L15: W'tree 5B **80**
Waldgrave Rd. L15: W'tree 5A **80**
Waldron Cl. L3: Liv 3C **76** (2D **4**)
Walford Cl. CH63: Spit 5F **141**
Walk, The L24: Speke 5F **145**
 L28: Stock V 4C **60**
Walker Av. WA9: Sut M 3B **88**
Walker Dr. L20: Boot 1C **54**
Walker Gallery, The 4D **77** (3F **5**)
Walker M. CH47: Tran 1D **119**
Walker Pl. CH42: Tran 1D **119**
Walker Rd. L21: Lith 1A **34**
Walker's Cft. CH45: Wall 1F **73**
Walkers La. WA9: Sut M 3A **88**
Walker St. CH42: Tran 1D **119**
 CH47: Hoy 4B **90**
 CH62: Port S 1C **142**
 L6: Liv 3A **78**
Walker Way L9: Walt 2F **35**
Wallace Av. L36: Huy 2A **84**
Wallace Dr. L36: Huy 2F **83**
Wallace St. L9: Ain 2A **36**
 WA8: Wid 4A **132**
Wallacre Rd. CH44: Wall 2E **73**
WALLASEY 1E **73**
Wallasey Bri. Rd. CH41: Birk . . .5F **73**
Wallasey Grove Road (Rail) 5E **51**
Wallasey Rd. CH44: Wall 2F **73**
 CH45: Wall 2F **73**
Wallasey Village CH44: Wall 5E **51**
 CH45: Wall 5E **51**
Wallasey Village Station (Rail) . .1E **73**
Wallcroft CH64: Will 5A **170**
Waller Cl. L4: Kirk 4E **55**
Waller St. L20: Boot 2A **34**
Wallgate Rd. L25: Gate 2F **103**
Wallgate Way L25: Gate 3F **103**
Wallingford Rd. CH49: Upton 5F **93**

Wallrake CH60: Hes 3F **157**
Wallsend Ct. WA8: Wid 1F **131**
Walmer Rd. L22: Water 5E **17**
Walmesley Rd. WA10: Eccl 3A **44**
Walmsley St. CH44: Wall 1C **74**
 WA8: Wid 4C **132**
Walney Rd. L12: W Der 3A **58**
Walney Ter. L12: W Der 3A **58**
Walnut Av. L9: Walt 5C **36**
Walnut Gro. L31: Mell 2A **22**
 WA9: St. H 3B **66**
Walnut St. L7: Liv 5F **77** (6J **5**)
Walpole Av. L35: Whis 3F **85**
Walpole Rd. WA7: Run 3B **166**
Walsall Gdns. WA9: St. H 5E **65**
Walsh Cl. L5: Liv 1C **76**
Walsh Rd. L14: B Grn 4C **80**
 (not continuous)
Walsingham Ct. CH44: Wall 3D **75**
 (off Liscard Rd.)
Walsingham Dr. WA7: Nort 5D **155**
Walsingham Rd. CH44: Wall 3D **75**
 L16: Child 5E **81**
Walter Beilin Ct. L17: Aig 4E **101**
Walter Gro. WA9: St. H 4F **67**
Walter St. L5: Liv 1B **76**
 WA8: Wid 3D **133**
Waltham Ct. WA7: Nort 3E **155**
Waltham Rd. L6: Liv 5C **56**
Waltho Av. L31: Mag 1E **13**
WALTON 1A **56**
Walton Breck Rd. L4: Walt 4F **55**
Walton Hall Av. L4: Walt 1A **56**
 L11: N Grn 1B **56**
Walton La. L4: Walt 4F **55**
Walton Lodge Rd. L9: Walt 4F **35**
Walton Pk. L9: Walt 4A **36**
Walton Pk. Gdns. L4: Walt 1A **56**
Walton Rd. L4: Walt 4E **55**
 WA10: St. H 2D **45**
Walton Sports Cen. 1B **56**
Walton Station (Rail) 4F **35**
Walton St. CH41: Birk 3E **97**
 WA7: Run 5A **152**
Walton Va. L9: Walt, Ain 2A **36**
Walton Village L4: Walt 1F **55**
 (not continuous)
Wambo La. L25: Gate 4C **104**
Wandsworth Rd. L11: N Grn. 2F **57**
Wandsworth Way WA8: Wid 1F **151**
Wango La. L10: Ain 4E **21**
Wantage Vw. L36: Roby 5C **82**
Wapping L1: Liv 1C **98** (7D **4**)
Wapping Quay L3: Liv 2C **98**
Wapshare Rd. L11: N Grn. 2E **57**
Warbler Cl. L26: Halew 2D **127**
Warbreck Av. L9: Walt, Ain 1A **36**
Warbreck Moor L9: Ain 1B **36**
WARBRECK PARK 1B **36**
Warbreck Rd. L9: Walt 2A **36**
Warburton Hey L35: R'hill 2B **86**
Warden St. L4: Kirk 3E **55**
Wardgate Av. L12: Crox 5E **39**
Ward Gro. CH42: R Ferr 4F **119**
Ward Rake L30: N'ton 5A **8**
Ward Rd. L23: Blun 5C **16**
Ward St. L3: Liv 4E **77** (4G **5**)
 L34: Prsct 4D **63**
 WA10: St. H 4A **46**
Wareham Cl. WA11: Hay 2C **48**
Wareing Rd. L9: Ain 2C **36**
Waresley Cres. L9: Faz 4E **37**
Warham Rd. L4: Walt 4C **56**
Waring Av. CH42: Tran 2D **119**
 WA9: St. H 1B **68**
Warkworth Cl. L36: Huy 1B **106**
 WA8: Wid 1C **130**
Warmington Rd. L14: K Ash 3C **80**
Warner Dr. L4: Walt 3C **56**
Warnerville Rd. L13: Liv 5B **80**
Warnley Cl. WA8: Wid 1D **131**
Warren, The CH49: Upton 4B **94**
 WA12: New W 5F **49**
Warren Cft. WA7: Nort 3C **168**
Warrender Dr. CH43: Bid 1F **95**

Warren Dr. CH43: Bid 3C **94**
   CH45: Wall, New B 3F **51**
Warren Hey CH63: Spit 5A **142**
Warrenhouse Rd. L22: Water 3B **16**
   L33: K'by 1A **24**
Warren Hurst CH45: New B 3A **52**
Warren Pk. CH45: Wall 4F **51**
Warren Rd. CH47: Hoy 4A **90**
   L23: Blun 5A **8**
Warren St. L3: Liv 5E **77** (5H **5**)
Warren Way CH60: Hes 1D **157**
Warrington New Rd. WA9: St. H . .5B **46**
Warrington Old Rd. WA9: St. H . .1B **66**
Warrington Rd. L34: Prsct 5D **63**
   L35: Prsct, Whis 5D **63**
   L35: R'hill 2B **86**
   WA7: Cas 5E **153**
   WA7: Mnr P 3A **154**
   (not continuous)
   WA8: Bold H 1F **109**
   WA8: Wid 4C **132**
Warrington St. CH41: Tran 5E **97**
Warton Cl. L25: Wltn 2C **126**
Warton St. L20: Boot 2A **34**
Warton Ter. L20: Boot 2B **34**
Warwick Av. L23: C'by 2D **17**
Warwick Cl. CH43: O'ton 4C **96**
   L36: Huy 3A **84**
Warwick Ct. L8: Liv 3A **100**
Warwick Dr. CH45: Wall 5C **52**
   CH48: W Kir 1C **134**
Warwick Gro. WA7: Cas 1F **167**
Warwick Rd. CH49: Upton 4E **93**
   L20: Boot 4D **35**
   L36: Huy 3A **84**
Warwick St. L8: Liv 3D **99**
   WA10: St. H 5D **45**
Wasdale Av. L31: Mag 5E **7**
   WA11: St. H 5B **30**
Wasdale Rd. L9: Walt 3A **36**
Washbrook Av. CH43: Bid 5C **72**
Washbrook Cl. WA10: Eccl 4B **44**
Washington Cl. WA8: Wid 1F **131**
Washington Dr. L33: K'by 4D **15**
Washington Pde. L20: Boot 4C **34**
Washington Rd. L27: N'ley 5F **105**
Washway La. WA10: St. H 1F **45**
   WA11: St. H 1F **45**
Wastdale Cres. CH46: More 5C **70**
Wastdale Dr. CH46: More 5C **70**
Wastdale M. CH46: More 5C **70**
Wastle Bri. Rd. L36: Huy 1E **83**
Waterdale Cres. WA9: St. H 4D **67**
Waterdale Pl. WA9: St. H 4D **67**
Waterfall Dr. L4: Walt 5A **36**
   L9: Walt 5A **36**
Waterfield Cl. CH63: High B 2D **141**
Waterfield Way L21: Lith 4A **18**
Waterford Rd. CH43: O'ton 4F **95**
   L27: N'ley 3C **104**
   (not continuous)
Waterford Way WA7: Murd 4C **168**
Waterfront WA4: Pres H 4F **169**
Waterfront Bus. Area Parliament St. Nth.
   L1: Liv 2D **99**
   (off Bird St.)
   L1: Liv 2D **99**
   (off Watkinson St.)
Waterfront Bus. Area Parliament St. Sth.
   L8: Liv 2D **99**
Watergate La. L25: Wltn 2B **126**
Watergate Way L25: Wltn 2B **126**
Waterhouse Cl. L6: Liv 5B **56**
Waterhouse St. L1: Liv 1F **77**
Waterland La. WA9: St. H 1F **67**
Water La. L35: Tar G 5C **106**
   WA8: Cron 5C **106**
WATERLOO 4E **17**
Waterloo Cen. WA8: Wid 1A **152**
Waterloo Cl. L22: Water 5D **17**
Waterloo Ct. CH63: Beb 1A **142**
Waterloo Docks L3: Liv 3B **76** (1A **4**)
WATERLOO PARK 4F **17**
Waterloo Pl. CH41: Birk 4E **97**
Waterloo Quay L3: Liv 3A **76** (1A **4**)

Waterloo Rd. CH45: New B 2B **52**
   L3: Liv 2B **76** (1A **4**)
   L21: Sea 1F **33**
   L22: Water 5E **17**
   WA7: Run 5F **151**
   (not continuous)
   WA8: Wid 2A **152**
Waterloo Station (Rail) 4E **17**
Waterloo St. L15: W'tree 2A **102**
   WA10: St. H 5F **45**
Watermead Dr.
   WA7: Pres B 5F **169**
Waterpark Cl. CH43: Pren 3F **117**
Waterpark Dr. L28: Stock V 3F **59**
Waterpark Ho. CH42: Tran 2B **118**
Waterpark Rd. CH42: Tran 3F **117**
   CH43: Pren 3F **117**
Watersedge WA6: Frod 3D **173**
Watersedge Apartments
   CH45: New B 2C **52**
Waterside L30: N'ton 5E **11**
   WA9: St. H 4B **46**
Waterside Cl. WA7: Run 4E **151**
   WA9: St. H 4B **46**
Waterside Dr. WA6: Frod 3C **172**
Waterside La. WA8: Hale B 2C **150**
Waterside Pk. L36: Roby 4D **83**
Waterstone Cl. L11: N Grn. 5B **38**
Water St. CH41: Birk 3F **97**
   CH44: Wall 2D **75**
   CH62: Port S 2C **142**
   L2: Liv 5B **76** (5C **4**)
   L3: Liv 5B **76** (5B **4**)
   L22: Water 5D **17**
   L23: Thorn 4B **10**
   WA7: Run 4A **152**
   WA8: Wid 1A **152**
   WA10: St. H 5F **45**
Waterway Av. L30: N'ton 2B **20**
Waterworks La. CH66: Hoot 4E **171**
Waterworks St. L20: Boot 4D **35**
Watery La. WA9: St. H 3E **67**
   WA10: Windle 2B **44**
   WA11: Windle 1F **43**
Watford Rd. L4: Walt 4A **56**
Watkin Cl. L30: N'ton 4B **20**
Watkins Av. WA12: New W 5F **49**
Watkinson St. L1: Liv 2D **99**
Watkinson Way WA8: Wid 1F **109**
Watling Av. L21: Lith 4A **18**
Watling Way L35: Whis 5A **64**
Watmough St. L5: Liv 2E **77** (1H **5**)
Watson St. CH41: Birk 2D **97**
Watton Beck Cl. L31: Mag 5F **7**
Watton Cl. L12: Crox 1A **60**
Watts Clift Way WA9: St. H 5B **46**
Watts Cl. L33: K'by 1A **24**
Watts La. L20: Boot 2E **35**
Wauchope St. L15: W'tree 1E **101**
Wavell Av. WA8: Wid 4C **130**
Wavell Rd. L36: Huy 2E **83**
Waverley Dr. L34: Prsct 1F **83**
Waverley Gro. CH42: Tran 2C **118**
Waverley Ho. L19: Aig 5F **123**
Waverley Rd. CH47: Hoy 4C **90**
   L17: Aig 5C **100**
   L23: Blun 1C **16**
Waverley St. L20: Boot 5B **34**
Waverton Av. CH43: O'ton 2E **117**
WAVERTREE 2E **101**
Wavertree Athletics Cen. 2F **101**
Waver Tree Av. WA8: Wid 4F **131**
Wavertree Av. L13: W'tree 5E **79**
Wavertree Blvd. L7: Liv 5D **79**
Wavertree Blvd. Sth. L7: Liv 5E **79**
Wavertree Bus. Pk. L15: W'tree . .1F **101**
Wavertree Gdns. L15: W'tree 2F **101**
WAVERTREE GREEN 3A **102**
Wavertree Grn. L15: W'tree 2A **102**
Wavertree Ho. L13: Liv 5A **80**
   (off Binns Rd.)
Wavertree Nook Rd. L15: W'tree . .5B **80**
   (not continuous)
Wavertree Retail Pk. L7: Liv 5C **78**
Wavertree Rd. L7: Liv 5B **78**

Wavertree Technology Pk.
   L7: Liv 4E **79**
   L13: W'tree 5E **79**
Wavertree Technology Park Station (Rail)
   . . . . .5F **79**
Wavertree Trad. Est.
   L15: W'tree 2E **101**
Wavertree Va. L15: W'tree 1D **101**
Wayford Cl. WA6: Frod 4B **172**
Waylands Dr. L25: Hunts X 5B **126**
Wayville Cl. L18: Moss H 2A **124**
Weardale Rd. L15: W'tree 3E **101**
Weasdale Cl. WA9: St. H 4D **67**
Weates Cl. WA8: Wid 1E **133**
Weatherby CH49: W'chu 5B **94**
Weaver Av. L33: K'by 4F **15**
   L35: R'hill 3B **86**
Weaver Ct. L25: Gate 1C **126**
Weaver Cres. WA6: Frod 4D **173**
Weaver Gro. WA9: St. H 5A **48**
Weaver Ho. L25: Gate 1C **126**
   (off Woodsome Pk.)
Weaver Ind. Est. L19: Gars 3C **144**
Weaver La. WA6: Frod 3B **172**
Weaver Pk. Ind. Est.
   WA6: Frod 3D **173**
Weaver Rd. WA6: Frod 4D **173**
   WA7: West 4A **166**
Weaverside Av. WA7: Sut W 1F **173**
Weavers La. L31: Mag 4F **13**
Weaver St. L9: Walt 5F **35**
Weaver Vw. WA7: West 4F **165**
Webb Cl. L7: Liv 5C **78**
Webb Dr. WA5: B'wood 5F **69**
Webber Rd. L33: Know I 4B **24**
Webb St. L7: Liv 2C **100**
   WA9: St. H 2D **67**
Web Complex L33: Know I 5C **24**
Webster Av. CH44: Wall 1D **75**
   L20: Boot 4E **35**
Webster Dr. L32: K'by 3E **23**
Webster Rd. L7: Liv 2C **100**
Websters Holt CH49: Upton 3F **93**
Webster St. L3: Liv 4D **77** (3E **5**)
   L21: Lith 1B **34**
Wedge Av. WA11: Hay 3A **48**
Wedgewood Gdns. WA9: St. H . . .5B **64**
Wedgewood St. L7: Liv 4B **78**
Wedgwood Dr. WA8: Wid 4B **110**
Weightman Gro. L9: Ain 2A **36**
Weirside WA9: St. H 5D **67**
Welbeck Av. L18: Moss H 4F **101**
Welbeck Ct. L22: Water 4D **17**
   (off Mt. Pleasant)
Welbourne Rd. L16: Child 5C **80**
Weld Blundell Av. L31: Lyd 2B **6**
Weldon St. L4: Walt 1F **55**
Weld Rd. L23: Blun 2C **16**
Welfield Pl. L8: Liv 5A **100**
Welford Av. CH43: Pren 2F **117**
Welland Cl. L26: Halew 1E **147**
Welland Rd. CH63: High B 2D **141**
Wellbank Dr. L26: Halew 3A **128**
Wellbrae Cl. CH49: Upton 4D **93**
Wellbrook Cl. L24: Speke 3D **147**
   WA7: Brook 5C **168**
Wellbrook Grn. L24: Speke 4D **147**
Wellbrow Rd. L4: Walt 1A **56**
Wellcroft Rd. L36: Huy 2E **83**
Weller St. L8: Liv 4F **99**
Weller Way L8: Liv 5A **100**
Wellesbourne Pl. L11: N Grn. 1A **58**
Wellesbourne Rd. L11: N Grn. 5A **38**
Wellesley Gro. CH63: Beb 1A **142**
Wellesley Rd. CH44: Wall 2B **74**
   L8: Liv 5A **100**
Wellesley Ter. L8: Liv 5A **100**
Wellfarm Cl. L9: Ain 5D **37**
Wellfield WA7: Pres B 5D **169**
   WA8: Wid 1A **132**
   WA11: R'ford 1A **28**
Wellfield Av. L32: K'by 4E **23**
Wellfield Rd. L9: Walt 4A **36**
Wellgreen Rd. L25: Gate 2F **103**
Wellgreen Wlk. L25: Gate 2F **103**

Wellington Av. L15: W'tree 3D 101
Wellington Cl. CH63: Beb 1A 142
  L10: Ain 2C 20
Wellington Flds. L15: W'tree 3D 101
Wellington Gdns. L22: Water 4D 17
  (off Wellington St.)
Wellington Ga. L24: Hale 5D 149
Wellington Gro. L15: W'tree 1E 101
Wellington Rd. CH43: O'ton 4A 96
  CH45: New B 2A 52
  CH63: Beb 1A 142
  L8: Liv 5F 99
  L15: W'tree 2E 101
  L21: Lith 1A 34
Wellington St. L3: Liv 2D 77 (1E 5)
  L19: Gars 1C 144
  L22: Water 4D 17
  WA7: Run 4A 152
  WA8: Wid 1A 152
Wellington St. Ind. Est.
  WA8: Wid 1A 152
  (off Wellington St.)
Wellington Ter. CH41: Birk 4B 97
  L8: Liv 4A 100
  WA10: St. H 3A 46
Well La. CH42: Tran 1D 119
  CH49: Grea 1C 114
  CH60: Hes 4A 158
  CH63: High B 1D 141
  L16: Child 2F 103
  (not continuous)
  L20: Boot 5D 35
  L25: Gate 2F 103
Well La. Gdns. L20: Boot 5D 35
Wells St. L15: W'tree 2F 101
Wellstead Cl. L15: W'tree 1A 102
Wellstead Rd. L15: W'tree 1A 102
Wellstead Wlk. L15: W'tree 1A 102
Welsh Rd. CH66: Lit Sut 5F 171
Welton Av. L5: Upton 4F 93
Welton Cl. L24: Speke 4D 147
Welton Grn. L24: Speke 4D 147
Welton Rd. CH62: Brom 5D 143
Welwyn Cl. WA9: St. H 5F 65
Wembley Gdns. L9: Walt 2F 35
Wembley Rd. L18: Moss H 4B 102
  L23: C'bry 2F 17
Wendell St. L8: Liv 2C 100
Wendover Av. L17: Aig 1C 122
Wendover Cl. CH43: Noct 5D 95
  WA11: Hay 1D 49
Wendron Rd. L11: Crox 3D 39
Wenger Rd. WA8: Wid 4B 110
Wenlock Cl. L26: Halew 5E 127
Wenlock Dr. L26: Halew 5E 127
Wenlock Rd. L4: Walt 4B 56
  WA7: Beech 1A 174
Wenning Av. L31: Mag 5E 7
Wensley Av. L26: Halew 5E 127
Wensley Dale L9: Walt 1A 36
Wensleydale Av. CH62: East 5E 163
Wensleydale Cl. L31: Mag 5B 6
Wensleydale Dr. L35: R'hill 3D 87
Wensley Rd. L9: Walt 1A 36
Wentworth Av. CH45: New B 4B 52
Wentworth Cl. CH43: Noct 5D 95
  WA8: Wid 4A 110
Wentworth Dr. CH63: Brom 5B 162
  L5: Liv 2F 77
Wentworth Gro. L36: Huy 4B 82
Wernbrook Cl. CH43: Noct 5D 95
Wernbrook Rd. L4: Walt 4C 56
Wervin Cl. CH43: O'ton 2E 117
Wervin Rd. CH43: O'ton 2E 117
  L32: K'by 4D 23
Wervin Way L32: K'by 4C 22
Wesley Av. CH44: Wall 1C 74
  WA11: Hay 1E 49
Wesley Gro. CH44: Wall 3E 75
Wesley Hall Gdns. WA9: St. H 5D 65
Wesley Pl. L15: W'tree 1F 101
Wesley St. L22: Water 5D 17
W. Albert Rd. L17: Aig 5B 100
W. Alfred Ct. CH43: O'ton 4C 96
West Allerton Station (Rail) 3B 124

WEST BANK 3A 152
Westbank Av. CH45: New B 4C 52
W. Bank Dock Est. WA8: Wid 2E 151
W. Bank Rd. L7: Liv 4E 79
Westbank Rd. CH42: Tran 1C 118
W. Bank St. WA8: Wid 2A 152
Westbourne Av. CH48: W Kir 4B 112
  L23: Thorn 4B 10
Westbourne Gro. CH48: W Kir 4B 112
Westbourne Rd. CH43: O'ton 4C 96
  CH44: Wall 2F 73
  CH48: W Kir 4A 112
  L25: Gate 4C 104
Westbrook Av. L34: Prsct 5B 62
Westbrook Rd. CH46: More 2C 92
  L25: Gate 4C 104
West Brow Gdns. CH43: Bid 1C 94
Westbury Cl. L17: Aig 3C 122
  L25: Hunts X 4D 127
Westbury St. CH41: Tran 5E 97
Westcliffe Cl. WA8: Wid 5B 110
Westcliffe Rd. L12: W Der 4F 57
West Cl. CH43: Noct 4D 95
  L34: Ecc P 4A 64
Westcombe Rd. L4: Walt 4C 56
Westcott Rd. L4: Walt 5B 56
Westcott Way CH43: Noct 5D 95
Westdale Rd. CH42: R Ferr 2E 119
  L15: W'tree 1F 101
Westdale Vw. L15: W'tree 1F 101
WEST DERBY 5C 58
W. Derby Rd. L6: Liv 3A 78
  (Brunswick Rd.)
  L6: Liv 1D 79
  (Rocky La.)
  L13: Liv 5E 57
W. Derby St. L7: Liv 4F 77
WEST DERBY VILLAGE 4B 58
W. Derby Village L12: W Der 4B 58
West Dr. CH49: Upton 4A 94
  CH60: Hes 3A 158
West End Gro. WA11: Hay 2F 47
West End Rd. WA11: Hay 2F 47
Westerhope Way WA8: Wid 1F 131
Western Approaches Mus.
  (Underground Wartime Mus.)
  . . . . .4C 76 (4C 4)
Western Av. CH62: Brom 3D 143
  L24: Speke 5C 146
  L36: Huy 3A 82
Western Dr. L19: Gras 5A 124
Westerton Rd. L12: W Der 5E 59
Westfield Cres. WA7: Run 1E 165
Westfield Dr. L12: Crox 5E 39
Westfield M. WA7: Run 1F 165
Westfield Rd. CH44: Wall 5D 75
  L9: Walt 2E 35
  WA7: Run 1E 165
Westfield St. WA10: St. H 5F 45
Westfield Wlk. L32: K'by 3B 22
West Float Ind. Est. CH41: Birk 4B 74
Westgate WA8: West 5B 130
Westgate Rd. CH62: Port S 3B 142
  L15: W'tree 4A 102
West Gro. CH60: Hes 2F 157
Westhead Av. L33: K'by 3F 23
Westhead Cl. L33: K'by 4A 24
Westhead Wlk. L33: K'by 3F 23
  (not continuous)
Westhouse Cl. CH63: Brom 5C 162
WEST KIRBY 4A 112
West Kirby Concourse 4A 112
West Kirby Marine Lake 5A 112
W. Kirby Rd. CH46: More 3C 92
West Kirby Station (Rail) 4A 112
West Knowe CH43: O'ton 5F 95
West La. WA7: Pal F 3E 167
Westleigh Pl. WA9: Sut L 1C 88
W. Lodge Dr. CH48: W Kir 3A 112
West Mains L24: Speke 4A 148
West Meade L31: Mag 5B 6
Westminster Av. L30: N'ton 1E 19
Westminster Cl. L4: Kirk 2E 55
  WA8: Wid 4B 130
Westminster Ct. CH43: O'ton 4F 95

Westminster Dr. CH62: Brom 3D 163
  WA11: Hay 1F 49
Westminster Gro. L34: Prsct 1A 84
Westminster Rd. CH44: Wall 2B 74
  L4: Kirk 2D 55
Westmoreland Rd. CH45: New B 4C 52
Westmorland Av. L30: N'ton 2C 18
  WA8: Wid 3B 132
Westmorland Pl. L5: Liv 1D 77
Westmorland Dr. L3: Liv 3C 76 (2D 4)
Westmorland Rd. L36: Huy 4E 83
W. Oakhill Pk. L13: Liv 4A 80
WESTON 4F 165
Weston Ct. L23: Blun 2B 16
  WA7: West 3F 165
Weston Cres. WA7: West 4F 165
Weston Gro. L26: Halew 1A 148
  L31: Mag 4D 13
WESTON POINT 3D 165
Weston Point Docks
  WA7: West P 3D 165
Weston Point Expressway
  WA7: Run, West 1E 165
Weston Rd. WA7: Run, West 2E 165
Weston Vw. WA7: Clftn 1D 173
W. Orchard La. L9: Ain 5D 21
Westover Cl. L31: Mag 1C 12
Westover Rd. L31: Mag 1C 12
WEST PARK 1D 65
West Pk. Gdns. CH43: Bid 1B 94
West Pk. Rd. WA10: St. H 1D 65
Westport Bus. Pk. L20: Kirk 4C 54
West Rd. CH43: Noct 4D 95
  L14: B Grn 4C 80
  WA7: West P 3D 165
Westry Cl. CH46: More 1B 92
West Side WA9: St. H 1C 66
W. Side Av. WA11: Hay 2A 48
Westside Ind. Est. WA9: St. H 1C 66
West St. CH45: Wall 1B 74
  L34: Prsct 5C 62
  WA10: St. H 2D 65
WESTVALE 3C 22
West Vw. CH41: Tran 5F 97
  CH45: New B 3A 52
  L36: Huy 4B 84
West Vw. Av. L36: Huy 4B 84
West Vw. Cl. L36: Huy 4B 84
Westview Cl. CH43: Noct 5D 95
Westward Ho. CH48: Caldy 3D 135
Westward Vw. L17: Aig 1A 122
  L22: Water 3B 16
West Way CH46: More 5E 71
Westway CH43: Noct 5D 95
  CH49: Grea 5E 93
  CH60: Hes 4F 157
  L15: W'tree 1B 102
  L31: Mag 5A 6
  WA7: Pal F 3E 167
W. Way Sq. CH46: More 5E 71
Westwick Pl. L36: Huy 3B 82
Westwood WA7: Wind H 1C 168
Westwood Cl. CH43: O'ton 4F 95
Westwood Gro. CH44: Wall 2A 74
Westwood Rd. CH43: Bid 3C 94
  L18: Aller 4C 124
Wetherby Av. CH45: Wall 1E 73
Wetherby Ct. L36: Huy 1C 82
Wethersfield Rd. CH43: Noct 1E 117
Wetstone La. CH48: W Kir 5C 112
Wexford Av. L24: Hale 5D 149
Wexford Cl. CH43: O'ton 5E 95
  WA11: Hay 1D 49
Wexford Rd. CH43: O'ton 5F 95
Weybourne Cl. CH49: Upton 2A 94
Weyman Av. L35: Whis 3E 85
Weymoor Cl. CH63: Spit 5F 141
Weymouth Av. WA9: St. H 2F 67
Weymouth Cl. L16: Child 1F 103
  WA7: Murd 4E 169
Weymouth Rd. WA5: B'wood 5F 69
Whaley La. CH61: Irby 1F 137
Whalley Av. WA10: St. H 1E 45
Whalley Ct. L30: N'ton 1D 19
Whalley Gro. WA8: Wid 1D 133

Whalley Rd. CH42: Tran 4D 97
Whalley St. L8: Liv 5F 99
Wharf, The WA7: Pres B 4F 169
Wharfedale WA7: Pal F 4B 168
Wharfedale Av. CH42: Tran 2B 118
Wharfedale Dr. CH62: East 5F 163
　　L35: R'hill 3D 87
Wharfedale Rd. CH45: Wall 5F 51
Wharfedale St. L19: Gars 2E 145
Wharford La. L37: Nort 4E 155
Wharf Rd. WA12: New W 5E 49
Wharmby Rd. WA11: Hay 2E 49
Wharncliffe Rd. L13: Liv 3A 80
Wharton Cl. CH49: Upton 3D 93
Wharton St. WA9: St. H 2B 66
Whatcroft Cl. WA7: Run 4D 167
Wheatcroft Rd. L18: Aller 2C 124
Wheatear Cl. L27: N'ley 5E 105
　　L30: N'ton 2B 20
Wheatfield Cl. CH46: More 2F 93
Wheatfield Rd. WA8: Cron 4C 108
Wheatfield Vw. L21: Ford 3B 18
Wheat Hill Rd. L36: Huy 2E 105
Wheathills Ind. Est. L27: N'ley 3E 105
Wheatland Bus. Pk. CH44: Wall 4D 75
Wheatland Cl. WA9: Clock F 2C 88
Wheatland La. CH44: Wall 3D 75
Wheatland Rd. CH60: Hes 3C 158
Wheatlands WA7: Run 1E 167
Wheatley Av. L20: Boot 3E 35
Wheatsheaf Av. WA9: Sut L 5D 67
Wheeler Dr. L31: Mell 2B 22
Whelan Gdns. WA9: St. H 1E 87
Wheldon Rd. WA8: Wid 1F 149
Whernside WA8: Wid 1C 130
Whimbrel Cl. WA7: Beech 5F 167
Whimbrel Pk. L26: Halew 3E 127
Whinberry Dr. L32: K'by 4D 23
Whinbury St. WA9: Clock F 2C 88
Whincraig L28: Stock V 4C 60
Whinfell Gro. WA7: Beech 5E 167
Whinfell Rd. L12: W Der 1B 80
Whinfield Rd. L9: Walt 2F 35
　　L23: Thorn 4A 10
Whinhowe Rd. L11: N Grn. 1A 58
Whinmoor Cl. CH43: Noct 3D 95
Whinmoor Rd. L10: Faz 1A 38
　　L12: W Der 1C 80
Whinney Gro. E. L31: Mag 4C 12
Whinney Gro. W. L31: Mag 4C 12
WHISTON .3E 85
WHISTON CROSS 3D 85
Whiston La. L36: Huy 2A 84
WHISTON LANE ENDS 4E 85
Whiston Station (Rail) 3E 85
Whitburn Rd. L33: K'by 1A 24
Whitby Av. CH45: Wall 1E 73
Whitby Rd. WA7: Run 1A 166
Whitby St. L6: Liv 5D 57
Whitchurch Way WA7: Run 4D 167
Whitcroft Rd. L6: Liv 3D 79
Whitebeam Cl. L33: K'by 4F 15
　　WA7: Wind H 1C 168
Whitebeam Dr. L12: Crox 5D 39
Whitebeam Gdns. WA9: St. H 5C 64
Whitebeam Wlk. CH49: Grea 2B 114
Whitechapel L1: Liv 5D 77 (6E 4)
Whitefield Av. L4: Kirk 3E 55
Whitefield Cl. CH49: W'chu 1B 116
Whitefield Dr. L32: K'by 3B 22
Whitefield La. L35: Tar G 4A 106
Whitefield Rd. L6: Liv 2A 78
　　WA10: St. H 3D 45
Whitefield Sq. L32: K'by 3C 22
Whitefield Way L6: Liv 2A 78
White Friars WA10: Eccl 5A 44
Whitegate Cl. L34: Know 4D 41
Whitehall Cl. L4: Kirk 2E 55
Whitehall Pl. WA6: Frod 5B 172
　　　　　　(not continuous)
Whitehart Cl. L4: Walt 2B 56
Whitehaven Rd. L5: Liv 5F 55
Whiteheath Way CH46: Leas 3F 71
Whitehedge Rd. L19: Gars 5B 124

White Ho. Cl. WA11: Hay 2B 48
Whitehouse Expressway
　　WA7: Brook, Pal F 4E 167
Whitehouse Ind. Est.
　　WA7: Pres B 1E 175
　　　　　　(not continuous)
Whitehouse La. CH60: Hes 1C 158
　　CH63: Brim 1C 158
Whitehouse Rd. L13: Liv 4B 80
Whitehouse Vale WA7: Pres B 5F 169
Whitelands Mdw. CH49: Upton 4E 93
White Lodge Av. L36: Huy 3D 83
White Lodge Cl. CH62: Brom 5D 163
Whitely Gro. L33: K'by 5F 15
White Mdw. Dr. L23: Thorn 4A 10
White Oak Lodge L19: Gras 5F 123
White Rock St. L6: Liv 2B 78
Whiteside Av. WA11: St. H 3E 47
Whiteside Cl. CH49: Upton 5A 94
　　L5: Liv 1D 77
Whiteside Rd. WA11: Hay 2B 48
Whitestone Cl. L34: Know 1C 60
White St. L1: Liv 1D 99
　　WA8: Wid 2A 152
Whitethorn Dr. L28: Stock V 3B 60
Whitewell Dr. CH49: Upton 3F 93
Whitewood Pk. L9: Ain 2D 37
Whitfield Cl. CH42: Tran 5D 97
Whitfield Gro. WA11: Hay 2A 48
Whitfield La. CH60: Hes 1A 158
Whitfield Rd. L9: Walt 3A 36
WHITFIELDS CROSS 1E 133
Whitfield St. CH42: Tran 5D 97
　　　　　　(not continuous)
Whitford Rd. CH42: Tran 5C 96
Witham Av. L23: C'by 2F 17
Whithorn St. L7: Liv 1D 101
Whitland Rd. L6: Liv 2D 79
Whitley Cl. WA7: Run 2F 165
Whitley Dr. CH44: Wall 1C 74
Whitley St. L3: Liv 2B 76
Whitman St. L15: W'tree 2E 101
Whitmoor Cl. L35: R'hill 5E 87
Whitney Pl. L25: Wltn 2C 126
Whitney Rd. L25: Wltn 1C 126
Whitstable Pk. WA8: Wid 5E 109
Whitstone Cl. L18: Aller 2E 125
Whittaker Cl. L13: Liv 5F 79
Whittaker St. WA9: St. H 2D 67
Whittier St. L8: Liv 2C 100
Whittington Ho. L21: Lith 1A 34
　　　　　　(off Beach Rd.)
Whittle Av. WA11: Hay 3A 48
Whittle Cl. L5: Kirk 5E 55
Whittle St. L5: Kirk 5E 55
　　WA10: St. H 2D 65
Whittlewood Cl. L33: K'by 1F 23
Whitworth Ct. WA7: Mnr P 3D 155
Wicket Cl. L11: Crox 3D 39
Wickham Cl. CH44: Wall 4D 75
　　WA8: Wid 1F 131
Wicksten Dr. WA7: Run 5C 152
Widdale Av. L35: R'hill 3D 87
Widgeons Covert
　　CH63: Thorn H 5F 159
　　CH63: Beb 2A 142
Widmore Rd. L25: Gate 5C 104
WIDNES .5A 132
Widnes Crematorium WA8: Wid . . .1A 132
Widnes Rd. WA5: Cuerd, Penk 2F 133
　　WA8: Cuerd, Wid, Penk 2F 133
　　WA8: Wid 5A 132
　　　　　　(not continuous)
Widnes Station (Rail) 1A 132
Widnes Vikings RLFC 4F 131
Wiend, The CH42: R Ferr 3D 119
Wightman St. L6: Liv 3B 78
Wignall Cl. L32: K'by 1E 39
Wilberforce Rd. L4: Walt 2B 56
Wilbraham Pl. L5: Liv 1D 77
Wilbraham St. CH41: Birk 3E 97
　　L5: Liv 1D 77
　　WA9: Clock F 3E 89
Wilburn St. L4: Walt 2F 55

Wilbur St. WA9: St. H 4E 67
Wilcock Cl. L5: Liv 1D 77
Wilcote Cl. WA8: Wid 5C 110
Wildbrook Dr. CH41: Birk 4D 73
Wildcherry Gdns. WA9: St. H 4B 64
Wilde St. L3: Liv 4E 77 (3G 5)
Wilding Av. WA7: Run 5B 152
Wild Pl. L20: Boot 1E 35
Wilfer Cl. L7: Liv 1C 100
Wilfred Owen Dr. CH41: Birk 2E 95
Wilkes Av. CH46: Leas 3B 72
Wilkie St. L15: W'tree 2D 101
Wilkinson Cl. WA8: Wid 2A 152
Wilkinson Ct. L15: W'tree 1D 101
Wilkinson St. CH41: Birk 4C 96
Wilkin St. L4: Kirk 4E 55
Willan St. CH43: O'ton 5B 96
Willard St. L20: Boot 2D 35
WILLASTON 5A 170
Willaston Dr. L26: Halew 1A 148
Willaston Grn. M. CH64: Will 5A 170
Willaston Rd. CH46: More 5D 71
　　CH63: Raby 5D 161
　　L4: Walt .1B 56
Willedstan Av. L23: C'by 2E 17
William Brown St. L3: Liv . . .4D 77 (4F 5)
　　　　　　(not continuous)
William Harvey Cl. L30: N'ton 2F 19
William Henry St. L3: Liv . . .3E 77 (1H 5)
　　L20: Boot 1B 54
William Jessop Way
　　L3: Liv 4B 76 (3A 4)
William Morris Av. L20: Boot 3E 35
William Moult St. L5: Liv 1D 77
William Rd. WA11: Hay 2F 47
William Roberts Av. L32: K'by 3C 22
Williams Av. L20: Boot 3E 35
Williamson Art Gallery & Mus. 4B 96
Williamson Ct. L25: Wltn 3C 126
　　L26: Halew 3A 128
Williamson Sq. L1: Liv 5D 77 (5E 5)
Williamson St. L1: Liv 5D 77 (5E 4)
　　WA9: St. H 4C 46
Williamson Student Village
　　L7: Liv 5A 78
Williamson Tunnels Heritage Cen.
　　. . . . . .5A 78
　　　　　　(off Old Stable Yd.)
Williams St. L34: Prsct 5D 63
William St. CH41: Birk 3E 97
　　CH44: Wall 4E 75
　　WA8: Wid 2C 132
　　WA10: St. H 4A 46
Williams Way WA6: Frod 5A 172
William Wall Rd. L21: Ford 3B 18
Willingdon Rd. L16: Child 5E 81
Willington Av. CH62: East 2E 171
Willink Rd. WA11: St. H 1C 46
Willis Cl. L35: Whis 4D 85
Willis La. L35: Whis 4D 85
Williton Rd. L16: Child 4E 103
Willmer Rd. CH42: Tran 4C 96
　　L4: Walt .4B 56
Willoughby Dr. WA10: St. H 3B 64
Willoughby Rd. CH44: Wall 2F 73
　　L14: B Grn 4E 81
　　L22: Water 4E 17
Willow Av. L32: K'by 2C 22
　　L35: Whis 3E 85
　　L36: Huy 1E 105
　　WA8: Wid 2B 132
Willowbank Cl. L36: Huy 1C 82
Willowbank Rd. CH42: Tran 1D 119
　　CH62: New F 1B 142
Willow Cl. WA7: Run 3B 166
Willow Ct. CH63: High B 1D 141
Willowcroft Rd. CH44: Wall 3C 74
Willowdale Rd. L9: Walt 4A 36
　　L18: Moss H 4F 101
Willow Dene L11: Crox 2D 39
Willow Grn. L25: Wltn 5F 103
Willow Gro. CH46: More 2D 93
　　L15: W'tree 1A 102
　　L35: Prsct 1E 85
Willowherb Cl. L26: Halew 2D 127

Willow Hey. L31: Mag 3E 13
Willow Ho. L21: Sea 2A 34
Willow Lea CH43: O'ton 5A 96
Willowmeade L11: N Grn. 5B 38
Willow Moss Cl. CH46: More 4A 72
Willow Pk. CH49: Grea 5C 92
Willow Rd. L15: W'tree 1D 101
   WA10: St. H 5C 44
   WA11: Hay 1E 49
Willows, The CH45: Wall 4E 51
   WA6: Frod 5C 172
   WA9: Clock F 2C 88
Willow Tree Av. WA9: Sut L 2D 89
Willow Way L11: Crox 3D 39
   L23: C'by 5E 9
Wills Av. L31: Mag 5C 6
Willsford Av. L31: Mell 2B 22
Wilmere La. WA8: Wid 4A 110
Wilne Rd. CH45: Wall 5A 52
Wilsden Rd. WA8: Wid 3B 130
Wilson Av. CH44: Wall 2E 75
Wilson Bus. Cen. L36: Huy 5A 84
Wilson Cl. WA8: Wid 3D 133
   WA10: St. H 5E 45
Wilson Gro. L19: Gars 1C 144
Wilson Rd. CH44: Wall 2E 75
   L35: Prsct 2D 85
   L36: Huy 4F 83
Wilson's La. L21: Lith 5B 18
Wilstan Av. CH63: High B 2D 141
Wilton Grange CH48: W Kir 2A 112
Wilton Gro. L13: Liv 4A 80
Wilton Rd. CH42: R Ferr 3A 120
   L36: Huy 5D 83
Wilton's Dr. L34: Know 5C 40
Wilton St. CH44: Wall 2B 74
   L3: Liv 3E 77 (2H 5)
Wiltshire Dr. L30: N'ton 2D 19
Wiltshire Gdns. WA10: St. H 1F 65
Wimbald Cl. L25: Gate 4C 104
Wimbledon St. CH45: Wall 1B 74
   L15: W'tree 2E 101
Wimborne Av. CH61: Thing 2A 138
Wimborne Cl. L14: K Ash 5B 60
Wimborne Pl. L14: K Ash 1B 82
Wimborne Rd. L14: K Ash 5A 60
Wimborne Way CH61: Irby 5D 115
Wimbrick Cl. CH46: More 1F 93
Wimbrick Hey CH46: More 1F 93
Wimpole St. L7: Liv 4B 78
Winchester Av. L10: Ain 2D 21
   L22: Water 3C 16
Winchester Cl. L25: Wltn 4B 126
Winchester Dr. CH44: Wall 2F 73
Winchester Pl. WA8: Wid 4C 130
Winchester Rd. L6: Liv 5C 56
Winchester Wlk. L36: Huy 2A 84
Winchfield Rd. L15: W'tree 3F 101
Windbourne Rd. L17: Aig 2B 122
Windermere Av. WA8: Wid 5B 110
   WA11: St. H 5A 30
Windermere Ct. CH41: Birk 4C 96
   (off Penrith St.)
Windermere Dr. L12: W Der 2C 58
   L31: Mag 5E 7
   L33: K'by 1D 23
Windermere Ho. L17: Aig 2D 123
Windermere Pl. WA11: St. H 5A 30
Windermere Rd.
   CH43: Noct 4C 94
   WA11: Hay 2B 48
Windermere St. L5: Liv 4B 100
   WA8: Wid 5B 110
Windermere Ter. L8: Liv 4B 100
Windfield Cl. L33: K'by 4F 15
Windfield Grn. L19: Gars 4C 144
Windfield Rd. L19: Gars 4C 144
WINDLE .2B 44
Windle Ash L31: Mag 5C 6
Windle Av. L23: C'by 1A 18
Windlebrook Cres.
   WA10: Windle 2B 44
Windle City WA10: St. H 2F 45
Windle Gro. WA10: Windle 2C 44
Windle Hall Dr. WA10: St. H 1E 45

WINDLEHURST 1F 45
Windlehurst Av. WA10: St. H 2E 45
WINDLES GREEN 5B 10
Windleshaw Rd. WA10: St. H 3D 45
Windle St. WA10: St. H 3F 45
Windle Va. WA10: St. H 3E 45
Windmill Av. L23: C'by 5F 9
Windmill Cl. L33: K'by 5E 15
Windmill Gdns. CH43: Bid 1C 94
   WA9: St. H 4D 47
WINDMILL HILL 5C 154
Windmill Hill Av. E.
   WA7: Wind H 5D 155
Windmill Hill Av. Nth.
   WA7: Wind H 4D 155
Windmill Hill Av. Sth.
   WA7: Wind H 1C 168
Windmill Hill Av. W.
   WA7: Wind H 5C 154
Windmill La. WA4: Pres H 4F 169
Windmill Shop. Cen.
   WA8: Wid 4B 132
Windmill St. WA7: Run 5B 152
Window La. L19: Gars 3C 144
Windsor Av. L21: Lith 5A 18
Windsor Cl. CH49: Grea 1D 115
   CH62: New F 5A 120
   L30: N'ton 5F 11
Windsor Ct. L8: Liv 3F 99
   (off Windsor St.)
   L20: Boot 3E 35
Windsor Dr. L36: Huy 3A 82
Windsor Gro. WA7: Run 2B 166
Windsor M. CH62: New F 5A 120
Windsor Pk. Rd. L10: Ain 2E 21
Windsor Rd. L9: Walt 2A 36
   L13: Liv 5D 57
   L20: Boot 3E 35
   L23: C'by 5D 9
   L31: Mag 1C 12
   L35: Prsct 2F 85
   L36: Huy 4A 82
   WA8: Wid 5A 110
   WA10: St. H 5D 45
   WN5: Bil 1F 31
Windsor St. CH43: O'ton 4C 96
   CH45: New B 2B 52
   L8: Liv 2E 99
Windsor Vw. L8: Liv 2B 100
Windus St. WA10: St. H 5E 45
Windwood Dr. L24: Speke 3F 145
WINDY ARBOR 1B 106
Windy Arbor Brow
   L35: Whis 1C 106
Windy Arbor Cl. L35: Whis 5D 85
Windy Arbor Rd. L35: Whis 4D 85
Windy Bank CH62: Port S 1A 142
Wineva Gdns. L23: C'by 2F 17
Winfield Way WA8: Wid 4B 132
Winford St. CH44: Wall 3D 75
Winfrith Cl. CH63: Spit 4F 141
Winfrith Dr. CH63: Spit 5F 141
Winfrith Rd. L25: Gate 5C 104
Wingate Av. WA9: St. H 5D 65
Wingate Cl. CH43: Noct 5E 95
Wingate Rd. CH62: East 5E 163
   L17: Aig 2E 123
   L33: K'by 1F 23
Wingate Towers L36: Huy 2D 83
Wingate Wlk. L33: K'by 2F 23
Wingfield Cl. L29: Seft 2D 11
Wingrave Way L11: N Grn. 2B 58
Winhill L25: Wltn 5A 104
Winifred Rd. L10: Faz 1B 38
Winifred St. L7: Liv 5B 78
Winkle St. L8: Liv 4F 99
Winmoss Dr. L33: K'by 5F 15
Winnington Rd. CH47: Hoy 1A 112
Winnipeg Dr. L27: N'ley 4E 105
Winnows, The WA7: Run 1D 167
Winser St. CH62: Port S 1B 142
Winsford Cl. WA11: Hay 1F 49
Winsford Dr. WA5: B'wood 4E 69
Winsford Rd. L13: Liv 5E 57
Winsham Cl. L32: K'by 5E 23

Winsham Rd. L32: K'by 5E 23
Winskill Rd. L11: N Grn. 2A 58
Winslade Ct. L4: Walt 1B 56
Winslade Rd. L4: Walt 2B 56
Winslow Cl. WA7: Nort 2D 169
Winslow St. L4: Walt 2F 55
Winstanley Ho. CH62: New F 5B 120
   (off Winstanley Rd.)
Winstanley Rd. CH62: New F 5B 120
   L22: Water 3E 17
Winster Dr. L27: N'ley 5A 106
Winston Av. WA9: St. H 1B 68
Winston Dr. CH43: Noct 4C 94
Winstone Rd. L14: K Ash 2A 82
Winston Gro. CH46: More 1E 93
Winterburn Cres. L12: W Der 4C 58
Winterburn Hgts.
   L12: W Der 4D 59
   (off Winterburn Cres.)
Winter Gdns., The CH45: New B . . .3A 52
   (off Atherton St.)
Winter Gro. WA9: St. H 5B 48
Winterhey Av. CH44: Wall 3B 74
Winterley Dr. L26: Halew 1A 148
Winter St. L6: Liv 3A 78
Winthrop Pk. CH43: O'ton 4E 95
Winton Cl. CH45: New B 3F 51
Winton Gro. WA7: Wind H 1D 169
Winwick Vw. WA5: C Grn 2D 69
Winwood Hall L25: Wltn 3A 126
Wirral Bus. Cen. CH41: Birk 5C 74
Wirral Bus. Pk., The
   CH49: Upton 1F 115
Wirral Cl. CH63: Beb 4F 141
Wirral Country Pk. 4A 136
Wirral Country Pk. Vis. Cen.
   . . . . .5F 135
Wirral Gdns. CH63: Beb 4F 141
Wirral Intl. Bus. Pk.
   CH62: Brom 1F 163
Wirral Leisure Pk.
   CH62: Brom 4E 143
Wirral Little Theatre 4C 96
Wirral Mt. CH45: Wall 1F 73
   CH48: W Kir 4D 113
Wirral Mus. 3F 97
Wirral Sailing Cen. 4A 112
Wirral Tennis & Sports Cen. 4D 73
Wirral Transport Mus. 2E 97
Wirral Vw. L19: Gras 5F 123
Wirral Vs. CH45: Wall 5E 51
Wirral Way CH43: Noct 4C 94
Wisenholme Cl. WA7: Beech 1E 173
Wisteria Way WA9: Bold 4A 68
Witham Cl. L30: N'ton 1A 20
Withburn Cl. CH49: Upton 4E 93
Withens, The L28: Stock V 4B 60
Withensfield CH45: Wall 5B 52
Withens La. CH45: Wall 5B 52
Withens Rd. L31: Lyd 4D 7
Wither Av. CH63: High B 4D 119
Withington Rd. CH44: Wall 3C 74
   L24: Speke 4F 147
Withins Rd. WA11: Hay 1E 49
Withnell Cl. L13: Liv 4B 80
Withnell Rd. L13: Liv 4B 80
Withy Cl. WA6: Frod 5C 172
Witley Av. CH46: More 5E 71
Witley Cl. CH46: More 5E 71
Witney Cl. CH49: Grea 1C 114
Wittenham Cl.
   CH49: Upton 5F 93
Wittering La. CH60: Hes 2D 157
Witton Rd. L13: Liv 5D 57
Witt Rd. WA8: Wid 5A 132
Wivern Pl. WA7: Run 4B 152
Woburn Cl. L13: Liv 1F 79
   WA11: Hay 1F 49
Woburn Dr. WA8: Cron 3D 109
Woburn Grn. L13: Liv 2F 79
Woburn Hill L13: Liv 2F 79
Woburn Pl. CH42: R Ferr 2F 119
Woburn Rd. CH45: Wall 5B 52
Wokefield Way WA10: St. H 4C 44
Wokingham Gro. L36: Huy 1E 105

Wolfenden Av. L20: Boot 3E 35
Wolfe Rd. WA9: St. H 1E 67
Wolferton Cl. CH49: Upton 2B 94
Wolfe St. L8: Liv 4E 99
Wolfrick Dr. CH63: Spit 1B 162
Wolseley Rd. WA10: St. H 3F 45
Wolsey St. L20: Kirk 2C 54
Wolstenholme Sq.
  L1: Liv 1D 99 (7F 5)
Wolverton Dr. WA7: Wind H 1D 169
Wolverton St. L6: Liv 5B 56
Womack Gdns. WA9: St. H 5E 65
Wood Av. L20: Boot 3E 35
Woodbank Cl. L16: Child 1F 103
Woodbank Pk. CH43: O'ton 5F 95
Woodberry Cl. CH43: Noct 5D 95
  L33: K'by 4F 15
Woodbine St. L5: Kirk 4D 55
Woodbourne Rd.
  L14: K Ash 2D 81
Woodbridge Av. L26: Halew 2D 127
Woodbrook Av. L9: Walt 1F 35
Woodburn Blvd.
  CH63: High B 4E 119
Woodburn Dr. CH60: Hes 4F 157
WOODCHURCH 2B 116
Woodchurch Ct. CH42: Tran 1C 118
Woodchurch La. CH42: Tran 2B 118
  CH49: W'chu 4C 116
Woodchurch Leisure Cen. 1C 116
Woodchurch Rd. CH41: Birk 1C 118
  CH42: Tran 3B 116
  CH43: Pren 3B 116
  CH49: W'chu 3B 116
  L13: Liv 2A 80
Woodchurch Sports Barn 5C 94
Wood Cl. CH41: Birk 2D 97
  L33: K'by 3D 23
Woodcote Bank CH42: R Ferr . . .5F 119
Woodcote Cl. L33: K'by 1A 24
Woodcotes, The CH62: Brom 4D 163
Woodcot La. CH60: Hes 1F 157
Woodcroft Dr. CH61: Hes 5F 137
Woodcroft La. CH63: High B 4E 119
Woodcroft Rd. L15: W'tree 2D 101
Woodcroft Way
  WA9: Clock F 2C 88
WOODEND 1B 152
Woodend CH61: Pens 2F 137
  L35: Whis 1E 107
  WA7: Murd 3E 169
Woodend Av. L23: C'by 4E 9
  L24: Speke 1C 146
  L25: Hunts X 1C 146
  L31: Mag 3C 12
Woodend Ct. WA8: Wid 2D 133
Woodend Ind. Est.
  L24: Speke 2D 147
Woodend La. L24: Speke 3C 146
WOOD END PARK 5F 123
Woodene Cl. L32: K'by 1A 40
Woodfarm Hey L28: Stock V 3A 60
Woodfield Av. CH63: High B 4E 119
Woodfield Rd. CH61: Pens 3E 137
  CH63: Beb 4A 142
  L9: Walt 3F 35
  L36: Huy 4C 82
Woodford Cl. WA7: Run 4B 166
Woodford Rd. CH62: New F 4B 120
  L14: K Ash 2E 81
  WA10: Windle 2C 44
Woodgate L27: N'ley 3C 104
Woodger St. L19: Gars 2C 144
Wood Grn. CH43: Bid 1C 94
  L34: Prsct 5C 62
Woodgreen Rd. L13: Liv 2A 80
Wood Gro. L13: Liv 4F 79
Woodhall Av. CH44: Wall 2D 75
Woodhall Rd. L13: Liv 3A 80
Woodhatch Rd. WA7: Brook 5A 168
Woodhead Rd. CH62: Port S 1C 142
Woodhead St. CH62: New F 5B 120
Wood Heath Way
  CH62: East 3F 163

WOODHEY 5E 119
Woodhey Ct. CH63: High B 4F 119
Woodhey Gro. CH63: High B 5F 119
Woodhey Rd. CH63: High B 5F 119
  L19: Gras 4A 124
Woodholme Ct. L25: Gate 5B 104
Woodhouse Cl. L4: Walt 4E 55
Woodhurst Cl. L36: Huy 5C 60
Woodhurst Cres.
  L14: K Ash 2A 82
Woodin Rd. CH42: R Ferr 4A 120
Woodkind Hey CH63: Spit 5A 142
Woodland Av. CH47: Meols 2D 91
  WA8: Wid 3F 131
Woodland Dr. CH45: New B 4C 52
  CH49: W'chu 1A 116
Woodland Gro. CH42: R Ferr 4F 119
Woodland Rd. CH42: R Ferr 4F 119
  CH48: W Kir 4E 113
  CH49: W'chu 1A 116
  L4: Walt 3C 56
  L21: Sea 1F 33
  L26: Halew 5E 127
  L31: Mell 1A 22
Woodlands, The CH41: Birk 4D 97
  CH49: Upton 4F 93
  L34: Ecc P 4F 63
Woodlands Dr. CH61: Barn 3C 138
Woodlands La. CH48: W Kir 5D 113
Woodlands Pk. L12: W Der 1A 80
Woodlands Rd. CH61: Irby 2D 137
  L9: Ain 1D 37
  L17: Aig 2E 123
  L36: Huy 4B 82
  WA11: St. H 2B 46
Woodlands Sq. L27: N'ley 5A 106
                (off Winster Dr.)
Woodland Vw. L23: Thorn 3A 10
Woodland Wlk. CH62: Brom 1C 162
  WA7: Cas 3E 167
Wood La. CH45: Wall 5E 51
  CH49: Grea 4D 93
  CH64: Will 4A 170
  L27: N'ley 4F 105
  L34: Prsct 1B 84
  L36: Huy 4B 84
  WA7: Murd 4C 168
  WA7: Sut W 1F 173
Wood Lea L12: Crox 5E 39
Woodlea Cl. CH62: Brom 5D 163
Woodlee Rd. L25: Gate 5C 104
Woodleigh Cl. L31: Lyd 2B 6
Woodley Rd. L31: Mag 4C 12
Woodpecker Cl.
  CH49: Upton 4D 93
  L12: W Der 2F 59
Woodpecker Dr. L26: Halew 2E 127
Woodridge WA7: Wind H 1C 168
Wood Rd. L26: Halew 5E 127
Woodrock Rd. L25: Wltn 2B 126
Woodruff St. L8: Liv 5F 99
Woodside Av. CH46: More 2E 93
  WA11: St. H 5F 29
Woodside Bus. Pk. CH41: Birk . . .2F 97
Woodside Cl. L12: W Der 3B 58
Woodside Ferry App.
  CH41: Birk 2F 97
Woodside Rd. CH61: Irby 1E 137
  WA11: Hay 1E 49
Woodside St. L7: Liv 5B 78
Woodside Way L33: K'by 5F 15
Woodsome Pk. L25: Gate 1C 126
Woodsorrel Rd. CH41: Birk 2F 95
  L15: W'tree 2B 102
Woodstack St. WA9: St. H 4E 67
Woodstock Gro. WA8: Wid 2D 131
Woodstock Rd. CH44: Wall 3A 74
Woodstock St. L5: Liv 1D 77
Wood St. CH41: Birk 2D 97
  CH47: Hoy 4B 90
  CH62: Port S 2B 142
  L1: Liv 5D 77 (6F 5)
  L19: Gars 1C 144
  L21: Lith 1B 34
  L34: Prsct 5D 63

Wood St. WA8: Wid 3C 132
  WA9: St. H 4C 46
Woodthorn Cl. WA4: Dares 3F 155
Wood Va. WA9: St. H 5E 65
Woodvale Cl. CH43: Bid 1C 94
Woodvale Ct. CH49: W'chu 3A 116
Woodvale Rd. L12: Crox 5F 39
  L25: Wltn 2B 126
Woodview L34: Know 5E 41
Woodview Av. CH44: Wall 4D 75
Woodview Cres. WA8: Wid 4A 130
Woodview Rd. L25: Wltn 5F 103
  WA8: Wid 4A 130
Woodville Av. L23: C'by 2D 17
Woodville Pl. WA8: Wid 3D 131
Woodville Rd. CH42: Tran 5C 96
Woodville St. WA10: St. H 4B 46
                (not continuous)
Woodville Ter. L6: Liv 1B 78
Woodward Rd. CH42: R Ferr 4A 120
  L33: Know I 1C 24
Woodway CH49: Grea 5E 93
Woodyear Rd. CH62: Brom 3E 163
Woolacombe Av.
  WA9: Sut L 1C 88
Woolacombe Rd. L16: Child 3D 103
Wooler Cl. CH46: More 1C 92
Woolfall Cl. L36: Huy 2B 82
Woolfall Cres. L36: Huy 2B 82
WOOLFALL HEATH 1C 82
Woolfall Heath Av. L36: Huy 1C 82
Woolfall Hgts. L36: Huy 1C 82
Woolfall Ter. L21: Sea 2A 34
Woolhope Rd. L4: Walt 1B 56
Woolley Cl. WA6: Frod 3D 173
Woolmoore Rd.
  L24: Speke 1C 146
Woolston Rd. WA11: Hay 1D 49
WOOLTON 2A 126
Woolton Cinema, The 2A 126
WOOLTON HILL 1E 125
Woolton Hill Rd. L25: Wltn 5E 103
Woolton M. L25: Wltn 2F 125
Woolton Mt. L25: Wltn 1A 126
WOOLTON PARK 5A 104
Woolton Pk. L25: Wltn 5A 104
Woolton Pk. Cl. L25: Wltn 1A 126
Woolton Rd. L15: W'tree 2A 102
  L16: Child 4D 103
  L19: Aller, Gars 1C 144
  L25: Aller 4E 125
Woolton St. L25: Wltn 2A 126
                (not continuous)
Woolton Swimming Pool 2A 126
Woolton Views
  L25: Hunts X 4D 127
Worcester Av. L13: Liv 4D 57
  L22: Water 3C 16
Worcester Cl. WA10: St. H 1F 65
Worcester Ct. L20: Boot 5D 35
Worcester Dr. L13: Liv 4D 57
Worcester Dr. Nth. L13: Liv 4D 57
Worcester Rd. CH43: Bid 1D 95
  L20: Boot 4D 35
Wordsworth Av. CH42: R Ferr 3F 119
  WA8: Wid 4F 131
  WA9: Sut M 3A 88
Wordsworth St. L8: Liv 2B 100
  L20: Boot 3A 34
Wordsworth Wlk.
  CH48: W Kir 1B 134
Wordsworth Way L36: Huy 5F 83
Wordworth Ct. L32: K'by 5C 22
World of Glass, The 5A 46
Worrow Cl. L11: N Grn. 5B 38
Worrow Rd. L11: N Grn. 5B 38
WORSLEY BROW 2E 67
Worsley Brow WA9: St. H 3E 67
Worsley St. WA11: Hay 2F 47
Worthing St. L22: Water 3C 16
Worthington Cl. WA7: Pal F 3A 168
Worthington St. L8: Liv 3D 99
Wortley Rd. L10: Faz 1E 37
Wray Av. WA9: Clock F 2D 89
Wrayburn Cl. L7: Liv 1C 100

Wray Ct. WA9: Clock F 2D **89**
Wrekin Cl. L25: Wltn 3B **126**
Wrekin Dr. L10: Ain 3E **21**
Wrenbury Cl. CH43: O'ton 2F **117**
    WA7: Sut W 1F **173**
Wrenbury St. L7: Liv 4C **78**
Wren Cl. WA7: Pal F 4A **168**
Wrenfield Gro. L17: Aig 2C **122**
Wren Gro. L26: Halew 3E **127**
Wright Cres. WA8: Wid 2A **152**
Wrights La. WA5: Cuerd 2F **133**
Wrights Ter. L15: W'tree 2A **102**
Wright St. CH44: Wall 2D **75**
    L5: Liv .1D **77**
Wrigley Rd. WA11: Hay 2E **49**
Wroxham Cl. CH49: Upton 5A **94**
Wroxham Ct. CH49: Upton 4A **94**
Wroxham Dr. CH49: Upton 5A **94**
Wroxham Way CH49: Upton 5A **94**
Wryneck Cl. WA10: St. H 4B **64**
Wrynose Rd. CH62: Brom 2E **163**
Wulstan St. L4: Kirk 4D **55**
Wycherley Rd. CH42: Tran 1D **119**
Wycherley St. L34: Prsct 5D **63**
Wychwood CH41: Birk, Tran 4D **97**
    CH49: Upton 4F **93**
Wycliffe Rd. L4: Walt 4C **56**
    WA11: Hay 1E **49**
Wycliffe St. CH42: R Ferr 2F **119**
Wye Cl. CH42: R Ferr 1F **119**
Wyedale Rd. WA11: Hay 1C **48**
Wye St. L5: Liv 5F **55**
Wykeham St. L4: Kirk 3D **55**
Wykeham Way L4: Kirk 4D **55**
Wyken Gro. WA11: St. H 3C **46**
Wyke Rd. L35: Prsct 1E **85**
Wyllin Rd. L33: K'by 3A **24**
Wylva Av. L23: C'by 2A **18**
Wylva Rd. L4: Walt 5A **56**
Wyncroft Cl. WA8: Wid 5C **130**
Wyncroft Rd. WA8: Wid 5C **130**
Wyncroft St. L8: Liv 5A **100**
Wyndale Cl. L18: Moss H 1B **124**
Wyndcote Rd. L18: Moss H 4B **102**
Wyndham Av. L14: B Grn 4F **81**
Wyndham Rd. CH45: Wall 1D **73**
Wyndham St. L4: Walt 1F **55**
Wynne Rd. WA10: St. H 3E **45**
Wynnstay Av. L31: Lyd 4D **7**
Wynnstay St. L8: Liv 3A **100**
Wynstay Rd. CH47: Meols 3C **90**
Wynwood Pk. L36: Roby 4C **82**
Wyre Rd. L5: Liv 4F **55**

Wyrescourt Rd. L12: W Der 1D **81**
Wyresdale Av.
    WA10: St. H 1E **45**
Wyresdale Rd. L9: Ain 1B **36**
Wysall Cl. WA11: St. H 3D **47**
Wyswall Cl. L26: Halew 2E **127**
Wythburn Cres. WA11: St. H 5B **30**
Wythburn Gro. WA7: Beech 5E **167**
Wyvern Rd. CH46: More 1F **93**

X

X Building L3: Liv 3C **4**

Y

Yanwath St. L8: Liv 2B **100**
Yarcombe Cl. L26: Halew 3F **127**
Yardley Cen.
    L33: Know I 4C **24**
Yardley Dr. CH63: Spit 1A **162**
Yardley Rd.
    L33: Know I 4C **24**
Yarn Cl. WA9: St. H 3F **67**
Yarrow Av. L31: Mag 5F **7**
Yates Cl. L34: Prsct 1D **85**
Yates St. L8: Liv 4E **99**
Yeadon Wlk. L24: Speke 4B **146**
Yellow Submarine 5C **76** (6D **4**)
Yelverton Cl. L26: Halew 3F **127**
Yelverton Rd.
    CH42: Tran 1D **119**
    L4: Walt 4C **56**
Yeoman Cotts. CH47: Hoy 5C **90**
Ye Priory Ct. L25: Aller 3E **125**
Yew Bank Rd. L16: Child 2D **103**
Yewdale Av. WA11: St. H 4B **30**
Yewdale Pk. CH43: O'ton 5B **96**
Yewdale Rd. L9: Walt 4B **36**
Yew Tree Av. WA9: St. H 5C **66**
    WA12: New W 4F **49**
Yew Tree Cl.
    CH49: W'chu 2A **116**
    L12: W Der 5E **59**
Yew Tree Grn. L31: Mell 1B **22**
Yew Tree La. L12: W Der 1E **81**
Yewtree La. CH48: W Kir 3B **112**
Yew Tree Rd. CH46: More 4F **71**
    CH63: High B 3E **141**
    L9: Walt 4F **35**
    L18: Aller 1D **125**

Yew Tree Rd. L25: Hunts X 4C **126**
    L36: Huy 5D **83**
Yew Tree Trad. Est.
    WA11: Hay 1F **49**
Yew Way CH46: More 5F **71**
YMCA 4A **46**
Yorkaster Rd. L18: Aller 3C **124**
York Av. CH44: Wall 3D **75**
    CH48: W Kir 1B **134**
    L17: Liv 3D **101**
    L22: Water 5D **17**
    L23: C'by 1D **17**
York Cl. L30: N'ton 5F **11**
    WA10: St. H 4F **45**
             (not continuous)
York Cotts. L25: Gate 5B **104**
York Ho. L17: Aig 4D **101**
York Pl. L22: Water 5D **17**
    WA7: Run 5B **152**
York Rd. CH44: Wall 4D **75**
    L23: C'by 1E **17**
    L31: Mag 3D **13**
    L36: Huy 3A **84**
    WA8: Wid 4C **130**
Yorkshire Gdns.
    WA10: St. H 1F **65**
York St. CH62: Brom 2D **143**
    L1: Liv 1D **99** (7E **5**)
    L9: Walt 5F **35**
    L19: Gars 3C **144**
    L22: Water 5D **17**
    WA7: Run 5A **152**
York Ter. L5: Liv 5E **55**
York Way L19: Gars 3D **145**
    L36: Huy 3A **84**
Youatt Av. L35: Prsct 2E **85**
Youens Way L14: K Ash 2E **81**
Yoxall Dr. L33: K'by 5D **15**

Z

Zander Gro. L12: Crox 5F **39**
Zante Cl. L5: Liv 5E **55**
Zara Ct. WA11: Hay 1C **48**
Zenith Wlk. L25: Gate 2A **104**
Zetland Rd.
    CH45: Wall 4F **51**
    L18: Moss H 4F **101**
Zetland St. CH41: Birk 4D **97**
Zig Zag Rd. CH45: Wall 5B **52**
    L12: W Der 1D **81**
Zircon Cl. L21: Lith 5C **18**

HOSPITALS and HOSPICES
covered by this atlas.

N.B. Where Hospitals and Hospices are not named on the map, the reference given is for the road in which they are situated.

ALDER HEY CHILDREN'S HOSPITAL 2C **80**
Eaton Road
West Derby
LIVERPOOL
L12 2AP
Tel: 0151 2284811

ARROWE PARK HOSPITAL 3A **116**
Arrowe Park Rd.
WIRRAL
CH49 5PE
Tel: 0151 6785111

ASHTON HOUSE HOSPITAL 5B **96**
26 Village Road
Oxton
PRENTON
CH43 5SR
Tel: 0151 653 9660

ASHWORTH HOSPITAL 1B **14**
Parkburn
LIVERPOOL
L31 1HW
Tel: 0151 4730303

BROADGREEN HOSPITAL 4C **80**
Thomas Drive
LIVERPOOL
L14 3LB
Tel: 0151 7062000

CARDIOTHORACIC CENTRE (BROADGREEN HOSPITAL), THE
.... 4C **80**
Thomas Drive
LIVERPOOL
L14 3PE
Tel: 0151 2281616

CLAIRE HOUSE CHILDREN'S HOSPICE 1D **161**
Clatterbridge Rd.
WIRRAL
CH63 4JD
Tel: 0151 3344626

CLATTERBRIDGE HOSPITAL 1E **161**
Clatterbridge Rd.
WIRRAL
CH63 4JY
Tel: 0151 3344000

FAIRFIELD HOSPITAL 3E **29**
Crank Road
Crank
ST HELENS
WA11 7RS
Tel: 01744 739311

HALTON GENERAL HOSPITAL 4F **167**
Hospital Way
RUNCORN
WA7 2DA
Tel: 01928 714567

HALTON HAVEN 5C **168**
Barnfield Av.
Murdishaw
RUNCORN
WA7 6EP
Tel: 01928 719454

LIVERPOOL WOMEN'S HOSPITAL 1A **100**
Crown Street
LIVERPOOL
L8 7SS
Tel: 0151 7089988

LOURDES HOSPITAL 4F **101**
57 Greenbank Road
LIVERPOOL
L18 1HQ
Tel: 0151 7337123

MARIE CURIE CENTRE, LIVERPOOL 2B **126**
Speke Road
Woolton
LIVERPOOL
L25 8QA
Tel: 0151 801 1400

MOSSLEY HILL HOSPITAL 5E **101**
Park Avenue
Mossley Hill
LIVERPOOL
L18 8BU
Tel: 0151 2503000

MURRAYFIELD BUPA HOSPITAL 2D **139**
Holmwood Drive
Heswall
WIRRAL
CH61 1AU
Tel: 0151 6487000

PARK LODGE HOSPITAL 1D **79**
Orphan Drive
LIVERPOOL
L6 7UN
Tel: 0151 3308934

RATHBONE HOSPITAL 4A **80**
Mill Lane
Old Swan
LIVERPOOL
L13 4AW
Tel: 0151 2503000

ROYAL LIVERPOOL DENTAL HOSPITAL 4F **77** (4J **5**)
Pembroke Place
LIVERPOOL
L3 5PS
Tel: 0151 7062000

ROYAL LIVERPOOL UNIVERSITY HOSPITAL
.... 4F **77** (3J **5**)
Prescot Street
LIVERPOOL
L7 8XP
Tel: 0151 7062000

Hospitals & Hospices

ST BARTHOLOMEW'S DAY HOSPITAL 4C **82**
Station Rd.
Huyton
LIVERPOOL
L36 4HU
Tel: 0151 4896241

ST CATHERINE'S HOSPITAL (BIRKENHEAD) 5D **97**
Church Rd.
BIRKENHEAD
CH42 0LQ
Tel: 0151 6787272

ST HELENS HOSPITAL (MERSEYSIDE) 2C **66**
Marshalls Cross Road
ST HELENS
WA9 3DA
Tel: 0151 4261600

ST JOHN'S HOSPICE IN WIRRAL 1E **161**
Mount Rd.
Higher Bebington
WIRRAL
CH63 6JE
Tel: 0151 3342778

ST JOSEPH'S HOSPICE 2F **9**
Ince Road
LIVERPOOL
L23 4UE
Tel: 0151 9243812

SCOTT CLINIC 1C **86**
Rainhill Road
ST HELENS
WA9 5BD
Tel: 0151 4306300

SIR ALFRED JONES MEMORIAL HOSPITAL
. . . . .1C **144**
Church Road
Garston
LIVERPOOL
L19 2LP
Tel: 0151 2503000

SMITHDOWN HEALTH PARK .3D **101**
Smithdown Road
LIVERPOOL
L15 2HE
Tel: 0151 33080/54/74/10

UNIVERSITY HOSPITAL AINTREE 1E **37**
Longmoor La.
LIVERPOOL
L9 7AL
Tel: 0151 525 5980

VICTORIA CENTRAL HOSPITAL .2B **74**
Mill La.
WALLASEY
CH44 5UF
Tel: 0151 6785111

WALTON HOSPITAL 5F **35**
Rice Lane
LIVERPOOL
L9 1AE
Tel: 0151 525 3611

WATERLOO DAY HOSPITAL 4E **17**
Park Rd., Waterloo
LIVERPOOL
L22 3XR
Tel: 0151 9287243

WHISTON HOSPITAL 2F **85**
Warrington Rd.
PRESCOT
L35 5DR
Tel: 0151 4261600

WILLOW HOUSE RESOURCE CENTRE 3E **85**
168 Dragon La.
PRESCOT
L35 3QY
Tel: 0151 4306048

WILLOWBROOK HOSPICE 4A **64**
Portico La.
PRESCOT
L34 2QT
Tel: 0151 4308736

WOODLANDS HOSPICE 2D **37**
Longmoor La.
LIVERPOOL
L9 7LA
Tel: 0151 5292299

ZOE'S PLACE - BABY HOSPICE 1E **81**
Yew Tree La.
LIVERPOOL
L12 9HH
Tel: 0151 2280353